M000251177

SOUTH-WESTERN

Microsoft® Visual Basic® 6.0

Introduction to Programming

Michael Sprague
Computer Science & Programming Instructor
Libertyville, IL

Amelia Phillips
Spokane Falls Community College
Spokane, WA

Dorothy L. Nield
Microsoft Certified Professional
Microsoft Certified Solutions Developer
San Leandro, CA

VISIT US ON THE INTERNET
www.swep.com
www.thomsonlearning.com

Australia • Canada • Denmark • Japan • Mexico • New Zealand • Phillipines
Puerto Rico • Singapore • South Africa • Spain • United Kingdom • United States

Managing Editor: Carol Volz
Editor: Mark Cheatham
Consulting Editors: Janet Andrews, Brenda K. Lewis, David B. Lewis
Production Coordinator: Angela McDonald
Art/Design Coordinator: Mike Broussard
Marketing Manager: Larry Qualls
Cover Design: Kim Buening Torbeck
Production Services: David Leiser, Electro-Publishing

South-Western Educational Publishing is a division of Thomson Learning.
Thomson Learning is a trademark used herein under license.

ISBNs: 0-538-68818-1 (hardcover); 0-538-68821-1 (soft cover)

3 4 5 6 7 8 9 0 CK 05 04 03 02 01 00

Printed in the United States of America

South-Western can meet your programming needs with these exciting new products!

From Visual Basic to Java, South-Western is your programming solutions provider.

Microsoft Visual Basic 6.0: Introduction to Programming by Sprague & Phillips
75+ hours of instruction. Supports the Microsoft Certified Professional exam criteria.

- Student book, soft cover 0-538-68821-1
- Student book, hard cover. 0-538-68818-1
- Certification Guide 0-538-69137-9
- Activities Workbook. 0-538-68916-1
- Electronic Instructor CD-ROM Package 0-538-68820-3
- Testing Package. 0-538-69461-0

Microsoft Visual Basic Programming Projects by CEP, Inc. & Sestak.
This generic computer programming projects book supplements other textbooks that teach Visual Ba
Includes over 30 projects.

- Student Book, soft cover 0-538-6889
- Electronic Instructor CD-ROM Package 0-538-688

Microsoft Visual Basic BASICS by Knowlton & Collings.
Provides the groundwork for immediate understanding of the theory and practice of Visual Ba

- Text workbook/data disk (soft cover). . . . . 0-538-)86-0
- Text workbook (hard cover spiral) 0-538-083-6
- Activities Workbook. 0-539084-4
- Electronic Instructor CD-ROM Package 0-5 69085-2
- Testing CD . . . . . 0- -69243-X

Introduction to Computer Science Using C++ by Knowlton.
75+ hours of instruction. Covers computer science fundamentals using C++; appropria for a variety of C++ courses. On-line support is available for this text through the Internet tance Education (IDE) program offered by Knowlton & Associates, Inc.

- Textbook (hard cover) 0-538-67600-0
- Text/Data Disks Package (IBM/Mac) 0-538-67601-9
- Manual/Data/Solutions Disk Package (IBM/Mac). 0-538-67605-1
- Workbook 0-538-67841-0
- MicroExam Test Bank (IBM) 0-538-67604-3
- MicroExam Test Bank (Macintosh) 0-538-67990-5
- AP Exam Study Guide 0-538-67922-0
- Electronic Instructor CD-ROM. 0-538-68799-1

For information call 1-800-354-9706.

Join Us On the Internet **http://www.swep.com**

PREFACE

Welcome to *Microsoft Visual Basic 6.0: Introduction to Programming!* The text you hold in your hands is part of a family of products designed with three goals in mind:

1. To lead the learner to mastery of Visual Basic 6.0 starting with fundamentals for the beginner and working through a number of advanced topics including
   - objects and classes;
   - the creation of ActiveX controls and Documents;
   - linking applications to Databases using ActiveX Data Objects; and
   - using the functions of the Application Programming Interface.
2. To guide the the learner toward developing good programming practices and techniques.
3. To allow the learner to pursue Microsoft Certification in Visual Basic.

   The product family includes these items:
   - The textbook (described below).
   - The *Activities Workbook* that contains dozens of problems for each lesson in several different formats. Use this workbook to help learners master material presented in the text. Workbook pages make great homework assignments. Each section in the workbook corresponds to a section in the text. The workbook also contains additional programming problems for each lesson.
   - The *Certification Guide* that addresses topics necessary for Visual Basic certification that are not covered in the textbook or that need additional emphasis. The Guide also includes questions written in the same general style that users will find on the actual exams.
   - The *Electronic Instructor* CD-ROM package that includes lesson plans, instructional strategies, and solution files for the programs presented in the text. Also included are programming solutions to application programming problems and the answers to all the exercises and questions in the text. PowerPoint slides are provided on the Instructor's CD to provide illustrations for classroom presentations. Slides include screen captures, code samples, and diagrams.

The defining feature of the text is the extensive use of step-by-step exercises. These exercises guide learners through each sample program. Explanations along the way help the learner understand what is happening as the sample program is developed. The samples are not only used as a vehicle for instruction, they are patterns for programmers to follow as they write their own programs. Samples are chosen with an eye to holding the reader's interest as well as illustrating new programming concepts.

Each lesson starts with Lesson Objectives that define the purpose of the lesson. Review the objectives to outline what the learners can expect to accomplish by studying the lesson. Included with the objectives is a time estimate of how long it may take to cover the material presented in the lesson (the actual time will vary for each individual depending upon aptitude and experience).

A listing of key terms presented at the beginning of each lesson gives learners a clue about where they are going. Use the key terms list both at the beginning and end of each lesson to ensure mastery of the material.

The body of each lesson explains programming concepts and methodology as well as the structure and meaning of the Visual Basic 6.0 programming language.

Following each section, a number of questions check learner understanding and recall.

Hundreds of screen illustrations show steps in the development of the sample programs and help the learner master new concepts.

Sidebars appear throughout the text with special information for learners:

- Building Programming Skills provides suggestions for resolving common problems that a new learner may encounter.
- Computer Ethics presents ethical and legal concerns in relation to technology.
- Building Communication Skills emphasizes the importance of developing communication skills within a work setting.
- Historically Speaking includes significant historical benchmarks in the development of computer technology and programming.

End of chapter features include:

- Chapter Summary summarizes and reviews chapter content.
- Review Questions thoroughly review the chapter content and require answers in both objective and written formats.
- Application Problems are presented at two levels—approximately 4 review problems then 2-4 advanced problems per chapter requiring learners to extend beyond what they have learned.
- Programming at Work is an ongoing project that presents a programming problem within the context of a business setting. As new language features are presented in a lesson, they are added to the ongoing project.

Use *Microsoft Visual Basic 6.0: Introduction to Programming* for a one semester introduction to programming or a two or three semester course that covers most of the language features of Visual Basic. Concentrate on objects and classes to prepare learners for the AP Computer Science course. With the addition of the *Certification Guide*, use the textbook to prepare learners for Microsoft Visual Basic certification.

Who Can Use This Book

This book and its ancillaries (the *Activities Workbook* and *Certification Guide*) can be used for learners at all levels. It is best suited for a two- or three-semester course. The book can be used alone as an introduction to programming or with its ancillaries can be used for learners with some programming experience who would like to study for the Microsoft Certified Professional Exams.

The Step-by-Step exercises provide an excellent hands-on, guided introduction to programming as well as a review for experienced users. Quick Check questions throughout the lessons as well as the Review Questions at the end of the lessons reinforce concepts presented in the Step-by-Step exercises.

The end-of-chapter Programming at Work activities are guided exercises that reinforce code and Visual Basic features presented in the lesson. In Lesson 4 the Programming at Work begins a Music Collection program that is built upon in the Programming at Work section in Lessons 5-10 and again in Lessons 13-15. The final program in Lesson 15 is a very sophisticated program that can be used on any system.

In addition to guided exercises and written review questions, critical thinking skills are developed in the end-of-lesson Application Problems. These Application Problems have two levels, an easier set of problems and a more difficult set of problems. In these problems, learners are challenged to create programs that incorporate code and Visual Basic features from all previous lessons. They are also encouraged to add their own variations of the code and features. Depending on the ability of the learner and the time available, these application problems can be skipped; they can be completed with additional instructor assistance; or the programs can be created by small groups of students working together. Ideally they will be created by individuals with trial and error to see what works best.

Just as real-life programming applications, no two learners will create exactly the same programming solution for these problems! None of the Application Problems are required to complete later activities in the book so beginners can skip them and come back and try them when they feel more comfortable with their programming skills. They provide valuable programming experience for all learning levels.

How to Use this Book

What makes a good instructional text? Sound pedagogy and the most current, complete materials. That is what you will find in *Microsoft® Visual Basic® 6.0: Introduction to Programming*. Not only will you find an inviting layout, but also many features to enhance learning.

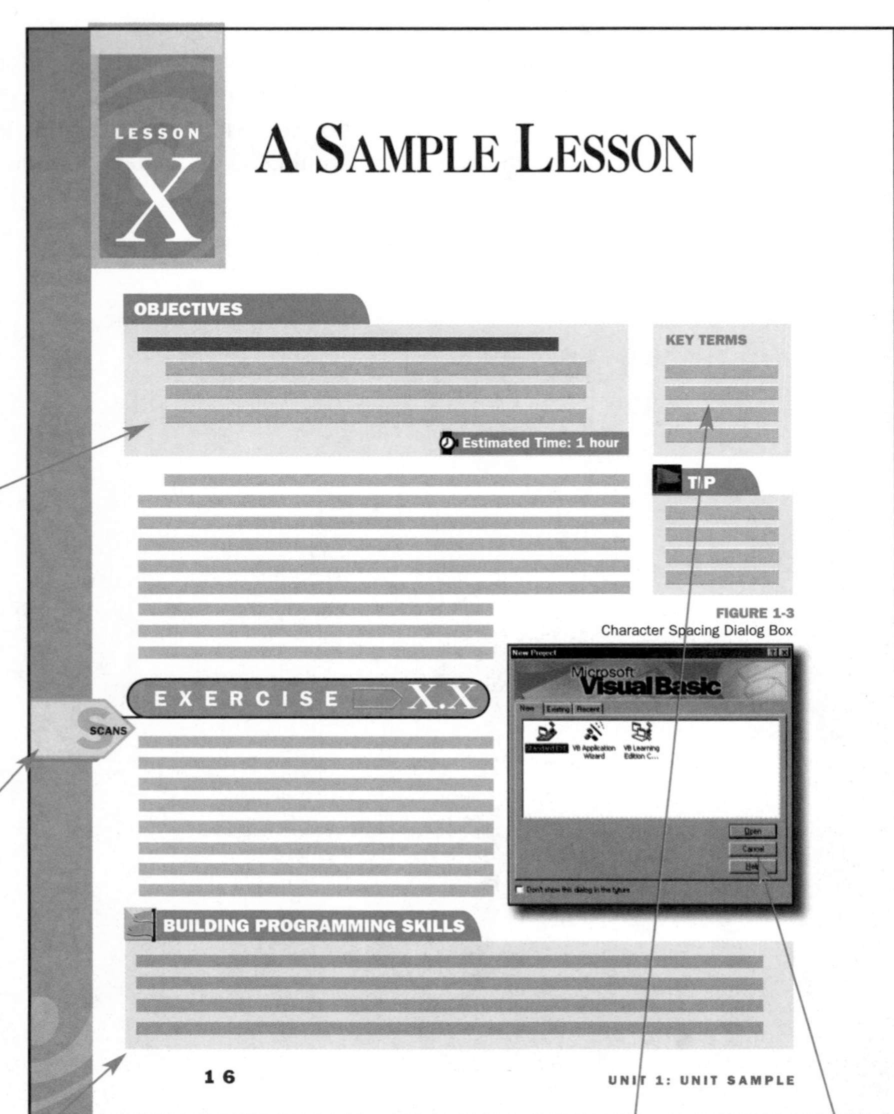

Objectives– Objectives are listed at the beginning of each lesson, along with a suggested time for completion of the lesson. This allows you to look ahead to what you will be learning and to pace your work.

SCANS (Secretary's Commission on Achieving Necessary Skills)–The U.S. Department of Labor has identified the school-to-careers competencies. The eight workplace competencies and foundation skills are identified in the exercises where they apply. More information on SCANS can be found on the *Electronic Instructor.*

Sidebar Items— These sidebar items provide additional information.

- *Historically Speaking* presents the history of computers and programming.
- *Building Programming Skills* introduces the student to programming issues and processes.
- *Computer Ethics* provides ethical guidelines.
- *Building Communication Skills* suggests sound methods for creating documentation.

Enhanced Screen Shots– Screen shots now come to life on each page.

Vocabulary– An emphasis is placed on building a vocabulary of programming terminology.

How to Use this Book

Summary– At the end of each lesson you will find a summary to prepare you to complete the end-of-lesson activities.

Review Questions– Review material at the end of each lesson enables you to prepare for assessment of the content presented.

Application Problems– End-of-lesson hands-on critical thinking problems.

Programming at Work– A step-by-step progressive project allows you to build a sophisticated program.

Appendices– Appendices include information on Windows and installing Visual Studio.

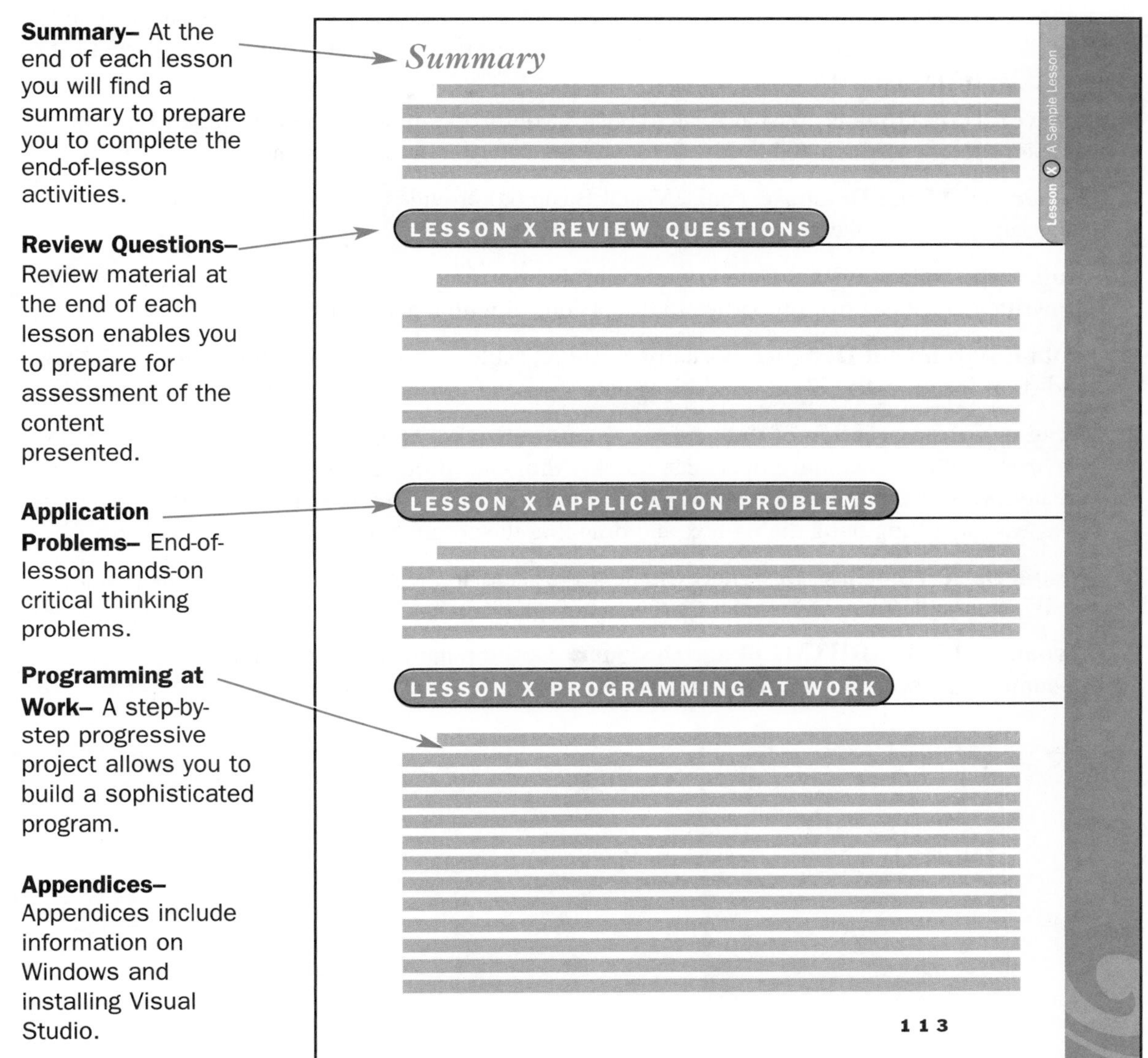

What's New

Microsoft Visual Basic 6.0 is an extremely powerful language with a wide range of capabilities and applications. Its programming environment is the best for ease of use and availability of tools. With each new version, its capabilities and ease of use are enhanced. Here is a partial list of features new to Version 6.0.

- **ActiveX Data Objects.** Visual Basic 6.0 uses Microsoft's powerful new standard for data access. Drivers are included to interface with many common data formats.
- **Integrated Visual Database Tools.** Visual Basic 6.0 provides a complete set of tools for integrating databases with any application.
- **Automatic Data Binding.** Data-bound controls provide access to database information with no written code. Set two properties to link a control with a data field.
- **Data Environment Designer.** Visually create reusable recordset command objects with drag-and-drop functionality. Bind to multiple data sources for data aggregation and manipulation.
- **Drag and drop creation of data-bound forms and reports.** Using the new Data Environment designer, developers can quickly drag-and-drop custom data-bound controls to create forms or reports with the new Data Report designer. Creation of custom data hierarchies is as easy as filling out a dialog box and dragging the command to the form.
- **Visual Basic WebClass Designer.** Create server-side applications and components that are easily accessible from any Web browser on any platform.
- **Dynamic HTML (DHTML) Page Designer.** Develop multimedia-rich applications using the document object model and Dynamic HTML design surface.

Start-Up Checklist

Hardware (for Visual Basic 6 Professional Edition)

- PC with a 486DX/66 MHz or higher processor: Pentium or higher processor recommended.
- 16 MB of RAM for Windows 95 or later (32 MB recommended); 24 MB for Windows NT 4.0 (32 MB recommended).
- Hard-disk space required: Typical installation: 76 MB; maximum installation: 94 MB
- Additional hard-disk space required for the following products:
  - Internet Explorer: 43 MB typical, 59 MB maximum
  - MSDN: 57 MB typical, 493 MB maximum
  - Microsoft Windows NT 4.0 Option Pack: 20 MB for Windows 95 or later; 200 MB for Windows NT 4.0
- CD-ROM drive
- VGA or higher-resolution monitor; Super VGA recommended.
- Microsoft Mouse or compatible pointing device.

Software

- Microsoft Windows 95 or later operating system.
- Microsoft Internet Explorer 4.01 Service Pack 1 (included with Visual Basic).

GUIDE FOR USING THIS BOOK

Please read this Guide before starting work. The time you spend now will save you much more time later and will make your learning faster, easier, and more pleasant.

Recommended Software

Visual Basic 6.0 Professional Edition or Enterprise Edition is recommended for use with this text.

Conventions

The different type styles used in this book have special meanings. They will save you time because you will soon automatically recognize from the type style the nature of the text you are reading and what you will do.

WHAT YOU WILL DO	TYPE STYLE	EXAMPLE
Program code you will key	`Courier`	`Option Explicit`
Individual options you will select	**Bold**	Click **Open** to add a new module
Text you will key	**Bold**	Name the module **modMymodule**.

WHAT YOU WILL SEE	TYPE STYLE	EXAMPLE
Program and file names	**Bold upper and lowercase**	Open the **MusicColl** project.
Glossary terms in book	*Italics*	The *menu* contains menu titles.
Words on screen	*Italics*	Highlight the word *pencil* on the screen.
Menus and commands	**Bold**	Choose **Open** from the **File** menu.

Electronic Instructor® CD-ROM

The *Electronic Instructor* contains a wealth of instructional material you can use to prepare for Visual Basic instruction. The CD-ROM stores the following information:

- Solution files for this course.
- Figures that appear in the text which can be used for PowerPoint presentations.
- Grids that show skills required for Microsoft Certified Professional (MCP) certification and the SCANS workplace competencies and skills.
- Additional instructional information about individual learning strategies, portfolios, and career planning.

Additional Activities and Questions

An *Activities Workbook* is available to supply additional paper-and-pencil exercises and hands-on application problems for each chapter of this book. In addition, testing software is available separately with a customizable test bank specific for this text.

A separate *Certification Guide* is available that provides tips for taking the exams and additional activities and problems correlated to each exam skill. Review Questions imitate the type of exam questions the user may encounter on the actual exams.

SCANS

The Secretary's Commission on Achieving Necessary Skills (SCANS) from the U.S. Department of Labor was asked to examine the demands of the workplace and whether new learners are capable of meeting those demands. Specifically, the Commission was directed to advise the Secretary on the level of skills required to enter employment.

SCANS workplace competencies and foundation skills have been integrated into *Microsoft Visual Basic 6.0 Introduction to Programming*. The workplace competencies are identified as 1) ability to use *resources*, 2) *interpersonal* skills, 3) ability to work with *information*, 4) understanding of *systems*, and 5) knowledge and understanding of *technology*. The foundation skills are identified as 1) basic communication skills, 2) thinking skills, and 3) personal qualities.

Exercises in which learners must use a number of these SCANS competencies and foundation skills are marked in the text with the SCANS icon.

Microsoft Certification

What is Certification?

After mastery of the textbook and the *Certification Guide* you will be ready to take the test to become a Microsoft Certified Professional (MCP). This certification, provided by Microsoft, demonstrates to customers and employers your mastery of Microsoft Visual Basic 6.0. This means you have the skills needed to develop and maintain applications using Visual Basic.

Obtaining the Microsoft Certified Professional credential makes it easier to pursue other Microsoft certification programs like Microsoft Certified Systems Engineer (MCSE), Microsoft Certified Database Administrator (MCDBA), and Microsoft Certified Solution Developer (MCSD).

Becoming a MCP also makes you eligible for special services from MSDN, the Microsoft Developer Network. It gives you free access to valuable resources and services provided through the MSDN Web site. You can also download technical and product information directly from a secured area of the MCP Web site, hosted by Microsoft. You receive a free subscription to Microsoft Certified Professional Magazine, as well as certificate, wallet card, and lapel pin to identify your MCP status to colleagues or clients.

What About the Test?

The textbook and *Certification Guide* are designed to present material needed to take Exam 70-175, *Designing and Implementing Distributed Applications with Microsoft Visual Basic 6.0* and Exam 70-176, *Designing and Implementing Desktop Applications with Microsoft Visual Basic 6.0.* The test questions are in several formats. Sample tests from previous versions of Visual Basic may be available at the Microsoft web site. Although your score on the practice test may not reflect what your score will be on a certification exam, the practice test gives you a good idea of the format of the questions.

You take the test at Sylvan Prometric or Virtual University Enterprises. To register with Sylvan, call (800) 755-EXAM (755-3926). To register online, visit Sylvan's web site.

TABLE OF CONTENTS

UNIT 1 MASTERING THE BASICS

UNIT 2 COLLECTIONS

UNIT 3 CREATING AND USING NEW CONTROLS

UNIT 4 LIFE OUTSIDE OF VISUAL BASIC

KYOTO
1582 Battery St.
San Francisco, CA 94702

MASTERING THE BASICS

UNIT 1

Estimated Time for Unit 1: 11.5 hours

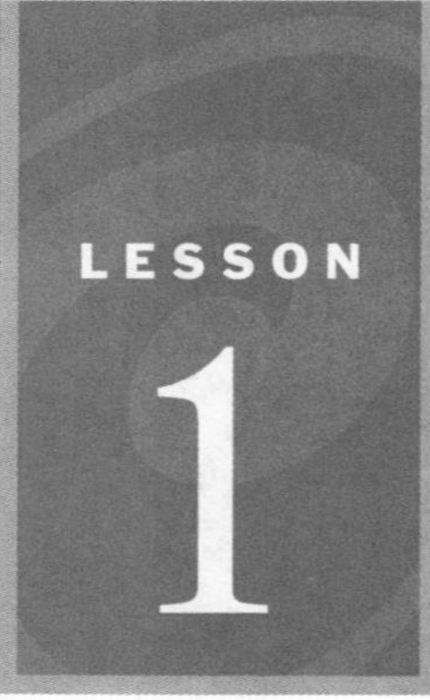

THE BASICS

OBJECTIVES

When you complete this lesson, you will be able to:

- Define Microsoft Visual Basic and identify the common features of Windows applications.
- Identify and use the basic tools in the Visual Basic Integrated Development Environment.
- Create a form and add objects to it.
- Explain the meaning of "event driven" and program an event procedure.
- Understand the Help system.

Estimated Time: 1 hour

KEY TERMS

Graphical User Interface (GUI)
menu
event-driven
object
Integrated Development Environment
controls
ToolTip
Dynamic Link Libraries (DLL)
forms
file extension
event procedure

Introduction to Microsoft Visual Basic

Microsoft Visual Basic is a set of programming tools that allows you to create applications for the Windows operating system. With Visual Basic, even a beginner can create professional-looking applications.

Visual Basic combines the BASIC programming language used by programmers all over the world with a *Graphical User Interface,* or *GUI.* A GUI lets you use both text and graphics to communicate with the computer. Programming languages of the past involved entering tediously long strings of code to create something as simple as a button that responds to a mouse click. Microsoft's Visual Basic simplifies many routine programming tasks. Instead of writing pages of code to have the window respond to the mouse, Visual Basic provides a set of prebuilt objects that can be placed on the screen, keeping most of the tedious code behind the scenes. This frees the programmer to concentrate on the application's features instead of worrying about how to make a mouse click work. Because of this, even new users can create useful applications after learning just a few simple commands. Built to simplify creating applications in the Windows environment, Visual Basic draws a wide crowd of enthusiasts.

If you performed a search on the World Wide Web for the term Visual Basic, the resulting list would be staggering. The most amazing part of the list would be the number of jobs advertised for Visual Basic programmers. Several hundred jobs are listed not only in the United States, but also worldwide.

Programs created in Visual Basic cover such diverse uses as tracking income, accessing databases, calculating currency exchange rates, multimedia, and more. Visual Basic is a very versatile language.

Programming Concepts

Programming for the Windows environment brings with it a list of user expectations. Because Visual Basic is a Windows development language, it is important to be familiar with the common features found in many Windows applications. In most Windows applications, a user expects to see things that are familiar, such as *menus*, toolbars, and Minimize and Maximize buttons, as shown in Figure 1-1. Before you start Visual Basic, let's look at a few of the common features that people expect to find.

FIGURE 1-1
Common Windows objects

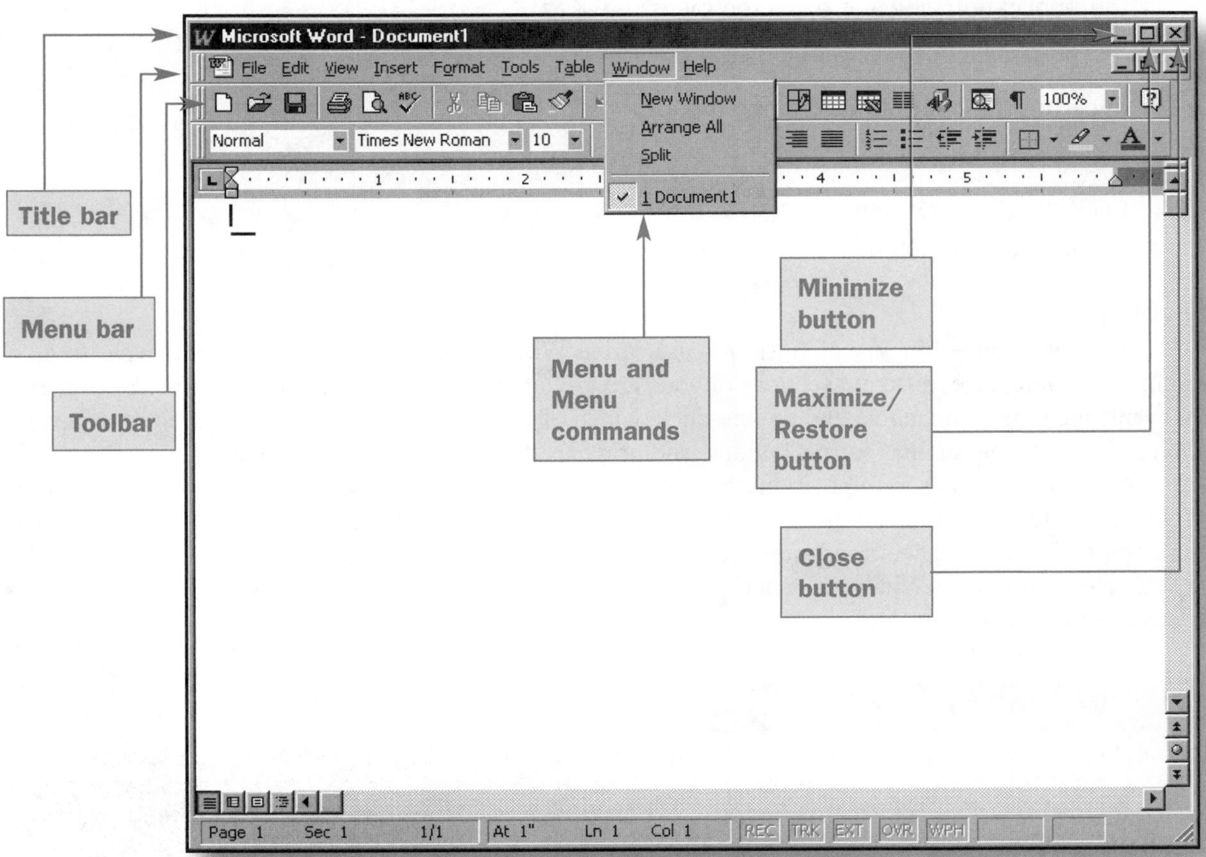

STEP-BY-STEP 1.1

1. Start Microsoft Word.

2. Click the various entries on the menu bar to display the menus.

3. Click the **Help** menu and select **About Microsoft Word**. This feature is known as an About box and is found in many Windows applications. Click **OK** to close the dialog box.

4. Click the **File** menu. Notice that it has Open, Save, and Exit commands.

5. Select the **Save As** command. Details such as the title bar on the dialog box are all taken care of in the design of the application which is expected by users.

6. Click the **Cancel** button to close the dialog box.

7. Click the **File** menu again. Notice that some of the commands have shortcut keys listed to the right of them (see Figure 1-2). For example, the shortcut key for the Save command is typically Ctrl+S. Some users prefer to use the keyboard rather than the mouse.

8. Quit Microsoft Word.

FIGURE 1-2
File menu with commands

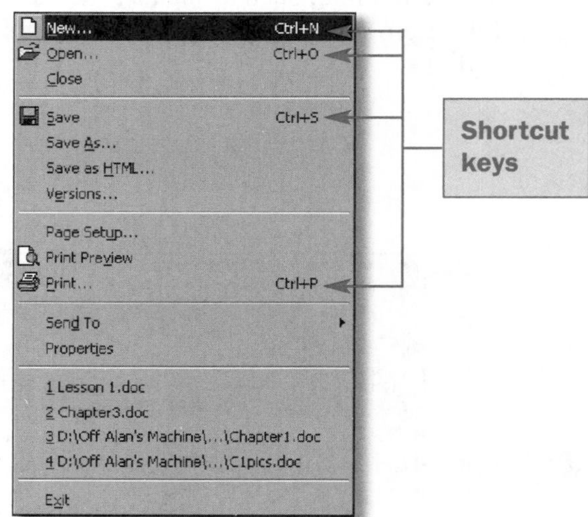

Programs created in Visual Basic for use in the Windows environment are *event driven*. In an event driven language, different sections of code are executed based upon the user's actions. Examples of events are drag, drop, click, and double-click. Much of the code in Visual Basic is linked to *objects*. Objects are controls such as forms, buttons, and graphics that you add to your program.

A programmer has to think about the order in which the user accesses the forms. What happens if the user accesses a form in a different way than the assumed design? Will the results be catastrophic? Should a warning message be given? These questions and more must be considered when programming in Windows or any other environment. You will explore and build upon these ideas throughout the text.

Historically Speaking

The first general-purpose computer of the modern age was the ENIAC—The Electronic Numerical Integrator and Computer. It was invented to do only one thing, calculate firing tables for missiles in the Second World War. The ENIAC consisted of more than 18,000 vacuum tubes and filled a large room. To program the ENIAC, it had to be completely rewired. It was a far cry from what we have today. Its inventors, J. Eckert and John Mauchley, went on to found the first American computer company called UNIVAC.

The Visual Basic Integrated Development Environment

All the tools that you need to create professional Windows applications can be found within Visual Basic's *Integrated Development Environment (IDE)*. Before you can get started programming in Visual Basic, you need to become familiar with navigating the environment. Figure 1-3 shows some of the essential parts of the Visual Basic workspace. Begin by opening Visual Basic and exploring the menu bar.

FIGURE 1-3
Visual Basic workspace

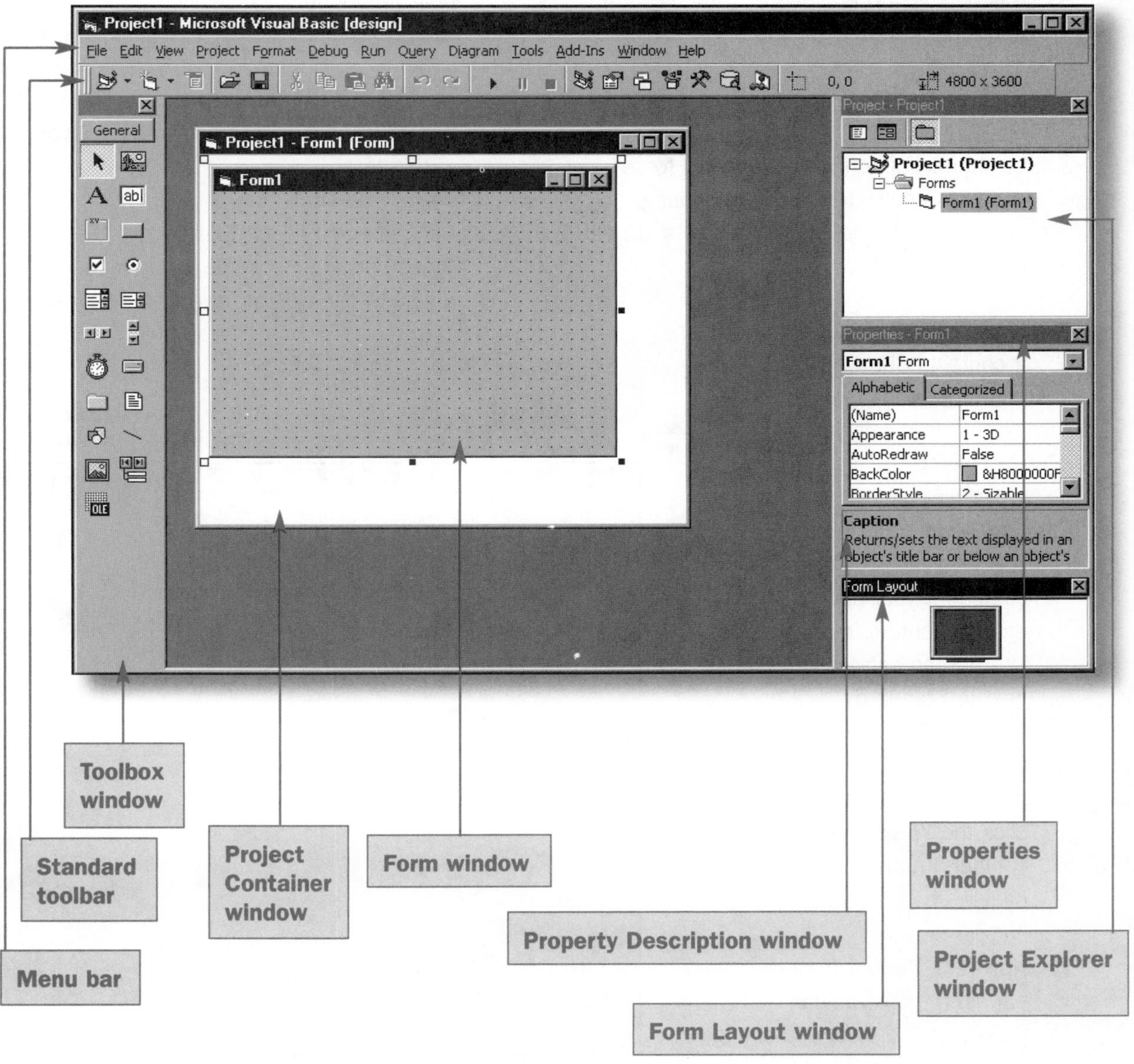

STEP-BY-STEP 1.2

1. In Windows, click the **Start** button. Point to **Programs** and then select the **Microsoft Visual Basic 6.0** program icon.

2. The New Project dialog box appears. Select **Standard EXE** (see Figure 1-4) from the dialog box and click **Open**.

3. A new project opens. Look at the windows and tools that appear.

4. Click **File** on the menu bar. Notice that it has many of the commands that are commonly found in the File menu for any Windows application. Saving, printing, opening, and creating new projects are all done from here.

5. Now click **Edit** from the menu bar. It contains Cut, Copy, and Paste, and other commands that are useful for editing your application.

6. Click **View** from the menu bar. The View menu lets you customize your development environment. Point to **Toolbars**. There is probably a check mark next to Standard. Click once on **Standard** to deselect it. Notice that the Standard toolbar does not appear. To retrieve it, simply click the **View** menu, point to **Toolbars**, and click **Standard** again.

7. Now click **Project** from the menu bar. From here you can add new files to your project and change or add components.

8. Click **Format**. The Format menu contains commands that are used to change the layout of forms and objects of the forms.

9. Click **Debug** to look at the options in this menu. As you begin programming later in this book, you will run into errors in your programs. Commands in the Debug menu help you identify, locate, and fix problems with your code.

10. Look at the remaining entries on the menu bar. Their uses will be explained later on in this text.

11. Click **File** and select **Exit** or click the Close button on the title bar to close Visual Basic. Do not save any changes.

FIGURE 1-4
New Project dialog box

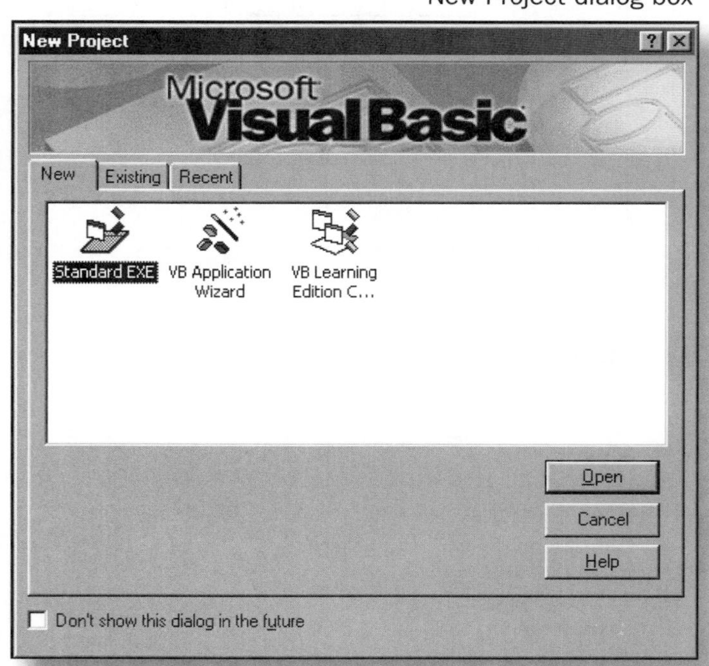

The Tools menu may vary from system to system due to different system configurations.

Quick Check 1.a

1. Visual Basic is a set of __________________ tools.

2. A graphical user interface uses both __________________ and __________________ to communicate with the computer.

3. __________________ are controls that you add to your programs.

4. Examples of events are __________________ , __________________ , and __________________ .

5. The __________________ menu is used when tracking down errors in your program.

Exploring the Standard Toolbar

When you open a project in Visual Basic, the Standard toolbar is usually visible. As with most Windows applications, the toolbar provides easy access to frequently preformed commands. Figure 1-5 shows the Standard toolbar. You may have additional buttons on the toolbar, depending on which version of Visual Basic you have installed.

There are three other toolbars in the View menu (Debug, Edit, and Form Editor) that you may want to take some time to look at. For now you will only be looking at the Standard toolbar.

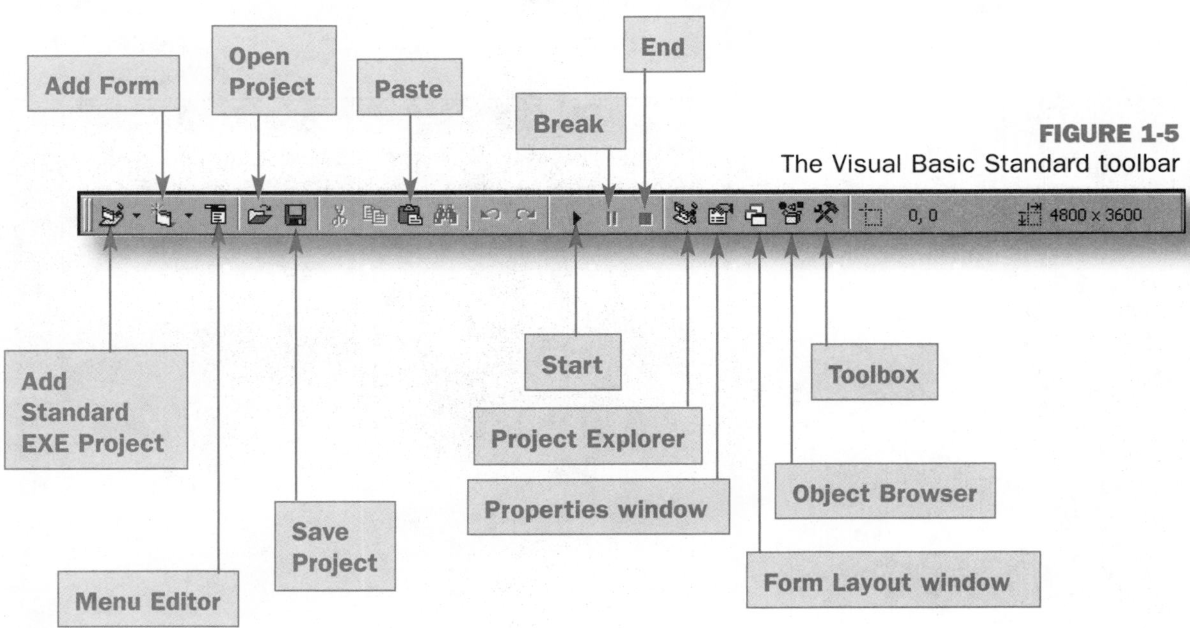

FIGURE 1-5
The Visual Basic Standard toolbar

STEP-BY-STEP 1.3

1. Start Visual Basic and click **Cancel** from the New Project dialog box.

2. Position the mouse pointer on a **Standard toolbar** button. A ToolTip will appear (see Figure 1-6).

3. Find and click the **Add Standard EXE Project** button. A Standard Project and Form window display and the other tools become active. If you click the list arrow to the immediate right of it, a list of project types appears.

4. Click the list arrow next to the **Add Form** button and a list of form types appears.

5. Click the **Add Form** button now. The Add Form dialog box appears. Under the **New** tab, select **Form** and click **Open**. There are two forms open in your workspace now. You can use this command anytime a new form is needed.

6. Take a few minutes to explore the other buttons on the toolbar. You will use most of these features as you create your programs.

7. Exit Visual Basic, and do not save changes.

TIP

Menu commands and buttons appear in color when they can be used and are grayed out when they cannot be used.

FIGURE 1-6
Standard toolbar ToolTip

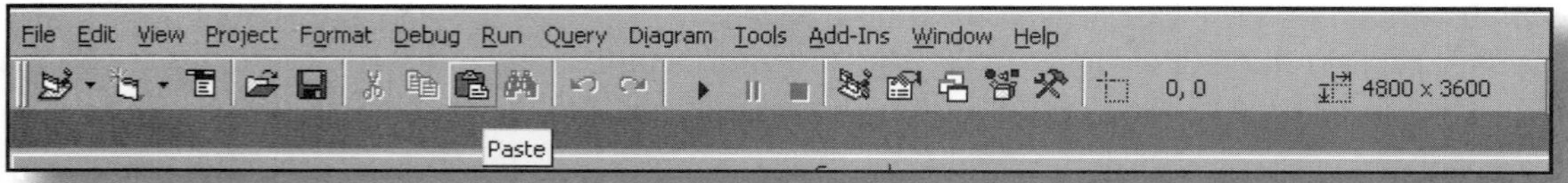

TIP

ToolTips give a short explanation of what a control does. They appear as yellow boxes near a control when your mouse pointer rests over the control. If ToolTips do not appear, they need to be activated (see Figure 1-7). Click Tools from the menu bar and select Options. Click the General tab and then select the Show ToolTips check box, as shown in Figure 1-7.

FIGURE 1-7
Activating ToolTips

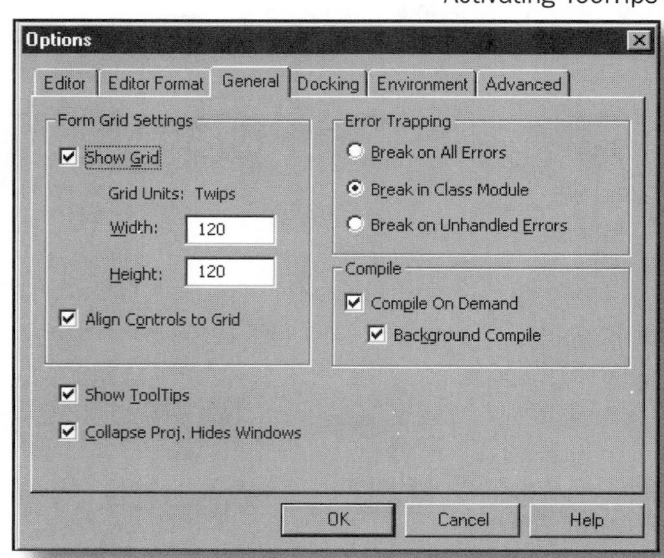

Exploring the Toolbox

The toolbox contains the tools that are available for use in designing the forms used in your applications. The tools allow you to place objects, also called *controls,* on forms. A set of basic tools is provided for you when you start a new Visual Basic project. The toolbox is normally located on the left side of the screen, but can be moved if you want it in another location. Some of the controls you can add are buttons, labels, list boxes, and scroll bars. To see what each of the tools does, look at its *ToolTip*. Simply place the mouse pointer over the tool for a few moments and the ToolTip appears. Refer to Figure 1-8 as you go through this section.

FIGURE 1-8
The Visual Basic toolbox

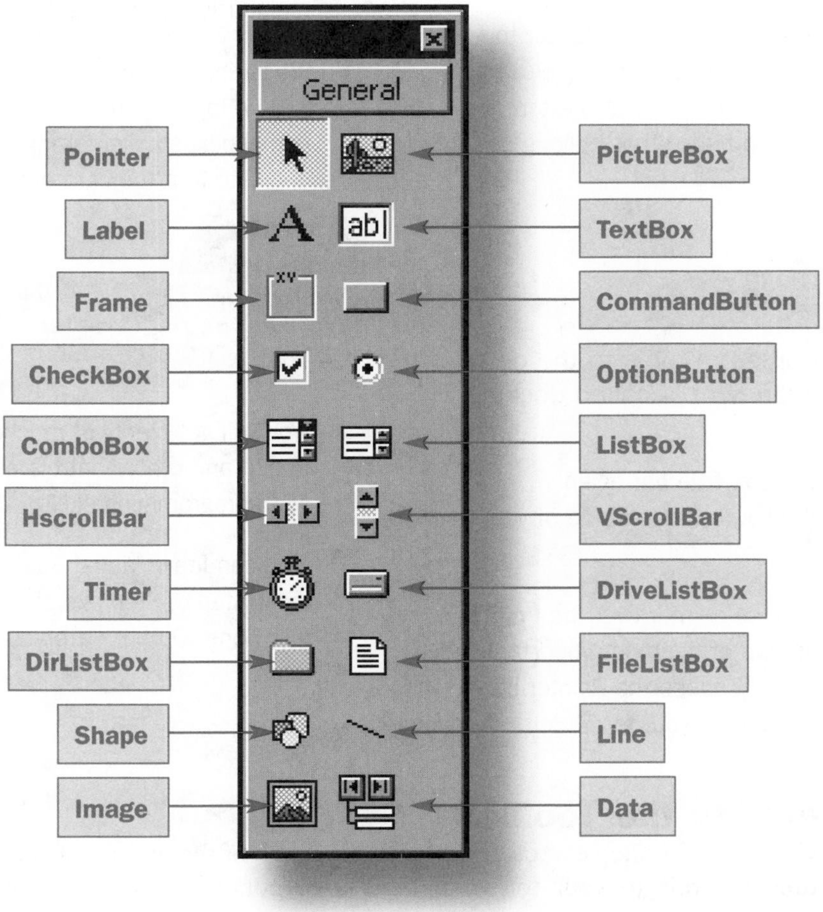

Building Communication Skills

Before starting any project, it is important to make sure that you, the programmer, understand exactly what your client expects from the program. One of the best ways of making this happen is to interview the client or the client's users. Do not assume that just because you think something should be done one way, that the client thinks the same thing.

STEP-BY-STEP 1.4

1. Start Visual Basic and double-click **Standard EXE**.

2. Make sure the toolbox is visible. If it isn't, click the **View** menu and select **Toolbox**. Don't worry if yours doesn't look exactly like the one shown in Figure 1-8. The toolbox can be moved to different locations.

3. Click and drag the **toolbox title bar** to move it around your workspace. Move it near the Standard toolbar at the top of your screen and notice that it elongates. Drop it in place.

Attaching your program tools to the development environment is called docking.

4. Click the **toolbox title bar** again and drag it back to the left side of your screen.

5. Move the mouse pointer over the **Pointer** tool. This is one of the most important tools. You must choose the Pointer before selecting objects on your form.

6. The tool to the right of the Pointer is the **PictureBox**. It is used to add graphics to your forms. These graphics can be decorative or functional in nature. Move the mouse pointer over this tool to view its ToolTip.

7. Click the **Label** tool. Move the mouse pointer over the form. Notice that the pointer is now a crosshair.

8. Click and drag the crosshair to draw a box. A label control appears with eight small boxes called sizing handles to indicate that the control is selected.

You can also double-click a tool in the toolbox and a default size control appears in the center of the form.

You will get plenty of practice working with these and other controls as you refine your programming skills.

9. You can leave Visual Basic open for the next Step-by-Step exercise or exit if you are done. Do not save your work at this time.

Adding Items to the Toolbox

In the previous Step-by-Step exercise you looked at a few of the basic tools in the Visual Basic toolbox for adding controls to your forms. Believe it or not, there are still a large number of components or tools that are available to you. In this next Step-by-Step exercise you add components to your toolbox. Adding a single component may add multiple controls to the toolbox.

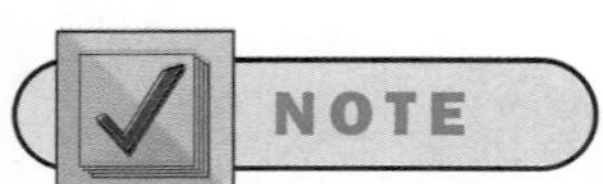

As you add tools, you may find that the toolbox extends beyond the bottom of the screen. Simply resize the toolbox window by dragging the right edge of the window and stretching it until you can see all of the controls.

STEP-BY-STEP 1.5

1. Start Visual Basic, if needed, and double-click **Standard EXE**.
2. Click the **Project** menu and select **Components**.
3. Select the **Controls** tab. Scroll through the selections. Do you recognize any of the programs listed here?
4. Click the check box next to **Acrobat Control for ActiveX** and click **OK**. If you do not have the Acrobat control, choose another one.
5. The Acrobat tool should now be on your toolbox. This control allows you to put files created with the program Adobe Acrobat on your forms.
6. Resize the toolbox, if necessary.
7. Open the **Components** dialog box again and deselect the **Acrobat Control for ActiveX**. This removes the control from the toolbox.
8. Open the **Components** dialog box again and click the **Insertable Objects** tab.
9. Scroll down and select **Microsoft Excel Chart**, then click **OK**. The Chart tool appears in the toolbox.
10. Leave Visual Basic open for the next Step-by-Step exercise, or exit Visual Basic without saving changes if you are done for the day.

Understanding the Project Explorer Window

The Project Explorer window lists all of the forms and modules used in a particular project. This window is provided to help you manage all of the different files for your project (see Figure 1-9). As you have seen in earlier steps, when you open a new project, Visual Basic creates a new project file with the default name Project1. The name appears in the Project Explorer's title bar and List window. The new project contains one form file with the default name Form1. If you do not change the default names, these are the names that will be used when you save a project. In the next Step-by-Step exercise you experiment with how this window works.

FIGURE 1-9
The Project Explorer window

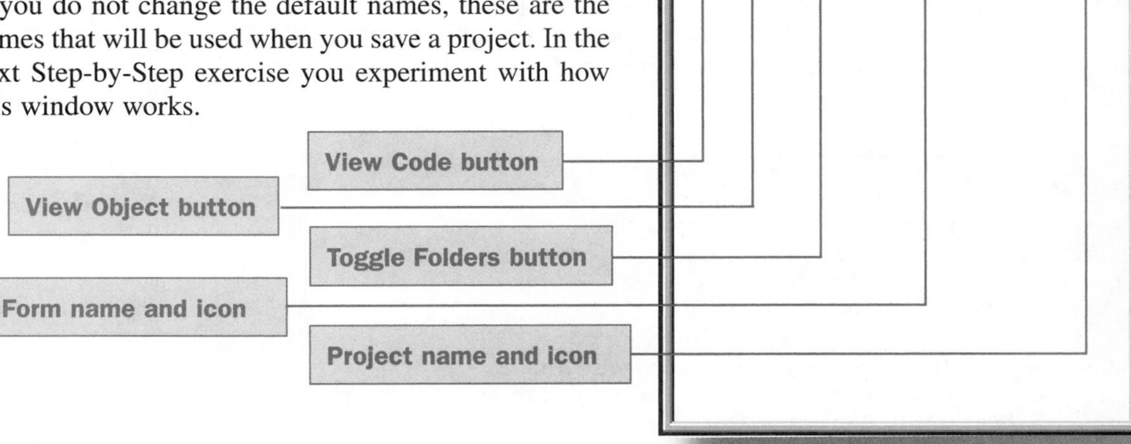

STEP-BY-STEP 1.6

1. Start Visual Basic, if necessary, and double-click **Standard EXE**.

2. Make sure that the Project Explorer window is open. If it is not, click the **View** menu and select it.

3. Move your mouse pointer over the three buttons on the Project Explorer's toolbar. Notice how ToolTips identify the View Code, View Object, and Toggle Folders buttons.

4. Right-click in the **Project Explorer** window and check out the pop-up menu that appears. Notice that it has some of the same commands that you find on the Standard toolbar.

5. Select **Add** and notice that a submenu appears, listing items you can add to your project.

6. Click **Form** and the Add Form dialog box appears. Select **Form** and click **Open**. A second form is added to the program and is listed in the Project Explorer window.

7. Click the **minus** sign to the left of the Forms icon. The branches collapse.

8. Now click the **plus** sign to the left of the Forms icon. The branches expand to reveal all the forms contained within your project.

9. Exit Visual Basic without saving because you need a fresh project for the next Step-by-Step exercise.

Learning the Properties Windows

Each object in Visual Basic has a set of characteristics such as name, color, behavior, size and position, or the state of an object such as enabled or disabled. The Properties window lists the characteristics for the selected form or object. The left column displays the properties associated with the selected object and the right column displays the current setting for that property. These properties are an important part of developing an application. Visual Basic assigns default settings to the properties of each object, but you can change these properties in the Properties window, or you can change them through the code you write (see Figure 1-10). You will do both throughout this text.

FIGURE 1-10
Properties window

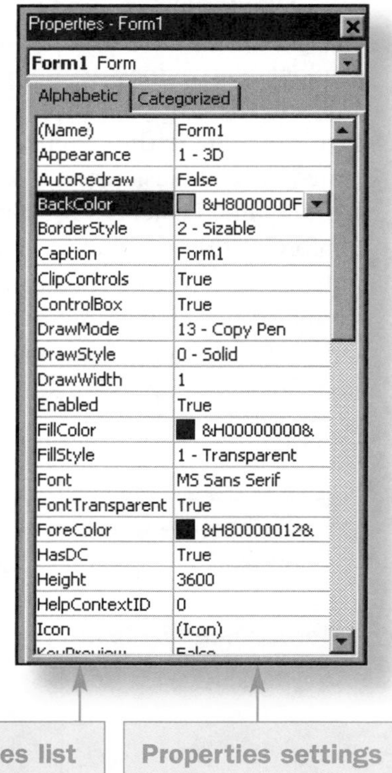

Building Programming Skills

Despite legal battles that have embroiled Microsoft over the last few years, the company has brought a level of continuity to the PC environment. Windows users, as a result, have come to expect certain things when they launch a Windows application. It would be unwise for a programmer who wanted to sell an application to deviate from industry standards.

TIP

An easy way to change a Property setting is to double-click the Property item in the left column. The Property setting is selected and ready to be replaced.

STEP-BY-STEP 1.7

1. Start Visual Basic and double-click **Standard EXE**.

2. Make sure the Properties window is open. If it is not, click the **View** menu and select **Properties**. Make sure the **form** is selected and look at its Properties window. Its title bar displays Properties – Form1.

3. Scroll to the top of the Properties list to find the Name property. Highlight **Form1** and change it to **frmPropertiesCheck**. The Properties title bar now reads Properties - frmPropertiesCheck because you changed the form's Name property.

4. Go to the Caption property. Highlight **Form1** and change it to **Checking Out Properties**. Notice that the Caption property setting displays in the form's title bar.

5. Click the **Categorized** tab, then click the **Alphabetic** tab. You can access the properties either alphabetically or by categories such as Appearance, Font, and Behavior.

6. Click **BackColor**. A list arrow appears in the settings column. If the property has pre-defined settings, a list arrow or ellipsis appears in the settings area. Click the **list arrow**, select the **Palette** tab, and choose a light blue color. The form's background color changes.

7. Exit Visual Basic without saving because you need a fresh project for the next Step-by-Step exercise.

Did You Know?

You can search for employment in Visual Basic Programming on the Internet. Knowledgeable Visual Basic programmers are in great demand by companies worldwide.

Information on Microsoft's Visual Basic can be found at

http://msdn.microsoft.com/vbasic/.

TIP

The properties are listed in alphabetical order with the exception of Name, which is at the top. While each object has its own unique set of properties, every one has a Name property. Visual Basic automatically gives each object a Name when it is created, but the values tend not to be particularly descriptive (for example, Form1). It is a good idea to give each object a more descriptive Name after adding it to the project because you use the object's Name property when writing code.

Computer Ethics

As a programmer, it is important to remember to give credit where credit is due. If you use someone else's work, make sure you have permission to use their work and give them credit for it.

When naming a control, it is recommended that you start the name with a three-letter prefix that helps you identify what kind of control you are referencing. For example, the form in the previous Step-By-Step exercise was called frmPropertiesCheck. The three-letter prefix is .frm. Table 1-1 lists the standard prefixes for commonly used controls.

TABLE 1-1
Standard prefixes for commonly used controls

STANDARD PREFIXES

PREFIX	CONTROL	PREFIX	CONTROL
ani	Animation button	hsb	Horizontal scroll bar
cbo	Combo box	img	Image
ch3	3D Check box	ils	Image list
chk	Check box	lbl	Label
clp	Picture clip	lin	Line
cm3	3D command button	lst	List box
cmd	Command button	mci	Multimedia MCI
ctr	Control (specific type unknown)	mnu	Menu
dat	Data	opt	Option button
dir	Directory list box	pic	Picture box
dlg	Common dialog box	prg	Progress bar
drv	Drive list box	shp	Shape
fil	File list box	sli	Slider
fr3	3D frame	spn	Spin button
fra	Frame	tlb	Toolbar
frm	Form	tmr	Timer
gpb	Group push button	tre	Tree view
gra	Graph	txt	Text box
grd	Grid	vtb	Vertical scroll bar

An object's name must begin with a letter and it cannot exceed 40 characters or use spaces. It must only contain letters, numbers, and the underscore character. By now you should have a pretty good feel for the features and functions that are available to you as you begin to work in the Visual Basic programming environment.

Quick Check 1.b

1. The ___________________ provides easy access to frequently performed commands.
2. Only the ___________________ menu items or buttons can be used.
3. The Visual Basic toolbox is normally located on the ___________________ side of the screen.
4. With the exception of ___________________, properties are listed in alphabetical order.
5. You should use a three letter ___________________ when naming a control.

The Visual Basic Project

A Visual Basic project is composed of all the forms, controls, code, and other items that make up the entire application. In some instances, you may need to create or add what are called *Dynamic Link Libraries* (DLLs). These are sets of routines that are called by an application. They are loaded and linked to the application at run-time. You may also want to add prebuilt components to your application. By using all of the tools available to you, powerful applications can be created quickly and efficiently.

File organization and consistency are important because of the number of items you create and save to design a complete application. As mentioned earlier, projects are typically made up of forms and modules. Because you may end up with several files for one application, it is a good idea to save all of the project files in a unique folder. Let's say you have created a project called Summer Vacation. It is a good approach to create a folder called Summer Vacation and save all relevant files in that folder.

Creating a Form

In Visual Basic you use forms to create the program interface for your users. The form may have buttons, scroll bars, menus, list boxes, and any of the other features that are common to Windows programs. Forms are the main building blocks of an application. You begin by creating the forms, adding the controls, writing the code, testing the application, and then finally using it in its actual setting. Proper planning helps ensure that users will be able to quickly find their way around a program. It is the programmer's responsibility to consider the multitude of users that may access their program and anticipate all of the different options that they may need.

When you start Visual Basic, a default form appears. The following Step-by-Step exercise explores a Visual Basic form.

STEP-BY-STEP 1.8

1. Start Visual Basic and double-click **Standard EXE**.

2. Notice that Visual Basic automatically creates a form with the default name and caption Form1 for the new project.

3. Click the **Form window's** title bar (that says Project 1 – Form1 (Form)) to select the form, and drag it around your screen.

4. Click the **Minimize** button in the upper right-hand corner of the title bar. The form is reduced to an icon. Click the **Icon** to restore the form.

5. Click the **Maximize** button in the upper right-hand corner of the title bar. This maximizes your form and changes the button to a **Restore Window** button. Click the **button** once to restore the form to standard size.

6. Notice the border around the form. Place your mouse pointer on the **border**. When the pointer becomes a double-headed arrow, click and drag to resize your form.

7. Leave Visual Basic open for the next Step-by-Step exercise, or exit without saving changes if you are done for the day.

Saving the Program

This is a good time to learn how to save your project. It is important to save the project files often. Power outages, emergencies, and even simple design mistakes can cause you to lose work. To make saving a form easier, it is a good idea to set the Name property first. The computer will use the Name property as the form's file name if you do not give it a different file name. Remember, the Name property you assign cannot have any spaces or periods in it. Visual Basic saves all of the form's code and objects in one file and the project components in another. This will come in handy in the future as you work on new projects, because you can add existing files to new projects. The file name, a period, and the *file extension* designate files. The file extension lets the program know what type of file it is. See Table 1-2 for a list of common file extensions and their uses in Visual Basic. Knowing the file extensions will make it easier to search for a file. In the next Step-by-Step exercise you name a form and save it.

TABLE 1-2
Common file extensions

FILE EXTENSIONS			
.frm	Forms	.mak	Visual Basic Project in versions 2 and 3
.vbp	Visual Basic Project	.bas	Module

STEP-BY-STEP 1.9

1. Start Visual Basic, if needed, and double-click **Standard EXE**.

2. In the form's Properties window, double-click **Name** to select the default setting Form1.

3. Change the name property to **frmMyFirst**. Then click the **Save Project As** button on the toolbar. The Save File As dialog box opens. Navigate to the **C:** drive (or the drive you are using) and create a new folder called **Lesson01.** Double-click this **folder** to move it to the Save in box.

4. Notice that the dialog box prompts you for the file name of the form first and that the Name property for the form now appears in the File name box with the extension **.frm** added. Change the file name to **MyForm.frm** and click **Save**.

5. The computer now prompts you to save the project. Highlight the file name, key **MyFirst**, and click **Save**. Note that the extension **.vbp** is added automatically to the project's file name.

6. You have just saved your first project. Close the project by clicking **File** and selecting **Remove Project**.

Adding Controls to Forms

The form is mainly a vehicle to present other controls. In this section you will begin to add the essential elements of a useful program. The first one is the label. A label tells the user what something is. Your labels, therefore, should be meaningful. The user cannot change a label while the program is running. There are six properties of a label that you initially need to know: Caption, Name, Alignment, Font, BackColor, and ForeColor. The Caption property appears on the label. The Name property, as with any object's Name, is how the label is referenced in the programming code. The Alignment property determines how the text appears on the label. You have the choice of left justified, right justified, or centered. The Font property allows you to select from a wide variety of fonts. Font features include size, boldface, italic, and underline. The BackColor property refers to the color of the label itself. The ForeColor property sets the color of the Caption text.

In the next Step-by-Step exercise you'll see how easy it is to add label controls to your form and change their properties.

STEP-BY-STEP 1.10

1. Start Visual Basic, if necessary, and click **Cancel**.

2. Open the previously saved **MyFirst** project. There are several ways of doing this. One way is to click the **File** menu. Notice that at the very bottom is a list of the most recent files you have used in Visual Basic. Click **MyFirst.vbp** and the project opens. Other ways include choosing **Open Project** from the **File** menu, clicking the **Recent** tab, and double-clicking **MyFirst.vbp**. Or choose the the **Existing** tab from the Open Project dialog box and navigate to **MyFirst.vbp** by selecting the appropriate drive and folder.

3. The Project Explorer window for MyFirst project appears. If it does not appear, click the **Project Explorer** button on the Standard toolbar.

(continued on next page)

4. If your toolbox is not visible, click the **View** menu and select **Toolbox**.

5. If the form is not displayed, select the **frmMyFirst** form in the Project Explorer window and click the **View Object** button.

6. Select the **Label** tool in the toolbox. Starting in the upper left corner of the form, click inside the form and drag down to the right to draw a Label control. The right edge of the Standard toolbar shows the dimensions and the position of the upper left corner of the object as you draw it on the form.

7. Make sure the label is selected and set the **Name** property to **lblHello.**

8. At this point, the label is pretty dull looking. With the label selected, set the **Caption** property to **Hello World**. Notice that the caption appears in the label, but doesn't really convey the excitement of an enthusiastic hello.

9. Now click the **Font** property box. Notice the ellipsis (. . .) in the button that appears in the **Properties** settings box. Click once on the ellipsis. The Font dialog box appears.

10. Select **Times New Roman** and **20** point size. Click **OK**. Now the enthusiasm of the greeting is conveyed. If needed, drag on a sizing handle to make the label large enough to read the caption.

11. To change the label's text color, select the **ForeColor** property box. Click the **list arrow** to the right. Choose the **Palette** tab and select a shade of **red**.

12. Click **BackColor** and set it to **white** to change the color of the label.

13. Click **Alignment** and select **2-Center** to center the caption in the label.

14. Save the project by clicking the **Save Project** toolbar button.

Quick Check 1.c

1. A Visual Basic project is composed of ____________________, ____________________, and ____________________.

2. DLL stands for ____________________.

3. ____________________ are used to create the program interface for your users.

4. When you start Visual Basic, a ____________________ appears.

5. The file name, a period, and the ____________________ designate files.

Programming an Event

Before you go any further, it is important to understand a bit about Windows messaging and Visual Basic event handling. Messages make Windows applications work. Whenever any user action happens in an application, Windows generates one or more messages that are sent to the application.

The user actions are called events. For example, if the user clicks a command button, Visual Basic sends a Click event. If the Space key is pressed, Visual Basic sends a KeyPress event. If a form is loaded, Visual Basic sends a FormLoad event. There are many different events that you will run into as you program. The programmer has to handle the event by writing code (explicit instructions) on how to handle the user action or event. This code is called an *event procedure* and is written in an object's Code window. This is why Visual Basic is called an *event-driven* programming language: A user triggers the running of a piece of code by clicking an object or pressing a key. Now you'll look at an object's Code window.

STEP-BY-STEP 1.11

1. If necessary, open the **MyFirst** program.

2. Double-click the **form**. This opens the form's Code window.

3. The box at the top left of the Code window is called the Object list box and should contain the word Form because you opened the form's Code window (see Figure 1-11).

FIGURE 1-11
Object list box

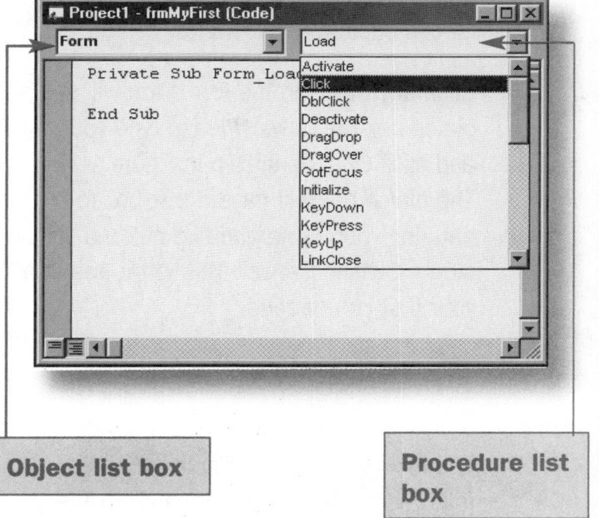

If you click the Object list box, you will see three choices: Form, lblHello, and General. Form and lblHello correspond to the objects that are available to this application at this point. If you were to add additional controls, they would be listed here as well. We will discuss General later in this text.

4. The box at the top right of the Code window is called the Procedure list box. Click the **list arrow** to display the events that correspond to the chosen object. Look them over and then select **Click**.

The following lines appear in the Code window:

```
Private Sub Form_Click()
End Sub
```

5. Press **Tab** and key the lines in **Code Step 5** after Private Sub Form_Click(). You will see the results in the next Step-by-Step exercise.

6. Check your work and save your program. Close the Code window by clicking its **Close** button.

CODE STEP 5

```
strName = InputBox("Please key your name and click OK.")
lblHello.Caption = "Hello " & strName & "."
```

Running and Testing a Visual Basic Program

Testing your program is quite easy to do. There are three buttons on the Standard toolbar for this. They are the Start, Break, and End buttons. Start and End are self-explanatory. Break comes in handy when you want to temporarily stop the program and then start up again at the same point. Before you test your program you should always save your work. You will test the MyFirst application now.

1. If necessary, open the **MyFirst** program.
2. Click the **Start** button from the Standard toolbar. The form displays, showing the label's caption "Hello World."
3. Click anywhere on the form. You will see a dialog box that says "Please type your name and click OK," as shown in Figure 1-12. The dialog box will have a text box for entering your name and two buttons on the side – OK and Cancel. This is the result of your first line of code.
4. Enter **your name** and click **OK** as the prompt requests.
5. The label should now display "Hello," followed by the name you entered. The second line of code you wrote changed the label's Caption setting from "Hello World" to "Hello Your Name."
6. If the program does not work as expected, go back and check that you entered the code exactly as stated. If there is no space between "Hello" and your name, add a space between the "o" and the quotation on the second line of the code.

It doesn't matter right now if you don't understand how the code works. You will get to that later.

7. Click the **End** button to stop the program. Congratulations. You have written your first event procedure in Visual Basic.
8. Exit Visual Basic and save the project if requested.

FIGURE 1-12
TheDialog Box etc.

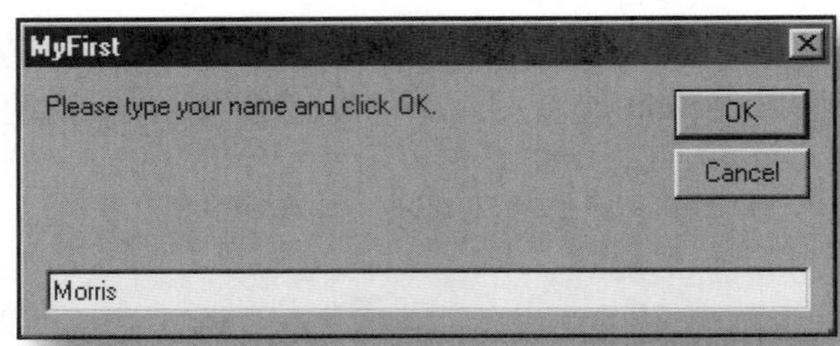

Getting Help in Visual Basic

The Professional and Enterprise Editions of Visual Basic come with a CD containing on-line help. The Help files on this CD can be loaded onto your computer, or accessed via the CD whenever you need them. Help is extensive and there are different ways of using it.

Visual Basic's on-line documentation references almost all aspects of Visual Basic. This includes a language reference, feature information, links to Visual Basic on the Web, and Microsoft Product support services. With it you should be able to find answers to most issues that you run into.

In order to access the on-line help, go to Help, and choose either Contents, Index, or Search, depending on what you want help on. Contents help brings you to a list of topics on Visual Basic, from the basics like building your first form, to the complex like using the new Data Tool and building ActiveX components. This section contains a language reference and examples, including usable code samples. Index help allows you to key in a keyword and lists the matching topics. Search help searches for all instances of an entered word or words in the on-line documentation and lists links to those instances.

One particularly nice feature is referred to as context-sensitive help. Any window, control, object, property, keyword, or error message has context-related help available. To access this help, select the item in question and press F1. This automatically displays Help information about the item.

It is important to remember that none of these items are available without loading the Help files on your computer or without accessing them from the CD. If you are without the CD but do have a connection to the Internet, you can access much of the same information by going to http://msdn.microsoft.com/vbasic/.

One last type of help that doesn't require the CD and that has already been discussed is the ToolTip. If you place your mouse over any object in the Visual Basic window, a ToolTip displays, giving a brief explanation of the object's role. This is particularly helpful when you are learning the toolbox controls.

Summary

- Microsoft Visual Basic is a set of programming tools that allow you to create applications for the Windows operating system.
- Programs in Visual Basic are event-driven.
- The toolbar provides easy access to frequently performed commands.
- The toolbox contains many controls that you can add to your forms. More controls can be added to the toolbox to give you even greater capabilities.
- The Properties window lists the property information for a selected form or object.
- Standard prefixes have been developed for commonly used controls.
- It is important to give all objects descriptive names.
- A Visual Basic project is composed of all the forms, controls, code, and other items that make up an application. Use the Project Explorer to view those components.
- Files are designated by the file name, a period, and the file extension.
- Programs in Windows work based on messages that generate events for the application.
- The three buttons used to run a program are Start, Break, and End.
- To exit Visual Basic, choose Exit from the File menu or click the Close button on the title bar.

LESSON 1 REVIEW QUESTIONS

FILL IN THE BLANKS

Complete each of the following statements by writing your answer in the blank provided.

1. Visual Basic ____________ many routine programming tasks.
2. In an event-driven application, sections of ____________ are executed, depending upon the user's actions.
3. The ____________ toolbar is usually visible when you open a project in Visual Basic.
4. ToolTips can be activated from the ____________ menu.
5. Attaching your toolbox to the development environment is referred to as __________ .
6. The Project Explorer lists all of the ____________ and ____________ used in a project.
7. Except for ____________ , properties are listed in alphabetical order.
8. You should start the name of a control with a ____________.
9. It is important to ____________ your files often in case of power outages.
10. ____________ makes searching for files easier.

WRITTEN QUESTIONS

Write your answers to the following questions.

11. Why is the Name property important?
12. List three properties that can be set in the Properties window.
13. Why should you create a separate folder for each Visual Basic project?
14. Describe the importance of file extensions.
15. What are some common features that users expect to find in a Windows application?
16. Name two things that a programmer must consider when creating a program.
17. Where is the toolbox normally located?
18. What does the Project Explorer window show?
19. List the four types of file extensions that are used in Visual Basic.
20. Describe what the Font dialog box allows you to do.

LESSON 1 APPLICATION PROBLEMS

Level One

THE INFORMATION COLLECTION PROGRAM

Create an application that allows users to enter their name, address, and phone number. Include option buttons at the top of the form for the user to choose Mr., Mrs., or Ms. Insert labels to the left of each text box and use them to describe what the user is to input. Name all of your objects using the appropriate three-letter prefix.

Level Two

THE CONGRATULATIONS PROGRAM

Create an application that contains two command buttons. One should ask the user to click it. Add the following code to that button so that it displays a message when the user clicks it:

```
MsgBox ("Congratulations on your success!")
```

The other should be an exit button. Add the following code so that the program stops when the user clicks the exit button:

```
End
```

Name all objects appropriately.

LESSON 1 PROGRAMMING AT WORK

In this section you will start an application that will be completed over the first three lessons.

On paper, design a program interface for determining the payments for an auto loan. When completed, it will calculate monthly payments based on purchase price, interest rate, and number of months. Keep in mind the following items:

- How do you want the user to enter the information?
- How do you want to present the results to the user?
- What basic commands will make the program more user-friendly (For example, the ability to reset or clear text boxes and a method for exiting the program).

LESSON 2

FORMS

OBJECTIVES

When you complete this lesson, you will be able to:

- Customize the look and feel of a form.
- Develop standard forms that can be reused in other applications.
- Create forms that react to user events like clicking a button and pressing a key.
- Use variables and pass information from one part of the project to another.
- Import graphics to a form.

Estimated Time: 1.5 hours

KEY TERMS

syntax
keyword
End statement
twip
load and unload
assignment statement
variable
constant
data type
modules

The Form

In this lesson you will learn about the basic building block in Visual Basic—the form. In Lesson 1 you learned that a basic form is created when you create a Standard project. This lesson continues to show you how to add controls and code to the forms, allowing you to build more powerful applications.

In the daily life of a programmer, there are certain forms and dialog boxes that are needed on a regular basis—no matter what the application. The earlier programming languages were focused primarily on solving problems—not on making the life of the programmer easier. Modular languages introduced the concept that replacing small sections of code is easier than rewriting an entire program. Visual Basic takes this concept one step further by allowing you to use the same code and forms in several different projects. Wouldn't it be nice if, after just a few months of programming, you had a personal library of forms and the needed code so you didn't have to reinvent the wheel every time you sat down to create an application?

One of the objectives of this lesson is to start creating some of the forms that you will use throughout the text in the applications you create. By planning ahead, you will be able to save yourself a lot of time and aggravation. This means thinking about forms that are reusable or easily adapted to other projects. It is a good idea to keep track of the form name and its current location so that you can import it into your library collection at a later date.

The heart and soul of any Windows application are the forms or user interface. As the programmer, you need to gather information about the user such as:

- What is the best way to present the application?
- What are their needs? (What do they need to see to do their job?)
- How are they accustomed to seeing the information?
- What colors or objects will help them do their job?

Have you ever seen some color combinations on the screen that after a few minutes begin to hurt your eyes? How about a screen that is too "busy" or just has too much information on it to be user-friendly? The list of things that must be considered is quite lengthy.

The Programming Code

All programming languages allow programmers to create applications that input, process, and output information. The standard structure of a program, no matter what language it is written in, is the following:

```
Start program
    Declare the variables you will use to make calculations
    Initialize values
        Get the information
        Process the information
        Show or save the answers
End program
```

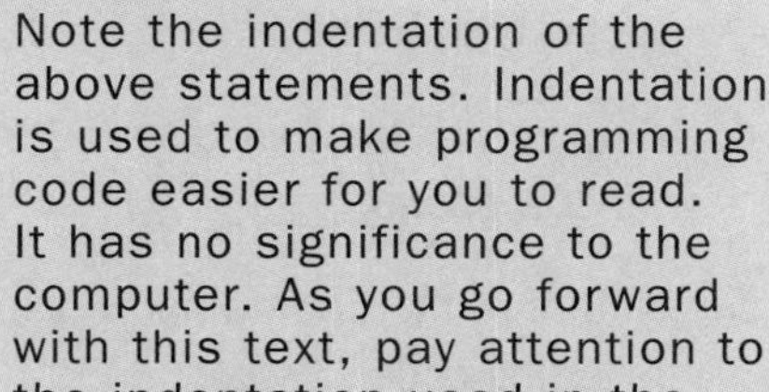

TIP

Note the indentation of the above statements. Indentation is used to make programming code easier for you to read. It has no significance to the computer. As you go forward with this text, pay attention to the indentation used in the Step-by-Step exercises.

As you may have noticed, when you first add a control button to a form, it acts like a light switch without the wires hooked up to it. You can click it on and off, but it doesn't actually do anything. The programming code is what makes it work. While there are a lot of things to learn about programming, you are going to approach programming one control at a time. Many people take for granted that Windows does things for them by the simple click of a button. You, as the programmer, have to be concerned with the code that is behind each of the controls and forms.

The OK and Cancel buttons are two of the most common command buttons used on forms in any application. The OK button typically means you accept what the application tells or asks you and signals the program to continue with what it is doing. The Cancel button typically means do not accept what the application tells or asks you. In the next Step-by-Step exercise you will look at how this works. As you saw when creating the MyFirst project, accessing the Code window is simple. Double-click any object on the form and the Code window for that object opens. You may also access the Code window by clicking the View Code button in the Project Explorer (see Figure 2-1).

Note that when you access the Code window, you see at least one Private Sub and End Sub statement. The Private Sub statement starts a routine that runs the code. Most of your code will be placed in between Private Sub and End Sub commands. Every programming language has a set of rules called *syntax* for building instructions. Each instruction has its own rules or syntax. Most instructions use *keywords*, a word that has special meaning in a programming language. Private and Sub are keywords that indicate the beginning of a local event procedure. Another simple keyword is End. The *End statement* tells Visual Basic to terminate the application.

In the next exercise you will add a command button to a form and set its properties. Then you will open the button's Code window and add the End statement. You'll indent the code under the Private Sub keywords to make the code easier to read.

TIP

Visual Basic makes code easy to follow by color-coding various things. This helps visually organize the code and makes debugging easier.

FIGURE 2-1
View Code button in the Project Explorer window

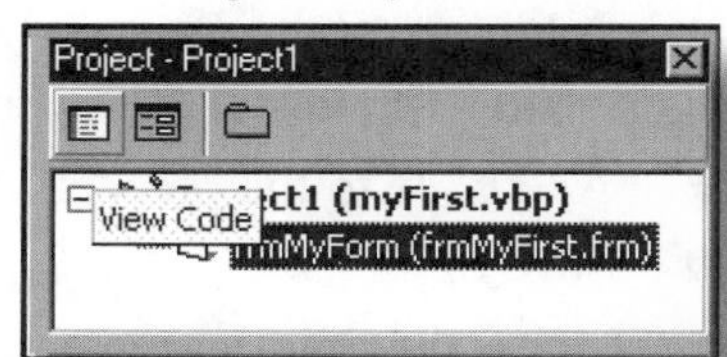

STEP-BY-STEP 2.1

1. Start Visual Basic and double-click **Standard EXE**.

2. Double-click the **CommandButton** tool to add a default size button to the middle of the form. Drag the button to the lower right corner of the form.

3. The default name and caption of this button is Command1. Set the Name property to **cmdExit** and the Caption property to **Exit**.

4. Double-click the **Exit** button. Its Code window opens.

5. Note that the Code window displays the following code:

```
Private Sub cmdExit_Click()
End Sub
```

6. Press **Tab**, key **End** between Private Sub and End Sub, and press **Enter**. You do not have to capitalize the first letter when entering keywords. When you press Enter, Visual Basic does it for you. If it does not change the case, check your spelling. The keyword is probably entered incorrectly.

7. Click the **Start** button on the Standard toolbar or press the **F5** key to run the program.

8. Click the **Exit** button. This causes the application to end. If it does not, check to make sure that you entered **End** correctly under the Private Sub cmdExit _Click statement.

9. There is no need to save this application, so click **File**, select **Remove Project**, and answer **No** to whether you want to save the project.

TIP

If you want to create code for a different object or event, you can use the Object or Procedure list boxes at the top of the Code window to open them.

NOTE

The keyword Private means that this event procedure can only be used within this form. The Sub keyword is an abbreviation for the word subprocedure (block of code). Sub is followed by the name of the control (cmdExit), an underscore (_), the name of the current event (Click), and parentheses.

Creating Simple Forms

You have now created a couple of simple forms, customized them for particular uses, and added various objects. The procedure is fairly simple.

- Start a Standard EXE, which creates a new form.
- Change the form properties as needed.
- Add controls such as text boxes, labels, and command buttons.
- Change the properties of the controls to convey information to the user.
- Add code to the objects.
- Save often.

By following these steps, you can create many useful applications.

In the next four Step-by-Step exercises you will continue to create forms, add controls you have not worked with yet, experiment with different properties, and expand your knowledge about the Visual Basic language.

Quick Check 2.a

1. Early programming languages were focused primarily on ____________________ .
2. The ____________________ and ____________________ buttons are two of the most common command buttons.
3. ____________________ is used to make code easier to read.
4. Double-click any object on the form to access the ____________________ window.
5. The ____________________ statement starts a routine to run the code.
6. Every programming language has a set of rules called ____________________ .

Fixing the Size and Location of a Form

The size and location of the form when it opens can be important, depending upon how you have laid out the application. Instead of using inches, Windows programmers often use the unit *twips* when describing size and location information. A twip is 1/1440 of an inch. You will recall that the areas at the far right of the Standard toolbar show location and size. These are given in terms of twips. The fine grid that shows up in design view is also in twips. This grid does not display when the form is running, but comes in handy when you start laying out objects on your form. If you prefer, there are other units of measure available to you such as inches, millimeters, and points. The unit of measure is selected in the form's ScaleMode property.

If you have the Form Layout window open you can view where the form appears when it runs.

Four new properties of the form that you need to become familiar with are Height, Width, Top, and Left. The values placed in these properties depend upon the unit of measure selected in the ScaleMode property. Height and Width are self-explanatory, with Height being the vertical size and Width being the horizontal size. Top and Left are how Visual Basic positions objects on the screen and in forms. Distance from the upper left corner of the form to an object is how an object's location is defined.

In the next Step-by-Step exercise you will experiment with the Height, Width, Top, and Left Property settings of a form.

Historically Speaking

In the late 1950s and early 1960s, computer scientists developed a way to write a program that would interpret everyday languages into machine language. This is known as the compiler. With the advent of the compiler, programming languages were developed that were far easier for humans to understand.

STEP-BY-STEP 2.2

1. Click **File**, select **New Project**, and double-click **Standard EXE**. Maximize the Project Container window.

2. First you'll experiment with the size of the form. In the Properties window, scroll down to **ScaleMode**. Click the **list arrow** in the settings box to view all the options available. Keep **ScaleMode** set to **1-Twip**.

3. Scroll up to **Height**, change the setting to **3000**, and press **Enter**. Notice that the height of the form becomes shorter.

4. Scroll down to **Width**, change the setting to **1680**, and press **Enter**. This time the form becomes too narrow to read the title bar. Change the width to **5000** and press **Enter**. Notice that the area on the far right of the Standard toolbar now reads **5000** x **3000**.

5. The location of a form when the program is running is based on the location of the upper left-hand corner of the form as compared to the upper left-hand corner of the screen. Scroll to the **Top** property and change the setting to **5000**. Run the program. The form drops toward the bottom of your screen. The coordinates of the location indicator on the inner right of the toolbar also change. Click **End** to stop the program.

6. Next change the value of **Top** to **500** (remember to press **Enter**). Run the program again. The form moves to the top of your screen. Stop the program and change **Top** to **1000**. Run it again and the form moves down a little. Stop the program.

7. To set the horizontal location of the form, you change the **Left** property. Scroll to the **Left** property and change it to **200**. Run the program. The form moves to the left of the screen. Stop the program.

8. Now change the **Left property** to **6000** and run the program. The form moves to the right of your screen. Stop the program.

9. Next change the value of the **Left** property to **2500** and run the program. This value places the form in the center area of the screen. You should now have an idea of how the computer "sees" the location of the object.

10. Stop the program and remove the project without saving.

Some things to consider when you are designing the size and location of forms are:

- What other forms will be open when this form opens?
- Will the user be able to use the other forms?
- Would it be more convenient to allow them to see the other forms?
- Should the user's attention be focused solely on one form?

Remember that your application must communicate with the user. For example, the warning messages that some applications give are particularly useful so the user does not corrupt data or lose their current document. You should send distinct messages to your user when there is a problem or even when a program has terminated successfully. A good programmer anticipates problems. An important aspect of this text will be to help you learn what questions to ask yourself when designing a program.

Creating the About Box Form

Now you are going to create a form that you can use in most of your applications. Another purpose of this text is to help you build your own library of forms and code. The About box is used by numerous applications to give the user information about who created it, what the copyright protection is, and even what version of the program is being used.

When creating a form, it is a good idea to make a list of the features you want on it before you start. Below is a short list of what you will need to do to create the About box form:

- Change the title bar.
- Disable the Minimize and Maximize buttons.
- Add a label to display the name of your company or program.
- Add a label to display your name.
- Add a label to display copyright protection information.
- Add an OK button.
- Add the code for the OK button.

The new properties you will use in this Step-by-Step exercise are a form's MaxButton and MinButton. If the properties are set to True, the buttons display on the title bar. If the properties are set to False, they are disabled and do not display on the title bar. You will also use a new statement, Unload, that is discussed after the Step-by-Step exercise.

STEP-BY-STEP 2.3

1. Click **File**, select **New Project**, and double-click **Standard EXE**. Save the form as **About.frm** and the project as **Library.vbp** in the Lesson02 folder.
2. Maximize the Project container window. Change the Caption property of the form to **About My Program**. The caption displays in the form's title bar.
3. Change the name of the form to **frmAbout**.
4. Scroll down to the **MaxButton** and **MinButton** properties and set them both to **False.** This removes them from the form's title bar.
5. Select the **Label** tool. Draw four labels on the form and place them in a column, as shown in Figure 2-2. Drag the bottom sizing handle to make the form longer.
6. Set the properties of the labels as shown in the table on the next page.
7. Save the application.
8. Click the **CommandButton** tool and add a button to the form centered underneath the labels. Name the button **cmdOK** and change the caption to **OK**.
9. Set the font to **Tahoma**, **8 point**.
10. Double-click the **OK** button to open the Code window.
11. Make sure that the Code window opens for the Click event of the cmdOK button. If not, change the window using the Procedure box. Press **Tab** and enter **Unload Me** between Private Sub cmdOK_Click and End Sub. Close the Code window.

(continued on next page)

You can select multiple controls on the form by holding down the Ctrl key as you click each control. Then you can move all the controls at the same time.

Label	Name	Caption	Width	Height	Font	Forecolor
Label1	**lblProgramInfo**	**My First Program Version 1.0**	**2535**	**735**	**Tahoma, 14 Point**	**Blue**
Label2	**lblCreated**	**Created by: Your name**	**4095**	**375**	**Tahoma, 14 point**	**Black**
Label3	**lblDate**	**Copyright Month Year**	**4095**	**375**	**Tahoma, 14 point**	**Black**
Label4	**lblCopyright**	**Warning: This program is protected by copyright laws and international treaties. Unauthorized reproduction or distribution may lead to severe penalties and will be prosecuted to the maximum extent of the law.**	**3855**	**975**	**Tahoma, 8 point**	**Black**

The recommended fonts may not be available on your computer. If that is the case, choose a font that pleases you.

12. Examine your form and make sure it looks good. Make any changes you think are needed. It should resemble Figure 2-2.

You can easily move a control one grid mark by selecting the control, holding down the Ctrl key, and pressing any of the arrow keys.

13. Save and run the application. Click the **OK** button. Notice that it closes the form.

14. Click **File** and select **Remove Project**. You have just started your own personal library of forms and code!

FIGURE 2-2
The About box

When an application runs, it automatically *loads* the starting form into memory and on the screen; in this case, the frmAbout form. (This form can be referred to as "Me.") The Unload statement removes, or *unloads,* a form from the memory and from the screen.

You have seen how forms are the primary interface, or way of communicating with the user.

Creating an Open File Form

Forms are used in a variety of ways. Another common form is the Open File form. To create one, you will be using three new controls—the Drive list box, the Directory list box, and the File list box. In the next Step-by-Step exercise you will add these three controls and become familiar with their uses. Then you will add some of the needed code.

You can set the value of a property with code. The syntax to set a property is:

```
object.Property = Value
```

Object is the name of the control for which you are setting the property. Property is the name of the property being set and value is the new setting for the property. This type of statement is called an *assignment statement* because the value on the right is being assigned to the object on the left.

TIP

One of the most important things programmers can do is document their code. Internal documentation is the easiest way of accomplishing this. This is called commenting. If you place an apostrophe (') at the beginning of a line, Visual Basic ignores the whole line and you can use it as a comment. As mentioned earlier, Visual Basic color-codes code. It marks comments in green.

STEP-BY-STEP 2.4

1. Click **File**, select **New Project**, and double-click **Standard EXE**. Save the form as **Open.frm** and the project as **FindFile.vbp** in the Lesson02 folder.

2. Change the caption of the form to **Open File** and the name to **frmOpenFile**.

3. Next, find the appropriate tools in the toolbox and add a Drive list box, Directory list box, and File list box, as shown in Figure 2-3. Name the Drive list box **drvMyDrives**, the Directory list box **dirMyDirectories**, and the File list box **filMyFiles**.

(continued on next page)

FIGURE 2-3
The Open File form

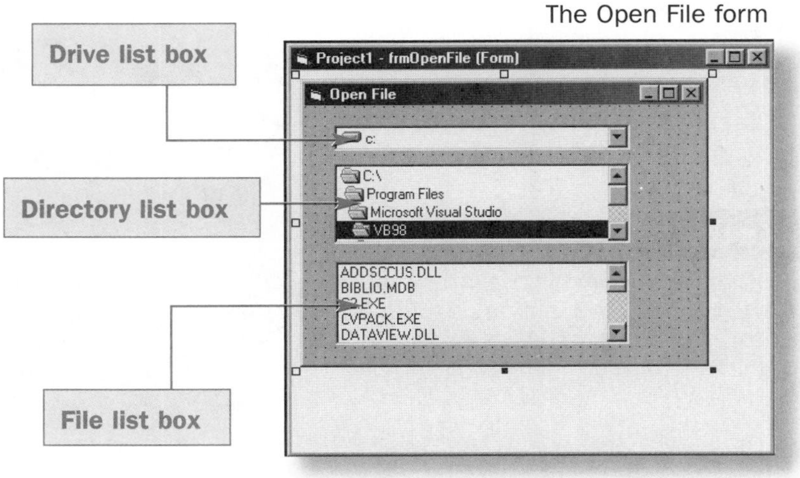

STEP-BY-STEP 2.4 CONTINUED

4. Save the project.

5. Run the program to see how the objects behave. Notice that the Drive list box allows the user to choose drives, and the Directory list box allows the user to choose directories (see Figure 2-4), but they are not linked to each other. You will add code to make this happen. Stop the program.

6. When the user chooses a drive, a Change event is triggered. So you need to add the code to the Drive list box's Change procedure. Double-click the **Drive list box** control to open the Code window.

7. Notice that the event procedure is labeled drvMyDrives_Change(?). First add an internal comment. Then add the code. Enter the code in **Code Step 7**, shown below.

   After you key dirMyDirectories and the . (period), a listing of the control's properties and methods appear. (A method is a predefined procedure.) You can either key Path or Select path and press Tab to enter the property.

8. If the directory changes, the files in the File list box should also change. Click the **Object box list arrow** and select **dirMyDirectories**. Enter the code and comment in **Code Step 8**, shown below.

9. Save your work and run the program. Change drives and directories and check that the program works as you expect. Later on you will add error handlers to deal with situations such as when a floppy disk is not in the drive.

10. Stop the program and remove the project.

CODE STEP 7

```
'Set the directory box path equal to the drive box path
dirMyDirectories.Path = drvMyDrives.Drive
```

CODE STEP 8

```
'Set the file list box path equal to the directory path
filMyFiles.Path = dirMyDirectories.Path
```

? Did You Know?

FORTRAN and COBOL were two of the first high-level or third generation languages created. FORTRAN was created almost exclusively for use by engineers and scientists. COBOL was created for the business world. Updated versions of both of these languages are still in use today.

Quick Check 2.b

1. The ____________________ gives the user information about who created the program.
2. When an application runs, it automatically ____________________ the starting form.
3. ____________________ are the primary interface with the user.
4. Instead of using inches, programmers often use the unit ____________________ .
5. The computer ignores any line of code that has an ____________________ placed in front of it.
6. You use an ____________________ to assign the value on the right to the object on the left.

More Controls

The next controls you will use are check boxes and option buttons. The Step-by-Step exercise that follows shows the difference between the two controls.

STEP-BY-STEP 2.5

1. Click **File**, select **New Project**, and double-click **Standard EXE**. Save the form and project as **Choices**.
2. Change the form caption to **Choices** and the name to **frmChoices**.
3. Select the **CheckBox** tool and draw three check boxes in a column on the left of the form. Use Figure 2-4 as a guide for placing the controls.
4. Set the Properties of the check boxes to the following:

CHECK BOX	NAME	CAPTION
Check1	chkPickles	Pickles
Check2	chkOnions	Onions
Check3	chkTomatoes	Tomatoes

5. Click the **Label** tool and add a label above the check boxes.
6. Change the Caption to **I want the following on my sandwich** and name it **lblChoices**.
7. Using the **OptionButton** tool, add three option buttons and place them in a column next to the check boxes.
8. Set the Properties of the option buttons to the following:

(continued on next page)

FIGURE 2-4
Unlinked Drive list and Directory list boxes

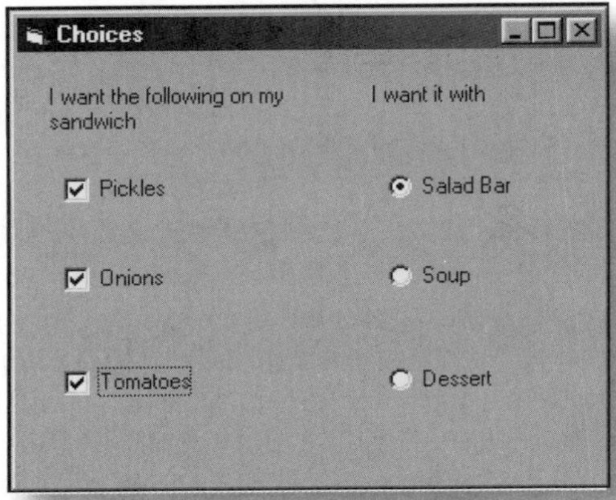

OPTION BUTTON	NAME	CAPTION
Option1	optSaladBar	Salad Bar
Option2	optSoup	Soup
Option3	optDessert	Dessert

9. Place a label above the option buttons, set the Caption to **I want it with**, and set the Name to **lblSides**.

10. Save and run the program. Click to select several of the check boxes. Now click several of the option buttons. Note that check boxes allow you to select any number of them. The option buttons, on the other hand, only allow one to be selected at a time. When you need to have more than one group of option buttons, you must put each group in a Frame control. This way, each option button group is mutually exclusive.

11. Stop and remove the program.

Unauthorized copying of software is considered stealing. It is illegal in many countries and people and corporations have been prosecuted and fired for "bootlegging" software.

Variables and Constants

Up to this point, the code that you have written has only stored data in properties of controls. In this section you use *variables* and *constants*, which allow you to temporarily store data in memory locations that can be used throughout your application.

A *variable* is a temporary storage location for data used in your application. Each variable has a name and a data type. The value of each variable, as the name implies, varies depending on different situations. For example, you can assign user input from a text box in a variable and use it to do calculations. Using variables like this also makes your code more efficient because data stored as a variable can be processed many times faster than data stored in the property of an object.

The value of a *constant*, on the other hand, remains the same. Constants are useful if you have a value that is used over and over, or if the code contains a number that is difficult to remember, such as the value of Pi. The use of constants makes it easier to read the code and also makes it easier to maintain the code.

Declaring Variables and Constants

Before you can use a variable or constant, you should declare it. Declaring a variable causes Visual Basic to reserve a spot in memory for the value of the variable. Visual Basic does not require that you declare your variables before you use them, but it is recommended that you do so. In fact, there is a line of code that can be put at the beginning of your program that causes Visual Basic to require you to declare all variables. The line is Option Explicit. It is recommended that you place this line in the General section of your code for every program.

You may wonder why it is important to declare your variables. If you declare them ahead of time, it reduces the chance of errors through misspellings. For example, if, when using Option Explicit, you declare the variable strUserName in the beginning of your application and later misspell this as strUseName, Visual Basic flags this as an undeclared variable, alerting you to the fact that you are not referencing the correct variable.

TIP

To set Visual Basic to force you to declare all variables, select "Require Variable Declaration" in the Editor tab under Tools-Options.

You declare a variable with the Dim statement. Dim stands for dimension, and this statement is usually found at the beginning of an event procedure. Declaring a variable reserves room in memory for the variable. The syntax of the Dim statement is:

```
Dim variablename [As data type]
```

The *data type* determines the type of data the variable can store. Table 2-1 gives a list of the types of variables you will use most often.

Specifying the data type is not mandatory, but it is a good practice to get into. By identifying the data type when declaring the variable, Visual Basic knows how much memory to set aside for the variable. Keep in mind that variables do not have to be numbers; they can also be what are called strings, which use alphanumeric characters. "In the state of" and "in your mind" are examples of strings, as is "$100.00." Notice that strings are in quotes. This helps the computer distinguish strings from commands.

TABLE 2-1
Data types

DATA TYPES

DATA TYPE	STORES	RANGE OF VALUES
Byte	Binary numbers	numbers 0 to 255
Boolean	Logical values	True or False
Integer	Integers	-32,768 to 32,767
Long	Integers	-2,147,483,648 to 2,147,483,647
Single	Floating Point numbers	Good to six decimal places in the range of E38 to E-45
Double	Floating Point numbers	Good to fifteen decimal places in the range of E308 to E-324
Currency	Numbers with up to 15 digits to the left of the decimal and 4 to the right of the decimal	± 922,337,203,685,477.5808
Date	Date and time	January 1, 100 to December 31, 9999
String	Text information	0 to approximately 65,400 characters

A few of these data types warrant an explanation. In declaring numbers, a programmer is typically concerned with the amount of storage space a number requires. The numbers that can be stored as a byte only need 8 bits of memory to be stored. A bit is a binary digit, 0 or 1. The Integer data type represents numbers that have no fractional portion, so they are whole numbers only. For example 1, 2, and 327 are integers. The number 238.58 is not an integer because it has a fractional portion. Notice that the Long data type holds larger values. That is because it uses 4 bytes of memory to the Integer's 2 bytes. The Single data type also uses 4 bytes of memory and is accurate to 6 decimal places. The Double data type uses 8 bytes of storage and is accurate to 15 decimal places. Currency uses 8 bytes of storage space. The String data type can store data that is comprised of the alphabet, dashes, or non-numeric characters. A good example of this is the Social Security Number 000-12-1111. If you do not assign a data type when declaring a variable, Visual Basic assigns it the Variant data type. The Variant data type can store different data types, so Visual Basic makes it the appropriate data type at run time. This is good when the data type is not known, but is less efficient than declaring the appropriate data type.

Assigning names to variables and constants takes a little consideration. Typically, you should select a name that is meaningful but not too long. It is helpful if you start the variable name with a three-letter prefix that identifies the data type; for example, str for String data type and int for Integer data type. You should not include spaces in the names of your variables or constants. Table 2-2 on the following page gives you a list of variable naming conventions.

When you declare a variable using one of the numeric data types, Visual Basic initializes it to the number 0 (zero). Visual Basic initializes String and Variant data types to blanks. You can use an assignment statement to store data in a variable.

You create a constant with Visual Basic's Const Statement. The syntax is:

```
Const constname [As datatype] = expressions
```

The rules for naming constants are the same as for variables except that you precede the constant's name with the prefix "con." Unlike variables, constants can't be changed while the program is running.

Building Programming Skills

Before you write the code, it is helpful to start by writing on paper what it is you want to accomplish. First, write what you want to accomplish in sentences. Then, change the sentences into short statements that use some of the commands you will be using, but do not worry about syntax. For example, if you wanted to write a program to decide if you should wear a jacket to work, you might start by thinking through the program like this:

```
    Check the temperature
        If it is warmer than 60 degrees, don't bring a jacket
        If it is colder than 60 degrees, bring a jacket
```

This could then be written as:

```
    Check the temperature
    If warmer than 60 degrees then
        Don't bring a jacket
    Otherwise
        Bring a jacket
```

This can easily be turned into the proper syntax for your program.

TABLE 2-2
Variable naming conventions

DATA TYPE PREFIX		
DATA TYPE	**PREFIX**	**EXAMPLE**
Boolean	bln	blnMyBooleanVariable
Byte	byt	bytMyByte
Collection object	col	colMyCollection
Currency	cur	curMyCurrency
Date(Time)	dtm	dtmMyDate
Double	dbl	dblMyDouble
Error	err	errMyError
Integer	int	intMyInteger
Long	lng	lngMyLong
Object	obj	objMyObject
Single	sng	sngMySingle
String	str	strMyString
User-defined type	udt	udtMyUDT
Variant	vnt	vntMyVariant

Building Communication Skills

In this lesson you started using the apostrophe ' to designate a comment line. When the computer reads a line of code that starts with an apostrophe, it ignores that line. Comments are important for documenting what is done in the code and why. Well-commented code is easier for people new to the project to follow, and also makes it easier for you as the programmer to recall what you were doing when you wrote a certain line of code.

STEP-BY-STEP 2.6

1. Click **File**, Select **New Project**, and double-click **Standard EXE**. Save the form and project as **UserInfo** in the Lesson02 folder.

2. Change the caption of the form to **Gathering User Information** and name it **frmUserInfo** (see Figure 2-5).

3. Add one label and one command button to the form.

4. Name the label **lblGreeting** and delete the text in the Caption property so that it is blank. Set the font property to **14** points.

5. Name the command button **cmdExit** and change the caption to **Exit**.

6. Double-click the **form** to open the Code window. Using the **Object box list arrow** at the top of the Code window, choose **(General)**. Enter the following line at the very top of the Code window:

```
Option Explicit
```

7. Again, using the **Object box list arrow**, choose **Form**. Choose **Load** from the **Procedure box list**. Press **Tab** and add the code in **Code Step 7** below **Private Sub Form_Load**.

8. Open the cmdExit Click event Code window. Add the following code below **Sub cmdExit_Click**:

```
End
```

9. Save and run the program. Enter **your name** when requested and click **OK**. What happens? When you start the program, the form is loaded and the Form Load code is executed. First, the Dim statement sets aside space in memory for a variable called strUserName with the String data type. Next, the InputBox function displays a dialog box to gather information. The InputBox function is discussed in detail later in this book. For now, you only need to know that when the user clicks OK, Visual Basic assigns the value of the Input Box to the variable on the left-hand side of the statement. Therefore, if you entered "Jane Doe," strUserName is now equal to "Jane Doe." Visual Basic stores this in the memory slot reserved earlier. The final line sets the Caption property of the label lblGreeting to "Welcome " and the value of strUserName. The addition of these two items is called concatenation and is also addressed in future lessons.

FIGURE 2-5
Gathering User Information form

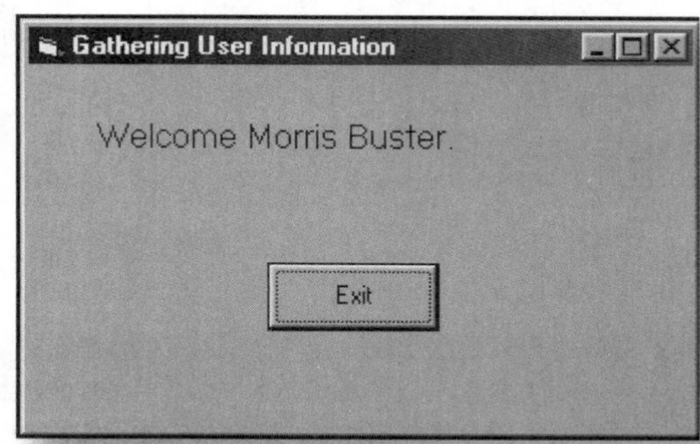

10. Click the **Exit** button to stop the program and remove the project.

CODE STEP 7

```
Dim strUserName As String
    strUserName = InputBox("Please enter your full name.")
    lblGreeting.Caption = "Welcome " & strUserName & "."
```

The Scope of Variables and Constants

The scope of variables and constants basically describes the lifetime of a variable, and what parts of the program are aware of each variable or constant. Setting scope for variables and constants works the same way. The variables you have declared so far have been local or procedure-level variables. These variables are only seen by the procedure in which they are declared. When the control's event procedure ends, Visual Basic removes the local variable from memory.

You can increase the scope of a variable by declaring it in the form's General Declarations section. All the procedures in that form can use variables declared in the General Declarations section, so they are called form-level variables. Form-level variables stay in memory until the application ends.

Code in Visual Basic is stored in *modules*. Up to this point, you have been working with form modules, which have the file extension .frm. Standard (basic) modules (file extension .bas) contain only code, functions, and procedures, and are where variables that are seen by more than just one form are declared. You use the Public statement to declare a variable in the General Declarations section of a Standard module. These variables are called global variables. You create a Standard module in the following Step-by-Step exercise.

STEP-BY-STEP 2.7

1. Click **File**, select **New Project**, and double-click **Standard EXE**. Do not save yet.

2. In the Project Explorer window, right-click **Project1**, point to **Add**, and choose **Module**. Click **Open** to add a new module. (This can also be done from the Project menu.) Note that the module's icon is different from the form's icon, that the module's only property is Name, and that adding the module automatically opens a Code window.

3. Name the module **modMyModule**.

4. Save the module as **MyModule.bas**, the form as **MyModule.frm**, and the project as **Module.vbp**. Leave the project open for the next Step-by-Step exercise.

INTERNET

There are many sites on the Internet that offer free and inexpensive controls that you can add to your Visual Basic applications. Before creating your own controls, you may want to see what is already available to you. There is no sense in reinventing the wheel.

Private and Public Variables

Private variables are variables that are only visible to the module in which they are declared. If your program uses more than one module, or, for example, a form and a standard module, the variables are only seen by the standard module. These are declared using the Private statement in the declaration section at the top of a module as follows:

```
Private strMyPrivateVariable as String
```

At the module level there is no difference in behavior between Private and Dim. However, it is recommended that you use Private in order to easily differentiate between procedure-level variables and module-level variables.

Public or global variables are available to all modules. They are declared using the Public statement in the declaration section at the top of a module as follows:

```
Public strMyPublicVariable as String
```

Public variables can only be declared in the declaration section of the code. You cannot declare public variables in a procedure.

STEP-BY-STEP 2.8

1. Open the **Module.vbp** project created in the previous Step-by-Step exercise, if necessary.

2. Add a label to the top of the form. Name the label **lblDisplay** and delete **Label1** from its Caption property so that nothing is displayed.

3. Add two command buttons to the form. Place them beneath the label. Name the first button **cmdGetName** and change its caption to **Get Name.** Name the second button **cmdDisplayName** and change its caption to **Display Name.** Double-click the **Get Name** button to open the Code window. In **Private Sub cmdGetName_Click**, press **Tab** and add the code in **Code Step 3**.

4. Click the **Object box list arrow** and select **(General)**. Add the following line of code to the top of the Code window (the General Declarations section) to force the declaration of variables:

   ```
   Option Explicit
   ```

5. Click the **Object box list arrow** and select the **cmdDisplayName_Click** event. Press **Tab** and add the code in **Code Step 5** to **cmdDisplayName_Click**.

6. Save the program and run it. Click the **Get Name** button, enter your name, and click **OK**. Your name is displayed in the message box. Click **OK**. Now click the **Display Name** button. What happened and

CODE STEP 3

```
Dim strName As String
    strName = InputBox("Please enter your name and click OK.")
    MsgBox "The name entered = " & strName & "."
```

CODE STEP 5

```
lblDisplay.Caption = "The strName variable = " & strName & "."
```

why? Click **OK** for the error message and stop the program.

When you enter your name in the input box, Visual Basic stores the entry in the local variable strName, displays it in the message box, then removes it from memory when the event procedure finishes. When you click the Display Name button, Visual Basic no longer knows about strName. This is because you changed procedures. How can you fix this? Try declaring strName in the cmdDisplayName_Click procedure to see what happens.

7. Add the following line to the cmdDisplayName_Click procedure above the lblDisplay.Caption code you added earlier:

```
Dim strName as String
```

Save and run the program. Click **Get Name**, enter **your name**, and click **OK**. Your name displays in the message box. Click **OK**. Now click **Display Name**. What happens and why? When you declared strName in the cmdDisplayName_Click procedure, Visual Basic put aside a new segment of memory for a variable called strName. This chunk of memory contains nothing at the moment. Visual Basic does not see the previously filled chunk of memory called strName stored during the cmdGetName_Click procedure.

8. Stop the program and try one more thing. Double-click the **Display Name** button and delete the line **Dim strName as String**. Delete this line from **cmdGetName_Click** as well.

9. Double-click **modMyModule** in the Project Explorer window to open the modMyModule Code window. Enter the following code at the top of this window:

```
Option Explicit
Public strName As String
```

10. Save the program and run it. Click the **Get Name** button and enter **your name**. Click the **Display Name** button. Your name is displayed on the label because you used a global variable.

11. Stop the program and remove the project.

You can achieve the same result by placing the code in the General Declarations section of the form module because all the procedures are in the same form module.

Quick Check 2.c

1. The __________ determines the type of data a variable can store.
2. A variable is a temporary ______________ location for data used in applications.
3. Before you use a _____________, you should declare it.
4. An ____________ data type combines numbers with other types of characters.
5. Code in Visual Basic is stored in _______________.

Adding Graphics to a Form

Graphics are what make GUIs so much fun to use. The idea that a picture speaks a thousand words is true even in this medium. Graphics can be used as a background for a form, as separate objects, or on other objects such as buttons. You can use either the Image control or the PictureBox control to add a graphic to a form. The Image control displays bitmaps, icons, metafiles, enhanced metafiles, JPEGs, or GIF. The PictureBox control can display the same files, and can also be used as a container for more than one object, including groups of option buttons. The Image control requires less resources than the PictureBox and redraws faster, but the PictureBox control has more properties to work with. Probably the most common use of graphics is to display company logos and symbols.

A large variety of icon and graphic files ship with Visual Basic and are located in its folder. In addition to importing an existing graphic, you can draw your own creation using the Shape and Line controls that come with Visual Basic or create a file in a graphics package and then import it. The most important thing to remember is that the graphic should convey a message to your user. Whether you want the form to just look nice or to evoke a response, the selected graphic should fit the situation. For example, a picture of a check and money bag might go well with a financial application.

Importing

Importing graphics is very easy. You simply draw a PictureBox or Image control the desired size and set the Picture property of the object to the file name and path of the graphic. If you want the Image control to automatically change size to fit the graphic, set the Stretch property to False. To accomplish the same thing with a PictureBox control, set the Autosize property to True. Since Picture is a property, the graphic can be changed during run time using code. In the next Step-by-Step exercise you'll see how simple importing a graphic is.

STEP-BY-STEP 2.9

1. Start Visual Basic and double-click **Standard EXE.** Save the form and project as **Messages**.
2. Change the Name of the form to **frmMessages** and its Caption to **The Graphics Program**.
3. Double-click the **Image** tool to add an image control to the form and name it **imgPhone**. Make sure its **Stretch** property is set to **False**.
4. Click the **Picture** property and click the **ellipsis** that appears.
5. Navigate to the **Lesson02** folder from the data disk and double-click **phone.bmp.** The graphic appears and the control changes sizes to fit it. Move the control to the left side of the form.
6. Double-click the form using the **PictureBox** tool to add a picture control and name it **picNotebook**. Set the **AutoSize** property to **True.** Click the **Picture** property and select the file **notebook.bmp** (also in the Lesson02 folder). The graphic appears and the control changes size to fit it. Move the control to the right side of the form.
7. Notice the difference in appearance between the two. Compare their Property lists.

8. Save and run the program.

9. Stop the program. Leave the project open for the next Step-by-Step exercise.

Attaching Code to a Graphic

A graphic can be used to perform various functions other than making the forms visually pleasing. As with all other objects, you need to plan the graphic's function. In the following Step-by-Step exercise, clicking the phone graphic displays a message to the user.

STEP-BY-STEP 2.10

1. If necessary, open the **Message.vbp** project.

2. Double-click the **imgPhone** image.

3. Press **Tab** and add the following code to the imgPhone_Click event:

```
MsgBox ("Ring!! Ring!!")
```

4. Save and run the program. Click the **phone graphic** and click **OK**.

5. Stop the program. Exit Visual Basic if you are done.

Summary

The basic elements of forms can be customized to fit their function. Title bars, Minimize/Maximize buttons, command buttons, etc., can be altered or in some cases, removed, depending on the needs of the programmer.

- Objects such as labels and text boxes are added to a form to give instructions to the user, retrieve information from the user, or for aesthetic reasons.
- The Properties window allows you to change an object's property settings. The color, caption, font type and size, and object size are changed with Property settings. Properties of objects can also be changed at run time with programming code.
- Many properties use True or False settings to determine if they can be used at run time. These settings can also be altered later with programming code.
- The programming code is what actually gives instructions to the computer to perform calculations, move objects, change properties, and print reports. In Visual Basic, programming code is typically associated with an object and is triggered by user events.
- Size and location of forms can be set by the programmer. Twips are the common unit of measurement used. A twip measures 1/1440 of an inch. The ScaleMode property allows you to set the unit of measurement to inches or centimeters. The size of an object is set by the Height and Width properties of the object, while the location is set by the Top and Left properties.

- Variables and constants should be declared before using them. A variable is declared by using the Dim statement. A constant is declared using the Const statement.
- Variables and constants have set lifetimes or scope. The scope is determined by where the variable or constant is declared.
- Internal documentation is used to explain in the programming code why something was done. Internal documentation is important for both the original programmer and the person who may have to make alterations to it later.
- The PictureBox and Image controls allow you to add graphics to a form.

LESSON 2 REVIEW QUESTIONS

TRUE/FALSE

Circle the T if the statement is true. Circle the F if it is false.

T F **1.** Indentation is used to make programming code easier to read.

T F **2.** The OK and Standard buttons are found on most forms.

T F **3.** The About box gives users information about who created the program.

T F **4.** Twips is the command used to end a program.

T F **5.** The Open File form is one of the most common forms.

T F **6.** The computer ignores any comment with a " placed in front of it.

T F **7.** Keywords have special meaning in a programming language.

T F **8.** A variable is a temporary storage location for data used in applications.

T F **9.** Code in Visual Basic is stored in modules.

WRITTEN QUESTIONS

Write your answers to the following questions.

10. Describe what is meant by the scope of a variable.

11. Explain why you indent some lines of code differently than others.

12. Describe the use of the About box.

13. Why are labels on forms important?

14. What are some of the things you should consider when deciding where a form should be when it opens?

15. What is an assignment statement?

16. Describe the use of internal documentation.

17. Describe the difference between a check box and an option button.

18. What are some things to consider when naming variables?

19. Why are graphics used so extensively in the Windows environment?

LESSON 2 APPLICATION PROBLEMS

Level One

THE RED CIRCLE PROGRAM

Create a project with a circle and two command buttons. When the user clicks one button, the color of the circle changes from black to red, and when the user clicks the other button, the color changes from red back to black. Use the Shape tool (prefix—shp) to create the circle. Change its Shape property to Circle and its FillStyle property to Solid. Remember that the statement for changing a property value of an object is ObjectName.PropertyName = Value. Set the shape's color by changing its FillColor property. Hint: You can set the value to the intrinsic constant vbRed instead of using the hexidecimal value for red. Use the Object Browser or the Help System to find names of the other Color constants.

Level Two

THE CHOICES PROGRAM

Create an application that lets the user choose only one of the following: Turkey, Ham, Roast Beef, or Veggie Sandwich, as well as any or all of the following options: Lettuce, Tomato, Pickles, Mustard, Mayonaise, Oil and Vinegar, and Salt and Pepper.

LESSON 2 PROGRAMMING AT WORK

Using the design that you created in Lesson 1, create a form with the necessary objects on it. Include a button that the user can click to exit the application.

LESSON 3

MENUS AND MDIs

OBJECTIVES

When you complete this lesson, you will be able to:

- Design a menu bar with menus and submenus.
- Create an operational application.
- Plan and document an application.
- Add forms from other projects.
- Use MDI forms.

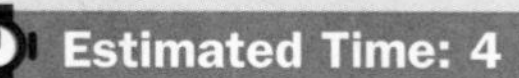

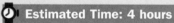

Estimated Time: 4 hours

KEY TERMS

access keys

shortcut keys

separator bar

Menu Editor

Multiple Document Interface (MDI)

personal library

cascade

tile

In this lesson you will learn about two items familiar to Windows users: menus and Multiple Document Interfaces. While you will find that menus are included in most applications, *MDIs* will be used only on occasion. When used properly, they improve the usability of your applications.

Menus are a common Windows tool that makes it easy to access commonly used commands. Imagine a Windows application with no menu bar. You would have to memorize a large number of key combinations and commands. This would drive most users to sheer frustration. Therefore, menus are an important part of most Windows applications. The menu bar is found at the top of the application window right under the title bar. Fortunately, in Visual Basic there is a tool called the Menu Editor that allows you to create menus quickly and easily. In this lesson you will learn not only how to create menus, but also how to plan menus. You should always start by asking critical questions such as:

- What commands and options do users need to access?
- In what order do they need to access them?
- What forms are required to handle their need?
- What information needs to be included in those forms?
- Where will this information come from?
- Do the forms need to transfer information elsewhere?

Planning is the most important stage of programming. Once the initial design is done, the rest should fall into place.

Basic Elements of a Menu

What exactly are the basic elements of a menu? Menus are made up of the menu bar, menu titles, menu commands, submenu titles, and submenu commands. Menu titles appear on the menu bar at the top of the form. When you click a menu title, its menu opens and displays a list of menu commands or submenu titles. Menu items usually have associated *access keys* that allow the user to quickly access them through the keyboard. And often menu items also have *shortcut key* combinations. Before creating your menu, it is a good idea to make a list of the forms that you will be using in your application. This will help you determine what menu commands will be needed in your application and with which forms they will be associated. Also, you should determine which menu commands logically belong together so that you can design menu groups. You should group menu items based on function. For example, it makes sense to group the commands Cut, Copy, and Paste together because they are all related to editing. *Separator bars*, thin lines that group like commands, are commonly used to show this type of relationship. But don't worry if you decide to make changes along the way. You will find that it is as easy to edit a menu as it is to create one.

The following is a list of basic conventions for creating Windows menus:

- Start all menu titles and menu commands with a capital letter.
- File and Edit are usually the first menu titles on a menu bar and Help is usually the last one.
- Use short, specific captions, preferably no more than two words each.
- Start the names of all menu items with the three-letter prefix "mnu."

Now that you have an idea of what makes up a menu, let's explore the Menu Editor.

The Menu Editor

The *Menu Editor* is a powerful graphical tool that manages menus in your program, making it easy to create new menu controls and edit existing ones. The Menu Editor can be accessed through the Tools menu. You can also open it using the shortcut key combination Ctrl+E or the Menu Editor button on the Standard toolbar. Figure 3-1 shows the Menu Editor and points out some of the key features. The top portion of the Menu Editor dialog box is where you set the properties of the menu control. At the bottom of the dialog box is a list box that displays the menu controls as you create them. In the middle are seven buttons that allow you to edit the menu controls. In the following four Step-by-Step exercises you will build a menu as you tour the Menu Editor dialog box.

? Did You Know?

In the early days of computers, the industry almost died because of a lack of programmers? The late 1950s and early 1960s programmers used assembly language, which is the obscure code-like language one level above machine language, or binary. It quickly became apparent that if something did not happen, the industry was doomed. To fill this need, high-level languages, more easily understood by humans than computers, were developed.

FIGURE 3-1
Visual Basic Menu Editor dialog box

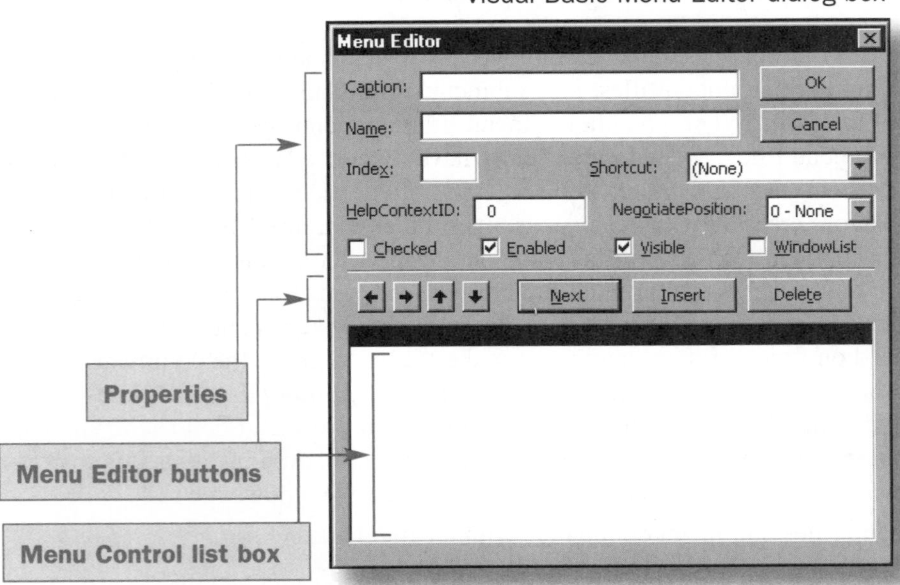

STEP-BY-STEP 3.1

1. Start Visual Basic and double-click **Standard EXE**. Save the form and project as **FrstMenu** in the Lesson03 folder.

2. Select **Tools** | **Menu Editor** or press **Ctrl+E**.

3. Enter **File** in the Caption box. Note that the caption also appears in the Menu Control list box. The caption is the menu title that appears in the menu bar.

4. Enter **mnuFile** in the Name box. This is the name of the menu control and is used to access it when writing code. You are required to name every menu item, even if you are not going to access it through code.

5. Click the **Next** button. This clears the property boxes so that you can add a new menu control.

6. In the Caption box, key **Edit** and name the control **mnuEdit**.

7. Click **OK** to exit the Menu Editor and view your menu.

8. Save and run the program. Click the **File** menu. Nothing happens because there is no code. Stop the program and leave it open for the next Step-by-Step exercise.

Adding Menu Commands and Submenus

So far, you have created a menu bar with two menu titles. If you click them, nothing happens. As you learned earlier, when you click a menu title, the menu opens and displays a list of commands or submenus. As with menus, submenu controls can have submenu titles, submenu items, and separator bars. You can have up to five levels of submenus. They are useful when you want to emphasize the relationship between two menu items, when the menu is full, or when an item is rarely used. However, you should create submenus with care. Too many submenus can cause confusion, as they are more difficult to navigate and hide controls from than the main menu items. If you think that you need more than one level of submenus, consider using a dialog box instead. Dialog boxes will be covered in Lesson 5 of this text.

You create menu commands and submenus that are associated with menu titles by indenting them in the Menu Control list box. You will do that next.

STEP-BY-STEP 3.2

1. Open the **FrstMenu** project, if necessary.
2. Press **Ctrl+E** to open the Menu Editor. Select the **Edit** control in the Menu Control list box.
3. Click the **Insert** button to insert a line between File and Edit.
4. Click the **right arrow** button above the list box to indent the next control.
5. Enter **Save** in the Caption box and **mnuFileSave** in the Name box.

   This creates a menu command associated with the File menu.

NOTE: Commands and submenus need to be indented under their menu titles.

6. Click the **Next** button and then the **Insert** button to make room for another control before Edit. Click the **right arrow** button to make this part of the File menu as well.
7. Enter a **single dash (-)** for the caption and name the item **mnuSep1**. This will create a separator bar (a horizontal line often used to separate items into logical groups).

TIP: Separator bars are created by entering a dash in the caption property of a menu control.

8. Click the **Next** button and the **Insert** button to put another item before Edit. Then click the **right arrow** button.
9. Enter **Exit** for the caption and name it **mnuFileExit**.
10. Select **Edit** in the list box. Click **Next** and then the **right arrow** button, and add a menu control with the caption **Color**. Name it **mnuEditColor**.
11. Click the **Next** button and the **right arrow** button. This will create a submenu under Color. Enter **Black** for the caption and **mnuEditColorBlack** for the name.
12. Click the **Next** button and add a submenu item with the caption **Blue**. Name it **mnuEditColorBlue**.

(continued on next page)

13. Add a third submenu item with the caption **Red** and the name **mnuEditColorRed**. Check your work with Figure 3-2.

14. Click **OK** to view your work in design view.

15. Save and run your program. Click **File** to open the menu and see the two commands. Click **Edit** to open the menu and view the submenu title. Point to **Color** to view the three subcommands. Stop the program and leave it open for the next Step-by-Step exercise.

To reorder a menu, select the item that you want to move in the menu object list box and click the up or down arrows to move it.

FIGURE 3-2
The menu controls for the FirstMenu project

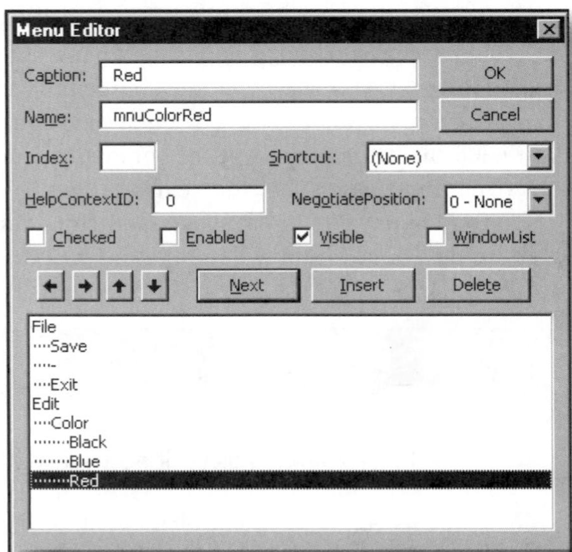

Adding Access Keys, Shortcuts, and Other Menu Features

You are probably familiar with access keys and shortcut keys. Access keys allow you to open a menu by pressing the Alt key and then the designated letter. Access keys also allow you to access a menu command once the menu is open by continuing to hold the Alt key and pressing its designated letter.

Shortcut keys are different. They run a menu command immediately after the shortcut key sequence is pressed. Shortcut keys with which you may be familiar are Ctrl+C for Copy and Ctrl+V for Paste (see Table 3-1). You cannot assign a shortcut key to a menu title. Other features that you may be familiar with are disabled (or grayed out) menu items and checked menu items. As you probably expect by now, the Menu Editor makes the creation of these features easy as well.

TABLE 3-1
Commonly used shortcut key combinations

SHORTCUT KEYS

COMMAND	SHORTCUT	COMMAND	SHORTCUT
Save	Ctrl+S	Paste	Ctrl+V
Print	Ctrl+P	Find	Ctrl+F
Undo	Ctrl+Z	Replace	Ctrl+H
Redo	Ctrl+Y	Spelling and grammer check	F7
Cut	Ctrl+X	Help	F1
Copy	Ctrl+C		

Quick Check 3.a

1. ____________________ are common features of Windows applications.
2. ____________________ allow users to quickly open menus.
3. The Menu Editor can be accessed through the ____________________ menu.
4. Keying an __________________ in front of a letter in the Menu Editor Caption property creates an access key.
5. Each menu can have up to ____________________ submenus.

STEP-BY-STEP 3.3

1. If necessary, open the **FrstMenu** program. Press **Ctrl+E** to open the Menu Editor.
2. Select **File** in the list box. In the Caption box, add an **ampersand (&)** in front of the word File. It should now look like this:

   &File

   The ampersand adds an access key to the File menu.

Placing an ampersand (&) before a letter tells Visual Basic to underline the letter and enable that as an access key.

3. Select **Save** in the list box. In the Caption box, add an **ampersand (&)** in front of Save. This will give the user access to the Save control by keying Alt+F+S.
4. Click the **Shortcut** list box and choose **Ctrl+S**. This adds a shortcut key that allows the user to run the Save control by keying Ctrl+S.
5. Select **Exit** in the list box. Change its caption to **E&xit**.
6. Select **Black** in the list box. Click **Checked**. This puts a check mark next to the Black control.
7. Select **Red** in the list box. Deselect **Enabled**. This disables, or grays out, the Red control. Check your work with Figure 3-3.
8. Click **OK**. Save and run the program. Press **Alt+F**. The File menu opens. The "F" in File, "S" in Save, and "X" in Exit are underlined. Save has a shortcut of Ctrl+S. Click **Edit** and point to **Color**. Black has a check mark and Red is disabled. Stop the program and leave it open for the next Step-by-Step exercise.

FIGURE 3-3
Changes made to the menu controls

How the Menu Helps

A properly designed menu gives the user some indication where to find certain commands. As noted, most Windows programs have commands located in specific areas. Users expect Cut, Copy, and Paste to be in the Edit menu. They expect the About box to be under the Help menu. By following such conventions when creating the menu system, your applications will be easier to use and therefore, more user-friendly.

Remember to name your objects as you create them.

Adding Code to a Menu

Now that you have created a menu, you must now add the code to make the menu options work. As you learned in Lesson 1, Visual Basic is driven by events. When a user clicks a menu control, a Click event occurs. All menu controls, with the exception of the separator bar, recognize the Click event. Coding for a Menu Click event works the same as coding for any other event procedure. You open the Code window, choose the menu control from the Object box on the left, and enter the code between the Private Sub and End Sub statements. The only difference is that you do not have a choice of events. The only event available from the Procedure box on the right is "Click."

STEP-BY-STEP 3.4

1. If necessary, open the **FrstMenu** program.
2. Open the **Menu Editor**. Select **Red** in the list box and click **Enabled** to re-enable this control. Click **OK**.
3. Using the **TextBox** tool from the toolbox, add a text box with the following properties:

PROPERTY	SETTING
Name	txtMenuTest
Alignment	2-Center
Text	Trying out the menu
Font	MS Sans Serif, Bold, 18 point

4. Size the **text box** so you can read all the text. Double-click the **form** to open the Code window.
5. Select **mnuEditColorBlack** from the Object box and add the code from **Code Step 5** to the Sub mnuColorBlack _Click event.

   As the comments indicate, the code for Code Step 5 first changes the ForeColor property of the txtTestMenu text box to black. Then it changes the Checked property of the mnuColorBlack submenu control to True, which displays a check mark to the right of the menu control. Finally, it sets the Checked property of the other two submenu controls to False, which means no check mark will display.
6. Select the **mnuEditColorBlue** control from the Object box and add the code from **Code Step 6** to the Sub mnuColorBlue _Click event.
7. Select the **mnuEditColorRed** control and add the code from **Code Step 7** to the Sub mnuColorRed _Click event.
8. Save and run the project. Click the **Edit** menu and select **Color**. Try choosing different colors. The color of the text in the text box changes and a check mark

displays next to the active submenu command.

9. Stop the program and click **File/Remove Project**.

CODE STEP 5

```
'Change the color of the text in txtMenuTest to black
txtMenuTest.ForeColor = vbBlack
'Check the Black submenu control
mnuEditColorBlack.Checked = True
'Uncheck the Blue submenu control
mnuEditColorBlue.Checked = False
'Uncheck the Red submenu control
mnuEditColorRed.Checked = False
```

CODE STEP 6

```
'Change the color of the text in txtMenuTest to blue
txtMenuTest.ForeColor = vbBlue
'Uncheck the Black submenu control
mnuEditColorBlack.Checked = False
'Check the Blue submenu control
mnuEditColorBlue.Checked = True
'Uncheck the Red submenu control
mnuEditColorRed.Checked = False
```

CODE STEP 7

```
'Change the color of the text in txtMenuTest to red
txtMenuTest.ForeColor = vbRed
'Uncheck the Black submenu control
mnuEditColorBlack.Checked = False
'Uncheck the Blue submenu control
mnuEditColorBlue.Checked = False
'Check the Red submenu control
mnuEditColorRed.Checked = True
```

You have probably noticed that the ForeColor property of a textbox in the properties window (or any other color property for any object) is listed with a strange-looking number. This is a hexadecimal number that equals a certain color in the palette. As you might imagine, it is a bit cumbersome to try to remember the hexadecimal number for each color that you may want to use. Luckily, there is a group of color constants for the most commonly used colors. Table 3-2 lists these colors.

TABLE 3-2
Commonly used constants

COLOR	CONSTANT	COLOR	CONSTANT	COLOR	CONSTANT
Black	vbBlack	Yellow	vbYellow	Cyan	vbCyan
Red	vbRed	Blue	vbBlue	White	vbWhite
Green	vbGreen	Magenta	vbMagenta		

The Multiple Document Interface (MDI)

The *Multiple Document Interface (MDI)* is another common item found in Windows applications. The Multiple Document Interface (MDI) allows you to create an application that has many forms that are contained within one main form. Applications like Microsoft Word, where you can open several different documents within the main Word program, are MDIs. These also can be referred to as parent and child forms. The main application is referred to as the parent and all of the forms contained within the application are called the children. MDIs allow the user to display several documents at the same time within the application, yet the documents are directly linked to the application. You may have noticed that, while you can move Word documents around within the confine of the main Word window, you cannot move a Word document outside of that main window. You may also have noticed that no matter how many documents you may have open, you always only have one main menu. These are features of the Multiple Document Interface. There can only be one MDI parent form per application. This cuts down on the possible confusion that could result from having more than one form in charge of the rest. The command to create a MDI is located under the Project menu. When you create a MDI form, the Properties box refers to it specifically as a MDI form rather than just a form. To have the application recognize that the other forms are children to the MDI form, you have to set their MDIChild property to True. Once they are set to be child forms, the forms will open inside the parent form.

The fun part comes in when you get to use some of the built-in features of MDI forms. When using various applications such as Microsoft Word, Microsoft Excel, and WordPerfect, you can have more than one document open at the same time. By clicking the Window menu, you can see a list of the documents that are open. You can even change the arrangement of the forms. All of this is easily accomplished by Visual Basic.

Quick Check 3.b

1. Users expect ____________________ , ____________________ , and, ____________________ in the Edit menu.

2. When a user clicks a menu control, a ____________________ occurs.

3. MDI stands for ____ .

4. ____________________ the form to open the Code window.

5. The MDI form is located in the ____________________ menu.

Building Programming Skills

A major problem that programmers run into is that they tend to design for their own use. It may seem obvious to you or another programmer how a program should flow. However, the end-user typically does not have the same perspective. Therefore, when designing a program, it is essential that you plan for alternate approaches. Murphy's law here is, "If users can figure out the one thing that would crash a program–they will."

Creating a MDI Application

In order to create a MDI application, you must create a MDI form. Creating a MDI form is similar to creating any other new form. After the MDI form is created, you can create as many child forms as necessary. In the following Step-by-Step exercise you will create a MDI application with one parent and two child forms. Then you will add a menu control to the parent form that will allow you to open both of the child forms.

STEP-BY-STEP 3.5

1. Start Visual Basic, if necessary, and double-click **Standard EXE**. Save the form as **FirstChild.frm** and the project as **FirstMDI.vbp** in the Lesson03 folder.
2. Set the Name to **frmFirstChild** and the Caption to **I am a child form**.
3. Click the **Project** menu, select **Add MDI Form**, and click **Open** to add the parent form.
4. Set the Name of this new form to **frmFirstMDI** and the caption to **My first MDI application**.
5. Click the **Project** menu, select **Add Form**, and click **Open** to add a standard form. Set the Name to **frmSecondChild** and the Caption to **I am also a child form**.
6. Click the parent form **frmFirstMDI** and press **Ctrl+E** to open the Menu Editor.
7. Enter **&File** in the Caption box and **mnuFile** in the Name box. Click **Next**, then click the **right arrow** button to indent one level.
8. Enter **E&xit** in the Caption box and **mnuFileExit** in the Name box. Click **Next**, and click the **left arrow** button to remove the indentation level.
9. Enter **Open** in the Caption box and **mnuOpen** in the Name box. Click **Next** and indent one level. Key **First Child** in the Caption box and **mnuOpenChild1** in the Name box. Click **Next** and leave the indentation as it is.
10. Enter **Second Child** in the Caption box and **mnuOpenChild2** in the Name box. Click **Next**. Remove the indentation by clicking the **left arrow** button. Check your work with Figure 3-4.
11. When you have finished, click **OK**.
12. Click **Save** and name the forms **SecondChild.frm** and **FirstMDI.frm**. Run the program. What happened?
13. Stop the program and leave it open for the next Step-by-Step exercise.

FIGURE 3-4
The menu controls

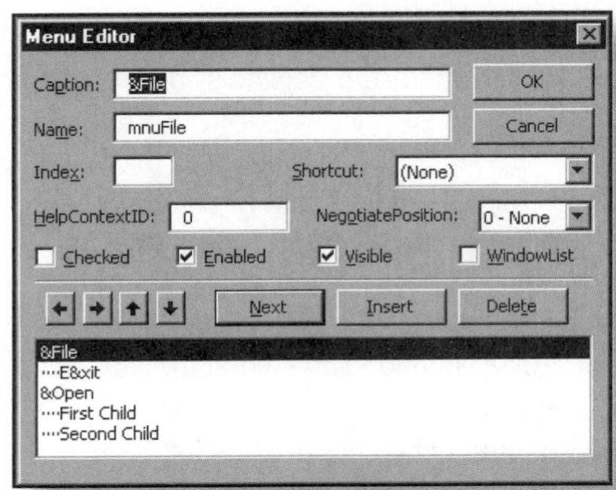

When you create a MDI application, you must set the MDIChild property of the child forms to True or else they will not be linked to the MDI form. This is why the parent form with the menu you created is unavailable and why the only form that shows is frmMDIChild. Next you will fix this and try again.

STEP-BY-STEP 3.6

1. If necessary, open **FirstMDI.vbp**. Select **frmFirstChild** and set its MDIChild property to **True** (see Figure 3-5).

2. Select **frmSecondChild** and set its MDIChild property to **True**.

3. Select **frmFirstMDI** and note that it does not have a MDIChild property.

4. Save and run the program. What happened this time? Stop the program and leave it open for the next Step-by-Step exercise.

FIGURE 3-5
Setting the MDIChild property to True

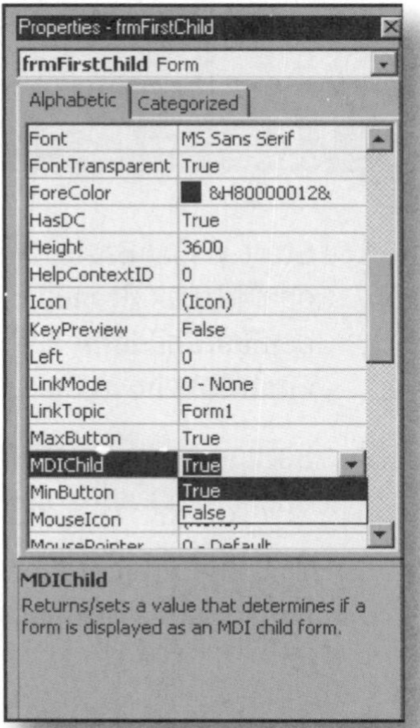

One last thing is needed to make the project run correctly. The MDI form must be set as the Startup Object. Currently, the program is starting with frmFirstChild. You set the Startup Object in the Project Properties dialog box.

STEP-BY-STEP 3.7

1. Click the **Project** menu and select **Project1 Properties**.

2. From the **General** tab, select **frmFirstMDI** from the Startup Object list box, as shown in Figure 3-6, and click **OK**.

3. Save the program and run it. Now the program displays frmFirstMDI with the menu bar.

   Next you'll add some code to this application so that you can open the different child forms.

4. Stop the application and open the Code window for **frmFirstMDI**. Select the **mnuOpenChild1_Click** event from the Object box. Press **Tab** and add the following code:

FIGURE 3-6
Changing the Startup Object

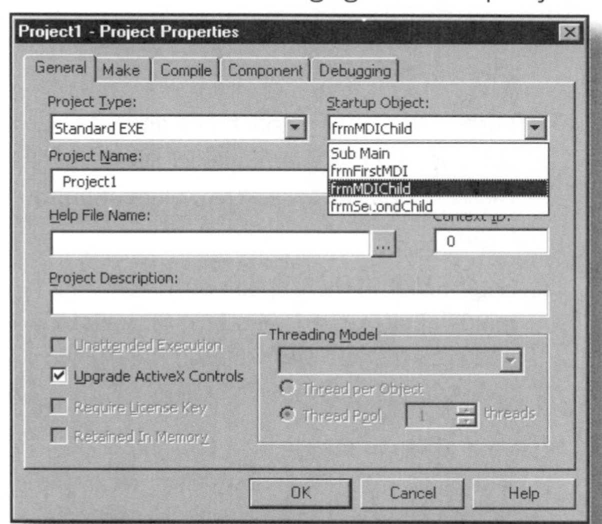

```
'Show the form frmFirstChild
frmFirstChild.Show
```

5. Select the procedure for the **mnuOpenChild2_Click** event. Press **Tab** and add the following code:

```
'Show the form frmSecondChild
frmSecondChild.Show
```

6. Save and run the program. Click **Open** and select **First Child**. Click **Open** and select **Second Child**. Notice that the forms stay within the confines of the MDI form. Stop the program and leave it open for the next Step-by-Step exercise.

Using Your Personal Library

As mentioned in Lesson 2, the use of your *personal library* makes your life easier. You can quickly and easily import ready-to-be-used files from other projects. Take the About box project that you created in Lesson 2, for example. With a little work, this could be reused in many applications by first importing the file into the current project using Project | Add Form | Existing tab. Then use File | Save As to save the form to the new project folder. By saving the forms as a new file, you can change the file without fear of affecting other applications. If you have a form that is exactly the same for multiple projects, you can attach it without making a new file. You will add the About form to your FirstMDI project.

STEP-BY-STEP 3.8

1. If necessary, open the **FirstMDI** project.
2. Click the **Project** menu, select **Add Form**, click the **Existing** tab and navigate to the **About.frm** from the **Library.vbp** project that you created in Lesson 2. Double-click the **About.frm** to add it.
3. Select **frmAbout**. Click **File**, select **Save About.frm. As**, and save it in the same folder as the rest of the FirstMDI project. Keep the same name if you wish.
4. Set the MDIChild property for frmAbout to **True**.
5. Click **frmFirstMDI** and open the Menu Editor. Click the first blank line in the Menu Control list box and key **&Help** in the Caption box and **mnuHelp** in the Name box. Press **Enter** and indent the next object. Key **&About** in the Caption box and **mnuHelpAbout** in the Name box and click **OK**.
6. Open the Code window and select the **mnuHelpAbout Click** event. Press **Tab** and add the following code:

```
'Show the form frmAbout
frmAbout.Show
```

7. Save and run the project. Click the **Help** menu and select **About**. The About box appears. You may need to size the forms to see all of the About box. Click the **OK** button to close it.
8. Stop the program and leave it open for the next Step-by-Step exercise.

Obviously you would want to make a few changes to the About form to customize it to your current project. You might change the copyright date and program name, for example.You have now seen how creating reusable forms can save you time and energy.

Adding Other MDI Windows Features

As mentioned earlier, there are some built-in features of Windows that you can take advantage of when creating MDI applications. One of these is a listing of all open windows. This listing is typically found under the Window menu. Create a Window list by clicking the WindowList check box in the Menu Editor.

STEP-BY-STEP 3.9

1. Open the **FirstMDI** project, if necessary.
2. Click **frmFirstMDI** and press **Ctrl+E** to open the Menu Editor.
3. Select **&Help** in the Menu Control list box. Click the **Insert** button to add a blank line above **&Help**.
4. Key **&Window** in the Caption box and **mnuWindow** in the Name box.
5. Click the **WindowList** check box to select it.
6. Click **OK** to exit the Menu Editor.
7. Save and run the program. Click the **Window** menu. Nothing happens.
8. Click **Open** and select **First Child**. Now click the **Window** menu. A list displays, showing which form is open.
9. Click **Open** again and select **Second Child**. Click the **Window** menu again. A list displays, showing that both forms are open. You can switch between the two files by selecting them in the Window menu.
10. Stop the program and leave it open for the next Step-by-Step exercise.

Users are also familiar with ways of displaying multiple documents within a parent Window. This property can be set using the Arrange method. Syntax for the Arrange method is:

```
object.Arrange arrangement
```

Settings for arrangement are shown in Table 3-3.

TABLE 3-3
Settings for arrangement

VALUE	DESCRIPTION	CONSTANT
0	Cascade all non-minimalized MDIChild forms	VbCascade
1	Tile all non-minimized MDIChild Forms horizontally	vbTileHorizontally
2	Tile all non-minimized MDIChild Forms vertically	vbTileVertically
3	Arrange all minimized MDIChild Form icons	vbArrangeIcons

Cascaded windows are displayed layered on top of each other offset left to right. Vertically *tiled* windows appear side by side. Horizontally *tiled* windows are arranged with no overlap from top to bottom. See Figures 3-7, 3-8, and 3-9 for examples of arranging windows.

FIGURE 3-7
Windows cascading

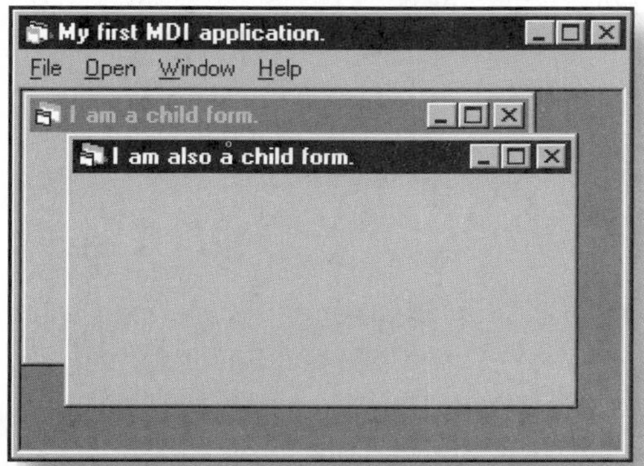

FIGURE 3-8
Windows tiled horizontally

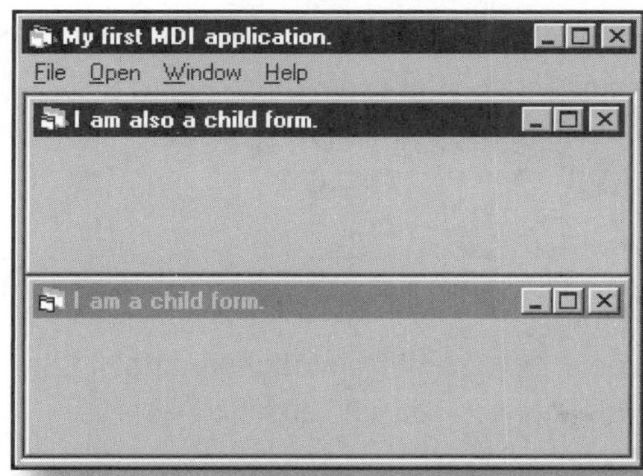

To get more ideas about the types of programs that people want to use, visit places on the Web such as http://www.shareware.com or http://www.freeware.com.

FIGURE 3-9
Windows tiled vertically

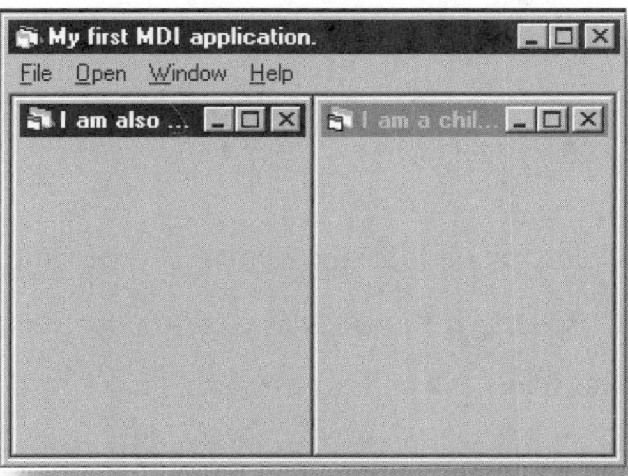

STEP-BY-STEP 3.10

1. If necessary, open the **firstMDI** project.

2. Select **frmFirstMDI** and open the **Menu Editor**.

3. Select **&Help** in the Menu Control list box and click the **Insert** button to add a blank line below **&Window**. Indent one level. Click **Insert** two times to add two more lines.

4. Enter **&Cascade** in the Caption box and **mnuWindowCascade** in the Name box. Click **Next**.

5. Enter **Tile &Horizontally** for the caption and **mnuWindowTileHorizontally** for the name. Click **Next**.

(continued on next page)

STEP-BY-STEP 3.10 CONTINUED

6. Enter **Tile &Vertically** for the caption and **mnuWindowTileVertically** for the name. Click **OK**.

7. Open the Code window and select the **mnuWindowCascade_Click** event. Press **Tab** and add the following code:

```
'Cascade windows
frmFirstMDI.Arrange 0
```

8. Select the **mnuWindowTileHorizontally_Click** event, press **Tab**, and add the following code:

```
'Tile windows horizontally
frmFirstMDI.Arrange 1
```

9. Select the **mnuWindowTileVertically_Click** event, press **Tab**, and add the following code:

```
'Tile windows vertically
frmFirstMDI.Arrange 2
```

10. Save and run the program. Click **Open** and select the **First Child** and **Second Child** windows. Click the **Window** menu and select **Tile Horizontally**. Then try **Tile Vertically** and **Cascade**. Stop the program and exit Visual Basic if you are done.

Multiple document interface applications can be very powerful, but use them wisely. The Single Document Interface is probably better suited for most applications that you develop.

Summary

- Menus make it easier for users to execute commands in their programs.
- The Menu Editor makes creating professional-looking menus easy.
- Shortcut keys and access keys help speed up access to commonly used menu commands.
- The Multiple Document Interface is made up of one parent form that contains many child forms.
- Previously created forms can be added from other projects.
- The Arrange method provides flexibility to the user to display child forms in different ways.

Building Communication Skills

In creating and editing programs, you will often forget why you did things a certain way or why a particular "fix" was used. That is why it is essential that you document your programs with explanations and dates for later reference. You may have already noticed that you have been using internal comments. This helps later when revisions are made and when the final documentation is done.

LESSON 3 REVIEW QUESTIONS

FILL IN THE BLANK

Complete each of the following statements by writing your answer in the blank provided.

1. ____________________ , ____________________ , and ____________________ commands are typically found under the File menu.

2. ____________________ are created to give users access to frequently used commands.

3. The Menu Editor is located under the ____________________ menu.

4. To create an access key, you must place an ____________________ in front of the letter.

5. There can only be one ____________________ form per project.

6. To add an existing form to your project, you click the ____________________ and choose ____________________ .

7. Use the Menu Editor ____________________ property to display a menu title, menu command, or submenu.

8. The ____________________ button is used to indent a Menu Object in the Menu Editor.

9. Use the Menu Item's____________________ property when writing code.

10. To open the form's Code window, ____________________ on the form.

WRITTEN QUESTIONS

Write your answers to the following questions.

11. Explain why it is important to know the standard shortcut keys used in the Windows environment.

12. What is the most common source of problems when trying to debug code?

13. Explain how to create menu titles, commands, and submenus.

14. How can colors prompt users?

15. Explain why menus are an important part of Windows applications.

16. Explain how to create a separator bar and when you would use one.

17. How do you create a Window list?

18. What is an MDI form and why is it used?

19. Why is it important to name objects?

20. When would you make changes to a menu?

LESSON 3 APPLICATION PROBLEMS

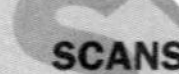

Level One

THE MENU PROBLEM

Create an application that has a menu bar containing the following menu titles:

- File
- Edit
- Help

Add the following menu items under the appropriate menu titles:

- Open
- Exit
- Cut
- Copy
- Paste
- About

Add the appropriate access keys and commonly used shortcut keys. Add code to the Exit command so that it terminates the program when clicked.

Level Two

THE COPY AND PASTE APPLICATION

1. Create an application that contains three forms: a parent form and two child forms as follows:

   a. Create frmMDIParent with the caption "The Cut and Paste Program." Add a menu bar containing the following menus:

      - File
        - Open
          - Copy Form
          - Paste Form
        - Exit
      - Edit
        - Copy
        - Paste

   Include a separator bar between Open and Exit.

   b. Create frmCopyFrom with the caption "Copy me." Add a text box named txtCopyFrom.

   c. Create frmPasteInto with the caption "Paste into me." Add a text box named txtPasteInto.

2. Set the properties so that frmMDIParent is the MDI parent form and frmCopyForm and frmPasteInto are both MDI child forms. When you start the program, frmMDIParent should open.

3. Add the ability to open each of the child forms from the parent form using the menu commands.

4. Declare a global (public) variable called gstrCopiedText.

5. Use the following code for the copy menu item so that it copies all text in the frmCopyForm text box:

```
'Save the text in the txtCopyFrom textbox
gstrCopiedText = frmCopyFrom.txtCopyFrom.Text
```

6. Use the following code for the Paste menu item so that it pastes the copied text into the frmPasteInto text box:

```
'Put the saved text into the txtPasteInto textbox.
frmPasteInto.txtPasteInto.Text = gstrCopiedText
```

Name all objects using the recommended naming conventions.

LESSON 3 PROGRAMMING AT WORK

SCANS

Using the CarBudget.vbp project created in Lessons 1 and 2, add a menu to the form that contains the following menus: File, Edit, and Help. Under the File menu, add the Exit menu control and add the appropriate code to it. Under the Edit menu, add a menu control with the caption "Clear All" and the name mnuEditClear. Add code to the Clear All menu control to clear all of the text boxes. (Use the txtTextBox.Text = "" statement to do this.) Under the Help menu, add an About menu control. Add the About form to this project, customize it so that it is appropriate for the application, and code the About control so that it calls this form.

LESSON 4

DECISIONS, LOOPING ARRAYS, AND SUBROUTINES

OBJECTIVES

When you complete this lesson, you will be able to:

- Plan the solution to a programming problem.
- Understand and apply the rules of logic to True/False expressions.
- Write If..Then..Else..End If statements.
- Write Do While and Do Until statements.
- Create program loops that depend on logical expressions.
- Declare and use arrays.
- Use built-in functions for a variety of tasks.

Estimated Time: 5 hours

KEY TERMS

user interface
algorithm
stepwise refinement
subroutine
event procedure
data structure
array
ListIndex
file extension
syntax
Boolean, or logical, expression
debug
program flow
relational operators
assignment operator
ASCII code
definite loop
indefinite loop
increment
body
sentinel
Mod
menu control array
element or member
index or subscript
scope
visability
lifetime
private variable
General Declarations
linear search
flag
concatenation
error trapping

Approaching a Problem

This lesson is about decisions: both the decisions you make as you plan a solution to a problem, and the decisions a program makes based on the data it is processing.

Start by considering how you solve problems you encounter in your daily life. Say you are ready to go to work. You go to your car, open the door, buckle your belt, and turn the key. Nothing happens. As you panic, you notice the headlight switch is turned to the "on" position. You left your lights on the night before and now your battery is dead. How do you approach the problem?

As you sit in your car, consider the alternatives. You can:

- call in sick,
- call a tow truck,
- call a coworker to come pick you up,
- ask a neighbor for a ride or to borrow a vehicle, or
- get your bike out of the garage and start pedaling.

Sometimes just making a list like the one shown above can help you make a good decision. Approaching a programming problem is not much different. The first rule is "Don't Panic." No matter how difficult a problem appears, it can usually be solved by good planning and sufficient information. The steps below are presented in order, but don't expect to completely finish one step before starting the next. Sometimes the steps overlap. You need to keep all the steps in mind through each part of the planning process.

Collect Information

Start by getting all the information you can about the problem. Talk to the users who will run the program. Find out what they want. Do not assume that you know more about their problems than they do. Gather as much information as you can, but expect to revise your solution later to meet unexpected or newly discovered needs.

Create the User Interface

Visual Basic gives you a unique way of communicating with the user whose problem you are trying to solve. Even before you know how to solve a problem, you can design the Visual Basic forms that become the *user interface*. The user interface is how the user will interact with the program. It is what the user keys and clicks. It is what the user sees as output. You can create a Visual Basic program that is "all show." Design the forms used to enter data. Design the forms that display the information. Once these samples are created, return to the user. Find out if your mock solution is what the user expects. Of course, your program won't actually process any data, and the results displayed will be simulated, but it is a great way to find out what the user expects and needs. Once you have designed the user interface, you are ready to solve the real problem.

Develop the Algorithm

Solve the problem completely on paper. If you cannot solve a problem with paper, a pencil, and a calculator, you probably will not be able to program the computer to solve the problem. The step-by-step solution to a problem is called an *algorithm*. The word *algebra* comes from the same root.

Subdivide the Problem

While solving the problem on paper, you have probably already started to break the main problem into a number of subproblems. This is a very powerful technique for solving problems. Subdivide each section into smaller and smaller tasks. Once the problem has been divided, each part can be approached individually. Usually these smaller problems are easy to solve. Even if they are not, at least the problem has been modularized and the tough parts can be puzzled out later in the process. This process is called *stepwise refinement.*

Part of the process of subdividing a problem is defining the *subroutines* your program will use. A subroutine is a self-contained portion of a complete program. It usually has a single task. The code that makes up the subroutines often exists in separate modules. You are already familiar with one kind of subroutine: As discussed previously, an *event procedure* is a subroutine connected with an object like a text box or command button. When a command button or menu item is clicked, the code associated with that event is executed. The Click event is one of many events that an object may respond to.

Choose Data Structures

A *data structure* is a way to organize data. The simplest way to represent data is to use variables. You've already learned about declaring variables in Lesson 2. Another important data structure is the *array*. An array is a list of values referred to by a single variable name. Values in an array may be numbers or strings, or they may represent complex data types that include many pieces of information.

Other data structures organize data according to relationships between the individual data items. Choosing an efficient method of representing the data your program will manipulate is very important. Such choices are not always easy to make; often tradeoffs are involved. Some data structures allow data to be accessed quickly but take a lot of memory space. Other data structures conserve memory but make recovering data a slow process.

Write the Code

Are you surprised? Writing the code may be the very last thing you do. Or it may not be. Be flexible. It may be wise to develop an algorithm and write the code to solve a particular piece of the problem before the user interface is designed or before a data structure is chosen. You may need to experiment with different solutions or different data structures to find the one that fits best. Things you discover in this process can affect other parts of the program. Don't be afraid to start over. The things you learn in your first attempt will make your second attempt better.

In the following Step-by-Step exercise you will set up the user interface for an application that lets a user search for a new water heater. The program should allow the user to search for a water heater based on its capacity, its power source, and its warranty period. The program lets the user specify minimum values from a suggested list and displays the information in a list box.

STEP-BY-STEP 4.1

1. Start Visual Basic and double-click **Standard EXE**.
2. Save your form and the project as **WaterHeater**. From now on, you can choose the folder in which to save your programs.
3. Change the name of the form to **frmWaterHeater**.
4. Change the caption of the form to **Choosing a Water Heater**.
5. Add **three combo boxes** and **three labels** to the form. Arrange the labels so one is above each combo box (see Figure 4-1).
6. Change the names of the combo boxes to **cboCapacity**, **cboPower**, and **cboWarranty**. Change the Text properties to **Capacity**, **Power Source**, and **Warranty Period**.
7. Change the captions of the corresponding labels to **Capacity**, **Power Source**, and **Warranty Period**, and the names to **lblCapacity**, **lblPower**, and **lblWarranty**.

8. Add a **list box** and a corresponding **label** to the form.

9. Change the caption of the label to **Qualifying Models** and name it **lblQualifying**. Name the listbox **lstQualifying**.

In many fonts, a lowercase L is nearly indistinguishable from the numeral 1. The context should tell you which to use.

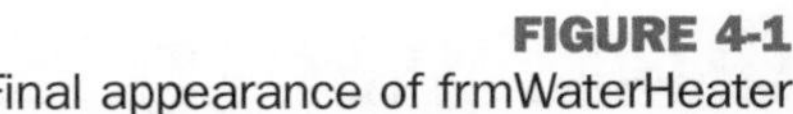

FIGURE 4-1
Final appearance of frmWaterHeater

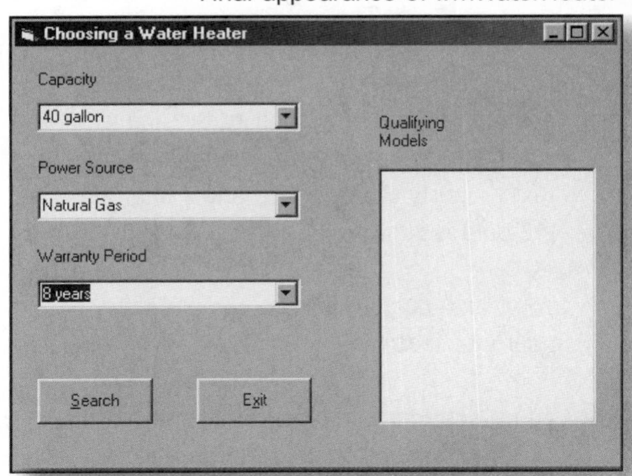

10. Add a **command button** to the form. Set its caption to **E&xit** and name it **cmdExit**.

11. Double-click the command button to open its Code window. Press **Tab** and enter the code **End**.

12. To add code to the form object, choose **Form** from the Object list, and then choose **Activate** from the Procedure list.

13. Press **Tab** and insert the following code:

```
cboCapacity.AddItem "30 gallon"
cboCapacity.AddItem "40 gallon"
cboCapacity.AddItem "50 gallon"
cboCapacity.ListIndex = 0
cboPower.AddItem "Natural Gas"
cboPower.AddItem "Electric"
cboPower.AddItem "LP Gas"
'cboPower.ListIndex = 0
```

The single quote character starts a comment. Comments are normally displayed in a green font.

```
cboWarranty.AddItem "1 year"
cboWarranty.AddItem "5 years"
cboWarranty.AddItem "8 years"
cboWarranty.AddItem "10 years"
cboWarranty.ListIndex = 0
```

A combo box is a text box with a list of predefined choices attached. The user can select the text for a combo box by displaying the attached list and selecting one of the entries. The code above adds items to the combo boxes' lists. The *ListIndex* property allows the programmer

To enter repetitive code, select the part of the code that repeats. Select Edit | Copy from the menu bar, or press Ctrl+C to copy the selected code. Move the cursor to the beginning of the next line and paste the code by selecting Edit | Paste or by pressing Ctrl+V. Once the code is copied a sufficient number of times, go back and edit each line.

(continued on next page)

to preselect an item from the list. Notice in the cboPower code, the ListIndex line is commented out by preceding the line with a single quote character. This allows the text property of the box to show when the program is run.

What else do you need to complete the user interface?

14. Add a **command button** to the form. Change its name to **cmdSearch** and its caption to **&Search**. When this button is clicked in the completed program, the program searches its water heater database for models that meet the criteria entered by the user. All qualified models are added to the list box. In this version of the program, there is no database, so the items chosen in each of the combo boxes are displayed in the list box.

15. To complete this Step-by-Step exercise, add the code shown in **Code Step 15** to the **Click** event for the **Search** button that copies the contents of the three combo boxes and displays their results in the list box.

16. Save and run the program. Select various options. Click the **Search** button. Quit the program.

17. Double-click the **form** to enter its Code window.

18. In the **Form_Activate** procedure, remove the single quote from the following line: **'cboPower.ListIndex = 0**

19. Save and run the program. What difference do you observe? Stop and remove the program.

CODE STEP 15

```
lstQualifying.Clear
lstQualifying.AddItem cboCapacity.Text
lstQualifying.AddItem cboPower.Text
lstQualifying.AddItem cboWarranty.Text
```

Quick Check 4.a

1. A(n) ____________________ is a step-by-step description of how to solve a problem.
2. It is entirely possible that the last step in writing a solution to a programming problem is to ____________________ .
3. The way a user interacts with a program is called the ____________________ .

4. To add an entry to a combo box, uses the box's ____________________ method.

5. Once a user has selected an item in a combo box, that item is available in the box's ____________________ property.

Program Decisions

When a database of heaters is added and the code is complete, the water heater program will select and display a list of qualifying water heaters based on the choices made by the user. The program uses If Then statements or Select Case statements to make those decisions. Leave the Water Heater problem now and look at the Four If statements and the Select Case statements.

The Four Ifs

There are four different forms of the If statement. The construction of a statement is called the statement's *syntax*. The simplest version of the If statement takes only a single line:

```
If condition Then statement
```

The one line If statement is its original form. Many early versions of BASIC were limited to this kind of If.

The condition in the If statement is called a *Boolean,* or *logical,* expression. It is an expression that, when evaluated, results in a True or False answer.

If the condition tested is True, the statement or statements following Then are executed. If the condition tested is False, the statements after Then are skipped. In either case, the statements following the If statement are executed.

Did You Know?

George Boole was a mathematician who worked out an entire mathematical system, an algebra, of variables that could only assume two values: True and False.

A second version is more useful because it makes the statements in the True branch easier to read:

```
If condition Then
    Statement(s)
End If
```

TIP

If you key Endif, Visual Basic will split the word into End If.

In this version, one or more statements may follow Then. The True branch of the statement is finished when the End If statement is encountered. In this syntax, each of the statements in the True branch occupies its own line of code. Although Visual Basic ignores spacing, the statements in the True branch are often indented. This makes the code easy to read. Code that is easier to read is easier to *debug*. Debugging is ridding code of errors.

The third version provides a place for statements that are only executed if the condition tested is False.

```
If condition Then
    Statement(s)
Else
    Statement(s)
End If
```

If the condition is True, the statements after Then are executed. When Else is encountered, *program flow* jumps to the statement following End If. Program flow means the order in which statements are executed. If the condition is False, the statements after Else are executed, skipping the statements after Then. When those statements are done, the flow of the program continues with the statements following End If.

A fourth variation is the ElseIf statement. This is useful if a number of conditions need to be tested.

```
If condition1 Then
    Statement(s)
ElseIf condition2 Then
    Statement(s)
Else
    Statement(s)
End If
```

ElseIf *condition* Then may be repeated as many times as necessary. The statements after Else are executed if none of the conditions tested are True.

Quick Check 4.b

1. If the condition tested in an If statement is True, the statements after ____________________ are executed.
2. In an If-Then-Else-End If statement, when the statements in the True branch have been executed, the program flow moves to ____________________ .
3. The order in which statements are executed is called ____________________ .
4. When several conditions have to be tested, use the ____________________ variation of the If statement.
5. ____________________ means to remove errors from program code.

Logical Expressions

The conditions tested in the If statement may be simple or very complicated. A simple condition may test the value of a variable.

```
If x = 3 Then ...
```

The value of *x* is compared with the constant 3. If they are equal, the condition is True. If they are not, the condition is False. Logical expressions are constructed with *relational operators*. The equal sign is a relational operator: It compares the value of the expression to the left, with the value of the expression to the right. It always returns a True or False.

Many of the commonly used relational operators appear in Table 4-1.

Using an equal sign as a relational op is not the same as using the equal sign as the *assignment operator*. Used as the assignment operator, the value of the expression to the right of the equal sign is evaluated and assigned to the variable to the left of the equal sign.

TABLE 4-1
Commonly used relational operators

=	True if the expression on the left and right have the same value
<	True if the expression on the left is "less than" the expression on the right
<=	True if the expression on the left is "less than or equal to" the expression on the right
>	True if the expression on the left is "greater than" the expression on the right
>=	True if the expression on the left is "greater than or equal to" the expression on the right
<>	True if the expression on the left and right are "not equal"

It is important to note that the relational operators work differently for different data types. If the left and right expressions represent numeric values, the meanings of the relational operators are clear. If the expressions are strings, then a string closer to the beginning of the alphabet is "less than" a string closer to the end of the alphabet. For instance, "apple" is "less than" "fritter." The comparisons are based on the *ASCII codes* of the characters. The *ASCII code* is a numerical code that represents each character as a value. "A" is 65. "a" is 97. The space character is 32.

More complicated and useful expressions are built by including the following operators: And, Or, and Not. These operators let you combine two or more conditions in the same expression.

```
' if True, ch is a lowercase character
If "a" <= ch And ch <= "z" Then
```

An And expression is True if both parts of the expression are True. If either part is False, the entire statement is False.

```
If x < 3 Or x > 7 Then ...
```

An Or expression is True if one part or the other or both parts are True. In the example above, it is not possible for both parts to be True.

The Not operator changes the truth-value of an expression. If an expression is True, a Not operator applied to the expression changes its truth-value to False.

```
If Not ( x > 3) Then ...
```

The previous condition is True if the value of *x* is less than or equal to 3.

Test out the four Ifs in the Step-by-Step exercise that follows. It tests the value of the Discriminant of a quadratic equation. The coefficients of the equation are a, b, and c. The discriminant is $b^2 - 4ac$. If the discriminant is positive, the equation has two real roots. If the discriminant is 0, the equation has a double root. If the discriminant is negative, the equation has no real roots.

STEP-BY-STEP 4.2

1. Start a new project by clicking **File**, selecting **New Project**, and double-clicking **Standard EXE**. Save the form and project as **FourIfs**.
2. Change the caption of the form to **The Four Ifs** and the name to **frmFourIfs**.
3. Double-click the **form** to open the Code window. Select **Activate** from the Procedure list to open the **Form Activate** procedure.
4. Press **Tab** and add the code shown in **Code Step 4**.
5. Save and run the program. The code you have typed will execute immediately. The second message box will be displayed (because b * b – 4 * a * c is not greater than or equal to 0).
6. Stop the program. Open the Code window and modify the code by changing the value of c from 10 to **3**.
7. Save and run the program. This time, the first message appears: "Two Real Roots".
8. Click **OK**. The second message appears: "No Real Roots". Both are not true. Since the tested condition is True, the first message box statement was executed. After that statement was executed, the flow of program execution jumped to the statement following the If statement. This displays the second message, even though it is incorrect.
9. Stop the program. Open the Code window and modify the code by changing the If statement. Use the code shown in **Code Step 9**.
10. Save and run the program. Using this code, the true message "Two Real Roots" displays. When you click **OK**, the subroutine is immediately terminated by executing Exit Sub. This is not a good solution either because you may have other code you want to execute.

CODE STEP 4

```
Dim a,b,c as Integer
a=1
b=6
c=10
If b * b - 4 * a * c >= 0 Then MsgBox "Two Real Roots", , "Quadratic"
MsgBox "No Real Roots" , , "Quadratic"
```

CODE STEP 9

```
If b * b - 4 * a * c >= 0 Then
  MsgBox "Two Real Roots" , , "Quadratic"
  Exit Sub
End If
MsgBox "No Real Roots" , , "Quadratic"
```

11. Stop the program. Open the Code window and modify the code by changing the If statement. Use the code shown in **Code Step 11**.

12. Save and run the program. The correct message, "Two Real Roots," is displayed. When **OK** is clicked, the second (incorrect) message is not displayed.

13. Stop the program. Open to the Code window and modify the code by replacing **c = 3** with **c = Val(InputBox("Enter a value for c:")).**

14. Save and run the program. The InputBox statement displays a dialog box that asks the user to enter a value from the keyboard. The Val( ) function converts the input to a numeric value. That value is assigned to the variable *c*. Enter **10** and click **OK**. The second message, "No Real Roots," displays because the expression evaluated to False. Stop and run the program again, enter **3**, and click **OK**. The expression evaluated to True, so the first message, "Two Real Roots," displays.

15. Stop the program. Open the Code window. Select all the **code** displayed between the Private Sub Form_Activate and End Sub statements. Cut and paste it to the **Form_Click** event procedure.

16. Add a command button to the form by double-clicking the **CommandButton** tool in the Toolbox. Change the caption to **E&xit** and name it **cmdExit**.

17. Double-click the **command** button to open its Code window. Press **Tab** and enter **End**.

18. Save and run the program. Click the **form**. Experiment with different values for *c*.

19. Stop the program by clicking the **Exit** button.

20. Open the Code window and change the IF statement. Use the code shown in **Code Step 20**.

21. Save and run the program. Click the **form** and experiment with different values for *c*. Try a value of **9**.

22. Stop and remove the program.

CODE STEP 11

```
If b * b - 4 * a * c >= 0 Then
  MsgBox "Two Real Roots", , "Quadratic"
Else
  MsgBox "No Real Roots", , "Quadratic"
End If
```

CODE STEP 20

```
If b * b - 4 * a * c > 0 Then     ' change >= to >
  MsgBox "Two Real Roots", , "Quadratic"
ElseIf b * b - 4 * a * c = 0 Then
  MsgBox "A Double Root", , "Quadratic"
Else
  MsgBox "No Real Roots", , "Quadratic"
End If
```

Quick Check 4.c

1. When comparing two strings with a relational operator, string A is "less than" string B if ___________________ .

2. The expression A and B is True if ___________________ is True and ___________________ is True.

3. An expression with an Or is False only if ___________________ .

4. One easy way to display a message to the user is to use a ___________________ .

5. Use an ___________________ function to gather input from the user.

The Select Case Statement

The ElseIf structure is powerful and convenient. But for certain situations, the Select Case statement is even more convenient. The structure of the Select Case statement is:

```
Select Case testexpression
Case expressionlist
    Statement(s)
Case expressionlist
    Statement(s)
Case Else
    Statement(s)
End Select
```

```
Select Case choice
Case 1
  txtShowOne.Visible=True
Case 2
  MsgBox "Show Two"
Case Else
  MsgBox "Not One or Two"
End Select
```

The *testexpression* is any expression that results in either a string or numeric value. The *expressionlist* is a particular value or range of values that the testexpression may assume. If the testexpression matches any part of the expressionlist, the statements that follow are executed.

The Case Else part of the statement is optional. If present and the testexpression does not match any of the previous expressionlists, the statements in this section are executed. When finished, execution resumes after the End Select statement.

In the next Step-by-Step exercise create a menu that allows the user to select a credit card from a menu of cards. Each menu item has the same name, so all the items, when selected, call the same event procedure. The Case statement is used within the event procedure to determine which menu item was selected and then to print the credit limit for that card on the form.

STEP-BY-STEP 4.3

1. Start a new **Standard EXE** project. Save the form and project as **Credit**.

2. Change the caption of the form to **The Select Case Statement**.

3. Change the name of the form to **frmCredit**.

4. Open the **Menu Editor** for the form.

5. In this example you will use a control array for the submenu items that will be in the Pick A Card menu. Each submenu item must be given a unique index number. All the submenu items will have the same name, and use the same event procedure. The index is used to tell the items apart when the program is running. Now enter the following **menu items**:

Caption	Name	Index
Pick a Card	**mnuCardList**	

To add additional items to the menu, click the **Next** button in the Menu Editor window. Indent the remaining items by clicking the **right arrow** button. This will make the following list into a submenu. Do not enter the leading dots shown in the table, they will be added automatically. When entering successive entries, it is not necessary to click the Next button. Just press the Enter key to add the next entry (see Figure 4-2).

Caption	Name	Index
....Discover	**mnuCard**	**0**
....MasterCard	**mnuCard**	**1**
....VISA	**mnuCard**	**2**
....VISA Gold	**mnuCard**	**3**
....Platinum	**mnuCard**	**4**

Press **Enter** and return to the main menu level by clicking the **left arrow** button. The dots disappear. Add the last menu item.

E&xit	**mnuExit**

6. Click **OK** to exit the Menu Editor. Click **Pick a Card**. Select **Discover**. This opens the Code window for **mnuCards_Click**. Look at the top line of the procedure. Following mnuCard_Click is a parenthesized expression. The variable declared in the parentheses is a *parameter*. Each subroutine creates its own local environment. To communicate, subroutines pass values called parameters. The Index parameter tells the subroutine the value of the Index property of the menu item that was selected by the user. Remember the index numbers you assigned in the Menu Editor dialog box? When the user clicks a particular menu item of this submenu, the Index parameter is set to the value of the Index property of that item.

FIGURE 4-2
The Menu Editor window for the Pick a Card exercise

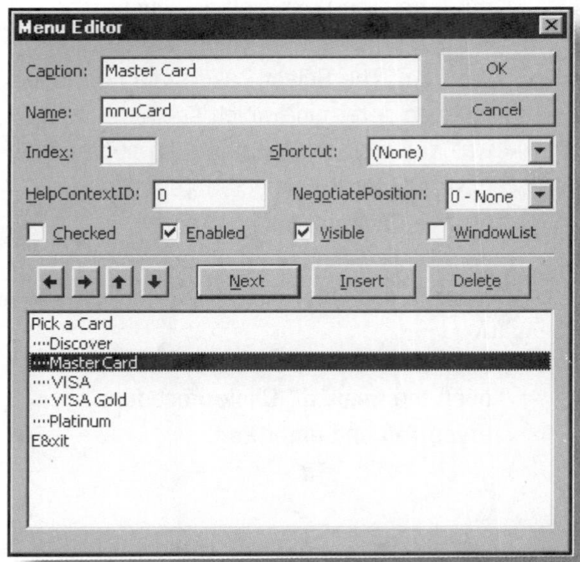

(continued on next page)

7. Enter the following code in mnuCard_Click(Index as Integer):

```
frmCredit.Cls
Print "Credit Limit:"
Select Case Index
Case 0 'discover
  Print "1500"
Case 1 'mastercard
  Print "2000"
Case 2 'visa
  Print "3000"
Case 3 'visa gold
  Print "3500"
Case 4 'platinum
  Print "5000"
End Select
```

This code will display its output on the form. The line frmCredit.Cls clears the form. Print "Credit Limit:" prints the message in the upper left-hand corner of the form. The Print method, when used without an object specified, will default to the form. The Select Case statement uses Index to determine which submenu item was selected. It then prints an appropriate message for the selected item. A Case Else statement is not necessary because no other value of Index is possible.

8. Select mnuExit in the Object box to open the **mnuExit_Click** procedure. Press **Tab** and enter **End**.

9. Save and run the program. Select **Pick a Card | Discover**. The credit limit for that card prints on the form. Select other cards. Click **Exit** to stop the program.

10. Cases can be combined. Open the Code window. Modify the Case 3 code using the code shown in **Code Step 10**.

11. Save and run the program. Select **VISA Gold**. Select **Platinum**. Both selections execute the same Case and therefore, Print statements.

12. Click **Exit** to stop the program.

13. A range of values can also be used. Open the Code window. Modify the Code Step 10 code using the code shown in **Code Step 13**.

14. Save and run the program. Select **VISA Gold**. Select **Platinum**. Again, both selections execute the same Case statement.

15. Stop and remove the project.

CODE STEP 10

```
Case 3, 4 'visa gold and platinum
  Print "3500"
```

CODE STEP 13

```
Case Is >= 3  'visa gold and platinum
  Print "3500"
```

Building Programming Skills

Characters or strings can also be used to select different cases.

```
Select Case FirstName
Case "Groucho"
   Statements(s)
Case "Harpo"
   Statements(s)
Case "Chicko"
   Statement(s)
Case "Else"
   Statements(s)
```

Quick Check 4.d

1. When giving several menu items the same name, it is required that each menu entry have its own ___________________ .
2. The last line in a Select Case statement is ___________________ .
3. If none of the conditions of a Select Case statement are matched, include a ___________________ to execute one or more default statements.
4. The Case ___________________ part of the Select Case statement allows the programmer to indicate a range of valid values.
5. If no object is specified, the Print method will display information on ___________________ .

A Lesson in Repetition

Executing the same statements over and over at almost inconceivable speeds is what makes computers so powerful. Visual Basic has a number of statements designed to control this repetition.

The first is the For loop. This is called a *definite loop* because its starting point, the upper limit, and the number of repetitions is generally known before the loop begins. *Indefinite loops* are sections of code whose repetitions are determined by conditions within the loop itself.

The syntax of the For loop is:

```
For control variable = start To end Step increment
    Body
Next x

Example:  For x = 1 To 100 Step 2
          ...
          Next x
```

In the example, the value of *x* is initialized to 1. The upper limit of *x* is 100. Each time through the loop, the value of *x* is incremented by 2. The loop counts: 1, 3, 5, 7, …, 97, 99. At the end of the last time through, when the value of *x* is 99, the Next x statement increments *x* to 101. The value of *x* is compared to the upper limit. Since 101 is greater than or equal to 100, the loop ends. When the loop ends, the statements following the Next *x* are executed. The Step increment is optional. If it is omitted, the loop automatically counts by 1. The starting point and upper limit do not have to be constants, as they are in the example. Any numeric expression or variable can be substituted.

```
For x = LowerLimit To 5 * LowerLimit
...
Next x
```

In the examples, the body of the loop is empty. There are no statements to execute. Normally, there are one or more statements in the body. Sometimes a For loop is used just to count. You may want to process 25 catalog items or 100 invoices. Other times the control variable (*x* in the example) is used as a part of the calculation.

The loop need not count by whole numbers.

```
For x = -5 To 5 Step 0.01
...
Next x
```

This loop initializes the value of *x* to –5 and increases its value by 0.01 each time through the loop. How many times will the body of the loop be executed? This kind of loop may be used to generate *x* values for the evaluation of a function in a graphing program.

Loops can count forward or backward.

```
For x = 10 To 1 Step -1
...
Next x
```

When the value of the control variable decreases each time through the loop, the Step increment must appear and the increment must be negative.

The value of the control variable should not be changed in the body of a For loop. The value is controlled by the For loop itself.

Indefinite Loops

It is not always possible to know the number of repetitions necessary for a loop before the loop begins. You may need to process records from a database until you run out of data. Or you may need to process data from the keyboard until a special ending value called a *sentinel* value is entered. For these situations, use an indefinite loop. Visual Basic has quite a variety of these.

```
Do While condition
    Body
Loop
```

This loop tests a condition and executes the statements in the body of the loop while the condition is True. If the condition is not True at the beginning, the statements in the body of the loop never execute.

```
x = 1
Do While x < 100
    x = 2 * x + 1
Loop
```

In the loop above, the value of *x* is initialized to 1 before the loop starts. The condition x < 100 is evaluated before the body of the loop is executed. Since the condition is True, the statement in the body of the loop is executed. The value of *x* is reassigned to 2 * 1 + 1, or 3. The Loop statement at the end sends the flow of control back to the top of the loop. At the top of the loop, the condition is tested again to see if it is True. Since it is still True, the loop repeats.

It is very important to provide a way for an indefinite loop to stop executing. In this case, the condition x < 100 must become False for the loop to stop. This occurs because the value of *x* increases each time through the loop.

Sometimes you want the body of the loop to execute before a condition is tested. In this kind of loop, the body of the loop is executed at least once no matter what the truth-value of the condition is.

```
Do
    Body
Loop While condition
```

This is identical to the first version except that the condition is tested at the end of the loop. The loop continues while the condition tested is True.

Another variation changes the way the condition is used to control the loop.

```
Do Until condition
    Body
Loop
```

In this statement, the loop continues until the condition is True. In other words, the loop continues while the condition is False. This is the opposite of the way the Do While loop uses its condition.

```
x = 1
Do Until x > 100
    x = 2 * x + 1
Loop
```

This loop will continue until the value of *x* exceeds 100. Often this kind of loop is used with the Until clause at the end of the loop.

```
x = 1
Do
    Body
Loop Until x > 100
```

The logic of the Until loop seems more sensible when you test the condition at the end of the loop rather than at the beginning, but either way is acceptable and useful.

There are a few additional loop variations. Some are included to be compatible with older versions of BASIC. Check the Help files if you are trying to interpret some old code.

The Step-by-Step exercise below shows how to use indefinite loops to illustrate a mathematical oddity called the Goldbach conjecture. Take any positive whole number. If the number is even, divide it by two. If the number is odd, multiply it by three and add one. Goldbach claimed that the series of numbers generated by applying these two rules always ends with a one.

How would you plan this program? The user should enter the number that starts the sequence. The numbers generated along the way should be displayed. If a text box is used, the numbers will flash by and no one will see them. Instead, use a list box to display the entire list. Provide a Command button to collect the input from the user and initiate the action. Watch as the program evolves.

STEP-BY-STEP 4.4

1. Start a new **Standard EXE** project. Save the form and project as **Gold**.
2. Change the caption of the form to **The Goldbach Conjecture**. Change the name of the form to **frmGold**.
3. Add a list box to the form. It should be taller than it is wide to display a list of values. Change the name of the list box to **lstDisplay**.
4. Put three command buttons on the form. Change the captions to **Enter Value**, **Clear List**, and **E&xit**. Change the names of the buttons to **cmdProcess**, **cmdClear**, and **cmdExit**. See Figure 4-3 to check the arrangement of the controls.
5. Double-click the **cmdClear** button to open its Code window. Press **Tab** and enter the following line of code: **lstDisplay.Clear**. The Clear method clears the contents of a list box.
6. Select **cmdExit** from the Object box. Press **Tab** and enter the following line of code: **End**.
7. Select **cmdProcess** from the Object box. Enter the code in **Code Step 7**.

   In this code, the InputBox function gathers input from the user. The input is converted to a value and assigned to the variable *x*. If the value of *x* is not positive, the InputBox function is displayed again. The user can not leave the loop until a valid value for *x* is entered.

   Once *x* is valid, it is displayed in the list box. The If statement in the loop determines whether the value of *x* is even or odd. The *Mod* operator divides one whole number by another and returns the remainder of the division. If two numbers are divided and the remainder is 0, the first number is divisible by the second. In the code above, the Mod operator divides *x* by 2. If the remainder is 0, *x* is divisible by 2; therefore, it is even. If even, *x* is divided by 2 and the result is assigned back to *x*. If *x* is not even, the value of *x* is multiplied by 3 and 1 is added to the result. The result is reassigned back to *x*. The result is

FIGURE 4-3
Final arrangement of controls on frmGold

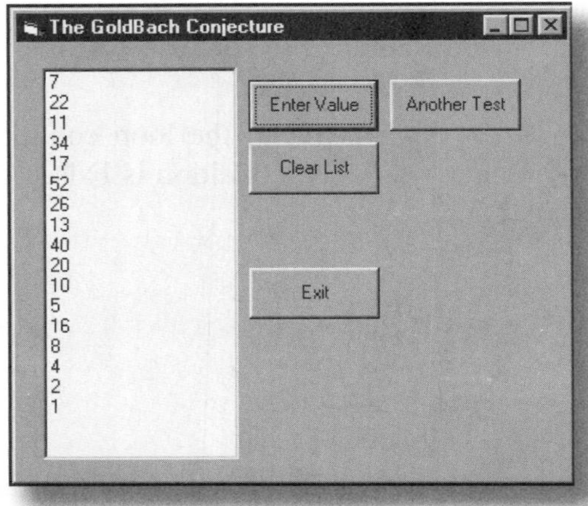

CODE STEP 7

```
Dim x As Integer
Do
   x = Val(InputBox("Enter a positive whole number:","Goldbach","7"))
Loop Until x > 0
lstDisplay.Additem x
Do While x <> 1
  If x Mod 2 = 0 Then
    x = x / 2
  Else
    x = 3 * x + 1
  End If
lstDisplay.Additem x
Loop
```

displayed in the list box and the process repeats. If the Goldbach conjecture were not correct, the loop might never end.

8. Save and run the program. Click **Enter Value** and enter various values. Clear the list box by clicking **Clear List**. Try entering a negative number. Then enter the number **7**. Whatever number you try, the sequence of numbers generated always ends in 1.

9. Now you will modify the program to try successive values of *x* until you find the smallest value of *x* that generates a number in its sequence that exceeds 1000. How would you do it? Add another **command button** to the form. Change its caption to **Another Test**. Change its name to **cmdOver**.

10. Press **Tab** and add the code in **Code Step 10** to **cmdOver**.

CODE STEP 10

```
Dim x As Integer, y As Integer, Largest As Integer
x = 1
Do
 x = x + 1
 Largest = x
 y = x
 lstDisplay.Clear
  lstDisplay.Additem y
  Do While y <> 1
    If y mod 2 = 0 Then
      y = y / 2
    Else
      y = 3 * y + 1
    End If
    lstDisplay.Additem y
    If y > Largest Then
      Largest = y
    End If
  Loop
Loop Until Largest > 1000
```

(continued on next page)

Building Programming Skills

A particular section of the code shown on the previous page is quite important:

```
If y > Largest Then
    Largest = y
End If
```

These lines compare the current value of y with a value stored in Largest. If the value of y exceeds the value of Largest, the value of y is saved in Largest. This allows the programmer to find the largest (or smallest) item in a list and save that value for later processing.

11. Save and run the program. Click **Another Test** and observe the results. Can you see the list box filling and clearing? What value was the first to generate a value in its series over 1000?

12. Stop the program and change the upper limit from 1000 to **10,000**. Save and run the program again. Click **Another Test** and observe the results.

13. Stop and remove the program.

Quick Check 4.e

1. To be sure that the body of a loop executes at least once, no matter what the truth-value of a condition is, put the While or Until statement at ____________________ .
2. A Do While loop continues executing the statements in the body of the loop while the condition tested is ____________________ .
3. The Mod operator divides two numbers and returns the ____________________ .
4. In a Do Until loop, the condition tested must be ____________________ for the loop to end.
5. If you know how many times a loop should execute before the loop begins, use a ____________________ loop. Otherwise, use a ____________________ loop.

Arrays

An array is a list of values referred to by a single name. The concept is very similar to giving multiple menu items the same name. All the menu items execute the same event procedure when selected. The menu items are distinguished by their unique index values. Such a group of menu items is sometimes called a *menu control array*.

You declare an array in a Dim statement by following a variable name with a number enclosed in parentheses.

```
Dim ClassList(45) As String
Dim Scores(10) As Integer
```

The first declaration declares an array ClassList with a capacity of 46 values of the String data type. The second defines an array of eleven integers and assigns to it the name Scores. When an array is first declared, the values of the array are assigned to 0 or the empty string "". To access a particular *element* or *member* of an array, state the name of the array with an *index* or *subscript* value in parentheses following the name. Normally, array subscripts start at 0. That is why ClassList has a capacity of 46 strings.

```
ClassList(7) = "Robinson, Oscar"
ClassList(12) = "The Grouch, Oscar"
```

The first statement changes the 7th entry of the array to "Robinson, Oscar." Until the value is changed, whenever ClassList(7) is used in an expression, it will return the value "Robinson, Oscar."

```
ClassList(Current) = ClassList(7)
```

This statement assigns the value of ClassList(7) to ClassList(Current). Current represents a whole number within the subscript range of the array. If that element is currently occupied, it will be replaced.

The valid subscripts of an array are determined when the array is declared. Change the default range of subscripts by specifying a starting value and an ending value.

```
Dim ClassList(1 to 25) As String
```

Here the valid subscripts are 1 to 25. The ending subscript must exceed the starting subscript. An array also may be initialized as follows:

```
Dim EngineSize As Variant
EngineSize = Array("3hp", "5hp", "8hp", "12hp")
```

A variable of Variant data type can be used as shown above to represent an array. The Array() function is used to initialize the elements of the array. Once the code is executed, EngineSize(1) is loaded with "5hp." The starting subscript defaults to 0.

Scope

Before you can start to use arrays in your programs, let's revisit the concept of the *scope* of a variable. The scope of a variable is a variable's *visibility* and its *lifetime*. The lifetime of a variable is when it does and does not hold valid values. Most variables have a limited life: They come into existence at the beginning of an event procedure and disappear when the procedure ends. They reappear when the procedure is again executed.

The visibility of a variable is where in the project the value of the variable is available to use or change. A variable declared with a Dim statement in one event procedure is normally not available (visible) in another event procedure. Such a variable is a *private variable*. When using an array in your project, you often want the values of the array to be visible to many or all of the event procedures in the form. To make the array visible to all the event procedures, declare the array in the form's *General Declarations* section. A variable or array declared in this section has a lifetime equal to the lifetime of the form and is visible to all event procedures in the form.

Explore arrays and learn about the *linear search* algorithm in the following Step-by-Step exercise. The Step-by-Step exercise creates an array with a capacity of 6 first names. One command button allows the user to enter names into the array. Names are displayed in a list box as they are entered. Another button lets the user clear the list box and the array. A third button lets the user search the array for the occurrence of a particular name. If the name is found, the index number of the name is displayed.

STEP-BY-STEP 4.5

1. Start a new **Standard EXE** project. Save the form and project as **Array**.

2. Change the caption of the form to **Exploring Arrays**. Change the name of the form to **frmArray**.

3. Add a list box and four command buttons to the form, arranged as shown in Figure 4-4. Change the names to **lstDisplay**, **cmdEnter**, **cmdSearch**, **cmdClear**, and **cmdExit**. Change the captions of the command buttons to **Enter a Name**, **Search**, **Clear**, and **Exit**. See Figure 4-4 for placement of controls on the form.

FIGURE 4-4
Final placement of controls on frmArray

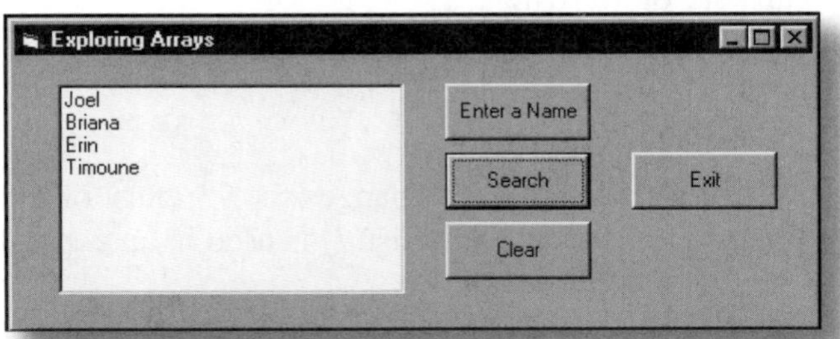

4. Double-click the **Exit** button to open the Code window. Select **(General)** from the Object list. The Procedure list should show **(Declarations)**. This is where you declare variables if you want the variable to be visible throughout the form. Enter the following code:

```
Dim FirstName(5) As String
Dim Current As Integer
```

   Current is used to keep track of the next empty space in the array. It is also used when names are added. When the value of Current exceeds the last valid array subscript, the program refuses to accept further input. Current is declared in General Declarations because its lifetime must equal the lifetime of the form. Its value is initialized in the Form_Activate procedure.

5. In the cmdExit_Click procedure, press **Tab** and enter **End**.

6. Select **cmdEnter** from the Object box. Enter the code in **Code Step 6**.

   In this code, names are added as long as the value of Current is valid — a whole number between 0 and 5. Current is checked, then used as a subscript to enter a name from the keyboard. The name is displayed in the list box and the value of Current is increased by one. Current always points to the next open space in the FirstName array.

7. Save and run the program. Click the **Enter a Name** button and enter a name. Repeat this several times. The names should

CODE STEP 6

```
If Current <= 5 Then
  FirstName(Current) = InputBox("Enter first name:")
  lstDisplay.AddItem FirstName(Current)
  Current = Current + 1
Else
  MsgBox "Array capacity exceeded!"
End If
```

appear in the list box. Keep entering names until you fill the array. Enter a seventh name. You should see the error message.

8. Click **Exit** to stop the program.

9. Open the Code window and select **cmdClear** from the Object list. The code you will add clears the list box and sets the elements of the array back to the empty string "". Enter the following code:

```
lstDisplay.Clear
For x = 0 To 5
  FirstName(x) = ""
Next x
Current = 0
cmdEnter.SetFocus
```

The For loop cycles through each entry in the array and sets it to "". Current is reset to 0.

10. Searching is the tough part. Select the **cmdSearch_Click** procedure in the Code window. The Search routine that you add gathers a name from the user. This name is the name you are looking for in the array of names. The name is assigned to the string variable Target. A Boolean variable, Found, is used as a flag. A *flag* is a variable used as an indicator. Most of the time, a flag can have one of two values: True or False. The Found flag is used in this program to indicate whether the Target string was found in the array. Press **Tab** and enter the **declarations** in the procedure:

```
Dim Target As String, x As Integer
Dim Found As Boolean
```

A Do Until loop is used to prevent the user from entering an empty string.

11. Continue by entering the code in **Code Step 11** below the previous code.

(continued on next page)

CODE STEP 11

```
Do
  Target = InputBox("Enter the name to search for:")
Loop Until Target <> ""
Found = False
For x = 0 To Current - 1
    If Target = FirstName(x) Then
       Found = True
       Exit For
    End If
Next x
If Found Then
    MsgBox (Target & " found at " & x)
Else
    MsgBox (Target & ": not in list.")
End If
```

This code starts by setting Found to False. If the target string is found, the flag is reset to True. A For loop cycles through all the occupied elements of the array. The If statement compares the Target string with each item in the array. If there is a match, the value of Found is changed to True and the For loop is exited. After the loop is over, Found is examined in an If statement to determine how the loop ended. If Found is True, the Target and its position in the array is reported to the user through a MsgBox. If Found is False, the Target is repeated and the "not in list" message is displayed.

12. Save and run the program. Enter several names. Click the **Search** button. Enter a name for which to search. Enter a name that is not in the list. Enter a name that is in the list.

13. Clear the list and reenter a few names. Test the **Search** button again. Stop and remove the program.

This kind of search is called a linear search. It is called this because the code examines each of the array entries in order from first to last. This is about the only kind of search that works with an unordered list. Imagine the search process you would have if the telephone book were not alphabetized.

Quick Check 4.f

1. The default for the starting value of a subscript for an array is ____________________ .
2. The number used to refer to particular elements of an array is called a(n) ____________________ or ____________________ .
3. Often a(n) ____________________ is used to indicate when a tested condition changes value.
4. To ensure the values of an array are visible to all the event procedures of a form, declare the array in the ____________________ ____________________ section of the form module.
5. The scope of a variable refers to its ____________________ and its ____________________ .

Commonly Used Math Functions

Visual Basic has a number of built-in functions. Some of these are like the functions built into a scientific calculator, although the notation is somewhat different. The values returned by a function can be assigned to variables or used in expressions. You can use a function in the right-hand expression of an assignment statement, but you cannot use a function to the left of the equal sign.

Following is a partial list of functions dedicated to mathematical uses:

Function Name	Use
Sqr( )	Returns the Double type square root of a number.
Abs( )	Returns the Absolute Value of a number.
Int( )	The greatest integer function. Int(7.9) = 7, Int(-3.3) = -4.
Fix( )	Like Int( ) except Fix(-3.3) = -3.
Round( )	Returns a properly rounded Double, VB6 only.
Sin( )	Calculates the Double sine of an angle measured in radians.
Cos( )	Calculates the Cosine of an angle measured in radians.
Tan( )	Calculates the Tangent of an angle measured in radians.
Atn( )	Calculates the radian measure angle whose tangent is specified.

You convert an angle from radians to degrees by multiplying by 180 and dividing by Pi, 3.1415927. You convert from degrees to radians by multiplying by Pi and dividing by 180.

If you have the entire MSDN Library installed with Visual Studio, you may get confused if you use the Help system to look up the use of functions. You may see multiple entries for each function because there are many different versions of each in the complete Microsoft family of products. There is a way to eliminate some of the confusion: Limit the Active Subset to Visual Basic Documentation. Other entries still appear in the Index list, but they are dimmed and cannot be selected.

Messing with Strings

Since manipulating strings is such a common programming application, Visual Basic 6.0 (VB6) provides a large number of functions for a number of purposes. Remember that a function returns a value that can be assigned to a variable, but the value of the original variable is not changed. You can, however, send a variable to a function and then assign the return value to the same variable: x = Sqr(x). This usage is common with the string functions. A partial list follows.

Function Name	Use
UCase(*string*)	Returns a string with all characters converted to uppercase.
LCase(*string*)	Returns a string with all characters converted to lowercase.
InStr(*val, str1, str2*)	Returns the position of *str2* in *str1*. The search starts at *val*.
InStrRev(*val*, *str1*, *str2*)	Same as InStr(), search starts at *val* and goes right to left, VB6 only.
Left(*string*, *length*)	Returns *length* characters of *string*, counting from the left.
Right(*string*, *length*)	Returns *length* characters of *string*, counting from the right.
Len(*string*)	Returns the number of characters in a *string*.
Mid(*string, start, len*)	Returns portion of *string* starting at *start* and consisting of *len* characters.
Trim(*string*)	Trims leading and trailing spaces from a string. Also LTrim and RTrim.
Chr(*value*)	Converts an ASCII value to its corresponding character.
Asc(*string*)	Converts the first character of *string* to its ASCII value.
Str(*value*)	Converts a value to a string representation of that value.
Val(*string*)	Converts a string to a value.
StrReverse(*string*)	Returns *string* with the characters in reverse order, VB6 only.

String *concatenation* is joining two strings together end to end. The concatenation operator is the ampersand (&). To remain compatible with older versions of BASIC, the plus sign (+) can also be used as a concatenation operator.

```
Dim First As String, Last As String
Dim FullName As String, LastFirst As String
First = "Oscar"
Last = "The Grouch"
FullName = First & " " & Last
LastFirst = Last & ", " & First
```

Notice that the order in which the strings are joined makes a difference in the results. In the example shown above, FullName = "Oscar the Grouch" and VLastFirst = "The Grouch, Oscar."

The next Step-by-Step exercise lets you test out some of the functions shown above. It uses a text box to enter a string that represents a name—first, middle, and last. The characters of the name are reversed and displayed in the first label. The second label shows the name rearranged so that the last name is listed first.

STEP-BY-STEP 4.6

1. Start a new **Standard EXE** project. Save the form and project as **Festival**.

2. Change the name of the form to **frmFestival** and the caption of the form to **Festival of Strings**.

3. Add a text box to the form. Name it **txtName**. Change the text property to **John Phillip Sousa**.

4. Add a label to the form below the text box. Clear its caption. Change the **BorderStyle** property to **1 – Fixed Single**. Select the **BackColor** property. Choose a **white background** from the Palette tab. Select the **Font** property. Open the Font dialog box and choose **12** as the FontSize.

5. Now that the label properties are set, right-click the label. Select **Copy** from the menu. Move the mouse pointer to the body of the form. Right-click the mouse. Select **Paste**. A message box appears with the warning: You already have a Control named "Label1." Do you want to create a control array? Answer **No**.

6. Move the new label to its proper place (see Figure 4-5). Copying and pasting a control is a great labor-saving device if the control is one of two or more controls that require identical Property settings. You still need to name each label. Name the first **lblReverse** and the second **lblLastNameFirst**. Remember, the lowercase "L" often looks like an "I" or a "1," depending on what font is used.

lblLastNameFirst must be large enough to display the entire name or it will cut off the entire part of the name that can not be fully displayed. In other words, if it is large enough to display the full last and first name, but not the full middle name, only last and first will be displayed. This might confuse the user.

7. Put another label next to each of the first two labels and enter the following captions: **Name Reversed** and **Last Name First**.

8. Add three command buttons to the form. Name them **cmdProcess**, **cmdClear**, and **cmdExit**. Change the captions to **Process**, **Clear**, and **Exit** (see Figure 4-5).

9. Double-click the **Exit** button to enter the form's Code window. Enter the **End** command.

10. Select **cmdClear** from the Object box. Enter the following code:

```
txtName = ""
lblReverse = ""
lblLastNameFirst = ""
txtName.SetFocus
```

11. Select **cmdProcess** from the Object box. Enter the code from **Code Step 11**.

12. Save and run the program. Click the **Process** button. Click **Clear**. Click **Process** while the text box is empty. Note the error message. Stop the program.

    The Trim function eliminates any extra spaces around the name entered by the user. If the txtName.Text property is assigned an empty string, the user is warned in a message box and the procedure is terminated by the Exit Sub statement. StrReverse( ) reverses the characters of the name. The result is displayed in lblReverse.

FIGURE 4-5
Final placement of controls on frmFestival

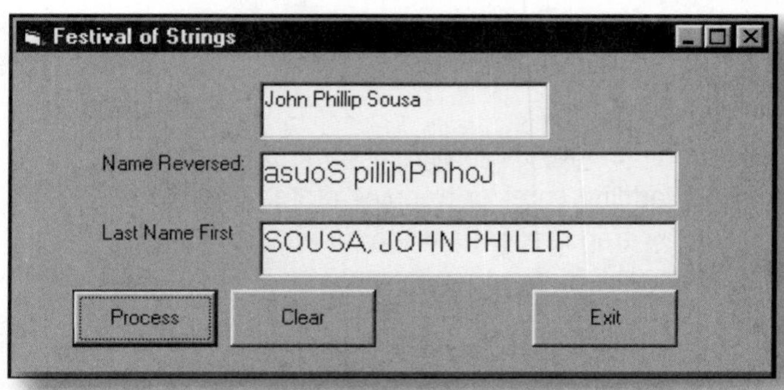

13. In **cmdProcess** at the end of the code from Code Step 11, enter the remaining code from **Code Step 13**.

14. Save and run the program. Click the **Process** button. Clear the form and enter your own name. Enter a name without a middle name. The program crashes.

    This program makes a bad assumption. The code is valid only for names with a first, middle, and last name. The program assumes that the user will know to only enter names with a first, middle, and last part.

CODE STEP 11

```
Dim Name As String
Name = Trim(txtName)
If Name = "" Then  ' no space between the quotes
  MsgBox "No name has been entered"
  Exit Sub
End If
' reverse the string. VB6 Only!
lblReverse = StrReverse(Name)
```

(continued on next page)

15. Stop the program.

16. You can give the program some protection by adding an error trapping statement. An error trap responds when an error occurs. The flow of program execution can be sent to special code written to handle the error, the program can end, or the program can skip the offending statement and try to continue. Add the statement **On Error Resume Next** after the FirstName = Left(Name, FirstSpace - 1) statement.

17. Save and run the program. Click the **Process** button. Click **Clear**. Click **Process** again. Note the error message. Enter a name without a middle name. Click **Process**. The program skips the offending statement and continues. Enter a name with two middle names. What happens?

18. Study the program carefully. Note how each function is used.

19. Stop and remove the project.

CODE STEP 13

```
Dim LengthName As Integer
Dim FirstSpace As Integer, LastSpace As Integer
Dim FirstName As String, MiddleName As String
Dim LastName As String
Const blank = " "   ' leave a space between the quotes
LengthName = Len(Name)
FirstSpace = InStr(Name, blank)
FirstName = Left(Name, FirstSpace - 1)
LastSpace = InStrRev(Name, blank) ' VB6 Only!
' LastSpace = InStr(FirstSpace + 1, Name, blank) use for VB5
LastName = Right(Name, LengthName - LastSpace)
MiddleName = Mid(Name, FirstSpace + 1, LastSpace - FirstSpace - 1)
lblLastNameFirst = UCase(LastName & ", " & FirstName & " " & MiddleName)
```

Quick Check 4.g

1. The Sin() function finds the sine of the given angle. The angle must be entered in ____________________ (what unit?).
2. In Visual Basic, the concatenation operator is the ____________________ .
3. To convert a string to a value, use the ____________________ function.
4. The InStr(*val, str1, str2*) function searches for ____________________ embedded in ____________________ , starting the search at the character at ____________________ .
5. To skip a line of code that causes an error, use an On Error ____________________ ____________________ statement.

Summary

- To solve a programming problem:

  Collect Information
  Create the User Interface
  Develop the Algorithm
  Subdivide the Problem
  Choose Data Structures
  Write the Code

- A combo box lets the user choose an item from a list.
- There are four If statements:

  If *condition* Then *statement*

  If *condition* Then
  statements
  End If

  If *condition* Then
  statements
  Else
  statements
  End If

  If *condition* Then
  statements
  ElseIf *condition* Then
  statements
  End If

- Relational operators let you build Boolean, or logical, expressions.
- Logical expressions can be combined using And, Or, and Not.
- The Select Case statement replaces a series of If Then statements.

  Select Case *textexpression*
  Case *expressionlist*
  statements
  Case *expressionlist*
  statements
  Case Else
  statements
  End Select

- Build a menu control array by giving two or more menu items in the same submenu the same name.
- The For statement is used to build definite loops that repeat statements a fixed number of times.
- The Do While and Do Until statements build indefinite loops. These loops are controlled by conditions within the loop itself.

- Arrays are lists of values referred to by the same name. The elements or members of the array are uniquely selected by specifying an index or subscript value.
- A linear search is used to search for a target value in an array.
- Visual Basic uses a large number of functions to handle special jobs involving mathematics and string manipulation.

LESSON 4 REVIEW QUESTIONS

TRUE/FALSE

Circle the T if the statement is true. Circle the F if it is false.

T F 1. The first step in solving a programming problem is to write the code.

T F 2. When solving a programming problem, communicate with the user by designing the user interface.

T F 3. A combo box lets the user select an item from a list of items.

T F 4. In an If statement, if the condition tested is True, program flow moves to the statement following the Else statement.

T F 5. When you have a number of conditions to test, you cannot use an If statement.

T F 6. The statements following the Case Else statement are executed if *testexpression* matches the *expressionlist*.

T F 7. For x = -5 to 5 … Next x is a definite loop that will execute the statement in the body of the loop 10 times.

T F 8. To be sure to execute the body of a Do While loop at least once, put the While part of the statement after Loop.

T F 9. Two array items may have the same subscript.

T F 10. The InStr( ) function is used to find the location of one string within another.

WRITTEN QUESTIONS

Write your answers to the following questions.

11. What are the steps to follow in solving a programming problem?

12. Why is it OK to start over when solving a programming problem?

13. What other control is the combo box most like?

14. Write the logical expression that would test to see if *x* is greater than 21 or less than -3.

15. Under what circumstances would you prefer to use a Select Case statement rather than an If statement with a number of ElseIf parts?

16. Write a For loop that generates the even numbers from 20 to 50. Write the equivalent loop with a Do While and a Do Until.

17. Write a statement to declare an array named ComputerCompanies of 10 strings. Write the code to display the contents of the array on the form. Assume the array is completely full and that the first index value is 0.

18. Write a statement that would extract the middle word of the string "oscar the grouch" and assign the result to Middle.

LESSON 4 APPLICATION PROBLEMS

SCANS

Level One

THE PRINTER PROGRAM

Write a program similar to the Water Heater program that lets a user choose a printer from a list of printers. The list should be displayed in a combo box and should include at least two printers. Include three command buttons, one to display the choice, one to clear the choice, and one to exit the program. After the choice is made, the user clicks a command button to display features of the printer in a list box. Either use printers known to you for examples or search the Internet for information about printers.

THE WEIGH TOO MUCH PROGRAM

To maintain a particular weight requires about 20 calories per pound per day. Write a program with a text box for a person's current weight and a second text box for a person's desired weight. Add three command buttons, one to calculate, one to clear, and one to exit the program. When a command button is clicked, the program should read the weights from the text boxes, calculate the number of calories needed to maintain each of the weights, and subtract one from the other. Subtract the calories needed to maintain the actual weight from the calories needed to maintain the desired weight. Use an If Then statement to determine if the value is positive or negative. If the value is negative, display a message that tells the user to increase his caloric intake. If the value is positive, display a message that tells the user to decrease his caloric intake. In either case, display the difference in calories.

THE UNIT CONVERSION PROGRAM

Write a program that allows a user to pick a unit conversion from a menu. For instance, Feet to Inches, or Miles to Meters. The menu items in the conversion submenu should all have the same name so that a menu control array is formed. Within the event procedure, determine which item was selected using a Select Case statement. Read a text box with the original value and display the new value with the units converted. If the user enters 36 in a text box and selects Inches to Feet, the program displays 3 feet. Here are some useful conversions. Use at least three in your program: 1 mile = 5280 feet, 1 lb. = 16. oz., 1 km = .62137119 mile, 1 inch = 2.54 cm, 1 kw = 1.341003 hp.

THE COOKING A TURKEY PROGRAM

Write a program to display a table of values that represent the cooking time in minutes for a turkey of *p* pounds. Assume that a turkey should be cooked 17 minutes per pound. Display the table (using a For loop) in a list box. The weight of the turkey should range from 8 pounds to 30 pounds.

Level Two

SCANS

THE UNTOLD WEALTH PROGRAM

Write a program to display the daily wealth of the founder of the MegaSoft computer company. The founder started with $50,000 and his wealth doubles every week. Write a program that starts at $50,000, displays the weekly total in a list box, and displays a special message when the founder's wealth exceeds $100 million. The message should say how many weeks it took for the amount to exceed that amount. Use a Do While loop to control the program flow.

THE RND FUNCTION PROBLEM

The Rnd function is used to generate a random number between 0 and 1. The Randomize statement is used to generate a different random sequence whenever the program is run. Use the Rnd function like this:

```
Dim x As Double
Randomize
x = Rnd
```

The value of *x* will be a random number between 0 and 1. To generate a random integer, use the following code:

```
Dim x As Integer
Randomize
x = CInt(100*Rnd)
```

This code starts with a value between 0 and 1, multiplies it by 100, and converts it to an integer. The result is an integer between 0 and 99. Use this latter code to generate 20 random integers between 0 and 99 and store them in an Integer array. Once the array is initialized with these values, display the contents of the array in a list box. Enter a target value between 0 and 99 in a text box and, when a command button is clicked, search the array for the target value. Use the linear search described in the text. If the value is found, display a message telling in what element of the array the value was found. If the value is not found, display a message that says the value was not in the list.

LESSON 4 PROGRAMMING AT WORK

SCANS

THE MUSIC COLLECTION PROJECT

This is the first part of an ongoing project called the Music Collection Project. The purpose of the program is to create a database for a music collection. A user will be able to add new entries to the database, display a table showing all the entries, search for a particular entry, or display a list of entries that all meet particular search criteria. In this lesson the data entry form will be developed.

Form and database design always begins with questions. What information should be stored? What information should be displayed? Should records of the database be displayed one at a time or in a grid or both? What is the easiest way for a user to make a new entry? How will the user designate search criteria to search the database?

To determine what information to store, look at a CD. The title, musician, and format (CD or tape) should all be included. What else is necessary? Do you have any classical CDs? If you do, you might want to store the names of the works. You will certainly want the name of the composer. The year published and the publisher's name might be important. The playing time is significant. If you were cataloging music for use in soundtracks, the key the music was played in would be important. A field for comments would help you remember something about the music. A field to categorize the music would make it easier to search the database for certain kinds of music. One of the purposes of having a database is to help you locate a particular work in your collection. A field describing the work's location is included.

Follow these steps to create the data entry form for the database:

1. Start Visual Basic and double-click **Standard EXE**. Save the form as **DataEntry** and the project as **MusicCo**.

2. Change the name of the form to **frmDataEntry** and the caption of the form to **Data Entry**.

3. Build the form shown in Figure 4-6. Use combo boxes to present a list of formats and musical categories. Use a font size of **10** instead of the default 8 in all the labels and text boxes. (Remember that some of the users may have trouble seeing small print.) Set the labels to **Autosize=True**. Clear the text from the text boxes. Build one sample text box and one sample label, and copy and paste the others.

4. Change the names of the text boxes and combo boxes to the caption of its label with the proper prefix added: **txtTitle**, **cboFormat**.

5. Add three command buttons as shown. Name them with their caption names with the **cmd** prefix added.

FIGURE 4-6
The Data Entry form

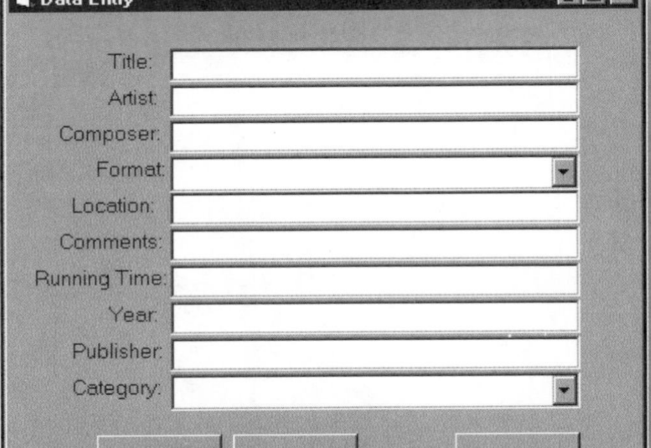

6. Double-click the form to enter its Code window. Enter the code below into the Form_Load event procedure to initialize the combo boxes. Add additional items to either combo box list to meet your needs.

```
cboFormat.AddItem "Standard CD"
cboFormat.AddItem "Mini CD"
cboFormat.AddItem "Tape"
cboFormat.ListIndex = 0
With cboCategory
      .AddItem "Bluegrass"
      .AddItem "Blues"
      .AddItem "Cajun"
      .AddItem "Classical"
      .AddItem "Folk"
      .AddItem "Gospel"
      .AddItem "Jazz"
      .AddItem "New Age"
      .AddItem "Rap"
      .AddItem "Rock"
      .ListIndex = 0
End With
```

7. Write code in the cmdClear procedure to clear the text boxes. Set the ListIndex property of the combo boxes back to **0**.

8. Save and run the program. Enter data in the text boxes. Make selections from the combo boxes. Click **Clear**.

9. Stop the program.

In the next lesson you will add some code, a pop-up menu, and a toolbar.

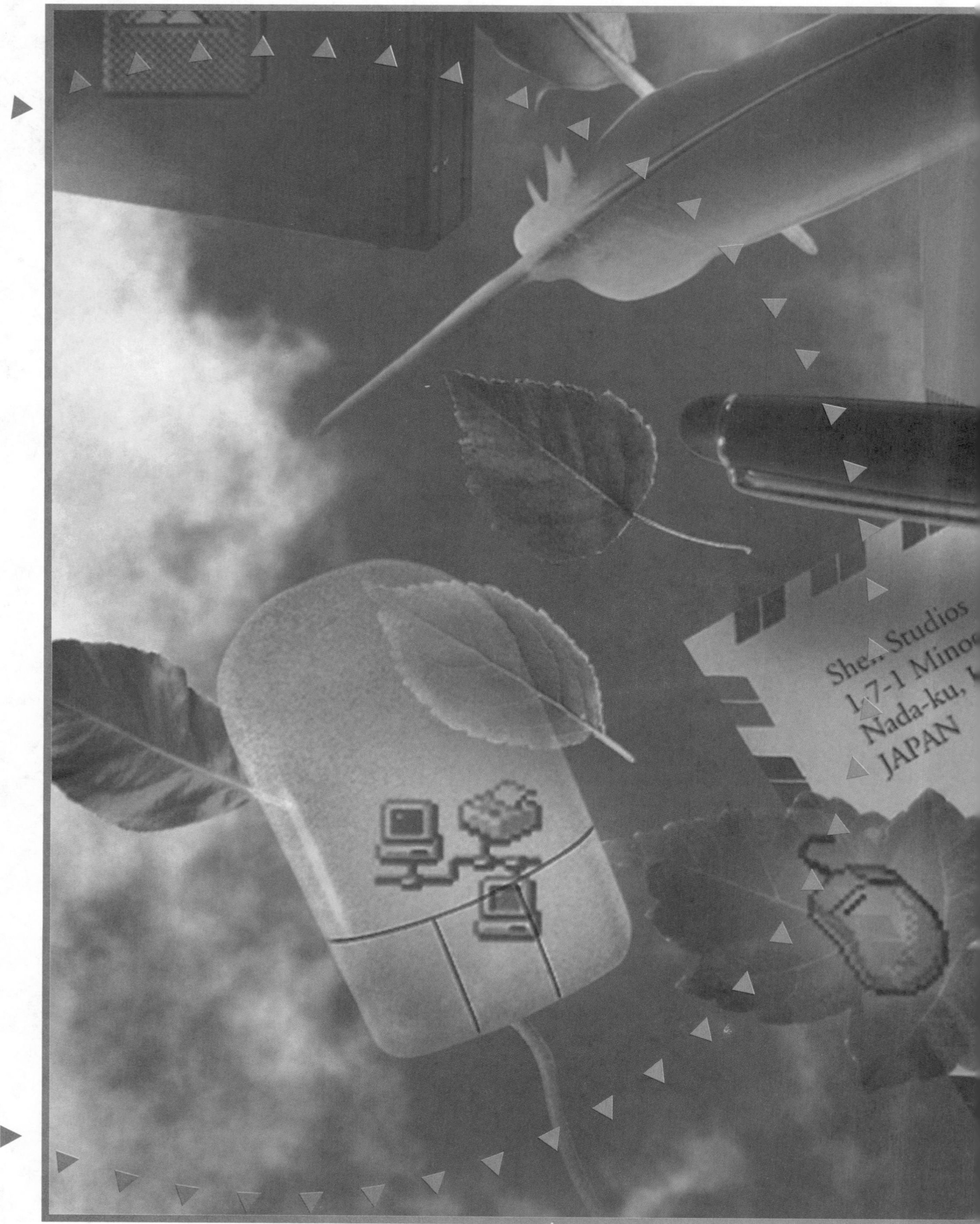
Studios
Nada-ku,
JAPAN

COLLECTIONS

UNIT 2

Estimated Time for Unit 2: 26 hours

LESSON 5

IMPROVING THE USER INTERFACE

OBJECTIVES

When you complete this lesson, you will be able to:

- Use several variations of the MsgBox and InputBox dialog boxes.
- Understand how to use Visual Basic built-in constants.
- Implement pop-up menus.
- Add a toolbar to your project.
- Use variations of the Common Dialog control to improve your program's user interface.

Estimated Time: 6 hours

KEY TERMS

MsgBox function
modal
InputBox function
null string
prompt
run-time error
pop-up menu
button
ImageList control
random access file
Common Dialog control
Open statement
FreeFile function
Print # statement
Close
Buttons Collection
Property Pages
sequential file
Input function
LOF( )

Communicating with the User

This lesson is about communication. Not the communication that starts at the beginning of a project—communication that helps you understand the definition of a problem. This lesson is about your program's interaction with the user: the user interface. You have already used some of the features discussed in this lesson. But here you will see variations and extensions that make simple dialog boxes like the message box and the input box even more useful. You will use pop-up menus, menus that are activated by a right-click of the mouse, and toolbars. A simple toolbar is a horizontal row of buttons marked with icons. The toolbars used in Windows use pictures, and can be oriented on any edge of the form. The Common Dialog control lets your program call and use the familiar dialog boxes common to many Windows programs, such as Open, Save As…, and Font dialog boxes.

The MsgBox Function

FIGURE 5-1
MsgBox function's dialog box

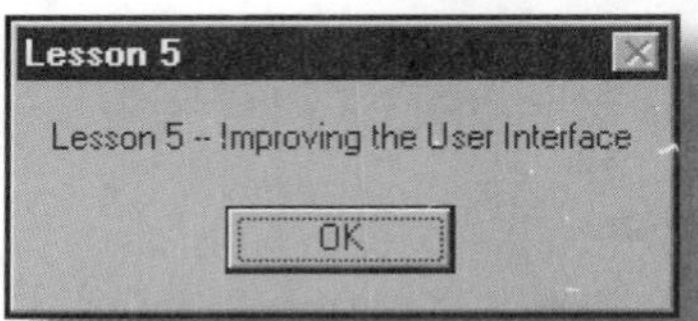

The *MsgBox function* interrupts the flow of the program and displays a message in a dialog box that the user must respond to. This dialog box is *modal*; the user must click one of the buttons before any other user-initiated event can be processed. The dialog box is displayed with either a MsgBox statement or function. As a function, it returns a value that corresponds to the button that is clicked by the user. The default is to display a message and an OK button for the user to click (See Figure 5-1).

When OK is clicked, the MsgBox function returns the value 1 which corresponds to the OK button.

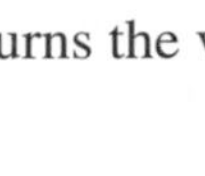

```
Dim x As Integer
x = MsgBox("Do you want to Exit")
```

After the line of code above is executed, the value of *x* is one. If MsgBox is used as a statement, the same dialog box appears, requiring the user to click OK. But the value corresponding to the button clicked is not assigned to a variable and is unavailable to the program. The MsgBox function has the following syntax:

```
variable = MsgBox(prompt[,buttons][,title][,helpfile,context])
```

In the syntax above, arguments in square brackets are optional. However, the arguments are positional, so the commas must appear: MsgBox("Enter a value:", ,"Sample Message box"). This statement displays a dialog box with the message "Enter a value:." The space for buttons is there between the commas, but is empty. The title is a string displayed in the title bar of the message box when it appears.

By changing the value of the button arguments, you change the type of box that appears. The button's parameter is an integer. MsgBox("Enter a value:", 0, "Sample Message box") puts an OK button only box on the screen. Change the button's parameter to 1 to put an OK and Cancel button box on the screen. This box has two buttons for the user to click: OK and Cancel. If the user clicks OK, the value returned by the function is 1. If the user clicks Cancel, the value returned is 2. When using a message box with more than one button, it is assumed the program will differentiate between the buttons and tailor a response to the button that is clicked.

A number of different boxes are available. Does the programmer have to remember the button's parameter value for each type of box? No, Visual Basic contains a vast number of built-in constants. Each constant has a descriptive name. The OK button only box uses a button value of 1. That value is stored in the constant, vbOKOnly. The constant for the OK and Cancel button box is vbOKCancel. Other boxes have similarly descriptive constants. Step-by-Step exercise 5.1 demonstrates the various message boxes and their constants. You will see as you enter the code that you do not even have to memorize the constant names because Visual Basic's Help system provides them for you.

STEP-BY-STEP 5.1

1. Start Visual Basic and double-click **Standard EXE**. Save the form and project as **Messages**.

2. Change the name of the form to **frmMessages**. Change the caption of the form to **Experimenting with the MsgBox Function**.

3. Select the **form** and open the **Menu Editor**. Enter the menu items shown in Table 5-1. The captions are shown in the first column, the names in the second, and the index values in the third.

4. Open the **Private Sub mnuExit_Click** procedure. Press **Tab** and key **End**.

5. Open **Private Sub mnuConstantsMsg_Click(Index As Integer)**, press **Tab**, and insert the code in **Code Step 5**. You get a pleasant surprise as you enter the MsgBox function. Once Visual Basic understands what you intend to do, it displays the syntax for the MsgBox function. When you enter the comma following the prompting message, Help supplies a list of constants that are legal button values. The names of the constants make it clear what kinds of message boxes are available.

TABLE 5-1

CAPTIONS	NAMES	INDEX VALUES
Trying Out the Constants	mnuConstants	
...OK Only	mnuConstantsMsg	0
...OK Cancel	mnuConstantsMsg	1
...Abort, Retry, Ignore	mnuConstantsMsg	2
...Yes, No, Cancel	mnuConstantsMsg	3
...Yes, No	mnuConstantsMsg	4
...Retry, Cancel	mnuConstantsMsg	5
...Critical	mnuConstantsMsg	6
...Question	mnuConstantsMsg	7
E&xit	mnuExit	

CODE STEP 5

```
Select Case Index
    Case 0
        x = MsgBox("This is the default style.", vbOKOnly, _
        "subtitle")
```

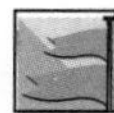

Building Programming Skills

The line above contains a continuation character, the underscore. When a line of code is too long to fit on a single line, you may continue the line by ending the first line with this underscore character. Leave a space in front of the character. You may want to continue a line just to make the code easier to read.

```
    Case 1
        x = MsgBox("Gives a choice of OK or Cancel.", vbOKCancel)
    Case 2
        x = MsgBox("The big three:", vbAbortRetryIgnore)
    Case 3
        x = MsgBox("Yes, No, Cancel", vbYesNoCancel)
    Case 4
        x = MsgBox("Yes or No ", vbYesNo)
    Case 5
        x = MsgBox("Retry or Cancel?", vbRetryCancel)
    Case 6
        x = MsgBox("Critical Message", vbCritical)
    Case 7
        x = MsgBox("Question", vbQuestion)
End Select
```

6. Save and run the program. Click **Trying Out the Constants**, select different items from the menu, and observe the results. Do you know which values are generated for *x*? Stop the program and add the code in **Code Step 6** under the existing Case statement to see.

   As you are entering the code, notice the differences from the code in Code Step 5.

The MsgBox statement immediately follows the Case statement on the same line. In the previous sample, each program statement occupied its own line. Generally, it is wise to give a separate line to each statement because it enhances readability. But sometimes, because it is clear what is being done, it makes sense to use a single line.

(continued on next page)

Historically Speaking

In the 1880s, it was predicted that it would take 11 years to count the 1890 census. Since a census comes every 10 years, clearly the situation was out of hand. The census bureau ran a contest for a new way to count the people of the nation. Herman Hollerith's machine used punched cards to record information and a machine that automatically counted the population based on the holes punched in the cards. Hollerith's machine was so successful he started a company, which became IBM, International Business Machines.

Another big difference is the way the MsgBox statement is used. In Code Step 5, MsgBox is used as a function returning its value to the variable *x*. The parameters of the MsgBox function are contained within parentheses. In the MsgBox statement, the value is returned but not assigned to a variable. When used as a statement, the parameters must not be enclosed in parentheses.

7. Save and run the program. Click **Trying Out the Constants** and select **Abort, Retry, and Ignore**. Click each of the three buttons to see the value returned by each. Select all of the styles of message boxes and study how the MsgBox works.

8. Stop and remove the program.

CODE STEP 6

```
Select Case x
    Case 1: MsgBox "The OK button: 1", vbInformation, "Value Returned"
    Case 2: MsgBox "The Cancel button: 2", vbInformation, "Value Returned"
    Case 3: MsgBox "The Abort button: 3", vbInformation, "Value Returned"
    Case 4: MsgBox "The Retry button: 4", vbInformation, "Value Returned"
    Case 5: MsgBox "The Ignore button: 5", vbInformation, "Value Returned"
    Case 6: MsgBox "The Yes button: 6", vbInformation, "Value Returned"
    Case 7: MsgBox "The No button: 7", vbInformation, "Value Returned"
End Select
```

Quick Check 5.a

1. A dialog box that must be clicked before the user can do anything else is said to be ____________________ .

2. When the OK button of a MsgBox function is clicked, the function returns the value ____________________ .

3. The constant ____________________ in the ____________________ parameter, is used to designate an OK button only style MsgBox.

4. To continue a long line of code on the next line, finish the first line with the ____________________ character.

5. The difference between the MsgBox statement and the MsgBox function is ____________________ .

The InputBox Function

The MsgBox statement is used to display information and elicit a response from the user. The response is limited to clicking one of the buttons. The *InputBox* function is also used to get information from the user, but it is not limited to a simple button click. An InputBox can accept up to 255 characters from the keyboard. Therefore, you can use it to prompt the user for a name or a value. When the InputBox function is executed, a box appears with a message prompting the user to enter a value or string. The box contains an area like a text box for the user to enter information. OK and Cancel buttons complete the box. The user enters data and clicks either OK or Cancel. If OK is clicked, the data entered by the user is returned to the calling program and is assigned to the variable. If Cancel is clicked, the *null string*, two quotes with nothing between them, is returned and assigned to the variable. The syntax of the InputBox function is shown below:

```
variable  = InputBox(prompt[,title][,default])
```

Typical *prompt* strings include "Enter a Value:" or "Enter the Last Name:." The title appears in the title bar of the box. The default value appears in the text box section. If the user clicks OK or presses the Enter key, the default value is returned and assigned to the variable. The title and the default strings are optional. To include a default string and omit a title, include the commas for a title, but omit the actual title. The statement below generates the InputBox shown in Figure 5-2.

```
x = InputBox("Enter the Last Name:", ,"Oscar")
```

"Clean Input" is what a novice programmer plans for: input from the user in the proper form. If programmers had their way, users would never key a number when a letter was expected. They would never add extra spaces or leave out necessary ones. Unfortunately, "clean" input is not always what happens, so you must protect your program from input that is not "clean."

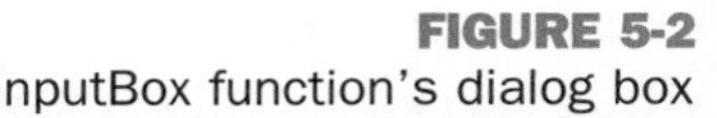
FIGURE 5-2
InputBox function's dialog box

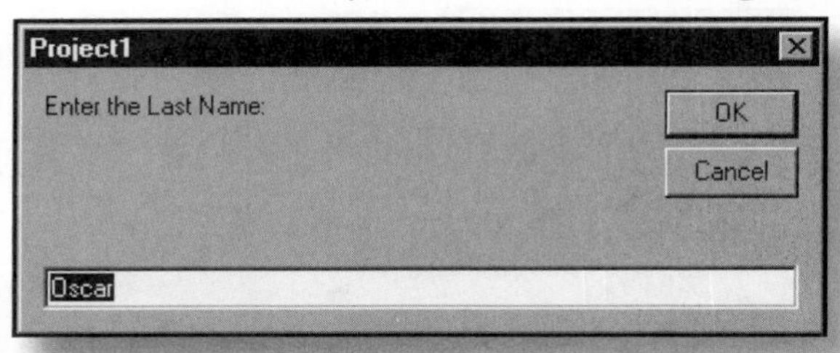

A *run-time error* occurs when a program cannot perform a task that it expects to be able to perform. Dividing by zero is common and easy to understand. A fraction with a denominator of zero does not exist, so anything that causes a program to try to divide by zero generates an error and stops the execution of the program. Not every run-time error causes a program to stop executing. Sometimes a run-time error is just something that is wrong. Maybe the user clicks the wrong option button when loading a program, or enters their age in the box where they are supposed to enter their name. What your program does in an error situation can make a real difference to the user. The next Step-by-Step exercise experiments with different uses of the InputBox function and how, with just a few lines of code, you can guard against mistakes in entered data.

STEP-BY-STEP 5.2

1. Start a new **Standard EXE** project. Save the form and project as **UserInput**.

2. Change the caption of the form to **Experimenting with InputBox** and the name of the form to **frmUserInput**.

3. Press **Tab** and enter the code in **Code Step 3** in the **Form_Click** procedure.

4. Save and run the program. Click the form and enter the following strings: **56.78**, **Answer=87**, **355/119**, and **87 is the Answer**. Each string is converted to a value, if possible. The first sample works as expected. The second, when converted to a value, returns a 0. A 0 is returned if the Val( ) function is unsuccessful in its attempt to convert the string. The third example, 355/119, shows that an operation will not be performed in the data entry portion of the InputBox: The first value encountered in the string, 355, is returned and assigned to *x*. The Val( ) function is able to convert the last string to a value. It returns the first value encountered: 87.

5. Stop the program and open the Code window. Replace the line "x=val..." with the lines in **Code Step 5**.

6. Save and run the program. Click the form and enter several values for *x*. If the value of *x* is between 1 and 5, it is accepted. Otherwise, the Do Loop keeps displaying the InputBox until a valid value is entered.

7. Stop and remove the program.

CODE STEP 3

```
Dim x As String
  x = Val(InputBox("Enter a value:"))
MsgBox x
```

CODE STEP 5

```
Do
  x = Val(InputBox("Enter a value between 1 and 5:"))
Loop Until 1 <= x And x <= 5
```

Another technique for protecting your input is to check the length of a string entered by the user. If you ask for a name in an InputBox and the string returned has a length of 0, the user has clicked Cancel or has clicked OK with nothing entered. Either way, your program should not treat the input as a valid entry.

The InputBox is useful for an occasional value or string entered from the keyboard, but generally you will design forms with combo boxes, text boxes, and menus to enter large amounts of data.

Quick Check 5.b

1. To gather up to 255 characters of input from the user, use the ____________________ function.
2. The InputBox function has three parameters (two of which are optional). They are ____________________ , ____________________ , and ____________________ .
3. "Nice Input" is ____________________ .
4. Dividing by zero when the program is running causes a ____________________ .
5. The Val( ) function converts a ____________________ to a ____________________ , if possible.

Pop-Up Menus

If used at all, *pop-up menus* usually appear when the user right-clicks the mouse button. It appears in the vicinity of the mouse pointer and floats over the form. Creating a pop-up menu is easy. It is designed like a normal menu using the Menu Editor and may even appear in the menu bar displayed on the form. What makes it a pop-up menu is a couple of lines of code usually included in the MouseUp event of the form.

The MouseUp event, executed when a mouse button has been clicked and released, passes a number of parameters to the routine. The first is the button parameter. If the value of this parameter is the built-in constant vbRightButton, the right button of the mouse has been clicked and released. The constant vbLeftButton designates the left button of the mouse. The second parameter is the shift parameter. This parameter communicates to the routine the status of the Shift, Alt, and Control keys. The final parameters, *x* and *y*, give the current position of the mouse pointer. You may want to tailor the code to respond certain ways when the mouse is positioned over a particular place on the form.

```
Private Sub Form_MouseUp(button As Integer,shift As Integer,x As Single,y As Single)
```

To use the MouseUp event to display the pop-up menu, check the *button* parameter. If the right button is clicked, execute the following line of code:

```
frmMain.PopupMenu  mnuMenuName
```

PopupMenu is a method that applies to the form object. If the name of the form is omitted, the form that currently has the focus is used. The name of the menu follows. The menu must have at least one submenu. When the menu displays, the Caption property of the menu called is not displayed. Only its menu items or commands are displayed. For instance, if you wanted the regular Windows File menu to pop up, the Caption "File" would not be displayed. Only File's submenu items would show.

In the Step-by-Step exercise that follows, a simple program to resize the form from a pop-up menu demonstrates some of the features of pop-up menus.

STEP-BY-STEP 5.3

1. Start a new **Standard EXE** project. Save the form and project as **PopUp**.

2. Change the caption of the form to **Trying Out Pop-Up Menus**. Change the name of the form to **frmPopUp**.

3. Open the **Menu Editor** and create the menu controls shown in Figure 5-3 and summarized below. Enter the menu controls shown in Table 5-2.

   Remember, the Menu Editor inserts the dots preceding the captions when you create a submenu by clicking the right arrow button.

4. Select **Size the Form** in the Menu Control list box and click the **Visible** property to deselect it, or set it to False. When set to False, the menu will not appear in the menu bar of the form. It will only appear when the body of the form is right-clicked. The default value of the Visible property is True and is not changed for the other menu items.

FIGURE 5-3
The Menu Editor with Visable set to False

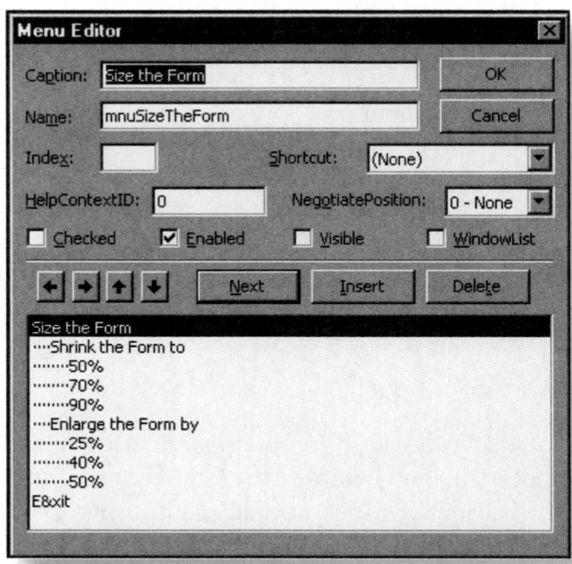

5. Click **OK** to exit the Menu Editor.

6. Double-click the body of the form and select the **Form_ MouseUp** procedure.

TABLE 5-2

CAPTION	NAME	INDEX
Size the Form	mnuSizeTheForm	
....Shrink the Form to	mnuShrink	
........50%	mnuShrinkAmt	1
........70%	mnuShrinkAmt	2
........90%	mnuShrinkAmt	3
....Enlarge the Form by	mnuEnlarge	
........25%	mnuEnlargeAmt	1
........40%	mnuEnlargeAmt	2
........50%	mnuEnlargeAmt	3
E&xit	mnuExit	

7. Press **Tab** and insert the code in **Code Step 7**.

8. Save and run the program. Click the **left mouse button**. Then click the **right mouse button**. The code you just entered executes when either mouse button is released while the mouse pointer is over the form. The If statement checks to see which button has just been released. If it is the right button, the PopupMenu method of the form is executed and the mnuSizeTheForm menu is displayed. If a regular menu or another pop-up menu is currently displayed, the new menu will not appear.

9. Stop the program and open the Code window. Press **Tab** and enter the following code in the **mnuEnlargeAmt_Click(Index As Integer)** procedure. When the user selects this option from the **Size the Form** menu, a multiplier is set corresponding to the enlargement percent. The multiplier is used to change the dimensions of the form.

```
Dim Multiplier As Single
Select Case Index
  Case 1:  Multiplier = 1.25
  Case 2:  Multiplier = 1.4
  Case 3:  Multiplier = 1.5
End Select
With frmPopUp
 .Height = Multiplier * .Height
 .Width = Multiplier * .Width
End With
```

The Height and Width properties of a form indicate the exterior dimensions of the form in twips, the basic unit of measurement used in Visual Basic. A twip is a twentieth of a point. A point is a unit of measure used by printers. It is equal to 1/72nd of an inch and is the measuring unit used for fonts.

10. Select the **mnuExit_Click** procedure, press **Tab**, and enter the command **End**.

11. Save and run the program. Right-click the body of the form. The **Size the Form** menu appears. Select **Enlarge the Form by** and choose a percentage. The size of the form changes.

12. Stop the program and open the Code window. Select **Private Sub mnuShrinkAmt_Click(Index As Integer)**, press **Tab**, and enter the following code:

```
Dim Multiplier As Single
Select Case Index
  Case 1:  Multiplier = 0.5
  Case 2:  Multiplier = 0.7
  Case 3:  Multiplier = 0.9
End Select
```

Building Programming Skills

The With statement simplifies code by letting the programmer get "inside" an object or data structure. Instead of referring to the Height property of the form as frmPopUp.Height, the With statement lets the programmer state the name of the object once. The object's properties are called by preceding the name of the property with a period.

CODE STEP 7

```
If Button = vbRightButton Then
  frmPopUp.PopupMenu mnuSizeTheForm
End If
```

(continued on next page)

```
With frmPopUp
  .Height = Multiplier * .Height
  .Width = Multiplier * .Width
End With
```

13. Save and run the program. Click the **right mouse button** and enlarge the form. Then click the **right mouse button** and shrink the form. Try several sizes.

14. Stop and remove the program.

Think about the pop-up menus you use in Windows applications. Most Windows editors use pop-up menus to provide editing functions like cutting and pasting. Visual Basic uses a number of pop-up menus. Try clicking the right button while in the Code window. Try again with the mouse pointer over the form. Experiment with menu selections. A number of the features have not been covered yet in this text, but with careful experimentation you can discover the use of several of them. As you write your own applications, think about how you can use this feature to simplify the user interface.

Quick Check 5.c

1. The parameters sent to the MouseUp event are the ____________________ parameter, the ____________________ parameter, and the ____________________ and ____________________ parameters.
2. The PopupMenu method is associated with the ____________________ object.
3. Each pop-up menu must have at least one ____________________ .
4. A pop-up menu may also appear in the ____________________ .
5. To get "inside" an object and simplify naming properties of the object, use the ____________________ statement.

Adding a Toolbar to a Form

It won't be the easiest thing you have done so far, but adding a toolbar is not too difficult and the payoff makes it worthwhile. Toolbars are everywhere in Windows programs. You often see them as rows of buttons with icons at the top or bottom of the active window in an application. In a word processor, the toolbar has buttons for opening a new file, saving a file, searching for text, cutting, pasting, copying, and many more functions. Your word processor probably has more than one toolbar. You may see a toolbar dedicated to fonts and paragraph formatting or drawing. Commonly used commands are the best candidates for inclusion in a toolbar. When designing your own applications, the most difficult part might be deciding what to include in the toolbar and which icon to use to symbolize the action.

The images for a toolbar come from an *ImageList control*. The ImageList is a place to store icons or pictures for the Toolbar control. You load the ImageList with icons or pictures during the design phase of the project, or dynamically while the program is running. The icons used in these lessons all come from the **Visual Basic\Common\Graphics\Icons** folder. The **Icons** folder contains a number of sub-folders of organized icons such as Arrows, Computer, Office, etc. You add the images to the ImageList control. The ImageList is then attached to a toolbar. The toolbar accesses each image stored in the ImageList by designating the image's Index number.

Take a look at the toolbox in Visual Basic. Do you see the Toolbar control or the ImageList control? They are not among the standard controls loaded by Visual Basic on start-up. Follow these instructions to add the controls to your project.

STEP-BY-STEP 5.4

1. Start a new **Standard EXE** project. Save the form and project as **ToolBarDemo**.

2. Change the name of the form to **frmToolBarDemo**, and the caption of the form to **Toolbars and Common Dialogs**.

3. Right-click the **Toolbox** window and click **Components**, or select **Project | Components** from the menu bar to open the Components dialog box.

4. Select **Microsoft Windows Common Controls 6.0** and **Microsoft Windows Common Controls-3 6.0** by clicking their check boxes (see Figure 5-4). Click **OK** to add the controls to the toolbox. In this section you will use the Toolbar and ImageList controls.

FIGURE 5-4
The Components dialog box with the proper choices selected

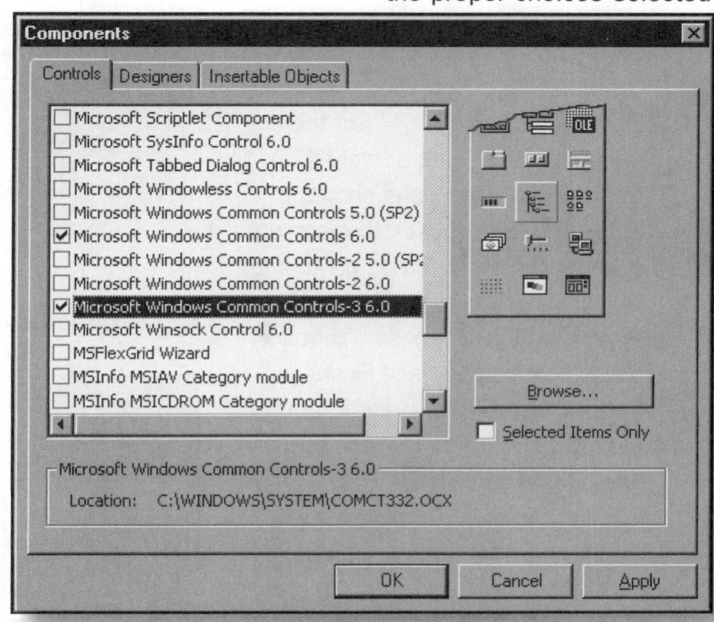

5. Notice the new controls at the bottom of the toolbox. Roll the mouse pointer over each new icon. Observe each ToolTip to see the name of each new control.

6. Add an **ImageList** control by double-clicking its icon in the toolbox. You may also draw the control on the form by single-clicking the icon in the toolbox and clicking and dragging your mouse pointer directly on the form. For some controls, this lets you control the size of the object. For the ImageList control, the size is not something you can control. It doesn't really matter because you can't see the ImageList when the program is running. The images stored in an ImageList are visible only if they are used in a toolbar.

7. Name the ImageList **ilsToolBarSupport**.

8. Add images to the ImageList by right-clicking the **control** on the form and selecting **Properties** from the pop-up menu. The Property Pages dialog box for

(continued on next page)

the control appears with three tabs: General, Images, and Color. Click the **Images** tab. Figure 5-5 shows the ImageList loaded with six icons. You may not see any icons yet.

FIGURE 5-5
The Images tab of the Property Pages of the ImageList control loaded with six images

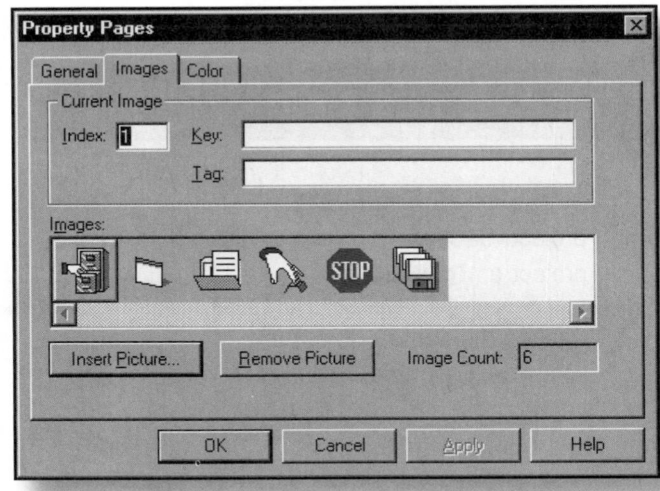

9. You need to know what is going to be on your toolbar before you can select images. For this demo, you will create a rudimentary text editor. The commands on the toolbar will be "Open a File," "New File," "Save a File," "Choose a Font," "Exit the Program," and "Edit a Recently Opened File." The icons shown in Figure 5-5 were chosen to represent those commands. To add an icon to the ImageList, click the **Insert Picture** button. The **Select picture** dialog box appears (see Figure 5-6). The icons shown are from the directory **C:\Program Files\Microsoft Visual Studio\Common\Graphics\Icons\Computer**. A normal installation installs with these folders. However, if not all the components are loaded, you may not find these particular images. If necessary, navigate to find a source of images.

FIGURE 5-6
The Select picture dialog box, a typical process for adding images to an ImageList control

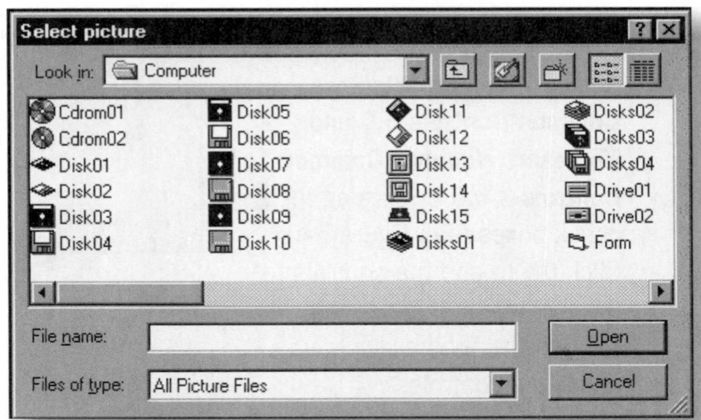

10. Double-click an **icon** and add six icons to the ImageList. The images in Figure 5-5 are from the **Computer** and **Office** folders. If you can't find these, add any icons you can find for the Step-by-Step exercise. Once the ImageList is attached to a toolbar, images cannot be added. To add images at that point, the ImageList must be detached from the toolbar, so be sure and add six icons.

11. Next, double-click the **Toolbar** tool in the toolbox to add it to the project. You can draw the control directly on the form, but it will migrate to its default position stretched across the top of the form. Name the toolbar **tlbMyToolbar**.

12. Right-click the **Toolbar** control and select **Properties** from the pop-up menu. The Property Pages dialog box for this control displays, as shown in Figure 5-7. Click the **ImageList** list arrow and select **ilsToolBarSupport**. This attaches the ImageList to the Toolbar control, making the icons stored in the ImageList available for use in the toolbar (see Figure 5-7).

FIGURE 5-7
The Property Pages dialog box for the Toolbar control

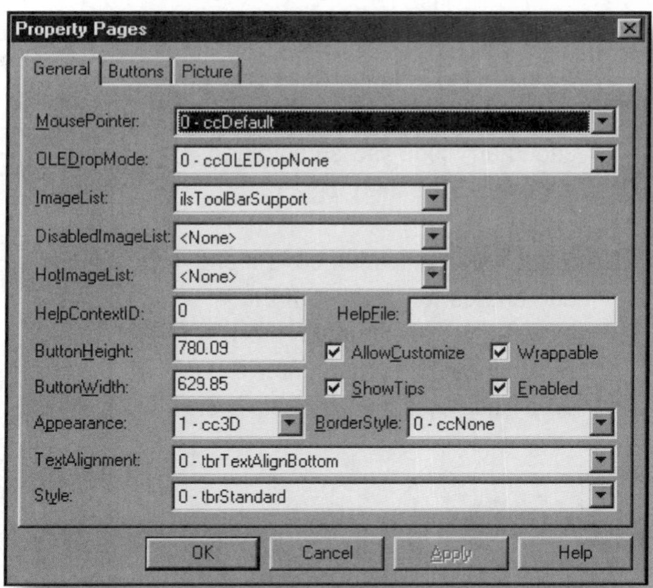

Following is a description of several of the important properties in this dialog box. The MousePointer property determines how the mouse pointer appears when it is over the area occupied by the toolbar. The default pointer is the familiar arrow pointing to the upper-left corner of the screen. As you already know, the ImageList property contains the name of the ImageList control that holds the icons used as images on the button faces. The ButtonHeight and ButtonWidth properties determine the dimensions of the button in twips. AllowCustomize, if selected, lets the user rearrange the buttons on the toolbar. Wrappable means the buttons are rearranged to fit on the form when it is resized. ShowTips allows the ToolTipsText to appear when the mouse pointer is hovering over a particular button. Since buttons have limited room for text and icons are not always easy to understand, you should always provide an entry in the ToolTipsText property. A toolbar button may have brief text in addition to an icon. By default, the text appears below the icon. The TextAlignment property allows you to change the alignment so the text is to the right of the icon.

13. To add buttons to the toolbar, click the **Buttons** tab. When the Buttons page is first displayed, all its entries are unavailable. Click **Insert Button** to add a button to the toolbar. Most of the text boxes and combo boxes are now available. An appropriate entry for the button's Index property is entered automatically. The complete entry for the first button on the toolbar is shown in Figure 5-8. The first button is the Open File button. Change the caption to **Open**. The Caption property displays below the icon on the toolbar. Enter **OpenFile** for the button's **Key** property. The Key property is how the button is identified in code. It is the button's most important property. Enter **Open a File** for the **Description** and the **ToolTipText** properties. Leave the entries for **Style** and **Value** at their default values. Make sure the **Index** property is set to **1**. It determines which image from the ImageList control is used for the button's icon. The entry of 1 uses the first image.

(continued on next page)

14. Save and run the program. The toolbar should appear with a single button. Click the button. You haven't added any code yet, so nothing happens. Stop the program.

15. Right-click the **Toolbar** control and add entries for the rest of the buttons. For each button, start by clicking **Insert Button**. Enter the properties as shown in Table 5-3.

It is likely that your Index values will be different unless you found the exact same (or similar) icons and put them into the ImageList in the same order.

FIGURE 5-8
The Buttons tab of the Property Pages of the Toolbar control

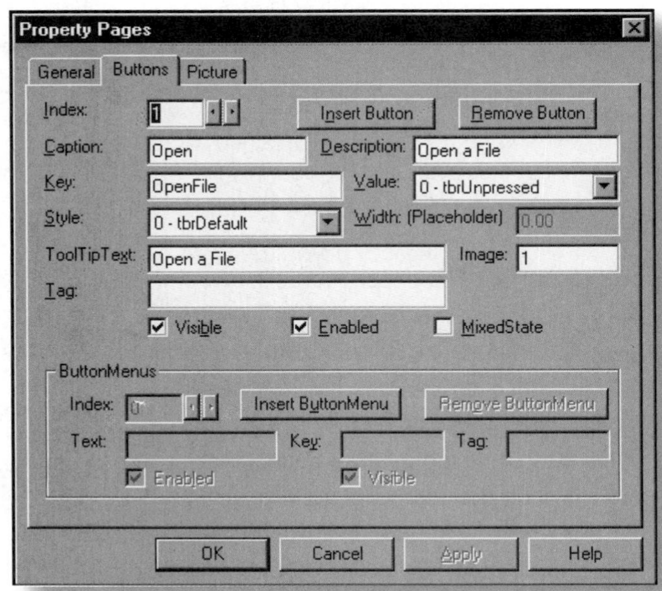

16. Next to the Index property are two small arrow icons. One points to the left, the other to the right. Use these buttons to move between the property pages for each of the buttons added to the toolbar. Test the arrows now by moving to the front and the back of the list of buttons.

17. Display the **property page** for the **fourth button**, **Recent**. This button is a different style from the others. The Drop-down style lets you add a drop-down list to the button. Add the list to the button by clicking the **InsertButtonMenu** button in the **ButtonMenus** frame at the bottom of the dialog box. Immediately, the dimmed text boxes become available.

18. This part of the page allows you to add menu items to the drop-down list attached to the button. For the first menu item,

TABLE 5-3

CAPTION	DESCRIPTION	KEY	STYLE	TOOLTIPTEXT	INDEX
New	New File	NewFile	0	Create a new document	2
Save	Save a File	SaveFile	0	Save a File	3
Font	Choose a Font	ChooseFont	0	Choose a Font	4
Recent	Recent Files	Recent	5	Edit a Recent File	6
Exit	Exit the Program	ExitProgram	0	Exit the Program	5

enter **Item One goes here** for the Text property and **ItemOne** for the Key property.

19. Click **Insert ButtonMenu** again and add a second menu item. Text: **Item Two**. Key: **ItemTwo**.

20. Save and run the program. Click the various buttons on the toolbar. Click the **Recent** button's list arrow and select the items shown.

21. Stop the program and leave it open for the next Step-by-Step exercise.

Save your work frequently. Typically, users run two or more programs at the same time. You might listen to a CD using CD Player while you edit a document. You may have a Help file open as well as a Solitaire game going. If any one of the programs crashes the computer, you may lose your work. Save your work whenever you step away from your machine. You never know when a power failure will occur.

In the previous Step-by-Step exercise you set up a toolbar. You may have tried to add code to a toolbar button by double-clicking the button. If so, you found that no matter what button you double-click, you wind up opening the Private Sub TblMyToolbar_ButtonClick(ByVal Button As MSComctlLib.Button) routine. This event procedure is executed when any of the buttons are clicked. The button clicked is sent as a parameter to this procedure. The variable "Button" represents the button clicked. The ByVal command means the value of Button cannot be changed by code in the procedure. The button's type is MSComctlLib.Button: Microsoft Common Control Library Button. This works a little like a control array where several menu items or controls share the same event procedure. In that situation, the Index parameter differentiates between the buttons. In the ButtonClick event of the toolbar, the button's Key property is used to choose between the items or controls. In the next Step-by-Step exercise you will add code to the project.

STEP-BY-STEP 5.5

1. Open the **ToolBarDemo** project, if necessary.

2. Double-click the **Toolbar** control on the form to open the **ButtonClick** event procedure. Press **Tab** and enter the code in **Code Step 2**.

3. Save and run the program. Click each button on the toolbar. Click the **Recent** button list arrow. Select a menu item. No code has been attached to these events yet.

4. Stop the program.

5. Double-click the **Toolbar** control to enter the Code window again. From the Procedure box, select the **ButtonMenuClick** procedure. The **ButtonMenu** parameter is used to identify which ButtonMenu item is clicked. The full name of the procedure is: **Private SubTblMyToolbar_ButtonMenuClick(ByVal ButtonMenu As MSComctlLib.ButtonMenu)**. Press **Tab** and enter the code in **Code Step 5**.

(continued on next page)

A problem may occur to you at this point in the program: What if more than one button is given a drop-down list? Is there a separate ButtonMenuClick routine for each? The answer to the second question is "No." All ButtonMenu items call the same event procedure. Can you give each of the menu items a different Index value? No, the first ButtonMenu item for each button will have the same Index value. To differentiate between the various first ButtonMenu items, you must use the Key property. For instance, If ButtonMenu.Key = "ItemOne" Then ... would be used in the Case statement to identify the first menu item of the Recent button.

6. Save and run the program. Click the **Recent** button list arrow. Select an item from its list.

7. Stop the program and leave it open for the next project.

INTERNET

Have you been to Carl and Gary's Visual Basic Home Page? Its URL is http://www.cgvb.com. It is a tremendous resource of current information about Visual Basic, downloads, book reviews, and links.

CODE STEP 2

```
Select Case Button.Key
    Case "OpenFile"
        MsgBox "Call the Open File dialog box."
    Case "NewFile"
        MsgBox "Create a new document."
    Case "SaveFile"
        MsgBox "Call the Save File dialog box."
    Case "ChooseFont"
        MsgBox "Call the Font dialog box."
    Case "Recent"
        MsgBox "Recent"
    Case "ExitProgram"
        End
End Select
```

CODE STEP 5

```
Select Case ButtonMenu.Index
    Case 1
        MsgBox "Item One of Recent"
    Case 2
        MsgBox "Item Two of Recent"
End Select
```

The next stage of the project is to give it a purpose. The images used in the toolbar were chosen to support the operation of a simple text editor. Luckily, many of the features of a text editor are already present in a normal text box. In the next Step-by-Step exercise you will add a text box to the project and enter code to position and resize the box in response to changes in the form.

STEP-BY-STEP 5.6

1. Open the **ToolBarDemo** project, if necessary.

2. Double-click the **TextBox** tool on the toolbox to add a control to the form. Change its name to **txtContent**. Don't worry about where it is located or what size it is. Just move it so it is not covering the ImageList control.

3. Set the **Text** property to **blank**, the **MultiLine** property to **True** and the **ScrollBars** property to **2-Vertical**.

4. Double-click the body of the form to open the Code window. In this Step-by-Step exercise you are creating a text editor program, so when the form is activated or resized, you want the text box to be sized to fit the interior dimensions of the form. You could enter the code into the form's Activate event, then copy and paste it into the Resize event. However, a better solution is to create a new procedure that is not linked to a particular object or event. From the menu bar, select **Tools | Add Procedure**. The Add Procedure dialog box appears, as shown in Figure 5-9. Enter **ResetTextSize** in the Name box, select the **Private** option button and click **OK**.

FIGURE 5-9
The Add Procedure dialog box

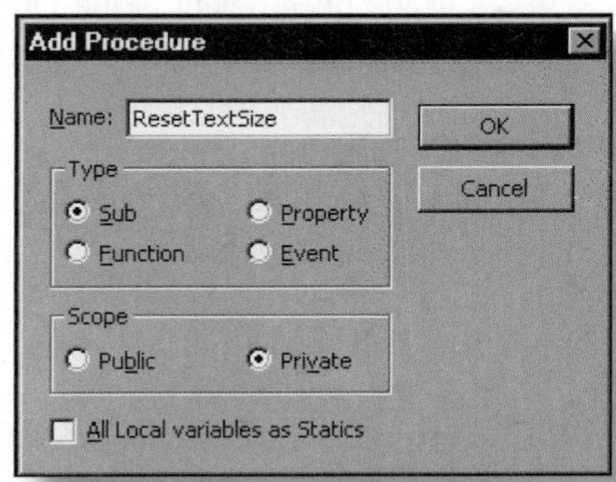

5. As soon as OK is clicked, an entry for the procedure is created and the text cursor is placed within the procedure. Press **Tab** and enter the code in **Code Step 5**.

   This code does the following: The coordinate for the Left property of the text box is calculated in relation to the interior space of the form. A value of 0 moves the text box to the far left edge. The top of the interior of the form is occupied by the

(continued on next page)

CODE STEP 5

```
With txtContent
    .Left = 0
    .Top = tlbMyToolbar.Height
    .Width = frmToolBarDemo.ScaleWidth
    .Height = frmToolBarDemo.ScaleHeight - .Top
End With
```

toolbar. The Top of the text box is set to the bottom of the toolbar. The Width of the toolbar is set equal to the ScaleWidth of the form. The Width of the form refers to its exterior dimension. The ScaleWidth property refers to the form's interior dimension. The Height of the text box is set to the ScaleHeight of the form minus the height of the toolbar.

6. Select **Form** from the Object list and **Activate** from the Procedure list. Enter the following line of code:

```
ResetTextSize
```

This line of code calls the procedure you defined in Code Step 5 when the form is activated.

7. Select the **Resize** event of the **Form**, press **Tab**, and enter:

```
ResetTextSize
```

This code calls the Code Step 5 procedure when the form is resized.

8. Save and run the program. The text box immediately fills the interior of the form. Resize the form several times.

9. Key some text into the text box. Enter a line long enough to note that the Word Wrap feature works. Select a portion of text and cut it from the text box. Move the cursor to another position and paste the text back into the document.

10. Stop the program. You will add even more features to the project in the next Step-by-Step exercise.

The project still lacks one of the most important features of a text editor: the ability to save and load files. In the section that follows you will add a Common Dialog control to the form and use it to get file names from the user.

Quick Check 5.d

1. The images used as icons for the buttons in a toolbar are stored in the ____________________ control.

2. Open the ____________________ dialog box to add the Toolbar control to a project.

3. An ImageList control does not appear on a form. It is attached to a ____________________ to provide images for its buttons.

4. To add an icon to the ImageList, click ____________________ in the Images tab of the Property Pages of the ImageList.

5. If activated, a ____________________ appears when a mouse pointer is hovering over an object or button to explain what the object is used for.

Adding the Common Dialog Control to the Form

In this section you not only learn how to add the familiar dialog boxes like Open a file, and Save As, you also learn how to save and load simple text files. The commands to manipulate text files are easy to learn. The statement's names describe their functions: Open, Input, and Print. A text file is saved as a series of characters. The characters are represented by their ASCII codes. If opened, a text file looks like a printout or screen display, though the line feeds may not be present. When entering data from a data file, the information comes into the program as if it were being keyed from the keyboard. The reason for the similarity is simple: The keyboard produces ASCII codes for each key pressed. There is no real difference between characters entered from the keyboard and characters entered from a text file.

The Common Dialog control is a standard part of Visual Basic, but it must be added to the toolbox in the same way you added the Microsoft Windows Common Controls.

STEP-BY-STEP 5.7

1. Open the **ToolBarDemo** project, if necessary.
2. Right-click the **toolbox** and click **Components**, or select **Project | Components** to open the Components dialog box.
3. Select **Microsoft Common Dialog Control 6.0** by clicking the check box. Click **OK** to add the control to the toolbox.
4. Locate the **CommonDialog** tool in the toolbox and double-click its icon to add it to the form. This is another of those controls whose size is not adjustable and doesn't matter because it is invisible at run time.
5. Name this Common Dialog control **cdlToolbarDemo**.
6. Save the project and leave it open for the next Step-by-Step exercise.

? Did You Know?

You can get a device for your computer that acts like a remote keyboard. It looks like a simple laptop with a small LCD screen that displays several lines of text. It has enough memory to store many pages of text. It doesn't run any programs and can't handle graphics. It lets you key and save the information to upload to your computer at a later time. It communicates with your computer through an infrared link connected to your keyboard cable. You open a word processor and spill the contents of your portable computer through the infrared link to the keyboard cable as if you were keying the text at that moment.

Commands and Functions for Handling a Text File

Normally, text files are *sequential files*. A sequential file stores characters one after the other like songs on a cassette tape. New characters are added to the end of the file. When a file is opened for Input, the characters are read one by one from the beginning of the file to its end. Another kind of file is a *random access file*. A random access file stores information in pieces called records. Each record is exactly the same length. If a record is 50 bytes long, the fourth record of the file is easily found by jumping over 150 bytes, the length of three records combined.

Sequential files are opened to enter data from them, as Input, to create and store data in them, as Output, and to add data to an existing file, as Append. The partial syntax of the *Open statement* is:

```
Open pathname For mode As [#]filenumber
```

Path name is the complete Windows path name of the file. It can be entered in an InputBox, but you will use a *Common Dialog box* to get the path name from the user. The mode is selected from the following: Input, Output, and Append. The file number is provided by the *FreeFile function*. The file number is like a channel number on a television set. Once communication is set up between a program and a file, the file is accessed through its file number. The FreeFile function keeps track of which numbers have been used and provides a free channel number when called. The sample below is a typical use of the Open statement:

```
Open "c:\temp\data\names.dat" For Input As #1
```

To read information from an open file, use the Input(*number*, [#]*filenumber*) function. The number shown is the number of characters to read. If the whole file is to be read, this number equals the number of characters in the file. The file number is the number associated with the file when it is opened. Once read, the characters have to be assigned to a variable or object. You will assign the characters of the file to a text box.

To find the number of characters in the file, use the *LOF*([#]*filenumber*) function. Use the three statements together, as shown in this sample:

```
Dim FileNumber As Integer, Characters As Integer
FileNumber = FreeFile
Open "c:\temp\data\names.dat" For Input As FileNumber
Characters = LOF(FileNumber)
txtContent = Input (Characters, FileNumber)
Close FileNumber
```

In an actual program, use a string variable to represent the path name of the file. The user, using the Common Dialog control, can enter the path name.

To put data into an open file, use the *statement* Print #.

Building Programming Skills

When reading the syntax of a statement in this text or in the Visual Basic Help system, a square bracket encloses optional parts of the statement. In many of the proceeding file statements, the number sign (#) is shown as an optional part of the statement. In the Print # statement, the number sign is not optional. The statement is left over from the earliest versions of BASIC and the number sign is necessary. If the number sign is omitted, there will be no error message, but the data will not be transferred to the file.

The syntax of the Print # statement is:

```
Print #filenumber, [outputlist]
```

The output list is a list of expressions, variables, or strings. Typical usage is shown below:

```
Dim FileNumber As Integer
FileNumber = FreeFile
Open "c:\temp\data\names.dat" For Output As FileNumber
Print #FileNumber, txtContent
Close FileNumber
```

In this sample, the entire contents of the text box, txtContent, is written to the file. If the file already exists, it is overwritten with new information. If the file does not exist, it is created when the Open statement is executed. Just like a barn door, you must *close* a file when you are done accessing its contents. If you don't, there is a risk of losing the information.

Entering the Code to Open a File

The Open file button prompts the user to enter a path name and then opens the file. The Recent button has a drop-down list that lets the user choose the file name of a recently opened file and open it. The actual code to open a file is the same for both, so it makes sense to create a separate routine to open the file and load its contents into the text box. The path name of the file is declared in the General Declarations section of the code so that the name of the file will be available to all the event procedures of the form. To create the drop-down list, each file name is added to the ButtonMenu list when it is loaded. To keep track of the next open space in the list, another variable, RecentFile, is used. The Activate event of the form is also modified to clear the ButtonMenu created at design time (in the last section).

STEP-BY-STEP 5.8

1. Open the **ToolBarDemo** project, if necessary. Double-click the form to open the Code window. Select the **General Declaration** section of the Code window. Press **Tab** and enter the declaration in **Code Step 1**.

2. Select the **Form_Activate** routine and add the code in **Code Step 2** below the existing code.

(continued on next page)

CODE STEP 1

```
Dim PathName As String, RecentFile As Integer
```

CODE STEP 2

```
Dim btnX As Button
Set btnX = tlbMyToolbar.Buttons("Recent")
btnX.ButtonMenus.Clear
RecentFile = 1
```

The first line of the new code declares a variable btnX as a Button type. The second line sets the value of the new variable to the Recent button of the toolbar. The buttons of the toolbar form a collection. The name of the collection is the *Buttons Collection*. This is like an array of the buttons of the toolbar. It grows and shrinks as buttons are added or deleted. The Set command allows you to assign an object, in this case, a Button object—to an object variable. The next line clears the ButtonMenu of the Recent button. Visual Basic guides you as you enter this line. As soon as you key the period following btnX, a list of possible entries appears in this position. The entries represent the properties of a Button object. Once a property is chosen, entering another period displays another list. This is a list of methods and properties that apply to the object. The last line sets the value of RecentFile to 1. The path name of the first file opened will be written to the text property of the first entry of the ButtonMenu of the Recent button.

3. Next, you will create a new subroutine to open a file and load it into the text box. In a previous Step-by-Step exercise you created a new procedure by selecting **Tools | Add Procedure** from the menu bar. This time, position the cursor after the Dimension statements at the top of the Code window and enter the following:

```
Private Sub LoadFile
```

   Press **Enter**. A new Sub entry is created.

? Did You Know?

In the earliest forms of BASIC, every assignment statement had to be preceded by the word Let. This was how the BASIC interpreter identified an assignment statement.

4. Enter the code in **Code Step 4** in **Private Sub LoadFile**.

CODE STEP 4

```
' This routine opens the file with the current
' PathName. It is called by "Open File" and when
' a file name is clicked in the "Recent" button.
    Dim FileNumber As Integer, Characters As Long
    On Error GoTo FileTooLarge
    FileNumber = FreeFile
    Open PathName For Input As FileNumber
    If Len(PathName) = 0 Then Exit Sub
    Characters = LOF(FileNumber)
    txtContent = Input(Characters, FileNumber)
    Close FileNumber
    Exit Sub
FileTooLarge:
    MsgBox "The File is too large to load.", vbCritical + vbOKOnly, "File Error"
```

Most of this code is similar to the sample code shown in the body of the lesson. The On Error GoTo FileTooLarge protects the program from trying to load a file that is too large to handle. If an error occurs, the program flow shifts to the program label FileTooLarge. The label itself consists of a string followed by a colon. This label marks code beyond the normal end of the routine. The normal end is marked with the Exit Sub command. If an error occurs, the MsgBox displays a "File Error" message. It is possible that the user clicked the Cancel command when presented with the Open a File dialog box (called in another routine). In that case, the path name returned is the null string with a length of 0. The Len( ) function counts the characters. If the value is 0, the Exit Sub command is executed.

5. Open the **tlbMyToolbar_ButtonClick** event. Above **Select Case Button.Key**, add the following:

```
Dim FileNumber As Integer
```

6. Locate the old MsgBox statement following the **Case "OpenFile"** statement and delete it. Enter the code in **Code Step 6** after Case "OpenFile."

Comments at the beginning of the routine document what the routine does and what other routines call it. Comments start with a single quote and can appear anywhere on the line. Despite the fact the Bill Gates claims to know sections of the code from his first version of BASIC by heart, most programmers forget the code they have written shortly after it is written. Internal documentation is very important.

The first two lines of this code are all that is needed to display the Open a File dialog box. The Filter property is set to preselect the file types that will display. This is a text processing program so .txt is the first filter. The filter has two parts. The first part is the text that appears in the Files of Type box. The vertical bar is called a pipe

(continued on next page)

CODE STEP 6

```
cdlToolbarDemo.Filter = "Text Files|*.txt|All Files|*.*"
cdlToolbarDemo.ShowOpen
PathName = cdlToolbarDemo.FileName
    ' If no PathName is entered, exit the subroutine.
      If Len(PathName) = 0 Then Exit Sub
      LoadFile
    ' Add file name to the Recent list.
      Dim btnX As Button
      Set btnX = tlbMyToolbar.Buttons("Recent")
      btnX.ButtonMenus.Add RecentFile, "File" & RecentFile, PathName
      RecentFile = RecentFile + 1
```

symbol and is required to separate each part of the Filter string. The second part sets the file name to a particular pattern. In this case, the pattern is files that end in ".txt." Since this is a type the box recognizes, it is not shown in the box. The third line reads the result of the dialog box. The FileName property of the Common Dialog control is assigned to the path name. If the PathName is the null string, the routine is ended. If the PathName is non-empty, the LoadFile routine is called to open the file and transfer its contents to the text box. When a file is opened, it is necessary to add the name of the file to the ButtonMenu of the Recent button. So btnX is declared as a Button type and assigned to the "Recent" button. The ButtonMenus property is accessed and the Add method is used to add an entry to the drop-down list. The Visual Basic Help system guides you through the process. A string for the Key field follows an index number, provided by RecentFile. The string is built by adding the value of RecentFile to the string "File." The path name is inserted into the ButtonMenus' text field.

7. The old code for the ButtonMenuClick routine assumed a couple of entries provided at design time were all there was to access. The code has to be changed to cope with an expanding and shrinking list. Delete the old code in Private Sub **tlbMyToolbar_ButtonMenuClick(ByVal ButtonMenu As MSComctlLib.ButtonMenu)** and enter the following code:

```
PathName = ButtonMenu.Text
LoadFile
```

There is only one drop-down list in this application, so there is no need to determine which list is used when a ButtonMenu item is selected. The Text property is assigned to the path name, and LoadFile is called to load the file clicked by the user.

8. In the **theMyToolbar_ButtonClick(ByVal ButtonAsMSCometLib.Button)** procedure, locate the old MsgBox statement following the **Case "NewFile"** statement and delete it. Enter the following code after **Case "NewFile"**:

```
txtContent = ""
```

9. Locate the old MsgBox statement following the **Case "SaveFile"** statement and delete it. Enter the code in **Code Step 9** after **Case "SaveFile."**

In this code, the ShowSave method displays the Save As dialog box. Once the

CODE STEP 9

```
cdlToolbarDemo.Filter = "Text Files|*.txt"
cdlToolbarDemo.ShowSave
PathName = cdlToolbarDemo.FileName
        If Len(PathName) = 0 Then Exit Sub
        FileNumber = FreeFile
        Open PathName For Output As FileNumber
        Print #FileNumber, txtContent
        Close FileNumber
```

path name is gathered, the file is opened for output and the entire contents of the text box is transferred to the file with the Print # command.

10. Save and run the program. Click the **Open** button and navigate to the **Windows** menu. There are a number of text files in this menu. Click **License** and click the **Open** button. (If license is not there, choose another text file.) Click the **Save** button and save the file as **License2**. Click the **New** button. The text box should clear. Click the list arrow of the **Recent** button. Select the entry for the **license** file to reload it. Open and save more files. Use the Recent list to reload files. Stop the program.

11. It is boring to look at the default font, so locate the MsgBox statement following the **Case "ChooseFont"** statement and delete it. Enter the code in **Code Step 11** after **Case "ChooseFont:"**

    In this code, the Flags property must be set before the Font dialog box can do anything. The predefined constant shown, cdlCFBoth, will load both the screen and printer fonts and make them available in the Font dialog box. The ShowFont method displays the dialog box. Once the user has made his/her choices, the With statement lets the programmer access the contents of the box without rekeying the name of the box each time a property is accessed. The format for similar properties is different for the text box and the dialog box.

12. Save and run the program. Open a text file. Click the **Font** button, choose a font for the text, and click **OK**. Experiment with different settings.

13. Stop and remove the program.

    Table 5-4 shows the dialog boxes available in the Common Dialog control and the methods that call them.

TABLE 5-4
Available dialog boxes

DIALOG BOX	METHOD
Open a File	ShowOpen
Save As	ShowSave
Font	ShowFont
Color	ShowColor
Printer	ShowPrinter

CODE STEP 11

```
cdlToolbarDemo.Flags = cdlCFBoth
cdlToolbarDemo.ShowFont
With cdlToolbarDemo
     txtContent.Font.Name = .FontName
     txtContent.Font.Size = .FontSize
     txtContent.Font.Bold = .FontBold
     txtContent.Font.Italic = .FontItalic
End With
```

There is lot more you could do with this project. You can provide a normal menu in addition to the toolbar; add a CoolBar to the form and cut and paste the toolbar into it; or add functions that are tailored to your particular needs.

Quick Check 5.e

1. Characters in a text file are represented by their ________________ codes.
2. To create a new text file, open the file for ________________ .
3. The number sign (#) before a *file number*, is optional for every file command except the ________________ statement.
4. The Buttons ________________ is a list of all the buttons on a toolbar.
5. To assign an object to an object variable, use the ________________ statement.

Summary

- The MsgBox function is used to communicate a short message to the user. Response from the user is limited to a button click. The syntax for MsgBox is:
  `variable = MsgBox( prompt [, buttons] [, title] [, helpfile, context])`
- Visual Basic provides many constants to simplify supplying parameter values to functions and procedures.
- The InputBox function gathers up to 255 characters from the user. The syntax for InputBox is:
  `variable = InputBox( prompt [, title] [, default])`
- The Val( ) function is often used to convert the string entered with an InputBox to a value.
- A pop-up menu usually appears when the user right-clicks the mouse button. It provides commonly used commands in a convenient package to facilitate user interaction with the program. The PopupMenu method is used to call the pop-up.
- Some important controls are not installed in the toolbox when Visual Basic starts. The Toolbar, ImageList, and Common Dialog controls must be loaded through the Components dialog box before they can be used in a project.
- The ImageList control is used to store images for the Toolbar control. Once the ImageList is loaded with images, it is attached to a toolbar where the images are used to label buttons.
- The toolbar contains buttons labeled with images from the ImageList control that provide commonly used commands to the user. Often the toolbar buttons mirror menu items.
- Right-clicking the object and selecting Properties opens the Property Pages of the ImageList and toolbar. These pages are used to set up images and buttons at design time. Buttons can be added and deleted at run time as well.
- Always supply ToolTipText for each button of a toolbar.
- A toolbar button may have a drop-down list attached. The list may be preloaded with options at design time, or items may be added at run time.
- The Common Dialog control is used to provide a project with a number of common Windows dialog boxes. These are dialog boxes any Windows user is familiar with: Open a file, Save As, Font, Printer, and Color.
- The Buttons Collection is a collection of the buttons on a toolbar. It can be used like an array of buttons.
- Text files are easily created and accessed through commands like Open, Input, and Print #. The LOF( ) function is used to count the number of characters in a text file.
- The syntax for the Open statement is:
  `Open pathname For mode As [#]filenumber`

- The *mode* parameter may have the values Input, Output, and Append. Other available options are described in the Visual Basic Help system.
- The syntax for the Input function is:
  `Input(number, [#]filenumber)`
- The *number* parameter is the number of characters in the file. The *file number* parameter associates the file with a channel number. All access to the file is through this identifying number.
- The syntax for the Print # statement is:
  `Print #filenumber, [outputlist]`
- The *output list* is a list of expressions, variables, or strings.
- A program label is a string followed by a colon that marks an area of code. Program flow can be directed to the label with a GoTo command.
- The On Error GoTo *program label* and the On Error Resume Next statements can trap errors and keep a program from abruptly ending by redirecting the program flow around offending statements.

LESSON 5 REVIEW QUESTIONS

TRUE/FALSE

Circle the T if the statement is true. Circle the F if it is false.

T F 1. A modal dialog box must be clicked or cancelled before the user can continue.

T F 2. A MsgBox function can collect up to 255 characters from the user.

T F 3. A MsgBox function must have an entry for the prompt parameter.

T F 4. When a MsgBox button is clicked, the function returns a string containing the name of the button.

T F 5. A cancelled InputBox returns a null string.

T F 6. A pop-up menu is usually triggered by a right-click by the user.

T F 7. Two pop-up menus can be displayed together.

T F 8. When designing a pop-up menu, prevent it from being displayed in the menu bar by setting its Enabled property to False.

T F 9. A toolbar can replace a menu.

T F 10. Predefine buttons for a toolbar by making entries in the Toolbar Property Pages.

WRITTEN QUESTIONS

Write your answers to the following questions.

11. Describe two situations in which you would use a MsgBox statement or function.

12. The InputBox function returns what kind of data?

13. What is a null string?

14. What property is set to be sure a pop-up menu doesn't appear on the menu bar?

15. What is the ImageList control used for and how is it loaded with images?

16. Describe the process of putting buttons on a toolbar at design time. Mention the important properties involved.

17. When an item from a button's drop-down list is selected, the ButtonMenuClick routine is called. How do you differentiate in code between items from different toolbar buttons?

18. Write an Open statement to create a file named c:\temp\names.dat. Describe each part of the Open command.

19. What methods of the Common Dialog control are used to open an Open a File dialog box? Save As dialog box? Font dialog box?

20. Describe the Buttons Collection and how it is used to add an item to a toolbar button's drop-down list.

LESSON 5 APPLICATION PROBLEMS

SCANS

Level One

THE GROCERY SHOPPING PROBLEM

Write a program to help users do their grocery shopping. Have users enter their total budget for shopping in a text box. In a second text box, have them enter the price of a particular item. Then click a button to check their budget. When the button is clicked, both values are read from the text boxes. The amount of the purchase is compared to the value remaining in the budget (using an If statement). If the purchase amount exceeds the budget, use a message box to warn the user that they are over their budget. If the amount is less than the amount remaining in the budget, subtract the purchase amount from the budget amount. Write the remaining budget amount into the budget text box. Clear the purchase amount text box and set the focus to that box. Include a button to clear both boxes and a button to exit the program.

THE MSGBOX PROGRAM

Write a program that lets the user build a custom message box. Have the form include a text box for the user to enter the message string. Use three combo boxes to let the user choose the different Button options available. Have the first combo box list the constants supplied by Visual Basic that control the number and types of buttons that display in the box. Have the second combo

TABLE 5-5
Building combo boxes

CONSTANT	VALUE	DESCRIPTION
vbOKOnly	0	Display **OK** button only.
vbOKCancel	1	Display **OK** and **Cancel** buttons.
vbAbortRetryIgnore	2	Display **Abort**, **Retry**, and **Ignore** buttons.
vbYesNoCancel	3	Display **Yes**, **No**, and **Cancel** buttons.
vbYesNo	4	Display **Yes** and **No** buttons.
vbRetryCancel	5	Display **Retry** and **Cancel** buttons.
vbCritical	16	Display **Critical Message** icon.
vbQuestion	32	Display **Warning Query** icon.
vbExclamation	48	Display **Warning Message** icon.
vbInformation	64	Display **Information Message** icon.
vbDefaultButton1	0	First button is default.
vbDefaultButton2	256	Second button is default.
vbDefaultButton3	512	Third button is default.
vbDefaultButton4	768	Fourth button is default.

box list the constants supplied by Visual Basic that control the appearance of the icon displayed the box. Have the third combo box list the options that allow the user to choose which button should be the default. Use Table 5-5 to build your combo boxes. The first combo box should display the first six entries of the table. The second combo box should display the next four entries. The third combo box should display the last four entries. A text box to enter the title should also appear on the form. Once the information is collected, use string concatenation (joining two strings with an &) and string assignments to make the following statement display your message box.

```
x = MsgBox Prompt, ButtonConst, Title
```

Prompt and Title should be declared as strings and assigned the values from the appropriate text boxes. The results of the combo boxes should be added together and assigned to ButtonConst.

SCANS

Level Two

THE ALTERNATE GROCERY PROGRAM

Change the grocery shopping problem so that in addition to the three command buttons, the user can right-click the form to check the budget, clear the text boxes, and exit the program.

ADDING A TOOLBAR PROGRAM

Add a toolbar to the grocery shopping problem. Choose appropriate icons (if possible). The toolbar should let the user check the budget, clear the text boxes, and exit the program.

THE PICTURE DISPLAY PROGRAM

The PictureBox control can display .jpg files. Write a program using a PictureBox control, a Common Dialog control, and a menu to let a user browse drives looking for .jpg pictures. The menu should have a File menu with Open and Exit commands with a separator bar between them. The Open command should call a routine that uses the ShowOpen method of a Common Dialog control to let the user browse the disk for .jpg files. Set the Filter property of the Common Dialog control to show just .jpg files. When a .jpg file is located, use the file name to load the picture into a picture box and the file name and path into a text box. To load a picture, use a line like the following:

```
Picture1.Picture = LoadPicture(FileName)
```

The Picture property receives the path name of the file, but it must be loaded using the LoadPicture function.

LESSON 5 PROGRAMMING AT WORK

THE MUSIC COLLECTION PROJECT

SCANS

In this installment of the Music Collection Project you will add a pop-up menu and a toolbar to the Data Entry form. Adding a pop-up menu starts by creating a normal menu for the form and setting the menu's Visible property to False. The pop-up menu shows the names of the buttons as submenu items on the form and allows the user to execute the button's code from the menu. Of course, the buttons don't do anything yet, but you will start by adding a message box statement to the click routine for each button.

1. Open the **MusicColl** project you started in Lesson 4.

2. Display the form and double-click the **Record** button to open its Code window. Enter the following code:.

   ```
   MsgBox "The Record Button is pressed.", , "Music Collection"
   ```

3. Open the Code window for the Return button and enter similar code. There is no need to enter a message box for the Clear button, because the Clear button is already coded.

4. Select the form and open the Menu Editor. Create the following menu controls:

   ```
   Commands
   É.Record
   É.Clear
   É.Return
   ```

   Name the menu items, **mnuCommand**, **mnuRecord**, **mnuClear**, and **mnuReturn**.

5. Set the Visible property of mnuCommand to **False**. Close the menu editor.

6. As you return to the form view, notice the menu is not visible on the form. Double-click the form to enter its Code window. Use the Object box to open the mnuRecord procedure. Enter the following code:

```
cmdRecord_Click
```

7. Enter a line in **mnuReturn** to call **cmdReturn_Click**. Executing the code this way is identical to clicking the control.

8. Select **Form** from the Object box and **MouseUp** from the Procedure box. Enter the following code into the Sub form_MouseUp procedure:

```
If Button = vbRightButton Then
      frmDataEntry.PopupMenu mnuCommand
   End If
```

   The If statement is True when the right mouse button is clicked over the active form. The PopupMenu mnuCommand statement displays the menu named mnuCommand. The three commands recorded in that menu will be shown. Selecting one of the commands is equivalent to clicking one of the buttons.

9. Save and run the program. Enter data in the text boxes. Click the **Record** button. Your message should be displayed. Click **OK**. Right-click the face of the form. Your pop-up menu should appear. Select **Clear** from the menu. Right-click the form again and select **Return** from the menu. Your other message box should appear.

10. Stop the program. Now you will add a toolbar to give the user a third way to execute the commands.

11. Select the form. Right-click the **toolbox** and click **Components** to open the Components dialog box.

12. Select **Microsoft Windows Common Controls 6.0** and click **OK** to add the controls to the toolbox.

13. Click the **View Object** button in the Project window. Double-click the **ImageList** control to add it to the form. Move the control to an out-of-the-way place on the form. Change the control's name to **ilsDataEntrySupport**.

14. Add images to the ImageList by right-clicking the control and selecting **Properties** from the pop-up menu. Click the **Images** tab of the Property Pages. You need images for Record, Clear, and Return. Navigate to an image source and find suitable icons. Add an icon for each of the buttons.

15. Make room for the toolbar on your form by enlarging the form at the bottom. Draw a box around all the form's controls using the **Pointer** control from the toolbox. The controls are all selected together as a unit. Click and drag on one of the controls and move the whole group down.

16. Add a toolbar to the form by double-clicking its icon in the toolbox. Identify its icon by reading the ToolTipText. Right-click the **toolbar** and select **Properties**. Click the **ImageList** list arrow and select **ilsDataEntrySupport**.

17. Click the **Buttons** tab and click **Insert Button**. A button appears on the toolbar. Fill in the following properties: Caption: **Record**, Description: **Record Data.**, Key: **RecordData**, ToolTipText: **Add the record to the database**. Set the Image property to the index of the appropriate icon in ilsDataEntrySupport. If the first icon is the correct one, set the Image value to **1**. Leave the other properties unchanged.

18. Add buttons for **Clear** and **Return**. Fill in properties as you did for the Record button. See Figure 5-10 for the final result.

19. Double-click the **toolbar** to open the ButtonClick event procedure. Enter the following code:

```
Select Case Button.Key
    Case "RecordData"
        cmdRecord_Click
    Case "ClearData"
        cmdClear_Click
    Case "ReturnPrevious"
        cmdReturn_Click
End Select
```

20. Save and run the program. Click each of the toolbar buttons. The appropriate message should display when Record and Return are clicked. Enter a title. Click the **Clear** button on the toolbar. The data should be cleared.

21. Stop the program.

All dressed up and no place to go. This form is ready to be linked to a database. That is what you will do at the end of the next lesson.

FIGURE 5-10
The Data Entry form in design view

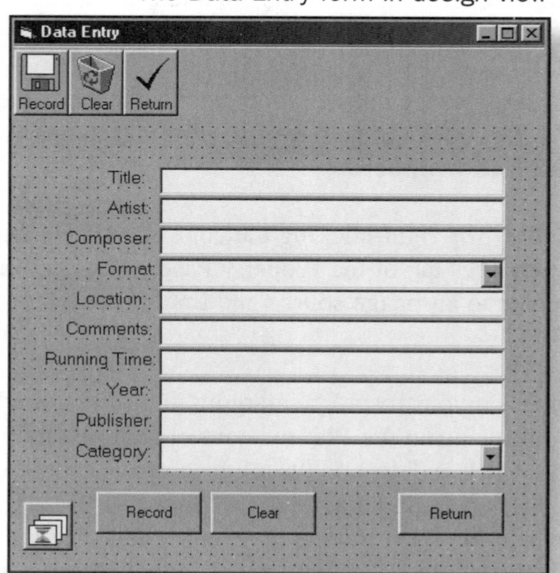

Building Communication Skills

Building a good user interface is all about communication. The forms of your projects are sometimes called the "face" of the project. It is that face the user sees and interacts with. As you design forms, try to keep the user's needs in mind. Make captions informative. When you run your program, look at your forms as if you are seeing them for the first time. Do they make sense? Can you tell what buttons to click or which menus to pull down? Your forms are the program's way of communicating with the user. Make sure they tell the user what he needs to know to run the program.

Computer Ethics

In this lesson you learned how to add additional components to the toolbox. All the components you added are included in Visual Basic. Other components are available on the Internet. Some are free and some are not. Even if they are free, you need to check to see if you can freely distribute an application written using the component without paying a royalty to the component's author.

LESSON 6

DATABASE PROGRAMMING

OBJECTIVES

When you complete this lesson, you will be able to:

- Explain what a database is and how to use it.
- Create a database using Visual Data Manager.
- Link a database to a Visual Basic project.
- Use a Visual Basic program to add and change records in a database.
- Link to external databases.
- Distinguish between the three kinds of modules: Standard, Class, and Form.
- Use User Defined Data Types.

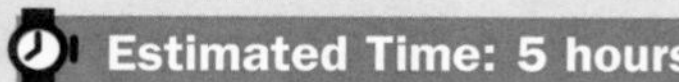

KEY TERMS

database
record
field
Jet database engine
VisData
Indexed fields
Recordset
dynaset
snapshot
Data control
DataSource property
DataField property
MSChart control
ChartData property
two-dimensional array
ActiveX Data Objects
profile
User Defined Data Types (UDT)
Standard module
Class module
fixed-length string
variable-length string
binary file

Using the Visual Data Manager

A *database* is an organized collection of related data. Data is facts, names, dates, and values. Once data is organized, it becomes information. An example of data that is not information is a telephone book that isn't alphabetized. The lack of organization makes it impossible to find a number. The actual database is organized in tables. In a school database, separate tables appear for teachers, course offerings, classrooms, class lists, students enrolled, etc. Within each table, data is organized into *records*. Each record is one complete entry. In the teacher table, a record exists for each teacher employed by the school. Each record is further subdivided into *fields*. In a teacher record, there are separate fields for first name, last name, address, etc.

In this lesson you will design and access databases using the Visual Data Manager and Visual Basic.

Computers and databases are like peanut butter and jelly. One without the other is incomplete. You may not realize yet how important databases are because a lot of the computing you have been involved with does not involve databases. In the real world, programmers spend most of their time figuring out how to interact with databases: how to keep them up-to-date, how to give access to users, and how to make data available over the Internet without compromising the security of the data.

One of the most challenging problems in this area involves database design. How should data be organized to give the most information and make it accessible in a reasonable amount of time? A policeman can not afford to wait for information about a stolen vehicle or a possible suspect. A retail customer can't be asked to wait too long for a credit approval. Database design decisions affect all these situations.

In Microsoft products, most databases are created with the *Jet database engine*. An engine in a car is the mechanism that makes the car go. But without the rest of the car—the electrical system, cooling system, wheels, etc.—the engine isn't going anywhere. A database engine is a unit of code that does all the work to create and access a database. Like a car engine, the Jet database engine does the database work for a number of Microsoft products, including Access.

Designing a Database

Suppose you want to design a database that is a buyer's guide for portable CD players. What kind of information should be recorded? How shall it be arranged? How will the user access the information? These are the questions that must be answered to design the database.

As a programmer, you may know little or nothing about the information for which you are designing a database. You may be asked to design a database about experimental cancer drugs or performance camshafts. If you know nothing about the information, you will be dependent on the users to help you determine what is important and what is not. This is the reason that communication with the users is

If a CD player database has information about each player, such as manufacturer, model number, and price, what else is necessary to make it into a buyer's guide? Normally a buyer's guide makes some sort of evaluation of the product. How would you evaluate a portable CD player? How good are the headphones? How does it stand up to shaking? How many CDs can it play on a set of batteries? What features does the unit have? As you ask these questions, the design of the database may start to resolve in your mind.

Once you arrive at a design, you use the Visual Data Manager, called *VisData*, to create your database and add data to it. In the following Step-by-Step exercise, that is what you will do. Keep in mind that this example is not the "definitive" portable CD buyer's guide and that you will make up information to enter just to learn database techniques. Creating a real buyer's guide takes a lot of research and testing.

STEP-BY-STEP 6.1

1. Start Visual Basic and double-click **Standard EXE**.

2. Click **Add-Ins | Visual Data Manager** from the menu bar. The VisData dialog box appears.

3. From VisData, click **File | New | Microsoft Access | Version 7.0 MDB**. (Choose Version 2.0 if you are interacting with a Windows 3.1 database.)

4. The Select Microsoft Access Database to Create dialog box opens. Navigate to a folder suitable for storing your database. It is customary to create a new folder for each database. You can create a new folder from the dialog box without starting Windows Explorer. Name your database **portableCD** and click the **Save** button. You are returned to the VisData dialog box, as shown in Figure 6-1.

5. The Database Window of VisData provides access to the database design functions. Right-click in the **Database Window** to add tables and fields to your database. Select **New Table**. The Table Structure dialog box appears. Enter **Portable CD Players** in the **Table Name** box. See Figure 6-3 on page 138 for a view of the Table Structure dialog box with the field names already defined.

Did you search the menu bar for an item that would let you build a new database by adding tables and fields? The menu bar does not provide those commands. They appear only by right-clicking the Database Window list box. When exploring Windows programs that are unfamiliar, remember to right-click various regions. You may find some commands useful to you.

FIGURE 6-1
The Visual Data Manager dialog box

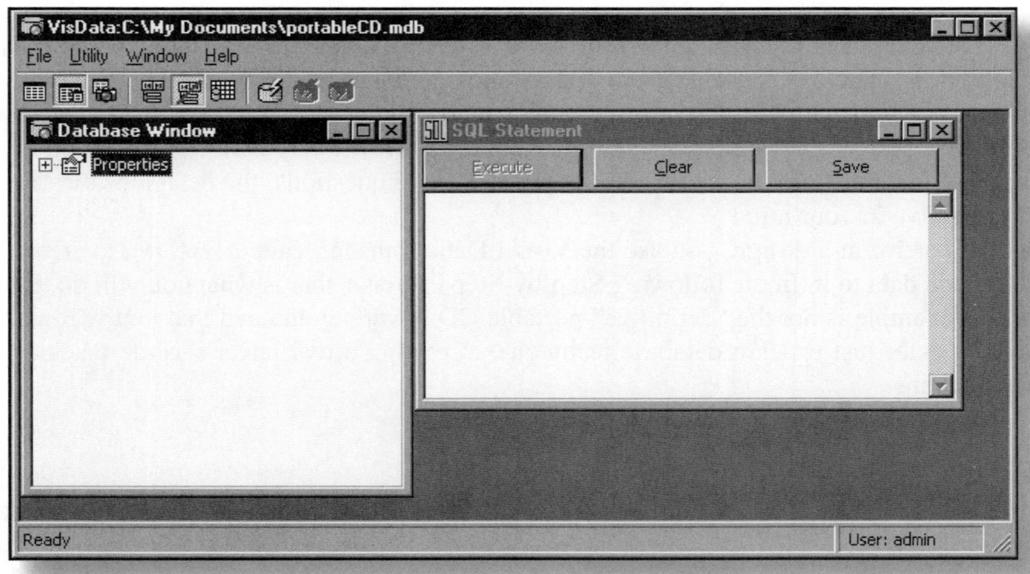

6. Click the **Add Field** button of the Table Structure dialog box.

   Each field requires a Name, a Type, and a Size, as shown in Figure 6-2. VisData provides a default Type and Size, but you must enter the Name. The Required check box must be selected if an entry is required for this field. Every CD player has a manufacturer, so it is a required field. To add the field entry to the table, you must click **OK**. When finished adding fields, you must click **Close**.

FIGURE 6-2
The Add Field dialog box adds new fields to a table

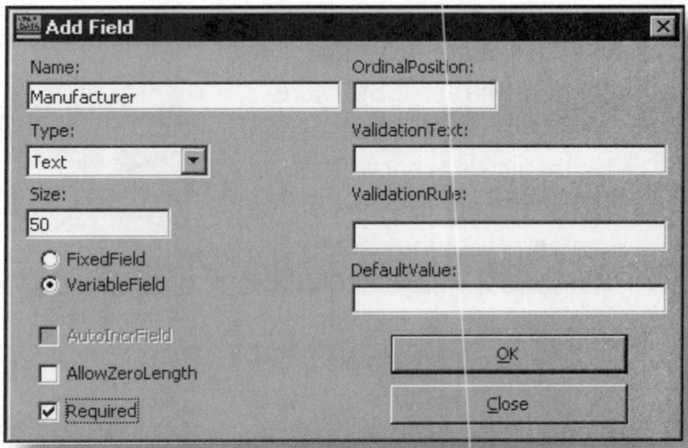

7. Now add the following seven fields to the table using the instructions above:

TABLE 6-1

FIELD ENTRIES

NAME	TYPE	SIZE	ALLOWZEROLENGTH	REQUIRED
Manufacturer	Text	50	Not checked	Checked
Model	Text	20	Not checked	Checked
Price	Currency	8	N/A	Checked
Headphone Rating	Integer	2	N/A	Not checked
Shaking Rating	Integer	2	N/A	Not checked
Battery Rating	Integer	2	N/A	Not checked
Features	Text	50	Checked	Not checked

8. Before you leave the Table Structure dialog box, click the **Add Index** button. Any database may be searched for information, but for a large collection of data, a search may take a long time. Fields that are *indexed* are kept in order in a special list. Each entry in the list contains a pointer to the actual record in the database. You should index any field that is used often to select a particular record from a database.

9. When **Add Index** is clicked, an Add Index to ... dialog box appears (see Figure 6-4). Enter **ModelIndex** in the **Name** box. (The font used shows that lowercase L and uppercase I are identical, but it is clear from the context what is meant.) Click **Model** in the **Available Fields** list to add the Model field to the **Indexed Fields** list. Click **OK** to add it and click **Close** to exit the dialog box. Once the Index has been added, it will display in the Table Structure dialog box, as shown in Figure 6-3.

(continued on next page)

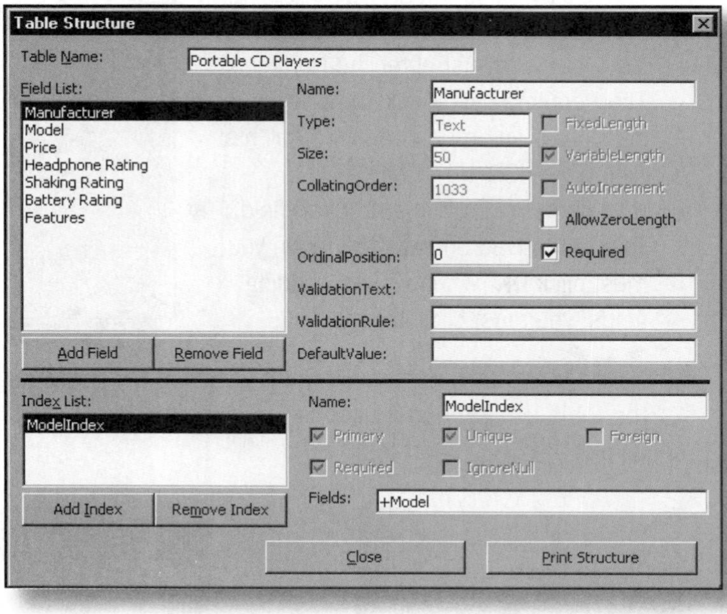

10. Click the **Build the Table** button. The Table Structure dialog box closes and VisData is the active window. The Database Window now shows an entry with the name Portable CD Players. Click the **+** to the left of the icon next to the name Portable CD Players. Click the **+** to the left of the Fields icon. A list of the fields just defined appears. Click the **+** to the left of the Indexes icon. The ModelIndex entry appears. Figure 6-5 shows the result.

11. Double-click the **icon** to the left of the name Portable CD Players. The Dynaset: Portable CD Players dialog box appears (see Figure 6-6). Each field you defined in the Table Structure dialog box is shown. You may have to enlarge VisData's window to see the whole dialog box.

12. Next you will enter seven records into the database using data from Table 6-2 on page 140.

    For this example, data simulates testing for the three rating fields. A single Features field is included for each record. To add a record, first click **Add**. Enter data into each field of the record. Once the

FIGURE 6-3
The Table Structure dialog box showing all the Field names

Table Structure
Table Name: Portable CD Players
Field List: Manufacturer, Model, Price, Headphone Rating, Shaking Rating, Battery Rating, Features
Name: Manufacturer
Type: Text
Size: 50
CollatingOrder: 1033
FixedLength / VariableLength / AutoIncrement / AllowZeroLength / Required
OrdinalPosition: 0
ValidationText:
ValidationRule:
DefaultValue:
Add Field | Remove Field
Index List: ModelIndex
Name: ModelIndex
Primary / Unique / Foreign / Required / IgnoreNull
Fields: +Model
Add Index | Remove Index
Close | Print Structure

FIGURE 6-4
The Add Index to Portable CD Players dialog box

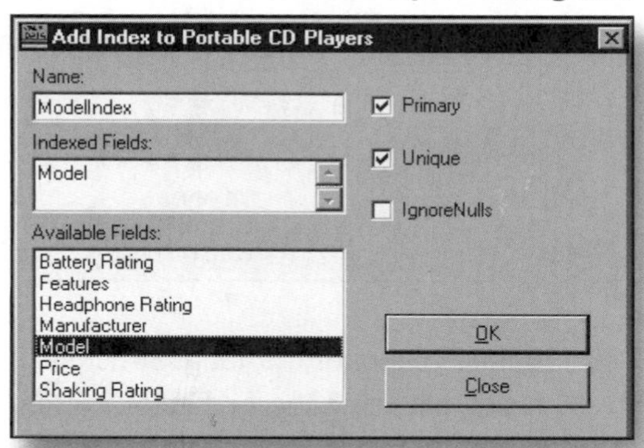

Building Programming Skills

A Recordset is a collection of records of a database. Visual Basic uses three kinds of Recordset: tables, dynasets, and snapshots. A table is a direct link to an actual table of data contained in the database. A dynaset is a set of pointers that point to particular fields of particular records from particular tables. A dynaset may be all the records of a particular table, or it may combine records and fields from several tables. A snapshot is a copy of a Recordset. It cannot be updated, but like a dynaset, it may be drawn from several tables.

record is complete, click **Update** to add the record to the table. Then click **Add** for the next entry. When finished, click **Close** to return to VisData. Don't forget to click **Add** for each record.

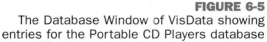

FIGURE 6-5
The Database Window of VisData showing entries for the Portable CD Players database

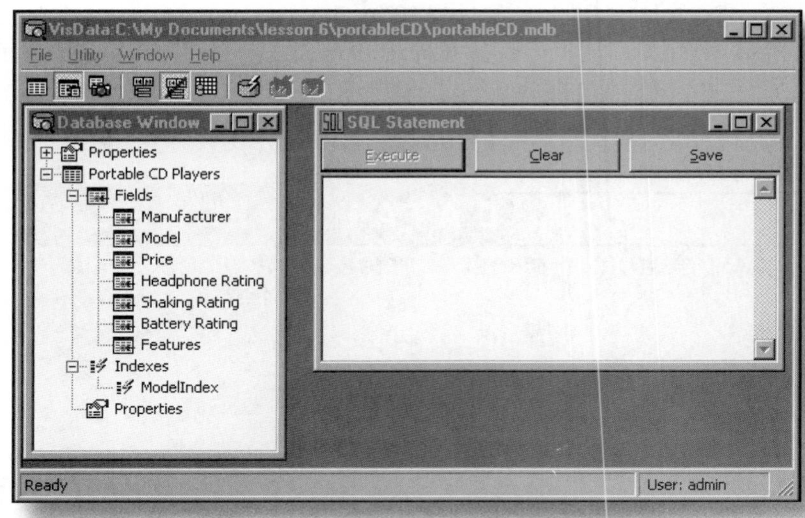

13. The Portable CD Players database is now complete. Now you will learn how to navigate and edit records. Double-click the **Portable CD Players** icon. Navigate from record to record by clicking the **left** and **right arrows** at the bottom of the Dynaset window. The records appear in the order in which they were recorded. To sort the list by Manufacturer, click **Sort**, enter the field name **Manufacturer**, and click **OK**. Navigate through the records. This time the records are arranged alphabetically by Manufacturer.

FIGURE 6-6
The Dynaset: Portable CD Players dialog box of VisData

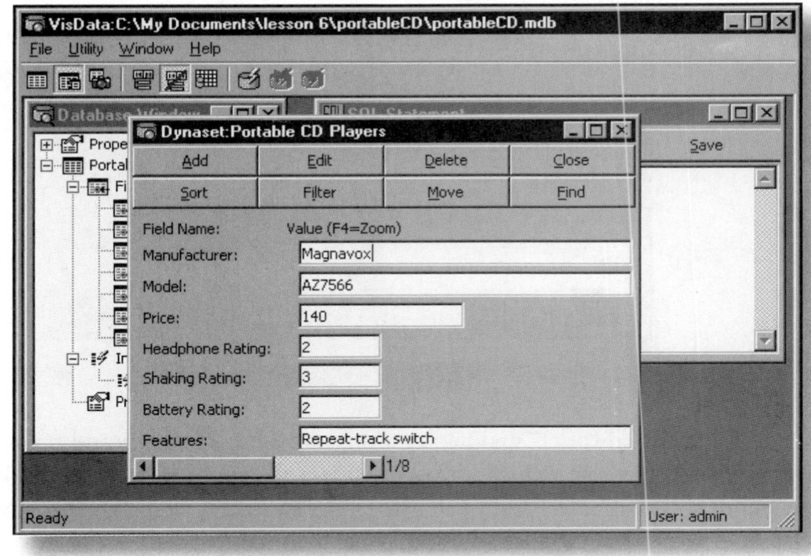

14. Sort the list by Price. Navigate the fields. Navigate to the Magnavox record. Try to enter a new price of **140**. The Price field cannot be changed until the Edit button is clicked. Click the **Edit** button. Change the **Price** to **140**. Click the **Update** button.

15. Click the **Find** button. The Find Record dialog box appears. On the left is a list of fields. In the middle is a list of comparison operators. On the right is a Value or Expression text box. Option buttons let you choose which record to find: first, next, previous, or last. Click the

(continued on next page)

Price field. Click **=**. Enter **140** for the value. Click **OK**. The window displays the first record matching the condition. It is the record you just edited.

16. Click **Close** and **File/Exit** to close the VisData dialog box. The data is already saved.

TABLE 6-2

DATABASE RECORDS

MANUFACTURER	MODEL	PRICE	HEADPHONE RATING	SHAKING RATING	BATTERY RATING	FEATURES
Sony	D-465	200	5	5	3	Hold lock
Sony	D-E301	110	4	4	4	AC adapter
Aiwa	XP-760	100	3	4	3	One-year warranty
Magnavox	AZ7566	120	2	3	2	Repeat-track switch
JVC	XL-P33	100	5	5	2	Auto power off
Panasonic	SL-S221C	100	5	4	3	Shuffle play
Panasonic	SL-S650	180	4	3	5	Bass-boost control
Craig	JC615K	100	3	4	3	Low battery indicator

FIGURE 6-7
A table of database information for the Portable CD Players database

Portable CD Players

Manufacturer	Model	Price	Headphone Rating	Features	Shaking Ratin	Battery Rating
Aiwa	XP-760	100	3	One-year warranty	4	3
Craig	JC6151K	100	3	Low battery indicator	4	3
JVC	XL-P33	100	5	Auto power off	5	2
Magnavox	AZ7566	140	2	Repeat-track switch	3	2
Panasonic	SL-S221C	100	5	shuffle play	4	3
Panasonic	SL-S650	180	4	Bass-boost control	3	5
Sony	D-E301	110	4	AC Adapter	4	4
Sony	D-465	200	5	Hold lock.	5	3

Add | Update | Delete | Refresh | Close

Record: 1

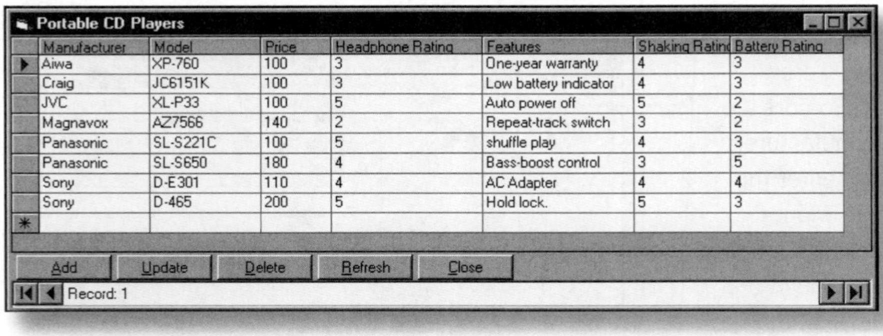

There is so much VisData can do that a full lesson could be written just about VisData. In this section you have seen how to use VisData to create a database and you have learned the extensive vocabulary associated with databases. In the next Step-by-Step exercise you will create a Visual Basic project that accesses the database you just created.

Quick Check 6.a

1. A database is a collection of records organized into one or more ____________________ .
2. A record is made up of related ____________________ , each of which contains one value, string, or data.
3. A ____________________ is a collection of records. The records may come from a single table or from several.
4. In this lesson you used ____________________ to create the Portable CD Players database.

5. After naming a database in VisData, you must _________________ in the Database Window to add a table to the database.

Using the Data Control

Before you see how it is done, it is hard to imagine how to link a database file with a Visual Basic project. Somehow you need to link particular fields of each record, one at a time, to text boxes or labels on a form. Using a text box implies you want to make changes to existing records or add new ones. Labels are used for displaying the contents of chosen fields of selected records. Some kind of grid would be helpful to display the data in a table.

The key to bringing this functionality to Visual Basic is the *Data control*. It links a database file with a Visual Basic project. It turns out that the ability to link a field from a database to a Visual Basic project is already built into the following controls: the TextBox, Label, CheckBox, PictureBox, and Image controls. These are the data bound controls. There are more data bound controls that can be added to the toolbox from the Components dialog box.

Once a Data control is added to a form, there are two properties that must be set: The DatabaseName property must be set to the name of the database file, and the RecordSource property must be given the information it needs to build a Recordset from the database. Other properties of the Data control that must be set are its name and caption properties. In the following Step-by-Step exercise you will create a Visual Basic project that displays the contents of the Portable CD Players database.

STEP-BY-STEP 6.2

1. Start Visual Basic and double-click **Standard EXE**. Save the form as **OneByOne** and the project as **CDplayers**.

2. Change the caption of the form to **The Portable CD Players Buyer's Guide**. Change the name of the form to **frmOneByOne**.

3. The Data control is in the bottom of the toolbox. It has a left and right arrow hovering over two tiny text boxes. The ToolTip for the control is "Data." Double-click the **Data** control to add it to the form. Change the Align property to **2-Align Bottom**. Change the name of the Data control to **datMyData**.

4. Change the caption of the data control to **First | Previous   Next | Last**. With the control aligned in the bottom of the form, the width of the control changes when the form is resized. At this point you don't know how wide to make the form. Later, when the width of the form has stabilized, you could change the space in the middle of the caption so the labels are closer to

(continued on next page)

Building Programming Skills

The Data control has two kinds of left arrows and two kinds of right arrows at the ends of the control. The leftmost button navigates to the first record in the database. The left arrow just to the right moves from the current record to the previous one. The right arrows are similar: the rightmost arrow navigates to the last record of the database. Clicking the adjacent button moves from the current record to the next record. One purpose of the Caption property of the Data control is for labeling these arrows.

the arrow buttons on the left and right ends of the control.

5. While in the Property window of datMyData, click the **DatabaseName** property. Click the ellipsis (...) and use the **DatabaseName** dialog box to navigate to your saved database. Double-click **portableCD.mdb**.

6. Click the **RecordSource** property. Click the **list arrow** to display a drop-down list. The list shows the table names defined in your database. Select the table name **Portable CD Players**. Once these two properties, DatabaseName and RecordSource, are set, the Data control links the database to the project and all the fields of the table are available to any data bound control.

7. In Figure 6-8 you see the completed (through Step-by-Step exercise 6-3), project, displaying a record from the database.

To bind a text box to the database, set the DataSource property of the box to the name of the Data control. To link the text box to a particular field, set the DataField property to the field name. Once the DataSource property is set and the Data control is properly set, the DataField property displays a list box giving access to all the possible field names.

8. Double-click the **TextBox** tool in the toolbox to add a text box to the form. Next, you will use Copy and Paste to create the other six text boxes. But first change the font to **bold**, click **DataSource**, and set it to **datMyData**.

9. Copy the text box by pressing **Ctrl+C**. Paste the box by pressing **Ctrl+V**. Visual Basic prompts you to create a control array. Press the **n** key to say no. Move the new box into position and resize it, if necessary. Paste by pressing **Ctrl+V** five more times for a total of seven boxes. Arrange and size them as shown in Figure 6-8. Change the names of the boxes to **txtManufacturer**, **txtModel**, **txtFeatures**, **txtPrice**, **txtHeadphones**, **txtShaking**, and **txtBatteries**. The Font and DataSource property of each text box is already set.

10. Select **txtManufacturers** and click its **DataField** property. Click the **list box** and bind the text box to the Manufacturers field of the database. Link each of the other six boxes to their corresponding fields of the database.

11. Add a label for each of the text boxes, as shown in Figure 6-8.

12. The menu and chart haven't been added yet, but the program is ready to run. Save and run the program. After a slight delay, the first record of your database is displayed. Use the arrows to navigate the records.

13. Stop the program.

14. Have you noticed? You haven't added a single line of code! This is a project that already lets a user navigate through a database and edit and update records without a single line of code. You will add a few lines now to get the chart working.

The contents of the fields can be permanently altered using your new Visual Basic project. If data in a text box is altered or deleted and you navigate to another record, the edited record is automatically saved in the database. The change, although it can be reversed, becomes permanent. This is not a bad thing. It lets you fix errors in the contents of the fields or change data. You cannot, however, add a new record to the database.

FIGURE 6-8
The Portable CD Players Buyer's Guide project displaying its first record

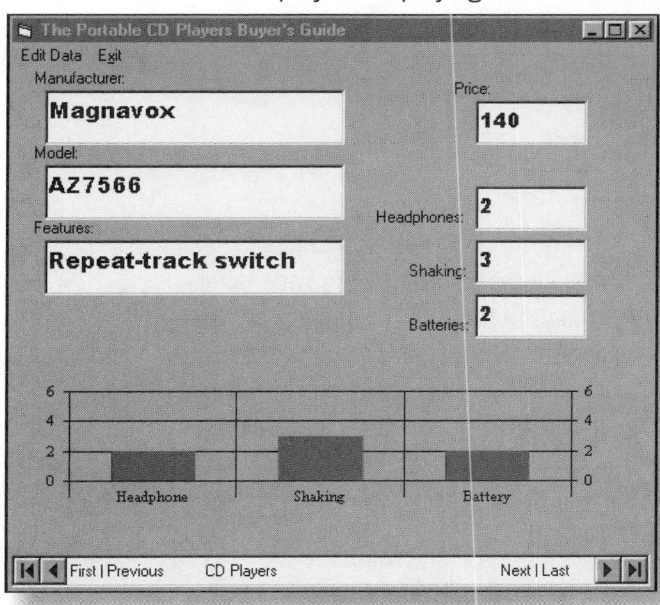

First right-click the body of the toolbox and select **Components** to open its dialog box.

15. Select **Microsoft Chart Control 6.0 (OLEDB)**. Click the **Apply** and **OK** buttons to add the control to the toolbox.

16. Double-click the **MSChart** tool to add it to the form, and size it to approximately the size shown in Figure 6-8. Name it **chCDchart**.

17. Right-click the **chart** and select **Properties**. Select the **Axis** tab. Select the **Axis** list arrow and select **Y-Axis**.

18. In the Axis Scale frame, deselect **Automatic Scaling**. Set **Minimum** to **0**, **Maximum** to **6**, **Major divisions** to **3**, and **Minor divisions** to **1**.

19. There is all kinds of fun to be had experimenting with the properties listed in the control's Property Pages, but for now, click **Apply** and **OK** to exit.

Read the following paragraphs to learn how to provide data to the MSChart control. Do not enter code until Step 20.

You provide data to the *MSChart control* with an array. Three pieces of data must be transferred: the Headphone Rating, the Shaking Rating, and the Battery Rating. The following statement draws a chart with bars representing the values 2, 4, and 3:

```
chCDChart.ChartData = Array(2, 4, 3)
```

The *ChartData property* is loaded with the contents of the array. You use the Array( ) function to build an array from the values 2, 4, and 3, declare a Variant type array variable, and assign values to the elements of the array. The code sample on the next page accomplishes the same thing as the statement above.

(continued on next page)

```
Dim arrRatings(1 To 3)
arrRatings(1) = 2
arrRatings(2) = 4
arrRatings(3) = 3
chCDChart.ChartData = arrRatings
```

It is not a good practice to display a chart without labels. You can provide label strings to the MSChart object by using a two-dimensional array. Think of a *two-dimensional array* as a chart of values with rows and columns. Use two index numbers to specify a cell of the array. To declare an array with two rows of three columns, use the statement:

```
Dim arrRatings(1 To 2, 1 To 3)
```

Which is first? The column or the row? You can think of it either way. The declaration makes it clear that the row is the first index and the column is the second. The value of the item in the third column of the second row of arrRatings is given by arrRatings(2, 3).

To load the chart with labels and data, put the label strings in the first row and the data values in the second row.

The simplest way to access the rating values is to read them from the text boxes after the Data control has provided the values to each bound control. The only problem is deciding where to put the code. How do you know when the record is fully transferred to the bound controls? One way to find out is to experiment by putting the code in the Change event of each of the text boxes used to represent the ratings: txtHeadphone, txtShaking, and txtBatteries.

20. Now enter the code shown in **Code Step 20** in the **txtHeadphones_Change** event procedure. Make sure the chart object is large enough to have room to display the labels.

21. Save and run the program. When the program starts, three bars should appear on the chart. If they do not, move the code to the Change event procedures of the other text boxes until three bars appear when the program starts. Navigate through the records.

22. Stop the program. Leave the project open for the next Step-by-Step exercise.

CODE STEP 20

```
Dim arrRatings(1 To 3, 1 To 2)
arrRatings(1, 1) = "Headphone"
arrRatings(2, 1) = "Shaking"
arrRatings(3, 1) = "Battery"
arrRatings(1, 2) = Val(txtHeadphones)
arrRatings(2, 2) = Val(txtShaking)
arrRatings(3, 2) = Val(txtBatteries)
chCDchart.ChartData = arrRatings
```

You have now used the Data control and the data bound controls to display the contents of the Portable CD Players database. You also learned that when an entry is edited, navigating to a different record automatically saves the record.

Quick Check 6.b

1. Data bound controls are controls that can automatically ___________________ .
2. The two properties of the Data control that must be set to link to a database are ___________________ and ___________________ .
3. To link the text box to a particular field, set the ___________________ property to the field name.
4. Provide data to the MSChart control by ___________________ .
5. A two-dimensional array accesses values using two ___________________ values.

Using the Visual Basic Data Form Wizard

Have you used a wizard yet? Many Microsoft products have wizards to help you build commonly used generic applications. Visual Basic has many wizards. The Data Form Wizard helps you create a form connected to a database that allows the user to view, modify, and add to the information contained in the database.

In the last section, the Data control was used to connect a database to a form. The Data Form Wizard uses the ADO Data control. It is much like the Data control used in the last section, but it uses *ActiveX Data Objects* (ADO) to create a connection between the data and the data bound controls. ADO is Microsoft's latest technology for accessing data. It is simple to use and gives more direct (hence, faster) access to the information stored in many kinds of database files.

In the following Step-by-Step exercise you will use the Data Form Wizard to build a form using a grid to display the data in the portableCD database. When you have finished, examine the code carefully to see how it works.

STEP-BY-STEP 6.3

1. Open the **CDplayers** project if it is not already open.
2. Click **Project | Add Form**. The Add Form dialog box displays, as shown in Figure 6-9.
3. Select **VB Data Form Wizard** and click **Open** to start the wizard.
4. Wizards guide you step by step through the process of creating your application. The Data Form Wizard - Introduction dialog box contains a brief description of the

(continued on next page)

wizard's purpose and prompts you for a name of a profile. The *profile,* if it existed, would contain information you saved in a previous use of the wizard. It is common to save commonly used settings so they do not have to be entered each time the wizard is called. Click **Next** to bypass this setting.

FIGURE 6-9
The Add Form dialog box lets you add a new form to your project

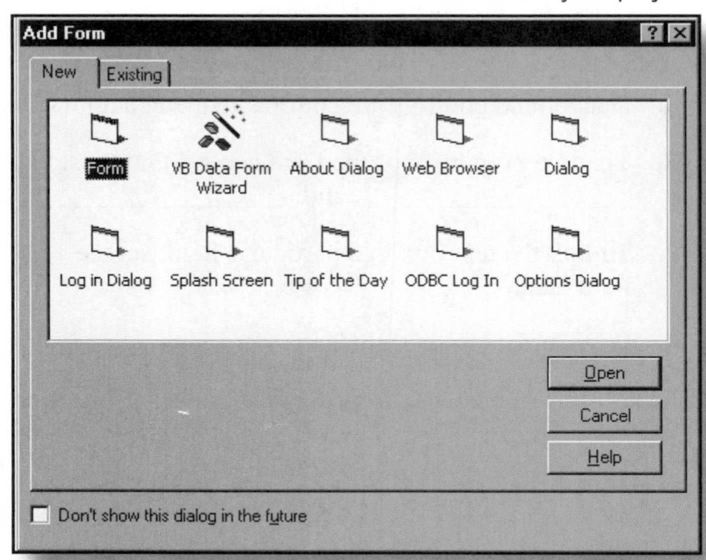

5. The Data Form Wizard - Database Type dialog box prompts you to enter a database type. Click **Access** and **Next** to go to the next screen.

6. The Data Form Wizard - Database dialog box prompts you to enter the name of the database. Click the **Browse** button and navigate to the **portableCD** database. When found, select it and click **Open**. The complete path name appears in the text box. Click **Next**.

7. The Data Form Wizard - Form dialog box appears. It prompts you for three pieces of information: the name of the new form, what should appear on the form, and how the data should be linked to the form. If you the leave the name blank, Visual Basic names the form with the same name as the database. Leave the name blank.

8. The default option in the Binding Type frame is **ADO Data Control**. Make sure that option is selected.

9. The default for the **Form Layout** is **Single Record**. This displays a single record at a time. Click **Grid (Datasheet)** to display the information in a table. Notice the preview area in the upper left changes to symbolize the form layout. Click **Next**.

10. The Data Form Wizard - Record Source dialog box prompts you to choose the source of the records. Click the list arrow of **Record Source** to see a list of available tables. Select **Portable CD Players**.

11. In the Available Fields list, a list of the fields of the table appears. Add all the fields to the display grid by clicking the **double right arrow button**.

12. You can arrange the way the fields are displayed in the table by selecting a field and moving it up or down with the up and down arrow buttons to the right of the Selected Fields list. Arrange the fields in the following order: Manufacturer, Model, Price, Features, Headphone Rating, Shaking Rating, and Battery Rating.

13. Click the list arrow for the **Column to Sort By** list and select **Manufacturer**. Click **Next.**

14. The Data Form Wizard - Control Selection dialog box shows the available controls. They are all selected by default. Click **Next**.

15. In the Data Form Wizard - Finished! dialog box, you are given a chance to save the settings you have used to build the form. Click **Finish**.

16. The wizard displays a message box telling you the form has been built, as shown in Figure 6-10. Click **OK**. The Project Explorer window shows that **frmPortableCDPlayers** has been added to the project.

17. In the **Project Explorer**, double-click **frmOneByOne** to select the form. Open the Menu Editor. Add the simple menu shown in Figure 6-8. Enter the captions **Edit Data** and **Exit**. Enter the names **mnuEditData** and **mnuExit**. Click **OK** to close the Menu Editor.

18. Click **Edit Data** to open its Code window. Press **Tab** and enter the following line of code in mnuEditData_Click:

```
frmPortableCDPlayers.Show.
```

When executed, this line of code displays the new form. As the form loads, it creates a link to the database and displays the data in a table.

19. Press **Tab** and enter **End** in the **mnuExit_click** procedure. Click **Save**.

FIGURE 6-10
The Data Form Created dialog box confirms the successful creation of the new form

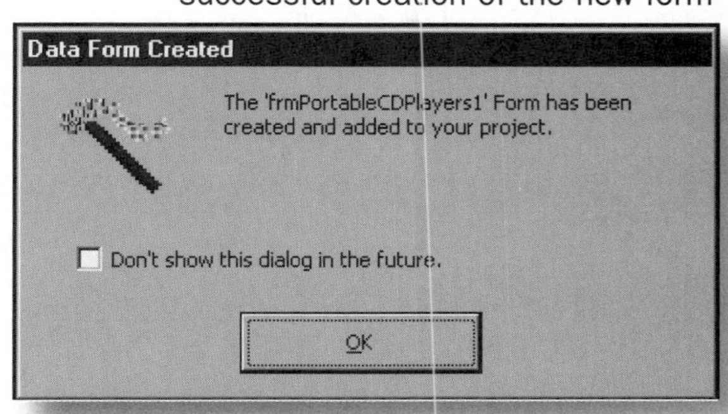

Visual Basic prompts you to enter a file name for the new form. Enter a name for the file or keep the default name. Be sure to save the new form file in the same directory as the rest of your project.

20. Run the program. Click **Edit Data** from the menu. The new form appears. Resize the form. Resize the columns to fit the data. Click the **Add** button. The first text box in the empty row prefixed with the asterisk is ready to accept new data. If you add data to this row and click **Update** or navigate to another record of the database, your addition becomes a new record in the database.

21. Click **Close** and the new form unloads itself from memory and you are back at the original form. Click **Exit** to stop the program.

22. Click **File | Remove project**.

Experiment with the process again. This time choose different options. The form you add doesn't have to access the portableCD database. Experiment with adding another database. You may find one or more in the Visual Basic directory. If you do add another form, remember to add it to the menu of the main program and write code to Show the new form.

Examine the code from the cmdAdd_Click event procedure. This is the code executed when the Add button is clicked:

```
  On Error GoTo AddErr
  datPrimaryRS.Recordset.MoveLast
  grdDataGrid.SetFocus
  SendKeys "{down}"
  Exit Sub
AddErr:
  MsgBox Err.Description
```

The On Error statement redirects program flow to the error handling code. If an error occurs, program flow is sent to the label AddErr. Find AddErr at the end of the event procedure. A single line of code follows. This line displays an error message. The Err object is created when an error occurs. Display its Description property to see an explanation for the error that occurred.

The name of the ADO Data control is datPrimaryRS. The PrimaryRS stands for Primary Record Set. The MoveLast method moves to the last entry in the Recordset. The SendKeys "{down}" statement sends one or more keystrokes to the active window as if keyed at the keyboard. Special codes are provided in the SendKeys Help file for keys that don't display characters when pressed. The code for the down arrow is down. These codes are enclosed in curly braces.

When the Delete button is clicked, the code in the cmdDelete_Click is executed:

```
On Error GoTo DeleteErr
With datPrimaryRS.Recordset
  .Delete
  .MoveNext
  If .EOF Then .MoveLast
End With
Exit Sub
DeleteErr:
  MsgBox Err.Description
```

The Delete method deletes the currently selected record. The MoveNext method moves the focus to the next record in the list. If the last record was deleted, there is no next record to move to, so the MoveLast method is used to change the focus to the current last record of the Recordset.

When the Refresh button is clicked, the statement datPrimaryRS.Refresh is executed. This statement reopens the database and refreshes the Recordset. Any changes made are saved and displayed.

The Update button executes datPrimaryRS.Recordset.UpdateBatch adAffectAll when clicked. Changes are stored in memory until this command forces all the changes to be written to the data file. The adAffectAll parameter updates all the records of the Recordset.

The Close button executes the code Unload Me. Me is a variable that represents the current form. The Unload statement unloads the form from memory. Focus is passed back to the form that initiated the call to the closed form.

The regular Data control has many of these same methods and capabilities but it is included for backward compatibility with older programs. Database access today should be through the ADO Data control. You will find that everything you did in the previous section with the regular Data control works the same way with the ADO Data control. The Data Form Wizard automatically added the ADO Data control to your project. To add it yourself, right-click the toolbox and click

Components. Click and add the Microsoft ADO Data Control 6.0 (OLE DB) and Microsoft DataGrid Control 6.0 (OLE DB). The abbreviation OLE DB stands for Object Linking and Embedding Database. This is the type of database that can be accessed with these controls.

In the last three Step-by-Step exercises you built a database and accessed it with both the regular Data control and the ADO Data control using a variety of data bound controls. Another subject related to this work is designing your own data types for use in your programs. In the next section you will work with UDTs, *User Defined Data types*.

Quick Check 6.c

1. ActiveX Data Objects are used to create a connection between the ____________________ and the ____________________ .
2. A ____________________ guides you step by step through the creation of commonly used generic applications.
3. To load another form into memory, use the form's ____________________ method.
4. The SendKeys statement is used to ____________________ .
5. To shift focus to the last record of the Recordset designated by datPrimaryRS.Recordset, use the ____________________ method.

User Defined Data Types

Visual Basic contains a number of very useful built-in data types: Byte, Boolean, Integer, Long, Currency, Decimal, Single, Double, Date, String, Object, and Variant. An array of the Variant type can hold almost any kind of information. You used a Variant array in Step-by-Step exercise 6.2 to hold both strings and values. A variable of the Variant type can also hold dates and times. As versatile as the Variant type is, it is often useful to design your own data types made of the other built-in types. These UDTs, *User Defined Data Types*, always hold data more efficiently (use less memory) than arrays of the Variant type.

User Defined Data Types are defined using a Type statement. A simple example follows:

```
Type Automobile
    Make As String
    Model As String
    Color As String
    Price As Currency
    HorsePower As Integer
    DateOfManufacture As Date
End Type
```

Not shown is an optional declaration of Public or Private preceding Type. More on that subject in a moment. Following Type is the name of the data type: Automobile. Between the Type statement and the End Type statements are the fields of the data type. The fields are the parts that make up the UDT. Each field in turn has its own data type. If a data type is not declared, the field is of the Variant type. Fields of another UDT may also be included in the type definition. Once a type is defined, variables of that type may be declared and used in the code.

A Type statement is only legal in certain places. A UDT may not be defined within an event procedure or function. A UDT declared in the General Declarations section of a form must be preceded with Private. This means the data type can only be used within the procedures and functions defined within the form. To create a UDT that can be used throughout a project, the code has to be placed within a Standard module.

All program code in Visual Basic is in one of three kinds of modules. The *Form module* is the foundation of all Visual Basic programs. It contains the code for the event procedures, functions, and variable declarations of the form. All the code you have written so far has gone into Form modules. UDTs must be declared at the module level: outside the procedures and functions of the module.

A *Standard module* is used to hold code that is accessed by other modules in the project. The procedures and functions in a Standard module are not linked to particular events or controls on a form. The module itself does not have a form. Procedures, functions, and variable declarations can be private to the module. That means they are only available internally. This is useful only if other procedures or functions of the module that are public to the project use the code.

Standard modules are saved in files with a .bas extension. In earlier versions of Visual Basic, they were called Code modules. You add a Standard module to a project by selecting Project | Add Module from the menu bar. The dialog box that opens prompts you to create a module or add an existing module to the project. Adding an existing module is common since the idea of a module is to contain code that is not linked to a particular form or control. Procedures and functions in a Standard module provide services that may be useful in many projects.

FIGURE 6-11
The Project Explorer window showing the presence of a Standard module

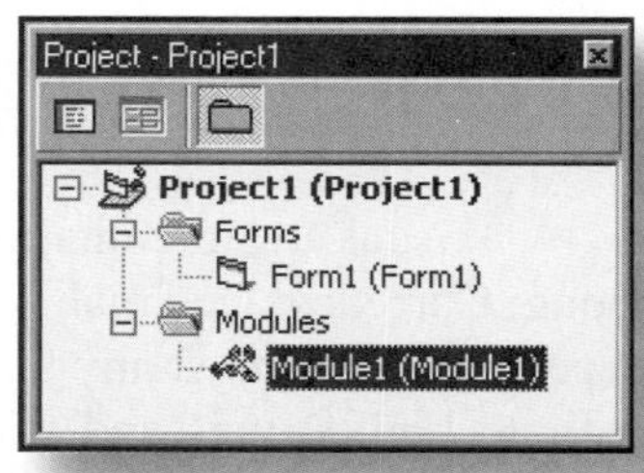

Once a Standard module has been added, you can see the result in the Project Explorer window, as shown in Figure 6-11. The project has not yet been saved, so none of the modules or the project itself has been renamed from their default names provided by Visual Basic.

The meaning of the icon for a Standard module is not readily apparent. It is meant to symbolize that a Standard module is a resource for any number of other modules (mainly Form modules) in a project. Public Type declarations made in a Standard module make the data type available to every procedure or function in every module in the project. Variables, data types, procedures, or functions with this kind of visibility are called global.

Class modules are the third kind of module in Visual Basic. Class modules contain definitions of new kinds of objects. Everything from text boxes to forms to fonts is a Visual Basic Object. Objects have properties and methods. Lesson 8 says a lot more about objects and Class modules.

UDTs are often defined with the Public keyword in a Standard module. A UDT so defined is visible everywhere in the project. In the following Step-by-Step exercise you will add a Standard module to a project, define the Automobile data type, and use it in a simple application. The application declares an array of the Automobile type, loads it with data, displays the information in a Microsoft Hierarchical FlexGrid Control on a separate form, and stores the result in a file.

STEP-BY-STEP 6.4

1. Click **File | Add Project** and double-click **Standard EXE**. This project will use a Multiple Document Interface, where the parent form is the container that holds the child forms of the project. A menu will be added to the parent to call the other forms and load and save data files. One child form is used to add data to the data file. The other contains a Hierarchical FlexGrid control to display the information collected.

2. Click **Project | Add MDI Form** from the menu bar and click **Open** to add a MDI form to the project. This form is the MDI parent form. Change the form's caption to **The Auto Lot**. Change the name of the form to **MDIAutoProject**.

3. Select **form1**, the default form provided by the project, and change its **MDIChild** property to **True**. Change its caption to **Add Data** and its name to **frmAddData**. When this form is active, it will appear in the client area of the MDI parent form. Save the child form as **AddData**, the MIDI form as **AutoProject**, and the project as **Autoproject**.

4. Select **Project | Add Form** from the menu bar. Select **Form** and click **Open** in the Add Form dialog box. Change the form's caption to **What's on the Lot?** and its name to **frmDisplayLot**. Change its **MDIChild** property to **True**. Save the form as **Displaylist**.

5. Select **Project | Add Module** from the menu bar. Select **Module** and click **Open** in the Add Module dialog box. Change the name of the module to **AutoSupport**.

6. Save the module as **AutoSupport**. Make sure you have saved all the files together in an appropriate directory.

7. Right-click the **toolbox** and select **Components** from the pop-up menu. In the Components dialog box, select **Microsoft Common Dialog Control** and **Microsoft Hierarchical FlexGrid Control 6.0 (OLEDB)**. Click **OK** to add these controls to the toolbox. The Common Dialog control is used to collect file names from the user to save and open data files. The FlexGrid control is used to display previously saved auto data.

8. From the **Project Explorer** window, select the **AutoSupport** module. Click the **View Code** icon in the window and insert the code in **Code Step 8**.

   The first line starts the type declaration for the Automobile data type. The Public keyword makes the data type visible throughout the project. The three strings, Make, Model, and Color, are declared as 20 character strings.

To specify a maximum length for a string, follow the keyword String with an * and a positive integer in the variable declaration. A fixed-length string, declared as described, has a capacity of up to 65,535 characters. A variable-length string, declared without the length specified, has a capacity of about 2 billion characters.

(continued on next page)

CODE STEP 8

```
Public Type Automobile
  Make As String * 20
  Model As String * 20
  Color As String * 20
  Price As Currency
  HorsePower As Integer
  DateOfManufacture As Date
End Type
Public Const MaxSpace = 50
Public Auto(0 To MaxSpace) As Automobile
Public LotNumber As Integer
```

It is necessary to fix the lengths of the strings in the data type because the information is to be stored in a *binary file*. When opening the file, the exact length of each record must be fixed and known. The maximum space available in the lot is recorded in the constant MaxSpace. Referring to this number as a named constant simplifies changes that must be made when the capacity of the lot changes. Make a single change to the value of the constant, and the change is made throughout the project. The Auto array is declared as type Automobile. Declaring it as a public variable in the module makes sure it is accessible to each of the child forms. LotNumber is used to keep track of the number of vehicles currently stored in the lot. This number is used to control access to the next empty space in the Auto array, and is used in loops that process the entire list.

9. Select **frmAddData** from the Project Explorer. Click the **View Object** icon to display the form. Add the controls shown in Figure 6-12 and listed in Table 6-3. Change the font size to **10** pts. for all the labels, text boxes, and the combo box.

   Change the **Sorted** property of the combo box to **True**.

FIGURE 6-12
The Add Data form

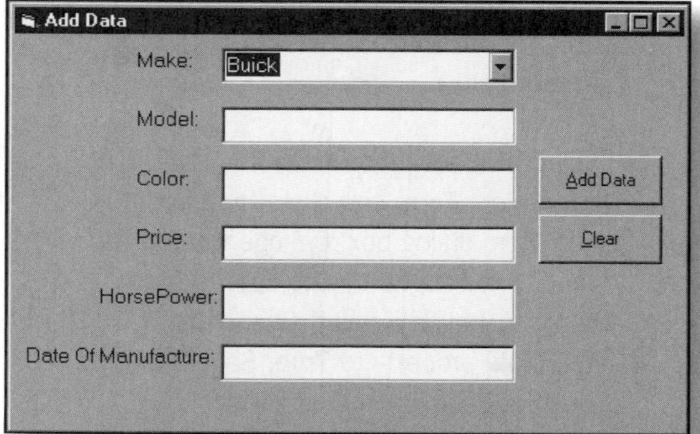

Building Programming Skills

To add several controls with similar properties to a form, first add a single control. Change the control's properties. Copy the control with Ctrl+C. Paste copies of the control with Ctrl+V. When prompted to create a control array, click N, for No.

TABLE 6-3

frmAddData CONTROLS

CONTROL	NAME	CAPTION OR TEXT
Combo Box	cmbMake	(see text)
TextBox	txtModel	none
TextBox	txtColor	none
TextBox	txtPrice	none
TextBox	txtHorsePower	none
TextBox	txtDate	none
Label	Label1	Make:
Label	Label2	Model:
Label	Label3	Color:
Label	Label4	Price:
Label	Label5	HorsePower:
Label	Label6	Date of Manufacture:
CommandButton	cmdAddData	&Add Data
CommandButton	cmdClear	&Clear

10. Double-click the body of the form to open its Code window. Add the following code to **Private Sub Form_Load**:

```
cmbMake.AddItem "Cadillac"
cmbMake.AddItem "Pontiac"
cmbMake.AddItem "Edsel"
cmbMake.ListIndex = 0
Me.WindowState = vbMaximized
```

One way to save time when adding similar code (like the three .AddItem lines) is to enter the first line, then copy and paste the line for each additional make. Next, you would change the string in each line to a different make. Since the Sorted property of the combo box is clicked, it doesn't matter in what order the entries are entered. The line **cmbMake.ListIndex=0** selects the first entry as the default text for the box. The **Me** object variable refers to the currently active form. The rest of the line maximizes frmAddData in its parent form.

11. Enter the code in **Code Step 11** to the **cmdAddData_Click** procedure:

Error checking is always tricky. Anticipating every possible error condition is often impossible. Trying to handle all the possible errors can add hundreds of lines of code to a large project. There is some error handling code in this program, but there are many error conditions that are not covered. Two kinds of errors are handled: exceeding the capacity of the lot and not filling in the necessary fields. The functions CCur( ), CInt( ), and CDate( ) coerce the strings from the text boxes into

(continued on next page)

the types—Currency, Integer, and Date, respectively.

12. Enter the following code in **cmdClear_Click** of **frmAddData**:

```
txtModel = ""
txtColor = ""
txtPrice = ""
txtHorsePower = ""
txtDate = ""
```

13. You could run the program now, but you cannot display the data, save, or load a file. In fact, the wrong form is called to open the program. FrmAddData was the original form of the project: It is still the start-up form. Select **Project | Project Properties** from the menu bar. The Project Properties dialog box appears. Change the start-up object in your project to **MDIAutoProject**, as shown in Figure 6-13, and click **OK**.

14. In the **Project Explorer** window, select **MDIAutoProject** and click the **View Object** icon. Open the Menu Editor. Add the following menu to **MDIAutoProject**:

CAPTION	NAME
&File	mnuFile
&Clear Current Data	mnuClearData
&Open File	mnuOpen
&Save As	mnuSave
-	mnuSeparator
E&xit	mnuExit
&Add Data	mnuAdd
&Display	mnuDisplay

CODE STEP 11

```
LotNumber = LotNumber + 1  ' next available space
  If LotNumber <= MaxSpace Then  ' more space available
  On Error GoTo FillAllBoxes
  With Auto(LotNumber)    ' load the data
    .Make = cmbMake.Text
    .Model = txtModel
    .Color = txtColor
    .Price = CCur(txtPrice) ' coerce to Currency type
    .HorsePower = CInt(txtHorsePower) ' Integer
    .DateOfManufacture = CDate(txtDate) ' Date type
  End With
  cmdClear_Click ' call Clear code
  cmbMake.SetFocus
  Else  ' capacity exceeded
  LotNumber = LotNumber - 1
  MsgBox "No Room on the Lot", vbCritical, "Error"
  frmAddData.Hide ' return to parent form
  End If
  Exit Sub
FillAllBoxes:    ' error handler
  LotNumber = LotNumber - 1
  MsgBox "Fill all fields before adding.", vbInformation, "Error"
```

Clear Current Data will call a routine that sets the variable LotNumber to zero. This effectively empties the array, even though old data may still be present. The old data cannot be accessed. Open and Save As will use the Common Dialog control to get a file name from the user. Add Data will call a routine that shows frmAddData. Display will call the form that displays data loaded from a file.

15. In the **General Declarations** section of the form, enter this line of code:

```
Dim FileName As String
```

16. In **Sub mnuAdd_Click**, add the following code:

```
frmDisplayLot.Hide
frmAddData.Show
```

When Add Data is selected from the menu bar, frmDisplayLot is hidden and frmAddData is shown.

17. In **Sub mnuClearData_Click**, add the following line of code:

```
LotNumber = 0
```

Setting this variable to 0 effectively empties the Auto array of data.

18. You will use frmDisplayLot to display saved data. If the form is called before the data is saved, an error message is returned. Enter the code in **Code Step 18** into **Sub mnuDisplay_Click**.

FIGURE 6-13
The Project property pages

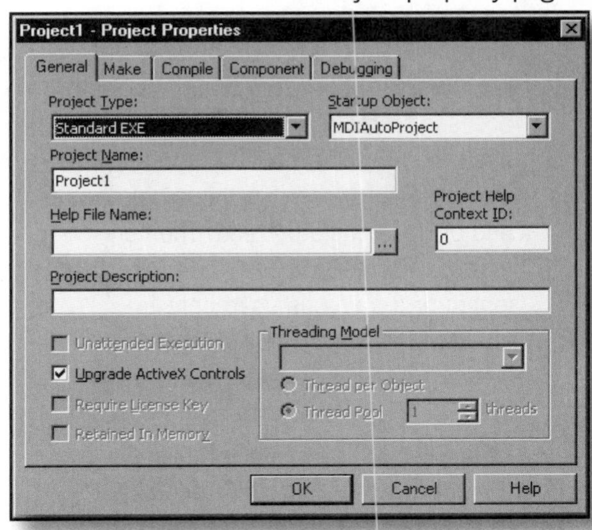

19. Double-click the **Common Dialog** tool in the toolbox to add it to **frmMDIAutoProject**. Name the control **cdlOpenSave**.

20. The **Open File** menu item will call a procedure that uses the Common Dialog control to get a file name from the user, open the file, and load the **Auto** array with data from the file. Enter the code shown in **Code Step 20** into **Sub mnuOpen_Click**.

The Open statement uses the fact that each record is the exact same length to open the file for Random Access. For instance, if each record is 100 characters long, the 0th record would start at byte

(continued on next page)

CODE STEP 18

```
If Len(FileName) <> 0 Then
  frmAddData.Hide
  frmDisplayLot.Show
Else
  MsgBox "First Open a file.", vbInformation, "Error"
End If
```

number 0, the 1st at byte number 100, etc. This allows any record of the file to be accessed directly. In a sequential file, each record would have to be read in order before a record in the middle or the end of a file could be read. The Len( ) function, formerly used to calculate the length of a string, is used here to calculate the length of a User Defined Data Type. The parameter sent to the Len( ) function is not the name of the type, but a particular declared variable of that type. The Get # statement gets a record from the file at the designated channel. The missing value is the record number. If no record number is supplied, records are read in order.

The record is assigned to the variable Auto(LotNumber). The EOF( ) function stands for End Of File. It becomes True when there is an attempt to read a record from beyond the end of the file. Since an attempt is made to read an extra record, the value of LotNumber must be adjusted downward by 1 to reflect the actual number of records read from the file.

A MsgBox reporting the number of records read from the file is commented out with a single quote character. The statement was used to help debug the program as it was written.

21. The Save As menu item will call a procedure that uses the Common Dialog control to save a file. Enter the code in **Code Step 21** into **Sub mnuSave_Click**.

22. Save and run the program. Select **Add Data** from the menu bar. Enter data for a sample record and click the **Add Data** button. The Add Data form has no menu of its own, so the parent's menu is still visible. Select **File | Save As** and enter a name for the file. The extension **.dat** is automatically supplied by the Filter property of cdlOpenSave. At the left end of the menu bar is an icon that represents the window menu of frmAddData. Click this menu icon and click **Close**. Click **Display**. The form shows, but there is no code to display the data. Stop the project.

23. Enter **End** in **mnuExit**.

CODE STEP 20

```
cdlOpenSave.Filter = "Auto Data | *.dat"
cdlOpenSave.ShowOpen
FileName = cdlOpenSave.FileName
If Len(FileName) <> 0 Then
  Open FileName For Random Access Read As #1 Len = Len(Auto(0))
  LotNumber = 0
  Do
    LotNumber = LotNumber + 1
    Get #1, , Auto(LotNumber)
  Loop Until EOF(1)
  Close #1
  LotNumber = LotNumber - 1
  'MsgBox LotNumber & " cars were loaded"
Else
  MsgBox "File name is invalid.", vbCritical, "Error"
End If
```

24. Select **frmDisplayLot** from the **Project Explorer**. Click the **View Object** icon.

25. Double-click the **MSHFlexGrid** tool in the toolbox to add a Hierarchical FlexGrid to the form. Change the name of the control to **grdCarLot**.

26. Open the **Menu Editor** and add the following menu:

CAPTION	NAME	INDEX
&Refresh	mnuRefresh	
&Sort	mnuSort	
By &Make	mnuSortBy	1
By &Horsepower	mnuSortBy	2

27. The code in mnuRefresh will set up the Hierarchical FlexGrid. It sets the number of rows equal to the number of records plus one. The number of columns corresponds to the number of fields in the record. The user is allowed to resize the width of the columns while the program is running. The TextMatrix property accesses the cells of the FlexGrid by specifying a row and column number for each cell. The code inserts data into the first row. This data becomes column headings for the grid. The data is then loaded from the Auto array into the FlexGrid. Once the data is loaded, all rows are selected and the Sort property of the FlexGrid is set to sort in order by column 0, the make of the auto. Enter the code in **Code Step 27** into **mnuRefresh_Click**.

28. The other menu items form a menu control array. They allow the user to sort by horsepower or by make. Enter the code in **Code Step 28** into **mnuSortBy**.

29. Enter the following line of code into the **Sub Form_Activate** procedure:

```
mnuRefresh_Click
```

This initializes the form to display the data when the form is made active.

30. Enter the following line of code into the **Form_Load** event procedure to maximize the form within its parent form:

```
Me.WindowState = vbMaximized
```

31. Save and run the program and exercise all its options. Enter data from cars you are familiar with and save and load the data.

32. Stop the program and exit Visual Basic if you have finished.

(continued on next page)

CODE STEP 21

```
Dim i As Integer
  cdlOpenSave.Filter="Auto Data|*.dat"
  cdlOpenSave.ShowSave
  FileName = cdlOpenSave.FileName
  If Len(FileName)<> 0 Then
    Open FileName For Random As #1 Len = Len(Auto(1))
    For i = 1 To LotNumber
      Put #1,,Auto(i)
    Next i
    Close#1
    'MsgBox LotNumber & " cars were saved."
  Else
    MsgBox "No file was opened.", vbCritical, "Error"
  End If
```

CODE STEP 27

```
If LotNumber = 0 Then Exit Sub ' no data to display
  grdCarLot.Rows = LotNumber + 1 ' one row for heading
  grdCarLot.Cols = 6
  grdCarLot.AllowUserResizing = flexResizeColumns
  Dim i As Integer
  ' Unlike the old MSFlexGrid, the MSHFlexGrid has
  ' a TextMatrix property that allows the programmer
  ' to access each cell with a single statement.
  ' The first index is the row; the second is the column.
  ' Headings:
  With grdCarLot
    .TextMatrix(0, 0) = "Make"
    .TextMatrix(0, 1) = "Model"
    .TextMatrix(0, 2) = "Color"
    .TextMatrix(0, 3) = "Price"
    .TextMatrix(0, 4) = "Horsepower"
    .TextMatrix(0, 5) = "Date of Manufacture"
    .ColWidth(5) = 2400
  End With
  ' Transfer data from the array to the grid.
  For i = 1 To LotNumber
    With Auto(i)
      grdCarLot.TextMatrix(i, 0) = .Make
      grdCarLot.TextMatrix(i, 1) = .Model
      grdCarLot.TextMatrix(i, 2) = .Color
      grdCarLot.TextMatrix(i, 3) = Format(.Price, "currency")
      grdCarLot.TextMatrix(i, 4) = .HorsePower
      grdCarLot.TextMatrix(i, 5) = Format(.DateOfManufacture, "long date")
    End With
  Next
  ' Initial display is sorted by Make.
  With grdCarLot
  .Row = 1  ' These two statements select all the rows
  .RowSel = LotNumber ' from 1 to LotNumber.
  .Col = 0  ' These statements select the column to sort by.
  .ColSel = 0
  .Sort = flexSortGenericAscending
  End With
```

CODE STEP 28

```
Dim SortCol As Integer
  Select Case Index
    Case 1
      SortCol = 0
      With grdCarLot
      .Row = 1
      .RowSel = LotNumber
      .Col = SortCol
      .ColSel = SortCol
      .Sort = flexSortGenericAscending
      End With
    Case 2
      SortCol = 4
      With grdCarLot
      .RowSel = 1
      .Row = LotNumber
      .Col = SortCol
      .ColSel = SortCol
      .Sort = flexSortNumericAscending
      End With
  End Select
```

In this section you created a UDT, a User Defined Data Type, and used it in an application. You used random files to save and load data of the Automobile data type. You declared an array of the Automobile data type. You used a Microsoft Hierarchical FlexGrid Control to display the data you collected and saved. There are times when this kind of data access and manipulation is better than using the ADO Data control.

Quick Check 6.d

1. To be visible throughout a project, the Public Type declaration for a User Defined Data Type must be in a ____________________ module.
2. The components of a User Defined Data Type are called ____________________ .
3. To fix the length of a string to 30 characters, follow the string declaration with ____________________ .
4. To display a form from its MDI parent, use the form's ____________________ method.
5. The ____________________ function is used to determine the number of characters in a record.

Summary

- A database is an organized collection of related data. It is divided into tables, records, and fields. Each field holds an individual piece of data, like a name or a value.
- The Jet database engine generates database files compatible with Access.
- The Visual Data Manager is a Visual Basic application that lets you create and access database files.
- To create a database, add fields to a named table. Each field must have a name and data type.
- A special list keeps the database in order by an Indexed field. You should index any field that is used often to select a particular record from a database.
- A Recordset is a collection of records of a database. A dynaset is a kind of Recordset. It is a set of pointers that point to particular records from particular tables.
- The Data control links a database file with a Visual Basic project. It is used to display information from database fields in a data bound control, like the text box or label controls.
- The DatabaseName property of the Data control must be set to the database's file name. The RecordSource property of the control must be set to a particular table of the database.
- The DataSource and DataField properties of a data bound control link the control to a particular field of the database.
- The Microsoft Chart control is used to display graphs of data. The control has a wide range of options that changes the appearance of the graph.
- A two-dimensional array uses two index values to store data in table form. Commonly, the first index represents the row and the second represents the column. An array of any data type may be defined.
- ActiveX Data Objects, like the ADO Data control, are used to create a connection between the data in a data file and a data bound control on a form.
- The Data Form Wizard guides a programmer step by step through the process of building a form that automatically accesses information in a database. The form is used in a project to add, display, and modify data.
- The On Error statement sends program flow to code that handles run-time errors.
- The SendKeys statement sends one or more keystrokes to the active window as if keyed at the keyboard.
- The Microsoft DataGrid control is used to add, display, and modify data.
- A User Defined Data Type, a UDT, is defined to provide a custom data type built from other built-in types or other UDTs. Variables of the UDT can be declared. Fields are accessed with the dot notation *Variablename.fieldname*.
- Three kinds of Visual Basic modules exist: the familiar Form module, the Standard module, and the Class module. The Standard module is used to store commonly used procedures, functions, and data type declarations.
- Variables declared with the Public keyword in the General Declarations section of a Standard module are visible throughout the project.

- The Me object variable refers to the currently active form. Me.WindowState = vbMaximized maximizes the active form.
- The functions CCur( ), CInt( ), and CDate( ), convert strings to Currency, Integer, and Date data types, respectively.
- The Get # statement is used to load a fixed-length record from a data file into an appropriate variable.
- The Put # statement is used to write a fixed-length record from a variable to a data file.
- The Start-up object, set in the Project Properties dialog box, determines which form is displayed when a project is executed.
- By specifying an exact record length, a Random file may be opened. Such a file gives direct access to the records saved in the file.
- The EOF( ) function is True when a program tries to read from an empty file.
- The Len( ) function is used to determine the exact length of a UDT.
- The MSHFlexGrid control is used to display information. You access the cells of the grid by using the grid's TextMatrix property. You sort the items in the grid by setting the Sort property to the proper value.

LESSON 6 REVIEW QUESTIONS

TRUE/FALSE

Circle the T if the statement is true. Circle the F if it is false.

T F 1. Once information is organized, it is called data.

T F 2. A database is made up of tables. Tables are further divided into records, and records are divided into fields.

T F 3. The purpose of the VisData program is to design Visual Basic Database forms.

T F 4. To add an Indexed field to a database, declare the field to be of the Index type.

T F 5. A dynaset is a type of Recordset.

T F 6. A Data control is used to connect a sequential data file to a Common Dialog control.

T F 7. A data bound control is filled with data before it is pasted onto a form.

T F 8. The RecordSource property is used to choose the table to get data from.

T F 9. The DataField property of a data bound control is used to define a new database file.

T F 10. The MSChart control is used to draw a graph of data used in a program.

WRITTEN QUESTIONS

Write your answers to the following questions.

11. Describe the relationship between data and information.

12. Describe the relationship between tables, records, and fields of a database.

13. What is the Jet database engine?

14. What is VisData used for?

15. Explain what a Recordset is.

16. Explain what a Data control is used for.

17. What two properties of the Data control connect it to a database file?

18. Explain what a two-dimensional array is. How are the elements of the array accessed?

19. What control has the RecordSource property? What is the property used for?

20. Describe the process of copying and pasting controls to replicate several controls at a time. Tell the specific keystrokes used.

LESSON 6 APPLICATION PROBLEMS

SCANS

Level One

THE GAME DATABASE—DESIGN PHASE

Use VisData to create a Game database with the following fields:

- Name of the game
- Controller required or desired to play the game
- Format of source (CD, disk, download, etc.)
- Price paid for source
- Rating 1-10

Choose an appropriate name for the table and file. Add at least five items to the database using VisData.

THE GAME DATABASE—DISPLAY PHASE

Write an application using the ADO Data control to display the items in the Game database. Your program should link the fields of the database to text boxes on the form. Use the Data control to navigate through the records of the database. Change the rating on one of the games and navigate to a different record. Exit the program. Run the program again and check to see if the change you made was saved.

THE GAME DATABASE—WIZARD PHASE

Modify your Game database program to have a menu to open a new form that adds, updates, and deletes records. Use the Visual Basic Data Form Wizard to create the new form that accesses the database. Instead of using the grid as you did in the CD Player application, use the wizard to build a form that accesses the records one at a time. Run the program and navigate through the records of the database. Add a new record to the database and check all the other options as well.

SCANS

Level Two

THE GAME DATABASE—UDT STYLE

Write a new program that creates a User Defined Data Type for the data described in the Game database problem. Declare your Game data type in a Standard module using the Public keyword. Declare an array of 100 games in the same place. Your program should use a form to add information to the game array. It is not necessary to use the Multiple Document Interface for this program. Let the user save the contents of the array by selecting a Save As menu item that uses the Common Dialog control to get a file name for the database. The user should also be able to select Open from the menu and get a dialog box that lets them open the data file. Display the data file record by record. Command buttons on the form should allow the user to navigate forward or backward through the array.

LESSON 6 PROGRAMMING AT WORK

SCANS

THE MUSIC COLLECTION PROJECT

In Lesson 5 you added a toolbar and pop-up menu to the Music Collection project. Now you will connect the Data Entry form to a real database. First you will build the database using VisData. Then you will add an ADO Data control to the form to link the text boxes and combo boxes to the database. Follow these steps to build the database.

1. Open the Music Collection project from Lesson 5. Select **Add-Ins** from the menu bar and click **Visual Data Manager**.

2. Select **File** and click **New**. VisData prompts you for a file name. Navigate to the folder you saved the Music Collection project in and name the data file **MusCol**.

3. Once the file is named, right-click the **Database Window** and click **New Table**. The Table Structure dialog box opens. Enter the table name **MusicCollection**. Click **Add Field** to open the Add Field dialog box. Enter the following field names, lengths, and data types:

Name	Type	Size	Required
Title	Text	50	Checked
Artist	Text	50	Not checked
Composer	Text	50	Not checked
Format	Text	15	Not checked
Location	Text	20	Not checked
Comments	Text	50	Not checked

Running Time	Text	10	Not checked
Year	Text	8	Not checked
Publisher	Text	50	Not checked
Category	Text	20	Not checked

4. Click **Build Table** to close the Table Structure dialog box. Right-click the entry **Music Collection** in the Database Window and select **Open** from the pop-up menu. The Dynaset:MusicCollection dialog box opens.

5. Add a record to the database. Remember to click the **Add** button. Once the entry is complete, click the **Update** button to add the record to the database.

6. Click **Close** to close the Dynaset:MusicCollection dialog box. Select **File | Exit** to close VisData. Now that the database has been designed and built, you will link it to the Data Entry form.

7. Right-click the **toolbox** and select **Components** from the pop-up list. Add the **Microsoft ADO Data control** to the toolbox. Double-click its icon to add it to the Data Entry form.

8. Change the caption of Adodc1 to **Music Collection**. Because the ADO Data control is more versatile than the original Data control, it is more complicated to set up. Right-click the control and select **ADOCD Properties** to open its Property Pages. Click the **General** tab. Click the **Use Connection String** option and the **Build** button to connect the Data control to a database. This opens the Data Link Provider dialog box. Click the **Provider** tab. Confused? See Figure 6-14.

9. An OLE DB provider is a program that gives you access to various kinds of databases. Select **Microsoft Jet 3.51 OLE DB Provider**. Click the **Connection** tab. Click the button with the ellipsis to navigate to the **MusCol** database file. Ignore the other choices offered in the dialog box. Click the **Test Connection** button to make sure everything is working. Click **OK** to return to the Data control's Property Pages.

10. Click the **RecordSource** tab. For the old Data control, you could choose a table name to create a table-type Recordset. For an ADO Data control, use an SQL Query to create a Recordset. SQL stands for Structured Query Language. SQL is designed to ask questions of databases. In the Command Text (SQL) box, enter the following query:

FIGURE 6-14
The Data Link Properties dialog box

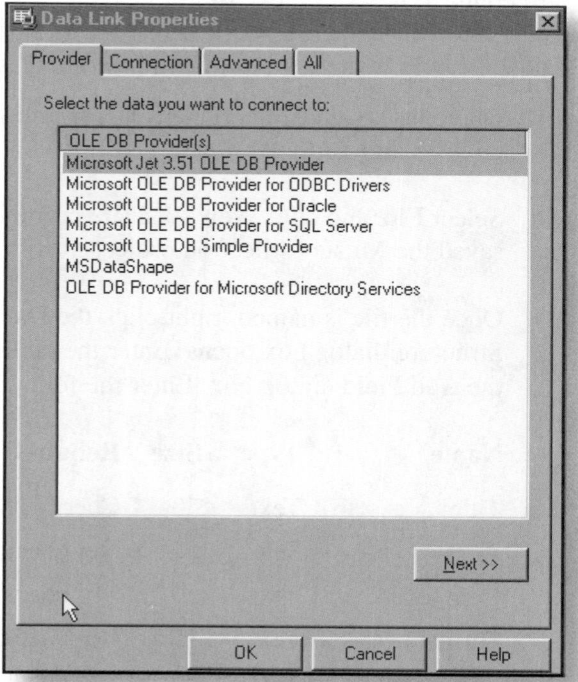

Select Title, Artist, Composer, Format, Location, Comments, [Running Time], Year, Publisher, Category from MusicCollection Order by Title

The query starts with *Select*. A list of the fields to import follows. Fields with spaces embedded in their names must be enclosed in square brackets. The name of the table follows the word *from*. Finally, the Recordset is put in order by the Title of the work. (see Figure 6-15).

11. Click the **Apply** button and the **OK** button to close the Property Pages.

12. Select **txtTitle**. Click its **DataSource** property from the Properties window. Click the **list arrow** and select **Adodc1**. Select the **DataField** property and click the **list arrow**. Choose **Title** from the list of fields. Select each of the text boxes and combo boxes on the form and link each to its appropriate field. Set the DataSource property for one control and select each of the other controls. As you select the new control, the DataSource property is automatically highlighted. Set this property for each of the controls. Set the DataField property in a similar way.

FIGURE 6-15
The ADODC Property Pages RecordSource tab

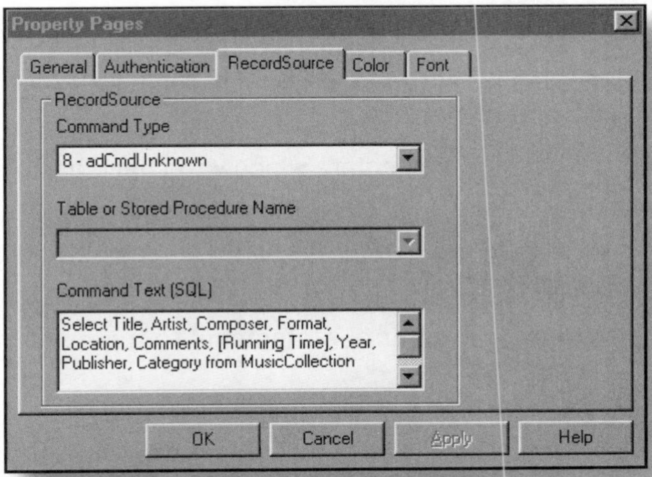

13. Save and run the program. The record you entered in VisData should appear.

14. Stop the program.

If there were more than one entry in the database, the Data Entry form could navigate from record to record. There is no way to add a record yet (except using VisData), but you will add that code at the end of Lesson 7. You will want to use some of the debugging methods you learn in that lesson to take the next step.

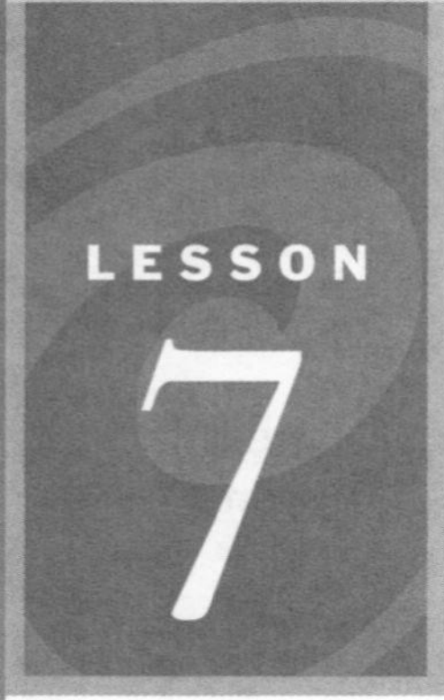

LESSON 7 UNDER THE HOOD

LESSON OBJECTIVES

When you complete this lesson, you will be able to:

- Use breakpoints and Watch windows to locate program errors.
- Use the Immediate window to check and change values.
- Check a program's logic by stepping through the program one line at a time.
- Use the On Error statements to trap run-time errors.
- Create a report using an ODBC driver.

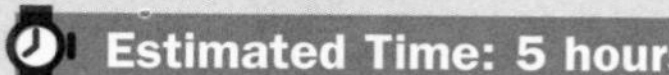
Estimated Time: 5 hours

KEY TERMS

bugs
error trapping
InterCap naming convention
Option Explicit
syntax errors
breakpoint
break mode
Watch expression
Watch window
Step Into
error handler
Err and Error
Err object
error log or log file
App object
ODBC Driver
data source name (DSN)

What's the Problem?

A program can fail in countless ways. The more complex the program, the more likely it is that hidden *bugs* are waiting to leap out and bite the unwary user. As a programmer, it is your job to keep the bugs at bay. If your programs are carefully thought out and tested, errors can be minimized. Every programmer should anticipate the creativity of the user to find ways to crash his program.

Some errors are purely programmer errors that should not occur. Some years ago, a C++ programmer misused a break statement and brought the national telephone system to a nine-hour halt. A simple data type error in a Fortran program sent an unmanned spacecraft off aimlessly into the unknown. A C programming error by an engineer encoded a math error in the first Pentium chips.

Luckily, there is a lot you can do to avoid such errors. Proper planning is the first, best defense against bugs. If you start writing a program without proper preparation, you can be sure errors will occur. On the other hand, properly planned programs with thousands of lines of code have been written with virtually no bugs.

Building Communication Skills

It is no surprise that communication with the user is an important part of preventing bugs. Programs that prompt the user for input should give the user something to look at that explains what input is required. A prompt to the user to enter their last name requires no explanation. A prompt to enter a date or dollar amount requires a pattern for the user to follow and an error trapping code if a mistake is made. *Error trapping* is rerouting program flow during a run-time error to code designed to handle the problem.

Visual Basic provides you with many tools to debug your programs. This lesson shows you how to use those tools.

Debugging with Variable Names

One of the debugging tools that is easiest to use is the *InterCap naming convention*. This means that when you define a variable or set a control's Name property, you should initial capitalize each part of the name. For example, using the InterCap naming convention, a text box used to enter an unpaid balance might be named txtUnpaidBalance. Then when you enter the name of the text box in code, you should key the whole name in lowercase characters. When you press Enter, Visual Basic changes the spelling to the correct capitalization if the name you entered matches a name in its list. If the capitalization is not changed, Visual Basic doesn't recognize what you keyed as a valid name and you should check your spelling.

Option Explicit

The *Option Explicit* statement, keyed in the General Declarations section of the Code window of a form, is the second line of defense. This statement requires all variables to be declared before they are used. As mentioned in Lesson 2, if the Option Explicit statement is not in the program, any misspelled variable name becomes an active variable in the program. It is initialized to 0 and probably will not behave as you want it to. If the Option Explicit statement is present in your program, the program flags a misspelled variable with an error message. Program execution is halted until the problem is solved.

Another way to include Option Explicit in your program is to select Tools | Options from the menu bar. Under the Editor tab, one of the settings is Require Variable Declaration. When selected, any new module automatically has Option Explicit in its General Declarations section (see Figure 7.1).

FIGURE 7-1
The Editor tab of the Options dialog box

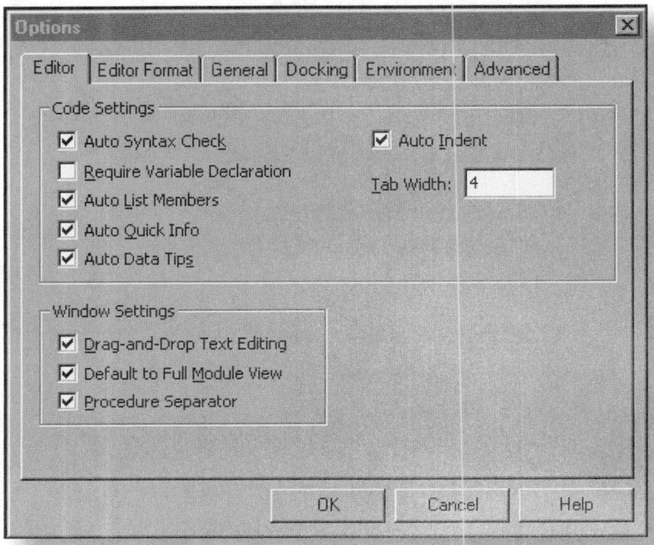

Syntax Errors

Visual Basic checks each line of code for *syntax errors* as soon as you press the Enter key. Syntax errors are errors in the structure of the statement itself. For example, if you misspell a command or omit a statement, that is a syntax error. The statement at the end of a Select Case statement is End Select. If you mistakenly key Select End, Visual Basic catches it immediately and prompts you for a correction.

Breakpoints

A *breakpoint* is a spot in the code at which the program pauses. With the program in break mode, you can examine and change values of variables. A program enters *break mode* automatically when it encounters a run-time error. In the next Step-by-Step exercise you will set breakpoints to pause program execution.

The program you will use to examine breakpoints is filled with potential errors. The program will ask the user to enter three values: the balance owed on a loan, the monthly payment for a loan, and the loan's yearly interest rate. From this data, the program calculates the number of payments left to pay off the loan.

STEP-BY-STEP 7.1

1. Start Visual Basic and double-click **Standard EXE**. Save the form and the project as **Payments**.

2. Change the caption of the form to **How Many More Payments?** and the name to **frmPayments**.

3. Add three text boxes, four labels, and three command buttons to the form, as shown in Figure 7.2. Name the text boxes **txtUnpaid**, **txtPayment**, and **txtRate** and set their Text properties to blanks. Set the captions of the labels that are above the text boxes to those shown in Figure 7-2. Name the lower label **lblPayments**, change its caption to **Payments**, change its BorderStyle to **1-Fixed Single**, and its alignment to **2-Center**. Name the command buttons **cmdCalculate**, **cmdClear**, and **cmdExit**. Change the captions of the command buttons to **&Calculate**, **C&lear**, and **E&xit**.

4. Double-click the **Calculate** button to open the Code window. Press **Tab** and enter the code in **Code Step 4**.

   Notice that you define the variables with initial capitals and that you enter the rest of the code in lowercase characters.

   This code reads the balance, monthly payment, and the interest rate from the text boxes. It initializes the variable Count to 0 and uses it to keep track of the number of payments. Each month the unpaid balance is calculated by adding interest and subtracting the monthly payment from the current unpaid balance. The program also converts the yearly interest rate to a monthly rate by dividing it by 12. If payments are more than interest, the unpaid balance is reduced each month until it is less than or equal to 0. Then the program reports the number of months it took to pay off the loan.

5. Enter the following code in Private Sub **cmdClear_Click**:

```
txtbalance = ""
txtpayment = ""
txtrate = ""
lblpayments = ""
txtunpaid.setfocus
```

   Did you notice a mistake as you entered the

FIGURE 7-2
The How Many More Payments? form

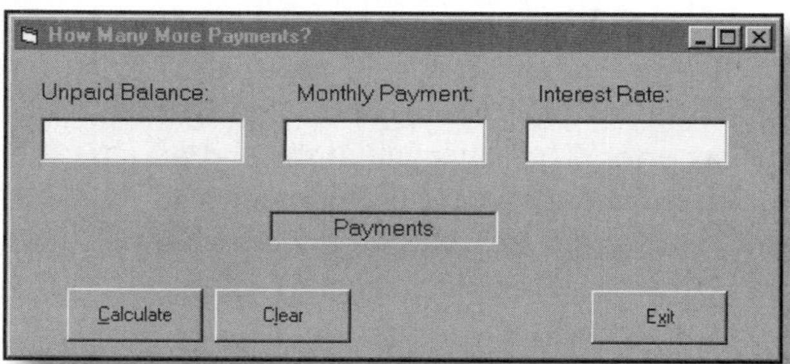

code? The name of the text box for the unpaid balance is txtUnpaid, but in the code it is referred to as txtbalance. Notice that Visual Basic did not capitalize the "b" in txtbalance as it did for the other variables and names. That is a tip to you that the code is incorrect.

6. Check the General Declarations section to be sure there is no Option Explicit statement. If one exists, add an apostophe as the first character to make it a comment. The program will run because Visual Basic thinks txtbalance is an undeclared variable.

7. Save and run the program (with the mistakes uncorrected). Enter the following data: Unpaid Balance as **5500**, Monthly Payment as **175**, Rate as **13**. Click **Calculate**. The program reports the number of payments as 1. Clearly, something is wrong. Stop the program.

8. To set a breakpoint, double-click the **Calculate** button. On the left edge of the Code window is a gray channel. Position the mouse pointer over the gray channel, even with the statement **Loop Until Balance <= 0**. Click once to establish a breakpoint. A brown ball appears in the channel and the line is highlighted in brown. Now when the program runs, the statements up to the marked statement execute. Then the program enters break mode. Another way to set a breakpoint is to use the Debug menu. To do that, you click the line where you want the break to appear, and click **Debug | Toggle Breakpoint**. The shortcut key is **F9**.

9. Save and run the program. Enter **5500**, **175**, and **13**. Click **Calculate**. When the program enters break mode, the form disappears and the Code window appears. The line with the breakpoint is highlighted.

10. Move the mouse pointer over various variables and object names. As the I-beam hovers over each one, a ToolTip appears, displaying the value of the variable or object. Check the Balance. The value *–175* appears. What happened to the value entered in the text box? Move the mouse pointer over each of the names of the text boxes. Two of the boxes are fine. They reflect the values entered when the program was run. But when the mouse pointer is placed over txtbalance, the ToolTip says the object is "Empty." By this time, the mistake should be apparent: The text box is misnamed in the program.

11. Now you will correct the error while still in break mode. Change txtbalance to **txtUnpaid** in both **cmdCalculate** and **cmdClear**. Enter it with a lowercase **u** and watch as it changes when you leave that line. Place the mouse pointer over txtUnpaid. Now the value displayed by the ToolTip is *5500*. Stop the program.

(continued on next page)

CODE STEP 4

```
dim Balance as currency, Payment as currency, Rate as single
dim Count as integer
balance = val(txtbalance)
payment = val(txtpayment)
rate = val(txtrate)
count = 0
do
     count = count + 1
     balance = balance + balance * rate / 12 - payment
loop until balance <= 0
lblpayments = count
```

12. Now that the problem is fixed, you will remove the breakpoint. Click the **brown ball** in the gray channel of the Code window, or put the cursor on the line with the breakpoint and press **F9**, or click **Debug | Toggle Breakpoint** from the menu bar.

13. Save and run the program, entering the same data as in Step 8. Oops. Not all the problems are fixed. A run-time error appears. Click **Debug** to enter break mode (see Figure 7-3).

14. When the Code window appears, make a note of where the program stopped. The line is highlighted in yellow. Move the cursor over Count. The ToolTip reports a value of *36,* and that value seems correct. Move the cursor over Balance. Something is wrong with the balance. Move the cursor over txtUnpaid. What happened to make the balance so large? It was initialized with the correct value. If the balance is increasing instead of decreasing, it means the amount of interest each month is larger than the amount of the monthly payment. The example data was chosen because it is reasonable, so the balance should be getting smaller each month.

    The answer is in how the Rate is used. The user enters a Rate of 13, intending 13 percent. The equation is using the value 13 as an Integer. Instead of a rate of 0.13, the rate is being interpreted as 1300%. No wonder the Balance is getting bigger instead of smaller!

15. While still in break mode, select **View | Immediate Window**. In this window you can view and change the values of variables.

FIGURE 7-3
The run-time error window

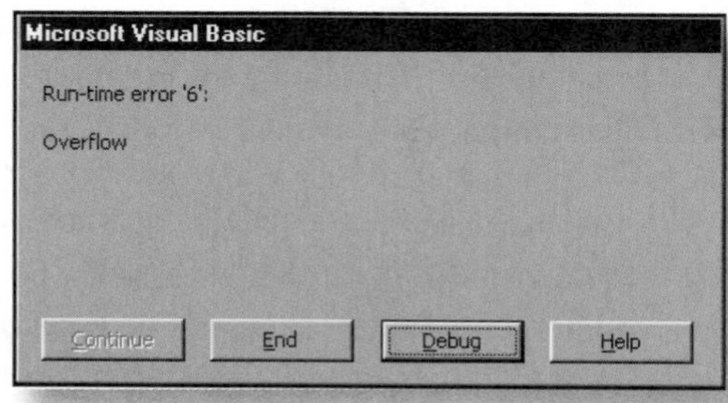

    Key **Print Balance** and press **Enter**. Note the wildly incorrect value. Key **Balance = 5500** and press **Enter**. Then key **Print Balance** and press **Enter**. This resets the value of Balance. Test your program logic by keying **Print Balance** * **Rate** / **12** and pressing **Enter**. Is this value a reasonable value for the interest charged on a loan with a monthly payment of $175? Key **Rate = .13** and press **Enter**, **Key Count = 0** and press **Enter**, and key **Print Balance, Rate, Count** and press **Enter**. All the values are reset. Press **F5** to resume execution of the program and note the number of payments.

16. Stop the program and open the Code window.

17. Change the line that calculates balance to the code shown in **Code Step 17**.

    This automates the process of changing Rate to a decimal. Add **End** to the **cmdExit** procedure.

18. Save and run the program. Enter **5500**, **175**, and **13**. Click **Calculate**. No error! The Payments label displays 39 payments.

19. Stop the program and leave it open for the next Step-by-Step exercise.

CODE STEP 17

```
Balance = Balance + Balance * Rate / 1200 - Payment
```

This section examined some of the ways Visual Basic helps you guard against common programming errors. Setting a breakpoint and using the mouse to examine the value of variables and objects is a very powerful technique for finding errors. Automatic capitalization of names is also very powerful. Maybe the first thing that should be done for any program is to enter Option Explicit in the General Declarations section of the code. If you have a program that doesn't work, enter Option Explicit in the General Declarations section and run the program again. In the next section you will learn about even more powerful tools to fix program bugs.

Quick Check 7.a

1. If you use the ____________________ convention to name variables, you can check for valid names by entering them all in lowercase when keying code.

2. The ____________________ statement, entered in the General Declarations section of a module, requires all variables to be declared before they are used in code.

3. You set a breakpoint by clicking in the ____________________ even with the statement.

4. ____________________ is the shortcut key for setting a breakpoint.

5. In break mode, a ____________________ appears when the mouse is hovering over a variable name.

Setting the Watch

Stopping a program and examining values with the mouse pointer is unmanageable if the program is large. Other tools let you set a *Watch expression*. The value of a Watch expression is displayed in the *Watch window* when the program enters break mode. You will use the program developed in the previous Step-by-Step exercise to implement a watch. You start by creating an error condition. As you know, the program logic does not work properly if the interest charged is greater than the monthly payment. By altering the data entered in the program, you can cause a run-time error. A run-time error automatically puts the program into break mode. The following Step-by-Step exercise shows you how to cause the error and then examine it with a Watch expression.

STEP-BY-STEP 7.2

1. Open the **Payments** project, if necessary.

2. Run the program. Enter **5500**, **175**, and **13**. Click **Calculate**. The program reports 39 payments. Change the monthly payment to **100**. Click **Calculate**. No error yet. The number of payments is increasing. Change the monthly payment to **70**. Click **Calculate**. Change the monthly payment to **60**. Click **Calculate**. Change the payment to **50**. Click **Calculate**. The program enters break mode and displays a run-time error showing an Overflow condition.

(continued on next page)

Click **Debug** to show the Code window. Note the line highlighted in yellow. Check the Balance with the mouse pointer. It is far out of any reasonable range.

3. Stop the program. Double-click any instance of the variable Balance to select it. Click **Debug | Quick Watch** or press **Shift+F9**. Click **Add** to add Balance to the list of Watch expressions. Run the program. Enter the data **5500**, **50**, and **13**, and click **Calculate.** The program crashes with a run-time error. The Watch window shows the variable name *Balance*, its value, its data type, and in which procedure of which module the error occurs. After checking the Watch window, stop the program.

Look around the screen. Can you find the Watch window? If not, select View | Watch Window from the menu bar. If it is too small to read, use the mouse to enlarge it. It shows the status of each Watch expression.

4. This is only one kind of watch and it is useful. Another kind of watch lets you set up more complex watch conditions. If the value of Count gets too large, there is probably something wrong with the data.

FIGURE 7-4
The Add Watch window

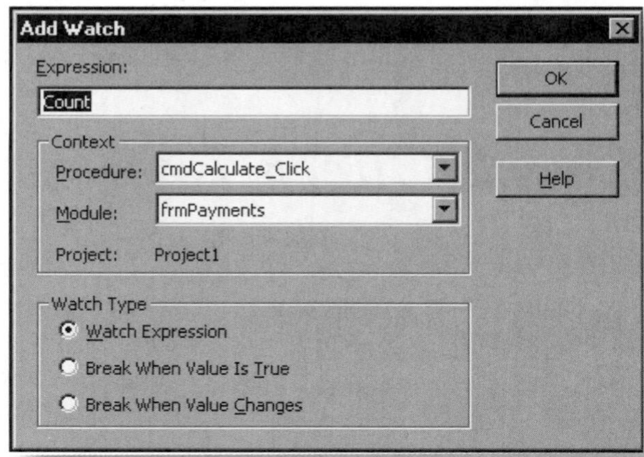

Click any occurrence of the variable **Count** in **cmdCalculate_Click**. Click **Debug | Add Watch**. The Add Watch window appears (see Figure 7-4).

5. The name of the variable appears in the Expression box. The names of the procedure and the module also appear. Change the Expression box from *Count* to **Count > 150**. Click the option **Break When Value Is True** in the Watch Type frame at the bottom of the dialog box. Click **OK** to close the dialog box.

6. Save and run the program. Enter **5500**, **60**, and **13**. Click **Calculate**. The program enters break mode. Examine the Watch

Building Better Programming Skills

The Step Into option steps into any procedure or function called in the code and executes it line by line. If you are certain there is no error in a particular procedure or function, execute the code by pressing Shift+F8, or select Debug | Step Over from the menu bar. With this command, the program will not show a line-by-line execution of a procedure or function called in the code. It executes the procedure or function in real time and returns to executing the lines of the calling procedure one at a time. Step Out or Ctrl+Shift+F8 finishes the execution of the current procedure or function and shifts program flow to the statement that follows the procedure. Use this option if you are sure the remaining code of a procedure or function is error-free.

window. Two expressions appear. One line shows the new Watch expression, *Count > 150*. The window shows its status: True, its data type, and its context (procedure). It also shows the current status of Balance. Notice that the value of Balance is much less than it was when it was so large that it caused an overflow.

This kind of information suggests that a program alteration is needed. For example, the program could check to see if the value of Count is getting unreasonably large. If it is, there is probably something wrong with the data and the program should stop (under control, not with a run-time error) and handle the error in some reasonable way.

7. When a program has a lot of changes in program flow caused by loops and If statements, you may have to you single-step through a program to find its errors. When the program is in break mode, you single-step through the lines of code by pressing **F8** or selecting **Debug | Step Into**. Press **F8** several times now to see the program execute one line of code at a time. You can watch the lines execute as the yellow highlighting moves from line to line. Check the value of Balance in the Watch window. It is changing as you step through the program.

   How would you fix this error condition? It only occurs if the calculated value of the monthly interest is larger than the monthly payment. You could add code to check this condition and alert the user if it occurs. If you do this, be sure and test your changes. If it doesn't work the way you expect, use the debugging techniques you have learned to troubleshoot the program.

8. Stop and remove the project.

In the next section you will look at how to gracefully deal with error situations. A run-time error is not acceptable.

Building Better Programming Skills

Part of the debugging process is to build a set of input data that tests all aspects of the program. Test the boundary conditions of the program (if any exist): the largest or smallest possible values, negative values, etc.

Quick Check 7.b

1. A run-time error automatically puts the program into ____________________ .
2. Values of expressions and variables can be viewed in the ____________________ when a Watch expression is set.
3. The shortcut for a Quick Watch is ____________________ .
4. Keying F8 in break mode will ____________________ through lines of program code.
5. The Step Over option in the Debug menu will not step into ____________________ while single-stepping through program code.
6. Selecting the Break When Value Is True option puts the program in break mode when ____________________ .

On Error

Years ago, computers were unforgiving. If you wrote a graphing program in BASIC and the program tried to plot a point outside the graphics area, the program crashed. You have probably used a graphing calculator and know that graphing outside the window doesn't cause an error. The worst thing than can happen on a graphing calculator is that a table entry may actually say "Error". In Visual Basic you can draw points with the PSet method. If you use PSet outside the graphics area, no error is generated. The system covers for your mistake by ignoring it.

You can set up your program to ignore run-time errors. It isn't the best way to deal with errors, but it is certainly the easiest. To ignore errors, use the statement On Error Resume Next. When a statement causes an error, it is ignored and the program continues with the next statement. No error message is generated and the program doesn't crash. But that does not mean everything is all right. The statement that generated the error did not execute correctly. That means whatever it was trying to accomplish is left undone. This certainly has an effect on the rest of the program.

In the next Step-by-Step exercise you will write a program to open a data file and transfer data from a text box into the file. You will introduce an error by trying to open the file in a nonexistent folder on the C drive.

STEP-BY-STEP 7.3

1. Click **File | New Project** and double-click **Standard EXE**. Save the form and project as **NoteSaver**.

2. Change the caption of the form to **Record a Note** and its name to **frmNoteSaver**.

3. Add a text box to the form. Change its name to **txtNotes**. Clear its **Text property**. Double-click **MultiLine** to change its value to **True**.

4. Add two command buttons to the form. Change the caption of the first to **Save Notes** and its name to **cmdSaveNotes**. Change the caption of the second to **E&xit** and its name to **cmdExit**.

5. Double-click **cmdSaveNotes**, press **Tab**, and enter the following code (remember to enter what you can in lowercase so Visual Basic can help you debug the code):

```
Dim FileName As String
FileName = "c:\notes\note.txt"
Open FileName For Output As #1
Print #1, txtNotes
Close #1
```

6. Select the **cmdExit_Click** procedure, press **Tab**, and enter the **End** command.

7. Save and run the program. Enter a line or two in the text box. Click **Save Notes**. Normally, opening a text file For Output creates a new file. But in this case, there is no path c:\notes. The file cannot be created and the program crashes.

8. Click **Debug** and make a note of the highlighted line. This is the line that caused the error. Stop the program.

9. Enter the following line of code after the Dim statement:

```
On Error Resume Next.
```

10. Save and run the program. Enter some data. Click **Save Notes**.

    There is no error, but the notes have not been saved and a file was not created. In other words, the program does not accomplish anything, but at least it doesn't crash. There is a better way. Instead of just executing the next statement, the On Error statement can send the program flow to special error-handling code.

11. Stop the program and open **cmdSaveNotes_Click**. Change On Error Resume Next to **On Error GoTo FileOpenError**. After the statement Close #1, add the statements shown in **Code Step 11**.

    The system automatically moves the label FileOpenError: to the edge of the left margin when you press Enter. A label (a string with no embedded spaces followed by a colon) is the name of a statement. This statement is called an *error handler*. When an error occurs, the On Error GoTo FileOpenError statement sends program flow directly to the MsgBox statement.

12. Save and run the program. Enter some text and click **Save Notes**. The error message appears. Now at least the user knows the notes have not been saved. Stop the program.

13. Change the path name to **C:\notes.txt**. If you are not able to access the C drive, use a diskette and change the drive letter to **A**. Now the program should work.

14. Save and run the program. Enter some text. Click **Save Notes**. The error message appears! Stop the program and open the Code window. Set a breakpoint on the Open statement.

15. Save and run the program. Enter some text. Click **Save Notes**. The program immediately enters break mode. Use **F8** to single-step through the program. Check the results of each step. There are no errors, but the error handler executes anyway because there is nothing to stop program flow after the Close #1 statement. The error message appears because of programmer error.

16. Stop the program and remove the breakpoint. Following the Close #1 statement, enter the line **Exit Sub**. This statement terminates the procedure without executing any of the remaining code.

17. Save and run the program. Enter some text. Click **Save Notes**. Now there is no error message! Stop the program.

18. Use **Windows Explorer** to check the C:\ for **note.txt**. Double-click **note.txt** to open the file in Notepad. You will see the text you entered saved in the file.

(continued on next page)

CODE STEP 11

```
FileOpenError:
MsgBox "File Open Error",  vbCritical, "File Error"
```

Historically Speaking

Labeling lines in BASIC code is not new. If fact, in the first versions of BASIC, every line was numbered and every program was a maze of GoTo's followed by statement numbers. It was possible to write code that was indecipherable even to the programmer. And the debugging capabilities of the language were far less sophisticated than they are today. The Tron command turned on Trace mode. In Trace mode, the line number of each line that was executed was listed. The result was an unmanageable list of line numbers that no one actually looked at.

Information is what a user wants and needs when an error occurs. What was the error? How can it be fixed? Your error handler should try to inform the user, maybe even correct the problem, and try to execute the code again. Three objects help you inform the user. They are system variables *Err*, and *Error*, and the *Err* object. When an error occurs, *Err* contains the error number. *Error* contains a description of the error. The *Err object* contains both and more besides.

19. Now restore the error to your program by changing the path name back to **c:\notes\note.txt**.

20. Edit the message box prompt to read **"File Open Error: " & Err**.

21. Save and run the program. Enter some text and click **Save Notes**. The error message displays the error number *76*.

22. Stop the program. Edit the message box prompt to read **"File Open Error: " & Error**.

23. Save and run the program. Click **Save Notes**. The error message displays the error description "Path not found."

24. Stop the program. Edit the message box prompt to read **"File Open Error: " & Err.** (Enter the period!) As soon as you enter the period following *Err*, you get a list of options. The Number property of the Err object gives you the error number. The Description property gives the same description as Error. Experiment with the other settings. Why might you want to know the Source of the error?

25. Save and run the program. Click **Save Notes**. Examine the results. Stop the program and repeat with a new value.

26. Stop the program and remove the project.

Log Files

Often an error handler saves error data in a file called an *Error Log* or *Log File*. This text file lists the errors and the time when they occur. A log file is usually a simple text file. Instead of opening the file **For Output**, as you did in the Note Saver program above, open the file **For Append**. This adds the new information at the end of an existing file. Follow these steps to create an error handler that logs error information.

STEP-BY-STEP 7.4

1. Start a new **Standard EXE** project. Save the form and project as **ErrorLog**.

2. Change the caption of the form to **Error Logging**. Change the name of the form to **frmErrorLog**.

3. Add a single command button to the form. Change the caption of the button to **Cause an Error**. Change the name of the button to **cmdCause**.

4. Double-click the button to open the Code window. Press **Tab** and enter the code in **Code Step 4**.

CODE STEP 4

```
On Error GoTo ErrorLog
  Open "c:\notes\note.txt" For Output As #1
  Close #1
  Exit Sub
ErrorLog:
  Dim Channel As Integer
  Channel = FreeFile
  Open "c:\ErrorLog.txt" For Append As #Channel
  Print #Channel, Err.Description, Err.Number, Err.Source, Now
  Close #Channel
```

This is a great place to use the FreeFile function. This function finds the next available channel number needed to open a file. Since this segment of code may be pasted into any program, the FreeFile function ensures an unused file number is always used.

5. Save and run the program. Click the **Cause an Error** button several times. The error number and description are written to the **ErrorLog.txt** text file, along with the date and time of occurrence of the error. Stop the program.

6. Use **Windows Explorer** to look for the file **ErrorLog.txt**. When you find it, double-click it to open it in Notepad. You will find the error messages, dates, and times.

7. Quit Visual Basic.

This program is not much by itself, but the error handling code could be pasted into any program. Be sure to adjust the name of the file and its path to suit each program.

Building Programming Skills

How can you distribute programs that open or append specific files on the hard-drive? You cannot know ahead of time how the user's drive is structured. If you hard code a specific path name to a file, the program will fail if the path doesn't exist. One thing you can be sure of is if a Visual Basic program is running on a system, it must be in a particular folder on a particular drive. If your data files are in the same directory as the program, you can find them by changing the program's default drive and directory to match where the program is. Change the default drive and directory by using the *App object.* The App object is the currently running program. Use the following statements:

```
ChDrive App.Path
ChDir App.Path
```

The first statement changes the current drive to the drive the application is running from. The second statement changes the default folder to the same folder the application is running from. If your data files are in the same directory with your application program, enter the names of the files without any other path information. Your program will look in its folder and find them there.

Quick Check 7.c

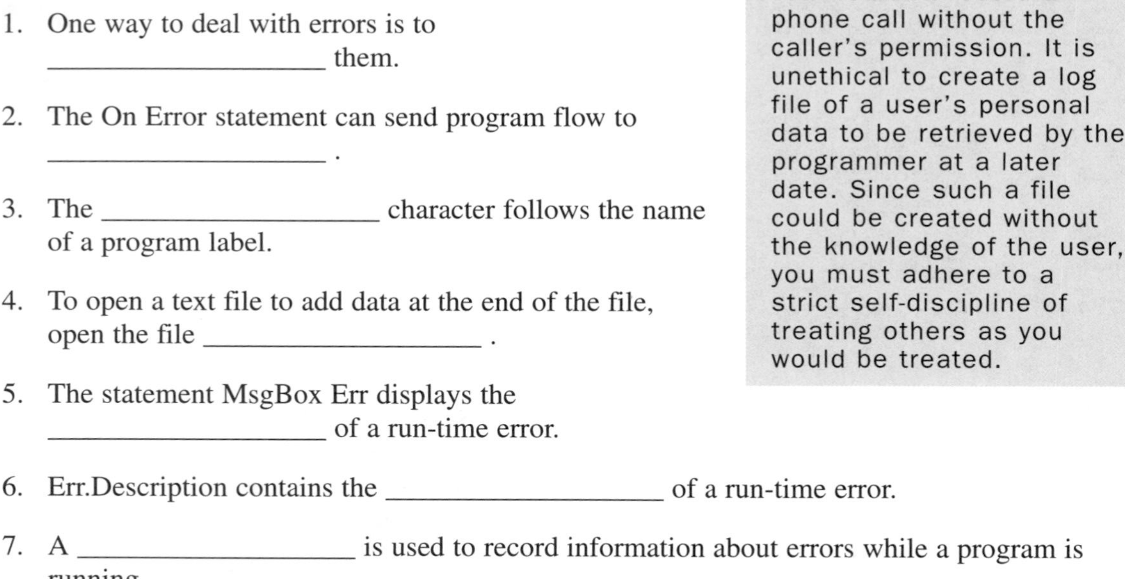

1. One way to deal with errors is to ____________________ them.
2. The On Error statement can send program flow to ____________________ .
3. The ____________________ character follows the name of a program label.
4. To open a text file to add data at the end of the file, open the file ____________________ .
5. The statement MsgBox Err displays the ____________________ of a run-time error.
6. Err.Description contains the ____________________ of a run-time error.
7. A ____________________ is used to record information about errors while a program is running.

Computer Ethics

You wouldn't record a phone call without the caller's permission. It is unethical to create a log file of a user's personal data to be retrieved by the programmer at a later date. Since such a file could be created without the knowledge of the user, you must adhere to a strict self-discipline of treating others as you would be treated.

Debugging a Data Report

Programmers are comfortable reading information from a computer monitor. But sometimes even programmers need to examine hard copy. For some reason, it is often easier to find coding errors when examining a hard copy. Formatting and appearance do not mean much if you are trying to find an error in program code. However, formatting and appearance mean everything if you are reporting to your boss.

In Lesson 6 you built a portable CD players database. You created your own data entry form using the Data control and you used the Data Form Wizard to build a form that displayed the items in grid form. Either form is suitable for interacting with the database on a computer's monitor. Neither format is suitable for hard copy. To get hard copy, you need to create a report.

To create a report, you need to:

- Create an ODBC, *Open Database Connectivity*, driver for the database.
- Set up an ADO Recordset for the source.
- Add a DataReport object to the project.
- Design the report using special controls added to the toolbox when the DataReport object is added to the project.
- Write code to display the form.

Creating an ODBC Driver

There are a couple of ways to access a database file from a Visual Basic project. In this example, a utility from the Windows operating system will be used to set up an ODBC driver for the database.

STEP-BY-STEP 7.5

1. Click the **Start** button on the taskbar. Point to **Settings** and click **Control Panel**. In the Control Panel, double-click **ODBC (32 bit)**. The ODBC Data Source Administrator dialog box opens, as shown in Figure 7-5.

FIGURE 7-5
The ODBC Data Source Administrator dialog box

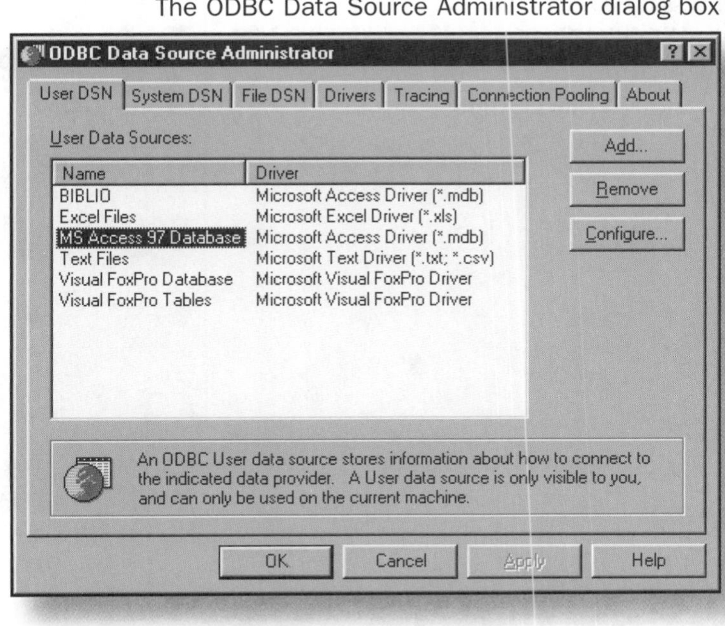

2. Click **MS Access 97 Database**, then **Add**, to open the Create New Data Source dialog box. The **portableCD** database of Lesson 6 is an Access database, so click **Microsoft Access Driver (*.mdb)** and **Finish**, as shown in Figure 7-6.

3. In the ODBC Microsoft Access 97 Setup dialog box, shown in Figure 7-7, click **Select** and navigate to **portableCD.mdb**, the database you created in Lesson 6. When you find it, select the database and click **OK**. Enter **portableCD** in the Data Source name box and **The Portable CD Database** in the Description box.

FIGURE 7-6
The Create New Data Source dialog box

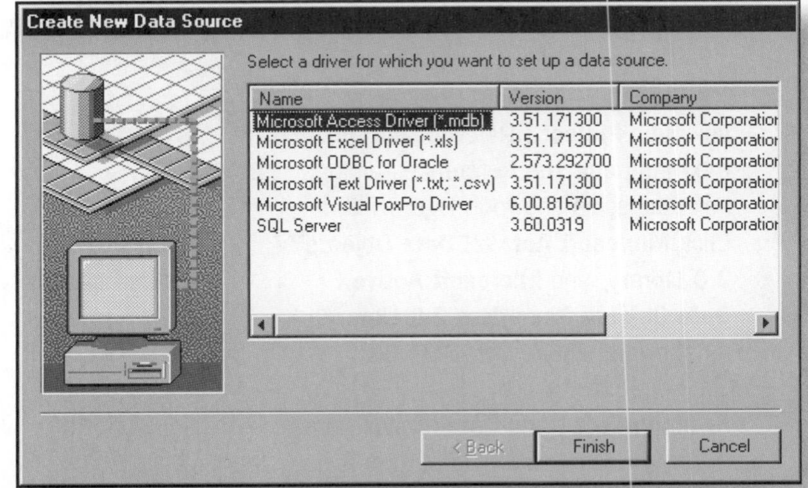

4. Click **OK** to return to the ODBC Data Source Administrator dialog box. Check that the database you set up appears in the User Data Sources list. Click **OK** to exit the ODBC Data Source Administrator dialog box.

Preparing the Project

Now that the data source is set up, you need to start a new Visual Basic project and add the components necessary to build the data report. In the next Step-by-Step exercise you will add the Microsoft ADO Data Objects and the DataReport object to the project.

FIGURE 7-7
The ODBC Microsoft Access 97 Setup dialog box, shown with data entered

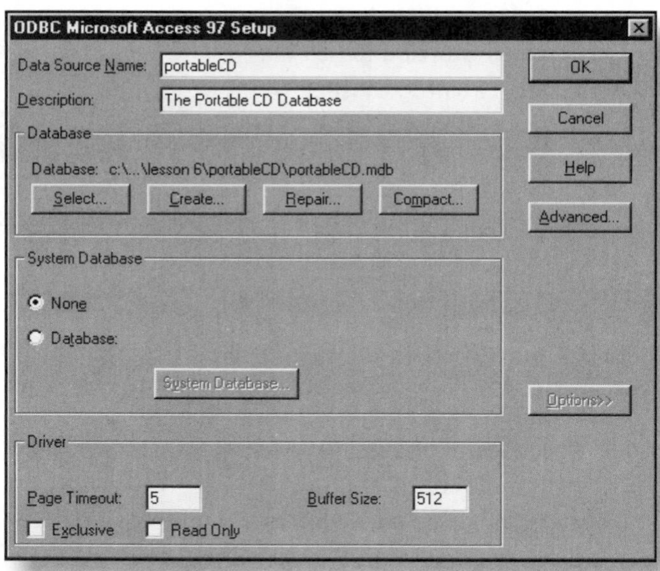

STEP-BY-STEP 7.6

1. Start Visual Basic and double-click **Standard EXE**. Save the form and project as **CDReport**.

2. Now add the ADO Data Objects by selecting **Project | References** from the menu bar. The References dialog box opens, as shown in Figure 7-8. Click **Microsoft ActiveX Data Objects 2.0 Library**, and **Microsoft ActiveX Data Objects Recordset 2.0 Library**, as shown in Figure 7-8. Click **OK**.

FIGURE 7-8
The References — Project 1 dialog box

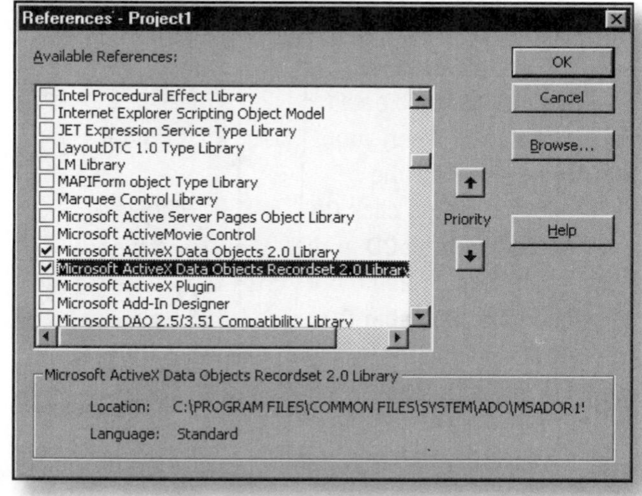

3. Select **Project | Add Data Report** from the menu bar. A new kind of form is added to the project called **DataReport object**, as shown in Figure 7-9. The Project Explorer also shows the addition of the DataReport object. In addition, new controls appear in the toolbox and the toolbox has grown a new bar to access them, as shown in Figure 7-10. While the DataReport object is selected, the old toolbox controls are dimmed because they cannot be used on a DataReport object.

4. Save the data report form as **CDReport.Dsr**. Save the project and keep the project open for the next Step-by-Step exercise.

FIGURE 7-9
The blank DataReport form

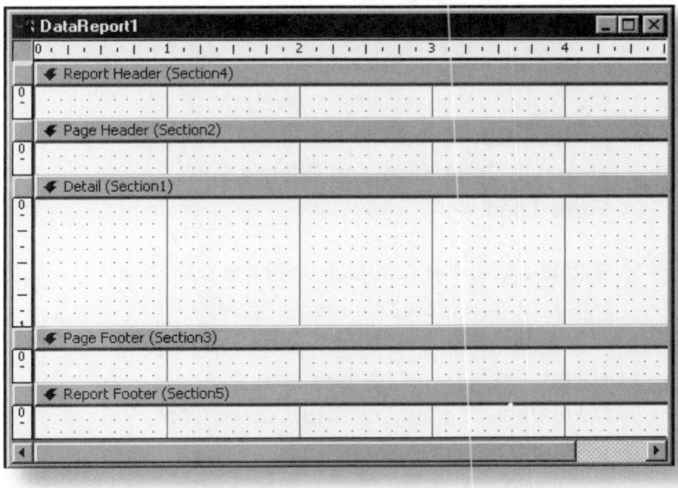

The DataReport form has the following five sections:

- The Report Header is where information displayed once at the top of the report will be defined.
- The Page Header is where information displayed at the top of every page of the report will be defined.
- The Detail Section is where what will be displayed for each record in the Recordset will be defined. This is the body of the report.
- The Page Footer is where information displayed at the bottom of each page will be defined.
- The Report Footer is where information displayed at the end of the report will be defined.

FIGURE 7-10
The DataReport toolbox

In Figure 7-10 from left to right across the top, the new toolbox controls are the Pointer tool, the RptLabel (used to display text that is not bound to the database), and the RptTextBox (a databound control that displays the contents of a database field). In the second row, RptImage displays images on the data report; it is not a databound control. The RptLine and RptShape controls allow you to draw simple figures on the report. The RptFunction control is valid only in the header or footer of the report. It is a databound control that finds the sum, average, or count of the elements in a data field.

Writing the Code to Set up the Recordset

You need two form level variables to set up the Recordset used in the project. One is for the connection to the database file and the other is for the Recordset created from the database.

STEP-BY-STEP 7.7

1. Open the **CDReport** project, if necessary. Select **Form1** in the Project Explorer window and click **View Object**. Change the name of the form to **frmCDReport**. Change the caption of the form to **CD Report**.

2. Double-click the form to open the Code window. Select the **General Declarations** section and enter the following lines of **code**:

(continued on next page)

```
Dim Connect As ADODB.Connection
Dim rsCD As ADODB.Recordset
```

3. Next, in the **Form_Load** procedure, you will add the lines that establish the connection between the Connect variable and the ODBC database driver created for **portableCD**. Press **Tab** and enter the code shown in **Code Step 3** in **Private Sub Form_Load**.

   In this code, the Connect object is set equal to a new connection to an ADO database. *DSN* stands for Data Source Name and it is set to the name given to the database when its ODBC driver was set up.

4. Press **Tab** and add the following lines of code to **Private Sub Form_Unload** to close the Recordset and to break the connection to the database when the form is unloaded:

```
rsCD.Close
Connect.Close
```

5. Click the **General** bar on the toolbox and display **frmCDReport**. Add a command button to the form. Change the name of the button to **cmdPrepare**. Change the caption of the button to **Prepare Recordset**. Double-click the command button, press **Tab**, and add the code in **Code Step 5**, needed to set up the Recordset from the Portable CD Players table of the **portableCD** database.

6. Save and run the program and click **Prepare Recordset**. If the connection is set correctly and the SQL string is right, you see the message *Recordset is Prepared.* If you do not see the message, set a breakpoint at the beginning of the **Form_Load** procedure and single-step through the program using the **F8** key to find the error.

7. Stop the program and leave it open for the next Step-by-Step exercise.

CODE STEP 3

```
On Error GoTo ConnectErr
Set Connect = New ADODB.Connection
Connect.Open "DSN=portableCD"
Exit Sub
ConnectErr:
  MsgBox "Error connecting to the database."
```

CODE STEP 5

```
Dim sqlCommand As String
On Error GoTo RecordsetErr
sqlCommand = "Select * from [Portable CD Players]"
Set rsCD = Connect.Execute(sqlCommand)
MsgBox "Recordset is Prepared"
Exit Sub
RecordsetErr:
 MsgBox "Error in constructing Recordset"
```

Adding Fields to the DataReport Object

As you learned earlier, fields that repeat for every record in the database are defined in the Detail section of the report. Next, you will add fields to the Detail section of the report to display the manufacturer, model, and price for each of the items in the **portableCD** database. You will also define column headings and calculate an average price that will print at the end of the report.

STEP-BY-STEP 7.8

1. Open the **CDReport** project, if necessary. In the **Designers** folder in the **Project Explorer**, click **DataReport1**, then click **View Object** to display the data report form.

2. Add a **RptTextBox** to the Details section of the report, as shown in Figure 7-12. Set the DataField property of the RptTextBox by entering **Manufacturer**. Add a second text box adjacent and to the right of the first one and set its DataField property to **Model**. Add a **third text box** adjacent and to the right of the second one and set its DataField property to **Price**. For the third box, double-click the **DataFormat** property, set the **Format Type** to **Currency**, and click **OK** (see Figure 7-11). Adjust the height of the Details section to eliminate wasted space below the text boxes.

FIGURE 7-11
The Property Pages dialog box called when the button on the DataFormat property is clicked

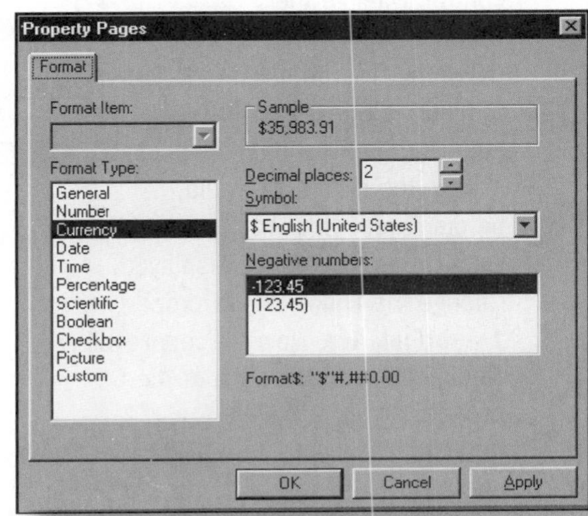

Since RptTextBox is a databound control, DataField is its most important property. Unless there is a particular reason to manipulate the contents of the text box in code, it is not necessary to give it a name.

3. Remember that items in the Page Header section of the data report appear at the top of every page, so this is where you usually define column headings. Add three **RptLabels** to the Page Header section. Change the captions of the labels to **Manufacturer**, **Model**, and **Price**. Change the font style to **Bold** and increase the size of the font to **9 pts**. Position the labels over the corresponding text boxes in the Details section of the data report, as shown in Figure 7-12.

4. Items in the Report Header section appear only at the beginning of the report. The label you will insert in this section will be changed in code, so you must name the section and the label. Click the **Report Header bar** in the data report. In the Property window, change the section name from *Section4* to **rptHeader**.

5. Add a label to the Report Header section. Change the name of the label to **lblPreparedBy**. Change the font size of the caption to **10** and delete the caption of the label.

(continued on next page)

6. Items in the Report Footer appear only at the end of the report. Add a **RptFunction** control to this section. A Function control is only valid in the Header or Footer of the report. Enter **Price** in the DataField property of the control. Change the DataFormat property to **Currency**. The default function is Sum( ), so the sum of the prices of each item in the database would be displayed. However, you want the average price displayed. Change the FunctionType property to **1 – rptFuncAve**. Now the report will display the average price of the CD players.

FIGURE 7-12
The finished data report

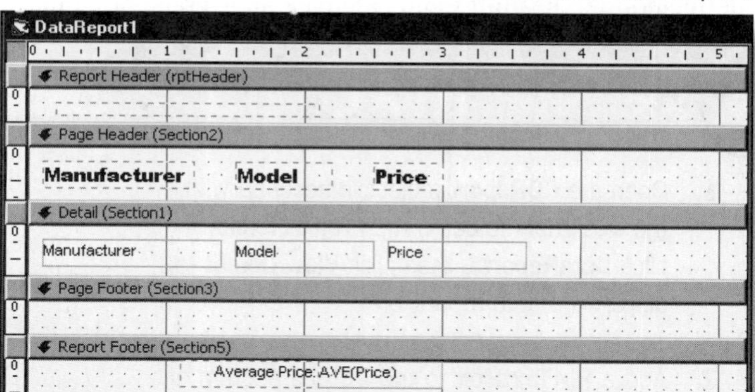

7. Add a **RptLabel** in front of the RptFunction control. Change the caption of the label to **Average Price:**. Change the Alignment property to **1 – rptJustifyRight**. Position the label so its right edge is just to the left of the RptFunction control. Check your work with Figure 7-12.

8. Select **frmCDReport** from the Project Explorer and click **View Object**. Add a command button to the form. Change the name of the button to **cmdDisplayReport**. Change the caption of the button to **Display Report**. Add the code in **Code Step 8** to the button's Click event.

   In this code, the InputBox prompts the user to enter their name. The DataSource property of the data report is set to rsCD, the name of the Recordset created by **cmdPrepare**. The data report is a collection of sections and each section is itself a collection of controls. The first part of the next line, **DataReport1.Sections("rptHeader").Controls("lblPreparedBy").Caption**, accesses the Sections collection of **DataReport1**. The name of the section (changed from its default name in Step 4), enclosed in double quotes, is used to identify the

CODE STEP 8

```
Dim Name As String
Name = InputBox("enter your name:")
Set DataReport1.DataSource = rsCD
DataReport1.Sections("rptHeader").Controls("lblPreparedBy").Caption = _
   "Prepared by " & Name
DataReport1.Show
```

particular section you want. The Controls collection of the **rptHeader** section is accessed by using the name of the label: **lblPreparedBy**. Its Caption property is changed to the string on the line **"Prepared by" & Name**.

The last line displays the data report. Once displayed, the report has a printer button that you can use to send the report to the printer.

9. Now add a third command button to the form. Change the name of the button to **cmdExit**. Change the caption of the button to **E&xit**. Add the line **Unload Me** to its Click event procedure.

10. Save and run the program. Click **Prepare Recordset**. Click **OK** when the message appears. Click **Display Report**, key **your name**, and click **OK**. Figure 7-13 shows the completed report.

11. Stop the program and exit Visual Basic.

FIGURE 7-13
The completed data report

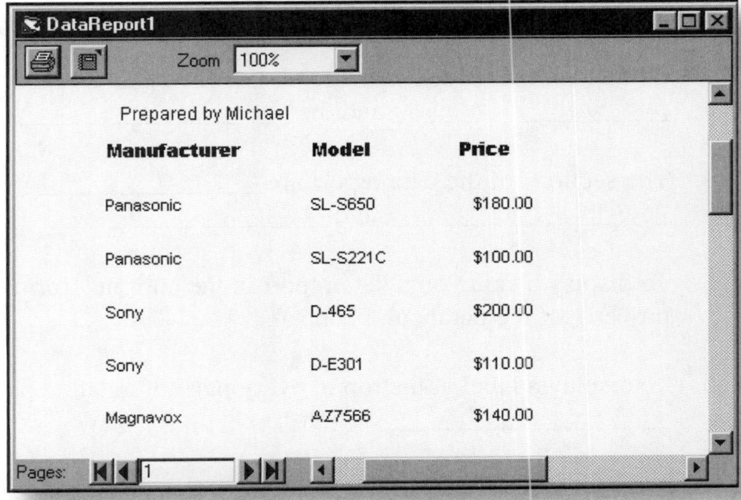

A Few Extras

The DataReport object has built-in codes that represent useful standard text. The codes can be included in a RptLabel to add these items to your report. The table below shows a list of the codes.

TABLE 7-1
A list of codes used as predefined placeholders in strings inserted into labels

CODES

CODE	DESCRIPTION
%p	Current page number. Use as follows: rptLabel1="Current page %p"
%P	Total number of pages
%d	Current date expressed in short date format: 5/27/78
%D	Current data expressed in long date format, including the name of the day
%t	Current time expressed in the short time format
%T	Current time expressed in the long time format
%i	Report title

In this section you have created a simple report using a DataReport object. This is one of the best ways to provide printer-ready output in Visual Basic. The error handling methods, also covered in this lesson, help you debug the program. Using On Error statements to anticipate errors makes it easy to properly handle errors when they occur.

Quick Check 7.d

1. To add ADO Data Objects to a project, select ____________________ from the menu bar.
2. To add a data report to a project, select ____________________ from the menu bar.
3. Of the controls added to the toolbox, when a data report is added to a project, only the ____________________ and the ____________________ controls are databound controls.
4. The sections of the data report are ____________________, ____________________, ____________________, and ____________________.
5. To display a value on a data report in the currency format, modify the ____________________ property of the databound control.
6. To display a label at the top of every page of a data report, include the label in the ____________________ section.

Summary

- Program bugs are errors and flaws in programming code. Debugging is the process of finding and eliminating bugs.
- Using the InterCap naming convention allows the object or variable name to be used in the debugging process. You enter a name with all lowercase letters when writing code. If the proper letters are not converted to uppercase when the cursor leaves the line, the names have not been recognized by Visual Basic.
- Use Option Explicit in the General Declarations section to force all variables to be defined before they are used. This is another technique to find misspelled names.
- Syntax errors, errors in statement structure, are identified by Visual Basic when the cursor leaves the line of a flawed statement.
- A breakpoint stops program execution while the program is running. While the program is stopped, it is in break mode. When in break mode, the values of variables can be examined and changed in the Immediate window.
- A Watch expression lets you examine particular values automatically in the Watch window when the program enters break mode. A Watch expression can also be set that puts the program in break mode when a particular condition is satisfied, or when a variable changes value.

- The On Error Resume Next statement skips any line of code that causes a run-time error. On rare occasions, simply ignoring a line is a sufficient fix for a problem. More often, however, the On Error statement is used to send program flow to error handling code.
- The GoTo statement sends program flow to code preceded by a label ending with a colon. GoTo's should be used sparingly.
- Use the Exit Sub command to exit a sound procedure and prevent the error handling code from being executed.
- Err and Error are system variables that contain the error number and description of the most recent error. The Err object also contains the error number and description, as well as the source of the error and additional information.
- An error log is a simple text file in which information about program errors is saved. The error number, description, and source, as well as the time the error occurred, are examples of the information saved.
- One way to prepare a database file for use in a Visual Basic program is to create an ODBC driver for the file.
- The DataReport object provides an easy way to generate hard copy from a database file.
- Databound controls in a data report are linked to particular fields of a database file.

LESSON 7 REVIEW QUESTIONS

TRUE/FALSE

Circle the T if the statement is true. Circle the F if it is false.

T F **1.** Programs that prompt the user for input should provide instructions or a sample about how to properly input data.

T F **2.** The InterCap convention for naming variables separates words in a name with the underscore character.

T F **3.** To check the syntax of a line of code, press F7.

T F **4.** The Immediate window is used to set a Watch expression.

T F **5.** Setting a Watch expression stops the program every time the Watch expression is positive.

T F **6.** Single-stepping through a program helps you trace a program's logic.

T F **7.** Ignoring a line that causes a run-time error usually is a good way to handle a problem.

T F **8.** The Err variable contains a description of the most recent run-time error.

T F 9. A log file is used to save data about a program's run-time errors.

T F 10. You add a DataReport object to a project through the Components dialog box.

WRITTEN QUESTIONS

Write your answers to the following questions.

11. What is the first best line of defense in fixing a program with bugs?

12. How does Option Explicit work to prevent or find program bugs?

13. What is the InterCap method of naming variables? How does it work to find program bugs?

14. How do you set a breakpoint in code?

15. How do you change the value of a variable while a program is in break mode?

16. How is the mouse and a ToolTip used to debug a program?

17. An option in the Watch window is Break When Value Changes. How would you use that option to debug a program?

18. How do you use the On Error statement to execute error handling code?

19. Describe the process of adding a DataReport object to a project.

20. List the steps required to find the average of a list of prices and display the average on a data report.

LESSON 7 APPLICATION PROBLEMS

Level One

ADDING A LIST BOX

Add a list box to the How Many More Payments program to display each calculation made in the While loop. Add a breakpoint to the beginning of the program. Single-step through the program to watch the values as they are added to the list box.

HOW MANY HORSES?

An engine is used to lift heavy crates on a truck loading platform. The horsepower needed to lift crates is found using this formula: the horsepower is equal to *f*, the weight of the crate in pounds, times *d*, the distance to raise the crate, divided by *t*, the time in seconds to raise the weight, divided by a constant 550. Write a program to enter a weight, *f*, and a distance, *d*, from text boxes. Use a For loop to calculate the horsepower needed to lift the weight, *f*, *d* feet, where the value for time goes from 1 second to 60 seconds. Display the results in a list box. A 660-lb. crate lifted 10 feet takes 4 seconds when the horsepower used is 3. Once the program is written, try to crash the program by choosing radical values for the weight and height. Try negative numbers. Set a breakpoint and single-step through the program noting possible errors.

Level Two

ANNUAL DEPRECIATION

Depreciation is the decrease in a tool's value. The annual depreciation is calculated with this formula: Annual depreciation = (cost – final value) / number of years of usefulness. Write a program to enter cost, final value, and number of years, and calculate the annual depreciation. Enter the values in text boxes. Display the result in a label. Set a breakpoint and single-step through the program with "reasonable" values. Experiment with values that defeat the purpose of the program. Single-step through the program to see the results. Change the program to detect conditions that cause the error (like a negative annual depreciation), and write code to prevent the mistakes or correct the mistakes.

ERROR LOGGING

Add an error handler to the Annual Depreciation program that stores the data that violates the conditions of the program in a simple data file along with the time of the occurrence. The errors possible in the program probably won't cause a run-time error, so don't use On Error statements. Check for an error with an If statement and execute the Error Log file code if there is an error.

DATA REPORT

Write a program to create a data report from the **Biblio.mdb** database included with Visual Basic. First, create an ODBC driver for the database. Select all records in the Authors table. Display the following three fields: Au_ID, Author, and Year Born. For fields with more than one word separated by spaces, enclose the field name in square brackets.

LESSON 7 PROGRAMMING AT WORK

THE MUSIC COLLECTION PROJECT

It is time to help the Data Entry form live up to its name. Now it only displays entries. After a few modifications, the user will be able to record entries using the Data Entry form. Before that, you will give the project a new start-up form. The start-up form will call the Data Entry form and a Data Grid form that you will also add in this lesson.

1. Open the **MusicCol** project from Lesson 6.

2. Add a new form to the project. Name the form **frmMusic**. Change the caption of the form to **Music Collection**.

3. Select **Project | Project1 Properties** from the menu bar. Change the Startup Object to **frmMusic**. Click **OK** to close the Project Properties dialog box.

4. Select the form. Open the **Menu Editor**. Build the menu illustrated in Figure 7-14 below. Use the following table to fill in the captions and the names of the menu items shown.

TABLE FOR THE MENU ENTRIES

CAPTION	NAME
View	mnuView
...Data Entry	mnuDataEntry
...Data Grid	mnuDataGrid
...-	mnuSeparator
...E&xit	mnuExit

5. Click **OK** to close the Menu Editor.

6. Click the **View** menu and double-click **Data Entry**. Enter the following line in **Private Sub mnuDataEntry_Click**:

```
frmDataEntry.Show
```

7. Enter the line **frmDataGrid.Show** in **Private Sub mnuDataGrid_Click**.

   NOTE: **frmDataGrid** does not exit yet.

8. In **Private Sub mnuExit_Click**, enter **Unload Me**.

9. Figure 7-14 shows an image in the background of the form. To insert a picture, select the form. Select the Picture property of the form in the Properties window. Click the ellipsis to open the Load Picture dialog box. Find an image in the Microsoft Office or Visual Basic Graphics directory. If there are no images on your system, go on-line to find an image.

FIGURE 7-14
The Music Collection form, showing the menu structure

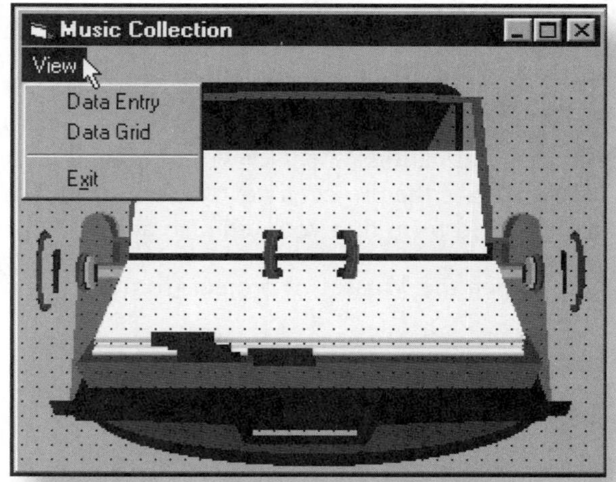

10. Use the **Project Explorer** to select **frmDataEntry**. Click **View Code** and open the **Private Sub cmdClear_Click** procedure. The clear command clears the text boxes in the normal way, but they are not normal text boxes. They are databound text boxes, set to display

information from the **portableCD** database. The AddNew method clears the boxes and gets the form ready to enter a new record in the database. Delete or comment out the following lines of code:

```
'txtTitle = ""
'txtArtist = ""
'txtComposer = ""
'txtLocation = ""
'txtComments = ""
'txtRunningTime = ""
'txtYear = ""
'txtPublisher = ""
```

11. Add the following line: **datCollectionRS.Recordset.AddNew**. The AddNew method clears all the databound controls and gets the form ready to receive new data.

12. Select the **Private Sub cmdRecord_Click** procedure. Delete its existing code and enter the following code:

```
 Dim x As Integer
 x = MsgBox("Record changes?", vbYesNoCancel, "Record")
 If x = vbCancel Or x = vbNo Then
  Exit Sub
 End If
 'On Error GoTo UpdateErr
 datCollectionRS.Recordset.UpdateBatch adAffectAll
 Exit Sub
UpdateErr:
    MsgBox Err.Description
```

This code first asks the user to confirm the change to the contents of the database. A message box is used and the user's response to the message box determines program flow. If the Cancel or No buttons are clicked, the changes are not recorded. If the Yes button is clicked, the UpdateBatch and adAffectAll method and parameter update all the records of the database. If there is an error, the UpdateErr section of the code displays the description of the error.

13. Save and run the program. Navigate to the Data Entry form. Click the **Clear** button. The text boxes clear of the current entry. Enter new data. Click **Record**. Confirm the changes.

14. Stop the program.

15. Run the program and navigate through the records of the database to confirm that your new record was recorded.

16. Click **Project | New Form**. Click **Data Form Wizard**. Skip the Profile window. In the Database Type dialog box, select **Access**. Click **Next** to advance to the next dialog box.

17. In the Database dialog box, browse to the Music Collection database file (with the *.mdb* extension). Click **Open** to add this entry to the *Database Name* text box. Click **Next**.

18. For the name of the form, enter **frmDataGrid**. For the Form Layout, enter **Grid**. Click **Next** to advance to the next dialog box.

19. Click the list arrow for the Record Source box and select **MusicCollection**. A list of available fields appears in the Available Fields list (see Figure 7-15).

FIGURE 7-15
The Record Source dialog box

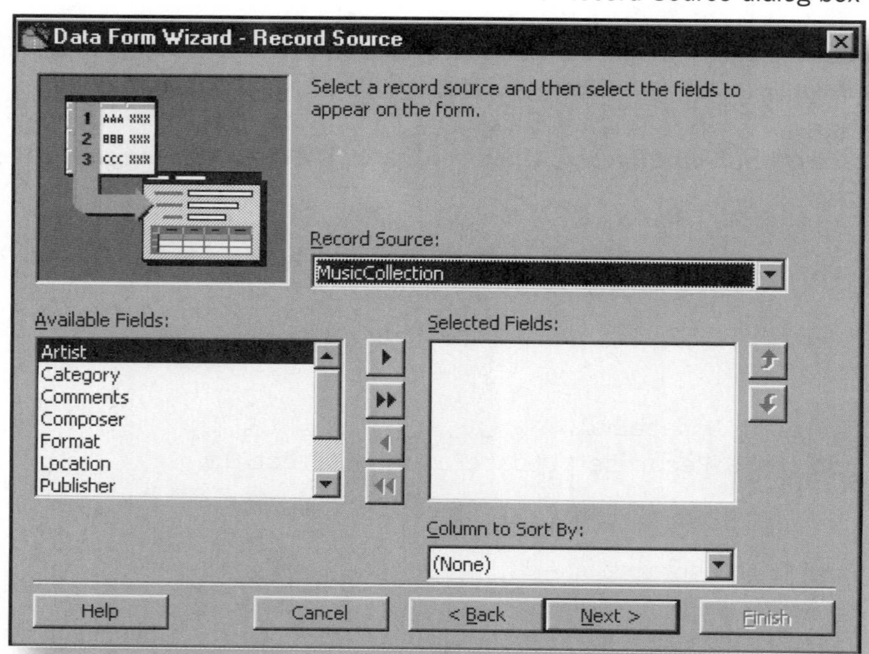

20. There are too many fields to include them all. Select **Title**, **Artist**, **Category**, and **Location**. Arrange the sequence in which the fields appear in the final product by rearranging them in the list box. Click **Next** to advance to the next dialog box.

21. Click **Next** to accept a full complement of buttons.

22. Click **Finish** to close the Data Form Wizard. The form is created and added to the project.

23. Save and run the program. From the start-up form, select **View | Data Grid**. The grid appears and displays the current records in the database.

If the data grid does not show the correct data, you may have linked it to the wrong database. In the course of working on the Music Collection project, you may have created more than one copy of the Music Collection database. To change the database the data grid is linked to, select frmDataGrid in the Project Explorer. Click **View Form**. Select the ADO Data control at the bottom of the form. In the Properties window, navigate to the Connection property. Open the Property Pages dialog box for the ADO Data control. On the General tab, click the **Build** button on the form. In Step 1 of the Connection tab, navigate to the database you want to display in the grid. Once it is added, click **Test Connection** to test the linkup between the form and the database. Click **OK**.

24. Stop the program.

The program is functional and is starting to look more like a professional application. In the next lesson you will add a Class to the project.

LESSON 8

WHAT'S THE OBJECT? PROGRAMMING WITH CLASS!

OBJECTIVES

When you complete this lesson, you will be able to:

- Use the Object Browser to explore classes and objects.
- Design and create class modules.
- Use class modules to declare and use objects.
- Add methods, events, and properties to created classes.
- Create an ActiveX DLL to distribute a class to other applications.

Estimated Time: 5 hours

KEY TERMS

platforms
reusable code
cross-platform
Object Oriented Programming
object
Data Encapsulation
Inheritance
Polymorphism
messages
data hiding
operator overloading
Object Browser
Visual Basic for Applications (VBA)
Class module
New
instance
Set
StrConv( )
Business Rules
ByVal
ActiveX DLL
Let
Get
References

OOP – What Is Object Oriented Programming?

Every programmer wants to be more productive. "Maximum effect with minimum effort" is an old saying that every programmer endorses. Programmers want a programming environment that makes it easy to write code. Programmers want to write one program to work on several different *platforms*. Programmers want to write *reusable code*.

You know enough about Visual Basic to know that it provides a friendly programming environment. It is easy to design a user interface and add code to the objects of that interface. It is easy to debug programs with problems. You appreciate Visual Basic even more when you try to write code in other languages.

Writing code that works on several different computers or similar hardware with different operating systems is the job performed by another language that will remain nameless. But even in this area, Visual Basic has a kind of universal capability. It does not cross to other computer hardware or operating systems, but it is the fundamental language of Microsoft's applications. You can write Visual Basic programs to power your Web page or customize your Excel spreadsheet. Write Word macros in Visual Basic and customize Access databases with Visual Basic code. This is not *cross-platform* code, but it does show that you can use Visual Basic in many situations.

Code reusability is a job in which Visual Basic excels. Code reusability is built into the language. In Lesson 6 you used a Microsoft Hierarchical FlexGrid. You gained familiarity with some of its features and you know the power of that single object. It is one of hundreds of objects that can be added to any program. When added, it brings to the program all of its functionality, all of its built-in programming. The ActiveX objects in Visual Basic's toolbox are a powerful form of code reusability. In a future lesson you will write new ActiveX objects.

Object Oriented Programming is a different kind of code reusability and Visual Basic, in its newest form, supports OOP better than ever. At the foundation of OOP is data—data and the operations that can be performed on the data. By now, you are accustomed to using variables and arrays. However, data in an array is passive. Statements in the program operate on the data in an array by adding and deleting elements, listing values, sorting, searching, etc.

An *object* contains both data and the operations that can be performed on the data. For example, a list box is an object. It contains data and operations that can be performed on the data. The operations are called methods. The AddItem method adds information to the list box. The Clear method removes data from the list box. A list box also has properties. When the list box's Sorted property is set to True, the data is displayed alphabetically within the list. A list box also responds to events such as the click and key-press events.

Three things characterize Object Oriented Programming: Data Encapsulation, Inheritance, and Polymorphism. *Data Encapsulation* means hiding certain kinds of information from the user and the programmer. How does a list box store information in memory? How does it sort its contents? In OOP, these are not concerns of the programmer. To communicate with an object, a programmer writes code that sends *messages* to the objects. The messages instruct the objects what operations to perform on themselves. Because communication is restricted to the messages, the internal working of the object is shielded from the user.

Data hiding is a good thing because it allows a programmer to worry about problem-solving rather than about writing code to handle details. The objects take care of the details for you.

When you create a new class based on a simpler existing class, the new class inherits all the properties of the original class. Those properties can be replaced or extended in the new class. This is called *inheritance*. The new class adds new methods and properties to the functionality of the old class, while gaining all the original class's functionality for itself. Visual Basic doesn't have this kind of inheritance.

Polymorphism is redefining methods, properties, and operations to behave differently with different objects. For instance, how many points is a field goal worth? A field goal in football is three points; in basketball, two or three points. A field goal's worth depends on the context—football or basketball.

The lowly plus symbol (+) has many functions: It adds integers, singles, doubles, and strings. Each operation calls a different section of code to execute the operation within the context in which it is found. When existing operators have more than one function depending on the context, it is called *operator overloading*. You can overload operations when you define new classes.

Objects are real things created from the templates provided by classes. They can be added to forms. Code can be written to manipulate objects and their data. Objects are cast in the image provided by classes. The class definition determines what data an object contains and how it is arranged in memory. The class definition determines the methods, properties, and events that are associated with an object.

Creating a class allows you to create objects from that class that all share the same characteristics and capabilities. This is a very powerful form of code reusability. Once a class is created, it can be added to any project, and objects of that class can be created within the project. It's not easy to create useful classes that can be used in more than one program without careful planning.

You must think about ways to make the class create objects that are generic enough to use in more than one program, but powerful enough to solve real problems.

The Object Browser

Enough theory! It is time to increase your understanding with the Step-by-Step exercises in this lesson. The *Object Browser* lets you look at classes and the properties of the objects created from the classes. In the following Step-by-Step exercise you will look at some familiar objects in the Object Browser.

STEP-BY-STEP 8.1

1. Start Visual Basic and double-click **Standard EXE**.

2. Click **View | Object Browser** or press **F2**. The Object Browser window displays, as shown in Figure 8-1. Maximize the window.

FIGURE 8-1
The Object Browser window

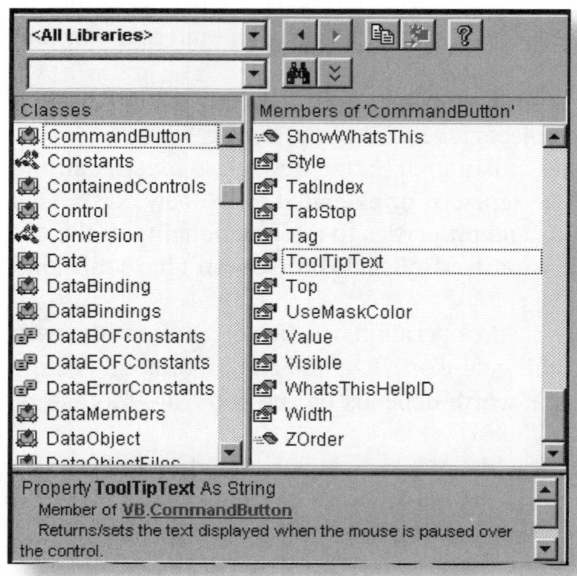

The box at the top left of the window shows that classes for all libraries are displayed. You change libraries by selecting the library name from the list. Choices of libraries include the VB library and the VBA library. *VBA* is the abbreviation for Visual Basic for Applications—the language used to program in most Microsoft applications. The left pane lists the names of the classes for the selected library. Since just about everything in Visual Basic is an object, it makes sense to see classes even for common objects like text boxes and command buttons. Whenever you add a text box to a form, it gets its properties from the class definition of a text box.

In Figure 8-1, the CommandButton class is selected, so the right pane lists the properties, methods, and events associated with a command button. The Description pane at the bottom of the window dislays a definition of the selected item. It also tells if the item is a property, event, or procedure (method), and to which library the class belongs.

The Member pane at the right is like the help that you see when you enter code for a particular command button. As you key the name of the command button and follow it with a period, the list displays to help you enter the proper code. The list contains the names of all the object's properties and methods.

3. Click the **library list arrow** and select **VB**. The VB library is much smaller. Most of

the classes are already familiar. Select **Clipboard** and observe its members in the right pane. Select several other classes and explore their members. Notice that there are different icons for properties, events, and procedures (methods). The brief explanations in the Description pane at the bottom of the window are very helpful for remembering important things about each object. No one can memorize everything about every object.

4. What about classes added later? Will they appear in the Object Browser? Right-click the **toolbox** and select **Components**. Select the **Microsoft Hierarchical FlexGrid Control**. Click **Apply** and **Close**. The MSHFlexGrid control appears in the toolbox.

5. Click the **library list arrow**. The **MSHierarchicalFlexGridLib** now appears in the list. Select it and observe its classes.

6. Select **MSHFlexGrid**, then select **BackColor** in the Member pane. Read the explanation that appears in the Description pane. Select several other members and read the descriptions. The Object Browser is a wealth of information.

7. Below the library box is the search box. Enter **Additem** and click the **Search** toolbar button with the binocular icon. This searches the current library for any class with an AddItem method. The Search Results pane appears with the results of the search. The current library has one occurrence of the AddItem method.

FIGURE 8-2
The Object Browser showing the results of a search for AddItem

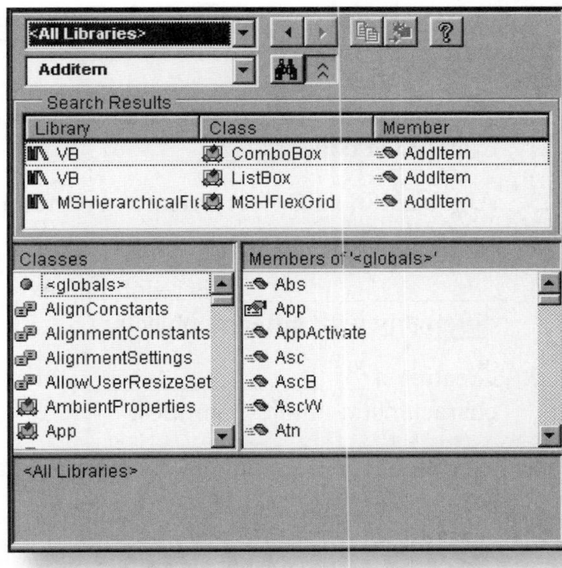

8. Select **<All Libraries>** from the library box. Immediately, the Search Results list expands to include all the classes that have the AddItem method, as shown in Figure 8-2.

9. Next to the Search button is the Hide Search Results button with a chevron icon. Click the **Hide Search Results** button. The Search Results pane disappears. Click the **Hide Search Results** button again. The Search Results pane reappears.

10. Right-click in the Object Browser window and select **Hide**. You are returned to normal design view.

What is really exciting is that you can easily add your own classes to a Visual Basic project—classes that create objects with properties, methods, and events, just like all the other Visual Basic objects. In the next Step-by-Step exercise you will create a class.

Quick Check 8.a

1. "Maximum effect with minimum ___________________" is an old saying that every programmer endorses.
2. The Hierarchical FlexGrid, an object that can be added to any Visual Basic project, is an example of code ___________________.
3. An object in an Object Oriented Programming language contains both data and ___________________.
4. ___________________ is redefining existing methods, properties, and operations to behave differently with different objects.
5. Creating a ___________________ allows you to create objects that all share the same characteristics and capabilities.
6. To examine a class's methods, properties and events, open the ___________________.

Creating a Class

Imagine that you are setting up a small business over the Internet. You determine that you need a customer database to keep track of names, addresses, and credit lines. In this Step-by-Step exercise you will create a *Class module*, define the clsCustomer class, and add it to a project that uses the class to create objects. You will also add the code to input the customer information and display it in a list box. The database will be saved in a text file in Step-by-Step exercise 8.3. In later Step-by-Step exercises you will add methods and events to the class.

STEP-BY-STEP 8.2

1. Start a new **Standard EXE** project, if necessary. Save the form and the project as **CustList**.

2. From the menu bar, select **Project | Add Class Module**. Select **Class Module** and click **Open**.

3. A new Code window opens. If the Project Explorer window is not visible, select **View | Project Explorer** from the menu bar. In the Project Explorer window, notice the default (still empty and unnamed) main form (the Class module) that has been added.

In previous versions of Visual Basic, the Project Explorer was called the Project Window.

4. Select the Class module and change its name to **clsCustomer**. The *cls* prefix indicates that the object contains a class definition. Save the Class module as **CustList.cls**.

5. Click the Code window of the Class module. If it is not visible, select the Class module in the Project Explorer window and click **View Code**.

6. Public variables declared in the General Declarations section of the Class module become the properties of an object created by the class. The customer object needs fields for name, title, address, and line of credit. So enter the following **code** in the General Declarations section of the Class module to declare them:

```
Public FName As String
Public LName As String
Public Address1 As String
Public Town As String
Public State As String
Public Credit As Currency
Private TitleNum As Integer
```

Before you can use these properties in a program, you must first declare a variable of the clsCustomer type. For example, you might declare a variable FirstCust with the statement, Dim FirstCust As New clsCustomer. In this statement, FirstCust is declared as a new object of the clsCustomer class. This is different from creating a variable of a particular type. It is creating a new object according to a template provided by clsCustomer. You would then access the properties as you would any other object's properties: FirstCust.Fname = "Oscar", or FirstCust.Town = "Chicago".

7. A variable declared with the Private keyword is not accessible to the user or to the programmer who uses the clsCustomer class in their code. The code you just entered uses a private variable to store a number that corresponds to the customer's title, such as Mr., Mrs., etc. The user will enter the title when inputting customer data and a special Property Procedure will convert the user input, a string, to the title's internal format, an integer. Select **Tools | Add Procedure** from the menu bar to add a Property

FIGURE 8-3
The Add Procedure dialog box

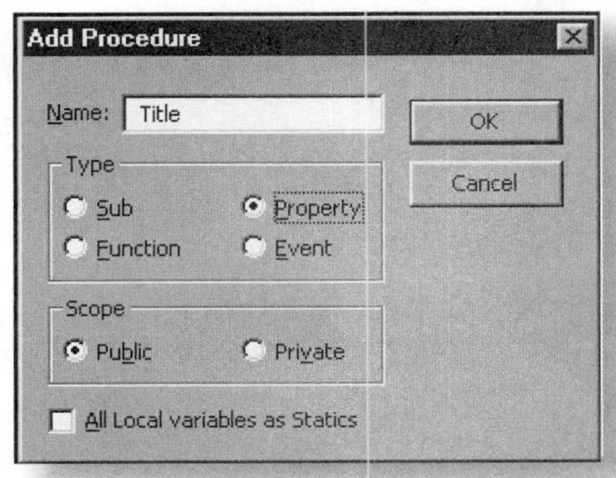

Procedure. The Add Procedure dialog box displays, as shown in Figure 8.3. Enter **Title** in the Name box, select **Property** and **Public**, and click **OK**.

This creates the skeleton code for two Property Procedures, as shown in **Code Step 7**. The Get procedure will be used when the property is accessed in code. For example, if used with the FirstCust variable described earlier, the statement Print FirstCust.Title & " " &

(continued on next page)

CODE STEP 7

```
Public Property Get Title() As Variant
End Property
Public Property Let Title(ByVal vNewValue As Variant)
End Property
```

FirstCust.LName would access the Title property of the FirstCust object. Internally, the data is stored as an integer. The integer value of TitleNum is used to return the actual title.

8. The code you will enter in the Get procedure uses the value of the private variable TitleNum as the test expression in a Case statement to select the property title string and return that string as the value of the Title property. Enter the following code in the **Public Property Get Title** procedure:

```
Select Case TitleNum
       Case 1
           Title = "Mr. "
       Case 2
           Title = "Mrs. "
       Case 3
           Title = "Ms. "
       Case 4
           Title = "Mr. & Mrs."
       Case Else
           Title = ""
  End Select
```

The **Public Property Get Title** statement was generated as a Variant data type. Change this to a **String** data type.

9. The Let procedure will be used when the user is inputting a title for a particular customer. The value entered by the user will come in as a parameter to the procedure. Then the parameter will be used as the test expression in a Case statement to determine which value will be stored internally in the Private variable, TitleNum. As with the Get procedure, vNewValue was generated as the Variant type. Change the *Variant* type to **String**, and change the name of the variable from vNewValue to *sNewValue* to reflect the change in data type. Enter the code shown in **Code Step 9** in the **Public Property Let Title** procedure. The first and last lines of the property procedure are shown as an example of the changes you are to make to the data type.

In the code you just entered, the Trim$( ) function trims any leading or trailing spaces, spaces at the beginning or the end of the input string. The UCase$

CODE STEP 9

```
Public Property Let Title(ByVal sNewValue As String)
    Select Case UCase$(Trim$(sNewValue))
        Case "MR."
            TitleNum = 1
        Case "MRS."
            TitleNum = 2
        Case "MS."
            TitleNum = 3
        Case "MR.& MRS."
            TitleNum = 4
        Case Else
            TitleNum = 0
    End Select
End Property
```

function converts the entire input string to uppercase. These functions help eliminate variations a user might make when entering the title. (It would have been wiser to use a combo box to gather user input for the title because a combo box can provide the exact characters required for each title. That way a user's keying error will not be a factor in recording the proper title. If the title is something unusual like "Your Excellency," it cannot be recorded. If an unusual title is necessary, you should write that specific title into the code and assign it a number.)

This completes the Class module.

FIGURE 8-4
The Customer List form showing placement of controls

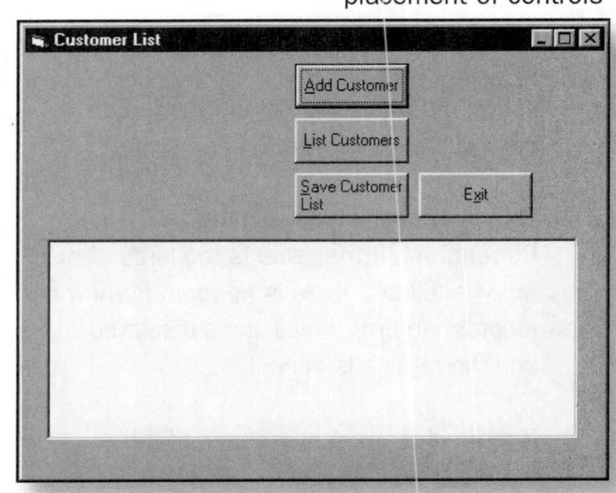

10. In the Project Explorer window, click **Form1**. Click the **View Object** button and select the form. Change the name of the form to **frmCustList**. Change the caption of the form to **Customer List**.

11. This form lets the user enter new records, display the records in a list box, and save the records in a file. Add four command buttons to the form, as shown in Figure 8-4. Change the captions to **&Add Customer**, **&List Customers**, **&Save Customer List**, and **E&xit**. Change the names of the command buttons to **cmdAddCustomer**, **cmdListCustomer**, **cmdSaveCustomer**, and **cmdExit**.

12. Add a list box to the form. Name the list box **lstCustList**.

13. Double-click the form to open the form's Code window. Select the **General Declarations** section and add the code shown in **Code Step 13**.

This code defines an array with a capacity of 51 objects of the clsCustomer type. The CurrentCust variable will be used to keep track of the next blank space in the array. The constant FileName will be used to provide a file name for the customer information file.

Check your hard drive to make sure you have a temp folder on the C: drive. You should also change the drive designation if you are not using the C: drive.

(continued on next page)

CODE STEP 13

```
Option Explicit
Dim CustList(50) As clsCustomer
Dim CurrentCust As Integer
Const FileName = "c:\temp\CustList.cus"
```

14. Select **cmdAddCustomer** to open its Code window. Press **Tab** and enter the code shown in **Code Step 14**, in **Private Sub cmdAddCustomer_Click**.

    This code checks the value of CurrentCust. If the value is too large, the array is full and there is no room for new records. An error message is displayed and the routine is ended.

    If there is room, a new object of the clsCustomer is created. You may have thought that you created 51 objects of the clsCustomer type when you declared the array. However, objects have to be intentionally created. To do that, you use the *Set* and *New* commands, as in Set CustList(CurrentCust) = New clsCustomer. The New command creates a new object called an *instantiation*, or *instance*, of the class. The Set command assigns the new object to the object variable declared in the previous Dim statement. One effect of this code is that you create new objects only if you really need them. This strategy means there are not a lot of empty objects sitting around unused.

    Simple InputBoxes are used to gather the data from the user. The *StrConv( )* function can convert ASCII code to Unicode and back, or work with Japanese characters. Here it is used with the built-in constant vbProperCase to convert the input string to a string where the first character is uppercase and the rest of the characters are lowercase.

    The With statement works as well with an object that is an element of an array as it does with a regular variable. Notice the line that resets CurrentCust. The variable is always pointing at the next empty entry in the array.

CODE STEP 14

```
If CurrentCust >= 50 Then
     MsgBox ("Error: too many customers!")
     Exit Sub
End If
Set CustList(CurrentCust) = New clsCustomer
On Error GoTo AddError
With CustList(CurrentCust)
    .FName = StrConv(Trim$(InputBox("Enter the first name:")), vbProperCase)
    .LName = StrConv(Trim$(InputBox("Enter the last name:")), vbProperCase)
    .Title = InputBox("Enter the title:", , "Mr.")
    .Address1 = InputBox("Enter the first line of the address:")
    .Town = InputBox("Enter the town:")
    .State = InputBox("Enter the state:")
    .Credit = CCur(InputBox("Enter the customer's line of credit:"))
End With
CurrentCust = CurrentCust + 1
Exit Sub
AddError:
MsgBox ("There has been an error in entering the data, please repeat step.")
```

15. Press **Tab** and enter the code in **Code Step 15** in the **Private Sub cmdListCustomer_Click** procedure. This code adds the current entries of the array to the list box on the form.

Since CurrentCust is always pointing at the next open spot of the array, one is subtracted in the For loop so that the program doesn't try to access an element outside the array. The data fields are added to the list box concatenated together to form a long string. The line adding the items to the list box is too long; a line continuation character is used to split the code to two lines.

16. Press **Tab** and enter the **End** command in the **Private Sub cmdExit_Click** procedure.

The line continuation character, the underscore, must be preceded by a space and it should be the last character in the line.

17. Save and run the program. Click **Add Customer** and enter data for a fictional customer. Click **ListCustomers** to display the entry in the list box. The record appears in the list box. The Save button does not have any code in it yet, so clicking it is useless.

18. Stop the program and leave it open for the next Step-by-Step exercise.

CODE STEP 15

```
Dim i As Integer
lstCustList.Clear
For i = 0 To CurrentCust - 1
   With CustList(i)
   lstCustList.AddItem i & ": " & .Title & .FName & " " & .LName & vbTab _
     & .Address1 & ", " & .Town & " " & UCase(.State)
   End With
Next i
lstCustList.Visible = True
```

In this Step-by-Step exercise you created your first class and a program to try it out. In the next Step-by-Step exercise you will add code to your program that saves the customer list to a file.

Quick Check 8.b

1. Three kinds of modules in Visual Basic are the Standard module, the ____________________ module, and the ____________________ module.

2. ____________________ declared in the General Declarations section of a Class module become the properties of an object created by a class.

3. A variable used internally by the object, but not available from the main program is declared in the Class module as a ____________________ variable.

4. The Get property procedure is used to __________________ the property value of an object.

5. The __________________ function converts a string to a string with the first character capitalized and the other characters lowercase.

6. A new object is called a(n) __________________ of a class.

Saving the Data

The next task is to save the customer data. It is tempting to use a random file to save each object. However, objects cannot be saved in random files. To save an object, you must save each piece of the object in a normal text file. To recover the pieces, you must read each piece into a separate variable and transfer it to the appropriate property of an object of the clsCustomer type.

The customer file is not static. The customer list grows and shrinks. One way to handle this is to read the entire customer list into memory when the program starts. Objects are created in the CustList array to handle each entry as it is read from the file. Customers can be added and deleted by updating the contents of the array. At the end of the session, the user will click the Save Customer List button to write the contents of the array back to the file.

STEP-BY-STEP 8.3

1. Open the **CustList** project, if necessary.

2. Enter the code shown in **Code Step 2** in the **Private Sub cmdSaveCustomerList_Click** procedure.

   In this code, the On Error statement sends program flow to the error handling routine called FileError: if a problem with the file occurs. The FreeFile function returns the next free channel number so you don't have to keep track of that. The Open statement opens a text file For Output. Remember Output mode always creates a new file or erases the contents before writing to an existing file. In order for you not to loose existing customer information in Step 3, you will add code to the Form_Activate procedure that loads the existing names into the list box.

   The For statement reads each entry in the list box and uses the With statement to write each property of CustList(i) to the file. Since CurrentCust points to the next open space in the array, one is subracted from it to end the loop with the last customer. Each part of the object is stored on a separate line in the text file. Once all the records have been written to the file, it is closed and a message box displays the file's path name and a message that it has been created.

3. Enter the code shown in **Code Step 3** in the **Private Sub Form_Activate** procedure.

   You cannot create an object and read a text string from a file into a property of the object. In other words, the statement Input #1, CustList(i).FName is illegal. Executing that statement results in the error message shown in Figure 8-5. Therefore this code reads the text string and stores it in a variable before moving it to the property of the object. Separate variables are declared to temporarily hold the values read from the file. An object is created with the New statement and the information is transferred into the object. The loop is controlled using the EOF function to detect the end of the file:

Do While Not EOF(FileNumber). The variable CurrentCust is advanced each time through the loop.

4. Save and run the program. When the program starts, the **Form_Activate** procedure is executed. The first time you run the program there is no file to open, so an error message appears. Click **OK** and ignore the message. Click **List Customers**. The list box is also empty the first time you run the program.

5. Click **Add Customer**. Enter data for a customer. Click **List Customers**. The data you just entered appears in the list box. Click **Save Customer List**. The contents of the array of objects are saved to the text file. A message box notifies the user of the completion of the task, as shown in Figure 8-6.

6. Add more customers to the program. Each time a customer is added, a new object is created.

FIGURE 8-5
Error message received when trying to read text from a file into a property of an object

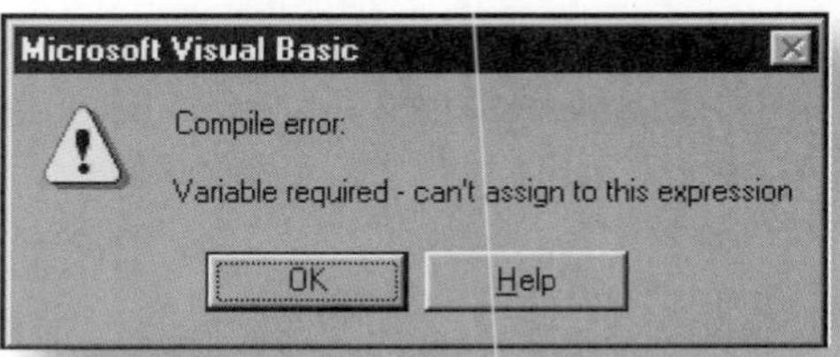

FIGURE 8-6
Message box signaling the creation of the customer text file

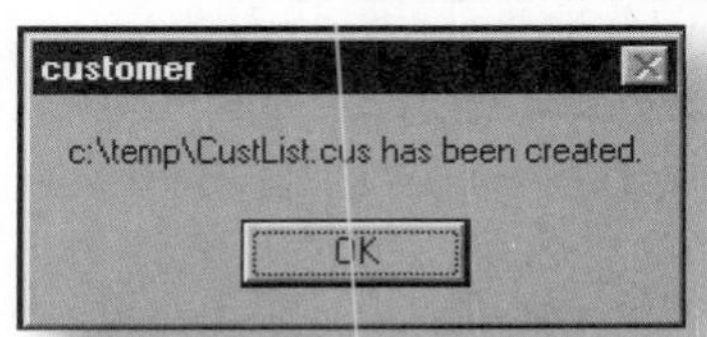

7. Click **List Customers** and **Save Customer List**. Exit the program.

(continued on next page)

CODE STEP 2

```
Dim FileNumber As Integer, i As Integer
On Error GoTo FileError
FileNumber = FreeFile
Open FileName For Output As #FileNumber
For i = 0 To CurrentCust - 1
   With CustList(i)
      Print #1, .FName
      Print #1, .LName
      Print #1, .Address1
      Print #1, .Town
      Print #1, .State
      Print #1, .Title
      Print #1, .Credit
   End With
Next i
Close FileNumber
MsgBox FileName & " has been created."
Exit Sub
FileError:
   MsgBox Err.Description
```

8. Run the program again. Click **List Customers**. Check the list to be sure every name entered is saved in the file. Stop the program.

   Many Windows programs prompt the user to save their work before the program is terminated. In the next step you will add some code to the Exit procedure to prompt the user to save the file.

9. Enter the code shown in **Code Step 9** in the **Private Sub cmdExit_Click** procedure.

   This code uses MsgBox as a function so that a value will be returned, and a YesNo box is displayed. If the user clicks Yes, the

CODE STEP 3

```
Dim First As String, Last As String
Dim Address As String, City As String
Dim St As String, sTitle As String
Dim Cred As Currency
CurrentCust = 0
Dim FileNumber As Integer
FileNumber = FreeFile
On Error GoTo FileError
Open FileName For Input As #FileNumber
Do While Not EOF(FileNumber)
         Input #1, First
         Input #1, Last
         Input #1, Address
         Input #1, City
         Input #1, St
         Input #1, sTitle
         Input #1, Cred
    Set CustList(CurrentCust) = New clsCustomer
    With CustList(CurrentCust)
        .FName = First
        .LName = Last
        .Address1 = Address
        .Town = City
        .State = St
        .Title = sTitle
        .Credit = Cred
    End With
    CurrentCust = CurrentCust + 1
Loop
Close FileNumber
Exit Sub
FileError:
  MsgBox Err.Description
```

Building Programming Skills

This would be a great time to experiment with single-stepping through a program. In any of the procedures, put a breakpoint at the top. Run the program and single-step through the code using the F8 key. Hover the mouse pointer over variables to see their values. Use Print statements in the Immediate window to view other values or execute assignment statements.

If statement is True and the **cmdSaveCustomer_Click** routine is executed. If the user clicks No, control goes to the statement following End If and the program is terminated.

10. Save and run the program and click **List Customers**. Click the **Exit** button. The message box shown in Figure 8-7 appears.

11. Click **Yes** to save the customer file and stop the program.

12. Leave the project open for the next Step-by-Step exercise.

FIGURE 8-7
The message box generated by the Exit button

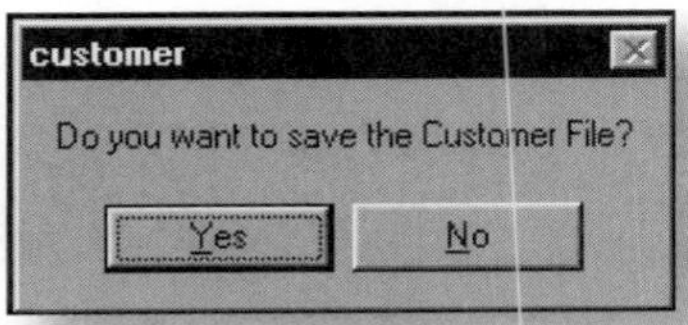

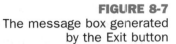

CODE STEP 9

```
Dim x As Integer
   x = MsgBox("Do you want to save the Customer File?", vbYesNo)
   If x = vbYes Then
      cmdSaveCustomer_Click
   End If
   End
```

In this Step-by-Step exercise you added file handling to the Customer List project. In the next Step-by-Step exercise you will add Methods to the clsCustomer Class definition.

Quick Check 8.c

1. An object cannot be saved in a ____________________ file.
2. The FreeFile function provides a ____________________ for the program to use.
3. The variable CurrentCust always points to the ____________________.
4. Loading the customer data file into memory is performed in the form's ____________________ event procedure.
5. Each time a customer is added, a new ____________________ is created.
6. When the Save Customer List button is clicked, the contents of the array of objects are ____________________.

Adding Methods and Events to a Class

Defining public variables in a Class module is equivalent to adding properties to the objects created with the class. Adding public procedures to a Class module is equivalent to adding methods to the objects created with the class.

Remember, a method is an action that can be performed by an object. For example, the list box object can execute the Clear method to clear its contents, or the AddItem method to add a new entry to the list.

In the next Step-by-Step exercise you will add methods to the clsCustomer class. The first method displays the customer's credit rating when their name is clicked in the list box used to display the customer list. Adding a method is a two-stage process. First you add a public procedure to the Class module. Then you add code to the main project that executes the object's method.

STEP-BY-STEP 8.4

1. Open the **CustList** project, if necessary.
2. Select the **clsCustomer** Class module from the Project Explorer. Click the **View Code** button to open its Code window.
3. Click **Tools | Add Procedure** from the menu bar. See Figure 8-3 for a review of the Add Procedure dialog box.
4. Enter **DisplayCredit** in the Name box. Click **OK**. The procedure's skeleton appears in the Code window. Press **Tab** and add the following line of code:

   ```
   MsgBox "Credit Line: " & Credit
   ```

5. Select **frmCustList** from the Project Explorer. Click **View Object** to display the form. Double-click the list box to open the **CstCustList** Click event procedure.
6. Press **Tab** and add the line of code in **Code Step 6** to **Private Sub lstCustList_Click**.

   This code uses the ListIndex property to identify the name that is selected in the list box. The ListIndex property corresponds to the item's position in the CustList array of objects. That object now has a DisplayCredit method that displays a message box showing the current credit limit. This line of code executes that method.

7. Save and run the program. Click **List Customers**. Click the first customer in the list box. The customer's credit limit appears in a message box. Click **OK**.

CODE STEP 6

```
CustList(lstCustList.ListIndex).DisplayCredit
```

8. Stop the program without saving the data file. Leave the project open for the next Step-by-Step exercise.

Business Rules

So far most of this lesson has revolved around the idea of a customer database for an Internet business. If you really were to start a business, both employees and customers would be subject to various rules. For your employees there might be rules about raises. For example, each employee is entitled to a raise each year. Another example could be if the employee has worked for the company for more than three years, they are entitled to a 1.5% raise; or if the employee has worked for three years or less, they are entitled to a 0.5% raise.

A rule for customers might be that you would not accept credit orders from customers with a credit limit under $5,000. These are all examples of *Business Rules*. Implementing these rules in programs is more interesting than ever. One way to implement the rules in a program is to write code for each rule into the program itself. The more interesting way is to build Business Rules into the classes used to create the objects the program manipulates. The rules pertaining to employees would be written into clsEmployee. The rules pertaining to customers can be written into clsCustomer. Putting the rules into the class definition makes it easy to change, and these kinds of rules change all the time.

You will implement the rule concerning credit limits in the next Step-by-Step exercise. The steps for implementing a Business Rule are the same as the steps for adding a method to a class.

To find out more about Business Rules and the new ways of integrating Business Rules into databases, use any Internet search engine and search on the string "Business Rules." Unlike many searches, this yields valuable information about Business Rules.

Computer Ethics

Building Business Rules into class definitions makes it easier to enforce those rules. If every programmer in the shop is required to use the same unmodified class definitions, all are compelled to use the same Business Rules.

STEP-BY-STEP 8.5

1. Open the **CutList** project, if necessary.

2. Select the **clsCustomer** Class module and click the **View Code** button to open the Code window.

3. Click **Tools | Add Procedure** from the menu bar. Enter **CreditCheck** in the Name box and click **OK**. Press **Tab** and enter the code shown in **Code Step 3** in **Public Sub CreditCheck**.

4. Select **frmCustList** and click **View Code** to open its Code window.

5. Open **Private Sub lstCustList_Click** and change the existing code to the code in **Code Step 5**.

   This code first displays the credit limit in a message box, then, once the user has clicked **OK**, it displays a second message box indicating the customer's credit status.

(continued on next page)

6. Save and run the program. Click **List Customers**. Click each customer in the list box. Add a few new customers so that you have some who pass the credit check and some who do not pass. Click **List Customers** again and click various customers in the list. Each click displays two message boxes, one with the credit limit and the other with an OK or a Warning. Click **Save Customer List**.

7. Stop the program and leave it open for the next Step-by-Step exercise.

CODE STEP 3

```
If Credit <= 5000 Then
   MsgBox "Not a good risk!", vbCritical, "Warning"
Else
   MsgBox "Credit OK", vbExclamation, "AOK"
End If
```

CODE STEP 5

```
With CustList(lstCustList.ListIndex)
   .DisplayCredit
   .CreditCheck
End With
```

Building Programming Skills

Displaying a customer's credit rating on the screen may be less important than returning a value about that credit rating to the calling program. It makes sense to write the method (or a separate method) as a function that returns a value. If written as a function, the return value is used in code to determine whether a customer is granted credit or not. It may be used to determine the nature of an e-mail to the customer, confirming or denying the customer's order.

Adding an Event

Adding an event to a class is no more difficult than adding a new method or property. But there is some work to do in preparation. Remember what an event is—when a user or the program takes some action on an object or a control, an event is triggered. For example, the MouseDown event occurs when the mouse button is clicked. Like any event procedure, if the programmer doesn't write code to respond to the event, nothing is executed and the event passes by unnoticed. In the next Step-by-Step exercise you will add an event to clsCustomer that executes its code when the user enters a last name that is blank.

Adding an event to the clsCustomer class is a multistage process. First, you must declare an event in the Class module, then you must write code in the Class module itself to raise the event. Lastly, in the calling program, you must declare object variables using the WithEvents keyword and write an event procedure to respond to the event when it occurs.

STEP-BY-STEP 8.6

1. Open the **CustList** project, if necessary.

2. Open the Code window for **frmCustList**. Add the following line of code at the end of the **General Declarations** section:

```
Dim WithEvents Customer As clsCustomer
```

This line does two things. First it declares an object variable Customer, of the clsCustomer type. Second, it declares it with the keyword WithEvents. This keyword allows the object so created to respond to events defined in the Class module. The CustList array cannot be declared with the WithEvents keyword. The program will be changed in the next few steps to read data into the Customer object first, and then transfer it to the CustList array of objects. This allows the events defined in the class to execute their event procedures.

3. Add the following line of code before the statement in the **cmdAddCustomer_Click** event procedure:

```
Set Customer = New clsCustomer
```

This line creates a new object of the clsCustomer type and assigns it to Customer.

4. In the same procedure, change the line **With CustList(CurrentCust)** to **With Customer**. This allows any events associated with Customer to execute.

5. Add the following line of code after the End With statement:

```
Set CustList(CurrentCust) = Customer
```

6. Later, you return to the Form module to write the code that responds to the event. For now, select the **clsCustomer** Class module from the Project Explorer.

7. Open the **clsCustomer** Code window. In the **General Declarations** section of clsCustomer, add the line of code shown in **Code Step 7**.

The name of the event is LNameError, Last Name Error. It fires when the last name entered by the user is a blank. Two parameters are sent. The first is an error message. The second is an object of the clsCustomer type. The object is sent so that the LName property of the object can

The ByVal keyword in a parameter list sends a parameter's value to the function. Because the parameter's address is not known to the function, the actual value of the parameter cannot be changed. It can be used in the function and the variable that represents the parameter can be changed, but the value of the parameter itself in the calling program cannot be changed.

(continued on next page)

Building Programming Skills

As the class is written, the last name of the customer is put into the LName variable without any code to check its validity. You cannot trigger an event without code that handles the property in some way. The class has to be altered to use Let and Get procedures to load the LName property.

be set to "Error". The idea is that the user will delete that entry and reenter the customer data with the proper information.

8. Delete or comment out the line **Public LName As String**. Click **Tools | Add Procedure**. Enter **LName** in the Name box, select the **Property** option, and click **OK**. Two property procedure skeletons appear.

9. Add a new line of code to the **General Declarations** section:

```
Private Last As String
```

This private variable will be used to hold the customer's last name. To the user (and to the code that is already written), the LName property of the class shows no change.

NOTE:

Step 9 illustrates an important concept. You can change the inner workings of a class, and if you don't change the public properties or methods, the existing code that uses the class does not need to be changed.

10. In the **Public Property Let LName(ByVal vNewValue As Variant)** procedure, change the variable type to **String** and the name to **sNewValue**. Add the code in **Code Step 10**.

In this code if sNewValue, the last name entered by the user, is blank, an event is raised. The RaiseEvent keyword fires the LNameError event. An error message is passed back to the calling program, along with a reference to the object that caused the error.

CODE STEP 7

```
Public Event LNameError(ByVal sMessage As String, ByVal CObj As clsCustomer).
```

CODE STEP 10

```
If sNewValue = "" Then
  RaiseEvent LNameError("An entry for Last Name is required!", Me)
Else
  Last = sNewValue
End If
```

CODE STEP 12

```
Private Sub Customer_LNameError(ByVal sMessage As String, ByVal CObj As clsCustomer)
  MsgBox sMessage, vbCritical, "Error"
  CObj.LName = "Error"
End Sub
```

11. Add the following line of code to the **Public Property Get LName() As Variant** procedure and change the data type to **String**:

```
LName = Last
```

This line reads the private variable Last and returns its value to the calling program as the value of the object's LName property.

12. Click **frmCustList** in the Project Explorer and open its Code window. At the end of the **General Declarations** section, enter the code in **Code Step 12**.

Notice that in this code, the parameters listed in the first line match the parameters in the Class module. The parameters must agree in number and type. The procedure's code will display the error message in a message box and set the object's LName property to "Error."

13. Save and run the program. Click **Add Customer**. Enter any first name and click **OK**. Click **OK** when prompted for the last name. The LNameError event fires and displays an error message. Click **OK** and the input process continues. The only error that crashes the data entry process is a blank entry for the credit limit. If a credit limit is entered, the input, however flawed, is processed normally. Enter a value for the credit limit.

14. Click **List Customers**. The new customer is added to the list box. Notice that the last name for the new customer is "Error."

15. Stop and remove the project.

This project is done for now, but save it, as you will modify it later when working the programming problems for this lesson. Conspicuous by its absence is any method for deleting customers from the database. That is not the only thing missing. As it stands, the project doesn't do anything beyond saving some customer information.

In the next Step-by-Step exercise you will package the class in an *ActiveX DLL* and call it from another program.

Quick Check 8.d

1. Putting Public procedure in a Class module is equivalent to adding ____________________ to the object created with the class.

2. The ListIndex property of a list box is used to identify the ____________________.

3. Giving a bonus to any worker who averages more than 45 hours of work a week is an example of a ____________________.

4. The first step in adding an event to a Class module is to ____________________.

5. The WithEvents keyword is used in the main program to ____________________.

6. The ByVal keyword is used to ____________________.

Creating an ActiveX DLL

Packaging your new class as an ActiveX DLL is the next logical step. If the customer class is useful in one application, it makes sense that it may be useful in other applications. Creating an ActiveX DLL of your class makes it available to other programs. By adding this DLL to other projects, the projects can declare and use objects of the clsCustomer class—called *references*.

The first step in the process is to build an ActiveX DLL from the clsCustomer Class module. Once that is built, a new Standard EXE is begun. Add the new DLL as a reference for the project and write code into the project that uses the clsCustomer class.

STEP-BY-STEP 8.7

1. Click **File | NewProject**, select **ActiveX DLL**, and click **OK**.
2. Right-click **Class Modules** in the **Project Explorer**. Point to **Add** and click **Class Module**. Click the **Existing** tab in the Add Class Module dialog box, as shown in Figure 8-8.
3. Navigate to the **CustList.cls** Class module created earlier in this lesson. Select it and click **Open**.
4. The name of the Class module now shows in the Project Explorer. Right-click the default Class module, **Class1**, and click **Remove Class 1** to remove it from the project. Click **No** to the save changes to the module prompt.
5. Set the Instancing property of **clsCustomer** to **5-MultiUse**. If it is not present, try to add the Class module again and check the name of the module to be sure you have the right one.
6. Click **View Code** in the **Project Explorer** to open the Code window for the clsCustomer class.

FIGURE 8-8
The Add Class Module dialog box

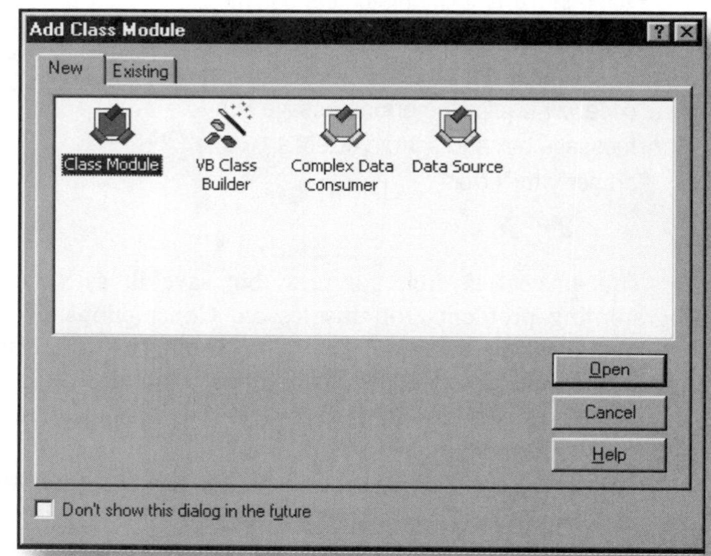

7. Click **Project1** in the **Project Explorer**. Change the Name property of the project to **CustDLL** and press **Enter**.
8. Select **File | Make CustDLL.DLL**. The Make Project dialog box displays, as shown in Figure 8-9. Click **OK** to accept the file name **CustDLL.dll** and create the DLL file.
9. Remove the project without saving it.

10. Click **File | New Project** and double-click **Standard EXE**.

11. Click **Project | References**. Scroll through the Available References list until you see **CustDLL**. Select **CustDLL** and click **OK** to close the References dialog box (see Figure 8-10).

12. Press **F2** to open the Object Browser. Select **CustDLL** in the Library list at the top of the Browser window. Select **clsCustomer** in the Classes pane. The properties, methods, and event of the clsCustomer class display in the Members pane. These members are available to the new project. Close the Object Browser.

13. Finish this project on your own by declaring a variable of the clsCustomer class in the General Declarations section of the form. Remember to use the **WithEvents** keyword. Add three command buttons and two text boxes to the form. Name and caption each control appropriately. Have the first command button read the two text boxes and assign the contents of the first text box to FName and the contents of the second text box to LName. The second command button should concatenate the names in the sequence last name, comma, first name, and then display the result in a message box. To create an object of the clsCustomer class, use Set and New. The third command button should exit the project.

14. Save the new project as **CustDisplay**. Enter a first name in the first text box and a last name in the second text box. Click **Get Data**, then click **Display**. Click **OK** to close the message box. When you have finished, exit Visual Basic.

FIGURE 8-9
The Make Project dialog box, showing the name of the CustDLL.dll file

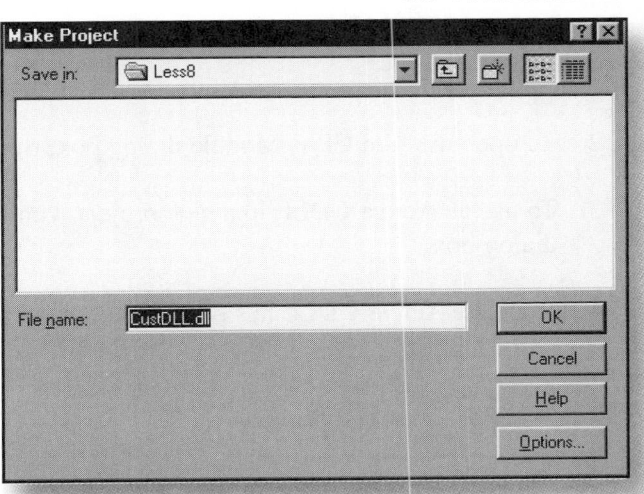

FIGURE 8-10
The References dialog box

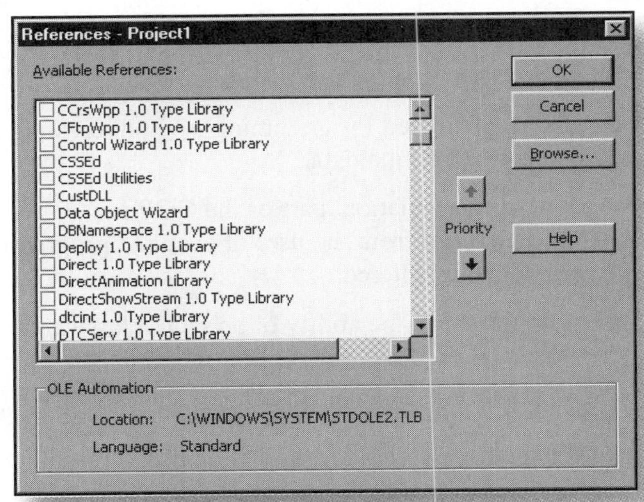

In this lesson you created a new class with its own properties, methods, and events. You packaged it as a DLL and used it in another project. This is a very powerful form of code reusability.

Quick Check 8.e

1. One way to make a class available to other applications, is to convert it to an ____________________.

2. To open the Add Class Module dialog box, right-click ____________________.

3. To use an ActiveX DLL in a new project, you must select it in the ____________________ dialog box.

4. Once the ActiveX DLL has been added to the references for the project, you can open the ____________________ to view the class(es) that have been added.

5. To create an object of a particular class in a project, use ____________________ and ____________________ in an assignment statement.

Summary

- Programmers want better programming environments, cross-platform applications, and reusable code modules.
- Visual Basic is the root language of many Microsoft products, including Microsoft Office.
- Object Oriented Programming is about creating objects that include data and the operations performed on the data.
- Data Encapsulation, part of the OOP paradigm, is the ability of an object to hide data and methods from the user or even the programmer. This protects data from being accidentally altered.
- Inheritance is the ability of an OOP class to inherit properties and methods from other classes. Visual Basic does not support inheritance.
- Polymorphism is the ability to define multiple uses for the same operators and methods.
- Objects are created from the templates provided by classes.
- The Object Browser lets the programmer look at classes and the properties of the object created from the classes.
- Classes added through the Components dialog box also appear in the Object Browser.
- You add classes to Class modules, one of the three types of Visual Basic modules: Form, Class, and Standard (or Code).
- Public variables declared in the General Declarations section of the Class module become the properties of objects created with the new class.
- Private variables declared in the General Declarations section of a Class module are available within the module but cannot be accessed outside the module.
- Property Procedures are used to gather and provide properties to objects. The procedures are also used to modify or process the properties.

- The StrConv( ) function can be used to convert an input string to a string where the first character is capitalized and the other characters are lowercase.
- A new object created from a class is called an instance, or an instantiation, of the class.
- Objects can be saved in text files by saving each part of the object as text in the file.
- Public procedures recorded in a Class module become methods of the objects created with the class.
- Private procedures in a Class module may provide functions only within the module. They are not available to an outside application.
- A Business Rule is a rule of the workplace written into the code of a program. When put into class definitions, Business Rules are easy to manage and implement.
- The ListIndex property of a list box contains the index value of the currently selected item in the list.
- To add an event to a Class module, first declare the event in the General Declarations section of the module, then write code to raise the event. The code initiates the event when some condition is satisfied (or not satisfied) in the Class module.
- To use event definitions in a Class module, use the WithEvents keyword to declare an object variable of that class in an application.
- The ByVal keyword in a parameter list sends a parameter's value to a function, not the parameter's address.
- The RaiseEvent statement is used in a Class module to fire an event procedure.
- Open an ActiveX DLL project to package a class for use with other applications. Add your existing Class module or create new ones. Compile the project as a DLL and use it in an application by clicking it in the project's References dialog box.

LESSON 8 REVIEW QUESTIONS

TRUE/FALSE

Circle the T if the statement is True. Circle the F if it is False.

T F 1. The ability to write reusable code is one of the features of Visual Basic.

T F 2. Object Oriented Programming involves Data Encapsulation, Inheritance, and Polymorphism.

T F 3. An object is made up of data and all the classes that make up the data.

T F 4. Visual Basic applications are run on many different platforms.

T F 5. The Object Browser is used to load components from the Internet.

T F 6. Public variables declared in the General Declarations section of a Class module become the methods of an object created with the class.

T F 7. Private variables declared within a Class module are not available to the application programmer.

T F 8. The Property Procedures Let and Get are used to define methods and events for a class.

T F 9. An object can be saved in a random file.

T F 10. Writing a Business Rule into a class makes the rule easier to maintain and modify.

WRITTEN QUESTIONS

Write your answers to the following questions.

11. What are the goals of Object Oriented Programming?

12. Give an example of a statement that uses the StrConv( ) function and explain what it does.

13. How are properties and methods added to a class definition?

14. List the three types of Visual Basic modules and explain what each one does.

15. What is Polymorphism?

16. What is the Object Browser used for? How is it called?

17. Describe how you package a class to be used in other applications.

18. Give two examples of Business Rules.

19. What is the ListIndex property of a list box used for?

20. What does the ByVal keyword do?

LESSON 8 PROGRAMMING PROBLEMS

Level One

CARTOON CLASS

Define a class to create objects that store information about your favorite cartoon characters. Information should include the name of the character, a short description, and the date when you first saw the character. Once the class is defined, write an application that uses the class. The application should allow the user to add cartoon characters and list the information about the characters in a list box.

CARTOON CLASS METHODS

Add a method to the class created in the Cartoon Class project to display a description of the character in a message box. For instance, if the class name is clsCartoonChar, declare an object with the statement: Dim WithEvents CChar As clsCartoonChar. Later, create an instance of the class with the statement: Set CChar = New clsCartoonCar. The method DisplayDesc would be called like this: CChar.DisplayDesc. Also add code to display the description of a character when the user clicks a button or an item in the list box.

THE COMPUTER CLASS

Define a computer class to store information about computer systems. Properties should include model, manufacturer, RAM size, processor, processor speed, hard drive capacity, price, etc. Write a program to enter and display entries of this class type.

COMPUTER CLASS METHODS

Add a method to the Computer Class project to return the value of a computer's price. For instance, CPrice = Computer.ReportPrice returns the price of the computer referred to by the object variable Computer. Use the method to display a list of the names of all the computers whose price is less than $1,000.

Level Two

AN EVENT FOR THE COMPUTER CLASS

Certain standards have been determined for computers purchased for the company. Each computer must have at least 64MB RAM, a 3 gigabyte or larger hard drive, and a Pentium II processor. Add an event to the Computer Class Methods project that fires whenever at least one of these conditions is violated. Write code to respond to the event by displaying a message box that describes the problem.

AN ACTIVEX PACKAGE FOR THE COMPUTER CLASS

Package the Computer Class project in an ActiveX DLL. Write a second application that uses the class by referencing the DLL. The application should collect and display information about computers and save the information in a text file. Use the Object Browser to examine the imported class.

SCANS

THE MUSIC COLLECTION PROJECT

In this lesson you will add a listener profile to the Music Collection project. The simple listener profile will allow you to record the listening preference for a number of different listeners. You will change the main form of the project to allow listeners to be added and selected. Once a listener is selected, the listener's musical preference can be used to select those items from the music database.

The listener profile will consist of a nickname and a musical preference. The information will be stored in a simple text file. Menu selections will let the user add new listener profiles. When exiting the program, the profile data file will be updated. Once a listener has been selected from a list box, the listener's preference can be used to select only those records in the Data Entry form of the project. You will also add new toolbar buttons to restore the selection of records to show all the records and to limit the selection of records to the listener's preference.

1. Open the **MusicColl** project from Lesson 7.

2. Select **Project | Add Class Module** to add a new class definition to the project. Change the name of the module to **clsListener**. Add the following code to the module:

```
Public NickName As String
Public Preference As String
' method to create a new SQL query
Public Function PruneSQL() As String
  PruneSQL = "Select * from MusicCollection where _
    Category ='" & Me.Preference & "' Order by Title"
End Function
```

The class has two simple properties—NickName and Preference, both strings. A single function builds an SQL query from the user's preference and returns the query as a string. You use this string to set the RecordSource property of the ADO Data control in the Data Entry form.

NOTE: The quotation marks are confusing because the SQL query requires the category to be enclosed in single quotes. The actual string is built in Visual Basic by surrounding it with double quotes. Me.Preference is the preference string of the current object of clsListener type.

3. Select **frmMusic**. This is the start-up form of the Music Collection project. Open the **Menu Editor**. Change the menu to be like that shown in the following table:

Caption	Name	Caption	Name
&View	mnuView	....E&xit	mnuExit
....Data & Entry	mnuDataEntry	&User	mnuUser
....Data & Grid	mnuDataGrid	....&Add a User	mnuAdd
....-	mnuSeparator	....&Retrieve a User	mnuRetrieve

4. Add a frame to the form, as shown in Figure 8-11. Name the frame **fraAddUser**. Add two labels, a text box, a combo box, and a single command button within the frame.

FIGURE 8-11
Modifications to frmMusic

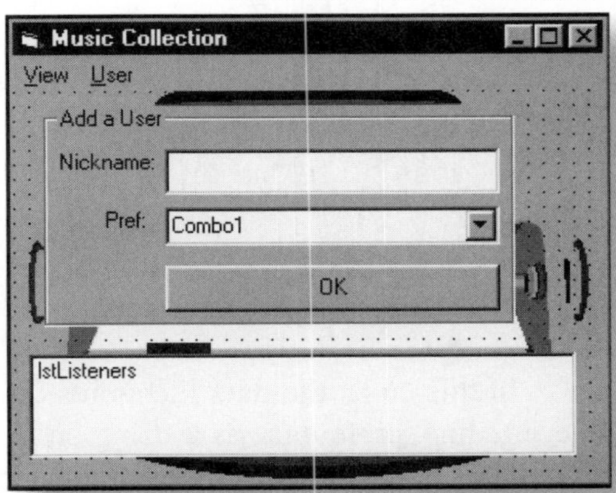

5. Change the captions of the labels to **Nickname:** and **Pref:**. Change the name of the text box to **txtNickName**. Delete the text box's text. Change the name of the combo box to **cboPref** and the name of the command button to **cmdOK**. Change the caption of the command button to **OK**.

6. Add a list box to the form. Change the name of the list box to **lstListeners**.

You will add code to the **Form_Load** procedure to look for a data file with listener profiles when the project starts. If the file is not found, an error message appears. If the file is found, its data is read and displayed in the list box. To select a listener, the user clicks the listener's nickname in the list box. This sets the variable CurrentUser, of clsListener type, to the listener selected by the user. The Data Entry form accesses this data to restrict the records displayed.

7. Add the following line to the General Declarations section of frmMusic: **Const FileName = "MusListnrs.dat"**. This defines the name of the listener's data file.

8. Add the following code to the **Form_Load** procedure of frmMusic:

```
ChDir App.Path
Dim lstnrAs clsListener
Dim Nick As String, Pref As String
Dim FileNumber As Integer
With cboPref
  .AddItem "Bluegrass"
  .AddItem "Blues"
  .AddItem "Cajun"
  .AddItem "Classical"
  .AddItem "Folk"
  .AddItem "Gospel"
  .AddItem "Jazz"
  .AddItem "New Age"
  .AddItem "Rap"
  .AddItem "Rock"
  .ListIndex = 0
End With
' Open the Listener data file and load data.
FileNumber = FreeFile
On Error GoTo FileOpenError
Open FileName For Input As FileNumber
```

```
  Do While Not EOF(FileNumber)
   Input #FileNumber, Nick
   Input #FileNumber, Pref
   lstListeners.AddItem Nick & vbTab & Pref
  Loop
  Close FileNumber
  Exit Sub
 FileOpenError:
  MsgBox Err.Description
```

In this code, the data file stores information in the following format: nickname as a string on the first line, preference as a string on the second line. The pattern is repeated for each listener. The data items added to the list box are separated with a tab character.

NOTE: The ChDir App.Path line is very important. When installing a program on another system, you must provide a way for the project to find any data files included with the project. The ChDir statement changes the active directory. The App object is a built-in object that identifies the currently running project. Together they set the current directory to the directory from which the current application is running. You need to make sure the data file is in the same directory as the application. You also need to delete any reference to a particular path from the project; just include the file name. In particular, delete the path in the DataLink properties of the ADO Data control in the Connection tab.

9. Add the following code to the **Form_UnLoad** procedure of frmMusic. This copies the data stored in the list box and recreates the listener's data file.

```
Dim x As Integer, TabPos As Integer
Dim Listener As String, FileNumber As Integer
FileNumber = FreeFile
On Error GoTo fileopenerror
Open FileName For Output As FileNumber
For x = 0 To lstListeners.ListCount - 1
 Listener = lstListeners.List(x)
 TabPos = InStr(1, Listener, vbTab)
 Print #FileNumber, Left(Listener, TabPos - 1)
 Print #FileNumber, Mid(Listener, TabPos + 1, Len(Listener))
Next x
Close #FileNumber
End
fileopenerror:
MsgBox Err.Description
```

The ListCount property contains the number of entries in the list box. The entries are recorded in the list box starting with index number 0, so the number of entries is adjusted by subtracting one. Listener is a temporary variable used to store the line of data from the list box. The Instr( ) function (see Lesson 4) is used to find the location of the tab character in the line copied from the list box. Once found, the Left and Mid functions are used to peel out the nickname and the preference of the listener. These are written into the text file.

10. Open the **cmdOK_Click** procedure and add the following code. These lines are executed after a new listener's nickname and listening preference are added.

```
Dim Lstnr As clsListener
Set Lstnr = New clsListener
Lstnr.NickName = txtNickName.Text
Lstnr.Preference = cboPref.Text
With Lstnr
 lstListeners.AddItem .NickName & vbTab & .Preference
End With
Set Lstnr = Nothing
lstListeners.Visible = True
fraAddUser.Visible = False
```

In this code, a new Lstnr of the clsListener type is declared and an instance is created with the New keyword. The NickName and Preference properties are set from the text box and combo box. The data is added to the list box. The memory occupied by the Lstnr object is returned to the pool of free memory by setting the object to Nothing. The Visible property of the list box is set to True so the data appears on the form. The Visible property of the frame is set to False to remove it from sight.

11. Enter the following code in **mnuAdd_Click**:

```
fraAddUser.Visible = True
txtNickName = ""
txtNickName.SetFocus
```

12. Enter the following code in **mnuRetrieve_Click:** `lstListeners.Visible = True`

13. Change the code in **mnuExit_Click** to **Unload Me**.

14. When the user selects a listener from the list box, the data will be loaded into a Public variable named CurrentUser. Enter the following code in **lstListeners_Click**:

```
Dim TabPos As Integer
Dim Listener As String, FileNumber As Integer
Listener = lstListeners.List(lstListeners.ListIndex)
TabPos = InStr(1, Listener, vbTab)
CurrentUser.NickName = Left(Listener, TabPos - 1)
CurrentUser.Preference = Mid(Listener, TabPos + 1, Len(Listener))
lstListeners.Visible = False
```

This code is similar to the code in the **Form_UnLoad** procedure. It reads a line of data from the list box and cuts it into pieces. The first piece is used to initialize CurrentUser.NickName. The second piece initializes CurrentUser.Preference. Once a listener is selected, the list box's Visible property is set to False.

The changes to frmMusic are complete.

15. Select **Project | Add Module** to add a Standard module to the project. Change the name of the module to **MusCol8**. Add the following line to the module: **Public CurrentUser As New clsListener**.

16. Use the **Project Explorer** to select **frmDataEntry**. Click **View Object**. Right-click the toolbar and open its Property Pages. Click the **Buttons** tab. Navigate to the last button. Click the **Insert** button. Change the following properties:

Caption	Refresh
Description	Refresh Recordset
Key	Refresh
ToolTipText	Refresh Recordset

17. Click **Insert Button**. Change the following properties:

Caption	Prune
Description	Prune Selections
Key	Prune
ToolTipText	Limit Selections

18. Add the following lines of code to the Select Case statement in **Private Sub Toolbar1_ButtonClick(ByVal Button As MSComctlLib.Button)**:

```
Case "Refresh"
  datCollectionRS.RecordSource = "Select * from MusicCollection Order by Title"
  datCollectionRS.Refresh
Case "Prune"
  If CurrentUser.NickName <> "" Then
    datCollectionRS.RecordSource = CurrentUser.PruneSQL()
    datCollectionRS.Refresh
  End If
```

This code sets the RecordSource property of the Data control to the SQL query required to either select all the records of the database or a restricted set based on the user's preference. The PruneSQL( ) method of the clsListener type is used to supply the modified SQL string.

19. Add the following lines to the end of the **Form_Load** procedure of frmDataEntry:

```
datCollectionRS.RecordSource = "Select * from MusicCollection Order by Title"
datCollectionRS.Refresh
```

20. Save the project, remembering to give appropriate names to the new modules added to the project.

21. Run the program. Ignore the error message concerning a file not found: It is the listener file. Select **User | Add a User** from the menu. Enter a nickname and music preference and click **OK**. Add a second user with a different preference. Select a listener's name from the list box. Select **View | Data Entry** from the menu. Click the **Refresh** button on the toolbar. Navigate through the entries in the database. Click the **Prune** button on the toolbar. Depending on the preference recorded for that listener and the records in the database, the selected records change. Navigate through the records. Click **Refresh** to return to the selection of the entire database.

22. Click the **Return** button to return to the start-up form. Select **View | Exit**.

    Add some records to the database with a variety of music classifications. Experiment with different listener preferences and make sure each part of the program works as expected. Think about the changes required to modify the Data Grid form in a way similar to the modifications made to the Data Entry form.

LESSON 9

WE'VE GOT A BUNCH OF THOSE!

OBJECTIVES

When you complete this lesson, you will be able to:

- Add and modify members of Visual Basic's Native Collections: forms and controls.
- Add and delete toolbar buttons based on user input.
- Enable and disable toolbar buttons based on user input.
- Create a collection of user-created objects.
- Create a collection of collections.
- Iterate through collection hierarchies to get and set object property values.
- Display and explain the object model of the created classes.

Estimated Time: 5 hours

KEY TERMS

collection
object
Forms collection
Controls collection
Printers collection
For Each statement
element
group
New function
Set command
Shell function
parallel arrays
boundary conditions
flag
Count property
Item method
Add method
Remove method
object model
robust
ListIndex property
List method

Collections

In a previous lesson you used the Visual Basic Data Form Wizard to build a form that accessed a database. The form built by the wizard used a grid to display the data. Another choice in the wizard creates a form populated with text boxes and labels for each field of the database. How does the wizard build a form at run time?

When you build a form, you anticipate the user's needs and put the proper number of text boxes, labels, and command buttons on the form while in design mode. You may, during design mode, set the Visible property of some of the controls to False so they do not appear when the program starts. Later, based on user input, the program can change the Visible property to make the controls appear. But this is not what happens when a wizard designs and builds a form. The wizard determines the number of text boxes and labels needed for the application while the wizard itself is running. It then creates text boxes and labels and places them on the form.

In this lesson you will write programs that create and place controls on a form while the program is running. It is just as easy to write a program that creates new forms while the program is running. The problem with creating a lot of new controls is that the code to make the controls do something useful has to be in place before the program runs.

The idea of a collection is what lets Visual Basic add controls or forms while a program is running. A *collection* is itself an object that contains a number of related objects. An *object* is actually just a pointer. It is a 4-byte memory address that points to something. What it points to is almost anything because just about everything in Visual Basic is an object. Controls are objects. Controls include text boxes, labels, and command buttons, as well as everything else you find in the toolbox. Remember running the Object Browser? Everything is listed there because everything in a Visual Basic project is an object.

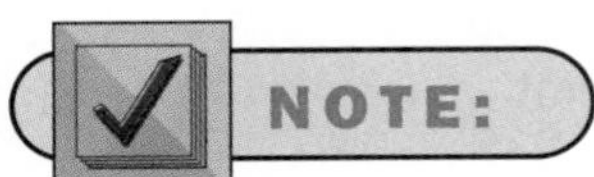

NOTE:

The idea of an object in Visual Basic is not exactly like the idea of an object in OOP, Object Oriented Programming. Lesson 8 describes the differences. Basically, the difference is that new Visual Basic objects can't inherit all the properties and methods of a previously defined object.

Visual Basic has three built-in collections: the *Forms collection*, the *Controls collection*, and the *Printers collection*. The Forms collection is a collection whose elements represent each of the loaded forms of an application. The Controls collection is a collection that contains each of the controls on a particular form. The usefulness of a collection lies in the fact that you can add members to the collection while a program is running. A collection also allows you to change the characteristics of all or some of its members with special looping statements. The following Step-by-Step exercise takes you through some manipulation of the Forms and Controls collections.

STEP-BY-STEP 9.1

1. Start Visual Basic and double-click **Standard EXE.** Save the form and project as **Exploring**.

2. Change the caption of the form to **Exploring Collections** and the name of the form to **frmExploring**.

3. Add four text boxes, four labels, and two command buttons to the form, as shown in Figure 9-1. Set the captions of the command buttons to **Click Me** and **Exit**. Name the command buttons **cmdClickMe** and **cmdExit**. Give each text box a unique name and text. Give each label a unique caption.

4. Add a list box to the form in the bottom right corner and name the list box **lstControls**. Figure 9-1 shows a possible result.

(continued on next page)

FIGURE 9-1
Exploring Collections form, showing placement of controls

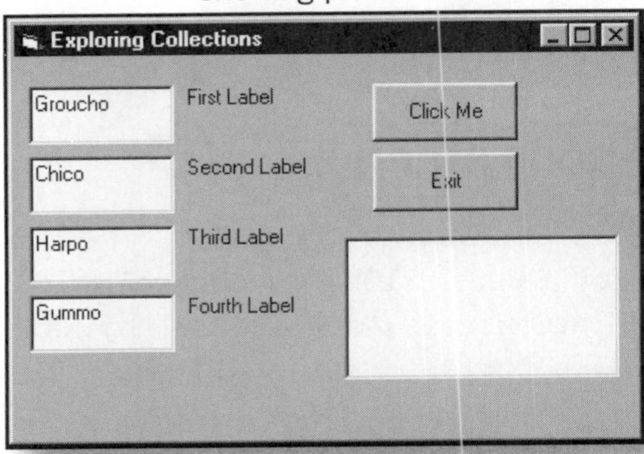

5. Double-click the **Click Me** button to open its Code window. Press **Tab** and add the code shown in **Code Step 5**.

   In the code you just entered, the Dim statement declares a variable CtrlObj as a Control type. When declared, the variable doesn't point to any specific control on the form, but it can point to any text box, label, command button, or list box. The For statement is barely recognizable, but it is related to the For statement you have used in the past. It is a special version of the For statement used for processing the items in a collection. It creates a loop using the variable CtrlObj. The In keyword initializes CtrlObj to the first item in the Controls collection. The Next statement advances CtrlObj to the next item in the Controls collection. In the body of the loop, the name of each control is added to the list box.

6. Press **Tab** and enter the **Unload Me** command in **cmdExit_Click**.

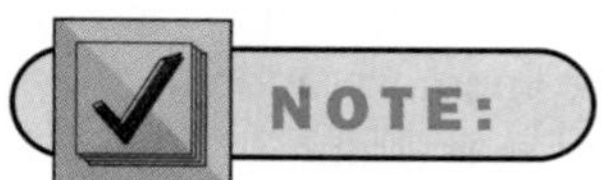

Unload Me removes the current form from memory. This stops program execution, but its action is limited to that form. The project, which may contain many forms, is not necessarily terminated.

7. Save and run the program. Click **Click Me**. The names of the controls appear in the list box.

8. Stop the program.

   The properties of the controls can be set using the same kind of loop. In addition, an If statement with a special kind of logical expression can distinguish between controls of different types.

9. Add the code shown in **Code Step 9** to the end of the statements in **cmdClickMe_Click**.

Building Programming Skills

The syntax of the For Each statement is:

```
For Each element In group
        Statement(s)
Next element
```

A valid way to exit the loop is to put the Exit For statement in the body of the loop. Element is usually an object variable. Group is the name of a collection. The Next element statement at the end of the loop sets element equal to the next item in the collection.

CODE STEP 5

```
Dim CtrlObj As Control
For Each CtrlObj In Controls
 lstControls.AddItem CtrlObj.Name
Next CtrlObj
```

CODE STEP 9

```
For Each CtrlObj In Controls
    If TypeOf CtrlObj Is TextBox Then
        CtrlObj.FontSize = 13
    End If
Next CtrlObj
```

In this code, the For loop is the same as the previous one. The If statement has a special kind of condition that is designed for use with objects. The TypeOf *objectname* Is *objecttype* expression is True when the object pointed to by *objectname* is of *objecttype*. The *Objecttype* may not be a standard data type like Integer or Single. In this case, the condition is used to select just the text boxes from the Controls collection.

10. Save and run the program. Click **Click Me**. The font size for the text in each text box is changed to 13 points, as shown in Figure 9-2.

FIGURE 9-2
The Exploring Collections program

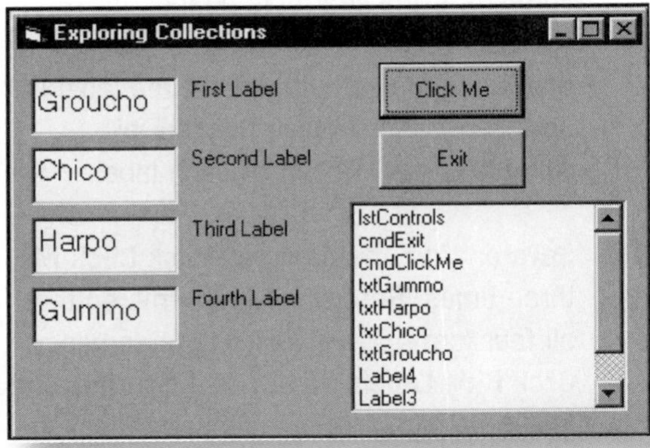

11. Stop the program.

It may seem annoying to save the project after each modification, but it is not as annoying as losing code when a program crashes the system before the code is saved.

12. Add the following lines of code at the end of the statements in **cmdClickMe_Click**:

```
Dim frmNewForm As New frmExploring
frmNewForm.Show
```

In this code, the Dim statement accomplishes two purposes: It declares the variable frmNewForm as a variable that represents a form of the type you have just designed, and the *New* keyword creates a new instance of the form. Like all created controls, the form is not visible when created. The Show method makes the form visible.

13. Save and run the program and click **Click Me**. The code in the routine executes as usual. The names of the controls appear in the list box and the font size changes in the text boxes, but the new instance of the form appears and covers results of that code. The new form has all the controls and characteristics of the original

(continued on next page)

Building Programming Skills

Usually the New function is separated into another statement. The following works, as well as what is shown above, and is considered better programming practice:

```
Dim frmNewForm As frmExploring
Set frmNewForm = New frmExploring
frmNewForm.Show
```

The Set command is a necessary part of the assignment statement when assigning a value to an object variable.

form. The original form is the mold from which the new form is built.

14. Click **Click Me** several times. As new instances of the original form are created, they are staggered on the screen so you can see the previously created forms. Use your mouse to move the top form by clicking and dragging the form's title bar. Underneath you see the previously created form with the text box fonts changed and a list of the form's controls in the list box.

15. Click **Exit** on the most recently created form. The form is unloaded from memory and disappears. Press **Alt+F4**. This key combination closes the currently active form. Close each of the active forms and stop the project.

16. In the next part of this Step-by-Step exercise you will use the Forms collection to access each form created by the Click Me button, and hide each label on each form by setting the label's Visible property to False.

17. Add a new command button to the form. Change the name of the button to **cmdHideLabels**. Change the caption of the button to **Hide Labels**. Double-click the button to open its Code window and add the code shown in **Code Step 17**.

    As in the code you added earlier, Dim CtrlObj As Control declares the variable CtrlObj as a variable capable of pointing at various controls. The Forms collection is accessed by the Forms object variable. The Count method returns the number of forms in the collection. Each individual form of the collection is accessed by its index number. The For i statement generates an index number for each form of the Forms collection. The For Each statement sets CtrlObj to each of the controls on the form. The form itself is Forms(i). If the control is a label, its Visible property is set to False. Notice that using the actual name of the label is not necessary because the CtrlObj variable is set to point to each label.

18. Save and run the program. Click **Click Me** three times. Reposition the forms so that all four forms are visible on the screen. Click **Hide Labels** on any of the forms. The labels on all the forms disappear because their Visible property is set to False.

19. Stop and remove the project.

CODE STEP 17

```
Dim CtrlObj As Control, i as Integer
    For i = 0 To Forms.Count - 1
      For Each CtrlObj In Forms(i)
        If TypeOf CtrlObj Is Label Then
            CtrlObj.Visible = False
        End If
      Next CtrlObj
    Next i
```

In this Step-by-Step exercise you used the For Each statement and the TypeOf conditional statement to manipulate the objects on the forms and the forms themselves. You used the Controls collection to change the properties of the controls on the form. You used the Forms collection to change the properties of controls on each form, and you added new forms to the project while the program was running. In the next Step-by-Step exercise you will add new controls to a form while the program is running.

Quick Check 9.a

1. A ____________________ is itself an object that contains a number of related objects.
2. An ____________________ is a 4-byte memory address that points to something.
3. The ____________________ ____________________ statement iterates through a collection by setting a variable to each element in the collection.
4. Examples of items you might find in a Controls collection are ____________________, ____________________, and ____________________.
5. You use the TypeOf ____________________ Is ____________________ to determine whether an object is a certain type.
6. The ____________________ creates a new instance of a form or object.

FIGURE 9-3
The Unit Conversion program starting screen

Adding Controls to a Form

In Step-by-Step exercise 9.2 you will add text boxes and labels to a program while it is running. The program will convert values from one unit of measurement to another. You will start with one set of text boxes. The left text box is for feet and the right text box is for inches. When the user enters a value in the box for feet and presses Enter, the value is converted to inches and is displayed in the right text box. Conversely, when the user enters a value in inches in the right text box and presses Enter, the value is converted to feet and is displayed in the left text box. Figure 9-3 shows the form with an example.

Notice the top button called Add a Conversion. When clicked, the user will be prompted to enter a left unit of measure, a right unit of measure, and a conversion factor. The program will create new text boxes and labels and add them to the form. The form itself will be enlarged and the conversion factor will be stored in an array and used to perform the conversion.

To add controls to a form, you start with a single control on the form and define it as a control array. Giving the same name to two controls of the same type creates a control array. In this program you create a control array with a single item by changing the control's Index property to 0. Once the control array is created, you add new controls to the form with the Load command. This is the same command used to load an instance of a form into memory. Each control added to the form is based on the original control. They have the same properties. Each control is added to a collection with a unique index. Visual Basic takes care of assigning sequential index numbers to the controls as they are created.

Like the forms added in the previous Step-by-Step exercise, the control's Visible property must be set to True to make the control appear on the form.

This Step-by-Step exercise starts by creating the application shown in Figure 9-3, without the ability to add new text boxes and labels.

STEP-BY-STEP 9.2

1. Start a new **Standard EXE** project. Save the form and project as **Convert**.

2. Change the name of the form to **frmConvert**. Change the caption of the form to **Unit Conversion**.

3. Add two text boxes and two labels to the form, as shown in Figure 9-3. It is important to make the text boxes long enough to show all the digits that are possible in the answers.

4. Name the text boxes **txtLeft** and **txtRight**. Set the **Index** property for each text box to **0**. This is an important step because it converts the text boxes to control arrays. You must use control arrays when you want to add new controls to a form.

5. Clear the text properties for both text boxes.

6. Name the labels **lblLeft** and **lblRight**. Set the **Index** property for each label to **0**. This converts the two labels to control arrays.

7. Set the caption of **lblLeft** to **ft** and the caption of **lblRight** to **in**. This is the only built-in conversion in the application. It is the pattern followed by the other conversions added by the user at run time.

8. Add three command buttons to the form. Change the captions of the buttons to **Add a Conversion**, **Calc**, and **E&xit**. Change the names of the buttons to **cmdAddConversion**, **cmdCalc**, and **cmdExit**.

9. Add the **End** command to **cmdExit_Click**.

10. The Calc button will be used to launch the Windows Calculator program. This will allow the user to calculate custom conversion factors and paste them into the conversion program. Enter the code shown in **Code Step 10** in **cmdCalc_Click**. This code launches the Calculator program.

    If you have a problem with this code, check the path to the calculator program on your system. The path for a normal Windows installation has been used, but yours may be different. If it is different, change the path in the code. The constant,

CODE STEP 10

```
Dim RetVal As Long
RetVal = Shell("C:\WINDOWS\CALC.EXE", vbNormalNoFocus)
```

Building Programming Skills

The Shell function runs an executable program and returns a Double value that represents the program's task ID number. The task ID is a unique number that identifies the running program. The syntax is:

```
shell(pathname[, window style])
```

The windowstyle argument has these values and purposes:

Constant	Value	Description
vbHide	0	Window is hidden and focus is passed to the hidden window.
vbNormalFocus	1	Window has focus and is returned to its original size and position.
vbMinimizedFocus	2	Window is displayed as an icon with focus.
vbMaximizedFocus	3	Window is maximized with focus.
vbNormalNoFocus	4	Window is restored to its most recent size and position. The calling program retains focus.
vbMinimizedNoFocus	6	Window is displayed as an icon. The calling program retains focus.

vbNormalNoFocus, runs the application in the size and position in which it was most recently run, and focus remains with the calling program.

11. Save and run the program. Click **Calc**. Enter a calculation. Click **Edit** in the menu bar and select **Copy**. The result of your calculation is copied and ready to paste. Close the Calculator.

12. Click **Exit** to stop the program.

When writing a long program, it is a good idea to test it as you write. Testing as you write the program helps isolate errors that may occur.

13. Code to execute the unit conversions will be in the KeyPress event procedure of each text box. The KeyPress event procedure of a text box is executed whenever the text box has the focus and a keyboard key is pressed. Typically, code in a KeyPress event procedure checks for the occurrence of a particular key. The ASCII value of the key is passed to the event through the KeyAscii parameter. Since the text box is part of a control array, two parameters are sent to the procedure, KeyAscii and Index. The Index parameter indicates which control of the control array has been activated.

14. Double-click the left text box to open its Code window. Select the KeyPress event

(continued on next page)

and enter the code shown in **Code Step 14** in the **txtLeft_KeyPress** procedure.

In this code, the If statement checks to see whether the Enter key is pressed. When the user enters a value in the box and presses Enter, the code in the routine is executed. The On Error statement is the simplest kind of error trap—it skips lines that cause errors. The variable Cnt is set to the number of controls in the txtLeft control array returned by the Count method. When the program starts, there is one item. The For statement iterates through the entries in the control array. The items in the array start with a subscript of 0, so the loop starts at 0 and its upper limit is the number of items in the array minus 1. If the left text box is empty, no processing is performed. Otherwise, the Result of the conversion is calculated by reading the contents of the left text box, converting it to a Double value, and multiplying it in a list of multipliers maintained by the program.

When a value is entered and Enter is pressed, each of the left text boxes are read and converted to their equivalents displayed in the right text boxes. The Multipliers array (a normal array of Double values) keeps track of the multipliers used in the conversions. The control array of text boxes and the array of Multipliers are *parallel arrays*. Parallel arrays use the same index value to indicate related values.

If the result is a very small number, the results are formatted using the Format function to display it in scientific notation. The Format function has two parameters: the first is the value to convert to a string, the second is the pattern used to convert the value. In the example above, the first pattern, "0.0####e-##", displays the value in scientific notation. It displays five digits to the right of the decimal point. Each number sign and each 0 stands for a single digit in the formatted result. The 0 is used when you want a 0 to appear if no digit would otherwise appear. The value

CODE STEP 14

```
Dim Cnt As Integer, i As Integer, Result As Double
If KeyAscii = 13 Then
On Error Resume Next
  Cnt = txtLeft.Count
  For i = 0 To Cnt - 1
  If Len(txtLeft(i).Text) <> 0 Then
   Result = CDbl(txtLeft(i).Text) * Multipliers(i)
   If Result < 0.00001 Then
    txtRight(i).Text = Format(Result, "0.0####e-##")
   Else
    txtRight(i).Text = Format(Result, "#,##0.#####")
   End If
  End If
  Next i
End If
```

.000000005 appears as 5.0e-9. The second format string, "#,##0.#####", displays large numbers with commas and five decimal places. Once the result is formatted, it is assigned to the right text box.

15. Select the **General Declarations** section of the form and enter this line to declare the Multipliers array:

```
Dim Multipliers(20) As Double
```

16. Select the **Form_Load** event procedure and enter the following line of code to initialize the Multipliers array:

```
Multipliers(0) = 12
```

17. Save and run the program. Enter **5** in the left text box and press **Enter**. The corresponding number of inches appears in the right text box. Try other values. Try changing the value in the right text box and pressing **Enter**. Nothing happens because there is no code in txtRight_KeyPress.

18. Stop the program.

19. From the **txtLeft_KeyPress** Code window, select all the code between the Sub statement at the top of the procedure and the End Sub Statement at the end of the procedure, and copy it to the Clipboard. (Do not copy the first or last lines of the procedure.)

20. Select the **txtRight_KeyPress** procedure and **paste** the code. Change all occurrences of *Left* to **Right** and *Right* to **Left**. Change the multiplication symbol to division. The code should appear as the code in **Code Step 20**.

21. Save and run the program. Enter a value in the right text box and press **Enter**. The corresponding value appears in the left text box. Experiment with very large and very small values. Experiment with entering values into the left and right text boxes.

22. Stop the program.

(continued on next page)

CODE STEP 20

```
Dim Cnt As Integer, i As Integer, Result As Double
If KeyAscii = 13 Then
On Error Resume Next
  Cnt = txtRight.Count
  For i = 0 To Cnt - 1
  If Len(txtRight(i).Text) <> 0 Then
 Result = CDbl(txtRight(i).Text) / Multipliers(i)
   If Result < 0.00001 Then
    txtLeft(i).Text = Format(Result, "0.0####e-##")
   Else
    txtLeft(i).Text = Format(Result, "#,##0.#####")
   End If
  End If
  Next i
End If
```

The rest of the code goes into the cmdAddConversion procedure. The code will start by collecting the names of the units for the left and right text boxes. A simple error handler will bail out of the procedure if no value is entered for the label or for the multiplier. This will handle the situation when a user realizes they clicked a button by mistake. It is always good to give the user a graceful way to exit the procedure.

The UBound method will give the value of the upper bound of the control array. If there are 3 items in the control array, the upper bound is equal to 2 (Remember, the array starts with an index of 0). The value returned by this method will be increased by one and is the index of the new text boxes and labels that will be added to the form.

The Load statement will use the name of the control array along with the new index number to create a new control on the form. When the control is created, it is identical to the original control except its Visible property is set to False. That means that it is the same size and in the same position. To be useful, it has to be repositioned and its Visible property has to be set to True.

Once two new text boxes and two new labels are created and positioned on the form, the form itself is resized to allow more room for more new conversions.

23. Double-click **Add a Conversion** to open its Code window and enter the code in **Code Step 23**.

24. Save and run the program.

25. Click **Add a Conversion**. Enter **in** for the left label and **cm** for the right label. Enter **2.54** for the conversion factor. Experiment by entering various values in the left and right text boxes. Press **Enter** when you are ready to execute the code.

26. Now click **Calc** to start the Calculator. Click **Add a Conversion**. Enter **ft** for the left label and **mi** for the right label. Activate the calculator and enter **5280**. Click the **1/x** key. Click **Edit | Copy** from the menu bar of the Calculator.

27. Return to the Unit Conversion application (still running) and paste (Ctrl+V) the value you copied from the Calculator into the InputBox prompting you for the multiplier. Click **OK**.

28. Enter **17**, **14**, and **746** into the three left text boxes. Press **Enter** after the last entry. The corresponding value for each measurement appears in the right text box. Your result should appear similar to Figure 9-4.

29. Experiment with different values in both the left and right text boxes. Add more conversions. Note the form grows with each additional conversion.

30. Stop the program and close the Calculator. Leave the project open for the next Step-by-Step exercise.

FIGURE 9-4
The Unit Conversion application with two conversions added

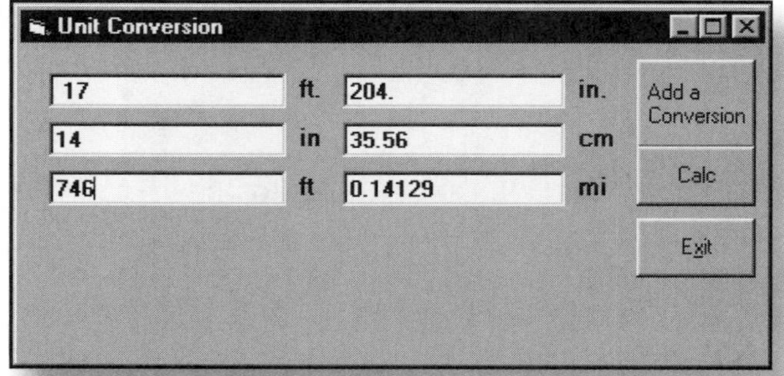

CODE STEP 23

```
Dim LeftUnit As String, RightUnit As String
Dim Factor As Double, NewUB As Integer
On Error GoTo BailOut
LeftUnit = InputBox("Enter left unit:")
If Len(LeftUnit) = 0 Then GoTo BailOut
RightUnit = InputBox("Enter right unit:")
If Len(RightUnit) = 0 Then GoTo BailOut
' Index for the new controls:
NewUB = txtLeft.UBound + 1
Multipliers(NewUB) = CDbl(InputBox("Enter the multiplier:"))
Load txtLeft(NewUB)  ' Creates a new left textbox.
With txtLeft(NewUB)
  .Top = txtLeft(NewUB - 1).Top + txtLeft(0).Height + 120
  .Text = ""
  .Visible = True
  .SetFocus
End With
Load lblLeft(NewUB) ' Creates a label to match the textbox.
With lblLeft(NewUB)
  .Top = txtLeft(NewUB - 1).Top + txtLeft(0).Height + 120
  .Caption = LeftUnit
  .Visible = True
End With
Load txtRight(NewUB) ' New right textbox.
With txtRight(NewUB)
  .Top = txtLeft(NewUB - 1).Top + txtLeft(0).Height + 120
  .Text = ""
  .Visible = True
End With
Load lblRight(NewUB)  ' New matching label.
With lblRight(NewUB)
  .Top = txtLeft(NewUB - 1).Top + txtLeft(0).Height + 120
  .Caption = RightUnit
  .Visible = True
End With
frmConvert.Height = frmConvert.Height + txtLeft(0).Height
Exit Sub
BailOut:
MsgBox "Try Again Later...", , "Bailing Out"
```

One thing that makes this application possible is the simple code needed to convert the value in one text box to a corresponding value in the other text box. The code is essentially the same for each conversion. Because the same code handles all the conversions, the user can add conversions until they run out of space. The conversions are not saved from session to session, however, and there is currently no way to recover from errors in conversion factors.

In review, use the following steps to add controls to a form while a program is running:

- Start with a control added at design time to be the pattern for all the other controls.
- Make the control into a control array by setting its Index property to 0.
- In code, use Load Ctrl(NextIndex) to create the new control on the form.
- Reposition the control on the form and set the control's Visible property to True.
- Use the appropriate subscript to access each control in its control array.
- Write code to process the new controls that automatically handle new additions to the control array.

Quick Check 9.b

1. You make a single control on a form into a control array by setting its ____________________ ____________________ to 0.
2. If there is a text box named txtName on the form and it is part of a control array, you use ____________________ ____________________ to create another control like txtName with the index NewUB.
3. You would use the ____________________ function to write a command that runs Notepad.exe.
4. The ____________________ event of a text box is executed when the text box has the focus and a keyboard key is pressed.
5. To display a decimal number with two decimal places, use the format string _______________.
6. ____________________ arrays are separate arrays that hold related information. Each related element in the array has the same Index value.

Removing Controls from a Form

What happens if the user makes a mistake? If the mistake occurs while the user is entering the unit labels or multiplier, clicking Cancel cancels the whole operation. However, once controls for another conversion are added to the form, there is currently no way to remove them. Adding code to remove the code is not difficult and you will do that next. Here are the steps to follow:

- Decide on the user interface. A command button would work, but the user would still have to indicate which conversion controls to remove. Instead of a command button, you could put the code into the DblClick event procedure of the left text box. When the user double-clicks the left text box, the index of the text box is sent to the DblClick event procedure. That index corresponds to the conversion to remove.

- Assuming the conversion controls to remove are somewhere in the middle of the list, you will have a loop in the DblClick event procedure move the items below the item to be removed up a notch. The controls to remove will now be at the bottom of the form. The loop must move the contents of the text boxes, the labels, and the corresponding multipliers.
- Next, you will remove the now unused boxes and labels by unloading them from the form. Since the contents of the boxes, the captions of the labels, and the values in the Multipliers array have been rearranged, the conversion controls just removed cannot be easily restored.
- Finally, you will resize the form to compensate for the boxes that have been removed.

Before you enter the code for this change, it is time for a confession. The program's main purpose is to make a conversion when the user enters a value in a text box and presses Enter. This is not a particularly good interface because most Windows programs don't use it. Users don't expect to press Enter to make a program work. In most Windows applications, the user enters a value and clicks a button. If desperate, the user might try to right-click the object looking for a pop-up menu.

Double-clicking an item to remove it from the form is also a bad interface because there are potential problems. When entering a value in the text box, the user might accidentally double-click. The text box, along with its label and the matching set, will disappear. Also, in many Windows applications you select the text in a text box by double-clicking the box.

With these user interface concerns in mind, you will have the project query the user about their

STEP-BY-STEP 9.3

1. Open the **Convert** project, if necessary.
2. Double-click the left text box to open its Code window and select the text box's **DblClick** event. Enter the code shown in **Code Step 2**.

   The top line of the code you just added is commented out; it is the On Error Resume Next statement. As you know, this statement can prevent program crashes due to careless errors, but it can also cover up errors that should not be allowed. It is hard to find errors that you don't know have occurred. You can remove the quote mark after you have tested the program.

   After declaring variables, an If statement checks the value of Index. This value will correspond to the text box clicked by the user. If the value of Index is 0, the user has clicked the first set of boxes on the form. The original text boxes and labels are the pattern used to create the collections. All the new text boxes and labels added to the form are based on these, so they cannot be removed. The If statement skips all the code if the value of Index is 0.

   The MsgBox function prompts the user with a message asking the user to confirm removal of the conversion controls from the form. The value returned by the function is compared with vbYes, a built-in constant equal to the value generated by the Yes button on the MsgBox. If they match, the If statements will execute.

   The code to move the contents of each text box and label up one level starts with the For statement: For x = Index + 1 To txtLeft.Count - 1. The Count method is

(continued on next page)

used to return the number of controls in the txtLeft text box collection. The Count is equal to the value of the last subscript plus one. That is because the subscripts of the control array start at 0. If the Count method returns a count of 5 items in the control array, the valid subscripts range from 0 through 4.

The loop must start at Index + 1, one item below the conversion controls to remove. Assignment statements actually move the data from the xth position to the (x-1)th position of the control array. This is why the For loop starts at Index + 1 instead of just Index.

The statement txtLeft(x - 1) = txtLeft(x) moves the entry at the xth item in the control array to the entry in the (x-1)th item of the array.

Once all the data is moved, the bottom set of boxes and labels is removed from the form. The Unload command removes the text boxes and the labels from the form. The code uses the Count of the txtLeft control array to remove items from all four control arrays. The code is arranged so that the item from the txtLeft collection of text boxes is removed last. If it is removed before any of the other controls, the value of txtLeft.Count is altered. The easiest way to fix this error is to remove the txtLeft text box last in the list of assignment statements. Another (possibly better) way is to use the Count method of each collection: Unload txtRight(txtRight.Count - 1) removes the dependency on the value of txtLeft.Count and makes the code less prone to error.

CODE STEP 2

```
'On Error Resume Next
Dim x As Integer, k As Integer
If Index <> 0 Then
 k = MsgBox("Remove the conversion?", vbYesNo, "Remove Conversion")
 If k = vbYes Then
  For x = Index + 1 To txtLeft.Count - 1
   txtLeft(x - 1) = txtLeft(x)
   txtRight(x - 1) = txtRight(x)
   lblLeft(x - 1) = lblLeft(x)
   lblRight(x - 1) = lblRight(x)
   Multipliers(x - 1) = Multipliers(x)
  Next x
  Unload txtRight(txtLeft.Count - 1)
  Unload lblLeft(txtLeft.Count - 1)
  Unload lblRight(txtLeft.Count - 1)
  Unload txtLeft(txtLeft.Count - 1)
  frmConvert.Height = frmConvert.Height + txtLeft(0).Height + 120
 End If
End If
```

Finally, the height of the form is readjusted to compensate for the removed controls.

3. Save and run the program. Enter a value in the left text box and press **Enter**.

4. Add three more conversions. Double-click the last left text box. The program prompts you to remove the conversion. Click **Yes**.

5. Double-click the top left text box. Nothing happened because you cannot remove this conversion.

6. Double-click the second left text box and the item just below the first item disappears.

7. Experiment with adding and deleting conversions from the program.

8. Stop the program and leave the project open for the next Step-by-Step exercise.

Building Programming Skills

To test the program, you have just checked the boundary conditions. The boundary conditions are what a program does at the edges of its functionality. You removed the item just below the top of the list. You also removed an item at the bottom of the list. Testing the boundary conditions of a program is very important. The boundary conditions are a very likely source of error.

intention before anything on the form is changed.

In this Step-by-Step exercise you used the UnLoad command to remove a created control from the form. You cannot remove a control created at design time, but it is easy to write code to remove a created control at run time.

Quick Check 9.c

1. Two issues that are important to consider when designing a ________________ ________________ are giving the user the ability to cancel an operation and an example of proper input.

2. The ________________ ________________ is not a good one to use to remove a text box from a form.

3. The expression txtLeft.Count returns the ________________ of items in the collection.

4. An On Error ________________ ________________ statement may not be a good idea because it can cover up errors in a program.

5. The upper and lower limits of acceptable input values are called ________________ conditions.

6. The ________________ command removes a control from a form.

Adding and Deleting Buttons from a Toolbar

In a previous lesson you added a toolbar to a program. To write code for the buttons, you learned that the buttons are part of a collection called the Buttons collection. Now you will use the Buttons collection to add buttons to and delete buttons from a toolbar while the program is running. As each conversion is added to the Unit Conversion project, a button will be added to the toolbar. When a conversion is removed, its corresponding button on the toolbar will also be removed.

Figure 9-5 shows the Unit Conversion project with a toolbar added. Two conversions have been added to the original feet to inches conversion that the project starts with.

FIGURE 9-5
The Unit Conversion program with a toolbar

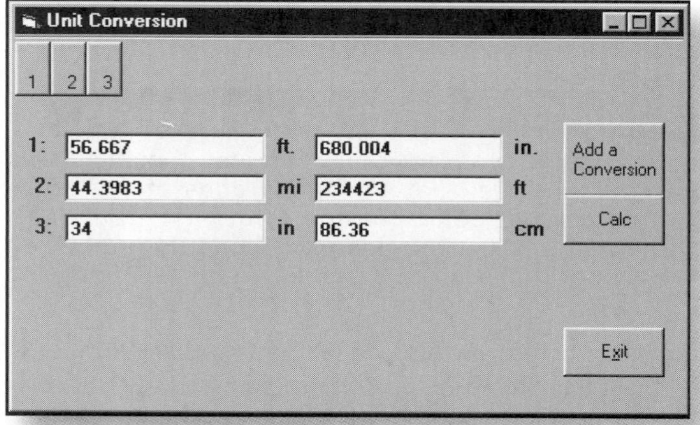

Labels to the left of each conversion pair have also been added, and the numbers in the labels correspond to the numbers on the buttons of the toolbar. Now when a user enters a value in either the left or right text box of a conversion pair and clicks the corresponding button, the value entered is converted and displayed in the other text box.

In the original program, when a value was entered into a left text box and Enter was pressed, all the values in the left text boxes were converted to their corresponding values and displayed in the right text boxes. The toolbar method will work a little differently. When a value is entered in a left text box and its corresponding button is clicked, just that value is read, converted to its corresponding value, and displayed in the right text box. A value entered into a right text box is treated the same way; it is converted and displayed in the corresponding left text box.

A Boolean variable called a *flag* will be used to determine if the left or right text box value is the one to convert. When a left text box receives the focus, the variable fLeft is set to True. When a right text box receives the focus, fLeft is set to False. When a button on the toolbar is clicked, the value of the flag is read and its value determines which code will be executed.

Unlike the toolbar added to a project in Lesson 5, the toolbar added to the Unit Conversion project doesn't use the ImageList control. Icons will not be attached to the toolbar. What icons would be appropriate? How would you add from a list of appropriate icons if they existed? Since conversions can be added in any order, there is no way to tell which icon to add. Not having icons simplifies adding the toolbar to the project.

All collections have the following method and property:

- The *Count property* reports the number of objects in a collection.
- The *Item method* retrieves a single object from the collection.

Most collections have the following methods:

- The *Add method* adds an object to a collection.
- The *Remove method* deletes an object from a collection.

In the next Step-by-Step exercise you will add a toolbar to the Unit Conversion project. Buttons will be added to the toolbar when conversions are added, and buttons will be removed from the toolbar when conversions are removed from the form. You will use the Add and Remove methods of the Buttons collection to accomplish this.

STEP-BY-STEP 9.4

1. Open the **Convert** project, if necessary.

2. Run the program. Enter and convert a few values. Add a conversion and test it. It is always a good idea to check a project to make sure it is running properly before adding anything else to it. Stop the program and select the project's form.

3. First you need to make room for the toolbar. Select the pointer tool in the toolbox. Click and drag a box around all the controls on the form. When the mouse button is released, all the controls the form are selected. Click and drag one of the controls to move the whole group down far enough to make room for the toolbar.

4. Right-click the toolbox and select **Components** or click **Project | Components** from the menu bar, to open the Components dialog box. Select **Microsoft Windows Common Controls 6.0** and click **Apply**. Click **Close** to close the dialog box.

5. A number of new controls appear in the toolbox. If you cannot see the additional controls, resize the toolbox to allow three columns of controls to display. Double-click the **Toolbar** tool to add the control to the form.

6. Change the Name property of the toolbar to **tlbMain**. Right-click the **Toolbar** tool and select **Properties**. Changes are not necessary under the General tab of the Property Pages. This is where you would normally connect an ImageList control to the toolbar, but this project does not use images.

7. Click the **Buttons** tab. Click **Insert Button**. Enter **1** (the digit one) in the Caption box and **B1** in the Key box. In the ToolTipText box, enter **ft to in**. Simple captions and Key properties for the button are easy to add at run time. The Caption, Key, and ToolTipText properties have to be set for every button added to the toolbar, as shown in Figure 9-6. Click **OK**.

8. Save and run the program. Click the toolbar button. Nothing happens because there isn't any code for the button yet.

(continued on next page)

FIGURE 9-6
The Buttons tab of the Property Pages for tlbMain, showing the entry for the first button of the toolbar

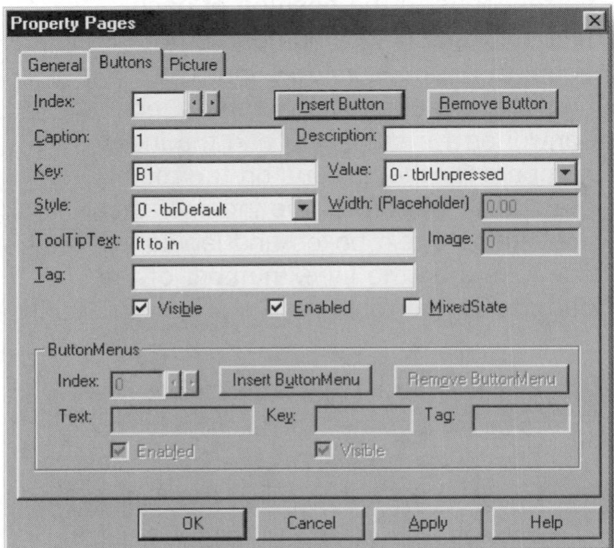

Stop the program.

Incremental programming is a programming technique where you make sure you have a correctly functioning program after every step in the program's development. In other words, whenever you add something to the project, or alter the project's code, run the program to make sure everything works as expected. It is far easier to find a mistake if you know the mistake is in the last item you added to the program.

9. Add **Option Explicit** to the **General Declarations** section to require all your variables to be declared. Add a label to the left of the left text box, as shown in Figure 9-5. Set the font to **Bold** and the font size to **10**. Change Autosize to **True**. Set the Index property of the label to **0**. Change the name of the label to **lblConvNumber** and set its caption to **1:**.

Each toolbar button has a number that corresponds to the position of each unit conversion. The number is not equal to the conversion's Index number because Index numbers for control arrays start at 0 and the index numbers for the buttons on the toolbar start at 1. Therefore, the Index of the conversion's text boxes and labels is one less than the Index number of the buttons on the toolbar.

10. A number of changes and additions have to be made to the code to add a toolbar. Start in the **General Declarations** section by adding the following line: **Dim fLeft As Boolean**. This variable will be used as the flag to indicate whether the left or right text box has received the focus. The program will assume that the most recent text box to receive the focus is where the user entered the value to be converted. If the user enters a value in the left text box, fLeft will be set to True. If the user enters a value in the right text box, fLeft will be set to False.

11. In **Private Sub txtLeft_GotFocus**(Index As Integer), enter the following line of code:

```
fLeft = True
```

12. In **txtRight_GotFocus**, enter the following line of code:

```
fLeft = False
```

13. Double-click the toolbar on the form to open the **Private Sub tlbMain_ButtonClick**(ByVal Button As MSComctlLib.Button) procedure. Enter the code shown in **Code Step 13**.

Much of the code in Code Step 13 is the same as the code from txtLeft_KeyPress. If you copy it from there, make sure to change all the occurrences of i to x.

A big difference between the code you just added and the code in the KeyPress event of the text boxes is the lack of a loop. This new code calculates and displays the result of a single conversion. It does not refigure the conversion of all the conversion pairs of the form, just the single conversion corresponding to the button clicked by the user.

14. Save and run the program. Enter a value in the left text box. Don't press Enter from the keyboard. Click the toolbar button **1**. The converted value is displayed in the right text box. Enter a value in the right text box. Click the button on the toolbar. The converted value appears in the left text box.

15. Stop the program.

    The next step in the process is to write code to add a button to the toolbar. Also, a new label has been added, so code must be written to add a new label for each new conversion. The code for adding the label is identical to the existing code for adding the other new labels and text boxes for each conversion. To add a button to the toolbar, you will use the Buttons collection's Add method. When the Add method is executed, a new button with all the properties of the original button is added to the toolbar.

16. Open the Code window for the **Private Sub cmdAddConversion_Click** procedure. The code in this existing procedure can be thought of as 3 or 4 subsections. The first section of code declares variables, the second section collects user input for the unit names and multiplier, and the third section adds new text boxes and labels and sets their properties. Following this third section, just before the line frmConvert.Height = frmConvert.Height + txtLeft(0).Height that adjusts the height of the form, add the code shown in **Code Step 16**.

(continued on next page)

CODE STEP 13

```
Dim x As Integer, Result As Double
  x = Val(Button.Caption) - 1
  If fLeft Then
    If Len(txtLeft(x).Text) <> 0 Then
     Result = CDbl(txtLeft(x).Text) * Multipliers(x)
     If Result < 0.00001 Then
      txtRight(x).Text = Format(Result, "0.0####e-##")
     Else
      txtRight(x).Text = Format(Result, "#,##0.#####")
     End If
    End If
  Else
    If Len(txtRight(x).Text) <> 0 Then
      Result = CDbl(txtRight(x).Text) / Multipliers(x)
     If Result < 0.00001 Then
      txtLeft(x).Text = Format(Result, "0.0####e-##")
     Else
      txtLeft(x).Text = Format(Result, "#,##0.#####")
     End If
    End If
  End If
```

17. Right after the line frmConvert.Height = frmConvert.Height + txtLeft(0), add the code shown in **Code Step 17**.

    In this code, the first line declares a Button type variable, btn, and a String type variable, BtnNumber. BtnNumber is set to the value of NewUB plus one, converted to a string. This number is the index number of the new toolbar button. The Set command that follows is one of those special assignment statements used to assign a value to an object variable. The value assigned to btn is generated by the Add method. The Add method of the Buttons collection generates a new button and places it on the toolbar. The Add method has four parameters:

    - The first parameter is the Index number of the new button.
    - The second parameter is the value of the Key property. In this case, the Key property is built from the letter B and the buttons index number.
    - The third parameter is the caption of the button. Often the caption is left blank because the button is loaded with an icon descriptive of its nature. When the caption or any other parameter is left blank, be sure to leave a comma in to hold the missing parameter's place.
    - The fourth parameter indicates the type of button to add. The following types are available using the predefined constants:
        - 0-tbrDefault is a constant for the default button. This button executes code that is independent of other code. Its icon, caption, and ToolTip all help to identify its purpose to the user.

CODE STEP 16

```
' code added for the addition of a toolbar
Load lblConvNumber(NewUB)
With lblConvNumber(NewUB)
   .Top = txtLeft(NewUB - 1).Top + txtLeft(0).Height + 120
   .Caption = Str$(NewUB + 1) & ":"
   .Visible = True
End With
```

CODE STEP 17

```
' Additional code used to add the toolbar buttons
Dim btn As Button, BtnNumber As String
BtnNumber = Str$(NewUB + 1)
Set btn = tlbMain.Buttons.Add(NewUB + 1, "b" & BtnNumber, BtnNumber, tbrDefault)
btn.ToolTipText = LeftUnit & " to " & RightUnit
```

- 1-tbrCheck is the constant for the Check button. It is used as a toggle to turn properties or program states on and off. The Bold button that sets text to boldface is a toggle.

- 2-tbrButtonGroup is the constant that indicates a button is a part of a button group. Buttons in a button group represent states or properties that are mutually exclusive. When one button is clicked, all others in the group are not.

- 3-tbrSeparator is the constant for a button used as a separator. Sometime it makes sense to put space between groups of buttons. The width of a separator button is 8 pixels.

- 4-tbrPlaceholder is the constant for a button used to make room in the toolbar for other controls. A list box or combo box can be added to a toolbar using this control to reserve the space. The width of the Placeholder button is adjustable.

18. Save and run the program and test it by adding a new conversion. Here are some conversions to add:

- **in** to **cm**, multiplier: **2.54**
- **mi** to **ft**, multiplier: **5280**
- **cm** to **mm**, multipler: **10**

19. Enter values in the left text boxes and click the corresponding toolbar buttons. Enter values in the right text boxes and click the corresponding toolbar buttons.

20. Stop the program.

The final step is to add code to delete buttons from the toolbar using the Button collection's Remove method. Recall that the code that removes a conversion is in the Private Sub txtLeft_DblClick(Index As Integer) procedure. This code moves all the data from conversions that follow the one to be deleted up a space. After the information is moved, the last entries in the text box and label collections are deleted. In this case, deleting a toolbar button is easier because there is no code in the button that is specific to a particular conversion. The code in the button converts the value in one text box to the corresponding unit and displays it in the other text box. That generic code is the same for all the buttons on the toolbar.

21. In the **Private Sub txtLeft_DblClick(Index As Integer)** procedure, add the code shown in **Code Step 21** following the line frmConvert.Height = frmConvert.Height + txtLeft(0).Height + 120 and before the first End If.

22. Once again, save and run the program and add and delete conversions. The toolbar buttons will appear and disappear when conversions are added and removed.

23. Stop and remove the project.

CODE STEP 21

```
Unload lblConvNumber(lblConvNumber.Count - 1)
tlbMain.Buttons.Remove tlbMain.Buttons.Count
```

In the Unit Conversion program you have used collections to add and delete controls to a form and buttons to a toolbar. In the next Step-by-Step exercise you will build a collection of objects from classes you define.

Quick Check 9.d

1. A flag variable is usually defined as a ____________________ data type.
2. If no icons are used in a toolbar, the ____________________ control may be omitted from the project.
3. All collections have a ____________________ property that reports the number of items in a collection and an ____________________ method that retrieves a single object from the collection.
4. The ____________________ and ____________________ methods of a collection add new items to the collection and remove existing ones.
5. The four parameters of the Add method of the Buttons collection are the ____________________, ____________________, ____________________, and the ____________________.
6. Two kinds of buttons that can be added to a toolbar are the ____________________ button, similar to a command button and the ____________________ button, used to toggle properties on and off.

More Collections

Collections make it easy to keep track of different kinds of objects. In the next Step-by-Step exercise you will write some simple classes and collections to store information about the structure of a school. Schools are divided into departments. Connected with each department are staff members and clerical information. Examine the diagram below to see the hierarchy of the organization of the data. Such a diagram is a way of displaying the relationships of an *object model.*

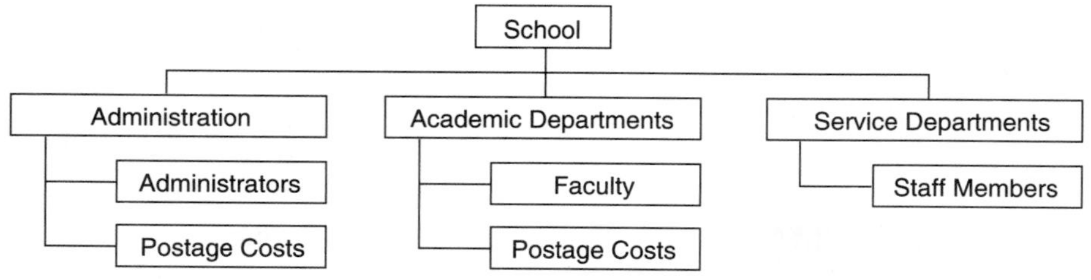

An easy way to reflect this hierarchy in a program is to create classes and collections for each category. The School class is built from an Administration class, a collection of entries for each Academic Department, and a collection of entries for each Service Department. In turn, each Academic Department is a collection of faculty members and each Service Department is a collection of staff members.

In the Step-by-Step exercise that follows, you will build enormously simplified versions of each of these classes and collections. The goal is to see how the relationships between the different classes and collections help you organize and manipulate the data.

STEP-BY-STEP 9.5

1. Start a new **Standard EXE** project. Save the form and the project as **SchoolData**.

2. Change the name of the form to **frmSchoolData**. Change the caption of the form to **School Data**.

3. Select **Project | Add Class Module** from the menu bar. From the Add Class Module dialog box, select **Class Module** and click **Open**. You will start by creating the classes that are on the lowest rung of the hierarchy in the diagram.

If you add a Class module accidentally, right-click the module in the Project Explorer. From the pop-up menu, select Remove, followed by the class's name. The default name is Class1.

4. Change the name of the class to **clsFaculty**. This class will be used to create objects that store data about faculty members. Eventually, this class will be used to define a collection that is a part of a larger class. The Academic Department class will contain a collection of clsFaculty objects. Using the principle of incremental programming, start by defining a collection of faculty members within frmSchoolData, test clsFaculty, and then define an Academic Department class that includes data about faculty members.

5. In order to see the relationships between the classes and collections of the project, most of the details that would make the classes do real work are omitted. In the **General Declarations** section of **clsFaculty**, enter the following code:

```
Private sFName As String
Private sLName As String
Public IDNumber As Variant
```

6. Select **Tools | Add Procedure** from the menu bar. Enter **FName** in the Name box and select the **Property** option in the Type frame. Click **OK** to close the Add Procedure dialog box, as shown in Figure 9-7.

7. Enter the two lines of code shown in **Code Step 7**, in the procedures that were just generated. The default data types generated in the Let and Get procedures are Variant type. For this application, also change all the references of *Variant* to **String**. Change the first character of

(continued on next page)

Building Programming Skills

The word *robust* means durable, tough, strong and complete. A program's robustness refers to the program's ability to cope with or recover from error conditions. A program that is robust is designed to prevent errors by making errors impossible. This is possible by writing code in such a way that mistakes cannot be made. Classes are a template for objects. A class definition determines how the properties and methods of an object are exposed to the programmer. A public variable declared in a class definition is fully exposed to the programmer. Any change can be made with a simple assignment statement. Writing Let and Get procedures expose an object's properties subject to the conditions written into the Let and Get procedures. Robust programs test data and raise errors if problems are found.

names of the variables that start with a lowercase **v** (indicating a variable of the Variant type) to a lowercase **s**. If you miss one of these changes, the program will crash when you try to run it.

8. Select **Tools | Add Procedure** from the menu bar. Enter **LName** in the Name box and select the **Property** option in the Type frame. Click **OK** to close the Add Procedure dialog box.

9. Enter the two lines of code shown in **Code Step 9** in the procedures that were just generated. Remember to change all references of **Variant** type to **String**.

Remember the StrConv(string, vbProperCase) function? It converts the first letter of every word in a string to uppercase.

FIGURE 9-7
The Add Procedure dialog box showing the entry for FName

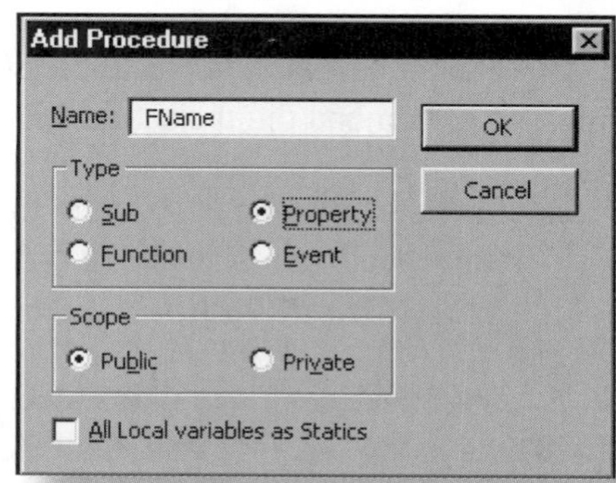

10. Select **frmSchoolData** in the Project Explorer and click **View Object**. Add three command buttons and a list box to the form, as shown in Figure 9-8. Change the names of the command buttons to **cmdAddFaculty**, **cmdSeeFaculty**, and **cmdExit**. Change the captions of the buttons to **&Add Faculty**, **&See Faculty**, and **E&xit**. Change the name of the list box to **lstFaculty**.

11. Open the Code window for frmSchoolData by clicking the **View Code** button in the Project Explorer window. Enter the

CODE STEP 7

```
Public Property Get FName() As String
  FName = sFName
End Property
Public Property Let FName(ByVal sNewValue As String)
  sFName = StrConv(Trim$(sNewValue), vbProperCase)
End Property
```

CODE STEP 9

```
Public Property Get LName() As String
  LName = sLName
End Property
Public Property Let LName(ByVal sNewValue As String)
  sLName = StrConv(Trim$(sNewValue), vbProperCase)
End Property
```

following declaration in the **General Declarations** section:

```
Dim FacultyList As New Collection
```

Later, this declaration will be replaced by a larger structure.

12. In **Private Sub cmdAddFaculty_Click**, press **Tab** and enter the code shown in **Code Step 12**.

In this code, NewFaculty is declared as a new object of the clsFaculty class. Data for the object is loaded using InputBox functions. The object is added to the FacultyList collection with the collection's Add method. The parameters of the Add method are the object's name and the object's key property. The key property is used to identify the object. It is unlike an array subscript because it does not have to be an integer or in any sequence at all.

FIGURE 9-8
The School Data form, showing arrangement of controls

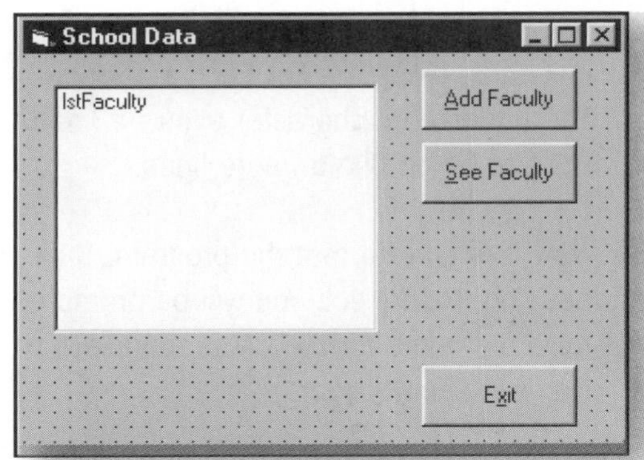

13. Press **Tab** and enter the **Unload Me** command in the **Private Sub cmdExit_Click** procedure.

14. In **Private Sub cmdSeeFaculty_Click**, press **Tab** and enter the code shown in **Code Step 14**.

In this code, the Dim statement declares an object variable capable of pointing to an object of clsFaculty type, but does not declare a new object of the type. Fac is

(continued on next page)

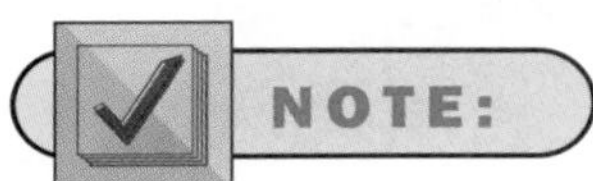

The End command is not a suitable way to end a program in a multiform project. The End command brings everything to a halt. Instead, use the Unload statement to remove each form as its job is finished.

CODE STEP 12

```
Dim NewFaculty As New clsFaculty
With NewFaculty
 .FName = InputBox("First Name:")
 .LName = InputBox("Last Name:")
 .IDNumber = InputBox("ID Number:")
End With
FacultyList.Add NewFaculty, NewFaculty.IDNumber
```

CODE STEP 14

```
Dim Fac As clsFaculty
For Each Fac In FacultyList
   lstFaculty.AddItem Fac.LName & ", " _
    & Fac.FName & vbTab & Fac.IDNumber
Next Fac
```

pointed to each object in the FacultyList collection using the For Each statement. The underscore character allows a line of code to be on two or more lines.

15. Now it is time to test the program. Save and run the project. You will be prompted for a file name for the Class module. Name it **Faculty.cls**.

16. Click **Add Faculty**. Enter names and ID numbers for two or three new faculty members. Click **See Faculty**. The entries you made appear in the list box, as shown in Figure 9-9.

17. Stop the program and leave it open for the next Step-by-Step exercise.

FIGURE 9-9
The School Data project

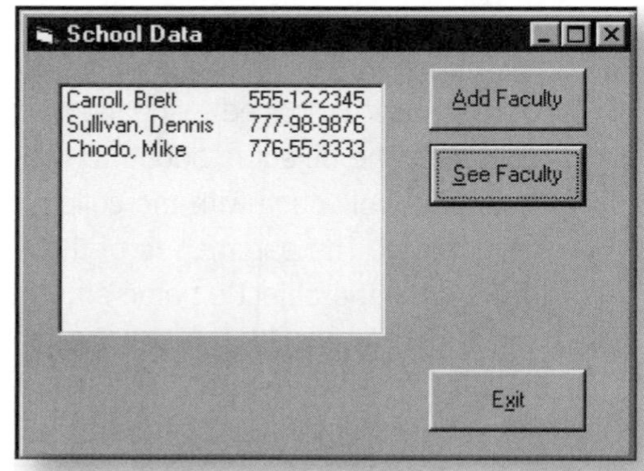

Now that this part of the program is working it is time to move up one step in the object hierarchy. Faculty members will be added to departments that are in turn parts of a school. You will create a new class for an Academic Department object.

STEP-BY-STEP 9.6

1. Click **Project | Add Class Module** from the menu bar. From the Add Class Module dialog box, select **Class Module** and click **Open**. Change the name of the Class module to **clsAcadDept**.

2. Add the code shown in **Code Step 2**.

   In this code, all the properties are fully exposed, bypassing any possibility for error trapping or correction. The Postage property is symbolic of the administrative and clerical detail that is a part of any department. The FacultyMembers collection will contain an entry for each faculty member of the department. The keyword New in the declarations means that when the property is accessed for the first time, a new collection will be created.

3. In the **Project Explorer** select **frmSchoolData** and click **View Code**. In the **General Declarations** section, make the following changes. Delete or comment out the line **Dim FacultyList As New Collection** because the collection of

CODE STEP 2

```
Public DeptName As String
Public Postage As Currency
Public FacultyMembers As New Collection
```

faculty members is now contained in the larger container of the Academic Department. Add the following line of code to the **General Declarations** section:

```
Dim adMusic As New clsAcadDept
```

The ad prefix indicates a variable of the clsAcadDept type.

4. Add the following line of code to **Private Sub Form_Load**:

```
adMusic.DeptName = "Music"
```

5. In **Private Sub cmdAddFaculty_Click**, change the reference to **FacultyList** to **adMusic.FacultyMembers**.

6. In **Private Sub cmdSeeFaculty_Click**, change the reference to **FacultyList** to **adMusic.FacultyMembers**. Enter the line shown in **Code Step 6** after the Dim statement.

7. Save and run the program. Save the new Class module file as **AcadDept.cls**. Enter a few names and ID numbers. Display the entries in the list box. The name of the department appears as the first entry in the list box. The user interface of the program is the same. The only difference is that faculty members are now stored in a collection contained in an object of the clsAcadDept type. Stop the program.

   This is a good opportunity to put together a number of programming techniques in a single sample that you will enter. The list box is used to display faculty members added to the department. The list box is also used to allow the user to select and process entries in the list box. The code you will enter displays just the last name of the faculty member when their entry is clicked. The name is displayed using a roundabout method to illustrate how members of a collection are retrieved. So far, you have iterated through the objects in a collection with the For Each command. In this next example, the object's key property is used to retrieve the object.

8. Double-click the list box on **frmSchoolData** to open the **Private Sub lstFaculty_Click** procedure. The code you will enter has two lines commented out. These lines were used to test the syntax as the code was entered. The program was run several times to test each new section of code. Debug lines are often commented out but left in the program in case further debugging is necessary. Enter the code shown in **Code Step 8**.

   In this code, the *ListIndex property* is set to the index number of the entry clicked by the user. If no item is selected, the ListIndex property is set to –1. Robust code would check for this condition and trap the possible error. The *List method* of the list box returns the line selected by the ListIndex property. The Trim function ensures there are no leading or trailing spaces. The InStrRev( ) function (VB6.0 only) searches the string from the right end looking for the tab character. The position of the tab is returned in the variable Start. The Right( ) function peels characters off the right side of the string. The IDNumber is separated from the entry and assigned to IDNumb. The IDNumber is used as the key property for the faculty objects in the collection of faculty

(continued on next page)

CODE STEP 6

```
lstFaculty.AddItem adMusic.DeptName
```

STEP-BY-STEP 9.6 CONTINUED

CODE STEP 8

```
Dim fac As clsFaculty
Dim IDNumb As Variant
Dim Entry As String
Dim Start As Integer
'MsgBox lstFaculty.List(lstFaculty.ListIndex)
Entry = Trim(lstFaculty.List(lstFaculty.ListIndex))
Start = InStrRev(Entry, vbTab)
IDNumb = Right(Entry, Len(Entry) - Start)
'MsgBox IDNumb
Set fac = adMusic.FacultyMembers.Item(IDNumb)
MsgBox fac.LName
```

members. The key is used as a parameter to the Item method. The Item method of a collection returns a pointer (remember, object variables are just pointers to the object's data) to the corresponding object in the collection. Fac is set to that object. MsgBox fac.LName displays the last name of the faculty member pointed to by fac.

9. Save and run the program. Enter two or more names. Click **See Faculty**. Click one of the entries displayed in the list box. The person's last name appears in a message box. Click **OK**.

10. Stop the program and leave it open for the next Step-by-Step exercise.

As a final stage you will add another class. The School class contains a collection of departments as well as information about the school itself. If you look back at the object model diagram at the beginning of the section, you see that this completes the steps up the ladder from faculty to departments to the school. In this next Step-by-Step exercise you add a class, two forms, and a module to declare variables needed throughout the project.

STEP-BY-STEP 9.7

1. Select **Project | Add Class Module** from the menu bar. From the Add Class Module dialog box, select **Class Module** and click **Open**. Change the name of the class module to **clsSchool**. Click **Save** and save the new Class module as **school.cls**.

2. In the **General Declarations** section, enter the code shown in **Code Step 2**.

3. Click **Project | Add Module**. Under the **New** tab, select **Module** and click **Open**. Change the name of the module to **mdlSchool**. Click **Save** and save the new

CODE STEP 2

```
Public SchoolName As String
Public Departments As New Collection
```

CODE STEP 3

```
Public LocalSchool As New clsSchool
Public Recent As String
```

module as **School.bas**. In the **General Declarations** section, enter the code shown in **Code Step 3**.

In this code, Recent will be used to recall a recently defined department that will be used to add faculty members to a department that has just been defined.

4. Select **Project | Add MDI form**. Make sure **MDIForm** is selected and click **Open**. The MDI form will become the new start-up form for the project. In this form, the user will be able to add a new department to the school, enter faculty members for the department, or list all the faculty members of each department. Change the name of the form to **mdiSchool**. Change the caption of the form to **Local School**. Click **Save** and save the MDI form as **School.frm**.

FIGURE 9-10
The Menu Editor dialog box for frmSchool

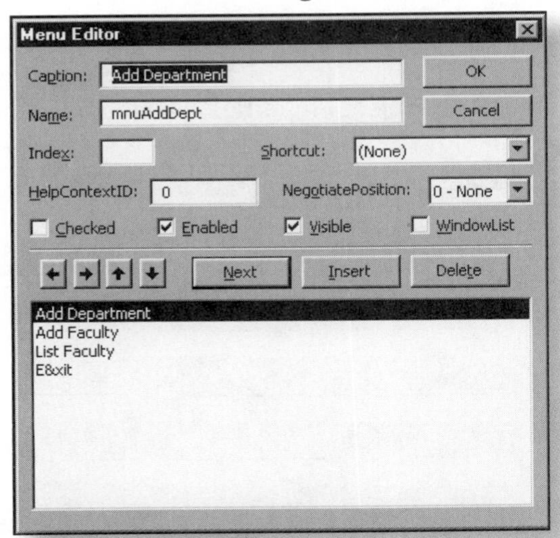

5. Open the **Menu Editor** and create the menu shown in Figure 9-10.

   The captions for the menu items are shown in Figure 9-10. Enter the following for the names: **mnuAddDept**, **mnuAddFaculty**, **mnuListFaculty**, and **mnuExit**.

6. Click **OK** to close the Menu Editor.

7. Press **Tab** and enter **Unload Me** in **Private Sub mnuExit_Click**.

8. In **Private Sub mnuAddDept_Click**, press **Tab** and enter the code shown in **Code Step 8**.

   In this code, NewDept is a temporary variable; a new object is created when it is used. Data is assigned to the object with Inputbox functions. The variable sDeptName is used in three places: first to set the DeptName property of NewDept, second as the key property of NewDept as it is added to the LocalSchool.Departments collection, and finally, to set the value of Recent.

9. In **Private Sub mnuAddFaculty_Click**, press **Tab** and enter the following line:

```
frmSchoolData.Show
```

10. In **Private Sub mnuListFaculty_Click**, press **Tab** and enter the following line:

```
frmAllFaculty.Show
```

(continued on next page)

CODE STEP 8

```
Dim NewDept As New clsAcadDept
Dim sDeptName As String
With NewDept
  sDeptName = InputBox("Enter department name:")
  .DeptName = sDeptName
  .Postage = CCur(InputBox("Enter Postage costs:"))
End With
LocalSchool.Departments.Add NewDept, sDeptName
Recent = sDeptName
```

This form hasn't been created yet!

Until now, frmSchoolData has been the whole show. It was the start-up form and it added faculty members to a single department. Now it has to be modified to serve as an input form for all the departments in turn. To minimize code changes, the variable adMusic will be used to refer to any department.

11. Select **frmSchoolData** in the Project Explorer window, and click **View Code**. In the **General Declarations** section, change the line Dim adMusic As New clsAcadDept to **Dim adMusic As clsAcadDept**. The New keyword you just deleted creates a new instance of clsAcadDept when adMusic is first used. Without the New keyword, adMusic is a pointer that points to an object of the clsAcadDept type.

12. In **Private Sub Form_Load**, delete or comment out the line adMusic.DeptName = "Music". Enter the code shown in **Code Step 12**.

    In this code, the first line sets adMusic to the most recently defined department. In a real application, the user would probably select the department name from a combo box. The Item method is used to retrieve the department object from its collection in the LocalSchool. The second line modifies the caption of frmSchoolData to reflect the department being modified.

    The changes to the General Declarations section and Form_Load allow the rest of the code to work unmodified. The big difference is in adMusic. With the changes, it just refers to a single department. Now the variable can be pointed to any of the departments defined in LocalSchool.

13. Click **View Form** in the Project Explorer. Click the body of **frmSchoolData**. In the Properties window, double-click **MDIChild** to set it to True and to make it a child form of mdiSchool that you created earlier.

14. Select **Project | Project1 Properties** from the menu bar. Select **mdiSchool** in the Startup Object combo box and click **OK** (see Figure 9-11).

FIGURE 9-11
The Project Properties dialog box, showing mdiSchool as the start-up form

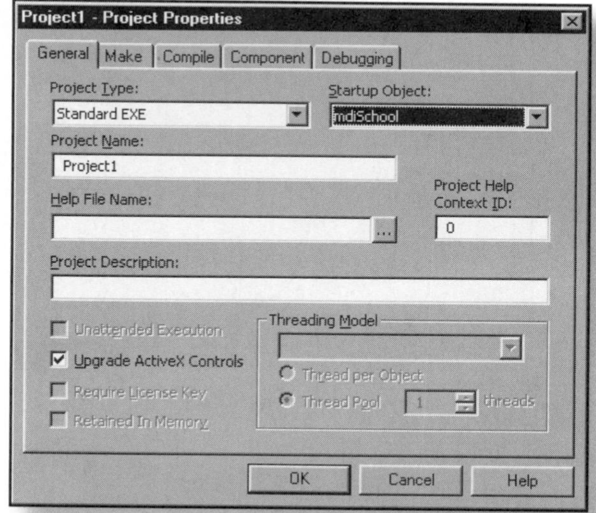

CODE STEP 12

```
Set adMusic = LocalSchool.Departments.Item(Recent)
frmSchoolData.Caption = "The " & Recent & " Department"
```

15. Save the project. You will be prompted for appropriate file names for each of the modules if you did not save them earlier. Be sure they are all being saved to the same directory.

16. Run the program. Click **Add Department** from the menu bar. Enter **Music** for the department name and **456.66** for the postage.

17. Click **Add Faculty** from the menu bar. Maximize **frmSchoolData** when it appears.

When a child form is maximized within a parent form, its menu bar (if it has one) replaces the menu bar of the parent and its caption is added to the title bar of the parent form.

18. Add some faculty members for the Music department. Click **See Faculty** to display the list, then exit the form.

19. Add the **Computer** department. Add some faculty members for the Computer department. Display their names and exit the form.

20. Stop the program.

21. Select **Project | Add Form**. Make sure **Form** is selected and click **Open**. Change the name of the form to **frmAllFaculty**. Change the caption of the form to **List All Faculty**. Click **Save** and save the form as **AllFaculty.frm**.

22. Select the form and open the **Menu Editor**. Enter a single menu item with the caption **E&xit**, the name **mnuExit**, and click **OK**.

23. Double-click **Exit** from the menu, press **Tab**, and enter the line **Unload Me** in its Code window.

24. Add a list box to the form. Change the name of the list box to **lstAllFaculty**.

25. Double-click the body of the form and enter the code shown in **Code Step 25** in **Private Sub Form_Load**.

    In this code, a couple of pointers are declared: dept to point to the department entry and fac to point to the faculty member of the department. For Each dept in LocalSchool.Departments iterates through the list of departments in the school. The name of the department is added to the list box. The next line For Each fac In dept.FacultyMembers iterates through each faculty member of the department. The name of each faculty member is added to the list box.

(continued on next page)

CODE STEP 25

```
Dim dept As clsAcadDept
Dim fac As clsFaculty
For Each dept In LocalSchool.Departments
  lstAllFaculty.AddItem dept.DeptName
  For Each fac In dept.FacultyMembers
    lstAllFaculty.AddItem fac.LName & _
      ", " & fac.FName
  Next fac
Next dept
```

26. Save and run the program.

27. Add a new department. Add faculty members to the department. Add another department and faculty members for the department. Click **List Faculty** from the menu bar. Each department's faculty appears in the list box.

28. Stop the program and exit Visual Basic if you are done.

This program shows how object relationships are captured when you implement an object model using classes and collections. To turn the program into a real application is still a big job.

Quick Check 9.e

1. An ____________________ ____________________ is a diagram that represents the hierarchical organization of classes and objects.
2. The characteristics of a ____________________ ____________________ refer to the program's ability to cope with or recover from errors.
3. With a multiform program, you should use ____________________ rather than ____________________ to terminate a form.
4. Writing small parts of a program and running the program each step of the way is called ____________________ ____________________.
5. When a child form is maximized within its parent form, the size of child form is ____________________ ____________________ to the interior dimensions of the parent form, and the ____________________ of the child is added to the title bar of the parent form.

Summary

- Controls can be added to and deleted from a form while a program is running.
- A collection is an object that contains a number of related objects.
- An object is a pointer to a Visual Basic object. Objects include forms, text boxes, labels, command buttons etc.
- Visual Basic has three built-in collections: The Forms collection is a collection whose elements represent each of the loaded forms of a project, the Controls collection is a collection that contains each of the controls on a particular form, and the Printers collection is a collection of all the installed printers.
- The For Each statement allows a program to iterate through the items in a collection.
- The New keyword in a Dim statement creates a new instance of the object as soon as the variable is accessed in the program.

- The special conditional expression TypeOf *ctrlObj* Is *Group* is true if the ctrlObj is the type of object contained in Group. For example, TypeOf obj Is Label is true if the object pointed to by obj is a label control.
- The Shell command is used to run a program from within a Visual Basic project.
- To add a new control to a form, the Load command creates a control from a model control that is already on the form. The model control must be defined as a control array.
- Parallel arrays contain information related through the common subscript value of the arrays.
- Format strings can be built and used in conjunction with the Format function to format dates, times, and values in an endless variety of ways. Typically, formatting of this type is used to set the number of decimal places in a displayed value.
- You remove a control from a form with the Unload command. You cannot remove a control put on the form at design time.
- Boundary conditions are the values at the extreme edges of the valid values. Testing a program's correctness at its boundary conditions is very important.
- The buttons of a toolbar form a Buttons collection. To add and delete buttons from a toolbar, use the Buttons collection's Add and Remove methods.
- A flag is a Boolean variable used to indicate a True or False condition.
- An object model shows the hierarchical relationships between classes and collections.
- A robust program is one that prevents errors by making them impossible.
- Incremental programming is writing small parts of the program and running the program each step of the way to confirm that everything is running correctly. Incremental programming helps localize errors to the statements most recently added to the project.
- The ListIndex property of a list box contains the Index number of an item selected by the user.
- The List method of a list box returns the item whose Index is supplied as a parameter to the List method.
- Nested For Each loops can cycle through items in collections of collections.

LESSON 9 REVIEW QUESTIONS

TRUE/FALSE

Circle the T if the statement is True. Circle the F is it is False.

T F 1. Once a form is designed, the number of controls shown on the form cannot be changed.

T F 2. A collection is an object that contains a number of related objects.

T F 3. The For Each statement is used to iterate through objects in a collection.

T F 4. As controls are created and added to the Controls collection of the form, the user must supply the correct index number for each control.

T F 5. To convert a control to a control array, set the control's ListIndex property to 0.

T F 6. Controls added at run time may be removed with the Unload command.

T F 7. A flag is set to equal the number of controls in the Controls collection.

T F 8. The Add method adds an object to a collection.

T F 9. The statement Dim Obj As clsAcadDept creates a new object of the clsAcadDept type.

T F 10. The Buttons collection is a built-in part of the toolbar.

WRITTEN QUESTIONS

Write your answers to the following questions.

11. Write the statements needed to change the font size of every control on a form to 12.
12. What kinds of things in Visual Basic are objects?
13. Write the statements needed to add a button to a toolbar.
14. Write a loop that changes the Visible property of every label on a form to False.
15. Make up an example that uses parallel arrays. Give name, data type, and purpose for each array.
16. Write a Format function that formats the value of PoundsPerUnit with three decimal places.
17. What statement removes a control from a form? A button from a toolbar?
18. How does Incremental Programming help control program bugs?
19. Name and describe each of the four parameters of the Add method.
20. What are the four methods and properties common to most collections?

LESSON 9 APPLICATION PROBLEMS

Level One

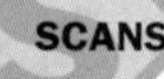

THE MOVING TEXT BOX PROBLEM

Write a program that moves text boxes. Add two text boxes and labels and three command buttons to the form. Program the first command button to add 120 twips to the Top property of each text box and label on the form. Use a statement like this to change the value of the Top property:

Ctrl.Top = Ctrl.Top + 120. Program the second command button to subtract 120 twips from the Top property of each text box and label. Have the third command button exit the program.

THE ALWAYS ANOTHER BOX TO FILL PROBLEM

Write a program with a single text box on the form. Whenever the user enters a string in the box and presses Enter, have the program add another text box below the first one, clear the text in the new text box, and adjust the size of the form to accommodate the new text box. If the user double-clicks the text box, have the program remove the text box from the form. Don't worry about filling in the gaps if the user double-clicks a text box in the middle of the column of text boxes.

COMPILING A LIST PROGRAM

Write a program to collect and display the names of wedding guests. As each name is entered in a text box and the user presses Enter, generate a new text box at the bottom of the list. If a guest's name is double-clicked, delete that text box from the form. When the user clicks a command button, have the names from the remaining text boxes displayed in a list box on the form.

MY VERY OWN BUTTON PROGRAM

Write a program to prompt the user to enter a person's first and last name when a command button is clicked. After both names are entered, have the program add a button to a toolbar for that person's name. Set the caption of the button to the first three letters of the person's last name. Use the Left function to return the first three letters of LName: Left(LName, 3).

SCANS

Level Two

CHAIN OF COMMAND PROGRAM

Write a program that captures the following simple object model: Principal, Teacher, Student. Have the program declare classes for Principal, Teacher, and Student. The Teacher class should include a collection of students. The Principal class should include a collection of teachers. Add three command buttons to the top of the form and a large list box under the buttons. Add an exit button below the list box. Program the first command button to prompt the user for the name of a single principal. Program the second command button to prompt the user for a teacher's name, followed by prompts for the students' names in that teacher's homeroom class. Program the third command button to list the principal, teachers, and their homeroom students.

THE MAGAZINE SUBSCRIPTION PROGRAM

Write a program to total the cost of the magazine subscriptions for a family. Define a class for the family that includes a collection of family members. Have the Person class include the person's name and a collection of magazines. Have the Magazines class include the title of the magazine and the cost of a subscription to the magazine.

Add three command buttons to the top of the form and a large list box under the buttons. Add an exit button below the list box. Program the first command button to prompt the user for the family's last name. Program the second command button to prompt the user for each family member's name, followed by the magazines they subscribe to and their price. Program the third command button to list each magazine and its cost for each family member. Have the program calculate the total amount for each family member and a grand total for the whole family.

LESSON 9 PROGRAMMING AT WORK

MUSIC COLLECTION PROJECT

SCANS

In this project, you will alter the Music Collection project to print a list of recorded users and their musical preferences.

1. Open the **MusicCol** project from Lesson 8.

2. Select the start-up form, **frmMusic** and open the **Menu Editor**. After the Data Grid menu item and before the separator, add the following menu item: Caption: **&Print User List**, Name: **mnuPrintUsers**.

3. Click **OK** to close the Menu Editor.

4. Open the form's Code window and enter this line in the **General Declarations** section: **Public Users As New Collection**. This declares a new collection used to store the user information.

5. In Lesson 8 you added the user preference file and handler. The contents of the user preference file is read when the form loads. The entire code for the revised Form_Load procedure is shown below. Enter only the changes marked as '*** add for lesson 9.

```
' all new for lesson 8
    ChDir App.Path
    Dim lstnr As clsListener
    Dim Nick As String, Pref As String
    Dim FileNumber As Integer
    With cboPref
         .AddItem "Bluegrass"
         .AddItem "Blues"
         .AddItem "Cajun"
         .AddItem "Classical"
         .AddItem "Folk"
         .AddItem "Gospel"
         .AddItem "Jazz"
         .AddItem "New Age"
         .AddItem "Rap"
         .AddItem "Rock"
         .ListIndex = 0
    End With

    'Open the Listener data file and load data.
    FileNumber = FreeFile
    On Error GoTo fileopenerror
    Open FileName For Input As FileNumber

    Do While Not EOF(FileNumber)
        Input #FileNumber, Nick
```

```
            Input #FileNumber, Pref
            lstListeners.AddItem Nick & vbTab & Pref
            ' *** add for lesson 9
            Set lstnr = New clsListener
            lstnr.NickName = Nick
            lstnr.Preference = Pref
            Users.Add lstnr
            Set lstnr = Nothing
            ' *** end of lesson 9 addition
        Loop
        Close FileNumber
        Exit Sub
    fileopenerror:
        MsgBox Err.Description
```

The additional lines copy information from the file into a variable of the clsListener type. The Add method adds the new user to the Users collection. When finished with the lstnr variable, the code sets the variable to Nothing to return its memory to the pool of free memory. You could run the program to check if there are any errors, but you would not learn much. There is no way yet to see if the listener profiles have been successfully added to the Users collection.

6. Next you will add a single line of code to **cmdOK_Click**. The entire procedure is shown below, with the line you are to add clearly marked as '*** add for lesson 9. Add the new line.

```
' all new for lesson 8
Dim lstnr As clsListener
Set lstnr = New clsListener
lstnr.NickName = txtNickName.Text
lstnr.Preference = cboPref.Text
With lstnr
   lstListeners.AddItem .NickName & vbTab & .Preference
End With
' *** add for lesson 9
Users.Add lstnr
' *** end of addition for lesson 9
Set lstnr = Nothing
lstListeners.Visible = True
fraAddUser.Visible = False
```

This line adds any new user to the Users collection.

7. An all-new procedure handles the printing duties. The procedure creates a new form using frmMusic as a pattern. The names and preferences are displayed on the form. Enter the following code in **Private Sub mnuPrintUsers_Click**:

```
' all new for lesson 9
Dim frmUsers As frmMusic
Dim lstnr As clsListener
Dim Answer As Integer
```

```
Set frmUsers = New frmMusic
With frmUsers
   .FontName = "Times New Roman"
   .FontSize = 14
   .FontBold = True
   .Height = 14 * 20 * (Users.Count + 7)
   .AutoRedraw = True
   .Show
End With
frmUsers.Print "User List"
frmUsers.Print
For Each lstnr In Users
    frmUsers.Print lstnr.NickName & vbTab & lstnr.Preference
Next lstnr
Answer = MsgBox("Confirm Print?", vbYesNo)
If Answer = vbYes Then
   frmUsers.PrintForm
End If
```

In this code, frmUsers is set to a new instance of frmMusic. This creates a new form in the project with all the properties (and code) of frmMusic. The font name and size are changed. FontBold is set to True. The Height is altered to accommodate the number of lines that will be displayed. Each line is set to 14 points. Each point is equal to 20 twips. The number of users is Users.Count. Several additional lines are added for proper spacing. The Height property of the new form is increased to make room for the names. Setting AutoRedraw to True means if the form is partly covered by another form and the other form is moved, the face of the form underneath redraws itself. A heading is printed on the form. The Users collection is used to control the printing of the users' names and preferences on the form. A confirmation is required before the form prints. The PrintForm method prints the client area of a form on the printer.

8. Save and run the program. Select **View | Print User List**. The new form appears with the user information on the face of the form (see Figure 9-12). A message box also appears, asking you to confirm the printing of the form. Click **Yes** if your system is connected to a printer.

9. Select **View | Exit** to stop the program.

This program uses two kinds of collections: It uses the Forms collection to create a new instance of an existing form, and it uses a Users collection to store information about user preferences. The PrintForm method is used to send a display to the printer.

FIGURE 9-12
The User List

CREATING AND USING NEW CONTROLS

UNIT 3

Estimated Time for Unit 3: 15 hours

LESSON 10

So That's How They Do It: The Microsoft Common Controls

OBJECTIVES

When you complete this lesson, you will be able to:

- Use each of the Microsoft Common Controls appropriately in application programs.

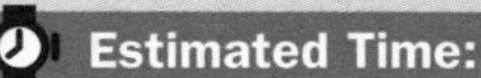

KEY TERMS

Windows Common Controls
ListImages collection
Stretch property
Static variable
ColumnHeaders collection
panels
Panels collection
tree metaphor
root
branch
leaf
family metaphor
parents
children
siblings
node
Nodes collection
hard-coded
ChDir App.Path
ChDrive App. Path
ZOrder

Images and Overview

What gives Windows programs their characteristic look and feel? It is the user interface. What makes the user interface possible? In part, the *Windows Common Controls*. You have already used a number of controls that package a lot of the Windows look in them. The Common Dialog control gives you access to a number of useful dialog boxes. The toolbar Control, a Windows Common Control covered in Lessons 5 and 9, not only introduces you to collections; it lets you easily add a toolbar with or without icons to any application.

In this lesson you will study the rest of the Windows Common Controls. The Windows Common Controls are listed in the table on the next page.

The ImageList Control

You used the ImageList control earlier in your first experience with the toolbar Control. In the following exercise, you will use the ImageList control as a source of images for a PictureBox control and an Image control. A PictureBox control can be used as a container for other Visual Basic controls or as a control to display images. An Image control is only used to display images on a form. Images can be stretched or shrunk to fit an Image control. In this exercise, you will use one command button to cycle through the images stored in the ImageList. You will use another button to display an Open dialog box, which allows the user to add images to the ImageList.

Building Programming Skills

Use white space to make your code more readable. Visual Basic tolerates all kinds of white space. You can leave spaces at the beginning of lines. You can also leave blank lines within the body of the code. Use both techniques to make your code more readable. Set related sections of code apart visually by skipping lines before and after the block. Use special comments to draw attention to sections of code. There is no penalty for including extra spaces and empty lines in your code.

WINDOWS COMMON CONTROLS

Control Name	Description
ImageList	Stores pictures for use with other Windows Common Controls.
TabStrip	Organizes controls in tabs that are selected by the user. Used in the Property Pages dialog boxes.
Toolbar	Uses captions and icons on buttons to provide an easy way to run commonly used operations.
StatusBar	Displays an informational bar, usually across the bottom of the form. The bar is organized into panels.
ProgressBar	Gives a visual display of progress through a lengthy process like loading or processing data files.
TreeView	Used as the left window in Windows Explorer, it gives a graphical display of information showing relationships between individual items.
ListView	The ListView control is similar in purpose to a list box but with many display enhancements. It is used as the right window in Windows Explorer.
Slider	An input device used to communicate a value within a particular range to the program.
ImageCombo	Adds images to a regular combo box.
Animation	Allows you to add silent video clips to your programs.
UpDown	An input device used to enter integer values into a program.
MonthView	Provides a box with a calendar-like display of a month.
DTPicker	Automates choosing a date.
CoolBar	Provides a frame for multiple toolbars.

STEP-BY-STEP 10.1

1. Start Visual Basic and double-click **Standard EXE**. Save the form and project as **Pictures**.

2. Change the name of the form to **frmPictureHolder**. Change the caption of the form to **Displaying Pictures**.

3. Before you can use the Windows Common Controls, they must be added to the toolbox. Right-click the toolbox and select **Components** from the pop-up menu. In the list of components, click the check boxes for **Microsoft Windows Common Controls**, **Microsoft Windows Common Controls-2**, and **Microsoft Windows Common Controls-3**. A version number may follow each name. At the time of this writing, it was version 6.0. Click **OK** to close the Components dialog box.

4. When the toolbox only displays two columns of controls, there may be too many controls to see them all on the

(continued on next page)

screen. If you can't see all of the controls click and drag the right border of the toolbox to resize the toolbox to display three or four columns of controls as shown in Figure 10-1. Hover the mouse pointer over each new control to read its name from the ToolTip.

FIGURE 10-1
The toolbox with the Windows Common Controls added

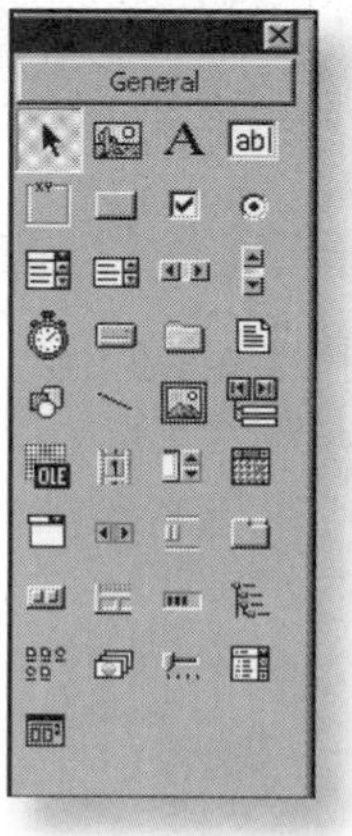

5. Double-click the **ImageList** control in the toolbox (not the Image tool) to add the control to the form. Leave the default name of the control, **ImageList1**, unchanged.

6. Normally, images are added to the ImageList at design time. In this project you will add images at design time and run time. Right-click the **ImageList** control and click **Properties** from the pop-up menu. From the Property Pages dialog box click the **Images** tab.

   Visual Basic comes with folders full of graphic images. In a full installation of Visual Studio, graphics are located in C:\Program Files\Microsoft Visual Studio\Common\Graphics\Icons. If they are not installed, they can be accessed from the Visual Basic program CD-ROM. If the graphic files are not loaded on your system, and you do not have access to the program disk, you can find some other source of picture files for this project.

7. Click **Insert Picture** at the bottom of the Image as tab. Navigate to the **Icons** folder and open the Computer folder. Select an image and click **Open**. (Remember any images will do.) Click **Insert Picture** again, select another image, and click **Open**. Continue until you have selected twelve images. Figure 10-2 shows the ImageList control loaded with 12 images. Click **OK** to close the dialog box.

FIGURE 10-2
The ImageList control loaded with 12 images

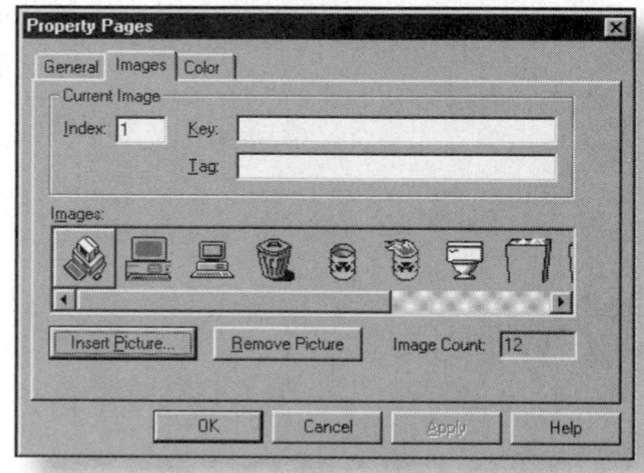

As you learned earlier the images are stored in the *ListImages collection* that is a part of the ImageList control. Like most other collections, the programmer does not have control over which index value an image receives. Not only do you not have control over the original index when images are removed from the ImageList control there is no telling how the indices of the remaining images are changed. Therefore when it is important to uniquely identify an image in the ListImages collection, you must use the image's Key property. In this application, however, images are displayed without regard to order.

8. Add **three command buttons** to the form as shown in Figure 10-3. Name the buttons **cmdCycle**, **cmdAddPicture**, and **cmdExit**. Change the captions of the buttons to **Cycle Picture**, **Add a Picture**, and **E&xit**. Open the Code window, select **cmdExit_Click**, press **Tab**, and add the code: **Unload Me**.

9. Select the **PictureBox** tool in the toolbox and draw a PictureBox control in the top right corner of the form. Name the picture box **picDisplay**. Select the **Image** tool and draw an Image control below the picture box. Change the name of the Image control to **imgDisplay**. Change the **Stretch** property of the Image control to **True**. With the *Stretch property* set to True, pictures are scaled to fit the Image control. This means that pictures larger than the Image control are made smaller to fit and pictures smaller than the Image control are enlarged. So using an Image control in your application can ensure that an image will fill a specified amount of space.

10. Select the **Slider** tool in the toolbox and add a Slider control between the PictureBox control and the Image control. (The Slider is one of the new controls that you added to the toolbox along with the other Windows Common Controls.) Leave the default name of the Slider control unchanged. You will use the Slider control as an input device in this project.

11. Right-click the **toolbox** and select **Components**. Click the check box for **Microsoft Common Dialog Control** and click **OK**. Double-click the **Common Dialog** tool in the toolbox to add the control to the form. Change the name of the Common Dialog control to **dlgGetPicture**.

FIGURE 10-3
The form layout for the Displaying Pictures project

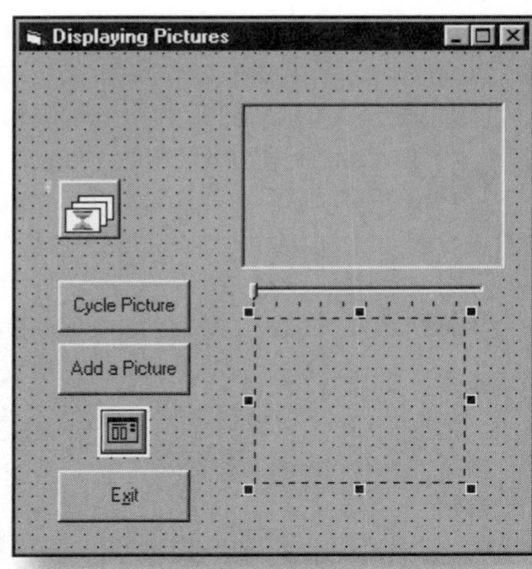

12. Open the Code window and select **cmdCycle_Click**. Press **Tab** and enter the code shown in **Code Step 12**.

This code uses the value of a variable to cycle through the images and display them in the two graphic controls.
The variable, CurrentIndex, is declared as a *Static variable*. The value of a Static variable persists beyond the end of the event procedure. This means that when the procedure is executed again, the old value of the Static variable is still present. Normally, variables created within an event procedure are re-initialized each time the event procedure is executed.

(continued on next page)

CODE STEP 12

```
Static CurrentIndex As Integer
CurrentIndex = CurrentIndex + 1
If CurrentIndex > ImageList1.ListImages.Count Then
    CurrentIndex = 1
End If
Slider1.Value = CurrentIndex
picDisplay.Picture = ImageList1.ListImages(CurrentIndex).Picture
imgDisplay.Picture = ImageList1.ListImages(CurrentIndex).Picture
```

ImageList1.ListImages.Count returns the number of images stored in the ImageList control. If the value of CurrentIndex exceeds the number of images, it is reset to one. The Value property of the Slider control is changed to set the indicator of the Slider control. This works the same way as a Horizontal Scroll Bar control. The last two statements copy the image from the ImageList control to the PictureBox and the Image controls.

13. Select **cmdAddPicture_Click**. Press **Tab** and enter the code shown in **Code Step 13**.

    In this code the first line displays the Open dialog box. The Open dialog box lets the user browse for and select picture files. The If statement is used to check the PathName. If it is empty, a message is displayed informing the user that they have entered an invalid file name.
    If the file name is valid, the LoadPicture function adds the picture to the ListImages collection of the ImageList1 control.

14. Select **Slider1_Click**, press **Tab**, and enter the code in **Code Step 14**.

    In this code you add the prefix "int" to the variable name Value to prevent confusion with the property name Value. The slider's Min and Max properties are set to the starting and ending index numbers of the images in the ImageList control. There must be two or more images in the ImageList control because if the slider's Max value is less than or equal to its Min value, an error is generated. The Value property of the Slider control reports the location of the pointer with reference to the Min and Max values set earlier. The position of the slider determines the value of the Value property of the control. The image that corresponds to the value of the slider is assigned to the PictureBox and the Image controls.

15. Save and run the program. Click the **Cycle Picture** button repeatedly to view each of the images stored in the ImageList

CODE STEP 13

```
dlgGetPicture.ShowOpen
Dim PathName As String
PathName = dlgGetPicture.FileName
If PathName <> "" Then
  ImageList1.ListImages.Add , , LoadPicture(PathName)
Else
  MsgBox "Invalid File Name"
End If
```

CODE STEP 14

```
Dim intValue As Integer
Slider1.Min = 1
Slider1.Max = ImageList1.ListImages.Count
intValue = Slider1.Value
picDisplay.Picture = ImageList1.ListImages(intValue).Picture
imgDisplay.Picture = ImageList1.ListImages(intValue).Picture
```

control. Click enough times to be sure the list is repeating. Use the mouse to drag the Slider. As the pointer comes to rest in a new position the images change.

If you prefer to click the slider rather than drag the pointer, adjust the Large Change property of the Slider control (the default is 5).

16. Click **Add a Picture**. Navigate to a source of pictures. One place to look is in the picture cache maintained by your Internet browser. Load a few pictures from the disk. Cycle through the pictures again to make sure the images you added are included in the ImageList.

17. Stop the program and leave the project open for the next Step-by-Step exercise.

This project used the ImageList as an anonymous collection of images. The images were displayed without consideration to what was being shown. To control the appearance of specific images in your applications, you must utilize the Key property of each image. The only sure way to access a particular image is to refer to it by its Key property.

Quick Check 10.a

1. You should not use the Index property to keep track of a particular image in an ImageList control because ___________________ .
2. Images in the ImageList control are contained in the ___________________ collection, a part of the ImageList control.
3. If the Stretch property of an ___________________ is set to True, images will be automatically sized to fit in the box.
4. The Slider control, part of the Windows Common Controls, works similar to the ___________________ control.
5. To load a picture into the Picture property of a PictureBox control or Image control, use the ___________________ function.
6. Write the expression that returns the number of images in the ImageList1 control: ___________________.

Viewing Lists and Status Bars

If you have used the Windows Explorer to examine drives and folders, you are already familiar with the ListView control because the right pane of the Explorer works like this control. You use a ListView control to display a list of items in one of four different views. Code included in an object's Click, DblClick, or ColumnClick event is executed when the user executes one of those actions. For example when a user double-clicks a document icon in the Explorer, a program opens and loads the document. A status bar can be added to a form to display the name of the view. The four views are:

- 0-lvwIcon displays each item in the list using a large icon provided by an ImageList control. A short description accompanies each icon. The item's subitems are not displayed.
- 1-lvwSmallIcon displays each item's description next to a small icon provided by a second ImageList control.
- 2-lvwList displays items arranged in a single column with a small icon accompanied by a short description.
- 3-lvwReport displays each item with a small icon, a short description and each of the subitems displayed in adjacent columns.

In the next Step-by-Step exercise you will program a button to cycle through the four views. To shorten the development time, you will add the ListView control to the application from the last Step-by-Step exercise because it already has an ImageList control. Other than that the ListView portion of the program is unrelated to the 10.1 exercise. The program also uses another shortcut by using the same ImageList for all three ImageList controls used by the ListView control. Normally, the control uses a separate ImageList for small icons, large icons, and icons shown in the column headings in the Report view.

STEP-BY-STEP 10.2

1. If necessary, open the **Pictures** project. Move and shrink the PictureBox control to make room for the ListView control. Select the **ListView** tool in the toolbox and draw a ListView control at the top of the form. In the Properties window, change the name of the control to **lvwImages**. Add two command buttons to the form. Name them **cmdLoadLV** and **cmdRotate**. Change the captions to **Load LV** and **Rotate View**. See Figure 10-4 for placement of controls.

FIGURE 10-4
Alterations to the Displaying Pictures project

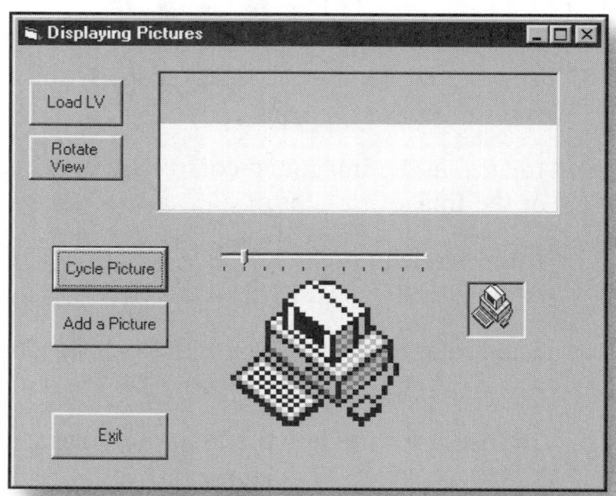

2. Right-click the **ListView** control and select **Properties**. Change the **View** property to **3-lvwReport**, as shown in Figure 10-5. The General tab of the Property Pages dialog box shows many of the ListView control's properties. You can set the properties while the form is being designed, or set the properties later when the program is running. Figure 10-4 shows the result of the change to the View property at run-time: The ListView control shows a gray upper edge. The upper edge will become the display area for the column headings in Report view. The white portion of the box displays the list. This application will set other properties for the control while the program is running. Other tabs in the Property Pages dialog box allow the designer to add text to the column headings and to set up the ImageList controls.

3. Click **OK** to close the Property Pages dialog box. Open the Code window and select **cmdLoadLV_Click**. Press **Tab** and enter the code shown in **Code Step 3**.

The first three lines of code set the ImageList resources for the large icons, small icons, and column header icons. As mentioned earlier this project uses the same ImageList for all three views. The Report view shows three columns. The width of the columns is found by, dividing the width of lvwImages (given in the Width property) by 3. You will use this value to set the width of the columns in the Add method that adds new columns to the ListView control. A variable, clmX, of the Column Header type is declared. The Add method then adds new column headers to the *ColumnHeaders collection* of the ListView control. The parameters of the Add method are:

FIGURE 10-5
The Property Pages dialog box for the ListView control

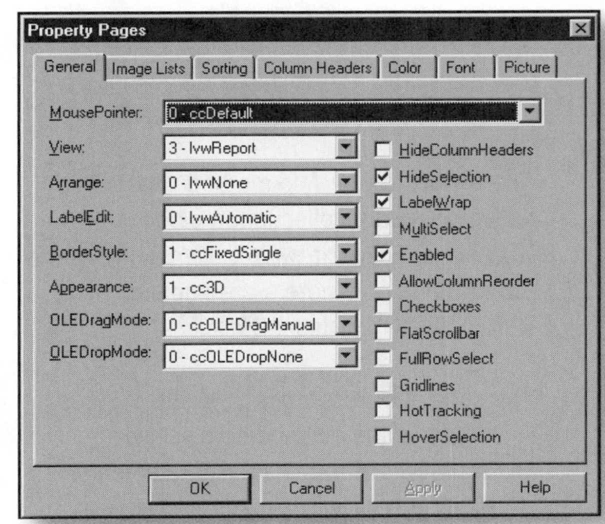

- Index—the number assigned to the new ColumnHeader object in the ColumnHeaders collection.
- Key—the best way to identify the new ColumnHeader.
- Text—the text that accompanies the icon in the column header (enclosed in quotation marks).
- Width—the width of the column in twips. The default value is 1440.0.
- Alignment—the alignment of the text in the column: lvwColumnLeft, lvwColumnRight, or lvwColumnCenter.

(continued on next page)

CODE STEP 3

```
lvwImages.Icons = ImageList1
lvwImages.SmallIcons = ImageList1
lvwImages.ColumnHeaderIcons = ImageList1

Dim W As Integer
W = lvwImages.Width / 3

Dim clmX As ColumnHeader
Set clmX = lvwImages.ColumnHeaders.Add(, , "First", W, , 1)
Set clmX = lvwImages.ColumnHeaders.Add(, , "Second", W, , 2)
Set clmX = lvwImages.ColumnHeaders.Add(, , "Third", W, , 3)

Dim itmX As ListItem
Set itmX = lvwImages.ListItems.Add(, , "magnetism", 4, 5)
itmX.SubItems(1) = "14"
itmX.SubItems(2) = "25"
lvwImages.GridLines = True
lvwImages.View = lvwSmallIcon
```

- Icon Index—the index number of the small icon to insert in the column heading.

The syntax for the Add method of the ColumnHeaders collection is *object.Add(index, key, text, width, alignment, icon)*. Blank parameters are supplied automatically by Visual Basic.

The code declares itmX as a ListItem types. A ListItem is the actual data displayed in the ListView control. The next statements provide the item with a name and an icon and two subitems: 14 and 25. The syntax for the Add method of the ListItems collection is *object.Add(index, key, text, icon, small icon)*. The SubItems and the item itself are meaningless examples used just to show how the ListView control works. The Gridlines property, when set to True, displays fine black lines separating the cells when the program is run and the display is set to the Report view.

4. Select the **cmdRotate_Click** procedure, press **Tab**, and enter the code shown in **Code Step 4**. This statement advances to the next image in the list, but always resets the image number back to 0 when 3 is exceeded.

5. Save and run the program. Remember the part of the program using the ListView control is separate and unrelated to the part of the program that illustrates the use of the ImageList control. Click **Load LV**. The last line of Private Sub cmdLoadLV_Click sets the control to display items using the small icon view mode. An icon flanked by the word *magnetism* appears in the ListView control on the form. Click the **Rotate View** button several times. Note the changes in the views. (If necessary, stop the program and adjust the size of lvwImages, save the change and run the program again.)

6. Click **Load LV** two or three more times. Each time the button is clicked, another set of identical column headers and another identical list item is added to the ListView control. Click the **Rotate View** button several times. With several list items in the control, you can better see the differences between the display modes.

7. Stop the program. Leave the project open for the next Step-by-Step exercise.

CODE STEP 4

```
lvwImages.View = (lvwImages.View + 1) Mod 4
```

The Status Bar Control

When the Rotate View button is clicked, there is no way to tell the name of the view that is being used to display the data. To fix this problem, you will add a status bar to the bottom of the form. The StatusBar control is part of the Windows Common Controls you already added to the toolbox. The status bar is a common feature of Windows programs. It usually appears across the bottom of the form with a number of *panels* used to convey different information to the user. For example the status bar called the taskbar, located across the bottom of the Windows 95 or 98 desktop displays the Start button (with its Windows icon) to the left of panels that display other active programs. The right-most panel shows the time and icons for programs that are running resident in memory.

STEP-BY-STEP 10.3

1. If necessary, open the **Pictures** project. Double-click the **StatusBar** tool in the toolbox. It will automatically position itself at the bottom of the form because this is its default position. Leave the name **StatusBar 1**. You can change the status bar's Align property in the Properties window at either design time or run time to change the position of the status bar on the form. For now, leave the status bar in the default position. The status bar also responds to the Click and DblClick events, as do each of its panels.

2. Right-click the body of the **status bar** and select **Properties** to open the Property Pages dialog box. The Style property determines the kind of status bar that will be displayed by the program. The sbrNormal style is the multipanel style you are used to seeing. The 1-sbrSimple style will display a single panel. In this Step-by-Step exercise you want the status bar to display two panels, so leave the Style property set to **0-sbrNormal**.

3. Click the **Panels** tab in the Property Pages dialog box (see Figure 10-6). Most of the property items shown on the tab are familiar by now; not because you have used panels before, but because the status bar's *Panels collection* is much like other collections you have used. Each panel has an Index Key, and Tag property. You could set a different minimum width so a panel does not disappear if there is no text in it. But for now, leave the default setting. The Picture frame lets you browse through directories, looking for appropriate icons to display in a panel. The icons would accompany any text included in the panel's Text property. The first panel is already a part of the Panels collection. The starting value for the Index property of a panel in the Panels collection is 1.

4. Click **Insert Panel** to insert another panel in the Panels collection. There are several styles of panels. Some come linked to useful information. Just add them to the status bar to display the status of the Num Lock key, the Caps Lock key, or the Date or Time. Click the **right arrow** for the Index property. With the Index property set to **2**, click the Style combo box's list arrow and select **5-sbrTime** for the panel's style. The table on the next page summarizes the available panel styles.

(continued on next page)

FIGURE 10-6
The Panels tab

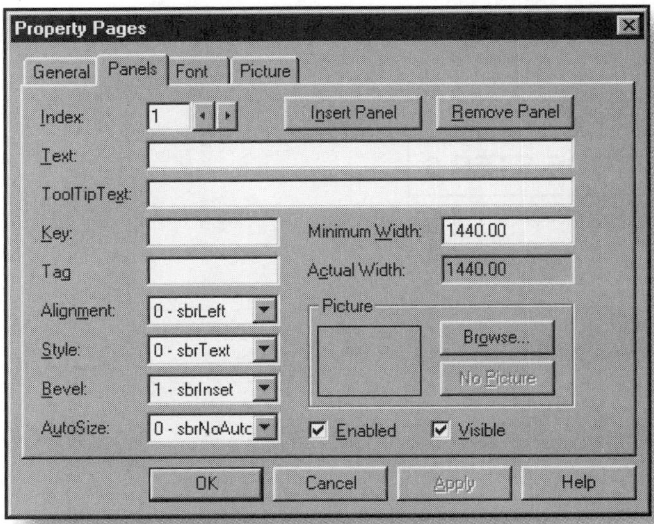

PANEL STYLES	
0-sbrText	Displays text or pictures inserted into the panel's Text property. The Text property is usually set while the program is running.
1-sbrCaps	Displays the status of the Caps Lock key.
2-sbrNum	Displays the status of the Num Lock key.
3-sbrIns	Displays the status of the Insert key.
4-sbrScrl	Displays the status of the Scroll Lock key.
5-sbrTime	Displays the current system time.
6-sbrDate	Displays the current date.

5. Click the **Font** tab in the Property Pages dialog box, change the font size to **12**, then click **OK**. You can probably see the effect of the font change immediately. If the font is too big, increase the height of the status bar. There are two ways you can change the height. In form design view, select the status bar, click the handle at the top of the control, and drag to resize the control to a new height. You can also change the control's Height property in the Properties window.

6. Open the Code window and select **cmdRotate_Click**. Enter the code shown in **Code Step 6** after the existing line of code.

   This code displays the current view of the ListView control in the status bar.

   You can access the panels using either the Index property or the panel's Key property. In this application, the Index property is used. The Text property of the panel contains the text displayed in the panel.

CODE STEP 6

```
Select Case lvwImages.View
    Case 0
        StatusBar1.Panels(1).Text = "0-lvwIcon"
    Case 1
        StatusBar1.Panels(1).Text = "1-lvwSmallIcon"
    Case 2
        StatusBar1.Panels(1).Text = "2-lvwList"
    Case 3
        StatusBar1.Panels(1).Text = "3-lvwReport"
End Select
```

7. Save and run the program. Click **Load LV** a few times to load some entries in the ListView control. Click **Rotate View** several times and note the text in the first panel in the status bar. The text most likely doesn't fit in the panel.

8. Stop the program. Right-click the body of the **status bar** and select **Properties**. Click the **Panels** tab. If necessary, change the Index property to 1. There are two ways to change the width of a panel. The first is to alter the value in the Minimum Width property of the panel. The second method is to change the panel's AutoSize property. Click the **list arrow** for **AutoSize** and select **2-SbrContents**. Click **OK** to close the dialog box.

9. Save and run the program. Click **Load LV** a few times. Click **Rotate View** several times. Notice that the size of the panel adjusts to fit the contents inserted in its Text property.

10. Stop the program and remove the project.

Building Programming Skills

Program documentation includes the following:

- Who wrote the program, when the program was written, and for what platform.
- What the program does and who will use the program.
- How to use the program.
- What values program variables represent.
- Explanations for each procedure and function, including a list of preconditions and post-conditions. Preconditions are the status and values of the parameters before the procedure or function is executed. Post-conditions are the status and values of the parameters after the procedure or function has executed.

Most people avoid writing documentation. Unfortunately, for any program longer than a page, documentation is necessary. After a month, even code you knew so well that you dreamed about it will seem incomprehensible unless there is documentation to remind you of what the code does and how it does it.

Quick Check 10.b

1. When an item in a ListView control is clicked, code in the control's ____________ , ____________ , or ____________ events is executed.

2. To provide images for the items in a ListView control, use one or more ____________ controls.

3. Properties of the ListView control are either set at design time or at ____________ .

4. The default value of a column in the ListView control is ____________ twips.

5. Rotate the views in the ListView control using a Mod operator. If x = 5, what is the value of x Mod 4? ____________

6. Information displayed in a status bar is contained in ____________ .

The TreeView Control

The TreeView control is next on the list for investigation. It is designed to display data that is hierarchical in nature, such as files and folders on a disk and organization tree structures. For example the TreeView control is at work in the left pane of the Windows Explorer. There it is used to display the relationship between the folders and files on a disk. A discussion of hierarchical data usually consists of a mixture of two metaphors: the tree metaphor and the familay metaphor. The **tree metaphor** uses the *root* as the first item in the hierarchy of the tree then the *branch* as an item in the tree that is neither a root nor a leaf, then the *leaf* as an item in the tree with no branches. The *family metaphor* uses *parents*, *children*, and *siblings*. Any entry on the tree is called a *node*. Two adjacent entries with the same parents are siblings. A descendant is a child. Traveling up the tree in the other direction, you find the parent of a node. The topmost level is called the root node. Each node in a tree is a programmable node object which belongs to the Nodes collection. As with other collections, each member has a unique Index and Key property. Each node typically consists of an image (set with the Image property) and a label (set with the Text property). There are two ways to add Node objects to Node Collections. You can use the Add method or you can declare an object variable of the type Node and then use the set statement with the Add method.

The next exercise demonstrates many of the properties and methods of the TreeView control. First you will initializes a tree from a simple text file. Once the tree is initialized and displayed, you can add or remove entries by clicking existing entries. In this example you will add code to give the user three choices when an entry is clicked: get information about the entry, add to an entry, or remove an entry from the tree. The Add option will further prompt the user to enter a spouse's name, a sibling's name, or a child's name. The tree will update automatically to show the new relationships. The Remove option will remove an item and all of its descendants from the tree.

STEP-BY-STEP 10.4

1. Start a new **Standard EXE** project. Save the form and project as **FamTree**.

2. Change the name of the form to **frmFamily** and the caption of the form to **Family Tree**.

3. Right-click the **toolbox** and select **Components** to open the Components dialog box. Select the three entries for the **Microsoft Windows Common Controls 6.0** by clicking the check box for each one. Click **OK** to close the Components dialog box.

4. If necessary, resize the toolbox to show the additional controls. Locate the TreeView tool using the mouse pointer and the ToolTip. Select the **TreeView** tool in the toolbox and draw a TreeView control on the form. Change the name of the TreeView control to **Tre1**.

5. Add three command buttons. Change the captions of the buttons to **Clear the Tree**, **Save the File**, and **E&xit**. Change the names of the buttons to **cmdClear**, **cmdSave**, and **cmdExit**.

6. Select the **ProgressBar** tool in the toolbox and add a progress bar below the command buttons. Change the name of the progress bar to **prg1**. See Figure 10-7 for the final appearance of the form. You use the progress bar to inform the user about the progress of any long process. Two examples are, the progress bar in an Internet browser is used to show the status of page loading and a progress bar is often used to show file transfer status. In this program, the progress bar will show the status of saving the nodes from the TreeView control in a text file.

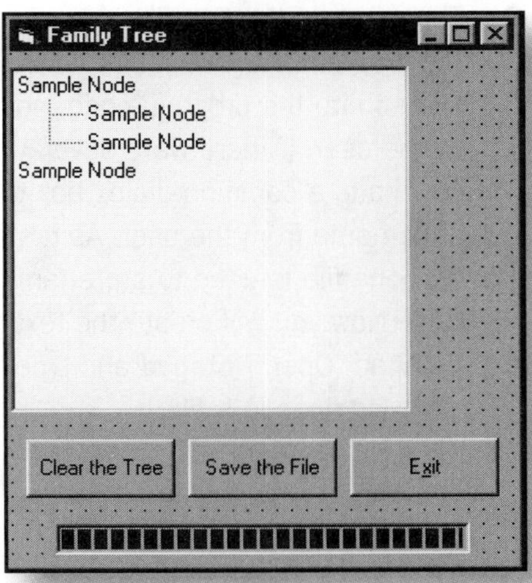

FIGURE 10-7
The Family Tree form showing placement of controls

7. Open the Code window and select **Form_Load**. Press **Tab** and enter the code shown in **Code Step 7**.

   The first step in this code is to declare variables for the fields in a text file that will be used to build nodes in the TreeView control. (The data in the text file is shown in Step 9.) Then the variable nodX is declared as a Node type. It will be used to point at various nodes added to the TreeView control. Then the text file is opened for input and the Input # statement reads the family name stored in the first record of the text file. Then the Add method creates the root node in the *Nodes collection* of the control. The parameters of the Add method are Relative, Relationship, Key, and Text. If a

(continued on next page)

CODE STEP 7

```
Dim Relative As String
Dim Relationship As String
Dim RShip As Variant
Dim Kee As String 'Use alternate spelling for Key.
Dim Txt As String 'Use alternate spelling for Text.
Dim nodX As Node
Dim FamName As String
prg1.Visible = False   ' Turn off the progress bar.
ChDrive App.Path         ' Change default drive.
ChDir App.Path           ' Change default directory.
tre1.Nodes.Clear           ' The Clear method clears sample nodes.
Dim FileNumber As Integer
FileNumber = FreeFile
Open "sprague.txt" For Input As FileNumber
Input #FileNumber, FamName   ' Family name for the root node.
Set nodX = tre1.Nodes.Add(, , "Root", "Grandpa_" & FamName)
Do While Not EOF(FileNumber)
   Input #FileNumber, Relative, Relationship, Kee, Txt
   If Relationship = "tvwChild" Then
         RShip = 4
   Else
         RShip = ""
   End If
   Set nodX = tre1.Nodes.Add(Relative, RShip, Kee, Txt)
   nodX.EnsureVisible
Loop
Close FileNumber
```

parameter is left blank, Visual Basic provides generic values. The first parameter, Relative, indicates to whom the entry is related. The second parameter, Relationship, specifies the relationship between the new node and the node named in Relative. The Key parameter is used to uniquely identify each node of the tree. In this example the key is generated from the first few letters of the person's name. The person's name is the fourth parameter in the list. Next a Do While loop reads the rest of the records in the file and adds a node to the control for each entry. The control sorts out the entries and adds each one in its proper relation to the other entries using the parameter properties. RShip=4 is the parameter that indicates the new node is to be added as the child of the previous node. For each item added to the control, the item is set equal to nodX whose EnsureVisible method is used to ensure the item appears in the TreeView control.

The complete syntax for the Add method of the TreeView control is *object*.Add(*relative, relationship, key, text, image, selectedimage*)

Besides the four parameters used and described, the optional Image parameter can provide an image number for an icon from an ImageList control to represent the item. The SelectedImage parameter can provide an image number for an icon to represent the item when it has been selected in the TreeView control. This project does not use an ImageList control.

8. Save the project.

9. The name of the text file is hard-coded in the program. *Hard-coded* means a value is written into the program code, not entered by the user. If there were several files you could add a common dialog box to collect a file name from the user. As it stands, only one file is used to store family tree data. Now you will create the text file in Notepad. Open **Notepad** and type the following lines in a file:

```
Sprague
Root, tvwChild,D, Dorothy
Root, tvwChild,B, Betty
Root, tvwChild,M, Mildred
Root, tvwChild,By, Byron
```

10. Save the file as **sprague.txt** in the same folder used to store the project file, then close Notepad. The *ChDrive App.Path* and *ChDir App.Path* lines in Form_Load make the drive and directory containing the application the default drive and directory. Putting the data file there ensures it will be found by the program.

11. Run the Family Tree project. The nodes are created and the relationships are displayed. Click the plus and minus signs to expand and collapse the tree. Stop the program.

12. The TreeView control has both Click and NodeClick events. The Click event is fired when the body of the TreeView control is clicked. The NodeClick event fires when an entry in the TreeView control is clicked. The NodeClick event reports which node is clicked in its parameter list. Next you will add code to the NodeClick event to allow the user to display information, add or delete nodes. Open the Code window and select **tre1_NodeClick**. Press **Tab** and enter the code shown in **Code Step 12**. (Do not run the program to test it until after Step 14.)

CODE STEP 12

```
Dim Msg As String
Dim SibNode As Node
Dim KidCounter As Integer
Dim Info As Integer
prg1.Visible = False
On Error GoTo ErrorHandler
Info = CInt(InputBox("Information, Addition, or Deletion? _ <Info=1, Add=2, Delete=3>"))
If Info = 1 Then
  If Node.Key = "Root" Then  'Special case
      Msg = "The Root Node, Patriarch"
  Else
      Msg = "Parent " & Node.Parent
  End If
  Msg = Msg & vbCr & vbLf
  If Node.Children = 0 Then
      Msg = Msg & "No children."
  Else
      Msg = Msg & "Children:"
      Msg = Msg & vbTab & Node.Child
      Msg = Msg & vbCr & vbLf
      Set SibNode = Node.Child
      KidCounter = SibNode.FirstSibling.Index
      Do While KidCounter <> SibNode.LastSibling.Index
         Msg = Msg & vbTab & tre1.Nodes(KidCounter).Next.Text
         Msg = Msg & vbCr & vbLf
         KidCounter = tre1.Nodes(KidCounter).Next.Index
      Loop
  End If
  MsgBox Msg
```

This part of the code handles the display information choice. It displays a message box showing the node's parents and children, if any exist. You build the message with several assignment statements. You add information to Msg with statements like Msg = Msg & .... If the root node is clicked, a special message is printed. When other nodes are clicked, a message with a list of the node's parents and children is displayed. The constants vbTab, vbCr, and vbLf represent the codes that display the tab, carriage return, and line feed characters. A carriage return and line feed together cause the message to split into a new line.

Visual Basic passes Node as a parameter to the event procedure. It identifies which node was clicked by the user. Node.Child returns a pointer to the node's first child. You access other child nodes as siblings of the first child. After the initial child's name is added to the message, you set the node variable SibNode equal to the child node. A Do While loop iterates through the child's siblings. The line KidCounter = tre1.Nodes(KidCounter).Next.Index advances KidCounter to its next value. The values assumed by KidCounter are not necessarily sequential.

(continued on next page)

The last line of code, MsgBox Msg, displays the complete message.

You may be tempted to replace the code shown with a simple For loop. The code seems to loop from the child node's first sibling's index value to the child node's last sibling's index value. It does not. The index properties of nodes are set by the order in which the node was added to the TreeView control. If you add a child to a particular node, add a child to another node, then return to the first node to add a sibling, the index numbers will not be sequential for siblings. As previously noted there is no way to guarantee a particular index value for a particular member of a collection.

13. Next enter the code shown in **Code Step 13** in the **tre1_NodeClick** event procedure below the code entered earlier.

    This section of code handles the addition of new nodes to the TreeView control. Each new node requires a relative, a relationship with the relative (child, sibling, etc.), a key value, and a text value. Spouses don't get separate nodes. They are added to the Text property of the node that was clicked. This line of code–Set NewNode = tre1.Nodes.Add(Node.Key, tvwNext, Left(SibName, 3), SibName)–adds a new sibling to an existing node. The relative of the new node is the key value of the clicked node. Visual Basic sends the clicked node as a parameter to the event procedure. The relationship constant, tvwNext, indicates that the new node is a sibling of the clicked node. The key value of the new node is the left three characters of the sibling's name. The scheme does not check for the uniqueness of the key. This would be a problem if more than one family member has the same name.

    The procedure to add a child to the control is in a Do While loop, so that more than one child can be added at the same time.

14. Now add the code shown in **Code Step 14** as the final installment in the **tre1_NodeClick** event pro-cedure below the existing code.

    If 3 is entered in the InputBox, the clicked node is removed from the TreeView control. The spouse and all of the node's children, if any exist, are also removed. The Remove method uses the node's index as a parameter to identify the node to remove.

    The error handler is a simple message box to display the description of the error.

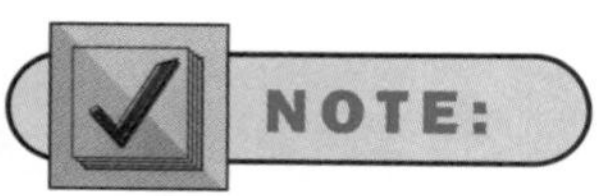

If an error condition exists in the code, the error handling code may actually hurt your chances of finding the error. When a run-time error occurs, you normally have the option of entering Debug mode. In Debug mode, the line that causes the error is highlighted and you can use the cursor to examine values of variables in the line. When the error handler is active, an error message (that may or may not be very informative) is displayed, but you may not be able to determine what line causes the error. If this happens, comment out the On Error line and let the program crash so you can enter Debug mode.

15. Save and run the program. Click a node and enter **1** to see information about the node. Click a node and enter **2** to add nodes. Add a spouse's name, a sibling's name, and a child's name. New nodes will appear. Click a node and enter **3** to remove the node.

16. Stop the program.

17. Open the Code window and select **cmdClear_Click**. Press **Tab** and enter the code shown in **Code Step 17**. The Clear method clears all nodes from the TreeView control.

18. Select **tre1_Click**. Press **Tab** and enter the code shown in **Code Step 18** to start a new family tree.

(continued on next page)

CODE STEP 13

```
ElseIf Info = 2 Then ' addition to the tree
 Dim NewNode As Node
 Dim SpouseName As String, SibName As String
 Dim ChildName As String
 Dim RShip As Integer
 RShip = MsgBox("Spouse?", vbYesNo)
 If RShip = vbYes Then
    SpouseName = InputBox("Enter the spouse's name:")
    Node.Text = Node.Text & "=" & SpouseName
 End If
 RShip = MsgBox("Sibling?", vbYesNo)
 If RShip = vbYes Then
    SibName = InputBox("Enter the sibling's name:")
    Set NewNode = tre1.Nodes.Add(Node.Key, tvwNext, Left(SibName, 3), SibName)
    NewNode.EnsureVisible
 End If
 RShip = MsgBox("Child?", vbYesNo)
 Do While RShip = vbYes
    ChildName = InputBox("Enter the Child's name:")
    Set NewNode = tre1.Nodes.Add(Node.Key, tvwChild, Left(ChildName, 3), ChildName)
    NewNode.EnsureVisible
    RShip = MsgBox("Child?", vbYesNo)
 Loop
```

CODE STEP 14

```
 ElseIf Info = 3 Then
     tre1.Nodes.Remove (Node.Index)
     Exit Sub
 End If
 Exit Sub
ErrorHandler:
 MsgBox Err.Description
```

19. Select **cmdExit_Click**, press **Tab**, and enter the line **Unload Me**.

20. Select **cmdSave_Click**, press **Tab**, and enter the code in **Code Step 20** to save the contents of the TreeView control in a simple text file.

    The progress bar has Min and Max properties that define the range of the bar. You initialize the Max property to the number of nodes in the TreeView control. As nodes are saved, you modify the Value property of the progress bar to indicate the progress of the save. You set the Value property from the Index property of the nodes as they are saved. The Visible property of the bar is set to False in the Form_Load procedure. Its Visible property is set to True in this procedure.

    The Family name is stored in the Text property of the root node. It is separated from the rest of the text string with the InStr( ) function. This function locates the position of the underscore character. That position is used in the Right( ) function to peel off the family name from the entire string. The family name is printed into the text file as its first entry.

    The For Each statement iterates through each item in the Nodes collection of the TreeView control. The root node is not added to the file since the family name is saved separately. Items are printed into the file separated by commas, so an Input statement can separate the different input fields.

A semicolon in a Print statement puts print items adjacent to each other. A comma separating items in a Print statement puts each print item in a separate print zone. Print zones are about nine characters wide.

CODE STEP 17

```
Dim Answer As Integer
Answer = MsgBox("Are you sure?", vbYesNo, "Clear the Tree")
If Answer = vbYes Then
   tre1.Nodes.Clear
End If
```

CODE STEP 18

```
Dim Answer As Integer
If tre1.Nodes.Count = 0 Then
 Answer = MsgBox("Would you like to start a new tree?", vbYesNo, "New Tree")
 If Answer = vbYes Then
   Dim nodX As Node
   Dim FamilyName As String
   FamilyName = InputBox("Enter the name of the Family's root:", "New Root")
   Set nodX = tre1.Nodes.Add(, , "Root", FamilyName)
 End If
End If
```

When all the nodes are processed, the file is closed.

If the Visible property of the progress bar was set to False immediately following the loop, there is a chance that you would never see it. On many of today's systems, the time it takes to save a modest file is negligible. Once a node in the tree is clicked, the Visible property of the progress bar is set to False and the progress bar disappears.

CODE STEP 20

```
Dim TreeNode As Node
Dim FileNumber As Integer
Dim FamName As String
Dim UnderScorePos As Integer
If tre1.Nodes.Count = 0 Then
    MsgBox "No nodes in the tree."
    Exit Sub
End If
' Set up the progress bar.
prg1.Min = 0
prg1.Max = tre1.Nodes.Count
prg1.Value = 0
prg1.Visible = True
' Open the file.
FileNumber = FreeFile
Open "sprague.txt" For Output As FileNumber
FamName = tre1.Nodes("Root").Text
UnderScorePos = InStr(1, FamName, "_")   ' Family name.
FamName = Right(FamName, Len(FamName) - UnderScorePos)
Print #FileNumber, FamName
' Process the rest of the nodes of the Tree.
For Each TreeNode In tre1.Nodes
   'MsgBox TreeNode.Text
   If TreeNode.Key <> "Root" Then
     Print #FileNumber, TreeNode.Parent.Key; ", tvwChild,"; _
       TreeNode.Key; ", "; TreeNode.Text
     prg1.Value = TreeNode.Index
   End If
Next TreeNode
Close #FileNumber
```

21. Save and run the program. Click **Clear the Tree** and the current nodes are removed. Click in the **Tree View** control and answer **Yes**. Enter a **root** name. Click the **root** name and enter 2. Try out each of the features of the program. Click **Save the File** to save your changes. Stop the program and restart it. The changes you saved should be visible. Stop the program again and remove the project.

Use the TreeView control to show relationships. Think about ways you can use the control to communicate with the user.

Quick Check 10.c

1. Talking about data displayed in a TreeView control usually involves two metaphors: the __________________ metaphor and the __________________ metaphor.

2. Each TreeView control can have __________________ root nodes.

3. The __________________ method is used to clear all nodes from the TreeView control.

4. The four parameters of the Add method used in this project are __________________, __________________, __________________ , and __________________.

5. You can not use a For loop to iterate through the children of a given node, because the index values of the child nodes are not necessarily __________________.

6. The __________________ method is used along with the node's index number to delete a node from the TreeView control.

More Common Windows Controls

The TabStrip control lets a user view and select different options. When another tab is clicked, the user is presented with a different set of options. A tab can display the equivalent of a dialog box: a mixture of text boxes, check boxes, command buttons etc. A tab can even display a TreeView control or ListView control. A tab can display anything, but unlike a frame or Picture Box control, the TabStrip control is not a container. A Container control actually contains objects within its boundaries. Controls are linked to the container and appear or disappear with the container. Typically, related controls such as option buttons are grouped in container controls and then are selected by user input.

One way to turn a TabStrip into a container is to put a frame or other container control in the TabStrip. The event procedure triggered by a click on a tab can then be used to turn the container on or off. If the container occupies the entire area of the TabStrip, you control the appearance of the containers with the *ZOrder* property of the container control. A ZOrder of zero brings an object to the forefront. A form is organized into three planes. The top plane has a ZOrder of zero.

In the following Step-by-Step exercise you will use a TabStrip control to demonstrate the difference between a regular combo box and an ImageCombo box. The ImageCombo box is another of the Windows Common Controls. It is similar to the regular combo box in that it lets the user select from a list of predefined options, and it also includes an icon with each text description. The ImageCombo control automatically sizes itself to accommodate the icon. It uses the ImageList control as a source of images.

Programming the ImageCombo box is different from writing code for the regular combo box. To add an item to the list of a regular combo box, you use the AddItem method. The ImageCombo uses a now familiar collection of objects to provide choices for the user. You add items to the collection with the Add method.

An additional Windows Common Control that you will add to the project in this exercise is the UpDown control. The UpDown control works with a "Buddy" control (a text box in this project). It increases or decreases the value in the Buddy control depending on which arrow the user clicks.

STEP-BY-STEP 10.5

1. Start a new **Standard EXE** project, Save the form and project as **TabDemo**.

2. Change the name of the default form to **frmTabDemo**. Change the caption of the form to **TabStrip and ImageCombo**.

3. Right-click the toolbox and select **Components** from the pop-up menu. In the Components dialog box select the three entries for the **Microsoft Windows Common Controls 6.0**. Click **OK** to close the dialog box.

4. Locate the TabStrip control in the toolbox using the mouse pointer and the ToolTip. Select the **TabStrip** control in the toolbox and draw a TabStrip control on the form. Leave the default name unchanged.

5. Right-click the **TabStrip** control and select **Properties** to open its Property Pages dialog box. Under the **General** tab, click the **HotTracking** option. When the program is running and the mouse is hovering over a tab, the tab is automatically highlighted when HotTracking is set to True.

6. Click the **Tabs** tab in the Property Pages dialog box. Enter the **Caption** of the first tab as **Combo Box**. Enter the **Key** property as **RegularCombo**. Enter the **ToolTipText** as **Demonstrating the Regular Combo Box**.

7. Click the **Insert Tab** button to insert a second tab. Enter the **Caption** and the **Key** property of the second tab as **ImageCombo**. Enter the **ToolTipText** to **Demonstrating the ImageCombo Box** as shown in Figure 10-8.

8. Click **OK** to close the Property Pages dialog box of the TabStrip.

9. Draw a regular Combo Box and an ImageCombo box on the TabStrip control as shown in Figure 10-9. (Single click the controls in the toolbox and draw the controls on the form. Do not double-click the controls in the toolbox.) Name the regular combo box **cboIndustry** and the ImageCombo box **imgcboImage**.

10. Add an **ImageList** control to the form. Right-click the **ImageList** control and select **Properties** to open its Property Pages dialog box. Click the **Images** tab. Click **Insert Picture** and navigate to a folder that contains icons. The images used in this Step-by-Step exercise were found in C:\Program Files\Microsoft Visual Studio\Common\Graphics\Icons\Industry. If this folder is not present on your system, find another source of icons and add them to the ImageList. Add at least **six images**. Write down the index number for each image you add. Click **OK**. This application uses four images in the Imagecombo box and two images on the tabs.

(continued on next page)

FIGURE 10-8
The Tabs tab of the TabStrip control, showing the addition of a second tab

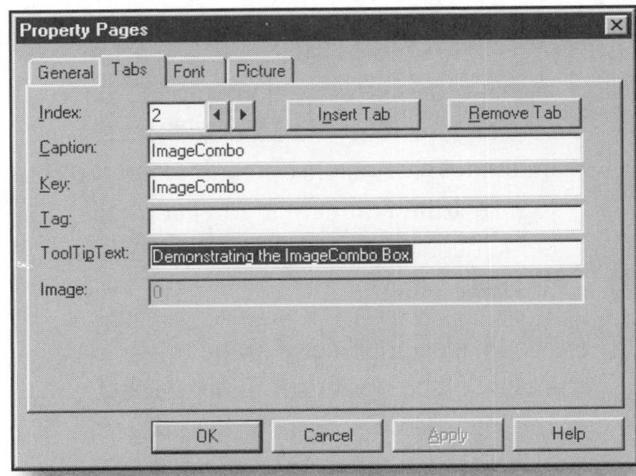

11. Add a command button to the form. Change the name of the command button to **cmdExit**. Change the caption of the button to **E&xit**.

12. Add a **text box** to the form. Change the name of the text box to **txtStyle**. Change the **Text** property to **0**. Add an **UpDown** control on the right side of the text box. The UpDown control icon in the toolbox looks like a vertical scroll bar icon next to a text box. Change the **AutoBuddy** property of the control to **True**. You want the UpDown control to work with the text box to provide a value for the style number used to control the appearance of the TabStrip control. So change the **BuddyControl** property to **txtStyle** if necessary. (It may change automatically when the AutoBuddy property is set to True.) Change the **SyncBuddy** property to **True**. Change the **Min** property to **0** and the **Max** property to **2** to represent the range of style settings for the TabStrip control. See Figure 10-9 for placement of controls.

13. Open the Code window and select the **Form_Load** procedure. Press **Tab** and enter the code shown in **Code Step 13** to set up the combo boxes and the TabStrip control. Substitute appropriate names for the images you loaded.

    In this code items are added to the regular combo box with the AddItem method. The ListIndex property is set to **0** to select the first item in the list as the default choice. The **Visible** property is set to **True**.

    The ImageList property of the ImageCombo box is set to **ImageList1**. This provides a source for the images used for each item. The collection of items are accessed with .ComboItems and the Add method is used to add four new entries (four of the six images you loaded). As usual, the first parameter is the Index. This is set automatically if the entry is blank. The second parameter is the Key . The third parameter is the Text. The fourth is the Image number. This number corresponds to an image in the ImageList control. Be sure to use the index numbers you wrote down for the appropriate images. A fifth parameter (not used in this application) specifies a second image from the ImageList control. This image is used when the item is selected by the user. A sixth parameter (also not used in this application) controls the indentation of the items in the ImageCombo box. Indentation is used to group entries under categories in the ImageCombo **control**.

    The code adds the items and then sets the Visible property to False.

    The exercise also uses images for each tab item. The last part of the code sets the TapStrip's ImageList property to the ImageList control. The tabs form a collection (surprised?). The line .Tabs(1).Image = 5

FIGURE 10-9
The Final placement of controls

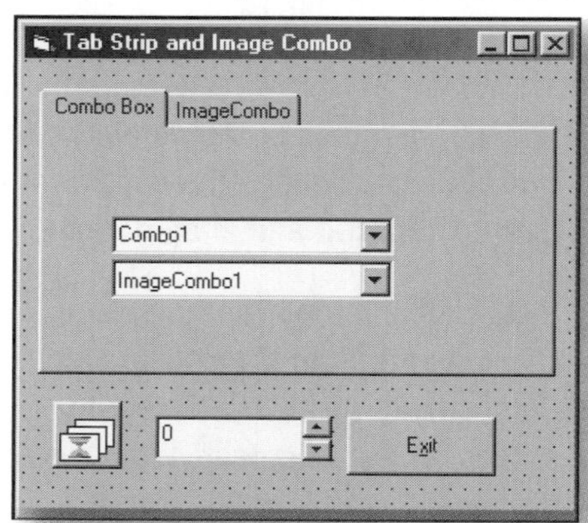

sets the Image property of the first item in the Tabs collection to the fifth image of the ImageList control. Be sure to use the correct index numbers for the images you loaded.

14. Select **cmdExit_Click**, press **Tab**, and enter **Unload Me**.

15. Select **txtStyle_Change**, press **Tab**, and enter the following code to change the appearance of the TabStrip control:

```
TabStrip1.Style = CInt(txtStyle)
```

There are three possible settings for the Style property: 0, 1, and 2. They correspond to the normal tab style, 3-D button style, and flat button style. The code reads the contents of the text box and converts it to an integer. The UpDown control allows the user to change the values.

16. When a tab is clicked, the **Private Sub TabStrip1_Click** event is executed. The index number of the selected tab is not sent as a parameter to the event, but it is available as a property of the TabStrip. Select **TabStrip1_Click**, press **Tab**, and enter the code shown in **Code Step 16**.

TabStrip1.SelectedItem returns the selected tab. The Index property is used to identify the tab that is clicked. The Key property could have been used to process the code. A Case statement is used (although an If-Then statement would be sufficient) to show how you would process a TabStrip with more than two tab items. Clicking the first tab makes the regular combo box visible and the ImageCombo box invisible. Clicking the second tab reverses the boxes. If a Container control had been used, the code could change the Visible control by resetting the ZOrder of the container to bring one or the other of the containers to the front.

(continued on next page)

CODE STEP 13

```
With cboIndustry
    .AddItem "Airplane"
    .AddItem "Cars"
    .AddItem "Factory"
    .AddItem "GasPump"
    .ListIndex = 0
    .Visible = True
End With
With imgcboImage
    .ImageList = ImageList1
    .ComboItems.Add , , "Airplane", 1
    .ComboItems.Add , , "Cars", 2
    .ComboItems.Add , , "Factory", 3
    .ComboItems.Add , , "GasPump", 4
    .Visible = False
End With
With TabStrip1
    .ImageList = ImageList1
    .Tabs(1).Image = 5
    .Tabs(2).Image = 6
End With
```

CODE STEP 16

```
Dim WhichTab As Integer
WhichTab = TabStrip1.SelectedItem.Index
Select Case WhichTab
    Case 1
        cboIndustry.Visible = True
        imgcboImage.Visible = False
    Case 2
        cboIndustry.Visible = False
        imgcboImage.Visible = True
End Select
```

17. Save and run the program. Select an item from the regular combo box. Click the **ImageCombo** tab. Select an item from the ImageCombo box. Select another item. Click the **UpDown arrows** button several times to see all the styles available for the TabStrip. While displaying a different style, select each of the tabs in turn. Everything works the same way it did before except the appearance is different.

18. Stop the program. Leave the program open for the next project.

Building Programming Skills

Write prompts that explain what is expected of the user. For example, InputBox should never have a prompt of "Enter:." Communicate to the user what he or she is to enter. Give the user an example of proper input.

When displaying data, write code to identify exactly what the output means. Display units along with values: Don't display 17 when the answer is 17 ft.

When displaying a table of data, use a control that organizes the data nicely into columns and rows, like the Microsoft Hierarchical FlexGrid. Use tab characters in list boxes to space data into columns.

The DateTimePicker Control

Users sometimes need to supply dates and times to a program. It is easy to provide the current date using the Now function, but supplying other dates can be more difficult. The Now function returns a Variant data type Date using the current date and time from your computer's system date and time. Converting the proper format is awkward and prone to error. The DTPicker control provides an easy way to help the user enter dates and times into a program. The DTPicker is like a combo box dedicated to dates and times. When the list arrow on the right edge of the control is clicked, a calendar showing the current date displays below the control. Then it is easy to select a date by clicking it with the mouse. When selected the date appears in the text box area of the control. The date is stored in the control's Value property and can be accessed and used at run-time.

In the next Step-by-Step exercise you add a new tab to the previous project. Then you add a DTPicker control and an UpDown control to the TabStrip. The UpDown control is linked to the DTPicker control so the user can alter the Format property of the control. The Format property controls the way dates and times display in the DTPicker control. A format value of 0 displays a short date. A value of 1 displays a long date. A value of 2 displays the time. You can change each part of the display by clicking on that part and entering new values. In the time display, click the hours and enter a new value. Just the hours value changes.

STEP-BY-STEP 10.6

1. If necessary, open the **TabDemo** project.

2. Select the form and right-click the **TabStrip** control. Select **Properties** from the pop-up menu to open the control's Property Pages dialog box.. Click the **Tabs** tab and click the right arrow next to the Index property to select the second tab. Click **Insert Tab.** Enter **DTPicker** for the Caption and the Key property. Enter **Date Time Picker Control Demo** for the ToolTipText property. Click **OK** to close the Property Pages dialog box of

the TabStrip control. The Tab Strip control now has three tabs. You may have to make both the form and the TabStrip control wider to accommodate the third tab item. Use the mouse to resize the form and TabStrip, if necessary.

3. The icon for the DTPicker tool is similar to the icon for the ComboBox tool. Single-click the **DTPicker** tool in the toolbox and draw a control on the TabStrip control. It is OK to partially cover one or both of the other controls already on the TabStrip. Change the name of the control to **dtpDate**.

FIGURE 10-10
The Property Pages for the DTPicker control

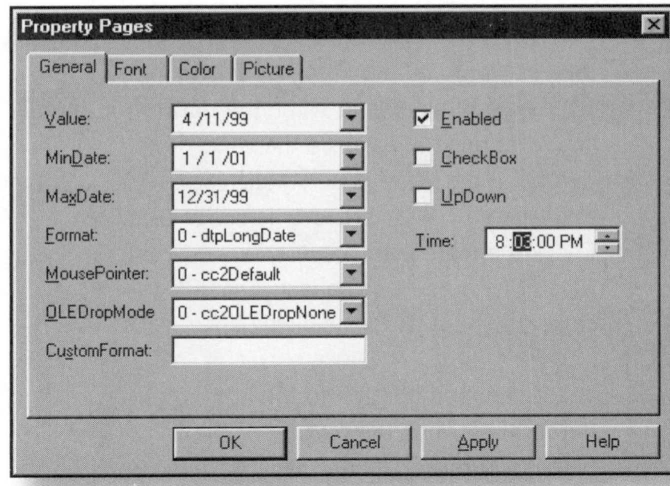

4. Right-click the **DTPicker** control and select **Properties** from the pop-up menu.

The Value property shows the current date. The Value property is the whole point of the control because it provides a date or time that can be used in the program. You use the MinDate and MaxDate properties to set a legal range of dates for the control. The default values cover a huge range of time because the MaxDate shown, *12/31/99*, actually refers to December 31, 9999.

The Format property determines how the date or time is displayed. The default is the Short Date (which does not display the first two digits of the year). Long Date, Time, and Custom formats are also available. If the CheckBox property is selected a check box appears in front of the date or time. If the UpDown property is selected, a tiny UpDown control is added to the DTPicker control. The UpDown control lets the user change the date or time by clicking the up or down arrows. The Time property determines the time that will be displayed. You will want to experiment with other settings in the tabs of the Property Pages dialog box – especially the color options.

5. Change the **Format** property to **0-dtpLongDate**. Change the default time by clicking on the **hour** in the **Time** property box. Just the two hour digits are highlighted. Enter **8**. Select the minutes digits and enter **3** as shown in Figure 10-10. Click **OK** to close the dialog box.

6. Draw an **UpDown** control to the right of the DTPicker control. This is the second such control on the form. Leave the default name, UpDown2, unchanged. Right-click the **UpDown** control and select **Properties** to open its Property Pages dialog box (see Figure 10-11).

7. Leave the setting in the General tab unchanged and click the **Buddy** tab. Select the **AutoBuddy** and **SyncBuddy** options. Change the **Buddy Control** property to **dtpDate**, if necessary. The Buddy control property determines which property of the Buddy control gets its value from the UpDown control. This application will use the UpDown control to change the value of the Format property of the DTPicker control. So select **Format** as the **Buddy Property**.

(continued on next page)

8. Click the **Scrolling** tab. Set the **Min** property to **0** and the **Max** property to **2**. Select the **Wrap** option. When the UpDown control is used to advance the value beyond 2, the Value is automatically reset to 0 when the Wrap property is set to True. Check the **Increment** property under Scroll Rate to be sure its value is **1**. Click **OK** to close the Property Pages dialog box.

FIGURE 10-11
The Property Pages of the UpDown control

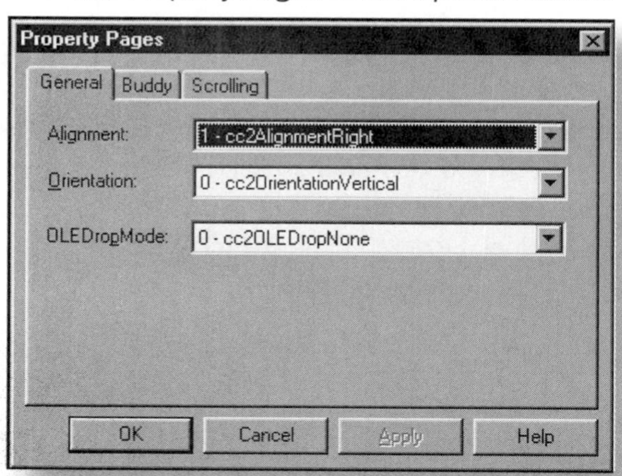

9. Add a command button to the bottom of the form. Change the caption of the button to **Read DTPicker**. Change the name of the button to **cmdReadPicker**. The final arrangement of controls on the form is shown in Figure 10-12.

10. Open the Code window and add the following code to the end of the **Form_Load** event procedure to accommodate the new controls added to the form:

```
With dtpDate
    .Visible = False
End With
UpDown2.Visible = False
```

FIGURE 10-12
The TabStrip and ImageCombo form, showing the addition of the DTPicker control

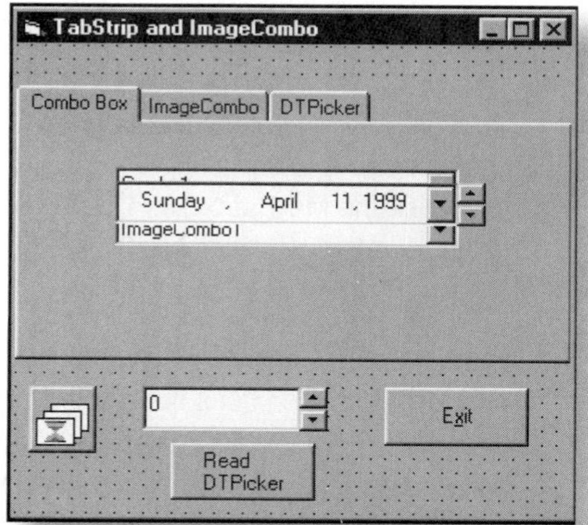

11. Change the code in **TabStrip1_Click** to match the code shown in **Code Step 11**. The new lines of code are shown in bold face. The new code turns the controls off and on by changing the value of their Visible properties.

12. Select **cmdReadPicker_Click**, press **Tab**, and enter the code shown in **Code Step 12**.

    This code reads the Format property of dtpDate to determine which format string to use to display the value of the control. In a real application, the value of the control might be used to record a time or date in a database. Or the date might be used to print an amortization table or calculate interest on a loan.

    The UpDown control was linked to the DTPicker control using the Buddy Control property so code is not necessary to make the make that connection.

13. Save and run the program. Select each tab in turn and work each of the controls displayed by the TabStrip. Use the UpDown control to change the display format of the DTPicker control.

14. Click **Read DTPicker**. A message box with the properly formatted value of the dtpDate control is displayed.

15. Stop the program and exit Visual Basic.

CODE STEP 11

```
Dim WhichTab As Integer
WhichTab = TabStrip1.SelectedItem.Index
Select Case WhichTab
   Case 1
      cboIndustry.Visible = True
      imgcboImage.Visible = False
      dtpDate.Visible = False
      UpDown2.Visible = False
   Case 2
      cboIndustry.Visible = False
      imgcboImage.Visible = True
      dtpDate.Visible = False
      UpDown2.Visible = False
   Case 3
      cboIndustry.Visible = False
      imgcboImage.Visible = False
      dtpDate.Visible = True
      UpDown2.Visible = True
End Select
```

CODE STEP 12

```
Dim FormatString As String
Select Case dtpDate.Format
Case 0
   FormatString = "Long Date"
Case 1
   FormatString = "Short Date"
Case 2
   FormatString = "Long Time"
End Select
  MsgBox Format(dtpDate.Value, FormatString), , "DTPicker.Value"
```

The Microsoft Windows Common Controls are fun and easy to use. They are part of what gives each Windows program its unique look and feel. In addition, they provide a lot of ways to make data input easier for the user. Anything that makes data input easier minimizes errors. But do not use the controls just because they are there. Use the controls every time it makes the user interface better.

Quick Check 10.d

1. Unlike frames and picture boxes, the TabStrip control is not a ________________.
2. Images for the ImageList control are provided by a ________________ control.
3. To add an item to an ImageList control, add the item to the ________________.
4. To link an UpDown control to a text box, set the ________________ property of the UpDown control.
5. The DTPicker control lets a user enter a ________________ or a ________________.
6. The Format property of the DTPicker control determines ________________.

Summary

- The look and feel of Windows programs is due, in part, to the Windows Common Controls used by Windows applications.
- Many controls use collections. The ImageList control uses the ListImages collection. The ListView control uses the ColumnHeaders collection. Mastering the syntax of collections (which varies slightly from control to control) is necessary to mastering the Windows Common Controls.
- The ImageList control provides images for each of the Windows Common Controls that use images.
- A picture box is both a Container control that can contain other Visual Basic controls, and a control used to display images.
- You use an Image control to display images on a form. Images can be stretched or shrunk to fit the control.
- You use the Slider control as a graphical input device. The Slider control is similar to the horizontal scroll bar.
- The ListView control displays lists of items in one of four viewing modes: large icon, small icon, list, and report. The right pane of Windows Explorer is a ListView control.
- The StatusBar control appears across the bottom of a form and displays program information to the user. The objects on a status bar are panels.
- Several built-in panel styles let the program designer build informative status bars.
- The TreeView control is used in the left window of Windows Explorer to display the folder structure of a disk.
- A TreeView control displays a number of Node objects. Each node is added to the Nodes collection by specifying the new node's Relative, Relationship, Key, and Text parameters.
- The ChDir App.Path and ChDrive App.Path lines in Form_Load make the directory and drive containing an application the default.

- The Index values of siblings in a TreeView control are not necessarily sequential.
- The TreeView control has a Click event and a NodeClick event. The Click event fires when the body of the TreeView control is clicked. The NodeClick event fires when an entry is clicked.
- You add nodes to a TreeView control with the Add method. You use the Remove method to remove a node from the control.
- The For Each statement iterates through items in a collection.
- The InStr( ) function locates the position of one string within another.
- The Right( ) function returns a fixed number of characters from a string counting from the right end of the string.
- A progress bar informs the user about the progress of a long process, such as loading a file.
- The Clear method removes all nodes from a TreeView control.
- The TabStrip control provides tabs for the user to make selections from the TabStrip control is not a container, though in use, it appears to be one.
- The ImageCombo control is similar to a combo box that provides a list for users to choose from. In addition it provides an icon for each description. Items added to the ImageCombo box are stored in a collection.
- The ZOrder of a control determines in which plane the control appears on the form. A ZOrder of zero brings a control to the front.
- The UpDown control works with a "Buddy" control. It adjusts the value in the Buddy control up or down depending on which arrow the user clicks.
- The DTPicker, DateTimePicker, control is a combo box dedicated to dates and times. Four formats are available: long date, short date, time, and custom.

LESSON 10 REVIEW QUESTIONS

TRUE/FALSE

Circle the T if the statement is true. Circle the F if it is false.

T F **1.** The primary purpose of the Windows Common Controls is to enhance the look and feel of the user interface.

T F **2.** The ListImages control provides images for most of the Windows Common Controls.

T F **3.** The ListView control is used in Windows Explorer to display the directory structure of a disk.

T F **4.** The items displayed in a TreeView control are called nodes.

T F **5.** A TreeView control has a single root node.

T F **6.** An ImageCombo Control is like a combo box with images added.

T F 7. You add an item to an ImageCombo box with the AddItem method.

T F 8. Setting a control's ZOrder to one (1) brings the control to the front display level of a form.

T F 9. To link an UpDown control with a text box, set the UpDown control's Buddy Control property to the name of the text box.

T F 10. A DTPicker control is a combo box for dates and times.

WRITTEN QUESTIONS

Write your answers to the following questions.

11. Name two Windows Common Controls that use collections. In each, what is the collection used for?

12. Describe how a Slider control is used as an input device? What property is used to provide the input value?

13. Why is the ImageList control an indispensable part of the Windows Common Controls?

14. Describe the difference between the Picture Box control and the Image control.

15. Use the LoadPicture function in a valid statement.

16. What are the four view modes of a ListView control?

17. Describe two of the predefined panel styles. In what control is a panel used?

18. Define the following terms in relation to the TreeView control: root, child, parent, node.

19. Explain what ChDir App.Path does. Why do we use it?

20. The TabStrip control is not a Container. Why is this important? How do you compensate for the fact that it is not a Container control?

Historically Speaking

FORTRAN, the FORmula TRANslating system, appeared in 1957. The language is designed and used mainly by engineers to solve math problems related to computing and science. A year later, Fortran II, capable of processing subroutines (event procedures and functions) appeared. FORTRAN is still in use today. One reason is the millions of lines of perfectly good code that still exist and can be called by newly written programs.

LESSON 10 APPLICATION PROBLEMS

Level One

THE CHANGING BACKGROUND PROGRAM

Start a new program. Put an Image control on the form. Put an ImageList control on the form and fill it with six images. Put a Slider control on the form. Write code that enables the Slider control to change the image in the Image control. In the Form_Load procedure, add code to set the range of values for the slider, add code to resize the Image control to fill the form, and add code to set the Stretch property of the Image control to True.

THE LISTVIEW CONTROL PROGRAM

Write a program using the ListView control (along with an ImageList control) to display a list of icons and names. Use the SmallIcon view of the ListView control to display an image as a small icon along with a text description (of a few words) of the icon.

THE STATUS BAR PROGRAM

Write a program with a status bar that demonstrates all the possible styles of panels available in a Status Bar control. Include the file name in the text panel.

Level Two

THE SCHOOL ORGANIZATION CHART

Write a program to display a school organization chart. Start with the district superintendent as the root. Use a text file describing the relationships to initialize the tree. When an item is clicked, give the user the option of viewing information on the person, adding names, or deleting the node from the tree.

THE TABSTRIP PROGRAM

Write a program using a TabStrip to display two option screens. In the first, use text boxes to collect information from the user about their favorite TV show. Collect the name of a show, as well as the day and time it is on, from the user. Use the DTPicker control to enter the time. In a second tab, use text boxes to collect information from the user about their favorite radio show. Collect the name of the radio personality and the date and day the user last listened to the show. Use a different DTPicker control to collect the date. (HINT: Draw two frame controls on the TabStrip control. Load the frames in the Form_Load procedure.)

COMBO JUBILEE

Write a program using a regular combo box, an ImageCombo box, and a DTPicker control to collect information from the user. Once the information is collected, a click on a command button should display all three pieces of information in a message box. Each piece of information should be on its own line in the message box. Load the regular combo box with five first names. Load the ImageCombo box with five icons from an ImageList control. Initialize the DTPicker to display the date. Preset the date to August 24, 2001.

LESSON 10 PROGRAMMING AT WORK

SCANS

In this project you will add a third display form to the Music Collection project. You do not need three forms, but each one illustrates a different strategy for displaying information from a database. In this new form, you will use tabs to display portions of the data instead of flooding the user with information they do not want. The first tab will display the Title, Artist, and Category. The second tab will display the Composer, Location, Comments, and Format.

1. Open the Music Collection project you saved at the end of Lesson 9.

2. Select **Project | Add Form** from the menu bar. Click **Form** in the New Form dialog box to add a normal form to the project. Change the name of the form to **frmTabbed**. Change the caption of the form to **Music Collection – Tabbed**.

3. Click the **Adodc** control in the toolbox and draw an instance of the control near the bottom of the form. (If the Adodc control is not in the toolbox, right-click the toolbox, select Components, click the check box for Microsoft ADO Data Control 6.0, and click OK.) Change the name of the control to **AdoForm3**. Its name refers to the fact that this is the third form in the project to display information from the database. Change the caption to **Click Arrows to Navigate the Collection**.

4. To connect the Ado Data control to the music collection database, right-click the control, and select **ADODC Properties**. Next to the Use Connection String option button (which should be selected), click the **Build** button. Enter the file name **MusCol.mdb**. Click the **Test Connection** button. Chances are the test will fail. The file **MusCol.mdb** is in the same directory as the Music Collection application. When the application runs (and its forms load), the ChDir App.Path and ChDrive App.Path statements alter the default directory to the one from which the application is run. If the application is not run before the connection is tested, Visual Basic looks for the file in the current directory. The current directory is the directory from which Visual Basic is run. Click **OK** twice to close the ADODC Properties dialog box.

5. To check the connection, run the project. The new form is not available—it is not finished and the menu on frm Music does not have an entry for it. Click one of the other display forms. Close everything and stop the program. This process resets the default directory. Use the Project Explorer to navigate back to frmTabbed (if necessary). Right-click the **Ado Data** control on frmTabbed and select **ADODC Properties**. Click **Build**. Click **Test Connection**. If the database file is in the default directory, the same directory as the application itself, the test succeeds. Click **OK**. If Visual Basic still cannot find the file, use the ellipsis button to navigate to a copy of the database. After you get a successful test, be sure the Connection tab shows only **MusCol.mdb** and not a full path. Test the connection again and click **OK** to close the message box and each dialog box.

6. Besides the connection string the RecordSource is the Ado Data control's most important property. If necessary, right-click the **Adodc** control and select **ADODC Properties**. Select the **RecordSource** tab in the ADODC Properties dialog box and insert the string **Select * from MusicCollection Order by Title** in the Command Text (SQL) box. (see Figure 10-13). Click **OK** to close the Property Pages dialog box.

7. Right-click the toolbox and select **Components**. Add Microsoft Windows Common Controls 6.0 by clicking the check box. Click **OK** to close the Components dialog box.

8. Click the **TabStrip** control in the toolbox and draw an instance of the control on frmTabbed. Right-click the **TabStrip** and select **Properties**. Click the **Tabs** tab. For the first tab, enter, **Main** for the Caption, **Main** for the Key and **Main Disk Information** ToolTipText.

9. Click **Insert Tab**. For tab 2, enter **Details** for the Caption, **Details** for the Key, and **All the Details** for the ToolTipText. Click **OK** to close the Properties dialog box.

10. Draw two frames on the form. Change the names of the forms to **fraMain** and **fraDetails**. Do not change the captions of the frames: They are not visible in the final program. These two forms are the containers switched on and off by the tab control.

FIGURE 10-13
The RecordSource tab of the Property Pages for the Ado Data control

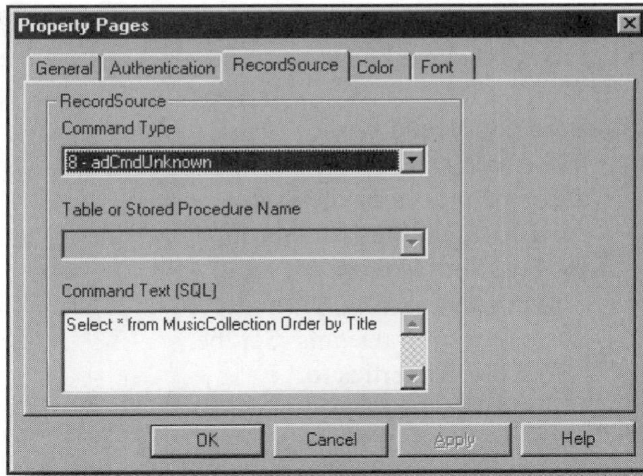

11. Move the second frame away from the first. Size the first so that it fits in the space allowed by the TabStrip. Adjust both, if necessary. Draw a text box on the frmMain frame. It must be directly on the frame. The name of the text box does not matter in this application; only its DataSource and DataField properties are important. Change the DataSource property to match the name of the Ado Data control: **AdoForm3**. Once this property is set, the DataField property of the box can be set.

12. Before setting the DataField property, be sure the text box is selected and copy it. Either right-click the text box and select **Copy** or select the text box and press **Ctrl+C** to copy the text box. Either right-click the body of the frame and select **Paste** from the pop-up menu or press **Ctrl+V**. Click **No** when prompted to create a control array. The new text box appears pasted in the upper left corner of the frame. Use the mouse to move it into position below the first text box. Right-click the body of the frame and select **Paste** to paste a second text box (total of three) on fraMain.

13. Select the top text box and select the **DataField** property. Click the **list box arrow** and select **Title:**. Change the **DataField** property of the second text box to **Artist:**. Change the **DataField** property of the third text box to **Category:**. You could key the entries, but there is less chance of error if you select the field names from the list box.

If there are no selections available in the list box of the DataField property, it means there is no valid connection to the database file. Three things have to be working: the Ado Data Control's connection string to the file name of the database, the Ado Data control's RecordSource property, and the text box's connection to the Ado Data control, set in the text box's DataSource property.

14. Draw three labels in the frame next to each text box. Change the captions of the labels to match the DataField names of each of the text boxes.

15. Drag the second frame, fraDetails, into view. Following the same processes of drawing the control on the frame, setting the DataSource property, and copying and pasting, put four text boxes on fraDetails. Set the DataField properties to **Composer:**, **Location:**, **Comments:**, and **Format:**. Set the captions of the labels to match (see Figure 10-14).

FIGURE 10-14
The Music Collection – Tabbed form showing layout in fraDetails

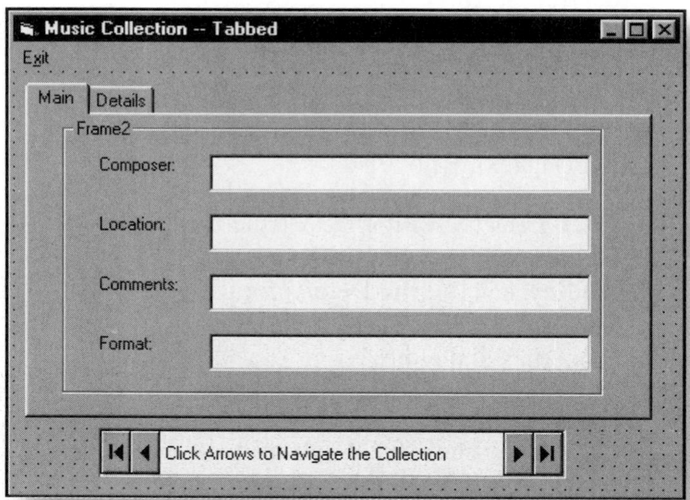

16. Select the form, **frmTabbed**. Open the **Menu Editor** and enter a single menu entry: Caption: **E&xit** Name: **mnuExit**

17. Open the Code window. Select **Form_Load**, press **Tab** and enter the following code:

```
fraMain.Visible = True
fraDetails.Visible = False
fraMain.BorderStyle = 0
fraDetails.BorderStyle = 0
```

18. Enter the following code in **mnuExit_Click**: `Unload Me`.

19. Enter the following code in **TabStrip1_Click**:

```
Dim WhichTab As Integer
WhichTab = TabStrip1.SelectedItem.Index
Select Case WhichTab
  Case 1
    fraMain.Visible = True
    fraDetails.Visible = False
  Case 2
    fraMain.Visible = False
    fraDetails.Visible = True
End Select
```

20. Save the form with an appropriate name.

21. Select the main form of the Music Collection project: **frmMusic** in the Project Explorer. Click **View Object**. Open the Menu Editor and modify the menu of the form by adding a menu item following ....Data &Grid. Be sure it is at the same level as the menu item above and below. Enter the caption **Data &Tabbed** and the name **mnuDataTabbed**. Click **OK** to close the Menu Editor.

22. Open the Code window and select **mnuDataTabbed_Click**. Press **Tab** and enter the following line of code: `frmTabbed.Show`.

23. Save and run the program. Select **Data Tabbed** and select different records of the database. Stop the program.

    Another application for the TabStrip control is to use it to display all the entries of a particular category of music. In that application, the code in the TabStrip Click event would resemble the code in the Prune Toolbar button. You would not need separate containers for each category; the TabStrip control would be used to select a category in much the same way the User system prunes the list to match the user's taste.

Historically Speaking

In 1959, COBOL, the COmmon Business Oriented Language, appeared. It was and is very good at processing the large text and data files used by large businesses. Every couple of years, it is declared dead, but it will continue into the next century.

BUILDING ACTIVEX CONTROLS

OBJECTIVES

When you complete this lesson, you will be able to:

- Build a new ActiveX control.
- Test the ActiveX control in a project group.
- Test the ActiveX control in a browser.
- Use the ActiveX control in a Standard EXE application.
- Enhance an existing control and package it as an ActiveX control.
- Create a user-drawn control.

Estimated Time: 5 hours

KEY TERMS

ActiveX controls
UserControl
project group
Get procedure
Let procedure
OCX
Compile
Make command
Dynamic Link Library (DLL)
Virtual Machine
parsing
Abs function
member
ActiveX Control Interface Wizard
PropertyBag
PropertyChanged event
Initialize

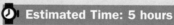

The LoanCalculator Control

Controls put a load of functionality into an easily used package. Pack commonly used functions and procedures into *ActiveX controls* to get consistent performance across applications. Use ActiveX controls to distribute commonly used procedures to other users.

There are three ways to build your own ActiveX controls: Combine existing controls and write code that binds them together, enhance an existing control to give it new functionality, or draw an original control to provide a new user interface.

In this section you will create a LoanCalculator control. The control collects the loan balance, the yearly interest rate, and the number of years of the loan, and calculates and displays the monthly payment. The monthly payment, as well as the total amount paid back and the finance charge, are also available as read-only properties of the control.

Design Considerations

When you first think about the design of the LoanCalculator control, you probably think of building an equivalent Visual Basic application. Such an application has text boxes to collect user input and a label to display the monthly payment. Should a control used from the toolbox collect data in text boxes, or should the control have no visible presence and let the programmer load information through properties of the control? A control with no visible presence, like a Timer control or the ImageList control, is a good choice if you want to give the programmer the most flexibility—and make him or her do the most work. The programmer sets the balance, interest rate, and years properties of the control with code. Once those properties are initialized, the programmer reads the monthly payment, the total payback amount, and the finance charge from read-only properties of the control.

A control with a visible interface makes it easier to put into a form or a Web page. The programmer does not worry about the appearance of the data entry portion of the application because it is included in the control.

The control designed in this lesson is a combination of the two: It provides a user interface to enter the balance, interest rate, and years of payment. It displays the monthly payment once all the data is loaded. It also exposes some calculated values through properties of the control.

Building Programming Skills

Check your output. After completing a program, check program output by hand, or at least estimate the result in your head or on paper to confirm that the program is displaying correct output. More than one contractor has been burned by spreadsheet estimates for jobs where the spreadsheet formulas were incorrectly entered, resulting in a bid that could not even cover expenses. It is embarrassing to hand over a defective product to the user.

STEP-BY-STEP 11.1

1. Start Visual Basic. Select **ActiveX Control** from the New Project dialog box. There are other selections with ActiveX in them, so be sure to select the proper one. Click **Open** to close the New Project dialog box.

Normally, you save your form and project as soon as you create them. In this lesson, do not save until you are instructed to do so. Save your forms, control, projects, and the group project (in that order) carefully at the times you are instructed to save. Select File | Exit or File | New to clear the screen. Do not select File | Remove to clear the screen; use this command only if you need to remove a single component from the group project you create in this lesson.

2. The "form" of an ActiveX control is called a *UserControl*. It looks like a form but it is not. There is no caption or menu bar and it does not support a normal menu. It does support a pop-up menu so when the UserControl is selected, the Menu Editor can be accessed. Change the name of the UserControl to **LoanCalculator**.

3. Put controls on the UserControl following the chart and Figure 11-1 on the next page. The yearly interest rate, balance, and the number of years are entered by the user text boxes. The monthly payment is then calculated and displayed in a label. Give all the labels names because some of their properties are altered in code. They are resized and repositioned when the control is put onto a form.

(continued on next page)

CONTROLS ON THE USER CONTROL

CONTROL	NAME	CAPTION/TEXT
label	lblRate	Yearly Interest Rate:
label	lblBalance	Balance:
label	lblYears	Years of the Loan:
label	lblPmtLabel	Monthly Payment:
text box	txtRate	(none)
text box	txtBalance	(none)
text box	txtYears	(none)
label	lblPmt	(none)

4. Change the **BorderStyle** of lblPmt to **1-Fixed Single** to make its appearance match the text boxes. Change the **BackColor** to **white** using the Palette tab.

FIGURE 11-1
The LoanCalculator UserControl, showing placement of controls

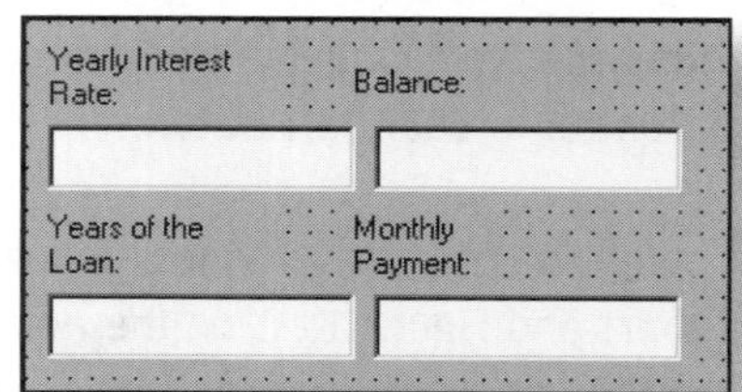

5. Right-click the body of the UserControl and select **View Code**. In the General Declarations section of the Code window, enter the following variable declarations:

```
Dim Balance As Currency
Dim Rate As Double
Dim Years As Integer
Dim Pmt As Currency
Dim TotalPayback As Currency
Dim FinanceCharge As Currency
```

When the necessary data is collected from the user, the monthly payment, total payback, and the finance charge are automatically calculated. Several event procedures require access to the values calculated by the control, so declare the variables with form-level visibility.

6. The code in Steps 6 and 7 is unavoidable. This code resizes the text boxes and labels when the UserControl is placed into an application. Unfortunately, the code is lengthy and cannot easily be shortened. Select **UserControl** from the Object list box in the Code window. Select **Resize** from the Procedure list box. Press **Tab** and enter the following code:

```
If UserControl.Width < 3870 Then
  UserControl.Width = 3870
End If
If UserControl.Height < 2115
Then
  UserControl.Height = 2115
End If
```

When the control design is finished (or nearly so), check the Height and Width properties of the UserControl. Make these the minimum sizes in the code for the Resize event (this application sets a minimum width of 3870 and a minimum height of 2115). If the user tries to set a smaller size (or if a programmer tries to draw the control on a form in another project in a smaller size), the control resizes to its minimum dimensions.

This discussion reveals an interesting fact: An ActiveX control has two run-time behaviors. When the control is put onto a form from the toolbox, it is running. The Resize event of the control fires when the programmer draws the control on the form of a Standard EXE project. The control has another run-time behavior that occurs when the application that contains the control is running.

7. Enter the code shown in **Code Step 7**. This code takes care of the rest of the resizing. Resizing the control involves changes to the width of each of the controls on the UserControl and re-spacing the controls to spread them across the form. Be sure to enter the code shown in Step 6 before entering the code in Code Step 7.

(continued on next page)

CODE STEP 7

```
Dim CtrlWidth As Integer     ' New width of each control.
Dim LeftEdge As Integer      ' New left edge of second column.
Dim VertSpacing As Integer   ' New up and down spacing.
CtrlWidth = UserControl.ScaleWidth / 2 - 400
Dim Ctrl As Control
For Each Ctrl In Controls    ' Resets the width of every control.
  Ctrl.Width = CtrlWidth
Next Ctrl
LeftEdge = UserControl.ScaleWidth / 2 + 200
lblBalance.Left = LeftEdge    ' Set the left edge of column two
txtBalance.Left = LeftEdge    ' controls.
lblPmtLabel.Left = LeftEdge
lblPmt.Left = LeftEdge
VertSpacing = UserControl.ScaleHeight / 4 - 160
lblRate.Top = 160            'Set a fixed distance from the top.
lblBalance.Top = 160
txtRate.Top = lblRate.Top + VertSpacing
txtBalance.Top = txtRate.Top
' Space second row of controls from a midline of the UserControl.
lblYears.Top = UserControl.ScaleHeight / 2 + 160
lblPmtLabel.Top = lblYears.Top
txtYears.Top = lblYears.Top + VertSpacing
lblPmt.Top = txtYears.Top
```

There is always some degree of experimentation involved in designing the appearance of a form. The figures used to determine the placement and the height and width of the controls in Code Steps 6 and 7 were calculated by trial and error.

8. With the UserControl selected, save it as **LoanCalculator.ctl** (the *.ctl* extension is added automatically). Save the project as **LoadCalculator.vbp**.

   You are going to want to run the control and test it—that is one of the main principles of incremental programming. If you click the Start button or press F5 to run the program, you may be in for a surprise. The ActiveX control project is not a normal Visual Basic program. An ActiveX control runs in the context of another program called a container. If you run the control and Internet Explorer is installed, it launches and displays the control in the Internet Explorer window. The only code that works is the code that resizes the control, and that code cannot be tested in the browser environment.

   To test the control, you need a new project. Visual Basic allows the creation of a *project group* for just this purpose. A project group has two or more projects. One project is designated as the start-up project.

9. Select **File | Add Project**. Select **Standard EXE** from the New Project dialog box and click **Open**. Both projects now appear in the Project Explorer and comprise a project group.

10. Right-click **Project2** (not the form) in the Project Explorer. Select **Set as Start Up** from the pop-up menu. Run the program. A blank form appears.

11. Stop the program. Select the form of the new project in the Project Explorer, and click **View Object**. The new form appears.

12. A grayed out generic UserControl icon appears in the toolbox. Click the grayed out button. Figure 11-2 shows the error message raised when the grayed out button is clicked. Click **OK** in the error message box.

FIGURE 11-2
The error message raised by clicking the grayed out UserControl icon

13. Double-click the **LoanCalculator** icon in the Project Explorer to return to the Loan-Calculator design window. Click the **Close** button in the upper right corner of the design window. If you have maximized the design window, be careful to click the Close button for the design window, not the Close button for Visual Basic (see Figure 11-3).

FIGURE 11-3
The Close button of the design window of the maximized LoanCalculator control

One way to tell what window you are in is to look at the title bar of the Visual Basic window. In Figure 11-3 you see a part of the title indicating the LoanCalculator design window is active. When you close it, the title reflects the name of the new project. Note that even though you closed the design window, the control and its code are still there loaded in memory.

14. Use your mouse pointer to identify the LoanCalculator control in the toolbox. It is no longer grayed out, and when the mouse pointer is over the control, the control's name appears. Double-click the **Loan-Calculator** control in the toolbox to add the control to the form. It appears in its default size on the form. Resize the control (not the form) several times. Note the change in the spacing of the controls, as well as the change in the width of the text boxes and labels when the width of the control is changed. Resize the control to a size smaller than its original size. The control's outline follows the pointer to whatever size you set, but if the size is smaller than the minimum dimensions, the control springs back to the minimum dimensions.

15. Double-click the **LoanCalculator icon** in the Project Explorer to return to the Loan-Calculator design window. The title of the window reflects you are back in the design window for the LoanCalculator control. This is how you return to the design window to change the control. In this phase of development you typically move back and forth from the control design window to the trial project several times.

16. Use the Project Explorer to return to Project2 without closing the LoanCalculator design window. If necessary, click **ViewObject** to see Project2's form. The space occupied by the LoanCalculator control is covered with a crosshatch pattern. You can use the mouse to resize the control, but, although the boundaries of the control appear to move, the Resize event of the control has not rearranged the text boxes and labels. The control is not running. It cannot run while its design window is open.

17. The best way to save all the files created in this Step-by-Step exercise is to save each file separately in the order given in this step.

    First, select **Form1** in the Project Explorer. Select **File | Save Form 1 As** and save the form as **LoanCalculator. frm**.

    Second, select **LoanCalculator** (the User-Control) in the Project Explorer and press **Ctrl+S** to save it with its existing name, **LoanCalculator.ctl**. (If you have not yet saved the UserControl, the dialog box appears for you to name your file).

    Third, select **Project 1** in the Project Explorer and press **Ctrl+S** to save it with its existing name **LoanCalculator.vbp**.

    Fourth, select **Project 2** in the Project Explorer. Select **File | Save Project 2 As**. Save the file as **LoanCalculator2.vbp**.

    Finally, to save the project group, select **File | Save Project Group As**. Save the project group as **LoanCalculator.vbg**. Leave the project group open for the next, Step-by-Step exercise or exit Visual Basic if you are done for the day. Do *not* select File | Remove.

In this Step-by-Step exercise you performed many of the basic skills necessary to get an ActiveX control working. You:

- Created an ActiveX control project.
- Added text boxes and labels.
- Added code to resize the control when the program designer uses the control on a form.
- Created a project group to test the control.

In the next Step-by-Step exercise you will add code to make the control functional, continue testing the control in a Visual Basic project, and test the control in the Internet Explorer.

Quick Check 11.a

1. The "form" of an ActiveX control is called a ___________________.
2. An ActiveX control has two run-time behaviors, one behavior when ___________________, and another when the program in which the control is placed is running.
3. An ActiveX control runs in the context of another program that is called a ___________________.
4. To test an ActiveX control in a Visual Basic project, create a ___________________.
5. The icon for the new ActiveX control is grayed until the control's ___________________ is closed.

Finishing and Testing the LoanCalculator Control

In this Step-by-Step exercise, make the LoanCalculator control functional by adding code to calculate and display the monthly payment. Make the monthly payment, as well as the total payback amount and the finance charge, available as properties of the control. Fully test the control by including it in a full application that uses the control.

STEP-BY-STEP 11.2

1. If necessary, start Visual Basic and open the project group file **LoanCalculator.vbg**. Enter the LoanCalculator design window by clicking the **LoanCalculator** icon under the **UserControl** folder in the Project Explorer.

Depending on your screen resolution, you may want more room on the screen to see the Code window. When you are not adding controls to a form or UserControl, close the toolbox by clicking its Close icon. Restore the toolbox by clicking its icon on the toolbar. The toolbox's icon is a crossed wrench and hammer.

2. Right-click the body of the **UserControl** and select **View Code**. Select **Tools | Add Procedure**. In the Add Procedure dialog box, enter the name **CalcPayment** and click the **Function** option button. Click the **Private** option button to make the function private to the control. If the function is Public, the programmer has access to the function (see Figure 11-4). Click **OK** to close the dialog box.

   The CalcPayment function does the work of calculating the monthly payment, the total payback of the loan, and the finance charge for the loan. Variables for each of these values were declared in the previous Step-by-Step exercise:

VARIABLES

NAME	DESCRIPTION
Pmt	The monthly payment.
TotalPayback	The total amount paid back on the loan.
FinanceCharge	The difference between the total amount paid back on the loan and the original loan balance.

FIGURE 11-4
The New Procedure dialog box, making the function CalcPayment a Private function

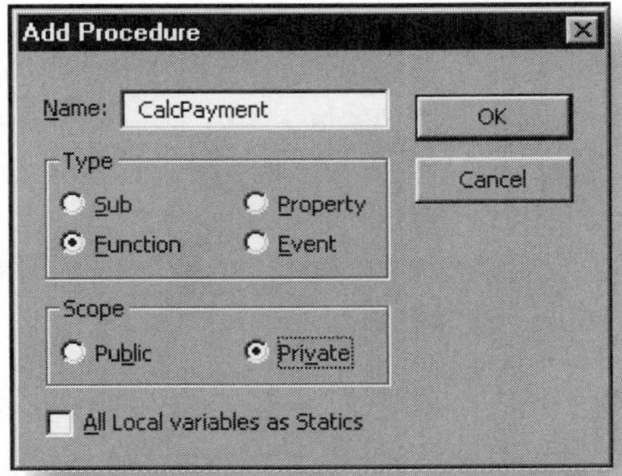

Once calculated, the monthly payment appears in the label named lblPmt. It and the other calculated values are exposed as properties of the control.

CODE STEP 3

```
Dim MRate As Double
Dim Payments As Integer
MRate = Rate / 1200
Payments = Years * 12
Pmt = Balance * MRate / (1 - (1 + MRate) ^ (-Payments))
TotalPayback = Pmt * Payments
FinanceCharge = TotalPayback - Balance
CalcPayment = Pmt
```

3. Enter the code shown in **Code Step 3** in **Private Function CalcPayment**.

   Enter the yearly interest rate as a percent. Enter eight percent as 8. Convert the percent to a decimal by dividing by 100. To convert the yearly interest rate to the monthly interest, divide by 12. The number of payments is the number of years times 12. Once the monthly payment is calculated, the total payback amount is equal to the monthly payment times the number of payments. The finance charge is calculated, and the monthly payment is passed back to the calling program as the value of the function.

   There is no command button in LoanCalculator. The CalcPayment function is called when all three values—yearly interest rate, balance, and years—have been entered by the user. Put code into the Change event of each of the three text boxes to do the calculation. Whenever there is a change in one of the text boxes, make a check to see if all three variables have a value. If they do have values, call CalcPayment.

4. Select **txtBalance_Change**, press **Tab**, and enter the code shown in **Code Step 4**.

   Whenever you see *On Error Resume Next*, you ought to wonder what deeper error is

(continued on next page)

being covered up. In this case, the On Error statement is used to handle an error condition that occurs when the user is backspacing to enter a new value. When the last digit is removed, the CCur( ) function attempts to convert the empty string to a currency value. This generates an error. The On Error statement steps around the error and allows program execution to continue.

Entering this code does not make the control ready for a test. The If statement checks three variables for values. If any of the three variables has no value, no calculation is performed. This code has to be copied to the Change event procedures of the other two text boxes before the control is functional.

5. Select and copy the code entered in **txtBalance_Change**. Paste the code in **txtRate_Change**, and **txtYears_Change**. In each, change the references to match the text box. In txtRate_Change, change *Balance = CCur(txtBalance)* to **Rate = CDbl(txtRate)**. In txtYears_Change, change *Balance = CCur(txtBalance)* to **Years = CInt(txtYears)**. Notice the convert function is changed to correspond to the datatypes of the variables.

6. Close the Code window, then close the LoanCalculator design window by clicking the **Close** button in the top right part of the window. The title bar of the Visual Basic window reflects the change. Save and run the program.

7. Enter **8** for the interest rate, **5000** for the balance, and **3** for the number of years. As soon as a value is entered for the number of years, a value appears in the box marked Monthly Payment. Enter other values in each text box. Putting the code in the Change event means it updates the monthly payment with every change, not just a complete change. Enter a balance of **8500**. With each change of digit, a new monthly payment is calculated.

8. Stop the program.

   If there is a problem with the performance of the control, this is where you start the process of re-entering the design window, fixing the code, closing the design window, running the test project, and checking the control. Repeat as necessary.

9. There is not a lot of investment in the test project at this point, so before going further, remove the test project so you can test the LoanCalculator control in a browser environment: Right-click **Project2** in the Project Explorer. Select **Remove Project**. This deletes the project from the project group, not from the storage device.

10. Run the program. If installed, Internet Explorer is launched with the LoanCalculator control loaded on the form.

CODE STEP 4

```
On Error Resume Next
Balance = CCur(txtBalance)
If Balance <> 0 And Rate <> 0 And Years <> 0 Then
   Pmt = CalcPayment
   lblPmt = Format(Pmt, "currency")
End If
```

If the Internet Explorer is not loaded, a dialog box appears, allowing you to choose a browser. Click **OK** if the dialog box appears. Test the control by entering several combinations of values. Close the browser window and stop the program.

Do not imagine the control is ready for stand-alone use—it is not. Although it appeared in a browser window and you could even save the HTML code that generates the window, the control does not have an existence independent of Visual Basic. Once the Visual Basic project stops, the control is no longer available.

11. If necessary, select **LoanCalculator** in the Project Explorer and click **View Code**. Add properties to the control by adding Get procedures for each property: Select **Tools | Add Procedure**. In the New Procedure dialog box, enter the name **MPmt**. Select the **Property** option. This is the Monthly Payment property. It is a property of the control, so be sure the Public option is selected. Click **OK** to close the New Procedure dialog box. As the dialog box closes, MPmt's Get and Let procedures appear in the Code window. The *Get procedure* is called when the user wants to read the property. The *Let procedure* is called when the user wants to set a value for the property.

12. Change the MPmt property to a read-only property: Select and delete the Public Property Let MPmt(ByVal vNewValue As Variant) procedure from the Code window.

13. Change the datatype of the MPmt's Get procedure from Variant to **Currency**. The procedure heading should now read Public Property Get MPmt( ) As Currency.

    The property has a value only if all three text boxes are filled by the user. An If statement similar to the one in the Change events of the text boxes is used to ensure there is valid data available. If valid data is not available, an error event is raised.

14. In the General Declarations section of the code, enter the line shown in **Code Step 14**.

15. Add the code shown in **Code Step 15** to **Public Property Get MPmt( ) As Currency**. If all three variables have values, assign the monthly payment to MPmt. If not, set MPmt to 0 and raise an error. The error event, DataError, begins when Pmt is invalid. Like any other event, if the programmer provides no code for the event, it passes unnoticed. In that event, the monthly payment of 0 speaks for itself.

(continued on next page)

CODE STEP 14

```
Public Event DataError(ByVal sMsg As String)
```

CODE STEP 15

```
If Balance <> 0 And Rate <> 0 And Years <> 0 Then
    MPmt = Pmt
Else
    MPmt = 0
    RaiseEvent DataError("Missing Data")
End If
```

You may remember the process of adding an event to a class. When using a class to declare variables in a project, you must declare the variable with the WithEvents keyword to use the events provided in the class definition. This is not necessary when adding an event to an ActiveX control.

16. Close the LoanCalculator Code window and, if necessary, close the LoanCalculator design window. The test bed project was removed to test the control's behavior in the browser. Add a new project by selecting **File | Add Project**. Select **Standard EXE** and click **OK**. Right-click the name of the project in the Project Explorer and select **Set as Start Up**. This ensures that Project2 runs when you click Start or press F5.

17. Put a LoanCalculator control on the form. Put a command button on the form below the control. Change the name of the command button to **cmdDisplayPmt**. Change the caption of the command button to **Display Payment**. Open the Code window and select **cmdDisplayPmt_Click**. Press **Tab** and enter the code shown in **Code Step 17**.

    The LoanCalculator control has its default name. This statement accesses the MPmt property of the control and displays its value in a message box.

18. Select **LoanCalculator1** from the Object list box and enter the following line of code: **MsgBox sMsg**. (If the list box does not display LoanCalculator1, close the Code window and double-click the form.)

19. Save the form as **LoanCalculator** and the project as **LoanCalculator2** (replace the existing file). Run the program. The LoanCalculator control appears along with the new command button. Click the command button. The DataError event begins, displaying the error message code. Click **OK**. The value of the MPmt property (0.00) appears. Click **OK** again.

20. Enter data into the three text boxes. Click **Display Payment**. The message box displays the same monthly payment shown in the label on the control. Click **OK**.

21. Stop the program.

22. Use Project Explorer to return to the Code window for LoanCalculator. Create new Property procedures for the total payback amount property and the finance charge property. Name the first **TPayback** and the second **FCharge**. Be sure to create both as Public Property procedures. Delete the Let procedures—this makes the properties read-only. Change the datatype of the two new Property procedures to **Currency**. Copy and paste the code from the MPmt Get procedure into the Get procedures for TPayback and FCharge. Change the variable names to match the properties.

23. Save the changes. Close the Loan-Calculator design window and return to Project2. Either add command buttons to the form to display the total payback amount and the finance charge, or add additional statements to cmdDisplayPmt to display each of the read-only properties. Save the form, the

CODE STEP 17

```
MsgBox Format(LoanCalculator1.MPmt, "currency")
```

control, the two projects, and the project group.

24. Run Project2 and thoroughly test the LoanCalculator control.

25. Make any changes necessary for the control to work properly, then save all the files and projects. Leave the project group open for the next Step-by-Step exercise or exit Visual Basic. Do *not* select File | Remove.

By now the control is doing all it is supposed to be doing. There are possibilities for enhancements. One would be a method that allows the programmer to change the font or font size of all the text boxes and labels on the control. This would let the programmer using the control customize the control for a particular project.

In the next section you will compile the control to get it ready for distribution.

Quick Check 11.b

1. To use a function within an ActiveX control and not make the function available to the programmer using the control, add the procedure as a ________________ function.

2. Putting code in a text box's Change event ensures the code executes with every ________________.

3. When you add a Property procedure to a project, a ________________ procedure and a ________________ procedure are created.

4. To turn a property into a read-only property, delete the ________________ procedure.

5. To ensure that Project2 runs when the Start button is clicked or when F5 is pressed, right-click the project name in the Project Explorer and select ________________.

Building Programming Skills

A great way to debug a program is to explain it to someone else. Formal "walk-throughs" are often used in industry to discover program bugs. Explaining program code to your peers helps you focus on problems and discover logical errors that you did not expect existed.

Print out code to review it. Often mistakes overlooked on a computer monitor jump out at you when you look at a printout.

Historically Speaking

In 1964, professors John G. Kemeny and Thomas E. Kurtz of Dartmouth University designed a programming language for incoming computer students: Beginners All-purpose Symbolic Instruction Code, BASIC. Eleven years later in 1975, Paul Allen and Bill Gates wrote a version of BASIC for the MITS Altair 8800 computer with 4K memory. Microsoft, the company founded by Gates and Allen, went on to write several versions of BASIC for many microcomputers of today.

Compiling the LoanCalculator Control

Lessons 14 and 15 discuss packaging Visual Basic projects to move to other machines and to use in different environments. This Step-by-Step exercise looks at compiling the LoanCalculator control to an *OCX* file. An OCX file can be used in other Visual Basic projects. In the first two exercises you used the control in the artificial test bed environment provided by the project group.

Before we get to the compilation of the control, look first at a partial list of properties of the LoanCalculator control. Many of the properties apply to several Visual Basic controls, and some have not been mentioned before in the text. Many properties work just fine loaded with their default values. You notice these properties only when you are trying to do something special with the control. The table below summarizes a number of properties of the LoanCalculator control. Note that each control has more properties than can be covered in this text. By examining properties and trying them out in sample programs, you can get ideas for programs of your own.

LOANCALCULATOR CONTROL PROPERTIES

PROPERTY	DESCRIPTION
AccessKeys	Sets or returns a string defining a control's hot keys. *object*.AccessKeys = "L" sets the object's hot key to Alt+L.
Alignable	A True/False property that determines if the Align method applies to a UserControl. If it does, a control can be set (like the toolbar) to align itself at the top, bottom, or sides of a form. Its default value is False.
Appearance	The Appearance property usually allows a choice between 3-D and flat. 3-D is the default value. A 3-D control has shading on two edges that makes the control appear to be three-dimensional.
AutoRedraw	When set to True, graphics on a control originally drawn by any of the graphics methods are automatically renewed when the control is resized, or when the control is revealed again after being covered by another control.
BackColor	The BackColor property sets the background color of the control. Most Visual Basic controls come in white or gray, but millions of colors are available. A useful palette of colors appears when the Palette tab is clicked while setting the BackColor property.
BackStyle	The BackStyle property is set to Opaque (the default) or Transparent. When Transparent, any image or color in the background of the control's container shows through the control. Only characters displayed in the foreground appear. When using a control with a transparent background, be sure the ForeColor and FontSize are set to make the control's content readable against the background of the form.
CanGetFocus	CanGetFocus is a True/False property that determines if the control can receive the focus. Usually, only controls that collect input from the user can receive the focus. If designing a control that only displays information, you may set CanGetFocus to False. The default value of the property is True.

LOANCALCULATOR CONTROL PROPERTIES

PROPERTY	DESCRIPTION
ControlContainer	When set to True, the ControlContainer property allows the UserControl to act like a picture box or frame: Other controls can be drawn on it. The default value of the property is False.
DataBindingBehavior	A DataBound control can be linked to a field of a database. If DataBindingBehavior is set to 1-vbSimpleBound, the UserControl can be bound to a field of a database through a data control. The default value of the property is 0-none.
DataSourceBehavior	If this property is set to 1-vbDataSource, the UserControl can be used to provide data for other Visual Basic controls. The GetDataMember event is added to the control's event procedures. If the property is set to 2-vbOLEDBProvider, the OnDataConnection event is added to the control's event procedures.
Enabled	If this control is set to False, no user-initiated events can affect the control. The default value, True, is used to allow the control to respond to user-initiated events.
Font	The Font property lets the program designer set the display font at design time or run time.
FontTransparent	The property's default value, True, allows color and graphics behind a font to be visible through the spaces in the characters.
ForeColor	The property used to set the color of characters and drawn objects on a control.
Height	The Height property is used to set or return the exterior height of the control in twips.
InvisibleAtRuntime	The default value of this property is False. If True, the control may be active in a project, but the control itself will not be visible. The Timer control and the ImageList control are both controls with the InvisibleAtRuntime property set to True.
Picture	Use the Picture property to display a picture file in the background of the control.
Public	When set to True (the default value), the ActiveX control is available for use by other applications. If False, the control cannot be seen outside of the ActiveX control project.
ScaleHeight	The ScaleHeight property is the interior height of the control in twips.

LOANCALCULATOR CONTROL PROPERTIES

PROPERTY	DESCRIPTION
ScaleLeft	Normally, the coordinate of the left edge of a control or form is 0. The ScaleLeft property sets the coordinate of the left edge according to the value written into the property.
ScaleMode	The ScaleMode property sets the units of the coordinate system. The default is twips. Also available are point, pixel, character, inch, millimeter, and centimeter.
ScaleTop	Similar to the ScaleLeft property. Sets the coordinate of the top edge of the control to a value determined by the programmer or user.
ScaleWidth	The ScaleWidth property is the width of the interior of the control in twips.
Tag	Stores extra data about the control. It is sometimes used to distinguish the control from other controls.
ToolboxBitmap	When the UserControl is first created, it is represented in the toolbox with a generic icon. Setting the ToolboxBitmap property to a 16-by-15-bit icon changes the control's representation.
Width	The measure of the exterior height of the control in twips.

Compiling the Control

To make the LoanCalculator control independent of the artificial test bed environment provided by the project group, the control must be *compiled*. Compiling an ActiveX control is the process of turning source code written in Visual Basic into object code and ultimately into machine code. When compiled, it becomes an OCX file. Once packaged as an OCX file, it can be added to a project's toolbox and be used in projects.

STEP-BY-STEP 11.3

1. If necessary, start Visual Basic and open the project group file **LoanCalculator.vbg**.
2. In the Project Explorer, click **LoanCalculator** in the **UserControl** folder, then click **View Object**.
3. In the Properties window, select **ToolboxBitmap**. Click the ellipsis to add a bitmap image to the toolbox. Find an appropriate bitmap (no small task). The bitmap icon you choose displays as an icon representing the LoanCalculator control when it is added to a new project. Save the project.

The *Make command* in the File menu builds executable files from project files. Executable files do not need the Visual Basic programming environment to run. They do need MSVBVM60.DLL, the Microsoft Visual Basic Virtual Machine 6.0. DLL stands for *Dynamic Link Library*. It is a collection of executable code used by other programs. You may have tried to transfer a program from one system to another and run into problems because you did not transfer the required DLL files.

A *Virtual Machine* is a program that turns one computer into another. In this case, the Visual Basic Virtual Machine turns a machine with Intel-compatible hardware and the Windows operating system into a machine that executes Visual Basic code.

The Make utility converts project files into EXE files, DLL files, or OCX files. To use an ActiveX control in another application, turn it into an OCX file.

4. If necessary, select **LoanCalculator** in the Project Explorer. Select **File | Make LoanCalculator.ocx**. The file name displayed in the menu will match the file name you gave the control when you saved it. When selected, the Make Project dialog box appears. This dialog box prompts you to navigate to a directory in which to save the control. Select a directory and provide a file name, then click **Save**. The default name is the name given to the LoanCalculator UserControl file, saved when you saved the projects and project group in the last section. You may accept the default name—the new file is saved with an OCX extension. This prevents it from overwriting your old file.

5. Even a fast computer takes a moment or two to compile the control. Open Windows Explorer by right-clicking the Windows **Start** button and selecting **Explore**. Navigate to the directory where you stored the OCX file. Note the length of the file. The sample OCX file is about 32K long. If you check the times of creation, you notice a couple of other files have also been created. The EXP and LIB files are used to communicate with other applications.

6. Close Windows Explorer. Leave the project group open for the next Step-by-Step exercise or exit Visual Basic. Do *not* select File | Remove.

Now that the control is compiled, use it in a project. The project that follows compares the finance charge for two loan scenarios. The LoanCalculator control provides calculations. Data is stored in a list box. When the user clicks an item in the list box, the difference in the finance charge between the clicked data and the data that precedes it is calculated and displayed.

STEP-BY-STEP 11.4

1. If necessary, start Visual Basic and open the project group **LoanCalculator.vbg**. Return to the design window and select **File | New Project**. If prompted to save files from the previous project, save them unless you made changes you do not want saved. The OCX file has already been saved.

2. Select **Standard EXE** from the New Project dialog box and click **OK**. Change the name of the form to **frmLoanInformation**. Change the caption of the form to **Figuring the Finance Charge**.

3. Right-click the toolbox and select **Components** to add the LoanCalculator control to the project. Select **Browse**. The Add ActiveX Control dialog box appears (see Figure 11-5).

(continued on next page)

The Add ActiveX Control dialog box defaults to the **System** folder. A number of other OCX files are visible in the figure. It is a good idea to put your OCX file in the **System** folder, but for this application, you may leave it in the folder in which you saved it.

FIGURE 11-5
The Add ActiveX Control dialog box

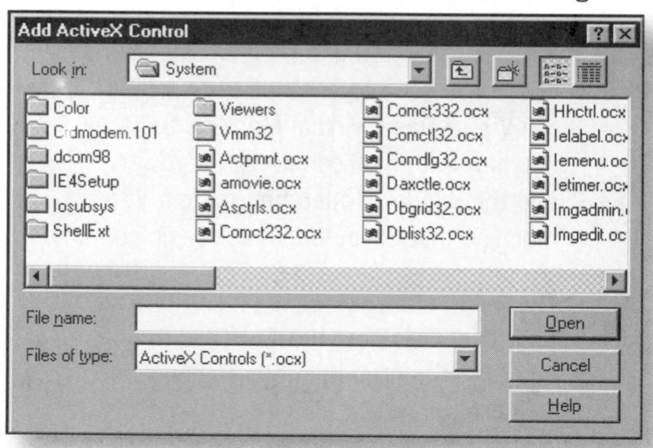

4. Navigate to the LoanCalculator's OCX file and select it. Click **Open**. The Components dialog box reappears. The name of the project, in this case Project1, appears in the Controls tab of the dialog box. It is already checked (see Figure 11-6). (Do not be concerned if you see more than one occurence of Project1. The checked Project1 should be your own UserControl. Check the path shown in the Project frame box.) Click **OK** to close the Components dialog box.

FIGURE 11-6
The Components dialog box, showing Project1 selected

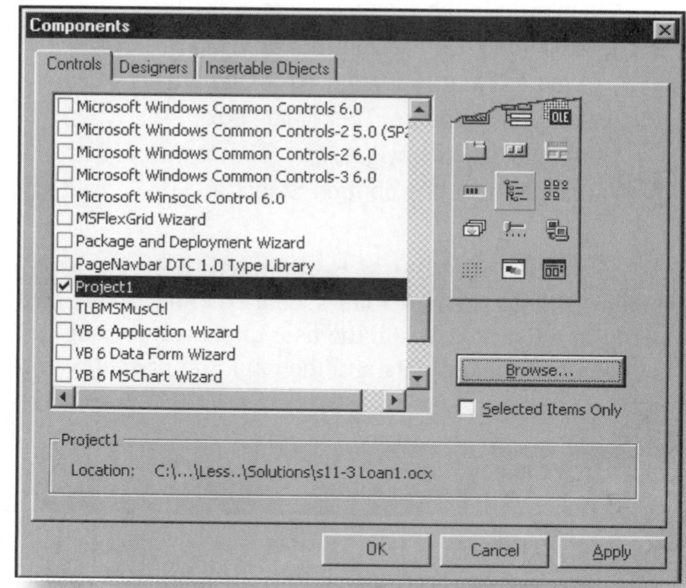

5. The icon you selected to represent the LoanCalculator control appears in the toolbox. Position the mouse pointer over the control. Its ToolTip reports the name of the control. Single-click the control's icon in the toolbox and place an instance of the control on the form. Size the control to occupy the top half of the form.

6. Check Figure 11-7 to see the placement of controls on the form. Add a list box to the form. Change the name of the list box to **lstCompare**. Add a label above the list box with the caption **Click to Compare**. Add three command buttons to the form. Change the captions to **&Store**, **C&lear**, and **E&xit**. Change the names of the buttons to **cmdStore**, **cmdClear**, and **cmdExit**.

7. Open the Code window and select **cmdStore_Click**. Press **Tab** and enter the code shown in **Code Step 7**. This code first checks to see if valid data has been entered into the LoanCalculator control. If

valid data exists, the calculated monthly payment and the finance charge are displayed in the list box. This information becomes the baseline to which new data is compared.

8. Enter the line **Unload Me** in **cmdExit_Click**.

9. Select **lstCompare_Click**, press **Tab**, and enter the code shown in **Code Step 9**.

   The Click routine of the list box begins when the user clicks an entry in the list box. The Index value of the item clicked is available in the list box's ListIndex property. If the ListIndex is 0, the first item was clicked: The event procedure ends. The program works by comparing the clicked item with the item above it.

   Read the clicked string from the list box using the List method. Save the string in First. Read the string above the clicked string from the list box and save it in Second. The statement FC1 = CCur(Right(First, Len(First) - InStrRev(First, vbTab))) looks complicated, but it has a simple job: It parses the finance charge

FIGURE 11-7
The Figuring the Finance Charge form, showing the final placement of controls

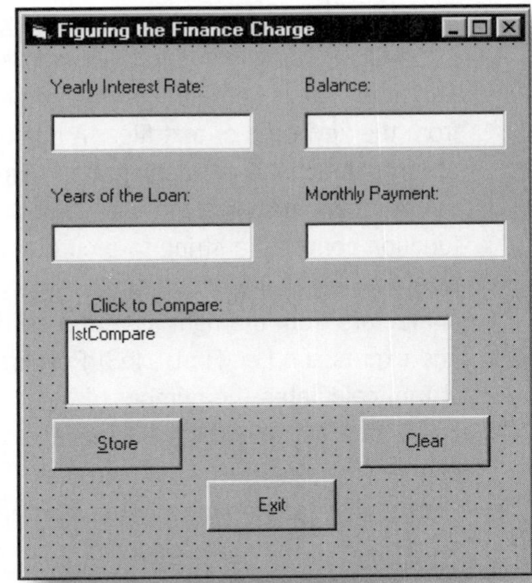

(continued on next page)

CODE STEP 7

```
With LoanCalculator1
  If .MPmt <> 0 Then ' valid value
      lstCompare.AddItem Format(.MPmt, "currency") & _
         vbTab & Format(.FCharge, "currency")
  End If
End With
```

CODE STEP 9

```
Dim Ind As Integer
Dim First As String, Second As String
Dim FC1 As Currency, FC2 As Currency
Ind = lstCompare.ListIndex
If Ind = 0 Then Exit Sub
First = lstCompare.List(Ind - 1)
Second = lstCompare.List(Ind)
FC1 = CCur(Right(First, Len(First) - InStrRev(First, vbTab)))
FC2 = CCur(Right(Second, Len(Second) - InStrRev(Second, vbTab)))
MsgBox "Difference in finance charge is " _
  & vbCrLf & Format(Abs(FC1 - FC2), "currency")
```

from the entry in the list box and assigns it to FC1. *Parsing* is separating commands and information from strings that come from the keyboard or text files. A number of string functions are designed to help the programmer parse strings. The CCur( ) function converts a string to a currency type. The Right( ) function peels characters from the right side of a string. The expression Len(First) - InStrRev(First, vbTab) calculates the number of characters occupied by the finance charge. The InStrRev( ) function (see Lesson 4) searches for a tab character starting from the right edge of the string. This function is available only in Microsoft Visual Basic 6.0. In version 5, use the InStr( ) function, which is identical but searches from the left edge of the string.

InStrRev( ) is used in this code because, at a future time, the list box might be modified to display the number of years of payments as well as the monthly payment and the finance charge. If that modification is made, it is easier to search starting from the right edge.

The MsgBox statement displays the message comparing the two finance charges. The built-in constant, vbCrLf, inserts both a carriage return and line feed character into the string. The *Abs function* finds the absolute value of the difference in the finance charges so that a positive value is always displayed.

10. Select **cmdClear_Click**, press **Tab**, and enter the line **lstCompare.Clear**.

11. Save the form and project as **Loan Information**. Run the program. Enter values for the interest rate, balance, and number of years. Click **Store** to transfer the data to the list box. Alter the interest rate by increasing it two percentage points. Click **Store** to transfer the data to the list box. Click the first item in the list box. Nothing happens. Click the second item in the list box. A message box appears, displaying the difference in the finance charges. Click **OK** to close the message box. Alter the number of years of the loan. Click **Store** to transfer the data to the list box. Click the third item of the list box. Note the difference in the finance charge.

12. Stop the program. Leave the project group open or exit Visual Basic. Do *not* select File | Remove.

In this Step-by-Step exercise you compiled the LoanCalculator control to an OCX file. You used the control in an application to compare the finance charges of loans. Along the way you may have noticed opportunities to enhance the original LoanCalculator control. When comparing finance charges, it would be nice to see the number of years along with the information about the monthly payment and finance charge. Seeing the number of years would make the comparison more meaningful. Unfortunately, there is no way to access the number of years. The text box used to enter that value is part of the LoanCalculator control. Its contents are not directly available to the user or to the programmer.

You cannot edit or modify a UserControl from an application that uses the control. To modify a UserControl, you need to open the project in which the control was developed. Another problem with the control becomes known when you want to clear the application form. Use the Clear method to clear the contents of the list box. How do you clear the text boxes of the LoanCalculator control? You cannot. A method to clear the control should be included.

Quick Check 11.c

1. ________________ is a True/False property that determines if the control can receive the focus.
2. When a UserControl is compiled, it becomes an ________________ file.
3. Right-click the toolbox and select ________________ to add the LoanCalculator control to a project.
4. Read a clicked string in a list box with the list box's ________________ property.
5. ________________ is a built-in constant that represents both a carriage return and line feed character.
6. To alter the behavior of a UserControl, you must ________________.

Modifying an Existing Control

Another way to create a unique ActiveX control is to modify an existing control. In this section you will add features to the text box. When the modified text box receives the focus, any value in the Text property of the box displays in General Number format. When the control loses the focus, the value in the box displays in a format chosen by the programmer.

Before you get too far in the project you will realize you need help. The *ActiveX Control Interface Wizard* automates the process of designing new ActiveX controls.

Building Programming Skills

Do you know everything you need to know to write the programs required for your job? Read the on-line documentation. Read publications dedicated to Visual Basic or Visual Studio. You will probably find program features and code that solve problems in different or better ways. Visual Basic is a large language. Chances are there is something more you can learn about it to improve programming skills.

Historically Speaking

In 1979, Dan Bricklin and Bon Frankston designed and wrote the first electronic spreadsheet program, Visicalc. They purposely did not seek patent protection for their creation. This act stimulated the computer industry greatly because it turned out that the spreadsheet was a wonderful tool for many different disciplines. Many other companies came out with their own products. Lotus bought the rights to Visicalc in 1985. The product disappeared shortly after.

STEP-BY-STEP 11.5

1. Start Visual Basic or select **File | New Project**. (Click Yes if prompted to save any changes from the preceding Step-by-Step exercise. The File | New Project command clears the screen.) Select **ActiveX Control** from the New Project dialog box and click **Open**. In the Project Explorer, right-click the **Project1** icon (not the **UserControl** folder or **UserControl 1**). Select **Project1 Properties**. In the Project1 - Project Properties dialog box, change the name of the project to **SpecialFormat**. Enter **Special Format Textbox** in the *Project Description* text box (see Figure 11-8). Click **OK** to close the dialog box, but not before clicking each of the other tabs and examining what you find there.

FIGURE 11-8
The Project1 - Project Properties dialog box

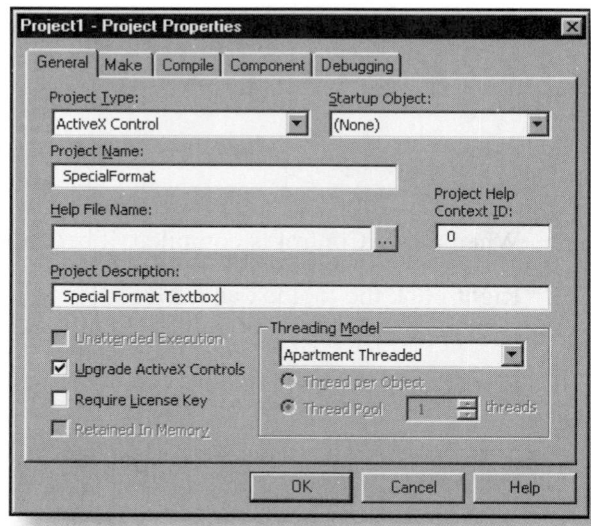

2. In the Properties window, change the name of the UserControl to **FormattedTextbox**. When compiled and put on a form in another application, the first instance of the control is named FormattedTextbox1.

3. Double-click the text box control in the toolbox to add a text box to the form. Change the name of the text box to **txtSpecial**. Delete the contents of the Text property of the box.

4. This is the only constituent control in the new UserControl, so you may close the toolbox if you want more room in the design window.

5. Right-click the body of the UserControl and select **View Code**. In the Object list box of the Code window, select **UserControl**. In the Properties list box, select **Resize**. Press **Tab** and enter the following code to resize and reposition the text box to fill the UserControl when it is put in an application:

```
With txtSpecial
  .Top = 0
  .Left = 0
  .Height = UserControl.ScaleHeight
  .Width = UserControl.ScaleWidth
End With
```

6. Select **File | Add Project** to add a test bed project to the project group. Select **Standard EXE** and click **Open** to close the dialog box. The new project appears in the Project Explorer. In the Project Explorer, select **Project1** (not the **Forms** folder or the form). Select **Set as Start Up**. When the program is run later in this Step-by-Step exercise, the test bed project starts.

7. Bring the toolbox back (if you closed it) by clicking its icon in the toolbar. Its icon is the crossed hammer and wrench. The UserControl icon appears grayed out in the toolbox because you are still in the User-Control's design mode. Double-click **Formatted Textbox** (the UserControl) in the Project Explorer to enter its design

window. Close the design window with the **Close** button. When the design window closes, you automatically return to the other project. The UserControl icon no longer appears grayed out in the toolbox.

8. Identify the UserControl with the mouse pointer hovering over its icon in the toolbox. The ToolTip that appears should read *FormattedTextbox*. Select the control by clicking it once in the toolbox. Draw an instance of the control on the form. Change the name of the control (not the form) to **txtFormatted**.

9. Put a command button on the form for experimenting with the UserControl. Change the name of the command button to **cmdExperiment**. Change the caption of the command button to **Try It**. Open the Code window and select **cmdExperiment_Click**. Press **Tab** and enter: **MsgBox txtFormatted.Text**.

   You probably know this is not going to work. As you enter the period following txtFormatted, a list of properties for txtFormatted appears. The Text property is not on this list. Your UserControl does not have a Text property. For now, finish the entry with the **.Text** and press **Enter**.

10. Save everything: the form, the UserControl, the projects, and the project group. Name the form **Test**, the UserControl **Formatted Textbox**, Project1 **Test**, the other project **Special Format**, and the project group **Special Format**.

11. Run the program. Click the button **Try It**. The error message shown in Figure 11-9 appears. Stop the program.

    The error message means the Text property does not exist for the UserControl. What kind of text box has no Text property? This is a big problem (with an easy solution). It would be almost impossible to write a property function for each of the dozens of properties and methods that work with a regular text box. Luckily, the ActiveX Control Interface Wizard automates the process of enabling existing properties of the old text box control in the new UserControl.

FIGURE 11-9
The Compile error message

The ActiveX Control Interface Wizard is an Add-In, just like VisData. Unlike VisData which is already loaded, you need to load the ActiveX Control Interface Wizard before you can use it.

12. Select **Add-Ins | Add-In Manager** from the menu bar. Figure 11-10 shows the Add-In Manager dialog box.

13. Double-click the entry for the **VB6 ActiveX Ctrl Interface Wizard** (you must double-click the entry to load it). Click **OK** to close the dialog box. Select **Add-Ins | ActiveX Control Interface Wizard**. The wizard starts executing.

14. Read the opening dialog box of information and click **Next** to advance to the next dialog box. In the Select Interface Members dialog box, choose names of properties, methods, and events that you want to be part of your control. This dialog box adds only the names. A *member* of an

(continued on next page)

ActiveX control is a property, method, or event of the control. In the right list box are standard names that are a part of almost every Visual Basic control. In the left list box is a list of available names. Most correspond to familiar properties, methods, and events. To select a name and add it to the control you can double-click the name in the left list box. It moves from the left list box to the right list box. You can also click the right arrow to transfer a selected name to the right list box. You may also click the double right arrow button to transfer all the names from the left list box to the right list box. For this Step-by-Step exercise, double-click only the **Text** property (see Figure 11-11).

FIGURE 11-10
The Add-In Manager dialog box

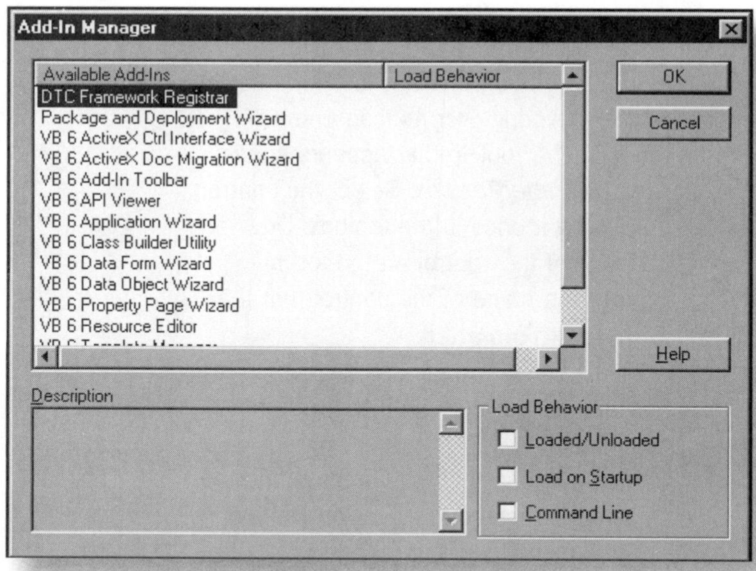

FIGURE 11-11
The Select Interface Members dialog box of the ActiveX Control Interface Wizard

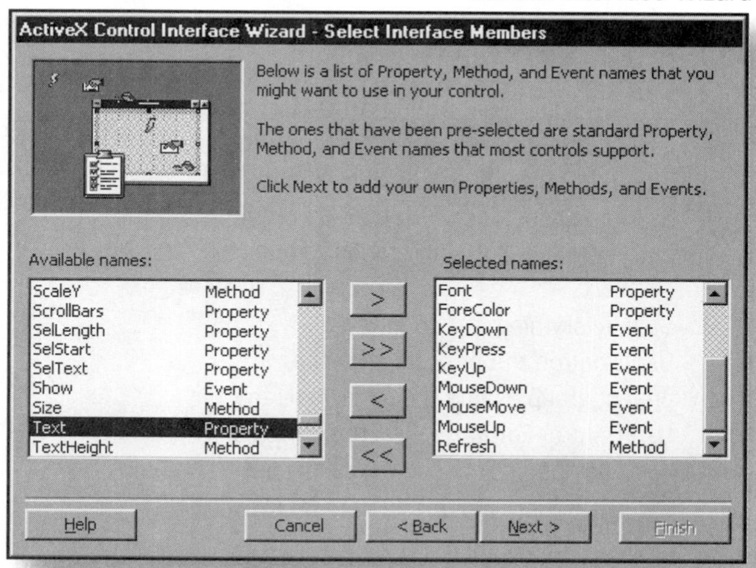

15. Click the **Next** button to advance to the next dialog box. This box collects the names of new properties, methods, or events you want to add to the control. The previous dialog box allowed you to add standard names. This dialog box lets you add any name at all. The control uses the Mode property to determine in what format to display values when the control loses the focus. Click the **New** button. Enter **Mode** for the Name property. The Property option button is already selected (see Figure 11-12).

16. Click **OK** to close the Add Custom Member dialog box, then click **Next** to advance to the next dialog box: the Set Mapping dialog box.

In this dialog box you map already existing properties, methods, and events of the constituent parts of the UserControl into the corresponding properties, methods, and events of the new UserControl. The caption, *Public Name*:, appearing above the left list box in the dialog box, refers to the fact that these are the Public properties of the new UserControl. Each must be provided with some kind of definition in code. The job of this window is to link the properties of the new UserControl with existing properties of txtSpecial.

FIGURE 11-12
The Create Custom Interface Members dialog box, showing the Add Custom Member dialog box

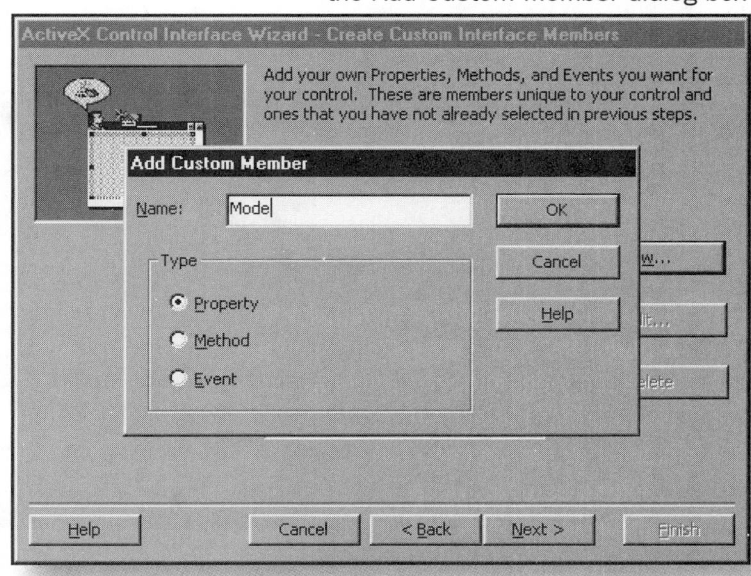

FIGURE 11-13
The Set Mapping dialog box

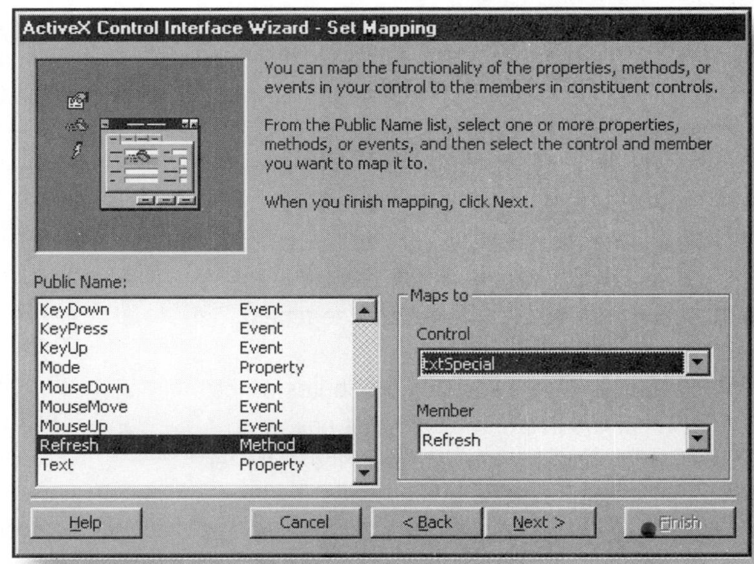

17. To link a single property, method, or event, select its entry in the left list box. For this application, select **Refresh** in the left list box. Click the list arrow for the Control combo box and select **txtSpecial**. Automatically, the Member box displays the corresponding entry of txtSpecial. Figure 11-13 shows the Refresh method of the UserControl mapped to the Refresh method of txtSpecial. You have to link the properties one by one when there is more than one constituent control from which properties are borrowed. In this case, there is only one control: txtSpecial. Click the first entry in the left list box, scroll down, hold down the **Shift** key, and click the last entry. All the properties are selected. Select **txtSpecial** from the Control combo box. The Member box

(continued on next page)

remains blank. Click **Next** to map the properties, methods, and events from txtSpecial to the new UserControl and advance to the next dialog box.

FIGURE 11-14
The Set Attributes dialog box

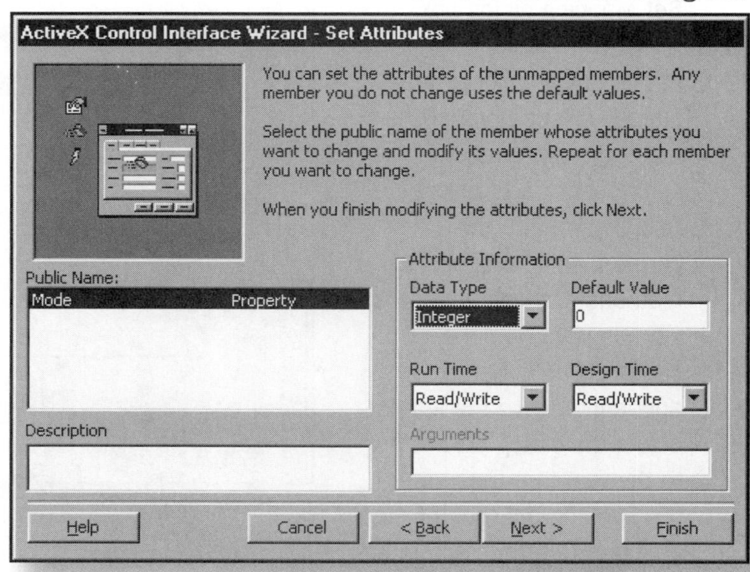

18. The Set Attributes dialog box appears. In the left list box appear any of the properties, methods, or events that did not get a mapping in the previous dialog box. These properties have no analog in the constituent control, txtSpecial. The BackStyle property serves no purpose for the UserControl. Click the **Back** button three times to return to the Select Interface Members dialog box. Select the **BackStyle** property in the right list box and double-click its entry. The BackStyle property shifts from the right list box to the left list box. This removes the BackStyle property from the UserControl. Return to the Set Attributes dialog box by clicking **Next** three times.

19. In this dialog box, set the attributes of the properties listed in the left list box, which now shows only Mode. Select the entry for the **Mode** property. Change the Data Type to **Integer** (see Figure 11-14). Click **Next** to advance to the final dialog box of the ActiveX Control Interface Wizard. The dialog box prompts you to View the Summary Report. Click the option (if it is not already selected) and click **Finish**. A window appears with the Summary Report. It explains how to test the new UserControl and what to do to finish it up. A Save button allows you to save the Summary Report for further reference. Click **Save** and save the report in the folder for this project.

20. Open the Code window for the UserControl. The ActiveX Control Interface Wizard adds a lot of code. Examine the code. The most mysterious is the code in Private Sub UserControl_ReadProperties (PropBag As PropertyBag) and Private Sub UserControl_WriteProperties(PropBag As PropertyBag). These event procedures save values of the UserControl's properties before they are changed. For instance, when a control is placed on a form, it is normal to set various properties of the control. An ActiveX control is running as soon as it is placed on the form. When a property value is set during design time, the value of the property is saved in the control's *PropertyBag*. If the value of the property is changed at run time, it is normal to return the property to its design-time value when the program stops. This is accomplished by restoring the design-time value of the property stored in the PropertyBag. The *PropertyChanged event* works with these procedures to be sure the values of properties are properly saved and restored.

21. In the General Declarations section of the UserControl code, enter the following line: **Dim sCurrent As String**. This variable holds the value of the text box. When a value like 0.000234 is displayed with four decimal places, it appears as the value 0.0002. When focus returns to the text box, the value is supposed to return to its original value. If 0.0002 is returned to the format "General Number," two digits of the original string are lost. Instead, the original string is saved in sCurrent. When focus returns to the text box, sCurrent is inserted into the Text property of the text box.

22. Select **txtSpecial_GotFocus**, press **Tab**, and enter the line **txtSpecial.Text = sCurrent**.

23. Select **txtSpecial_LostFocus**, press **Tab**, and enter the code shown in **Code Step 23** that reformats the value in the text box.

Do not change any of the entries made by the wizard. Do not even change the comments. The comments are a necessary part of the code generated by the wizard.

24. Close the UserControl design window by clicking the **Close** button for the design window. Select the form of the test bed project and click the **Menu Editor** button on the toolbar. Enter the following menu to select a mode:

MODE SELECT

CAPTION	NAME	INDEX
Select Mode	mnuMode	
....General	mnuModeSelect	0
....Currency	mnuModeSelect	1
....Percent	mnuModeSelect	2
....FourDecimals	mnuModeSelect	3
E&xit	mnuExit	

(continued on next page)

CODE STEP 23

```
sCurrent = txtSpecial.Text   ' Save the original string.
Select Case m_Mode   ' Internal value of the Mode property.
  Case 0
     ' default – no change
  Case 1 ' Currency
     txtSpecial.Text = Format$(sCurrent, "currency")
  Case 2 ' Percent
     txtSpecial.Text = Format$(sCurrent, "percent")
  Case 3 ' FourPlaces
     txtSpecial.Text = Format$(sCurrent, "#,0.####")
End Select
PropertyChanged "Text"
```

25. Click **OK** to close the Menu Editor. Double-click the **Exit** button and enter the line **Unload Me** in **mnuExit_Click**.

26. Select **mnuModeSelect_Click**, press **Tab**, and enter the code shown in **Code Step 26**.

27. Check to see that the procedure **cmdExperiment_Click** still has the line **MsgBox txtFormatted.Text**.

28. Run the program. Select **Select Mode | Currency** from the menu bar. Enter the value **1454.34759** in txtFormatted. Press **Tab** several times to shift the focus from txtFormatted to the command button and back. When txtFormatted loses the focus, the format of the value changes to represent a dollar amount. When the focus returns, the original string is restored. Test each of the other formats and experiment with shifting the focus with the Tab key.

29. Stop the program. Save the form, the project, the UserControl, its project, and the project group. If they have already been saved, click the **Save Project Group** buttton on the toolbar to save all at once.

30. To use the control in a future project, select the **Formatted Textbox User Control**. Select **File | Make** and compile the control to an ActiveX OCX file.

31. Leave the project open or exit Visual Basic Do *not* select File | Remove.

CODE STEP 26

```
txtFormatted.Mode = Index  ' Sets the Mode property.
```

If there is a problem with the code in the UserControl, open the UserControl's design window to make alterations. The debugging techniques involving breakpoints and single-stepping through code with F8 work in the ActiveX control.

It is not as easy as you might imagine to come up with significant improvements on existing controls. When you do think of a good improvement, the ActiveX Control Interface Wizard makes changes to existing controls straightforward.

Quick Check 11.d

1. Before using a UserControl in a test bed project, you must close the UserControl's __________________.

2. Use the __________________ dialog box to add the ActiveX Control Interface Wizard to the Add-Ins menu.

3. Use the Select Interface Members dialog box to select __________________ of the properties, methods, and events you want to add to the UserControl.

4. The Set Mapping dialog box of the ActiveX Control Interface Wizard has the job of __________________.

5. The PropertyBag is used to __________________.

Building a Custom Interface ActiveX Control

The common name for a Custom Interface ActiveX control is a User-Drawn ActiveX control. The normal controls found in the toolbox reflect Microsoft's interpretation of what the user interface should look like. The point of a User-Drawn control is that the programmer uses the control to create a unique or original interface.

The biggest difference between a User-Drawn control and a regular ActiveX control is that the User-Drawn control usually uses no constituent parts: It contains no text boxes, labels, or command buttons. Build the visual appearance of the control by using graphics methods in the control's Paint method. The Line method draws a line or draws and fills a rectangular box with color. The PSet method plots a single point. The Circle method draws and fills circles or ellipses with color. See the table below for a summary of each. Parts of the syntax appearing in square brackets are optional. Color is supplied by the QBColor( ) or RGB( ) color functions.

DRAW METHODS

METHOD	SYNTAX	DESCRIPTION
Line	*object*.**Line** [**Step**] **(***x1*, *y1***)** [**Step**] - **(***x2*, *y2***)**, [*color*], [**B**][**F**]	Draws a line from the first pair of coordinates to the second pair, or, if B is included, draws a box from corner coordinate to corner coordinate. If F is included, the box is filled with the same color used to draw the box.
PSet	*object*.**PSet** [**Step**] **(***x*, *y***)**, [*color*]	Plots a point on an object at coordinates (x,y).
Circle	*object*.**Circle** [**Step**] **(***x*, *y***)**, *radius*, [*color, start, end, aspect*]	Draws a circle at center (x,y) with radius radius. Start and end give the radian measure the starting point and the ending point of the arc drawn. Aspect specifies the aspect ratio of the circle. Any value but 1 results in an ellipse.

To put characters on a User-Drawn control, use the control's Print method. Define other properties or events in code or borrow them from the underlying UserControl object. The toughest part of designing a new kind of interface is conceiving something that is both different and useful. One reason the standard controls appear they way they do, is because they are easy to understand and to use.

The following Step-by-Step exercise guides you through the process of building the PictureFrame control. The control displays a message in a picture frame. The programmer sets the frame's colors and contents at design time or run time. Click the frame at run time to change the width of the frame.

STEP-BY-STEP 11.6

1. Start Visual Basic or select **File | New Project** to clear the screen. Select **ActiveX Control** and click **Open**. In the Project Explorer, right-click **Project1** and select **Project1 Properties**. In the Project1 Properties dialog box, change the Project Name to **PictureFrameLabel**. Enter **Label that looks like a picture frame** as the Project Description. Click **OK** to close the dialog box.

2. If necessary, click the body of the UserControl to select it. In the Properties window, change the name of the control to **PictureFrameCtrl**. Be sure the Public property of the control is set to **True**.

3. Open the UserControl's Code window. Enter the following declarations in the General Declarations section:

```
Dim lngFrameColor As Long
Dim lngBodyColor As Long
Dim nFrameWidth As Integer
```

   Color numbers are of the Long datatype. The FrameColor is the color of the edge of the frame. The BodyColor is the color of the interior of the frame. The FrameWidth is the width of the frame in twips.

4. Select **UserControl_Initialize**, press **Tab**, and enter the following code:

```
lngFrameColor = vbCyan
lngBodyColor = vbBlue
nFrameWidth = 300
```

   The *Initialize event* begins when the User-Control is put onto an application's form. It initializes the frame's colors and width.

5. The code in the UserControl's Paint method determines its appearance. Select **UserControl_Paint**, press **Tab**, and enter the code shown in **Code Step 5**.

   The FillStyle property controls the appearance of the inside of the drawn box. A FillStyle of 0 fills the box with a solid color. The default value of FillStyle, 1, makes the interior of the box transparent. The With statement works with properties, but not methods. To call the Line method, specify the object name.

CODE STEP 5

```
Dim nHeight As Integer
Dim nWidth As Integer
With UserControl
  nHeight = .Height
  nWidth = .Width
  .DrawWidth = 3
  .FillColor = lngFrameColor
  .FillStyle = 0
  .ForeColor = vbBlack
  UserControl.Line (0, 0)-(nWidth, nHeight), , B
  .FillColor = lngBodyColor
  UserControl.Line (nFrameWidth, nFrameWidth)-(nWidth - nFrameWidth,
    nHeight - nFrameWidth), , B
End With
```

Note: The lines shown in bold in this code should be entered on the *same* line.

The code draws one box inside the other using the specified coordinates. The first box is completely filled with lngFrameColor. The inner box is filled with lngBodyColor.

6. Add a project by selecting **File | Add Project**. Select **Standard EXE** and click **Open**. In the Project Explorer, select the name of the new project. Right-click the name of the project and select **Set as Start Up**.

7. Return to the design window of PictureFrameCtrl by double-clicking its entry in the Project Explorer. Close the design window with the **Close** button. The form for the new project appears.

8. Single-click the **PictureFrameCtrl** control in the toolbox. Draw an instance of the PictureFrameCtrl on the form. The form should appear similar to Figure 11-15 below.

FIGURE 11-15
Project2's form, showing an instance of PictureFrameCtrl

9. Save the form as **PictureFrame**. Select the UserControl and save it as **PictureFrameCtrl.** Select **Picture Frame Label** and save the project as **Picture Frame Label**. Select the new project and save it as **PictureFrame**. Save the project group as **PictureFrame**. If necessary, close the design window.

10. Run the project. The new control responds to no events. Stop the program by clicking the **Close** button in the right top corner of the window.

11. In the PictureFrame project form (not the UserControl), select the **PictureFrameCtrl1** control. The properties seen in the Properties window are the basic properties that almost all controls have. Before the control is functional, more properties must be added.

12. Double-click **PictureFrameCtrl** in the Project Explorer to open the control's design window. Add the ActiveX Control Interface Wizard, if it is not added. Start the wizard by selecting **Add-Ins | ActiveX Control Interface Wizard**. Click **Next** to enter the Select Interface Members dialog box. Click the double left arrow to remove all the property and event names from the Selected Names list box. In the left list box, Available Names, select and add the name **Font** and click the **right arrow**.

13. Click **Next** to enter the Create Custom Interface Members dialog box. Click **New** and enter **Caption** for the name of the new property. If necessary, select **Property** as the type. Click **OK**.

14. Click **Next** to enter the Set Mapping dialog box. If necessary, select **Caption** in the Public Name list box. Select **UserControl** in the Control combo box. A corresponding member does not appear in the Member combo box. The UserControl has no Caption property to loan its functionality to the new control. Select **Font** in the Public Name list box. Select **UserControl** in the Control combo box. A corresponding Member, Font, appears in the Member combo box. Click **Next** to enter the Set Attributes dialog box.

15. If necessary, select **Caption** in the Public Name list box. Select **String** for the Caption

(continued on next page)

property's Data Type. Enter **Caption displayed in PictureFrameLabel** as the Description. Click **Finish**. Close the Summary Report window.

16. The basic code for the Font and Caption properties is present in the Code window. Open the Code window and examine the code created by the wizard.

17. In the **UserControl_Paint** event procedure, enter the code shown in **Code Step 17** just prior to the line End With.

    This code positions the caption in the PictureFrameCtrl. The Print method displays a string at coordinates provided by CurrentX and CurrentY. The code calculates and sets these properties. The .TextWidth and .TextHeight methods calculate the space needed for the caption. CurrentX and CurrentY are set from these values. UserControl.Print m_Caption displays the caption centered in the UserControl.

18. Add the line **UserControl_Paint** to the following procedures:
    - Public Property Get Font( ) As Font
    - Public Property Set Font(ByVal New_Font As Font)
    - Public Property Let Caption(ByVal New_Caption As String)

    When the font or caption is changed, the UserControl must be redrawn. The control's Paint method renews the appearance of the control each time the font or caption is changed.

19. Click **View Object** in the Project Explorer. Click the **Menu Editor** button on the toolbar. The UserControl does not support a menu bar, but it does support a pop-up menu. Use the pop-up menu to let the user change the width of the frame while the application is running. Enter the following pop-up menu:

POP-UP MENU

CAPTION	NAME	INDEX
Adjust Width	mnuAdjWidth	—
....Increase	mnuAdjustWidth	1
....Decrease	mnuAdjustWidth	2
....Cancel	mnuAdjustWidth	3

20. Click **OK** to close the Menu Editor. Right-click the body of the UserControl and select **View Code**. Select **mnuAdjustWidth_Click** and enter the code shown in **Code Step 20.**

21. In **UserControl_Click**, enter the following code:

```
UserControl.PopupMenu mnuAdjWidth
```

22. Close the PictureFrameCtrl design window by clicking the **Close** button in the top right corner of the window. (Do not close Visual Basic!)

CODE STEP 17

```
'position the caption
.CurrentX = (.Width - .TextWidth(m_Caption)) / 2
If .CurrentX < 5 Then .CurrentX = 5
.CurrentY = (.Height - .TextHeight(m_Caption)) / 2
If .CurrentY < 5 Then .CurrentY = 5
.ForeColor = vbBlack
UserControl.Print m_Caption
```

23. Right-click the toolbox, select **Components**, select **Microsoft Common Dialog Control,** and click **OK**. Double-click the **Common Dialog** control in the toolbox to add it to the form below the UserControl. Add two command buttons to the form. Change the caption of the first command button to **Change Caption**. Change the name of the command button to **cmdCaption**. Change the caption of the second command button to **Change Font**. Change the name of the command button to **cmdFont**.

24. Open the Code window and select **cmdCaption_Click**. Press **Tab** and enter the code shown in **Code Step 24** to prompt the user to add a new caption to the PictureFrameCtrl.

25. Select **cmdFont_Click**, press **Tab**, and add the code shown in **Code Step 25**. The Flags property sets options for each of the dialog boxes supported by the Common Dialog control. The cdlCF Screen Fonts constant causes the Font dialog box to list only the screen fonts supported by the system.

26. Save all the parts of all the projects and the project group. Run the program. Click anywhere on the body of the PictureFrameCtrl. Select **Increase** or **Decrease**. Do it again. Each time the width of the Picture Frame changes. Click **Change Caption**. Enter a new caption. The new caption appears in the label. Click **Change Font**. Select a new font and font size. The format of the caption changes to match the selected font.

27. Stop the program.

28. Select **File | Make** to compile the new PictureFrameCtrl. It is now ready to use in other projects.

29. Exit Visual Basic (save changes if you are prompted).

CODE STEP 20

```
Select Case Index
 Case 1  ' increase
   nFrameWidth = nFrameWidth * 1.25
 Case 2  ' decrease
   nFrameWidth = nFrameWidth * 0.75
End Select
UserControl_Paint
```

CODE STEP 24

```
PictureFrameCtrl1.Caption = InputBox("Enter a new caption")
```

CODE STEP 25

```
CommonDialog1.Flags = cdlCFScreenFonts
CommonDialog1.ShowFont
With PictureFrameCtrl1
   .Font.Name = CommonDialog1.FontName
   .Font.Size = CommonDialog1.FontSize
   .Font.Bold = CommonDialog1.FontBold
End With
```

This completes the discussion of User-Created and Enhanced ActiveX controls. You have a powerful new tool for code reusability.

Quick Check 11.e

1. The common name for a Custom Interface ActiveX control is a ________________.

2. To put characters on a User-Drawn control, use the control's ________________ method.

3. The ________________ begins when the control is put onto an application's form.
4. The Paint method is used to ________________.
5. Select File | Make to ________________ the control and make it ready for use in other applications.

Summary

- ActiveX controls are a good way to pack commonly used functions and procedures into a portable package.
- There are three kinds of User-Created ActiveX controls: controls that combine existing controls, controls that enhance an existing control, and controls with a custom user interface. All three require code to make the functionality of the control available to the programmer.
- The UserControl object supports pop-up menus, but not normal menus.
- Just as all forms are called forms, all User-Created ActiveX controls are called UserControls.
- A major programming concern when designing a UserControl is handling the control's Resize event. The Resize event is triggered when the control is put onto an application.
- An ActiveX control has two run-time behaviors: one when the control is put on an application form, and another when the application containing the control is running.
- A project group is the easiest way to test an ActiveX control. It allows two projects to be open at the same time. One project is the ActiveX control, the other is the project used as a test bed for the ActiveX control.
- Running an ActiveX control with no project group or companion test bed project launches Microsoft Internet Explorer and runs the control within the browser window.
- Once a control is tested, it is ready to be compiled to an OCX file. Once compiled, it can be used in other Visual Basic projects.
- Each control has more properties than can be covered in a normal text. By examining the properties and trying them out in sample programs, you can get ideas for new programs of your own.
- The Make command in the File menu builds executable files from project files. To use an ActiveX control in a future project, select File | Make and compile the control to an ActiveX OCX file.
- Visual Basic projects need MSVBVM60.DLL to run outside the Visual Basic environment. This Dynamic Link Library contains the Visual Basic Virtual Machine, the program that turns a normal Windows computer into a Visual Basic computer.
- String functions parse commands and data from longer strings.
- The ActiveX Control Interface Wizard automates the process of building an ActiveX control. It supplies code skeletons for new properties, methods, and events. It also maps existing properties, methods, and events from constituent controls to the new control.
- Another name for a Custom Interface Active X control is a User-Drawn Active X control.
- Use graphics methods to draw the appearance of User-Drawn controls that have no constituent parts. This allows the programmer to design unique user interfaces.

LESSON 11 REVIEW QUESTIONS

TRUE/FALSE

Circle the T if the statement is true. Circle the F if it is false.

T F 1. An ActiveX control is a good way to package data for future use.

T F 2. The UserControl supports normal menus.

T F 3. When an ActiveX control is placed on an application form, its Resize event begins.

T F 4. Deleting a property's Let property procedure makes the property read-only.

T F 5. Select File | OCX to compile an ActiveX control to an executable file.

T F 6. A Virtual Machine is a program that turns one computer into another.

T F 7. Parsing a string means to build a string out of commands and data.

T F 8. One type of user-created ActiveX control enhances the features of an existing control.

T F 9. Use the Add-In Manager to load the ActiveX Control Interface Wizard.

T F 10. The PropertyBag is used to save values of properties changed at run time.

WRITTEN QUESTIONS

Write your answers to the following questions.

11. What are the three kinds of User-Created ActiveX controls?

12. Why is the Resize event so important in the process of designing and writing an ActiveX control?

13. What does it mean to say an ActiveX control has two run-time behaviors?

14. How do you test an ActiveX control during its design phase?

15. What does it mean to compile an ActiveX control?

16. What is the Visual Basic Virtual Machine?

17. What are some of the string functions used to parse a string to read its commands or data?

18. In the ActiveX Control Interface Wizard, what does mapping mean?

19. What is the difference between a User-Drawn ActiveX control and a regular ActiveX control?

20. What is the significance of the FillStyle property?

LESSON 11 APPLICATION PROBLEMS

SCANS

Level One

THE DISTANCE BETWEEN TWO CITIES ACTIVEX CONTROL

Create an ActiveX control similar to the LoanCalculator control to calculate and display the distance between two cities. The UserControl has four text boxes with corresponding labels so the user can enter the longitude and latitude of each city. The UserControl also includes a label for the mileage calculation results with a corresponding label. The UserControl resizes when added to an application. After the user inputs latitude and longitude, the control calculates the distance between the cities in degrees using the distance formula d = sqr((x1-x2)^2 + (y1-y2)^2), then converts to miles using the conversion factor 1 degree = 69 miles. The control displays the distance in miles in a label on the control and it exposes the Distance property to the programmer. The user clicks a command button to display a message showing the total mileage. Fully debug the control using a program group. HINT: Use the "fixed" format. This is a built-in pattern used by the Format function to display values with two decimal places.

COMPILING AND USING THE DISTANCE BETWEEN TWO CITIES CONTROL

Compile the control created in the first application above. Use the control in an application that calculates driving costs and time between two cities. The user enters the latitude and longitude of two cities and clicks a command button; the program displays the distance in miles and the cost and the time to drive between the cities. Use 24 cents per mile and 50 miles per hour for the average speed.

Level Two

THE PAYROLL CONTROL

Create a payroll calculator control. Write the control with no visible interface, so all access to the control is through properties. The control has the following write-only properties: wage rate in dollars per hour and hours. The control has two read-only properties: the regular wages and the overtime wage. Figure overtime at 1.5 times the regular hourly wage. Write, debug, and compile the control. Use the ActiveX Control Interface Wizard to automate the design of the control.

A PAYROLL EXERCISE

Use the Payroll control created in the third application above to write an application that calculates the weekly pay for the following workers:

PAYROLL		
WORKER NUMBER	WAGE PER HOUR	NUMBER OF HOURS
45	16.5	37
33	22.5	42
67	12.75	48

Use Notepad or Wordpad to create a text file with the above data. Separate each piece of data with a space. Put each worker's data on a separate line. Save the file.

Sample: 45 16.5 37

Use the Line Input statement to get the entire line of data for each worker and use the string functions discussed in the text to split the input line from the file into three separate pieces of data. Use the PayrollCtrl to provide wage information and write all the data to a new text file. The text file should have the following structure (each item separated with a tab character):

WorkerNumber, Wage, Hours, RegularPay, OTPay

A CUSTOM CONTROL

This control accepts a currency exchange rate and a number of dollars from the user and converts the dollar amount to another currency. ExchangeRate is a property of the Single type used to set the conversion factor. For instance, the ExchangeRate might be 148 escudos per dollar. (Escudos is the national currency of Portugal.) The user enters the number of dollars in the custom control and double-clicks the control to convert the dollar amount to escudos. The number of dollars is multiplied by the value of ExchangeRate and the result is displayed on the body of the control. The body of a UserControl accepts a picture as well as graphic methods. Load the control's Picture property with a picture. A Windows Metafile (*.wmf* extension) is a good choice because the picture scales to any size. Some WMF files are included on the Electronic Instructor CD-ROM.

To display characters on the body of the control, use the control's KeyPress event. Each time the event fires, check the parameter KeyAscii to confirm it is a numeral (ASCII codes 48 through 57, inclusive). If it is, concatenate it to a Caption string declared in the General Declarations section. Call UserControl_Paint to print the caption on the body of the control. Center the caption on the body of the control using the .TextWidth and .TextHeight methods.

The test bed project should prompt the user to enter the exchange rate. Labels on the form should direct the user to click the control and key numerals to enter values into the control. A second label should prompt the user to double-click the control to calculate the exchange.

LESSON 11 PROGRAMMING AT WORK

SCANS

In the Programming at Work for this lesson you are going to do something a little different. The Music Collection project is quite mature at this point, and it is hard to see the relevance of ActiveX controls. So instead of enhancing the Music Collection project, in this exercise you will build an ActiveX control capable of reading and displaying a database.

The SeeDatabase control lets the user select a database file with the extension *.mdb.* The user also selects a table from within the database. The control then generates a text box for each field of the table and connects the text box to the field. It also generates a label describing the field represented by the text box.

The new ActiveX control uses a DataControl to handle connections to the database. The important properties of the DataControl are DatabaseName and RecordSource. The DatabaseName is the name of the database file. Initialize the RecordSource property with the table selected by the user from a list box.

The control starts with a single text box with its Index property set to 0. This creates a control array. The text box is invisible and its DataSource property is set to the name of the DataControl at design time. When listing the fields of a database, new text boxes are loaded. For each, its DataField property is set to a field name from the table.

An invisible label is used as the basis for a control array to label each of the new text boxes.

1. Start Visual Basic. Select **ActiveX Control**. Click **Open**.

2. Right-click **Project 1** in the Project Explorer. Select **Project1 Properties**. Change the name of the project to **SeeDatabaseControl**. For the Project Description, enter **A control to view any database**. Click **OK**.

3. In the Properties window, change the name of the UserControl to **SeeDatabase**.

4. Right-click the toolbox and select **Components**. From the Components dialog box, check **Microsoft Common Dialog Control 6.0**. Click **OK**.

5. Put a DataControl along the top of the UserControl. Change its name to **dtaUniverse**. Add a Common Dialog control to the UserControl. Change its name to **dlgFile**.

6. Add a label and a text box to the UserControl. Set the Index property of each to **0**. This turns each into a control array. Set the Visible property of each to **False**. Set the DataSource property of the text box to **dtaUniverse**. Put a list box on the form. Change its name to **lstTables**. Set the Visible property of the list box to **False**.

7. Add a command button to the UserControl. Change its name to **cmdLoadDB**. Change its caption to **Load DB**. See Figure 11-16 for the final placement of the controls.

FIGURE 11-16
The SeeDatabase control showing final placement of controls

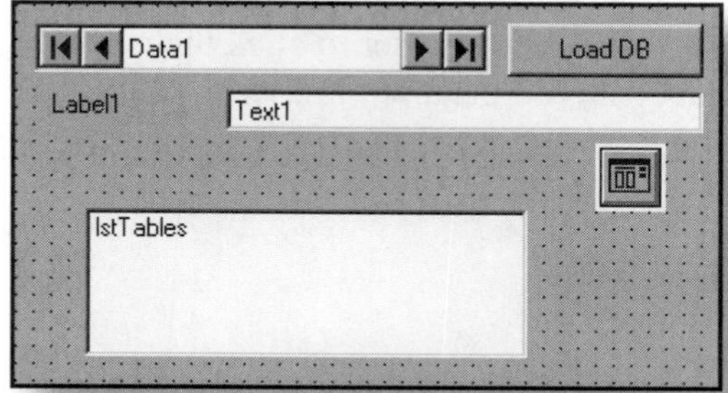

8. When a control is added to the UserControl, its height is altered to accommodate the control. When the control is removed, the UserControl returns to its original height. That value is saved in OrigHeight. Open the Code window of the UserControl. Enter this line in the General Declarations section of the UserControl: **Dim OrigHeight As Integer**.

9. In **UserControl_Initialize**, enter the following lines:

```
With UserControl   'Sets UserControl to minimum size.
  .Width = 4800
  .Height = 2670
End With
OrigHeight = UserControl.Height
```

10. Enter the following line in **UserControl_Resize**:

```
If UserControl.Height < 2670 Or UserControl.Width < 4800 Then
  UserControl_Initialize
End If
```

This calls the Initialize procedure if the control is sized smaller than its original height or width. It avoids redrawing the control when the control's height or width is altered by other parts of the code.

11. In the procedure **cmdLoadDB_Click**, enter the following code:

```
Dim x As Integer
lstTables.Clear
dtaUniverse.DatabaseName = ""
dtaUniverse.RecordSource = ""
If Text1.UBound > 0 Then
  For x = 1 To Text1.UBound
    Unload Text1(x)
    Unload Label1(x)
  Next x
End If
UserControl.Height = OrigHeight
```

The beginning of the code does not make sense until you realize that the user may click the button more than once. If clicked a second time, all the old data is cleared from the control. The code clears the list box, resets the DatabaseName and RecordSource of the DataControl to the null string, and clears all the text boxes and labels that were added to display the fields of the last database. The final step in the initialization is the restoration of the UserControl to its original height.

12. Continue by adding the following code below the code from Step 11:

```
'Set up the Common Dialog Control
dlgFile.Filter = "Database Files | *.mdb"
dlgFile.ShowOpen
Dim fn As String
fn = dlgFile.FileName   'Read filename from the dialog box.
```

```
If fn = "" Then Exit Sub  'Exit if no filename.
dtaUniverse.DatabaseName = fn
dtaUniverse.Refresh
```

The Refresh method makes the connection to the database file. The DataControl is loaded and ready to use.

13. Continue by adding the final section of code below the code from Step 12.

```
Dim db As Database
Set db = dtaUniverse.Database
'The TableDef is the definition of a database table.
Dim tb As TableDef
For Each tb In db.TableDefs
  If Left(tb.Name, 4) <> "MSys" Then
   lstTables.AddItem tb.Name
  End If
Next tb
lstTables.Visible = True
```

This code defines a Database object, db. It is set to the database exposed by the DataControl. Within the database is a least one table. Each table in a database has a table definition called a TableDef. Within the TableDef is a list of each field of the table. The variable tb, declared to be of the TableDef type, is used to probe the TableDef's collection. The name of each table is inserted into the list box. Some of the tables are used internally and are not accessible to the user, though their names appear in the TableDef. Those names all start with "MSys." Any table with an MSys prefix is omitted from the list box.

14. Enter the following code in **Private Sub lstTables_Click**:

```
Dim Table As String   'Holds the table name.
Dim RS As Recordset   'Refers to the Recordset.
Dim i As Integer
i = lstTables.ListIndex  'Table name clicked by user.
Table = lstTables.List(i)
lstTables.Visible = False  'Turn off list box.
With dtaUniverse
  .RecordSource = Table    'Set the RecordSource to the Table.
  .Caption = Table    'Put the Table name in the caption.
  .Refresh            'Refresh the connection to the database.
  Set RS = .Recordset
End With
```

The name of the table is stored in the TableDefs collection of the database. The name of each field is stored in the Fields collection of the table.

15. Enter the following code below the code you just entered:

```
Dim f As Field, x As Integer
x = 1
For Each f In RS.Fields
```

```
        On Error Resume Next
        Load Text1(x)    'Add a text box to the control array.
        With Text1(x)
          .DataField = f.Name    'Field name from Table.
          .Top = Text1(x - 1).Top + Text1(0).Height + 160
          .Visible = True        'Don't forget, control is invisible.
        End With
        'Load the matching label and fill with field name.
        Load Label1(x)
        With Label1(x)
          .Top = Text1(x).Top
          .Caption = f.Name
          .Visible = True
        End With
        x = x + 1    'x keeps track of the next control to add.
    Next f
    'Adjust the size of the control.
    UserControl.Height = x * (Text1(0).Height + 160) + 1000
```

16. Save the control with appropriate names.

17. Add a **Standard EXE** project to create a project group. Right-click the name of the new project in the Project Explorer and select **Set as Start Up**. Close the design window of the SeeDatabase control. Add the control to the new form. Run the program. Click **Load DB**. Navigate to a saved database file, such as the Music Collection database or the **portableCD** database. Click the file name of the database and click **Open**. The database's table(s) appear in the list box. Click a table in the list box. The list box disappears. Text boxes and labels appear. They contain the first record from the table in the database. You may have to resize the form to view all the fields. Click the arrows on the DataControl to look at the records.

18. Click **Load DB**. The text boxes and labels disappear. Again, the Common Dialog control prompts you for a file name. Navigate to a different database file. Select its name and click **Open**. The list box appears with the table names. Click a table and explore the resulting display. Stop the program.

19. Save the form, the UserControl, the project files, and the project group file (in that order).

    You are not done (although everything works) until the control is compiled and tested in a new application.

20. Select **File | Make SeeDatabase.ocx** (your file may not match this exactly). Click **OK** in the Make Project dialog box. When Visual Basic is finished, make sure everything is saved and open a new project. Select **Standard EXE** and click **OK**.

21. Right-click the toolbox and select **Components**. Click the **Browse** button. Navigate to your new OCX file. Double-click its entry to add it to the Components dialog box. The control's description appears in the dialog box: *A control to view any database*. Click **OK** to close the dialog box.

22. You are ready to test the control in your new application. It can stand alone with no other controls or code. Add the control to the form, then run the program.

23. Use your new control to view the Music Collection database (see Figure 11-17).

    An obvious modification in the future would allow the control to search for particular data or enter an SQL (Structured Query Language) string to filter the RecordSet.

24. Stop the program to exit Visual Basic. You do not need to save this new project.

FIGURE 11-17
The SeeDatabase ActiveX control, showing a record from the Music Collection database

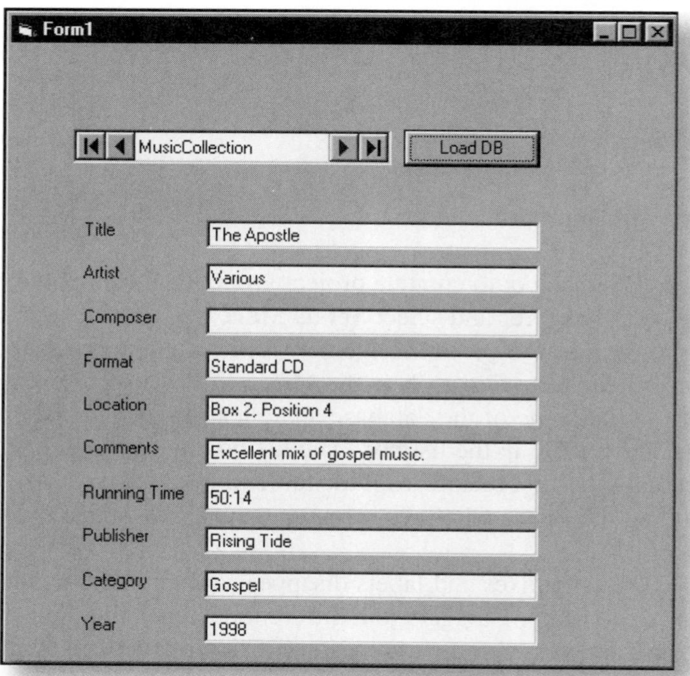

Historically Speaking

Steve Jobs is partly responsible for Visual Basic. Well, not directly. Steve Jobs and Steve Wozniak started the Apple computer company in a garage in the mid '70s. In 1979, Jobs visited the Xerox Palo Alto Research Center, PARC, and saw the Alto computer. It had a mouse and a graphical user interface. Jobs instantly recognized the future of computing in the graphical user interface. The Macintosh computer, presented in 1984, was the first Apple instantiation of this vision. The graphical user interface is now the standard of the industry and Visual Basic is the fastest and easiest way to deliver programs with that graphical user interface to customers.

API: Application Programming Interface

LESSON 12

OBJECTIVES

When you complete this lesson, you will be able to:

- Use the API viewer to View and copy API declarations to Visual Basic applications.
- Use an API function directly.
- Build a Visual Basic "wrapper" around an API function call.
- Use an API function call to play WAV files in an application.
- Use API function calls to build INI files for your applications.
- Access the Windows Registry Database.

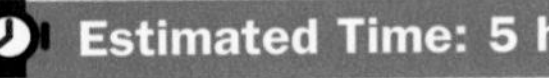

KEY TERMS

base-16
Machine Language
reentrant
Component Object Model (COM)
Application Programmiing Interface (API)
Win32api.txt
ByVal
handle
hWnd property
hexadecimal
WAV sound files
asynchronously
INI files
Windows Registry
parsing

The API Viewer

Years ago, when microcomputers first appeared, they provided extra opportunities for exploration and adventure. Each came with a different and incompatible built-in version of the BASIC programming language. For those that mastered their computer's version of BASIC, there was the shadowy and unknown world of operating systems. Almost every BASIC gave direct access to memory cells (a no-no today) with Peek and Poke commands. Some contained mechanisms to call machine language functions hidden in the operating system's Read Only Memories or hard coded in *base-16* codes by the programmer. Base-16 is a number system based on powers of 16 instead of powers of 10. It is closely related to the binary number system.

Some companies refused to divulge information about their operating system's internal workings. Others published fully commented assembly language listings. Either way, by using *Machine Language* routines directly from the computer's operating system, computer wizards were able to do things other programmers could not do.

Today, things are different. First, most code is *reentrant*. This means the code can be loaded and run from anywhere in memory and restarted several times simultaneously—no more direct Peeks and Pokes into specific memory areas. Another difference is that the languages of today make far more of the functions contained in the operating system available to the user. Not only are they available, each is neatly packaged as statements in the language itself: That is one reason programming languages are so large.

The Component Object Model

COM is the *Component Object Model.* This model is used to build almost all Microsoft software. It is the basis of the Windows operating systems. It allows programmers to build applications and systems from components supplied from many sources. The ActiveX objects you compiled in the last lesson are part of the Component Object Model. Compiled ActiveX objects are no longer tied to a source language: They are used as building blocks to make new applications in any language.

The entire Windows operating system uses modules of code stored in Dynamic Link Libraries (DLLs). These modules are the basis of much of Visual Basic. They define how Visual Basic interacts with the file system, multimedia applications, windows, the mouse, and other hardware devices. You already use the *API*, *Application Programming Interface*. It is built into Visual Basic. The API is a set of routines used by an application to access and execute the procedures of a computer's operating system. This lesson is about using API functions.

This lesson is not a comprehensive discussion of API calls. It would take several lessons to document and demonstrate even a small portion of the possible uses of API functions and Sub procedures. Part of the complexity of the subject is due to the many parameters that are a part of most API calls. The argument or parameter list may have zero to a dozen entries. To call the API function, you have to know what each parameter does and what default values to provide.

You can find default values in the list of constants displayed in the API Viewer. The problem with the list of constants is that they are undocumented. Only the name of the constant gives a clue to what its use is. For instance, constants that start with CB_ concern the combo box. You will use one of those to send messages to a combo box in one of the demonstrations later in the lesson.

The API Viewer

Some things do not change much. There is still a shroud of mystery hanging around API calls. The API Viewer helps demystify API calls, but it is not a comprehensive reference of what the API calls are. The API Viewer provides a listing of the API declarations. It makes them easy to use in a Visual Basic program. It copies the declaration needed to call an API function so that you can paste it into your application.

API functions are not much different from Visual Basic functions. They have a data type (unless they are Sub procedures), a name, and parameters. One difference is how the API functions use strings as parameters. A string passed as a parameter to an API function must be of fixed length, filled with spaces or nulls. When a value of a string is returned by the API function, it is terminated with ASCII code 0. This is common for many programming languages, but it is not the way Visual Basic terminates a string.

To use an API function in a program, you must declare it. The syntax of the Declare statement is:

[**Public** | **Private**] **Declare Function** *name* **Lib** "*libname*" [**Alias** "*aliasname*"] [([*arglist*])] [**As** *type*]

There is a whole language dedicated to expressing the syntax of programming statements. You see many of the language elements in the line above. Anything in a square bracket is optional. The vertical bar means "or." It separates different options: Public or Private, not both. Anything in boldface type is a "terminal symbol," actually part of the statement as it appears in code. Items in italics are like variables that refer to a specific item, like a particular name or path name. Some items in italics are themselves subject to expansion. Arglist (argument list) represents a syntax for entering a parameter list. The syntax for Arglist appears below:

[Optional] [ByVal | ByRef] [ParamArray] *varname*[( )] [As *type*]

As you suspected, the Arglist is just a list of variable names and types. The libname is the name of the file that contains the DLL. The name of the function (or Sub) is any legal Visual Basic function name. It is the name used in application code. The Alias is the actual name of the function used in the DLL. It may be different from the name given to the Visual Basic function. Some Function names in DLLs are illegal in Visual Basic. In this case, the Alias is necessary. It allows the Declare statement to find the actual function in the DLL.

STEP-BY-STEP 12.1

1. Start Visual Basic and double-click **Standard EXE**. Save the form and project as **APIDemo**.

2. Change the caption of the form to **API Demo**. Change the name of the form to **frmAPIDemo**.

3. Select **Add-Ins | Add-In Manager** from the menu bar. Double-click the entry **VB 6 API Viewer** (be sure the Load Behavior column shows *Loaded*). See Figure 12-1. Click **OK** to close the dialog box.

4. Select **Add-Ins | API Viewer** from the menu bar. The API Viewer opens. It shows no entries because the API data file has not been selected. Select **File | Load Text File** from the menu bar of the API Viewer. Figure 12-2 shows the Select a Text API File dialog box. Click the entry for **Win32api.txt**. **Win32api.txt** is a file of Declare statements, Constants, and Type declarations applying to API calls. The text files shown are loaded into the Winapi directory when Visual Basic or Visual Studio is loaded. Each text file shown in Figure 12-2 contains the Declare statements needed to use an API function in a program. Each file contains a different set of functions. This Step-by-Step exercise uses the **Win32api.txt** file.

FIGURE 12-1
The Add-In Manager dialog box showing the selection of VB 6 API Viewer

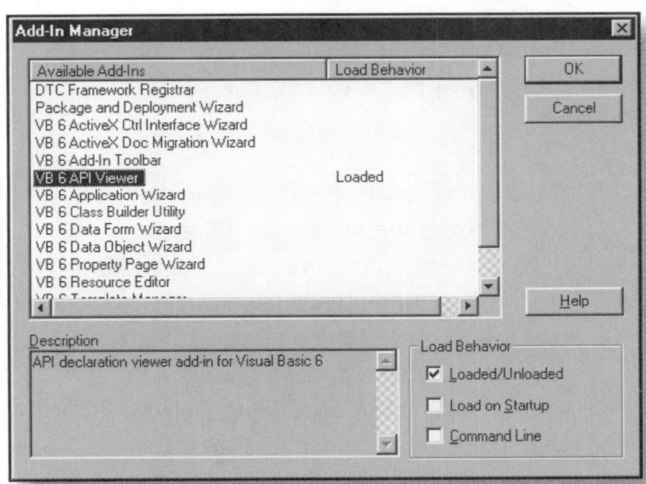

FIGURE 12-2
The Select a Text API File dialog box

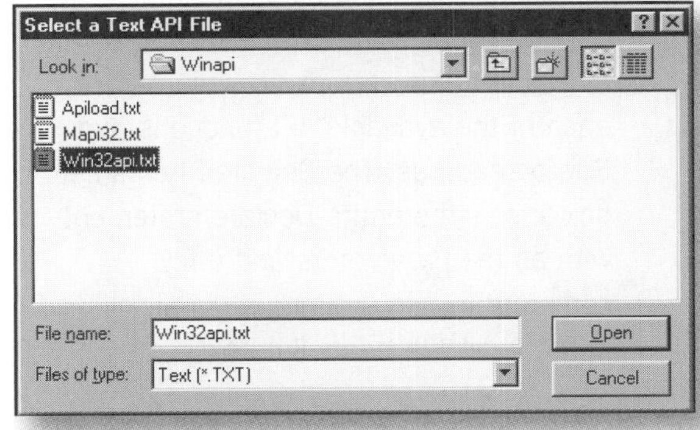

(continued on next page)

5. Click **Open** to select **Win32api.txt.** The Select a Test API File dialog box closes and the API Viewer appears (after a moment or two) with entries from **Win32api.txt**. Figure 12-3 shows the API Viewer as it first appears after the text file is loaded. Keep the API Viewer open as you read the following paragraphs.

FIGURE 12-3
The API Viewer with **Win32api.txt** loaded

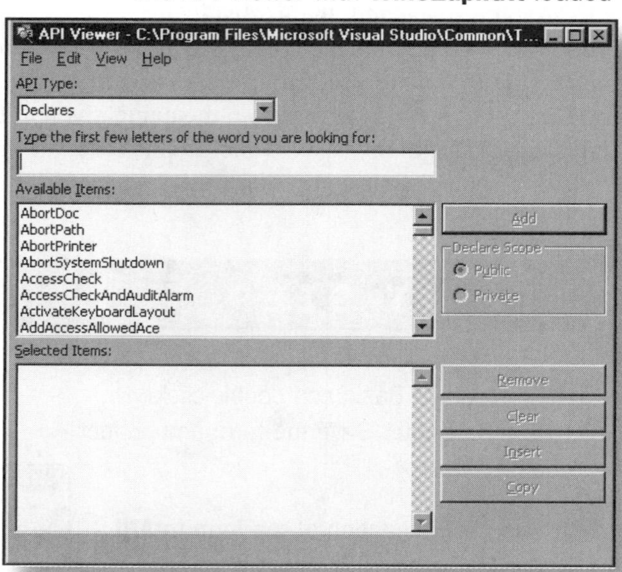

The API Viewer remains in the Add-Ins menu until you exit Visual Basic. Each time you start Visual Basic, repeat Steps 3-5 if you need to use the API Viewer.

There are three API Types listed in the combo box of the API Viewer: Constants, Declares, and Types. The most interesting are the Declare statements shown in Figure 12-3. The Declare statements are used to integrate operating system function calls into Visual Basic. Select, copy, and paste appropriate Declare statements directly into your Visual Basic application to execute its code. Enter characters of a particular API call to scroll quickly through the (long) list to the first item beginning with those characters. The Available Items list box lists the names of each of the available API functions and Sub procedures. The Selected Items list box shows the entire Declare statement with all the parameters and a few comments when an item is double-clicked in the Available Items list box.

Once the Declare statement for an item appears in the Selected Items list box, you can examine its parameters and data types closely and decide if that is the function you want. When you collect all the API Declare statements you need for a particular application, click the button to copy the Selected Items list box to the Windows Clipboard. Once copied to the Clipboard, it is easy to paste the Declares to the General Declarations section of the Code window for a form or standard (code) module.

API procedures are either Public or Private. If they are declared in the General Declarations section of a form module, they must be declared as Private. If you paste a Declare statement containing the Public keyword, just change the keyword to Private. If the API function is to have universal visibility in a project, put its Declare statement in a standard (code) module and use the Public keyword.

A second way to add a Declare statement to the Selected Items list box is to select the name of the API function in the

Available Items list box and click the Add button.

A third way to add a Declare statement to the Selected Items list box is to select the name of the API function in the Available Items list box and click the Insert button. The Insert button inserts the list of Declare statements into the Select Items list box and inserts them directly into a module. If you open a Standard EXE, which starts with only a form module, the Insert button inserts the Declare statements in the General Declarations section of the Code window of the form module.

If you add a standard module by selecting Project | Add Module from the menu bar, the Insert button inserts the Declare statements in the Selected Items list box directly into the code module.

The Clear button clears the entire Selected Items list box. Use the Remove button by clicking anywhere in an entry you want to remove and clicking the Remove button.

The option buttons, Public and Private, in the Declare Scope frame, determine how the entry will be copied into the Selected Items window.

At some point in the process, the API Viewer may show the message box in Figure 12-4. As a text file, the information in the file takes some time to break into pieces. If converted to a database file, access is much faster.

The **Win32api.txt** file is a file you can view in WordPad or Word. It is too large for Notepad. In fact, you should open the file in WordPad and look it over. Every

FIGURE 12-4
The API Viewer's request to convert the text file to a database

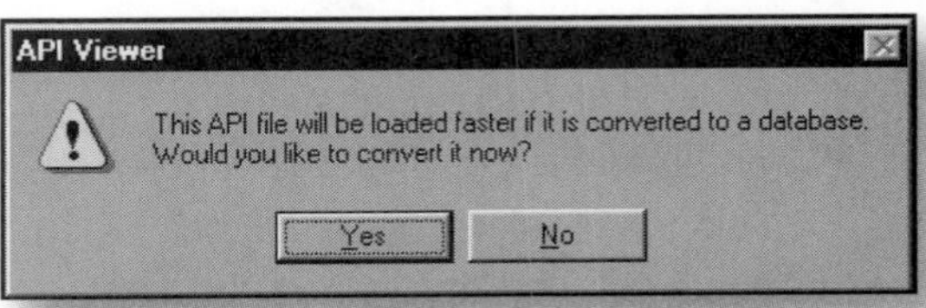

constant, type declaration, and Declare statement visible in the API Viewer is shown in the file. In addition, the file contains comments like the one shown below. Actually, many of the comments are very helpful.

```
'An attempt has been made to operate
'on an impersonation token by
'a thread that is not
'currently impersonating a client.
```

6. Be sure the word *Declares* is showing in the API Type combo box. If not, click its entry. In the search text box, enter **Charlower**. When CharLower is selected in the Available Names list box, click **Add** to add its declaration to the Selected Items list box (see Figure 12-5). The figure shows the selection of CharLower in the Available Names list box, and the Declare statement used to call the function in the Selected Items list box.

   The Declare statement is shown below:

```
Public Declare Function CharLower_
Lib "user32" Alias "CharLowerA" _
(ByVal lpsz As String) As String
```

   This is one of the easier Declare statements in the list. Use the keyword Public only if the Declare is placed in a standard (code) module. If put in the General Declarations section of a form module, change Public to Private. The Visual Basic name of the function is

(continued on next page)

CharLower. Its definition is found in user32.dll. Its internal name is CharLowerA. The line is continued using the underscore character. When copied to your application, Declare statements appear on a single line. Since most are very long, there is no way to see the entire line unless you break it up with line continuation characters.

The function sends a single parameter. The name of the parameter is lpsz. The first two letters, "lp," stand for long pointer. Long means a long integer, pointer means an address pointing to the value of the parameter, in this case a string. "s" in the parameter name stands for string and "z" means the string should be terminated with a null character (ASCII code 0). The parameter is sent *ByVal*, short for "by value." The value of the parameter sent ByVal cannot be changed by a Function or Sub. Variables sent by value cannot be permanently changed in the calling program. The return value of the function is itself a string. In this case, the string returned is the original string converted to all lowercase.

This is the function underlying the LCase( ) function already present in Visual Basic.

7. Click **Insert** to insert the Declare statement into the General Declarations section of the Code window for your current project. Since we forgot to click the Private option button, the Declare is written into the General Declarations section of the form module with the keyword Public. Figure 12-6 shows the prompting message that results when you click Insert. Click **Yes**, then close the API Viewer by selecting **File | Exit** from the API Viewer menu bar (not the Visual Basic menu bar).

FIGURE 12-5
The API Viewer, showing the entry for CharLower

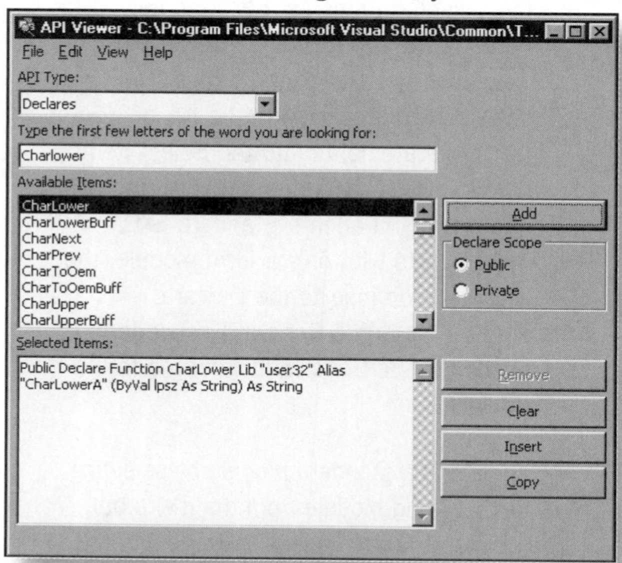

FIGURE 12-6
API Viewer confirmation message: Insert selected items

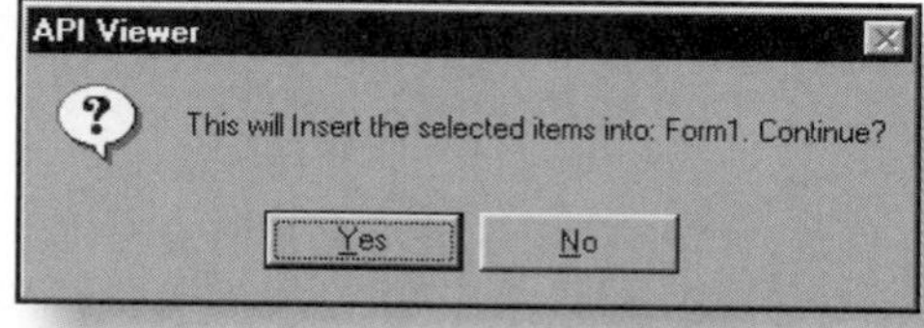

8. When the API Viewer closes, the project returns. Open the project's Code window. The copied Declare statement is present at the top of the Code window. Break the long line of code into three lines by inserting the underscore character, as shown in Step 6, and pressing **Enter**. Change Public to **Private**.

9. Click **View Object** in the Project Explorer to show the form. Add a command button to the form. Change the caption of the command button to **Convert to Lower**.

Change the name of the command button to **cmdConvertLower**.

10. Double-click the button to open the Code window to **cmdConvertLower_Click**. Press **Tab** and enter the code shown in **Code Step 10**.

As mentioned, API functions expect fixed length strings. TryThis and Result are declared as 40 character strings. The strings sent to API Functions are null terminated. ASCII 0 is concatenated to the end of the string TryThis. A message box displays the original string, CharLower( ) is called, and a message box displays the modified result.

11. Save the project. Run the program. Click **Convert to Lower**. The original message appears. Click **OK**. The characters in TryThis are converted to lowercase.

12. Stop the program and add the following line at the end of the code for **cmdConvertLower_Click**:

```
MsgBox "The original: " & TryThis
```

13. Save and run the program. Click **Convert to Lower**, then click **OK** when the original message appears. Click **OK** again when the modified message appears. Not only is the string labeled Result converted to lowercase, but so is the original. Surprised? Remember the description of the parameter, lpsz. The parameter is a pointer to the string. The pointer is sent by value (ByVal) and cannot change, but the string it points to can change, and does. The original string is converted to all lowercase characters.

14. Click **OK** and stop the program, then remove the project.

CODE STEP 10

```
Dim TryThis As String * 40, Result As String * 40
TryThis = "API Functions are COOL" & Chr$(0)
MsgBox "The original: " & TryThis
Result = CharLower(TryThis)
MsgBox "The modified: " & Result
```

All this to say, API function calls are risky. They are also fun.

Quick Check 12.a

1. API stands for ____________________.
2. COM stands for ____________________.
3. Declare the Declare statements in a form module with the keyword ____________________.
4. Terminate a string sent to an API function with a ____________________.
5. ByVal means that the value of the parameter sent "by value" ____________________.
6. The Insert button in the API Viewer copies ____________________ directly to ____________________.

Sending Messages to Controls

Object Oriented Programming works by creating programming objects that are both representations of data and the actions that can be performed on the data. Programming with objects means sending messages to objects and receiving messages from objects. Use the API function discussed in this section to send messages to Visual Basic controls, which are a kind of object.

The combo box was introduced in an early lesson. It is close kin to the text box. It is a deluxe text box because it gives the user a selection of appropriate choices. The choices appear in the form of a drop-down list, similar to a list in a list box. The combo box uses the AddItem method (like a list box) to add items to its drop-down list. It even uses the List property (like a list box) to allow array-like access to the entries in its list. Like a text box, its value is read in its Text property.

To open the list in a combo box, you must click the tiny down arrow on the right edge of the box. In this Step-by-Step exercise you will send a message to the combo box to open (drop down) its list when the box receives the focus.

STEP-BY-STEP 12.2

1. Start a new **Standard EXE** project. Save the form and project as **Combo**.

2. Change the name of the form to **frmComboMessage**. Change the caption of the form to **Sending a Message to the Combo Box**.

3. Double-click the **ComboBox** control in the toolbox to add a combo box to the form. Change the name of the combo box to **cboLanguages**. Put a text box on the form next to the combo box. The text box is used as a second object that can receive the focus. With two objects on the form when the program is running, it is possible to shift the focus back and forth by pressing Tab.

4. Open the Code window of the form and select **Form_Load**. Press **Tab** and enter the code shown in **Code Step 4** to initialize the combo box.

5. Save the project. Run the program. Click the list arrow of the combo box to show the drop-down list. Select an item from the list. Press **Tab** several times to shift focus back and forth between the text box and the combo box.

6. Stop the program.

7. Click **Add-Ins** on the menu bar. If API Viewer is in the menu, click **Add-Ins** again to close the menu. If API Viewer is not in the menu, select **Add-In Manager**. Double-click **VB 6 API Viewer** in the list of Available Add-Ins. The word *Loaded* should appear in the column headed Load Behavior. Click **OK** to close the Add-In Manager.

CODE STEP 4

```
cboLanguages.AddItem "Visual Basic"
cboLanguages.AddItem "Visual C++"
cboLanguages.AddItem "J++"
cboLanguages.AddItem "Microsoft Fortran"
cboLanguages.AddItem "MASM"
```

8. Select **Add-Ins | API Viewer**. In the API Viewer, select **File | Load Text File**. In the Select a Text API File dialog box, select **Win32api.txt** by double-clicking its entry. The file loads in the API Viewer. Enter **SendMessage** in the search window. Click the **Private** option button in the Declare Scope frame. Click **Add** to add the name SendMessage to the Selected Items list box. Click **Insert** to insert the Declare statement into the Code window of the project's form. Figure 12-7 shows the API Viewer message box, prompting the user to confirm the insert.

9. Click **Yes** to confirm the insertion. Leave the API Viewer open. In the Project Explorer, double-click **frmComboMessage** to return to the Visual Basic project. Open the Code window. Note the Declare statement. Reformat the single-line statement into four lines by inserting line continuation characters and using the Enter key. Format the statement so it is similar to the statement in **Code Step 9**.

   The name of the Visual Basic function is SendMessage. The function's name in its Dynamic Link Library, user32.DLL, is SendMessageA. The function is used to send messages to Visual Basic objects, including windows, forms, and controls. The function takes four parameters and returns a long value.

   The first parameter is hwnd. The *h* stands for *handle*. A handle is an integer value assigned to forms and many controls. The value of the integer is defined by the operating environment and is unique for

FIGURE 12-7
The API Viewer message box, asking for user confirmation of the insert procedure

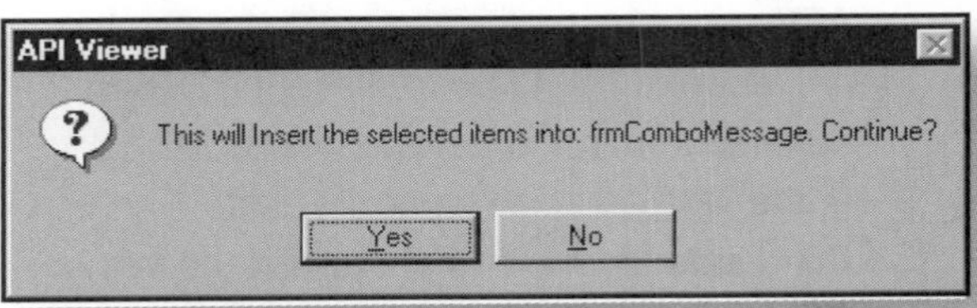

   each control and form. This property is commonly used in API calls to identify a particular object. The value of the *hWnd property* (when used as a property, it is spelled with an uppercase W) is not under programmer control. It is subject to change without notice, so do not store its value in a variable. The value stored may not always refer to the same control or form in the life of the project.

   The second parameter, wMsg, is a constant that represents the message sent to the object. Use the API Viewer to examine constants to find an appropriate message. The message itself is an integer value usually expressed in base-16, hexadecimal. Values in *hexadecimal*, hex for short, are identified by the "&H" prefix. Other letters in the constant are actually hex digits. The letters A through F represent the digits 10 through 15.

   The last two parameters are additional information that may be required by the message. In this project, these parameters are set to 1 and 0.

10. To find the message that tells the combo box to display its drop-down list, click the

(continued on next page)

CODE STEP 9

```
Private Declare Function SendMessage _
Lib "user32" Alias "SendMessageA" _
(ByVal hwnd As Long, ByVal wMsg As Long, _
ByVal wParam As Long, lParam As Any) As Long
```

APViewer icon on the taskbar to access the API Viewer. Click **Clear** to erase the Declare statement from the Selected Items list box. In the API Types combo box, select **Constants**. If you have not turned the text file into a database file for faster access, the API Viewer may remind you to do so. By examining the **Win32api** text file, you might discover that all the combo box messages start with the prefix CB_. That information is found as a comment in the text file. In the search text box, enter **CB_**. A list of message constants appears.

As you look over the list, you wonder: What do all these messages mean? When you find one you think you can figure out, more questions occur to you: What additional parameters are needed for the message? What value is returned? Is the return value returned in the function name or as a parameter? The API Viewer has no answers for these questions.

11. Select **CB_SHOWDROPDOWN=&H14F**. Click **Add** to add the constant to the Selected Items list box. Be sure **Private** is Selected under Declare Scope. Click **Insert** to enter the constant declaration to the General Declarations section of the form. Click **Yes** to confirm the insertion. Return to the Code window for the Visual Basic project. Leave the API Viewer open. Notice the constant declaration.

12. In the Code window, select **cboLanguages** from the Object list and **GotFocus** from the Procedure list. Press **Tab** and enter the code shown in **Code Step 12**. Note that par1 and par2 refer to the wParam and lParam parameters.

13. Save the project. Run the program. Since the combo box was placed on the form first, it receives the focus first. The drop-down list appears as soon as the form loads. Press **Tab** to shift focus to the text box. The drop-down list disappears. Press **Tab** several times. It is obvious that this API is used to display the drop-down list as if the down arrow on the combo box were clicked. Stop the program.

14. Do you feel adventuresome? Click the window for the API Viewer. Click **Clear** to clear the Selected Items list box. Enter **CB_ADDSTRING** in the search text box and select the constant for **CB_ADDSTRING**. Be sure the **Private** option button is clicked and click **Add** to add the constant to the Selected Items list box. Repeat the process for **CB_DELETESTRING**. Click **Insert** to insert the constants into your program. Click **Yes** to confirm the insertion and select **File | Exit** from the API Viewer menu bar to close the API Viewer.

Clearly, CB_ADDSTRING and CB_DELETESTRING are messages to add and delete an item from the combo box's drop-down list. But how shall the last two parameters be set? If you have the full MSDN libraries installed, or have access to the MSDN library disks, you may search for the answers. Alternatively, you may guess and check. The code for Step 17 is a result

CODE STEP 12

```
Dim Result As Long, par1 As Long, par2 As Long
par1 = 1
par2 = 0
Result = SendMessage(cboLanguages.hwnd, CB_SHOWDROPDOWN, par1, par2)
```

of both searching the MSDN libraries and guessing and checking.

15. Add a command button to the form. Change the name of the command button to **cmdAddItem**. Change the caption of the button to **Add a New Language**. Add a second command button. Change its name to **cmdDelete** and its caption to **Delete a Language**.

16. Add an Exit command button. Change its caption to **E&xit**, and its name to **cmdExit**. Figure 12-8 shows the completed form. Open the Code window and enter the statement **Unload Me** in **cmdExit_Click**.

17. Enter the code shown in **Code Step 17** in **cmdAddItem_Click**. Note that par1 refers to the lParam parameter in this code.

The code looks reasonable, but it will not work yet. AddThis is a fixed length string. Collect a value for the variable with the InputBox function. Add an ASCII 0 to the end of the string. Pass the string as the fourth parameter (lParam). To send the string as a parameter, the fourth parameter must be sent ByVal.

FIGURE 12-8
The complete form for the Sending a Message to Combo Box project

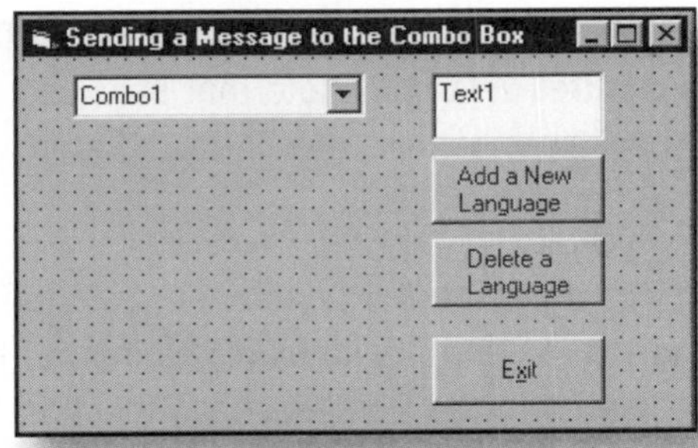

18. Locate the **SendMessage Declare** statement in the General Declarations section of the form. Insert the keyword **ByVal** and a space in front of the fourth parameter: **lParam As Any**.

19. Save the project. Run the program. Press **Tab** until the command button **Add a New Language** receives the focus. Press **Enter** or click the button. When prompted, enter **Pascal** for a new language and click **OK**. Press **Tab** until the combo box once again receives the focus. The language name entered in the InputBox appears as the last item in the combo box list. Stop the program.

(continued on next page)

CODE STEP 17

```
Dim Result As Long, par1 As Long
Dim AddThis As String * 40
par1 = 0
AddThis = InputBox("Enter the name of a computer language:")
AddThis = AddThis & Chr$(0)
Result = SendMessage(cboLanguages.hwnd, CB_ADDSTRING, par1, AddThis)
```

Building Programming Skills

Can you throw away a program and start over? Absolutely! Sometimes you realize an approach to a problem is just leading further and further down a road of complexity that you do not want to travel. After travelling that road often, you can see a better way. Start over. The things you learned on the cul de sac will make the second trip much faster.

20. Enter the code shown in **Code Step 20** in **cmdDelete_Click**. Note that par1 and par2 in this code refer to the wParam and lParam parameters.

This time, the third parameter (wParam) is used to send the index of the item to be deleted to the SendMessage function.

21. Save the project. Run the program. Press **Tab** until the **Delete a Language** command button receives the focus. Press **Enter** or click the button. When prompted, enter **2** to remove the third item of the list, then click **OK**. Press **Tab** until the combo box once again receives the focus. The third item (J++) from the drop-down list is gone. Press **Tab** until the focus is on **Delete a Language**, press **Enter**, and remove more of the items from the list. Check to confirm that the items are gone. Stop the program and exit Visual Basic.

CODE STEP 20

```
Dim Result As Long, par1 As Long, par2 As Long
par1 = CLng(InputBox("Enter Index number of language to delete:"))
par2 = 0
Result = SendMessage(cboLanguages.hwnd, CB_DELETESTRING, par1, par2)
```

In this Step-by-Step exercise, you got some ideas about how to make sense of the information in the API Viewer. Use the comments in the text file **Win32api.txt** to get clues about how to use the Declare statements, the Constants, and the Type decarations contained in the API.

Visual Basic already does almost anything you want to do. Now you know that just about anything the operating system can do, Visual Basic can do using an API function call. In the next section you will answer the question: Why can't Visual Basic do sounds?

Quick Check 12.b

1. Programming with objects means sending __________________ to objects and receiving __________________ from objects.

2. The combo box is a combination of features from two Microsoft controls: the __________________ and the __________________.

3. Base-16, or hexadecimal, numbers expressed in Visual Basic code as the value of a constant always have a prefix of __________________.

4. The hWnd property of a form or control is used to __________________.

5. Sometimes the best way to find out how to use a parameter in an API function or Sub procedure is to guess and __________________.

Playing WAV Sounds

Has it bothered you that the standard controls that ship with Visual Basic do not support any kind of sound? A control for sound was left out of the basic controls in the standard toolbox. To be sure, many controls now exist for playing sounds in Visual Basic. Add those controls to the toolbox with the Components dialog box. For this lesson you will use an API function instead, and package it as an ActiveX control.

The operating system uses *WAV sound files* to play the cute sounds you hear when you click your mouse in the wrong place, or when the system boots. This should tell you that a similar function is available to your Visual Basic program through an API function.

The PlaySound function plays WAV sound files. The best way to start talking about the PlaySound function is to launch the API Viewer and look over the Declare statement for the function.

STEP-BY-STEP 12.3

1. Start Visual Basic. Select **ActiveX Control** and click **Open**. Save the UserControl as **WAVPlayer.ctl** and the project as **WAVPlayer.vbp**.

2. Select **Add-Ins | Add-In Manager** from the menu bar. Double-click the **VB6 API Viewer**. Be sure the word *Loaded* appears in the column to the right of its entry. Click **OK**.

3. Select **Add-Ins | API Viewer**. Select **File | Load Text File** or, if you have converted the text file to a database file, **File | Load Database File**. Double-click **Win32api.txt**. Confirm that *Declares* is visible in the API Type combo box. In the search text box, enter **snd**. This is the prefix used for all entries concerning sounds. **sndPlaySound** appears in the Available Items list box. Click **Private** in the Declare Scope frame. Click **Add** to add the Declare to the Selected Items list box. The Declare statement is shown below:

```
Private Declare Function sndPlaySound_
Lib "winmm.dll" Alias "sndPlaySoundA"_
(ByVal lpszSoundName As String,_
ByVal uFlags As Long) As Long
```

The Visual Basic function name is sndPlaySound. Winmm.dll contains its definition. Winmm stands for Windows MultiMedia. Its real name in the DLL file is sndPlaySoundA. The first parameter, lpszSoundName, is a long pointer that points to a null terminated string. Null terminated means the string ends with an ASCII 0. The SoundName itself is usually a file name, but it can also refer to a system event or be a resource identifier. The uFlags parameter is a long integer. It is built by adding predefined constants. Each constant communicates a different message to the function.

Imagine you encoded a message as follows: The hundreds digit stands for the number of donuts in your lunchbox. The tens digit stands for the number of sandwiches, and the units digit stands for the number of napkins. If you have two donuts, one sandwich, and two napkins, you could build the message like this: 200 + 10 + 2. The first value, 200, is the two donut constant. The second value is the one sandwich constant. The third value is the two napkins constant. The message is

(continued on next page)

communicated as a single value: 212. This is the way the uFlags parameter works.

The first parameter of sndPlaySound usually represents the file name of the WAV file to play. It is also used to turn off a recurring sound. Passing the Null string in this parameter turns off a sound. The table below shows a selection of sound constants and an explanation of how they are used. They are added together to form the uFlags parameter of sndPlaySound.

The ActiveX control will expose many of these constants to the user as Boolean properties. A method of the control will stop a repeating sound.

4. Select **Constants** from the API Type combo box. Backspace to erase the entry in the search text box, then enter **snd** again in the search text box to find the sound constants. Select each of the constants below and click the **Add** button to add each to the Selected Items list box.

SND_ASYNC
SND_FILENAME
SND_LOOP
SND_NODEFAULT
SND_NOSTOP
SND_NOWAIT
SND_SYNC

SOUND CONSTANTS

CONSTANT	DESCRIPTION
SND_ASYNC	The sound is played *asynchronously* and sndPlaySound returns immediately after beginning the sound. Asynchronously means that sndPlaySound does not wait for any other process to finish before initiating the sound. It also does not wait until the sound is finished to let the program resume other processes.
SND_FILENAME	This constant, added to the uFlags parameter, indicates that the string in the first parameter, lpszSoundName, represents the name of a WAV file.
SND_LOOP	When added to uFlags, this causes the sound to repeat until stopped by another execution of sndPlaySound with lpszSoundName set to the Null string.
SND_NODEFAULT	Normally, when sndPlaySound cannot find a sound to play, it plays a default sound. Add this constant to uFlags to have sndPlaySound return silently if the designated sound cannot be found.
SND_NOSTOP	If another sound is already in progress, sndPlaySound, will not stop that sound to start a new one.
SND_NOWAIT	If this constant is added to uFlags and, if sndPlaySound finds the sound driver already in use, it returns immediately without playing the sound.
SND_SYNC	If set, program flow does not return to the project until the sound is finished. It is similar to a modal dialog box, a box that must be responded to before anything else can proceed.

5. Click **Insert** to put the Declare statement and all the constants into the UserControl. Click **Yes** for the confirmation message. Select **File | Exit** from the API Viewer menu bar to close the API Viewer.

6. Right-click **Project1** in the Project Explorer. Select **Project1 Properties**. Change the project name to **WAVPlay**. Change the description to **WAV File Player**. The description appears in the Components dialog box when the **OCX** file is added.

7. Click **OK** to close the Properties dialog box. Click the **UserControl** icon in the Project Explorer. Change the name of the UserControl to **WAVPlayer**. Change InvisibleAtRuntime to **True**. Change AutoRedraw to **True**. Change Border-Style to **1-Fixed Single**.

8. Add the following code to **Private Sub UserControl_Paint**:

```
Cls
Font.Size = 14
Font.Bold = True
Print "WAV file"
Print "Player"
```

   This code clears the body of the UserControl, sets the size and bold property of the font used to draw on the UserControl, and displays a message. The message appears only when the control is placed on a form.

9. Add the following line of code to Private Sub UserControl_Resize: **UserControl_Paint**. The line calls the Paint routine to renew the printing on the face of the control whenever it is resized.

10. Resize the body of the UserControl to a much smaller size. You want the control to expose several properties and two methods to the user. The properties include the sound constants and the file name of the WAV file. One method plays the sound; the other method turns the sound off. The easiest way to set up the control is through the use of the ActiveX Control Interface Wizard. Select **Add-Ins | Add-In Manager** from the menu bar. Double-click the entry **VB6 ActiveX Ctrl Interface Wizard**. Be sure the word *Loaded* appears in the right column. Click **OK**.

11. Select **Add-Ins | ActiveX Control Interface Wizard** from the menu bar. Click **Next** to leave the Introduction screen. In the Select Interface Members dialog box, click the double left pointing arrow to clear everything from the Selected names list box (see Figure 12-9).

12. Click **Next** to enter the Create Custom Interface Members dialog box. Add a new

(continued on next page)

FIGURE 12-9
The Select Interface Members dialog box, showing a cleared selected names list box

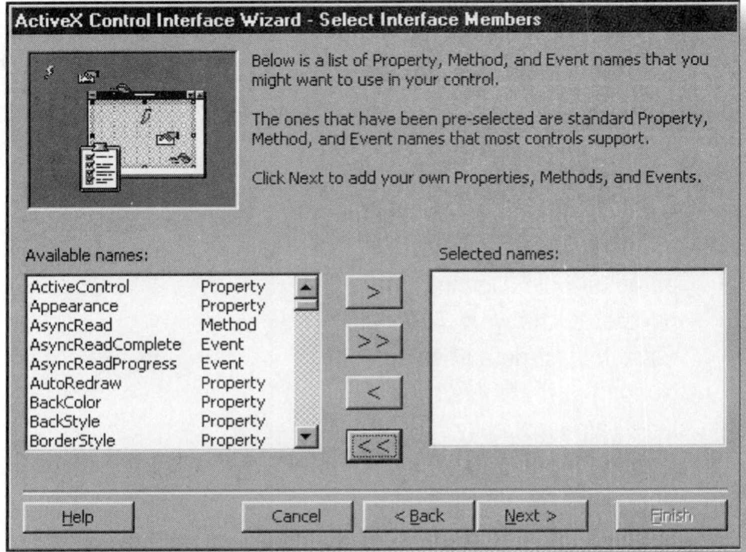

member according to the following table. For each new member, click **New**, then fill in the name and the Type and click **OK** (see Figure 12-10).

NEW MEMBERS

NAME	TYPE
Async	Property
FileName	Property
Repeat	Property
NoDefault	Property
NoStop	Property
NoWait	Property
Sync	Property
PlayWav	Method
StopWav	Method

13. Click **Next** to advance to the Set Mapping dialog box. This is the place to link your new properties to the underlying properties of the constituent controls of the UserControl. These are direct mappings, so click **Next** to advance to the Set Attributes dialog box.

14. In this dialog box, set the data type and the default value for each of the properties and the methods. Use the following defaults table. Change the number to the word *True* or *False* for the default value. Notice the members are now listed alphabetically.

15. Click **Next**. Uncheck the Print Summary Report check box

DEFAULTS

NAME	DATA TYPE	DEFAULT VALUE
Async	Boolean	True
FileName	String	the Null string (delete any entry)
NoDefault	Boolean	False
NoStop	Boolean	False
NoWait	Boolean	True
PlayWav	Boolean	(not applicable)
Repeat	Boolean	False
StopWav	Boolean	(not applicable)
Sync	Boolean	False

and click **Finish**. In a moment, the wizard fills in dozens of lines of code.

16. Open the Code window. Break up the long line of the Declare statement into four lines by inserting the line continuation character,

FIGURE 12-10
The Create Custom Interface Members dialog box

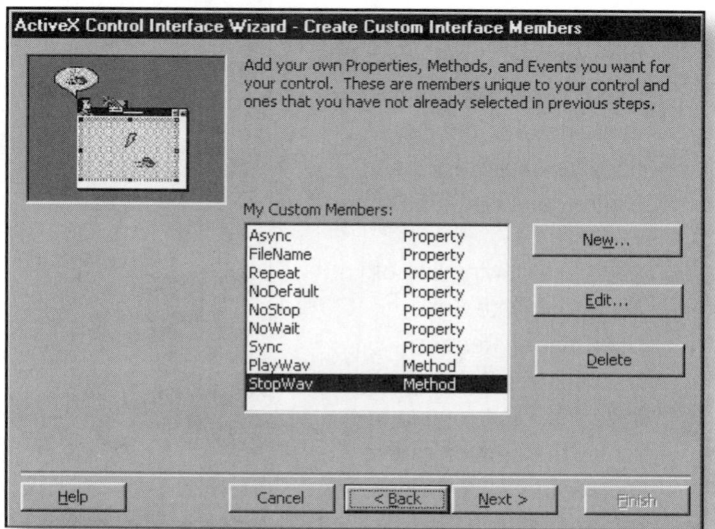

the underscore as shown in Step 3. Delete blank lines between the Constant statements. Look over the code generated by the wizard. The constants with the prefix m_def_ record all the default values entered in the wizard. When the UserControl is initialized, these values are used. The Dims that follow, declare the internal representation for each of the properties. The sound variable SND_LOOP is exposed as Repeat instead of Loop, because Loop is a Visual Basic keyword.

17. Most of the properties are already coded and require no modification. Enter the code shown in **Code Step 17** in **PlayWav( ) As Boolean**.

If the file name is set to the Null string, the Function returns a False. If the file name is not empty, the uFlags parameter is set up based on the values of the properties. If the value of the property is True, its corresponding constant is added to uFlags. The application is limited to playing WAV files, so uFlags is initialized to the constant that represents the presence of a file name, SND_FILENAME. An ASCII 0 is added to the end of the file name string and the parameters are sent to sndPlaySound. This function returns a Boolean value, indicating whether or not the sound was played successfully. The value of that Boolean is returned as the value of PlayWAV.

18. In the spirit of incremental programming, it is time to add a second project. Select **File | Add Project**. Click **Standard EXE** and click **Open**. Right-click the project name of the new project in the Project Explorer and select **Set as Start Up**. Click the **Save Project Group** icon on the toolbar. Save the new form as **WAVPlayer**. Save the new project as **WAVPlayer2**. Save the project group as **WAVPlayer**. The remaining components will be saved with their existing names.

19. Use the Project Explorer to return to the UserControl design window and close it. Double-click the **UserControl** in the toolbox to add the new UserControl, WAVPlayer, to the new project. Run the program. At this point, you are looking for errors—the program will not run yet. A blank form appears.

(continued on next page)

CODE STEP 17

```
Dim uFlags As Long, Result As Long
Dim SoundName As String * 256
If m_FileName = "" Then
  PlayWAV = False
Else
  uFlags = SND_FILENAME
If m_Async = True Then uFlags = uFlags + SND_ASYNC
If m_Repeat = True Then uFlags = uFlags + SND_LOOP
If m_NoDefault = True Then uFlags = uFlags + SND_NODEFAULT
If m_NoStop = True Then uFlags = uFlags + SND_NOSTOP
If m_NoWait = True Then uFlags = uFlags + SND_NOWAIT
If m_Sync = True Then uFlags = uFlags + SND_SYNC
  SoundName = m_FileName & Chr$(0)
  Result = sndPlaySound(SoundName, uFlags)
  PlayWAV = Result
End If
```

20. Stop the program. Use the Project Explorer to open the UserControl design window. Open the Code window and enter the following code in **StopWav( ) As Boolean**:

```
Dim Result As Long
Result = sndPlaySound("", 0)
StopWav = Result
```

21. Save the files and close the UserControl design window. Change the name of the test form to **frmTestWav**. Change the caption of the form to **Testing the WAVPlayer Control**. Add a command button to the form of the text project. Change the name of the control to **cmdPlaySound**. Change the caption to **Pick a Sound**.

22. Add a second command button to the form. Change the name of the control to **cmdTurnOff**. Change the caption of the control to **Turn It Off**.

23. Right-click the toolbox. Select **Components**. From the component list, check **Microsoft Common Dialog Control**. Click **OK**.

24. Double-click the **Common Dialog** control in the toolbox to add one to the form. Change the name of the control to **dlgFile**.

25. Open the Code window and select **cmdPlaySound_Click**. Press **Tab** and enter the code shown in **Code Step 25**.

26. Select **cmdTurnOff_Click**, press **Tab**, and enter:

```
WAVPlayer1.StopWav
```

27. Save the files. Run the program. Click **Pick A Sound**. Navigate to a WAV file. Some are included on the Electronic Instructor CD-ROM. There are also WAV files in the Windows\Media directory. Select a WAV file and click **Open**. The sound should play and repeat. Click **Turn It Off** to turn the sound off. Listen to several sounds, then stop the program.

28. Select the design window of the UserControl from the Project Explorer. Select **File | Make WAVPlayer.ocx.** Click **OK** in the Make Project dialog box. Now the control is ready to use in a new application.

29. Exit Visual Basic and make sure everything is saved. One of the application problems at the end of the lesson asks you to add check boxes and option buttons to give the user access to the sound constants.

CODE STEP 25

```
Dim Result As Boolean     'Value returned from WAVPlayer control.
WAVPlayer1.Repeat = True  'Set sound to repeat in a loop.
dlgFile.Filter = "WAV files | *.wav"
dlgFile.ShowOpen
WAVPlayer1.FileName = dlgFile.FileName
Result = WAVPlayer1.PlayWav  'Calls the WAVPlayer.
If Not Result Then           'Checks the result.
MsgBox "Error"
End If
```

This control is ready to use. Add it to a project. Most of the properties have initial values that you do not need to change. Give it a WAV file name and call the function. While building the control, you learned a lot about the constants that are necessary to make the API calls work. Finding information about the constants is tough, but it is fun to experiment.

In the next section you will wrap two API functions together.

Quick Check 12.c

1. In the API Viewer, all constants and Declare statements concerning sounds have the ________________ prefix.

2. In a message encoded as an integer, the hundreds digit represents the number of text boxes on a form. What value would you add to the message total to indicate four text boxes? ________________.

3. The string entered in the Description box of an ActiveX control's Properties dialog box appears in the ________________ dialog box when the user is adding the ActiveX control to the toolbox.

4. The ________________ constant added to uFlags repeats a sound until it is intentionally stopped.

5. When setting up properties and methods in the ActiveX Control Interface Wizard, the default value of a method is usually ________________.

6. The SoundName parameter of the PlayWav function usually refers to a ________________, but when trying to turn off a sound, its value is ________________.

Accessing INI Files with API Functions

Years ago, *INI files* were simple little text files. INI files, files that end with the *.INI* extension, store configuration information about applications. Items like initial values of variables or the location of data files are stored in INI files. An INI file is a logical place to store usernames or the high scores of a game. A small section of Win.ini appears below. It is somewhat different for each installation of Windows.

```
[windows]
load=
run=
NullPort=None
device=Canon Bubble-Jet BJ-200e,CANON800,LPT1:
[Desktop]
Wallpaper=(None)
TileWallpaper=0
WallpaperStyle=0
```

INI files have four components: Section names (also called Application names), Keys, Values, and Comments. Enclose Section names in square brackets. The Key is a unique string followed by an equal sign. The Key is the name of a configuration setting. The same Key name can appear in two or more sections. For instance, the Key StartUpFile may appear in more than one section.

The value is the start value given to the Key when the application starts. From the example above, you see that the value for a key may be omitted. Comments start with a semicolon. Visual Basic ignores everything following a semicolon. Often, alternate lines for the same key are commented out but left in the INI file.

INI files are still used to store configuration information, but things are not as simple as they were. Configuration information for most new applications is now stored in the *Windows Registry*. The Registry is a database maintained by the Windows operating system. It contains configuration information about the Windows operating system, all applications, and even ActiveX controls and databases.

You know if you double-click a file with a *.vbp* extension in the Windows Explorer window, Windows automatically starts Visual Basic and opens the project. The extension *.vbp* stands for Visual Basic Project. The link between the extension *.vbp* and the application program, Visual Basic, is maintained in the Windows Registry.

Which should you use? Today, use the Windows registry to store configuration information. Although the registry has all but replaced INI files, some applications still use them. In this lesson you will examine a pair of functions that use API calls to add and read information from an INI file.

The beauty of using an API call to manage an INI file is that the API function takes care of details. How is the file created? How is information separated from the text in the file? It does not matter, because the API function takes care of the actual mechanism used to read and write to the file. *Parsing* is separating commands from input strings. For instance, if the command is Drop the Amulet, the command Drop is parsed from the string and interpreted as a command to the program.

STEP-BY-STEP 12.4

1. Start Visual Basic and double-click **Standard EXE**. Save the form and project as **TestINI**.

2. Change the name of the form to **frmINIFileTest**. Change the caption of the form to **Testing INI Files**.

3. Select **Project | Add Module** from the menu bar. From the Add Module dialog box, select **Module** and click **Open**. Change the name of the module to **AccessINI**. Save the module as **AccessINI**.

4. Select **Add-Ins | Add-In Manager** from the menu bar. Double-click **VB6 API Viewer** from the Add-In Manager dialog box. Check to be sure the word *Loaded* appears in the right column of the window next to the API Viewer. Click **OK**.

5. Select **Add-Ins | API Viewer**. Select **File | Load Database File** from the menu bar of the API Viewer. Select **Win32api.mdb** from the Select a Jet Database dialog box. If **Win32api.txt** has not been converted to a database file, select **File | Load Text File** and select **Win32api.txt**.

6. Be sure that *Declares* is visible in the API Type combo box. Enter **GetPrivateProfileSt** in the search text box. There are so many similar names in the Available Items list box, you must enter nearly the entire string before you select the one you want.

If you key the entire string, the API Viewer selects the name following the one you want.

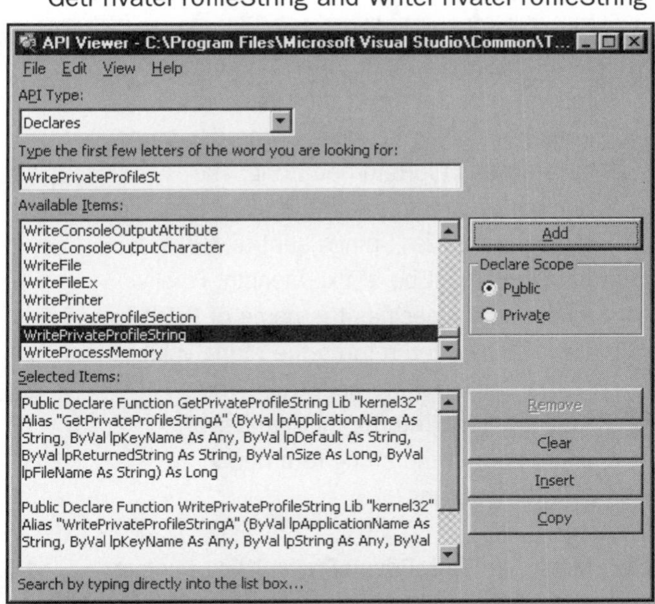

FIGURE 12-11
The API Viewer, showing the selection of GetPrivateProfileString and WritePrivateProfileString

7. The Declare statements are going into a standard (code) module, so be sure to select **Public** under Declare scope. This is the default value. Click **Add** to add the Declare statement for GetPrivateProfileString to the Selected Items list box.

8. Backspace to erase the entry in the search text box. Enter **WritePrivateProfileSt** in the search text box. Click **Add** to add the Declare statement for WritePrivateProfileString to the Selected Items list box (see Figure 12-11).

9. Click **Insert**. The API Viewer displays the message box shown in Figure 12-12. Click **Yes** to insert the functions into the module, then select **File | Exit** from the API Viewer menu bar to close the API Viewer.

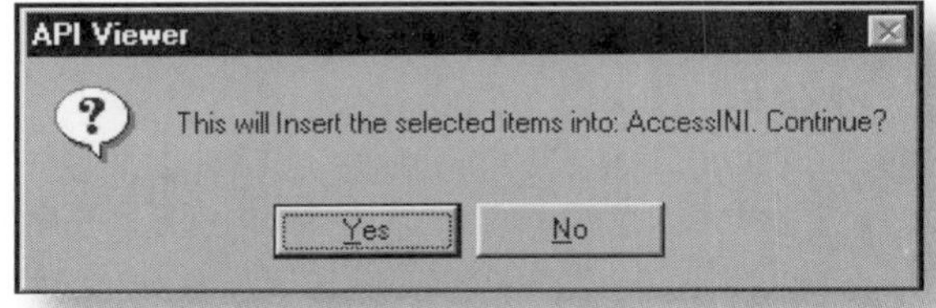

FIGURE 12-12
The API Viewer message box, prompting confirmation of the transfer

10. Open the Code window for the module. Modify the **Public Declare Function GetPrivate Profile String** statement with line continuation characters, as shown in **Code Step 10**.

The first parameter, lpApplicationName, represents what is now known as a Section name. The name of a section is contained in square brackets in the INI

(continued on next page)

CODE STEP 10

```
Public Declare Function GetPrivateProfileString _
Lib "kernel32" Alias "GetPrivateProfileStringA" _
(ByVal lpApplicationName As String, _
ByVal lpKeyName As Any, _
ByVal lpDefault As String, _
ByVal lpReturnedString As String, _
ByVal nSize As Long, _
ByVal lpFileName As String) As Long
```

file. lpKeyName is like a variable name. lpDefault is a default string provided for the value of the Key if the Get function somehow fails. The value of the Key string is returned in lpReturnedString. The number of characters in the string variable is sent as nSize. Strings sent to API functions must be of fixed length. Finally, lpFileName, specifies the name of the INI file. The function returns the string value of the Key in lpReturnedString. The function itself returns the number of characters in the string returned in lpReturnedString.

11. Modify the **WritePrivateProfileString Declare** statement with line continuation characters, as shown in **Code Step 11**.

    Many of the parameters in this function are the same as the function above. lpString is used to send the value of the Key. If the Section does not exist, it is created. If the INI file does not exist, it is created. The function itself returns 0 if the function is not successful, and a non-zero value (True) if the function is successful.

    The next step is to write a "wrapper" function to encapsulate the two API functions.

12. Select **Tools | Add Procedure** from the menu bar. Enter the function name **GetInfoINI**. Click the **Function** option button. This function returns the Key value returned from the INI file. Click **OK**.

13. Select **Tools | Add Procedure** from the menu bar. Enter the function name **WriteInfoINI**. This is a Sub procedure. Click **OK**.

14. Open the Code window. Add the parameter list shown in **Code Step 14** inside the parentheses for **Public Function Get Info INI**.

    The parameters are shown with line continuation characters to enhance readability in the Code window. The parameters have been rearranged from the order used in the API function. This order, showing the INI file name first, seems to make more sense. Add **As String** following the closing parenthesis of the Function declaration.

CODE STEP 11

```
Public Declare Function WritePrivateProfileString _
Lib "kernel32" Alias "WritePrivateProfileStringA" _
(ByVal lpApplicationName As String, _
ByVal lpKeyName As Any, _
ByVal lpString As Any, _
ByVal lpFileName As String) As Long
```

CODE STEP 14

```
INIFileName As String, _
Section As String, Key As String, _
Default As String
```

15. Enter the code shown in **Code Step 15** in the same function.

    The Space$( ) function returns a string of the indicated length with nothing but spaces. Use the string to initialize Temp. GetPrivateProfileString returns the number of characters in Temp. Use the value in the Left$( ) function to separate the characters from the ASCII 0 added by the function to the end of the string.

16. In **Public Sub WriteInfoINI( )** enter the parameter list shown in **Code Step 16** within the parentheses.

    The list is shown with line continuation characters for readability. WriteInfoINI has no return type.

17. Enter the code shown in **Code Step 17** in the same procedure.

    The Section name and Key name are set to all lowercase characters. If all characters are the same case, it makes it easier to match names with user input.

18. The code module is complete. Save the changes to the module.

    Later you can add this module to a project to give the project the capability of reading from and writing to INI files. Most applications from the Windows 3.1 era or earlier use INI files.

19. Select **File | Open Project** from the menu bar and, if necessary, click the **Existing** tab, Navigate to the location of your current project, select it, and click **Open**. Reloading the project from the version you just saved sets the App.Path to the path in which the project is saved. If the application is not reloaded from your application directory, the default directory probably remains the directory from which you run Visual Basic. The location of the INI file depends on the default directory being the same as the application directory.

20. Select **frmINIFile test** in the Project Explorer. Click **Viewobject**. Put two command buttons on the form. Name them **cmdTestINI** and **cmdExit**. Change their captions to **Reading an INI File** and **E&xit** (see Figure 12-13). Enter the code **Unload Me** for **cmdExit_Click** in the code window.

(continued on next page)

CODE STEP 15

```
Dim Temp As String * 256
Dim nLength As Integer
Temp = Space$(256)
nLength = GetPrivateProfileString(Section, _
Key, Default, Temp, 255, INIFileName)
GetInfoINI = Left$(Temp, nLength)
```

CODE STEP 16

```
INIFileName As String, _
Section As String, Key As String, _
Value As String
```

FIGURE 12-13
The Testing INI Files application

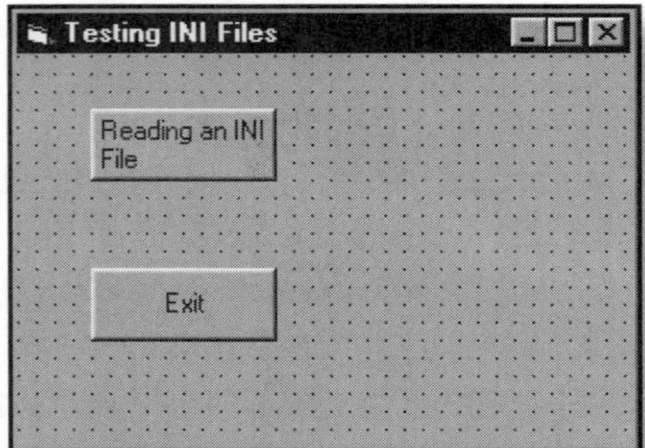

The TestINI button prompts the user for a Section name and a Key name. The routine reads the INI file and returns the Key value. If the Key value does not exist, or the Key does not exist in the file or indeed, if the file itself does not exist, it is created. Once created, the program prompts the user to enter a value for the new Key.

21. Open the Code window and select **cmdTestINI_Click**. Press **Tab** and enter the code shown in **Code Step 21**.

    It is not at all unusual to hard-code the name of the INI file in the application itself. Variables are declared for the INI file name, the Section name, Key name, and the Key value. InputBoxes are used to collect the Section name and the KeyName. GetInfoINI( ) is called to read the corresponding Key value. The question mark is the default value used if the read operation fails. If it fails, the user is prompted to enter a value for the Key. The value is written to the INI file using WriteInfoINI.

22. Save the project. Run the program. Click **Reading an INI File**. Enter **YardTools** for the Section name, click **OK**, enter **Mower** for the Key name, and click **OK**. GetInfoINI

CODE STEP 17

```
Dim n As Integer
Dim Temp As String  'String to write.
Dim Ch As String
Temp = ""    'Initialize to the null string.
'Replace any cr or lf characters with spaces.
For n = 1 To Len(Value)
  Ch = Mid$(Value, n, 1) 'Peel off a character
  If Ch = vbCr Or Ch = vbLf Then
    Temp = Temp & " "     'Add a space instead.
  Else
    Temp = Temp & Ch      'Just add the character.
  End If
Next n
Section = LCase$(Section)  'All lowercase characters.
Key = LCase$(Key)
'Call the API function.
n = WritePrivateProfileString(Section, Key, Temp, INIFileName)
```

fails because the INI file does not yet exist. The program moves to the True branch of the If statement and prompts the user for a name (the Key value). Enter **BigWheel** for the name.

23. Click **Reading an INI File**. Enter **Yard Tools** for the Section name and click **OK**. Enter **Mower** for the Key name and click **OK**. This time the INI file does exist with the Section name and the Key name. The Key value (Big Wheel) is read from the INI file and displayed in the message box. Click **OK**, then stop the program.

24. The next test involves Key values that span more than a single line. Add another InputBox to collect a second line of input from the user. In **cmdTestINI_Click**, enter the lines shown in **Code Step 24** following the line KeyValue = InputBox$("Enter name:").

This code collects a second name and concatenates it to the first with a carriage return and line feed to make a second line. The MsgBox displays the KeyValue to show it contains two lines.

25. Save the project. Run the program. Click **Reading an INI File**. Enter **YardTools** for the Section name. Enter **Chipper** for the Key name. Of course, no entry for Chipper exists. When the program prompts for a name, enter **YardMan**. For the last name, enter **Deluxe**. Figure 12-14 shows the first message box. The name of the Chipper appears on two lines.

26. Click **OK** to close the message box. Click **Reading an INI File**. Enter **YardTools** for the Section name. Enter **Chipper** for the Key name. This time the entries exist and a message box appears with the Key

(continued on next page)

CODE STEP 21

```
Dim INIFileName As String
Dim Section As String
Dim KeyName As String
Dim KeyValue As String
INIFileName = App.Path & "\MYAPP.ini"
Section = LCase$(InputBox("Enter the Section name:"))
KeyName = LCase$(InputBox("Enter the name of the Key:"))
KeyValue = GetInfoINI(INIFileName, Section, KeyName, "?")
If KeyValue = "?" Then
  KeyValue = InputBox$("Enter name:")
  WriteInfoINI INIFileName, Section, KeyName, KeyValue
Else
  MsgBox KeyValue
End If
```

FIGURE 12-14
The TestINI message box, showing the two-line Key value

CODE STEP 24

```
Dim LastName As String
LastName = InputBox$("Enter last name:")
KeyValue = KeyValue & vbCrLf & LastName
MsgBox KeyValue
```

value. Figure 12-15 shows the modified Key value.

FIGURE 12-15
The TestINI message box, showing the modified Key value

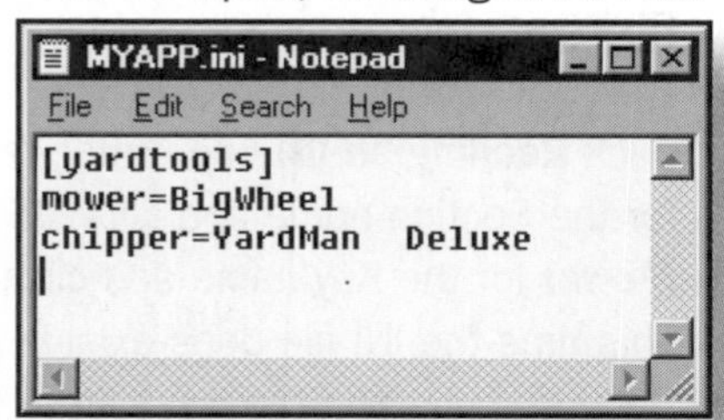

FIGURE 12-16
The Notepad, showing MYAPP.ini

27. Stop the program.

28. Right-click the **Start** button in the Windows taskbar at the bottom of the screen. Click **Explore** to open Windows Explorer. Navigate to your work folder. Look for the entry MYAPP.INI. When you find it, double-click it. Notepad opens and displays the INI file. It should look like Figure 12-16.

29. Close the Notepad and close Windows Explorer. Save the change to MYAPP.INI if prompted to do so.

What if there is more than one value for a particular Key? It cannot happen. The Key must be unique in each section. You will now make one more quick addition to the test program. Now that you know how to read from and write to INI files, how does the registry work? It is easier to use than INI files and you will recognize the similarity to working with INI files immediately.

In the following steps you will write an entry to the Windows Registry. Writing to the Registry requires great caution. If your instructor does not want you to alter the Registry, exit Visual Basic now and simply read the following steps.

30. Add two command buttons to frmINIFileTest. Change the names of the buttons to **cmdReadReg** and **cmdWriteReg**. Change the captions of the buttons to **Read the Registry** and **Write to the Registry** (see Figure 12-17).

FIGURE 12-17
The Testing INI Files application with the Read the Registry and Write to the Registry buttons

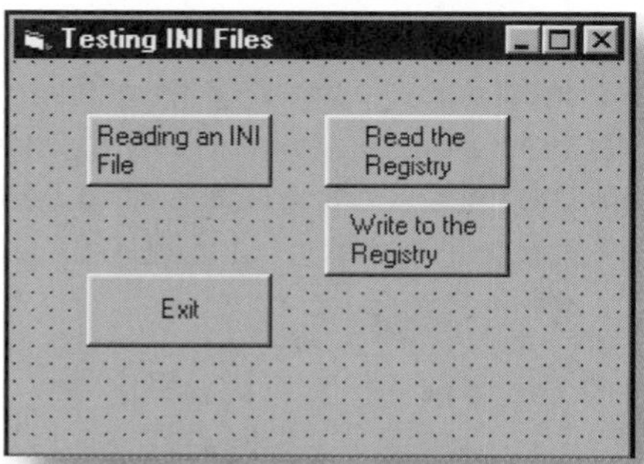

31. Open the Code window and select **cmdWriteReg_Click**. Press **Tab** and enter the code shown in **Code Step 31**.

The first five lines are copied from various parts of Private Sub cmdTestINI_Click. The SaveSetting command writes directly to the Windows Registry. A file name is not required. Each application gets its own area. The Application name is the first parameter of the SaveSetting command. The second parameter is the Section name, the third is the Key name, and the fourth is the Key value. Sound familiar? It does not matter where the Registry file is located. The SaveSetting and GetSetting commands take care of locating it.

32. Select **cmdReadReg_Click**, press **Tab**, and enter the code shown in **Code Step 32**.

    Copy the first five lines from Private Sub cmdWriteReg_Click. The GetSetting( ) function returns the key value. The first parameter is the Application name, the second is the Section name, the third is the Key name, and the fourth is the default value returned by the function if no value is read from the Registry.

33. Save the project. Run the program. Click **Write to the Registry**. Enter **OutputDevices** for the Section name. Enter **DefaultPrinter** for the Key name. Enter **Canon Bubble-Jet BJ-200e** for the Key value.

34. Click **Read the Registry**. Enter **OutputDevices** for the Section name. Enter **DefaultPrinter** for the Key name. Figure 12-18 shows the output.

FIGURE 12-18
The message box, showing the contents of OutputDevices, DefaultPrinter

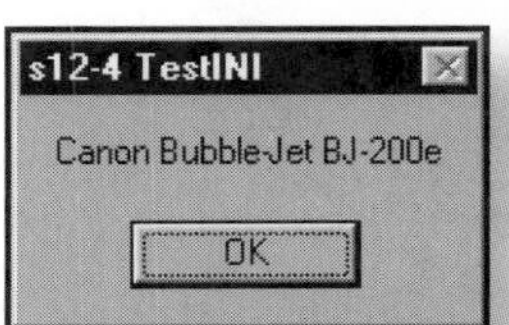

NOTE:

Case for the Section and Key names is ignored. Case is only retained for the Key value.

(continued on next page)

CODE STEP 31

```
Dim Section As String
Dim KeyName As String
Dim KeyValue As String
Section = LCase$(InputBox("Enter the Section name:"))
KeyName = LCase$(InputBox("Enter the name of the Key:"))
KeyValue = InputBox$("Enter the Key value:")
SaveSetting "TestINI", Section, KeyName, KeyValue
```

CODE STEP 32

```
Dim Section As String
Dim KeyName As String
Dim KeyValue As String
Section = LCase$(InputBox("Enter the Section name:"))
KeyName = LCase$(InputBox("Enter the name of the Key:"))
KeyValue = GetSetting("TestINI", Section, KeyName, "?")
MsgBox KeyValue
```

Building Communication Skills

No single event procedure should be too long. What is too long, and why is it a bad thing? Long segments of code are difficult to understand. Usually, code can be broken down into smaller, easier-to-understand segments. Call procedures defined in a standard module to hide the complexity of a difficult piece of code.

35. Click **OK**. Stop the program and exit Visual Basic. Make sure all changes are saved.

How do you read all the values of each Key name in a section? Use the GetAllSettings statement. This statement uses two parameters: the application name and the section name. It returns a two-dimensional array in a variable of the Variant type. In the 0th entry of each row of the array is the Key name. In the first entry of each row is the value for the Key name. The code below shows an example:

```
Dim TwoColumns As Variant
TwoColunms = GetAllSettings("TestINI","OutputDevices")
For x = 1 to UBound(TwoColumns,1)
  ...
Next x
```

The UBound( ) function returns the highest row number of any occupied row.

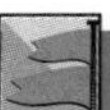

Historically Speaking

Donald Knuth, professor emeritus at Stanford, set out in 1962 to write a volume of 12 chapters entitled *The Art of Computer Programming*. He soon realized that depth rather than brevity was called for, and the work has grown to a planned seven volumes. While working on the second edition of the first volume, *Fundamental Algorithms*, he thought there was no reason for technical works to look bad. This began a ten-year hiatus from work on *Art*, during which he developed TEX, a typesetting language, and Metafont, an alphabet design system, and put them into public domain. During that time he also wrote six books to explain them. The *Art* has become a standard in the field. Many textbooks list *Art* as a reference.

Building Programming Skills

All Dim statements should be at the beginning of the procedure or function. Well, that is what some programmers say. It is generally a good idea to list the Dim statements at the top of the procedure. That way you know what values are going to be used in the code. Sometimes, it seems a good idea to declare a variable just before it is used. If you find yourself writing Dim statements in the middle of procedures, maybe you should break the procedure into pieces. Each piece then has its Dim statements at the top of the code.

There are still a lot of INI files around. Not everyone is running applications written in the last couple of years. Knowing how to deal with INI files is very helpful. You still have to know something about the internal structure of either the INI or the Registry for either to be really useful. You must know what the Section and Key names are and how the program uses them.

With the Registry file, you have a place to store data between runs of your applications. As you write applications, think about ways to use the Registry.

Visual Basic cannot do everything. It cannot expose every operation of every DLL file to the programmer. When Visual Basic cannot do the job, look at API functions to fill in the gap.

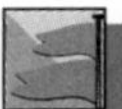

Building Programming Skills

Provide error-handling routines for invalid data values entered by the user. Validating input values is an important part of application programming. A lot of that kind of error-checking is omitted from this text so that each procedure demonstrates a single idea to the reader without searching through the necessary details of a real application.

Quick Check 12.d

1. INI files, files that end with the *.INI* extension, store __________________ about applications.

2. The __________________ , a "variable" in an INI or Registry file, is the name of a configuration setting.

3. Configuration information for most new applications is now stored in the __________________.

4. When putting an API Declare statement in a standard (code) module, the first word of the statement should probably be the keyword __________________.

5. When accessing an INI file with a WritePrivateProfileString API call, if the INI file does not exist, __________________.

6. To reset the App.Path to the directory in which your application is saved, you must __________________.

Summary

- Years ago, machine language functions written in base-16 machine code could be included in BASIC programs. Today, each function and subprocedure of the Windows operating system is exposed to the programmer, either through Visual Basic statements or API calls.
- COM is the Component Object Model. It allows programmers to build applications and systems from components supplied from many sources.
- API stands for Application Programming Interface. The API is a set of routines used by an application to access and execute the procedures of a computer's operating system.
- The API Viewer is used to view and write Declare statements, Constants, and Type declarations to application programs. The Declare statements are used to integrate operating system function calls into Visual Basic.
- There is a language dedicated to expressing the syntax of statements in a programming language.
- The Alias clause in an API Declare statement identifies the name of the function or sub as it is found in the DLL.
- Each library file accessed by the API calls is a file of routines, constants, and Type declarations. Each file has a DLL extension.
- API Declare statements in a standard module start with Public. Declare statements in the General Declarations section of a form module start with Private.
- The value of a parameter sent ByVal cannot be changed by a function or sub. Terminate strings sent as parameters to API functions with the ASCII code 0.
- A handle is an integer value assigned to forms and many controls. The value of the integer is defined by the operating environment and is unique for each control and form. It is found in the hWnd property of forms and most controls.
- The **Win32api.txt** file contains Declare statements, Constants, and Type declarations for API calls. Examine the file to view the sketchy comments describing some of the Constants.
- Select File | Make from the menu bar to turn an ActiveX control design, such as WAVPlayer, into a compiled control.
- INI files, files that end with the *.INI* extension, store configuration information about applications.
- INI files have four components: Section names (also called Application names), Keys, Values, and Comments.
- The Windows Registry is a database maintained by the operating system. It contains configuration information about the Windows operating system, all applications, and even ActiveX controls and databases.
- Parsing an input string means separating the words of the input string into individual commands.
- The SaveSetting and GetSetting commands are built into Visual Basic. They are used to access the Windows Registry database.

LESSON 12 REVIEW QUESTIONS

TRUE/FALSE

Circle the T if the statement is true. Circle the F if it is false.

T F 1. API stands for Applied Patent International.

T F 2. Finding explanations for the values of the parameters sent in API calls is part of the challenge of using API functions.

T F 3. Strings sent as parameters to API functions and subprocedures always have to be of fixed length.

T F 4. When describing the syntax of a language statement, a phrase in boldface type is called a "terminal symbol."

T F 5. The API Viewer is used to view and write Declare statements, Constants, and Type declarations to application programs.

T F 6. Since the handle of a form is defined by the operating environment when the form becomes part of a project, a form's handle changes whenever the form is added to or deleted from a project.

T F 7. Unfortunately, related constants in the **Win32api.txt** file do not always start with the same prefix symbols.

T F 8. To build the uFlags parameter of the WAVPlayer control, add one or more of the sound constants together.

T F 9. The configuration information that used to be stored in INI files is now stored in the Windows Registry database.

T F 10. Each API function must be wrapped alone in a corresponding Visual Basic function.

WRITTEN QUESTIONS

Write your answers to the following questions.

11. What is reentrant code?

12. Below is the syntax of the Declare statement. Describe some of the features of the language that is used to describe the syntax of the statement.

    [**Public** | **Private**] **Declare Function** *name* **Lib** "*libname*" [**Alias** "*aliasname*"] [([*arglist*])] [**As** *type*]

13. When using a Declare statement, why are there two function names: the legal Visual Basic name and the Alias?

14. What does it mean when a parameter is sent to a function "ByVal"?

15. Describe the four parameters of the SendMessage function.

16. In the hexadecimal number system, digits 10 through 15 are represented with the letters A through F. Each column in the Hex number represents a power of 16. If what we call the 10's column in the decimal number system is the 16's column in Hex, what is the value of &HAC?

17. For what is an INI file used? Why are they not still used today?

18. What are the parameters of the GetPrivateProfileString( ) function?

19. Why do you think the LCase function is used in the following statements?

```
Section = LCase$(InputBox("Enter the Section name:"))
KeyName = LCase$(InputBox("Enter the name of the Key:"))
```

20. Explain how to use the GetSetting and SaveSetting commands.

LESSON 12 APPLICATION PROBLEMS

SCANS

Level One

THE CHARACTER ANALYZER

Write a program to enter a string with an InputBox and analyze the characters of the string. Use the IsCharAlphaNumeric API function to evaluate whether an individual character of the input string is a countable alphabetic or numeric character or not. Send the function the ASCII code of the char (using the ASC( ) function to convert a single character to an ASCII code). Count each valid character as it appears and concatenate all the valid characters into a new string. Display the new string and the count of valid characters.

CHANGING THE DEFAULT DIRECTORY

Use the API Viewer to get the Declare statement for SetCurrentDirectory. The function takes a single parameter: the path name of a file. It changes the default directory to the path of the file. Add the Common Dialog control to the toolbox. Put a command button on the form. Change the caption to reflect the button's use: Use the button to get a path name from the user and change the default directory to that path. Show the Open dialog box and collect a path name from the user. Call the API function with the file name read from the dialog box as its parameter. The return value of the function, a long, returns a flag, indicating if the routine was successful. Check the return value and display an appropriate message. Finally, use a statement like Open "Text.txt" For Output As #1 and print a single line in the file: "This is only a Test!" With the path omitted, the text file is saved in the default directory. Run the program. Stop the program and use Window's Explorer to check the existence of the text file in the proper directory.

Level Two

USING THE WAVPLAYER

Note: If you use a different folder for applications than for the Step-by-Step exercises, copy the **WAVPlayer.ocx** file to the new folder.

Write a simple application with three text boxes and three command buttons. The three text boxes represent Distance, Rate, and Time. The three command buttons are Calculate, Clear, and Exit. In each of the three text boxes, put the following lines in the GotFocus event:

```
WAVPlayer1.FileName = "c:\data files\lesson 12\data files\ _
  Musical Question.wav"
Result = WAVPlayer1.PlayWav
```

Change the path name to the location of the data files provided for this lesson or to the location of the sound files on your system (probably C:\Windows\Media). Provide a different sound using similar statements for each command button. The program should divide the Distance by the Time and display the result in the Rate box.

USING THE REGISTRY

NOTE: Check with your instructor before doing this application.

Change the program written for the problem above to save data for particular drivers. The program should prompt the user for a username. The username, a string, should be stored in the Registry with the Application name "MPHFinder" and the Section name "Users." For the Key name, use the username. After the Miles per Hour is calculated in the program, write the new value to the Registry as the Key value.

Add a list box to the form. In the Form_Activate procedure, read the users from the Registry using the GetAllSettings command. Read the table of information into a variant type variable. Transfer the data from the two-dimensional array into a list box.

READING AND WRITING AN INI FILE

Write a program that stores and retrieves user information in an INI file. The program should store information using the following structure:

INI File Name:	"PersonalData.INI"
Section Name:	"Person1"
Key Names:	"FirstName"
	"LastName"
	"Address1"
	"City"
	"ZipCode"

One command button should record the data. When the form is activated, read the INI file and display the results in a list box. Use the code developed in Step-by-Step exercise 12.4 to access the INI file.

SCANS

MORE WORK ON THE SEEDATABASE CONTROL

In the next lesson, discussion returns to the Music Collection database. For this lesson, take care of some unfinished business concerning the SeeDatabase control created in the last lesson. When added to a project, it allows the user to navigate to any database, open it, choose a table from a list box, and view its records. The control automatically adds a label and a text box for each field of the table and links them to the Data control.

The result is a form that displays every field of a table of a database. Small databases are easy to navigate. If you have fewer than 50 records, you can search for a particular record by scrolling through each of the records. For a large database, this is impractical.

The answer is to install a search. To search for a particular record in a database, the user specifies what field to search and then enters a value on which to base the search. For instance, in the Music Collection database, the user may want to search for a particular title. The user clicks the Title label and then enters the title itself. If the record exists, it is displayed. If the record does not exist in the database, an error message appears.

The Recordset object has a method called FindFirst. When supplied with a properly structured search string, the FindFirst method moves to the first record that matches that value. FindFirst starts its search with the first record of the Recordset. The FindNext method moves to the next record that matches the search string.

The search string itself must have a precise structure. When trying to match a text field with a particular search criteria, the form is "*fieldname* = '*SearchCriteria*'" or "*fieldname* LIKE '*SearchCriteria*'". Enclose the SearchCriteria in single quotes. When using LIKE, the search criteria may contain wildcards. The asterisk (*) specifies any combination of characters. The code automatically appends an asterisk to the search criteria.

If searching for a long or integer value, the SearchCriteria is not enclosed in single quotes. If the SearchCriteria is a date, enclose it in pound (#) signs.

The user enters the search field by clicking the label for the particular field. The label contains the name of the field. Immediately, a problem arises: How do you tell the data type of the field? Each field in a database has a Type property. This property contains a constant that specifies its data type. A list of the available constants appears in the table below:

CONSTANTS		
dbBigInt	dbDecimal	dbMemo
dbBinary	dbDouble	dbNumeric
dbBoolean	dbFloat Float	dbSingle
dbByte	dbGUID	dbText
dbChar	dbInteger	dbTime
dbCurrency	dbLong Long	dbTimeStamp
dbDate	dbLongBinary	dbVarBinary

Who would have thought that there could be so many data types used in a database? You are going to simplify your program by considering only three types of data: Long or Integer, dates, and strings. The values of the constants represented in the table on the previous page can be found using debugging routines in the main code.

The control also gets a new command button. When a search string is specified and the first occurrence of the search criteria is found, a command button with the caption Next appears. Clicking this button finds the next record that matches the search string. The search string uses the LIKE operator and the * to search for all the records that match a pattern: spr* finds all the strings that match the first three letters exactly and have any character following.

Finally, if the field name contains a space, like Year Born, it must be enclosed in square brackets. The field name is examined and if a space is found, square brackets are added.

1. Start Visual Basic. Open the project group you used to develop and test the original SeeDatabase control in Lesson 11 (it has a *.vbg* extension). Do not open the individual project (with the *.vbp* extension); open the project group to facilitate testing.

2. At the end of Lesson 11, you compiled the SeeDatabase control to an OCX file. The easiest way to create a new version of the control is to change its name. Select **See Database** in the Project Explorer and click **View Object**. Select **Project 1 See Database Control Properties**. Change the **Project Description**, as shown in Figure 12-19, then click **OK**. This description appears in the Components window when loading the control in the toolbox of a new application.

FIGURE 12-19
The SeeDatabaseControl-Project Properties dialog box

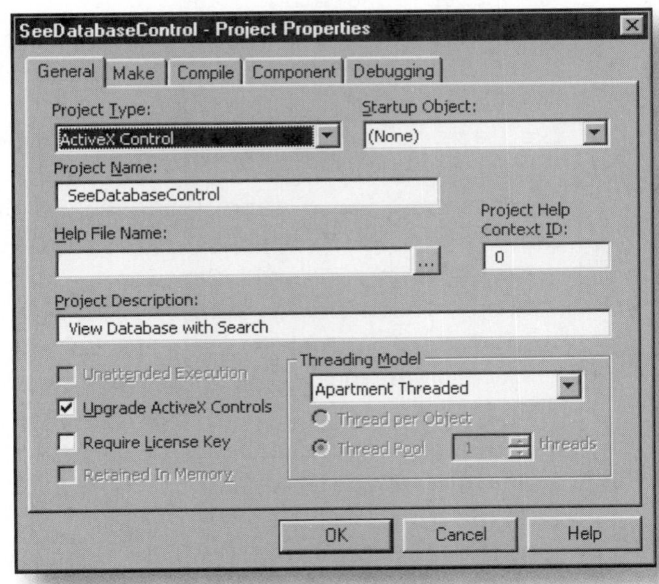

3. The Search Criteria string is used by the label Click procedure and by the Next command button, so it is declared in the General Declarations section of the form. Open the Code window and add this line to the General Declarations section: **Dim SearchString As String**.

4. View the UserControl by clicking **View Object** in the Project Explorer. Expand the control to make room for a new command button. Add a command button to the control. Change its caption to **&Next** and its name to **cmdFindNext**. See Figure 12-20 for final placement of controls.

FIGURE 12-20
The SeeDatabase control UserControl, showing final placement of controls

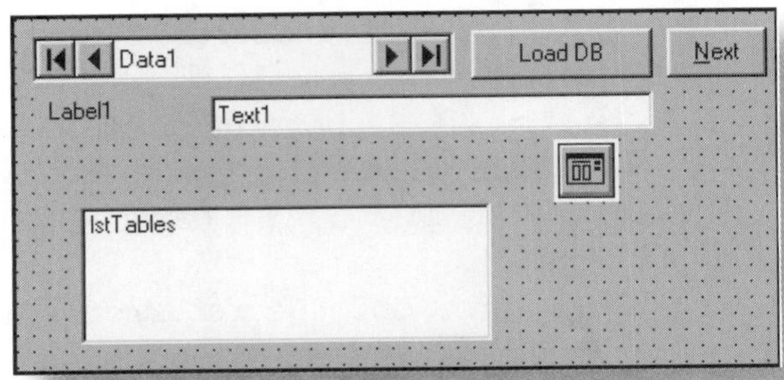

5. You resized the UserControl to accommodate the Next command button. Check the Properties window to check the new width. Open the Code window and make the changes shown below for Private Sub UserControl_Initialize. There are two changes: The Width is larger and a line is added to set the Visible property of cmdFindNext to False.

```
With UserControl
   .Width = 5600
   .Height = 2670
End With
OrigHeight = UserControl.Height
'added for 12
cmdFindNext.Visible = False
```

6. In the UserControl_Resize event procedure, change the number for the width to **5600**.

7. The next changes are made to Private Sub Label1_Click(Index As Integer). Add the following code:

```
'Search added for lesson 12
Dim Search As String
Dim NewCaption As String, Pos As Integer
'SearchString declared in General Declarations.
'The label contains the field name.
'The label's tag contains the datatype.
   With Label1(Index)
'Process the field name (put square brackets around
'the field name if necessary.
   NewCaption = Trim$(.Caption)
   Pos = InStr(NewCaption, " ")
   If Pos <> 0 Then        'If no space, then Pos=0.
      NewCaption = "[" & NewCaption & "]"
   End If
   'Collect search criteria.
   Search = InputBox("Enter Search Criteria<" & NewCaption & ">:")
   If Search <> "" Then
    If CInt(.Tag) = dbLong Or CInt(.Tag) = dbInteger Then
      SearchString = NewCaption & _
         " = " & Search      'No Single Quotes.
    ElseIf CInt(.Tag) = dbDate Then
      SearchString = NewCaption & _
         " = #" & Search & "#"      'Dates need pound signs.
    Else
     'The LIKE operator finds near likeness.
      SearchString = NewCaption & _
         " LIKE '" & Search & "*'"     'Asterisk finds all matches.
    End If
    On Error GoTo SearchError  'If SearchString does not work.
    dtaUniverse.Recordset.FindFirst SearchString
    If dtaUniverse.Recordset.NoMatch = True Then
```

```
            MsgBox "No Matching Record"
        End If
      End If
    End With
    'Turn on Next button to find next
    'occurrence of search item.
     cmdFindNext.Visible = True
     Exit Sub
   SearchError:
     MsgBox "No Search Available for Field.", vbExclamation
```

8. Enter the following line in Private Sub cmdFindNext_Click:

```
dtaUniverse.Recordset.FindNext SearchString
```

9. Add the following line to Private Sub lstTables_Click, between the lines With Label1(x) and End With. Its exact position within the With statement does not matter.

```
.Tag = f.Type  'added for lesson 12
```

This sets the Tag property to identify the data type of the data field.

10. Save everything. Close the UserControl design window. Run the program. The new version of the control is automatically used in the test bed project.

FIGURE 12-21
The test bed project, showing the list of tables in **Biblio.mdb**

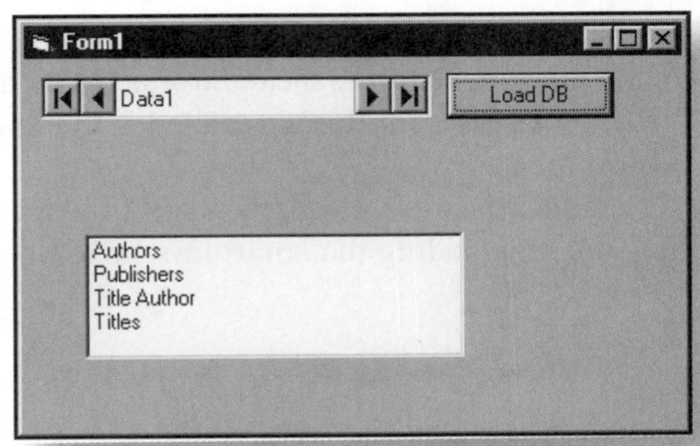

11. Click **Load DB**. Navigate to a database. If **Biblio.mdb** is present, select it in the Open File dialog box and click **Open**. (If it is not on your system, you can open a copy from the Electronic Instructor CD-ROM). Figure 12-21 shows the list box of tables present in the database. Click **Authors**.

FIGURE 12-22
The test bed project, showing the form generated to display the Author table of **Biblio.mdb**

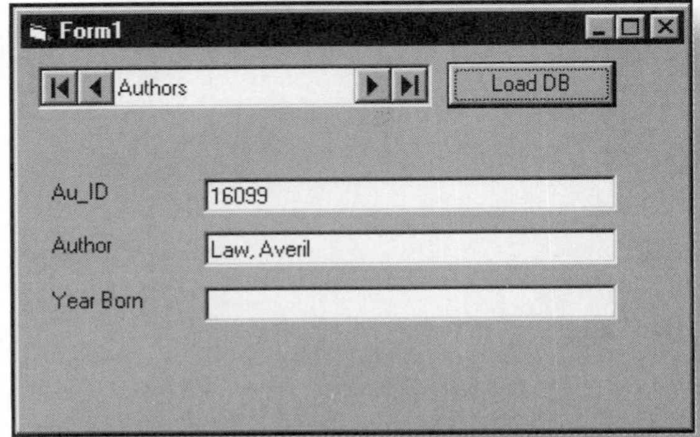

12. Click the right arrow of the Data control to access several of the records. Note the Au_ID field. It starts at 1. Click the right arrow with the bar to access the last record of the database (see Figure 12-22). In this version, the Au_ID exceeds 16000. It would be difficult to find a given author in such a large database.

NOTE: This is a database of real authors, books, and publishers. Look for some of your favorites.

13. Click the **Author** label. An InputBox prompts you for an entry for the search criteria. Enter **spr** and click **OK**. The code automatically appends an asterisk so the search is made for any name starting with "spr." Case does not affect the search. Click the **Next** button. Figure 12.23 shows the result.

FIGURE 12-23
Searching the database for spr*

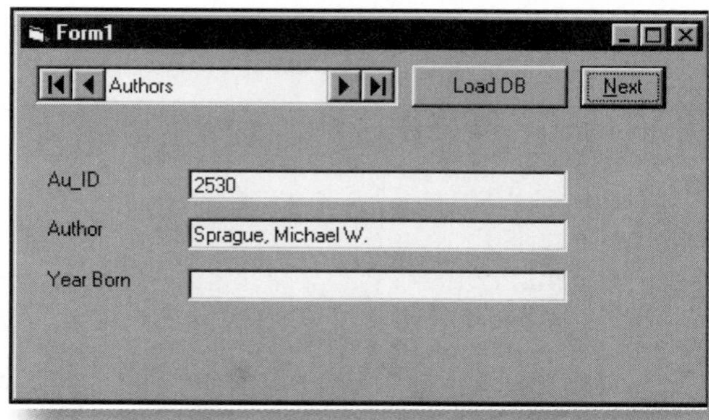

14. Open another database or open the same database and select a different table. Search on different fields. Use the control to search **Win32api.mdb**, the Music Collection database, or the **portableCD** database.

15. Stop the program. Save everything. Compile the control with **File | Make**.

Once the control is compiled and properly registered, it can be used in any Visual Basic application. Registering the control is covered in Lessons 14 and 15. One way to transfer it to another machine with Visual Basic installed is to copy the project files and recompile the control to the new environment.

Add the control to a new project by opening the Components dialog box, browsing to the OCX file, and then adding the control to the toolbox.

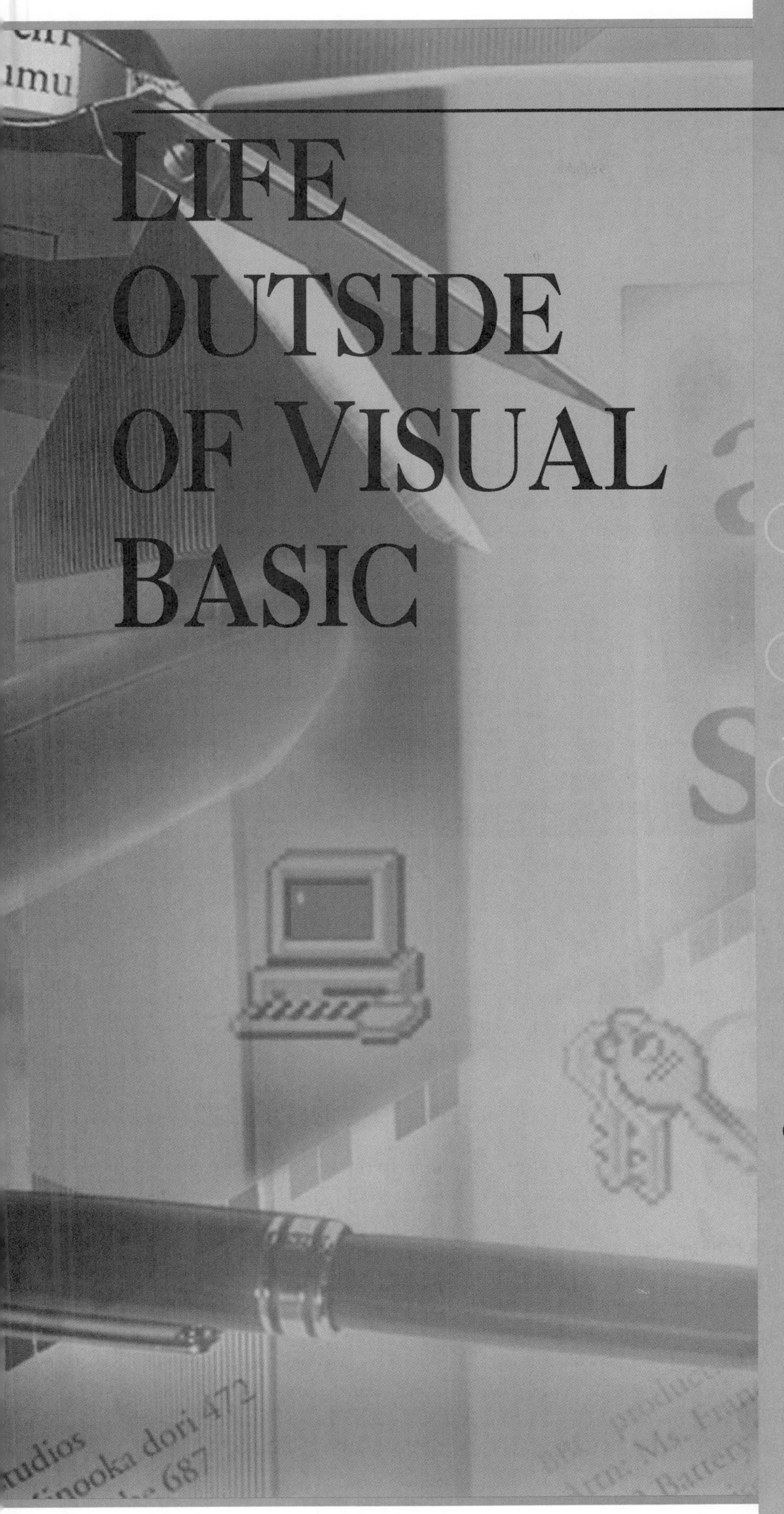

LIFE OUTSIDE OF VISUAL BASIC

UNIT 4

Estimated Time for Unit 4: 15 hours

LESSON 13

HELP

OBJECTIVES

When you complete this lesson, you will be able to:

- Build a topic file of help topics.
- Use the Microsoft Help Workshop to compile the topic file, map topic IDs to numbers, and compile the project to a help file.
- Use the What's This Help System to provide pop-up help to a user.
- Provide traditional Windows help for your application through WinHelp.
- Provide HTML help for an application.
- Convert an existing WinHelp System to HTML Help.

Estimated Time: 5 hours

KEY TERMS

WinHelp
HTML
topic file
Rich Text Format (RTF)
HelpContextID
WhatsThisHelpID
ScaleMode property
Scale method
Line method
PSet method
What's This Help
Microsoft Help Workshop
topic ID
jumps
HTML Help System
Internet Server
Internet Browser
World Wide Web
HTML tags

Context Sensitive Help

The most carefully crafted user interface occasionally needs help. As intuitive as you think your application is, there is someone who will be mystified by it. You may need help for your own program a month after you have written it.

The traditional Windows Help System, *WinHelp*, provides inter-linked Help topics with full-text search capabilities and tables of contents.

The newer HTML Help System provides the same features as WinHelp but uses *HTML* to build each Help topic entry. HTML is the hypertext markup language used to build documents for the World Wide Web.

To create context sensitive on-line help for your application, start by building a *topic file*. The topic file contains text and graphics used to explain a feature or instruct the user in how to use the application. Create the file in a word processor capable of writing a file in *Rich Text Format*. This format preserves formatting instructions: this is necessary to create a topic file.

Next, use the Microsoft Help Workshop to compile the .rtf (Rich Text Format) topic file and build the Help file (.hlp).

Finally, provide the links from your application to the Help file and Help topics. Each control has a property called the *HelpContextID*. This property connects a control with a Help topic when using WinHelp. Each control also has a *WhatsThisHelpID*. This property is also used to connect a control with a Help topic. It is used when the What's This Help System is active.

In this exercise you set up an application to work with throughout the lesson. The application provides an introduction to some of Visual Basic's graphic methods.

The next exercise looks at a minimal implementation of context-sensitive help using What's This Help. This system provides quick help to the user without opening the Help Viewer. It supports traditional WinHelp (.hlp) Help files and HTML Help (.chm) files.

Do not forget the lowly ToolTip. Most controls have the ToolTipText property. When the mouse hovers over a control, its ToolTip appears in a pop-up box next to the control. This is especially useful for labeling images.

STEP-BY-STEP 13.1

1. Start Visual Basic and double-click **Standard EXE**. Save your form and project as **Graphing**.

2. Before you design a Help system, you need an application. The application in this section draws graphs of quadratic and linear equations entered by the user. As you develop the program, plan the Help topics. Change the name of the form to **frmGraphing**. Change the caption of the form to **Graphing Quadratic and Linear Equations**. The first help topic is an explanation of the purpose of the application. It appears when the form is selected and F1 is pressed.

3. The Graphing program draws parabolas and lines. The user enters the data using text boxes in two frames whose appearance is controlled by a Tab Strip control. Right-click the toolbox. Select **Components**. In the Components dialog box, select **Microsoft Windows Common Controls 6.0**. The TabStrip control is in the first of the Common Control files. Click **OK** to close the Components dialog window. A tab is used for each kind of equation. One Help topic deals with entering quadratic equations and the other deals with entering linear equations. Click the **Tab Strip** control in the toolbox and draw a Tab Strip on the form. Leave the default name.

4. Put a picture box on the form. Change the name of the box to **picGraph**. Set the **Height** property to **2295** and the **Width** property to **2775**. The Scale property is set with code when the program runs.

The picture box (as well as the form) has a *ScaleMode property* and a Scale property. Each has to do with how the object is measured. The ScaleMode property allows choices among a number of predefined measuring standards: the twip, the pixel, the character, the millimeter, the centimeter, the inch, and the user defined mode. The *Scale method* is used to set a user defined measure for a form, picture box, or the printer. To use the Scale method, specify the coordinates of the top left corner of the object and the bottom right corner of the object. Visual Basic uses these coordinates to determine the scale of the drawing.

(continued on next page)

5. Select the form and enter the Menu Editor. Enter the following menu, then click **OK**.

MENU ITEMS

CAPTION	NAME	INDEX
Graph	mnuGraph	
....Draw the Graph	mnuDrawGraph	
....Clear	mnuClear	
....Zoom In	mnuZoom	0
....Zoom Out	mnuZoom	1
....-	mnuSeparator	
....E&xit	mnuExit	

The item below the Zoom Out entry is the menu separator character, the hyphen or minus character. The Zoom items form a menu control array. They call the same code and require an index number.

Each menu item has a HelpContextID property to connect the menu item with a Help topic. You set the HelpContextID property for each menu item after the Help file is built.

6. Put a command button on the form. Change the name of the command button to **cmdZoom**. It calls the same code as the menu items. Copy the control with **Ctrl + C** and paste it on the form with **Ctrl + V**. When prompted to create a control array, click **Yes**. Leave the name of the new button the same as the first button. Drag it below the first command button. Change the caption of the first button to **Zoom In** and the second to **Zoom Out**. You set the HelpContextID property of the Zoom command buttons to the same Help topic as the Zoom menu items after the Help file is built. Figure 13-1 shows the form layout.

FIGURE 13-1
The placement of controls on the Graphing project

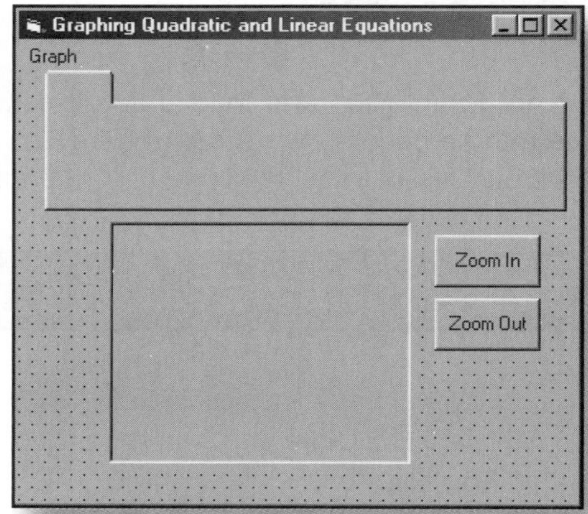

7. Draw a frame on the form. The dimensions of the frame should approximately fit the working area of the TabStrip. Change the name of the frame to **fraQuadratic**. Later you change the BorderStyle property to make the border of the frame disappear.

8. The next two steps draw the input form for entering data for the quadratic equation. The formula for the quadratic equation is $y = ax^2 + bx + c$. Draw a label in the frame. Select the **Font** property for the label and change the size of the font to **10** and its Font style to **Bold**, then click **OK**. Change the **AutoSize** property to **True**. Right-click the control and select **Copy**. If you press **Ctrl + V**, the control is pasted into the form. However, you want the control in the frame. Right-click the body of the frame and select **Paste**. Answer **No** to the prompt about creating a control array. The new label appears in the

upper left corner of the frame. Reposition the labels to match Figure 13-2. Right-click the body of the frame and paste a third label on the frame. Reposition the third label. Change the caption of the first label to **y =**, the second to **x^2 +**, and the third to **x+**.

FIGURE 13-2
The frame for entering the coefficients of a quadratic equation

9. Draw a text box on the frame. Change the Font Size to **10** and the Font style to **Bold**. Clear the **Text** property. Copy and paste the text box on the frame twice. Answer **No** to the prompt about creating a control array. Reposition the text boxes to match Figure 13-2. Change the names of the text boxes to **txtA**, **txtB**, and **txtC**.

10. Although the figure above shows the frame within the boundaries of the TabStrip, you know that unlike a frame or a picture box the TabStrip is not a container. The frame is sitting on the TabStrip. For now, move the frame away from the TabStrip and draw another frame within the bounds of the TabStrip. Name this frame **fraLinear**. The formula for the linear equation is: *ax + b*. Copy the appropriate labels and text boxes **y =** and **x +** from fraQuadratic and paste them onto fraLinear. Change the names of the text boxes to **txtLA** and **txtLB**. "L" stands for linear. This letter differentiates the text boxes from the ones used in the quadratic input frame. Match the new frame to Figure 13-3. You create a Help topic for each equation type in the next exercise.

FIGURE 13-3
The Graphing project form showing both frames

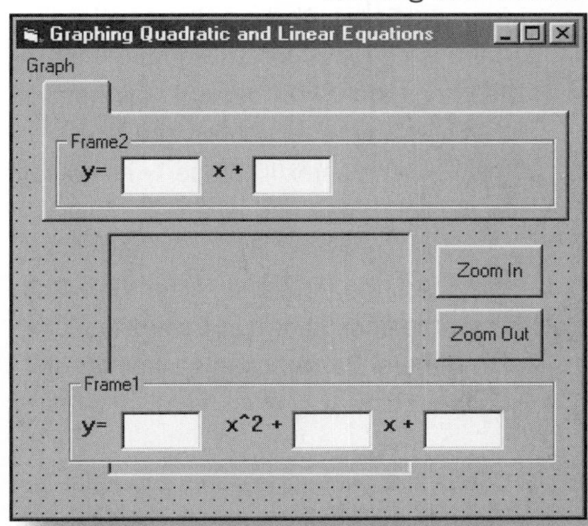

11. Set an appropriate ToolTipText for each textbox. For instance, for txtA and txtLA, set the **ToolTipText** property to **Enter A**.

12. Position the frames on top of each other within the confines of the TabStrip. Change the **BorderStyle** property for each of the frames to **0-None**. You may need to select one of the frames from the combo box at the top of the Properties window: it may not be possible to select it from the form once one frame is on top of the other.

13. Right-click the TabStrip (be careful not to right-click one of the frames—check the Properties window for the name of the selected item) and select **Properties**. Click the **Tabs** tab in the Property Pages dialog box. For the Caption of Tab 1, enter **Linear**. For the tab's ToolTipText, enter **Enter the coefficients for a linear equation**. Click **Insert Tab**. Enter **Quadratic** for the Caption and **Enter the coefficients for a quadratic equation** for the ToolTipText. Leave the Key property blank. Click **OK** to close the TabStrip's

(continued on next page)

Property Pages. You may have noticed there is no HelpContextID property for the TabStrip. That is OK because the frames that contain the text boxes and labels have a HelpContextID property as do each of the text boxes and labels.

14. Right-click the form and select **View Code**. Enter the lines shown in **Code Step 14** in the General Declarations section of the Code window.

    One of the neatest features of Visual Basic is the ability to use the Variant data type. If no type is specifically declared in a variable declaration, the variables are of the Variant type. Those coming from strongly typed languages like Pascal rebel at using variables of an indeterminate type, but they work quite nicely in Visual Basic. There is additional overhead in the form of memory: the Variant type takes more memory than many other types. The advantage is being able to write code that is not linked to a particular data type. xMax and yMax are of the Variant data type.

15. Enter the code shown in **Code Step 15** in **Form_Activate** to set the properties and the starting points of the graph.

16. Enter the code shown in **Code Step 16** in **TabStrip1_Click** to set up the TabStrip control.

    Index value one designates the Linear equation. Change the frame's Visible property to True. Change the Quadratic frame's Visible property to False. Set the Quadratic flag to False. Set the focus to the first text box of the Linear frame.

    If the Index value is 2, the Quadratic tab has been selected. Make its frame visible and the Linear frame invisible and set the Quadratic flag to True. Set the focus to txtA, the first text box of the Quadratic frame.

17. Most of the work is done in mnuDrawGraph_Click. Enter the code shown in **Code Step 17** as the first part of the code for **mnuDrawGraph_Click**.

CODE STEP 14

```
'Flag to determine which graph to draw.
Dim Quadratic As Boolean
Dim xMax, yMax 'Absolute values of max x and y.
```

CODE STEP 15

```
'Set quadratic frame and variable to Visible=False.
fraLinear.Visible = True
fraQuadratic.Visible = False
Quadratic = False
'Start points for dimensions of graph.
xMax = 10
yMax = 10
```

CODE STEP 16

```
'Set the Visible property and the focus
If TabStrip1.SelectedItem.Index = 1 Then
  fraLinear.Visible = True
  fraQuadratic.Visible = False
  Quadratic = False
  txtLA.SetFocus
Else
  fraLinear.Visible = False
  fraQuadratic.Visible = True
  Quadratic = True
  txtA.SetFocus
End If
```

CODE STEP 17

```
Dim a, b, c, x, y, Increment
'Set ToolTipText to reflect dimensions of Graph.
picGraph.ToolTipText = xMax & " by " & yMax
'Set the Scale of the graph.
picGraph.Scale (-xMax, yMax)-(xMax, -yMax)
'Draw the coordinate axes.
picGraph.Line (-xMax, 0)-(xMax, 0), QBColor(5)
picGraph.Line (0, yMax)-(0, -yMax), QBColor(5)
'Calculate a reasonable increment for the For loop.
Increment = 2 * xMax / 100
x = -xMax
If Quadratic Then
  'Gather data from the Quadratic frame.
  a = CDbl(txtA)
  b = CDbl(txtB)
  c = CDbl(txtC)
  'Calculate the coordinates of the first point of
  'the graph and plot the single point.
  y = a * x * x + b * x + c
  picGraph.PSet (x, y), QBColor(3)
  'Plot the remaining points.
    For x = -xMax To xMax Step Increment
      y = a * x * x + b * x + c
      'Draw a line from the last point to the new point.
      picGraph.Line -(x, y), QBColor(3)
      'Old degug line to show listing of x,y values generated
      'in the loop. Now commented out.
      'Debug.Print x, y
    Next x
```

(continued on next page)

The Line method has the following syntax:

object.**Line** [**Step**] **(***x1*, y*1***)** [**Step**] - **(***x2*, *y2***)**, [*color*], [**B**][**F**]

In the code for Step 17, xMax and yMax define the dimensions of the graph. A ToolTip displays the dimensions. The *Line method* draws a line on an object. The object can be a picture box or a form. Use Step when the coordinates are relative to the current graphic's position given by the CurrentX and CurrentY properties. In the variation of Line shown in the code for Step 17, the coordinate of the first point is omitted. In this case, a line is drawn from the current graphic's position given by the CurrentX and CurrentY properties to the new point. The optional color is specified with one of two color functions: QBColor( ), a function left over from the very old days, or RGB (red, green, blue) which picks out a color from a full 24-bit color palette. When the option [B] is specified, the two coordinates become the corners of a box. If [F] is included with the [B], the box is filled with the specified color. The increment is set in proportion to the scale of the picture box so connecting points for the lines are neither too close (thereby slowing down the drawing process) nor too far apart (which makes the graph look jagged.) To draw a graph in the boundaries of the picture box, xMax is used to control the For loop.

The PSet method has the following syntax:

object.**PSet** [**Step**] (*x*, *y*), [*color*]

The *PSet method* plots a point on an object. The object in this case is the picture box picGraph. It could also be the form. (x,y) is the coordinate of the point to graph. Color specifies a color provided by the QBColor( ) function or the RGB( ) function. The optional Step is used if the point is to be graphed relative to the current graphic's position given by the CurrentX and CurrentY properties.

18. Enter the code shown in **Code Step 18** for **mnuDrawGraph_Click**, below the code already entered in Step 17. (You can copy the 'Gather data... code from Step 17 and modify it for the Linear frame.)

19. Enter the code shown in **Code Step 19** in **mnuZoom_Click**. xMax and yMax are used to set the dimensions of the picture box. The code in step 19 makes the values smaller or larger to change the scale of the picture box. The picture box doesn't change size, but the relative scale of the picture box changes when xMax and yMax change.

20. Enter the code shown in **Code Step 20** in **cmdZoom_Click**.

CODE STEP 18

```
Else
  'Gather data from the Linear frame.
   a = CDbl(txtLA)
   b = CDbl(txtLB)
   y = a * x + b
   picGraph.PSet (x, y), QBColor(3)
   For x = -xMax To xMax Step Increment
     y = a * x + b
     picGraph.Line -(x, y), QBColor(3)
     'Debug.Print x, y
   Next x
End If
```

21. In **mnuClear_Click**, enter the following code to clear the text boxes of the frame with the focus.

```
If Quadratic Then
  txtA = ""
  txtB = ""
  txtC = ""
Else
  txtLA = ""
  txtLB = ""
End If
picGraph.Cls
```

22. In **mnuExit_Click**, enter **Unload Me**.

23. Save the project. Run the program. Click the **Quadratic** tab. Verify that there are Tool Tips for the text boxes. Enter the coefficients **1**, **-5**, and **–6**. Select **Graph | Draw the Graph**. The graph of the function appears. Verify that there is a Tool Tip for the graph.

24. Draw several graphs with different coefficients. Click each of the Zoom buttons several times. Click **Graph** on the menu bar and select the zoom items in the menu. Select **Graph | Clear** to clear the text boxes and clear the graph. Click the **Linear** tab and test with coefficients **–.5** and **–2**. Draw the graph and test zooming. Satisfy yourself that all the parts of the program work.

25. Stop the program. If necessary, correct the code, save your changes, test again, and stop the program. Leave the project open for the next exercise.

What do you do if the graph does not appear? Get out your debugging tools. Set a breakpoint and single-step through the code with F8. Remove the single quote (apostrophe) for the Debug.Print lines in the code so they are no longer comments. Check the output in the Debug window. Make sure Option Explicit is present in the General Declarations section of the form. Many errors are spelling errors. Check the names of each of your controls. Did you change them from their defaults? While debugging it is annoying to have to always re-enter test data. Since data is collected from text boxes, change the Text property for each of the boxes to reflect reasonable data. This saves the step of re-entering data for every test run. Often errors in graphing programs involve the Scale method.

CODE STEP 19

```
'Clear the current graph.
 picGraph.Cls
 If Index = 0 Then
  'Zoom In
  xMax = xMax / 1.5
  yMax = yMax / 1.5
 Else
  'Zoom Out
  xMax = xMax * 1.5
  yMax = yMax * 1.5
 End If
'Call DrawGraph to redraw the graph.
 mnuDrawGraph_Click
```

CODE STEP 20

```
'Calls the same code as mnuZoom.
 mnuZoom_Click (Index)
```

Have you thought about all the places Help files are needed to help the user? What about explaining the math itself? It is possible a user will run the program who does not understand the first thing about graphing.

In the next lesson add What's This Help to the application.

Quick Check 13.a

1. The traditional Windows Help System, __________________, provides inter-linked Help topics with full-text search capabilities and tables of contents.

2. The __________________ property chooses between a number of predefined measuring standards: the twip, the pixel, the character, the millimeter, the centimeter, the inch, and the user defined mode.

3. The Scale Method requires the coordinates of two points to set the scale for a picturebox or form. The two points are the coordinates of the __________________ and the coordinates of the __________________ corners of the object.

4. Unlike the picture box and the frame, the TabStrip is not a __________________.

5. To plot a point on a picture box or form, use the __________________ method.

6. The two color functions used in Visual Basic are __________________ and __________________.

What's This Help

The simplest kind of Help system to implement is *What's This Help*. In a way, it is a glorified ToolTipText system. When this Help system is enabled, a question mark icon appears in the place of the Minimize and Maximize buttons in the title bar of the form. The question mark is called the What's This Help button. To use the system, click the question mark icon and click a control. Any Help text connected to the control is displayed.

To make any kind of Help System work, you need to create a Help topic file. This is a multi-stage process that requires at least two additional programs: a word processor (such as Microsoft Word) that supports writing files in the Rich Text Format, and the *Microsoft Help Workshop* to compile the Help file from the topic files, mappings, and other data. The skills you learn here are used when building a full-blown Windows Help System.

STEP-BY-STEP 13.2

1. If necessary, start Visual Basic and open the **Graphing** project developed in the last exercise. Figure 13-4 shows the program drawing the graph of a quadratic function. Use the figure to plan Help topics.

2. Provide Help topics for the following: Linear equations, Quadratic equations, the Zoom In and Zoom Out buttons, and the picture box. To start the process, start **Microsoft Word**. (Click the **Start** button on

the task bar, point to **Programs**, and navigate to Microsoft Word.) Insert the following Help topics separating each paragraph with a page break. To insert a page break, press **Ctrl + Enter** or select **Insert | Break** from the menu bar, then select **Page break** and click **OK**. Use an 11-point font size.

HELP TOPICS

A linear function in x, a function of the form $y = ax + b$, expresses a rule for generating a set of ordered pairs, (x,y). The function uses an x term with x raised to the first power. The form used is called the *y-intercept* form. The value of a is the value of the slope of the line. The slope is a measure of the slant of the line. The value of b is the coordinate where the line intercepts (crosses) the y-axis.

A quadratic function in x, a function of the form $y = ax^2 + bx + c$, expresses a rule for generating a set of ordered pairs, (x,y). Quadratic functions are characterized by an x^2 term. If the coefficient of the x^2 term is 0, the function is not a quadratic function. Every quadratic function generates a set of ordered pairs, that, when graphed, draw a parabola. A parabola is a conic section generated by passing a plane through a cone parallel to the side of the cone.

The Zoom In function divides the current scale of the picture box by 1.5. The maximum values for the x and y axes change accordingly. If the original value of xMax and yMax is 10, after a Zoom In, the values are 2/3rd of the original value: 6.6666.

The Zoom Out function multiplies the current scale of the picture box by 1.5. The maximum values for the x and y axes change accordingly. If the original value of xMax and yMax is 10, after a Zoom In, the values are 1.5 times the original value: 15.

The picture box represents the coordinate axes, the xy plane. Each function entered represents a rule for generating tables ordered pairs. Each ordered pair is graphed on the coordinate axes represented by the picture box.

FIGURE 13-4
The Graphing Quadratic and Linear Equations project, showing the graph of a quadratic equation and the ToolTip that appears when the mouse pointer hovers over the picture box

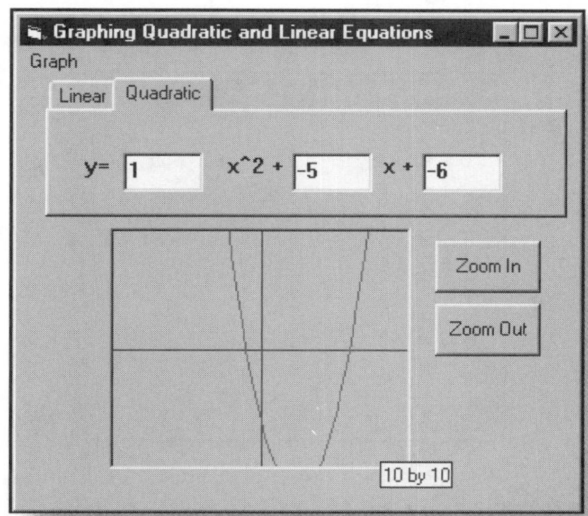

3. Make sure the Help topics are separated by page breaks. Save the Help topic file by selecting **File | Save As** from the menu bar. In the Save As dialog box, open the Save as type combo box. Select **Rich Text Format** from the combo box. Navigate to a directory (preferably the same directory as the Graphing application) and save the Help topic file with the name **GraphingHelp.rtf**.

4. Move the cursor directly in front of the first character of the first entry. The Help topic file provides information to the Help Workshop about each Help topic through footnotes. Different footnotes convey different information concerning the Help topic. Select **Insert | Footnote** from the menu bar. See Figure 13-5.

(continued on next page)

FIGURE 13-5
The Footnote and Endnote dialog box showing a Custom mark entry

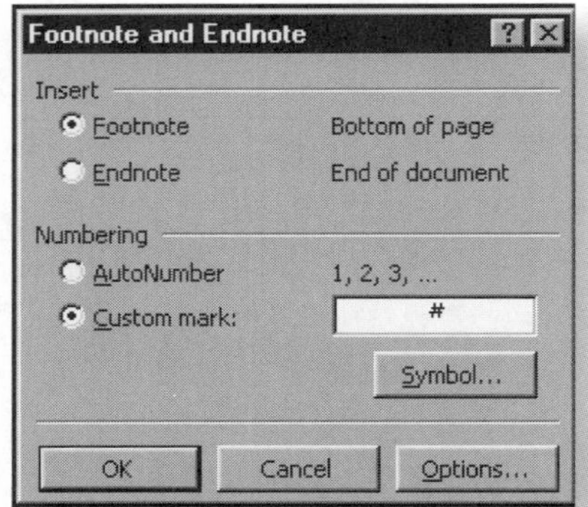

Footnotes are commonly used to record notes commenting on the contents of a text. In this application, footnotes are added to each Help topic to identify it in a Help file.

5. Enter the pound sign (#) in the Custom mark text box. This symbol identifies a *topic ID*. A topic ID is a string that identifies a Help topic or identifies a location within the topic to display. Click **OK**. The screen splits showing your original text in the top and the Footnotes window below. In the Footnotes window enter the topic ID, **IDH_Linear**. The Help compiler uses the prefix IDH_ to check the status of each Help topic. (Note: You can leave a blank line between footnotes as shown in Figure 13-6 if you press Enter but the blank lines are not necessary.)

The only footnote that is required for Help topics is the topic ID. Some other footnotes are added and explained in the next section.

6. At the beginning of each of the other Help topics insert a footnote. Supply the pound sign (#) as the custom mark for each. Supply the following topic ID names: **IDH_Quadratic**, **IDH_ZoomIn**, **IDH_ZoomOut**, and **IDH_PictureBox**. Figure 13-6 shows a portion of the resulting file.

Usually, if a file is open in Word, other applications cannot access it. This is not the case for a Help topic file. If you expect a lot of editing to fix or supplement the Help topic file, leave the file open. You may still add the Help topic file to the Graphing project in Visual Basic. Save the Help topic file to preserve changes.

FIGURE 13-6
A look at the Help topic file as it is being developed in Microsoft Word

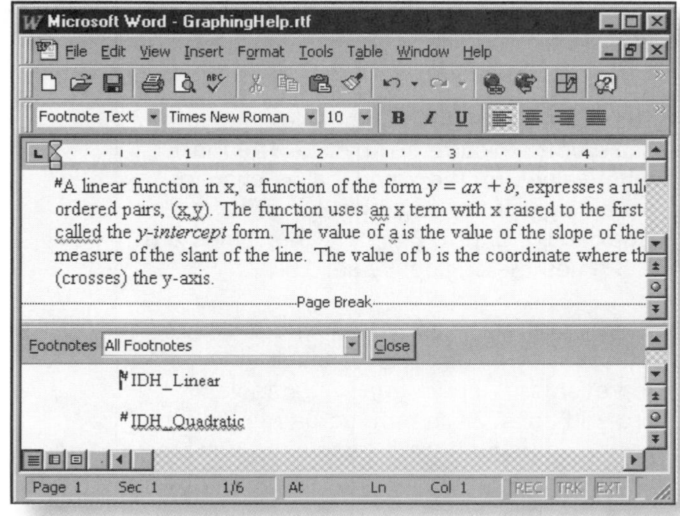

7. When each topic is properly footnoted, save the file. Exit Microsoft Word.

8. Start the Microsoft Help Workshop. If Visual Studio is installed, you can find the application in the Start menu. Click **Start** and select **Programs | Microsoft Visual Studio | Microsoft Visual Studio 6.0 Tools | Help Workshop**.

The filename of the executable file is HCW.exe. If it is not listed in the Start menu, right-click Start and select Find. Enter HCW.exe in the Named: text box. Change Look in: to C:\ or to whatever letter represents the drive on which application software is installed. Be sure Include Subfolders is checked. Click Find Now. If the file is not on your system it can be installed from the Electronic Instructor CD-ROM or downloaded from the Microsoft Web site on the Internet.

9. Once the Help Workshop is open, click the Tip to close it. Start a new Help project by selecting **File | New** from the menu bar of the Help Workshop. In the New dialog box, select **Help Project** and click **OK**. See Figure 13-7.

FIGURE 13-7
The New dialog box in the Help Workshop

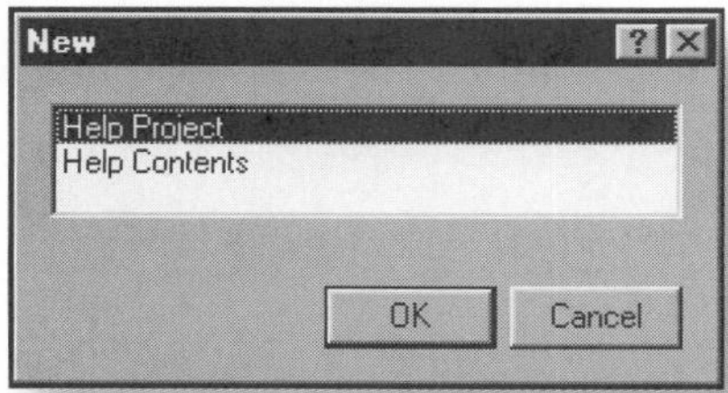

FIGURE 13-8
The Microsoft Help Workshop

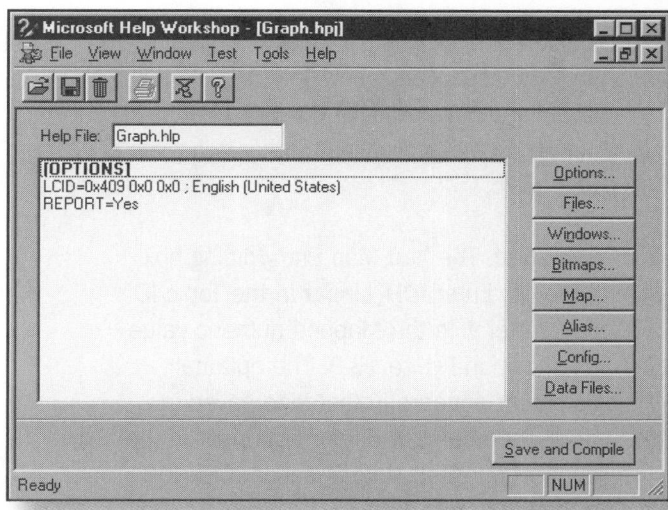

10. In the Project File Name dialog box, navigate to the directory that contains the Graphing application. Enter **Graph** for the name of the file and click **Save**. The .hpj extension is automatically provided. The .hpj extension is added to the name of the project file and a file with a .hlp extension is also created. Figure 13-8 shows the OPTIONS section of the new Help project displayed in the opening screen of the Help Workshop.

11. Click the **Files** button. Click **Add** in the Topic Files dialog box. In the Open dialog box, select **GraphingHelp.rtf**. Click **Open** to close the dialog box. Click **OK** to close the Topic Files dialog box. A FILES listing for the Help topic file appears in the Help Workshop window.

12. In the application, Help topics are accessed by using their WhatsThisHelpID numbers. In the Help topic file, each Help topic receives an identifying topic ID, which is a string. What connects the WhatsThisHelpId number of the application to the topic ID string of the Topic file? Click the **Map** button in the Help Workshop. The Map dialog box

(continued on next page)

appears. Mapping is the process of setting up a correspondence between the Help topic ID string and a particular number. Use the number in the application to refer to a given Help topic.

13. Click **Add**. The Add Map Entry dialog box appears. Enter **IDH_Linear** in the Topic ID box. Enter **1** in the Mapped numeric value as shown in Figure 13-9. The optional comment appears in the code saved in the Help project. It does not appear in the application when Help is called. Click **OK** to save the mapping.

FIGURE 13-9
The Add Map Entry dialog box showing the entry for IDH_Linear

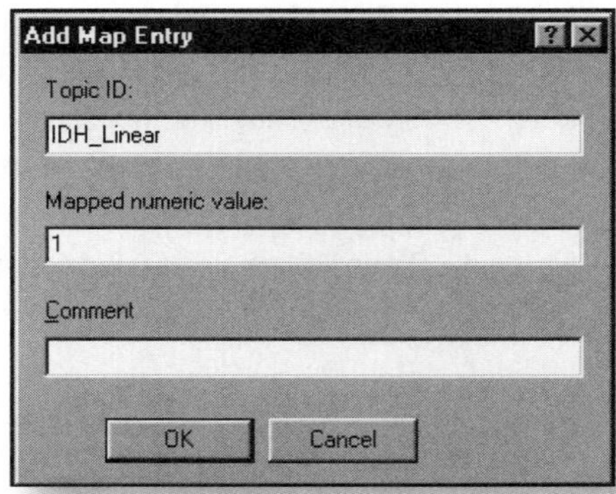

14. The value used for the numeric entry often conforms to a careful plan for numbering Help topics. In such a scheme, use multi-digit numbers where the value of each digit stands for something that helps identify the Help topic. In your application, there are five Help topics. Click **Add** and add the remaining Help topics. Number them 1 to 5 using the table below. The IDH_Linear topic has already been added. In the Map dialog box, the entries appear in alphabetical order. When finished, click **OK** to close the Map dialog box.

15. You now have the minimum information needed to create a Help file. Click the **Save and Compile** button. The Help Workshop builds a Help file with the name Graph.hlp. Figure 13-10 shows the report returned by the Workshop. If a Topic ID remains unmapped or a Help topic is unmarked, an error report appears.

16. To test the appearance of the Help topics, click the **question mark icon** (Run WinHelp) in the toolbar. The View Help File dialog box appears. You can view the Help generated by your Help file in two different ways. The filenames in the dialog box are set automatically. Select **IDH_Quadratic** from the Mapped Topic IDs: combo box. Click the option button **A pop-up** from the "Open Help file as if it were" frame. See Figure 13-11. Click **View Help**.

HELP TOPICS

TOPIC ID STRING	MAPPED NUMERIC VALUE
IDH_Linear	1
IDH_Quadratic	2
IDH_ZoomIn	3
IDH_ZoomOut	4
IDH_PictureBox	5

17. After viewing the pop-up Help for the Quadratic function, click the pop-up to close it. Click the option button **Invoked by a program** from the "Open Help file as if it were" frame and click **ViewHelp**. The Help topic appears in the traditional WinHelp window. Close the WinHelp window. Test the other Help topics in the Mapped Topic IDs combo box, then close the View Help File dialog box by clicking **Close**.

FIGURE 13-10
The Microsoft Help Workshop showing the result of the Save and Compile. Your paths are probably different, but the file names should be the same

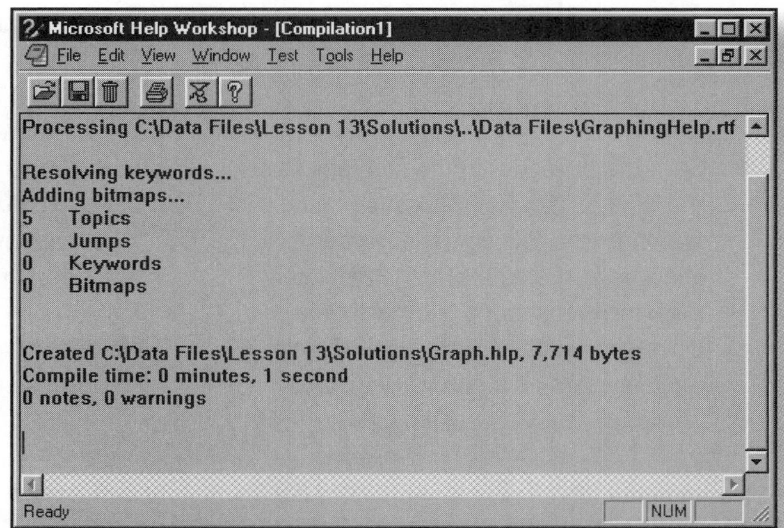

18. Select **File | Exit** on the Microsoft Help Workshop menu bar to close Microsoft Help Workshop. If necessary, open the **Graphing** application in Visual Basic. Right-click **Project1** in the Project Explorer. Select **Project1 Properties** to open the project's Property Pages. In the General tab, click inside the Help File Name box. Use the ellipsis button to navigate to the Help file, **Graph.hlp**, created by the Help Workshop. Select the Help file and click **Open**, then click **OK** to close the Property Pages for Project1.

FIGURE 13-11
The View Help File dialog box set up to view the Help topic for the Quadratic function as a pop-up

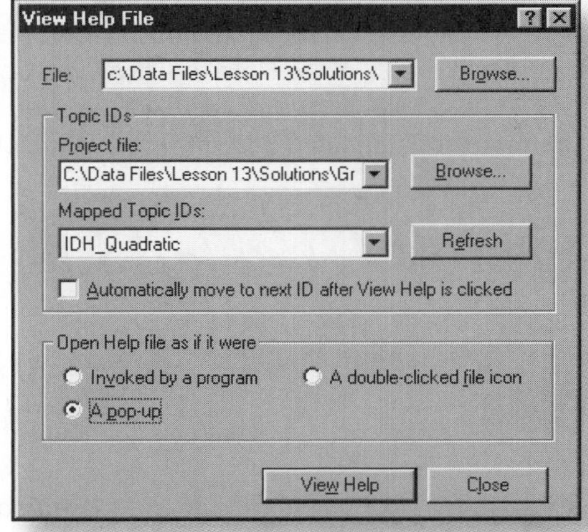

19. Double-click **frmGraphing** in the Project Explorer. With the form selected, select **BorderStyle** in the Properties window. Change the setting to **3-Fixed Dialog**. The Minimize and Maximize buttons on the form disappear. They are incompatible with the WhatsThisHelp System. Double-click the **WhatsThisButton** property to toggle its value from False to **True**. Automatically, the value of the **WhatsThisHelp** property changes to **True**. Where the form's Minimize and Maximize button would appear, the What's This Help question mark button appears.

20. In the combo box for the Properties window select **fraLinear**. Select the **WhatsThisHelpID** property and change the value of the property to **1**. Select **fraQuadratic** (you may have to select it in the combo box at the top of the Properties

(continued on next page)

window) and change its WhatsThisHelpID to **2**. Change the same property of the ZoomIn button to **3**, the ZoomOut button to **4**, and the picture box to **5**.

21. Save the project. Run the program. Click the **What's This Help** (question mark) button on the title bar. The pointer changes to the WhatsThisHelp pointer. Click the mouse on a text box in the Linear frame. The Linear function Help topic appears as a pop-up Help. Click What's This Help and Click each of the command buttons to test their Help. Click What's This Help and click the picture box to test its Help. Click the pop-up to close it. Click the Quadratic tab to switch to the Quadratic frame. Click the **What's This Help** button and click each of the controls that have Help available. Make sure everything is working.

22. Stop the program. Leave the project open for the next exercise.

It is common at this point to realize that you missed several opportunities to help the user run your application. For instance, there is no Help for entering values for the coefficients of the functions. There is no Help attached to the menu items. You may choose to go back to Word, open the Help topic file and add new topics. Remember to add the identifying footnotes. Open Microsoft Help Workshop and recompile the Help system. Insert new WhatsThisHelpID's in the application and test the program again.

It is common to generate a lot of paperwork as you develop any project. When you talk with users to define their needs, it is common to create files of information. With a little brushing up, the notes you create can become your Help topics. You do not need to create a whole new document for each Help topic. Write Help topics as you develop your application. Start before you write any code.

In the next Step-by-Step exercise, you turn the easy pop-up style Help of WhatsThisHelp into the more sophisticated and powerful WinHelp Help System.

Quick Check 13.b

1. The simplest kind of Help system to implement is ____________________.

2. Topic files are not saved as doc or txt files, but as ____________________.

3. Help topics in a topic file are identified with strings called ________________.

4. The Microsoft Help Workshop uses ____________________ to make the connection between the Help topic in the Help topic file and the application.

5. To work with WhatsThisHelp, set the form's BorderStyle property to ____________________.

6. To connect a control with a Help topic in the WhatsThisHelp Help System, change the control's ________________________ property.

Using the WinHelp Help System

Converting to the WinHelp Help System is easy. You even use the same topic file. Utilizing all the powerful features of the WinHelp Help System is a little more complicated. However, hard work pays off in a much more powerful Help system.

STEP-BY-STEP 13.3

1. If necessary, start Visual Basic and open the **Graphing** project.

2. Select the form. In the Properties window, Select **Whats This Help** and double-click to toggle the value for this property as well as **Whats This Button** back to **False**. Change the **BorderStyle** property for the form back to **2-Sizable**. This turns off the What's This Help Help System and the Minimize and Maximize buttons return.

3. In the Properties window, select **fraLinear** in the combo box at the top of the window. Change its HelpContextID to **1**. This identifies a Help topic for fraLinear in the same way that the WhatsThisHelpID identified a Help topic for fraLinear. Change the HelpContextID for the Quadratic frame and command buttons as shown in the table below. Menu items also have a HelpContextID property. Select the form, open the Menu Editor and set the property for the two Zoom menu items as shown, then click **OK** to close the Menu Editor.

HELP CONTEXT ID PROPERTY SETTINGS

NAME (OR CAPTION)	HELPCONTEXTID
fraQuadratic	2
cmdZoom(0)	3
cmdZoom(1)	4
picGraph	5
ZoomIn (menu item)	3
ZoomOut (menu item)	4

4. Save the project. Run the program. WinHelp can be used as a context sensitive Help system. Press **Tab** until the Zoom In button is selected. Press **F1**. The Help topic for the Zoom In button appears in the Help Viewer. See Figure 13-12. Note the Index and Back buttons at the top of the Help Viewer are grayed out. You provide information for an index later in this exercise. Press **Esc** to close the Help Viewer or close the Help Viewer window with the **Close box** in the top right corner of the window.

The default size of the Help Viewer Window is quite large. Like everything else, this size is adjustable. The size of the Help Viewer in the figure is reduced.

5. Select **Graph** from the menu bar. Position the mouse pointer on Zoom Out without clicking it. Press **F1**. The Help topic for Zoom Out is displayed. What looks OK as a pop-up in the What's This Help System, looks flat and dull in the Help Viewer. Press **Esc** to close the Help Viewer, then stop the program.

6. To improve the looks of the Help topics and add index items, start Microsoft Word (click

(continued on next page)

the **Start** button on the task bar, point to Programs, and navigate to Microsoft Word). Open the Help topic file saved in the previous exercise: **GraphingHelp.rtf**. When you select **File | Open** to open the file, remember to change Files of type: to Rich Text Format or else you may have trouble finding the Help topic file. Once the file is opened, select **View | Footnotes** to open the Footnotes window at the bottom of the document.

FIGURE 13-12
The Zoom In Help topic displayed in the Help Viewer

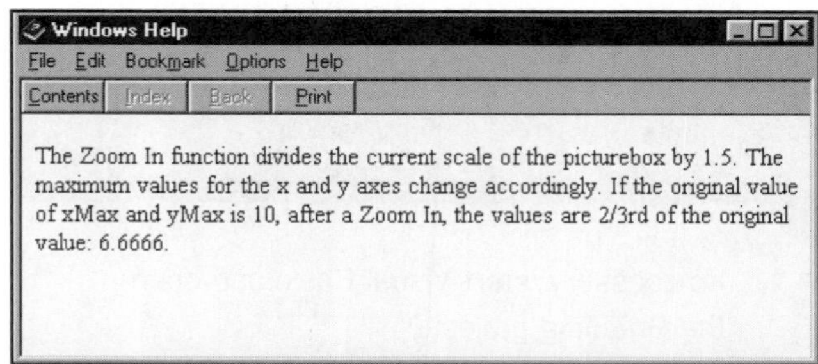

7. First, work on the appearance of the Help topic text. Add a Bold heading to each Help topic. To the Linear Function topic, add the heading **Linear Function**. Position the cursor between the footnote symbol (#) and the first letter of the first word in the Help topic text. In this case, it is the letter **A**. Enter the text: **Linear Function** and press **Enter**. Select the words just entered and change the font size to 14 and click **Bold** on the toolbar. Indent the first line of the Help topic text to make it look more like a normal paragraph.

8. Add Bold 14 point headings for each of the Help topic entries and indent the first line of the Help topic text for each Help topic. Use the heading **Coordinate Axis** for the picture box.

9. You could test the present changes, but it is a lengthy multi-step process to recompile the Help file. Instead, make the changes necessary to add index entries to the Help system. Position the cursor between the footnote symbol and the first letter of the new Linear Function heading. Select **Insert | Footnote**. For the Custom mark, enter **k** and click **OK**. This marks a footnote as a container of index key words. In the Footnotes window enter: **function; linear; line; graphing; slope; y-intercept**. Each item becomes an index entry in the compiled Help system. Each item is separated with a semicolon. Add as many index words as you like.

10. Add a **k** footnote for each of the four additional help topics using the table below. You may add additional index items

K FOOTNOTES

HELP TOPIC	LIST OF INDEX WORDS APPEARING AS A K FOOTNOTE
Linear Function	function; linear; line; graphing; slope; y-intercept
Quadratic Function	function; quadratic; parabola; graphing; conic section; cone
Zoom In	scale; xMax; yMax
Zoom Out	scale; xMax; yMax
Coordinate Axis	coordinate axis; xy plane; ordered pairs

to each list. The entry for the Linear Function topic repeats in the table.

11. It is also necessary to add topic names for each of the Help topics. To add a topic name, insert a footnote for each Help topic with the Custom mark $. Enter a topic name for each of the Help topics using the table below.

HELP TOPIC NAMES

HELP TOPIC	TOPIC NAME (USE CUSTOM MARK: $)
Linear Function	Linear Function
Quadratic Function	Quadratic Function
Zoom In	Zoom In
Zoom Out	Zoom Out
Coordinate Axis	Coordinate Axis

12. Figure 13-13 shows the Linear Function with all three footnotes. Save the Help topic file, then exit Microsoft Word. You may want to give the topic file a new name. It is a good idea to leave the original file unchanged in case there is a reason to return to the original.

13. Run Microsoft Help Workshop. Select **Start | Programs | Microsoft Visual Studio 6.0 | Microsoft Visual Studio Tools | Help Workshop**. Click the Tip to close it. Select **File | New** and select **Help Project** then click **OK**. Save the file with a different name than the original Help file. Click the **Files** button and click **Add** to add the Help topic file you just created and click **Open**. Click **OK** to return to the Help Workshop. The Help Workshop window shows the addition of the Help topic file.

14. Click **Map** and click **Add** to add a mapping between a Topic ID and a number. Map the five Topic ID's to the numbers 1 through 5. Use the table below.

TOPIC ID's

TOPIC ID	MAPPED NUMERIC VALUE
IDH_Linear	1
IDH_Quadratic	2
IDH_ZoomIn	3
IDH_ZoomOut	4
IDH_PictureBox	5

15. Click **OK** to return to the Help project window. The mappings appear in the list box of the Help Workshop in alphabetical order.

16. Click **Save and Compile** to build the new Help file. Figure 13-14 shows a portion of the report. The report of 21 keywords

(continued on next page)

FIGURE 13-13
A detail of the Help Topic file showing three footnotes: Topic ID, Topic name, and index entries

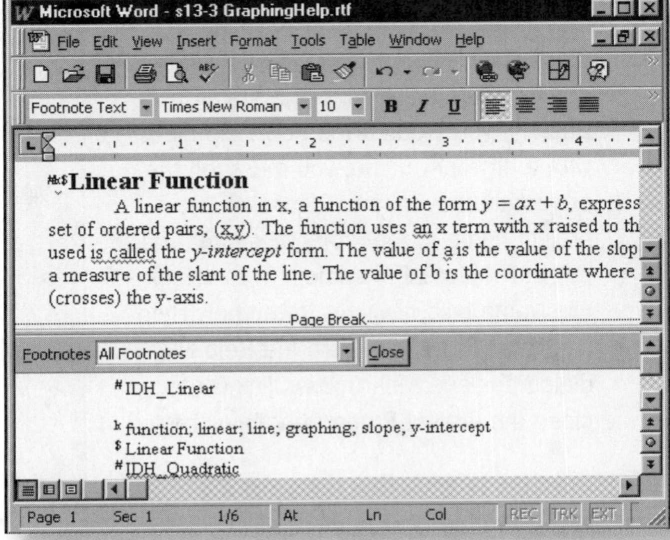

means the index entries were processed and added to the Help file.

If you have to make changes and save and compile the Help file again, close the report window by clicking the lower of the two Close boxes in the upper right corner of the Help Workshop window. Make your changes, then click Save and Compile. If you reopen the Help file you will see a sentence not to modify the Help file directly. Modify the Word document, add it in the Help Workshop and Save and Compile it. You may also see a warning about DOS compatibility. Ignore this warning and modify the file as needed.

FIGURE 13-14
A portion of the Help Workshop showing the report generated when the new Help file is compiled

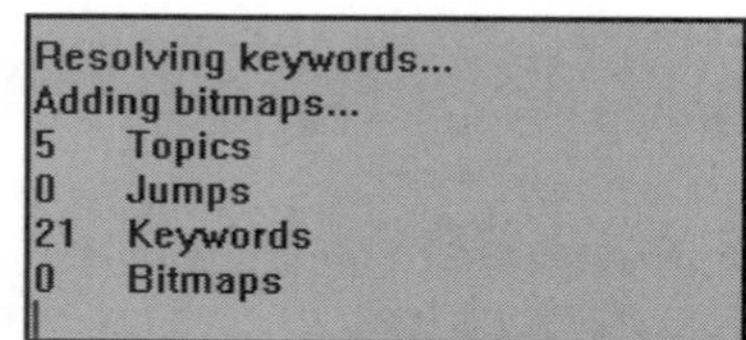

17. Close the Help Workshop. If necessary, open the **Graphing** project in Visual Basic. If you created the new Help file with a different name, you must tell the project the new name. Right-click the project name in the Project Explorer and select **Project1 Properties**. In the Help File Name box, navigate to the new Help file. Select its name from the Help File dialog box and click **Open**. Click **OK** to close the Project Properties dialog box.

18. Save the project. Run the program. Press **Tab** until the Zoom In button is selected. Press **F1**. The Help Viewer appears with the Help topic for that button. A significant difference is the Index button in the Help Viewer. It is no longer grayed out. Click the **Index** button. Figure 13-15 shows the Help Topics window. Included in the list is each of the keywords defined in the Help topic file.

19. Click **parabola** to select it and click **Display**. The Help topic for Quadratic Function appears. Test the other Help topics and several of the Index entries. If there is a problem, start the cycle again: edit the Help topic file, compile the Help file in the Help Workshop, and test the Help file in the application.

20. One thing is still missing. If necessary, run the program again and press **Tab** to select **Zoom In**. Press **F1**. Click **Contents**. At this point, the Contents button in the Help Viewer for the Help system displays the entry for Linear Function rather than the

FIGURE 13-15
The Help Topics window showing the Index entries made in the topic file

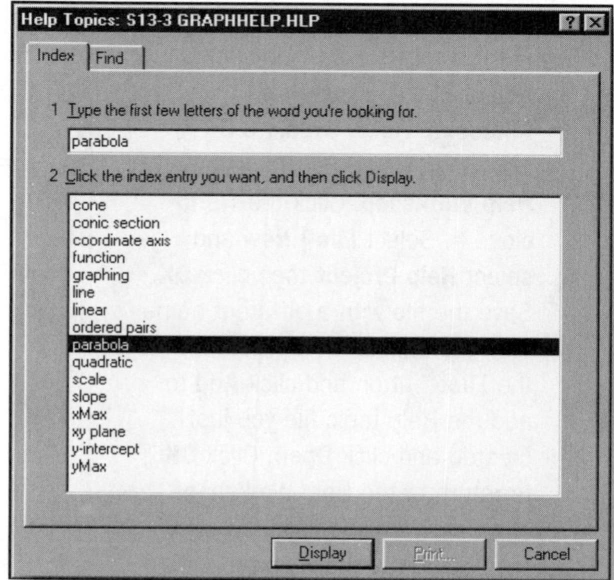

entry for Zoom In. Close the Help window and stop the program. In the next step, edit the Help topic file to add a table of contents.

21. Start Microsoft Word and reopen the Help Topic file. If the footnotes are not visible, select **View | Footnotes** from the menu bar. Position the cursor at the beginning of the file. Press **Enter** twice. Use the up arrow to move up a line. Press **Ctrl + Enter** to insert a page break (or select **Insert | Break**, select **Page Break** and click **OK**). Position the cursor above the page break. Enter the following text with the indentation shown. Change the font to 14 point Bold. Leave a blank line after the first entry only.

CONTENTS
Graphing Project Help
Linear Function
Quadratic Function
Zoom In
Zoom Out
Coordinate Axis

22. To make this into a table of contents, provide *jumps* to the appropriate Help topics. Jumps are links you click to "jump" from one area to another related area in a browser or in a Help file. First though, give the table of contents a topic ID. Position the cursor just before the G in Graphing. Select **Insert | Footnote**. Supply the pound sign (**#**) for the Custom mark. Enter the name **IDH_Contents** in the footnote. Add a topic name footnote **Contents** using the Custom mark $.

23. Position your cursor directly following Linear Function. Leave no space. Enter the topic ID: **IDH_Linear**. Repeat this for each of the five Help topics. (For Coordinate Axis enter IDH_PictureBox).

24. To turn the topic name into a jump to a Help topic, select just the name: **Linear Function.** (Click at the beginning of the name. Hold down **Shift** and press the **right arrow key** to select the name.) Select **Format | Font** from the menu bar. Select **Double** from the Underline combo box. Click **OK.**

25. Select just the topic ID following Linear Function: **IDH_Linear** (use Shift + right arrow). Select **Format | Font**. In the dialog box click **Hidden**. Click **OK.**

26. If the text is now hidden, click the paragraph symbol on the Microsoft Word toolbar. All hidden characters appear embedded in the text. Do not forget how to turn this view mode off; click the paragraph symbol to hide the text.

27. Repeat this procedure for each of the Help topics: 1) Select the topic name and double underline it, 2) Select the topic ID and make it hidden text. Make one change. For the Zoom In topic, instead of double underlining, select single underlining. Instead of jumping to the Help topic, the Help topic text displays as a pop-up. Save the topic file! Exit Microsoft Word.

28. Return to or run the Help Workshop. Return to the same Help project. If the former report is showing, close it with the lower of the two Close boxes in the upper right corner of the Help Workshop window. Click **Map**. Add a mapping for the Table of

(continued on next page)

FIGURE 13-16
A portion of the Help Workshop report showing the five jumps

```
Resolving keywords...
Adding bitmaps...
6    Topics
5    Jumps
21   Keywords
0    Bitmaps
```

Contents. Map its topic ID, **IDH_Contents** to the number **0** and Click **OK**. Click **OK** to close the Map dialog box.

29. Click **Save and Compile**. Notice that the report, a part of which is shown in Figure 13-16, now shows 5 jumps. Close the Help Work-shop.

30. Return to or reopen the Graphing project. There have been changes to the Help file, but no changes to the linkage between the Help file and application (unless you changed the name of the Help file). Run the program. Press **Tab** to select the **Zoom In** button and press **F1** to activate the Help system. Click the **Contents** button. See Figure 13-17. Use the table of contents to view the various Help topics. Click the **Back** button to return to the Contents window. Notice what happens when you click the Zoom In topic: the Help text displays as a pop-up. Click the pop-up to close it.

FIGURE 13-17
The Table of Contents

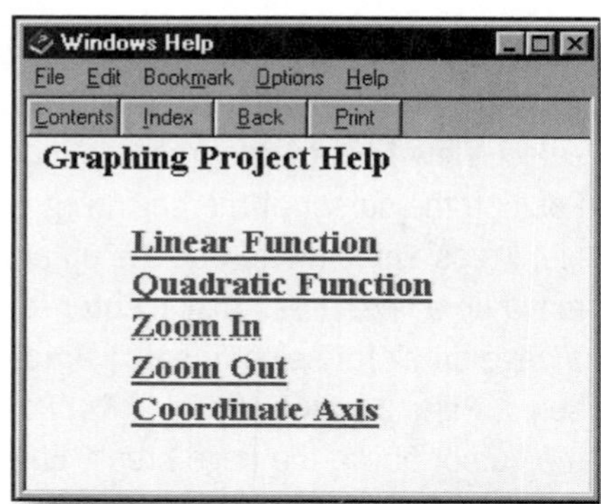

31. Close the Help window. Stop the program and exit Visual Basic.

It is a lot of work, but the results are worth it. A good Help system can really help the user understand and use your application. The quality of the system depends on the effort you expend to build it. Think like a user and try to remember the times you have been bewildered by a program. What kind of help have you needed (and not gotten)? Supply it for your user.

You need to budget time for writing Help systems. Part of your program development time must be set aside for work in this area.

In the next Step-by-Step exercise you look at the newest version of the Visual Basic Help, HTML Help.

Quick Check 13.c

1. When using WinHelp, connect a control with a Help topic using the control's ____________________ property.

2. To call context sensitive Help while an application is running, press ____________________.

3. The custom mark for an index keyword footnote is ____________________.

4. To insert a jump in a Help topic, the first thing to do is enter the ____________________ of the destination following the text that is the jump.

5. To create a pop-up window of Help text instead of a jump, set the jump text to ____________________ underline.

Using HTML Help

Microsoft's new standard of Help is its *HTML Help System*. It is part of a strategy to make information available to the user in a seamless natural way. Unlimited access to information has always been the dream we expect computers to fulfill. Years ago, main-frame computers had thousands of megabytes available on-line, filling rooms with disk drives the size of dishwashers that each held 256Mb of information.

When the first CD-ROMs came out, the text-only devices partly delivered on that promise of unlimited access to information: 550Mb of information per disk. It was enough to hold an entire encyclopedia and a complete index to every word in the encyclopedia. Today, that same CD holds an entire encyclopedia along with illustrations, video, audio, and multimedia presentations. Libraries use CD-ROM servers to make several disks available at the same time across a network.

Also hooked to most networks today is an *Internet Server*. With access to the Internet, the amount of information on-line goes up by several orders of magnitude, although it is not always easy to find what you are looking for. The *Internet Browser*, a piece of software used to view specially encoded Internet documents, is one of the most important pieces of software on your computer. The documents used in the *World Wide Web* (a collection of inter-linked documents stored on computers all over the world as a part of the Internet), are encoded in HTML, Hypertext Markup Language. It is a language used to build linked documents. These documents are stored on Internet servers, computers used to run the Internet software. Each of these documents can easily be linked to hundreds of other documents anywhere on the Internet or on local or network drives. Information is gathered, reorganized, stored, and displayed without regard to where the information is actually located. Using the Browser, a single Web document may display information from several different sources.

The Browser is very good at integrating information from different sources and presenting it to the user in ways that makes it easy to use. Microsoft decided to change many of its interfaces to make them as friendly and efficient as the Browser. Windows Explorer can be set to look like a browser. Even Microsoft Word can view Web pages from the Internet directly.

An HTML based Help system brings the full power of interlinked documents to Help files. Images and multimedia clips are easily included. Links to sites on the Internet itself give the Help system access to a much wider range of Help information.

The topic files used in the HTML Help System are normal HTML files. Use HTML to build files of any appearance and capability. To fully exploit the system, you must learn HTML code, although it is possible to use HTML documents created in any of the HTML editors, including Microsoft Word.

Loading HTML Help Workshop

Building an HTML Help System is not very difficult once you have the HTML Help Workshop. This product is similar to the Help Workshop you used in the last two exercises.

Although the documentation included with Microsoft Visual Studio mentions that the HTML Help Workshop is included with Visual C++, it is not found in a normal installation of Visual Studio nor is it available for the stand-alone Visual Basic 6.0 Professional version. To find if it is on your system, right-click the Start button and select Find**.** Change the Look In: combo box to the root directory of your main drive and search for the file name: hhw.exe. This is the executable file for the HTML Help Workshop.

If the file is not found you have to close the Find dialog box and get the install file from the Electronic Instructor CD-ROM or download the files from the Internet. The Web Workshop – Introducing HTML Help is at the address:
http://msdn.microsoft.com/workshop/author/htmlhelp/default.asp.

Read the Introduction and navigate to the next page using the link: Download HTML Help. Find the link to download the HTML Help Workshop on the second page and click it. The file size is somewhere around four megabytes, so if you are working with a slow modem, or Web traffic is high, be prepared for a 20 to 40 minute download time. You are downloading a self-extracting file with all the files necessary to run the HTML Help Workshop. Microsoft is committed to making the HTML Help Workshop available free for the foreseeable future.

Once saved on your local drive, double-click the self-extracting file html help.exe and follow the directions given in the setup program. The HTML Help Workshop loads by double-clicking the file named hhw.exe. When the installation is complete, you are ready to open the HTML Help Workshop.

STEP-BY-STEP 13.4a

1. Your first exercise is to convert the WinHelp Help System you designed in the last section to the HTML Help System. This is an automated process that works well for a simple WinHelp Help System. Run HTML Help, hhw.exe. The installation procedure probably installed HTML Help Workshop in your Start menu: click **Start**. Select **Programs | HTML Help Workshop | HTML Help Workshop** to run the program.

FIGURE 13-18
The New Dialog box showing the kinds of files that can be created by the HTML Help Workshop

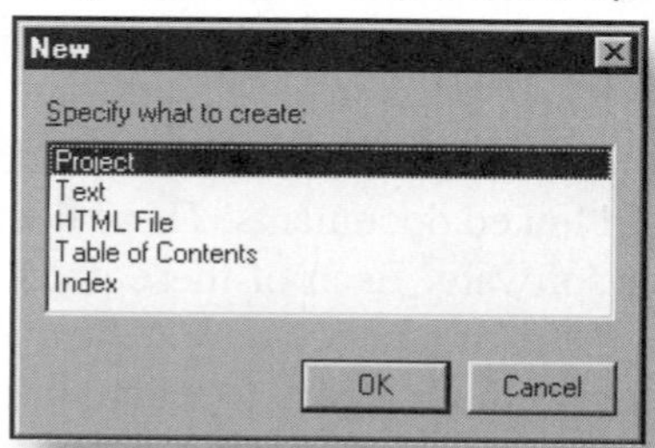

2. When the program starts, select **File | New**. Figure 13-18 shows the New dialog box. Note the contents of the box. The HTML Help Workshop can create project files, text files, HTML files, Table of Contents files and Index files. Many of these files remind you of various parts of the WinHelp Help System you used in the last exercise.

3. With **Project** selected, click **OK**. The New Project Wizard appears. The Wizard will help you convert your old WinHelp project. Click the **Convert WinHelp project** check box and click **Next** to proceed to the next dialog box.

FIGURE 13-19
The New Project – Source and Destination Project Files dialog box

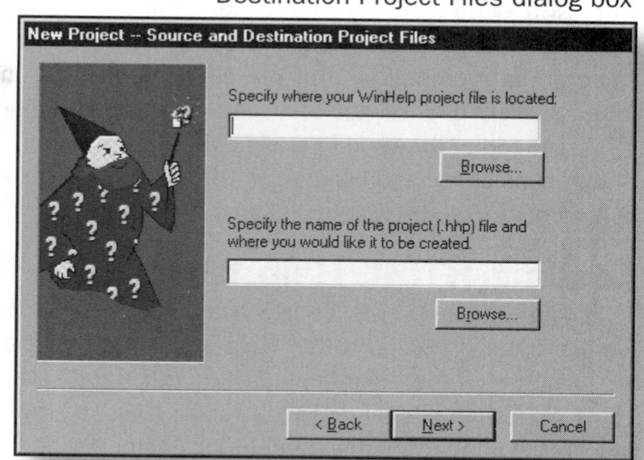

4. Figure 13-19 shows the New Project – Source and Destination Project Files. This window prompts you for the name and location of the old WinHelp project you want to convert. It also prompts you for the name and location of your new HTML Help project. Near the top text box, click **Browse** and navigate to the directory that contains the old WinHelp file. Once you locate the file (.hpj), select its name in the Open window and click **Open**. When you return to the New Project window, click the **Browse** button next to the lower text box and locate the directory that contains the

Graphing project. Enter a name for the new project: **HTMLGraphHelp**. Click **Open**, then click **Next** to go to the next dialog box.

5. The New Project – Finish window tells you it is going to build a new project from the WinHelp file. Click **Finish**. After some figuring, the HTML Workshop reports the results of the conversion. Figure 13-20 shows the report.

   The Compiled file parameter shows the name of the compiled HTML Help file: HTMLGraphHelp.chm. The Help file in the WinHelp Help System uses the extension .hlp. The HTML Help file uses the extension .chm. When you link the application to the HTML help file, be sure to use the file with the .chm extension.

   The Default topic parameter, if present, gives the name of the HTML file used for the default Help topic (your file name may not match the one shown in Figure 13-20). The default topic appears when F1 is pressed.

   The Index file parameter shows the name of the Index file created when HTML Help Workshop converts the old WinHelp Help System to HTML Help.

   The [FILES] section shows the HTML files generated for each Help topic. Unlike the WinHelp Help System that uses a single Help topic file with Help topics separated by page breaks, the HTML Help System uses a separate HTML document for each Help topic.

6. Click the **Index** tab. A list of the keywords originally defined in the WinHelp Help System appears. Double-click the keyword: **function**. A Topics Found dialog box appears. The keyword function is referenced for two Help topics. Each appears in the Topics Found dialog box. Select **Quadratic Function** and click **Display**. The new HTML code for the Quadratic Function Help topic appears in the right window. Scroll through the window. Within the HTML code, you recognize the original text. Close the topic in the right window.

Whenever you double-click a keyword entry or a file entry you enter an edit mode. This behavior is defined in the Preferences dialog box in the Contents and Index tabs. If you double-click an item on the left and the right window is blank, select File | Preferences from the menu bar. In both the Contents and Index tabs, under Action to take when double-clicking an entry, select Open the file for editing, then click OK. The file appears in the right window and and a second row of icons appears in the upper toolbar. You may edit the file in the right window, although it is probably unnecessary for this project. If you make any changes, click the Save icon on the second row of the toolbar along the top of the window.

(continued on next page)

FIGURE 13-20
The HTML Help Workshop showing the report on the conversion of the WinHelp file

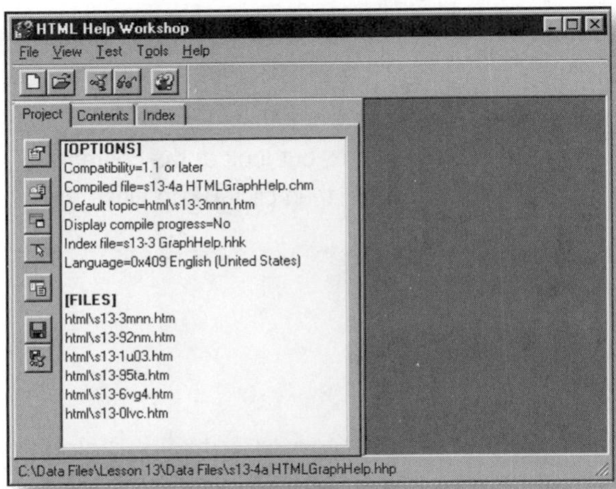

7. Click the **Project** tab. Double-click each HTML file listed in the [FILES] section. As you double-click each filename, its HTML code appears in the right window. Write down the filename you see in the title bar. Also, write down the associated Help topic (for example, Linear Function) that appears between <TITLE> and <TITLE> toward the bottom of the code. You need to match the filename to the Help topic later in this exercise. Double-click the first item in the [FILES] list. It displays the HTML code for the table of contents page for the WinHelp Help System. Scroll and look at the structure of the file. If you already know hypertext markup language, you recognize many simple language elements in the listing. Leave this HTML code window for the Contents page on the right open.

8. Double-click the entry **Compiled file** in the [OPTIONS] section of the report. The Options dialog box appears. If necessary, select the **Files** tab. The name of the compiled file is listed, but the compiled file has not been built. The Log file is currently empty as is the Contents file. Click the check box for **Automatically create contents file (.hhc) when compiling**. You cannot use the HTML Contents from the old WinHelp Help System as a real table of contents, because it is not in the correct format. In the next exercise you build a Table of Contents file from scratch.

9. At this time, change nothing else in the Options dialog box, but look at the contents of the other tabs, then click **OK** to close the dialog box.

Click Cancel if the Internet Autodial dialog box appears during the following step.

10. Select **View | in Browser** from the menu bar or click the **Display in Browser** button on the toolbar (the icon looks like a world with a magnifying glass). Along one side of the screen the Help screens appear. The display starts with the old Contents page. Click a link to another Help topic. Return to the Contents with the **Back** button of the browser. Notice that the link you clicked is now a different color. A color change indicates topics that have been accessed. Close the browser window with the **Close box** in the upper right corner of the window.

11. You are ready to save the project and compile the HTML Help file. Use the mouse pointer and the ToolTip generated by the mouse pointer to locate an icon whose ToolTip is Save all files and compile. This icon is the lowest of a column of icons along the left side of the Help display area. It is only visible when the Project tab is selected. The icon itself is a picture of a disk and a meat grinder. The disk represents the save function. The meat grinder implies that a lot of information is ground up together to create the HTML compiled help file. Click the **Save all files and Compile** icon.

12. A report appears in the right window in a Log. If an error occurs, the best thing to do is undo things and recompile until the problem clears up. For instance, if there is a problem with the table of contents, uncheck the checkbox that automatically creates the table. Once everything compiles, you can close the Help Workshop. You can also leave it open. Your application can access the Help file whether the Help Workshop is open or not. If you expect a lot of movement back and forth between the application and the Help Workshop, leave the Help Workshop open. Leave it open for now.

If you have an error in the compilation of the Help file and you fix the error and recompile, you may or may not get what you expect. Sometimes the Help Workshop gets confused and starts displaying increasingly disturbing error messages. Close the Help Workshop. Reopen the Help Workshop and load the old project. Try to compile it again.

13. The Table of Contents file (toc.hhc) that is created automatically when the Help project is compiled has a problem: all the items in the table link to the same html file (the Contents page). To fix this problem, you must edit each of the items in the Table of Contents (except Graphic Project Help which is already correct). Click the **Contents** tab and click **Yes** in the message box that appears. Select the second entry in the table: **Linear Function**. Click the **Edit Selection** button (the icon looks like a pencil) on the toolbar to the left of the Contents tab. This puts you in edit mode. See Figure 13-21. Unfortunately, the table has used the same filename (the one for the Graphic Project Help entry) in the Files/URLs box for each of the entries. You must select each of the entries and edit the filename so that the entry title is matched to the correct File/URL. Click **Remove** to delete the current entry under File/URLs. Click **Edit**, then click the topic name **Linear Function**. The File or URL name box is changed to the correct filename. Click **OK** in the Path or URL dialog box, then click **OK** in the Table of Contents Entry dialog box. For each remaining item in the Contents tab of the HTML Workshop window, click the entry (Quadratic Function, Zoom In, Zoom Out, and Coordinate Axis), click the **Edit Selection** button, click **Remove**, click **Edit**, click the topic name so that the File or URL name box is changed, then click **OK** in both the Path or URL dialog box and the Table of Contents Entry dialog box.

14. Click the **Save** button in the second row of the toolbar to save the log file with the suggested name. Click the **Project** tab. Click the **Change project options** icon (the top of the list of icons along the left edge of the tab). Click the **Files** tab and click the **Browse** button for the Contents file box. Select **toc.hhc** and click **Open**. Uncheck the **Automatically create** check box below the Contents file box.

15. Click **OK** to close the Options dialog box. Click the **Save all files and compile** icon. Close the HTML Help Workshop.

16. Start Visual Basic and click the **Recent** tab. In the list of Recent files, select the **Graphing** project and click **Open**. Right-click **Project1** in the Project Explorer. Select **Project1 Properties**. In the General tab, under Help File Name, click the browse button with the ellipsis. Change the Files of

(continued on next page)

FIGURE 13-21
The Table of Contents Entry dialog box

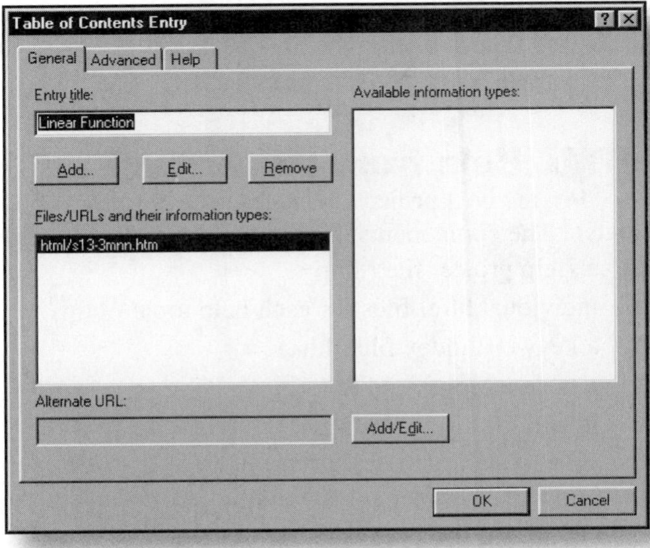

type entry to HtmlHelp Files (.chm). Navigate to the directory with your compiled Help file and select it in the dialog box. Click **Open**. Click **OK** to close the Project1 Properties window, then if necessary double-click **frmGraphing** in the Project Explorer.

17. The HTML Help file you have created is not set up to provide context sensitive help. There is no mapping between the HelpContextID numbers and the Help topics. To avoid an error message when calling Help from the application, select each control that has a non-zero HelpContextID number and change its value to 0. Change the HelpContextID number to **0** for the following controls and menu items: **Zoom In** menu item, **Zoom Out** menu item, **fraLinear**, **fraQuadratic**, the **Zoom In** button, the **Zoom Out** button, and the picture box, **picGraph**.

18. Save the project. Run the program. The Help system created by the HTML Help Workshop is a reference work about the application. Press **F1** to open the Help system. Check the Help topics as well as the keyword index. Figure 13-22 shows the HTML Help System after the cone entry is double-clicked in the index.

FIGURE 13-22
The HTML Help System displaying the Quadratic Function Help Topic

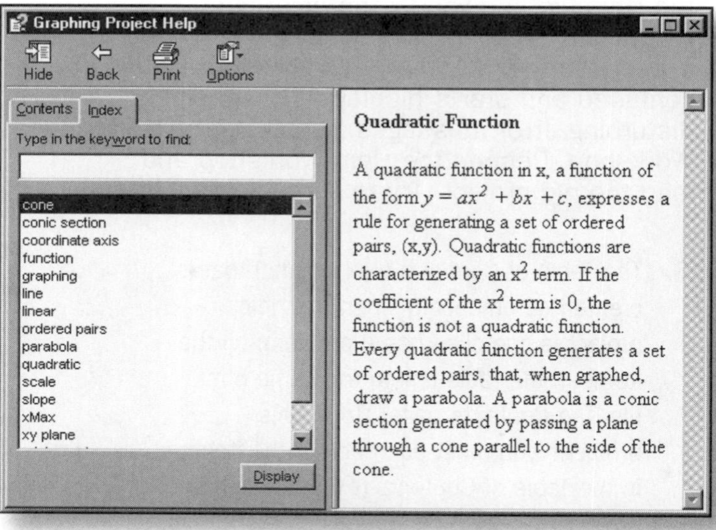

19. Click the **Hide** icon at the top of the Help window. The left side of the window with the keyword search disappears. Click **Show** to return to the original view. Click several links and use the **Back** button to return to the Contents page.

20. Close the Help window and remove the Graphing application.

HTML Help from the Ground Up

For the next project, instead of starting from an existing WinHelp Help System file, start from scratch. The components used to build the compiled file (.chm) of the HTML Help System are:

- a Help project file (.hhp)
- individual html files for each help topic (.htm)
- a keyword index file (.hhk)
- a table of contents file (.hhc)
- image files (.jpg, .gif, .png)

The system you design in this Step-by-Step exercise does not support context sensitive help. The project file brings together all the components of the Help system. It is the basis for building the compiled Help file.

Be very careful to use exact spelling, capitalization, and spacing in the following Step-by-Step exercise.

STEP-BY-STEP 13.4b

1. Run the HTML Help Workshop. Select **File | Close All** to close any Help project file that is automatically opened. Select **File | New** to open the New dialog box. Select **Project** to start the New Project Wizard and click **OK**. Click **Next** without clicking the check box to build a new HTML Help System from an existing WinHelp Help System. In the New Project – Destination dialog box, browse to an appropriate directory and supply a name for your Help project file: **GroundUp**, and click **Open**. Click **Next** to go to the New Project – Existing Files dialog box. You have no existing files to add to the project, so click **Next** to go to the New Project – Finish dialog box. Click **Finish**. The result should look like Figure 13-23.

FIGURE 13-23
The HTML WorkShop showing the beginning of the GroundUp Help project

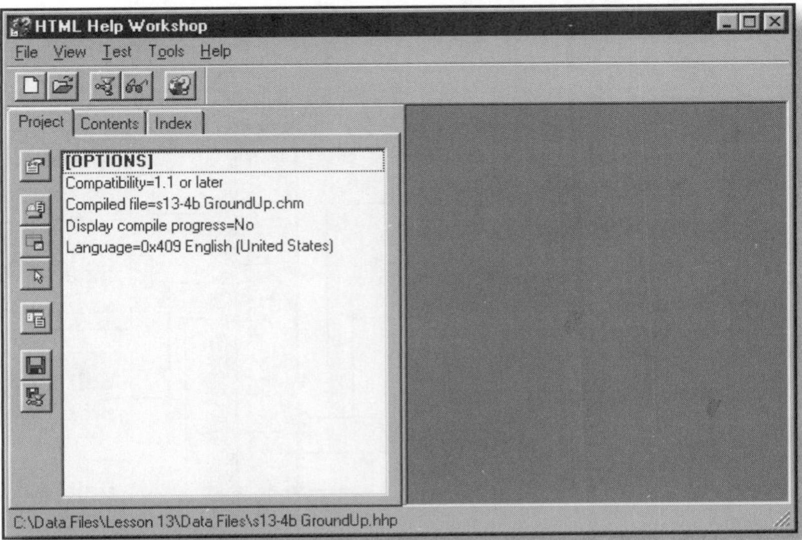

2. Click the **Contents** tab. The message box in Figure 13-24 appears. The Create a new contents file option button is already selected, so click **OK**.

FIGURE 13-24
The Table of Contents Not Specified message box

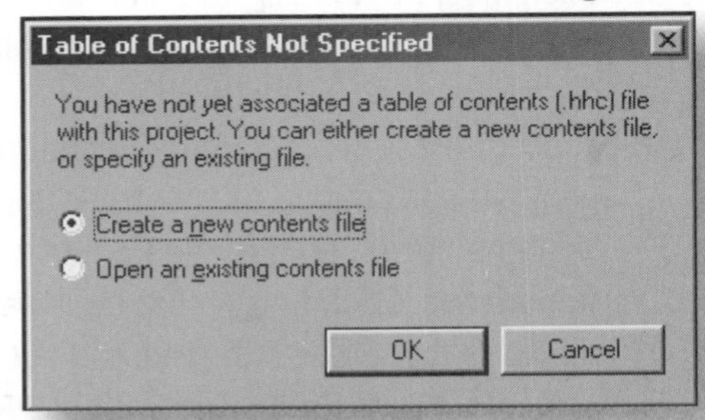

3. In the SaveAs dialog box that appears, navigate to the same directory as the Help

(continued on next page)

project file (if necessary — it may already be set to that directory) and replace the default name: Table of contents.hhc with the name **GroundUp**. Click **Save** to enter the edit window for the Table of Contents file. It is a blank window at this point.

The edit area takes over the left side of the Help Workshop. Use the icons along the left edge to create, edit, and move entries for the table. Figure 13-25 shows each of the buttons with a short explanation.

FIGURE 13-25
An explanation for the icons in the Create Table of Contents window of the HTML Help Workshop

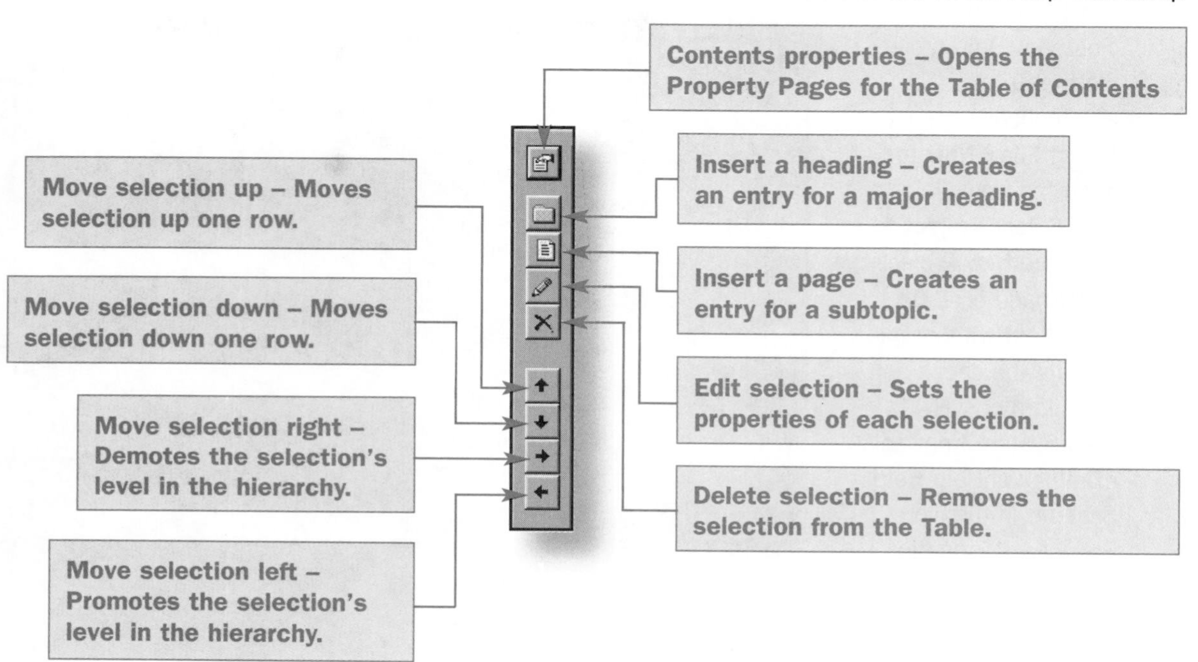
Contents properties – Opens the Property Pages for the Table of Contents
Insert a heading – Creates an entry for a major heading.
Insert a page – Creates an entry for a subtopic.
Edit selection – Sets the properties of each selection.
Delete selection – Removes the selection from the Table.
Move selection up – Moves selection up one row.
Move selection down – Moves selection down one row.
Move selection right – Demotes the selection's level in the hierarchy.
Move selection left – Promotes the selection's level in the hierarchy.

4. Click **Insert a heading** to enter the Table of Contents Entry dialog box. The Help system created in this exercise concentrates on program operation, not program explanation as the other Help systems have. For Entry title enter **Commands**. Each entry must be linked to a URL or file. Press **Tab**. The Add button is selected. Press **Enter**. The Path or URL dialog box appears. Click in the File or URL box near the bottom of the window and enter the full name of the htm file you will create for this entry: **MenuCommands.htm**. You need to include the file extension. Click **OK** to return to the Table of Contents Entry dialog box. The file you entered appears in the list box on the left. This action does not create the htm file. It links the entry you made in the Table of Contents to an htm file. If you compile the Help system now, the file name you entered would show as a dead link. Click **OK** to close the dialog box and return to the Table of Contents Editor (the main window of the HTML Help Workshop).

5. Click **Insert a page**. A message box queries if you want to add the entry at the beginning of the table of contents. If you say Yes, the entry is inserted above the heading. Click **No**. You are back in the Table of Contents Entry dialog box. Use the table below to create the rest of the Table of Contents. The process to build each item is a) click the **Insert a page** icon, b) enter the Entry title, c) click **Add**, d) enter the filename for the associated htm file at the bottom of the window, e) click **OK**, and f) click **OK** again.

The HTML Help System require names to be matched with exact capitalization, spelling and spacing. Key information carefully!

TABLE OF CONTENTS

ENTRY TITLE	FILENAME
Draw the Graph	DrawtheGraph.htm
Clear	Clear.htm
Zoom In	ZoomIn.htm
Zoom Out	ZoomOut.htm

6. There is a lot more that could be added, but you realize by this time that a really good Help system may take more development time than the project you connect it to. Click the **Project** tab and click the **Save project, contents, and index files** icon in the left edge of the Project tab. Click the **Change project options** icon at the top of the list of icons and click the **Files** tab. Note the name of the Contents file is already included in the project.

7. Click the **General** tab and enter a title for the project: **HTML Help from the Ground Up**. Click **OK** to close the dialog box. Note: in the project window an entry exists for the Contents file parameter.

8. Select **File | New** in the menu bar of the Help Workshop. If necessary select **HTML File** from the New dialog box and click **OK**. Enter the title: **Menu Commands** and click **OK**. In the right side of the Help Workshop window appears the skeleton for the HTML file you want to create. The cursor is positioned between <BODY> and </BODY> ready for you to enter the content of the help topic. See Figure 13-26.

9. At the cursor position enter: **After the user has chosen a function to graph and entered data for the coefficients of the function, the menu commands allow the user to Draw the Graph, Clear the coordinate axis, Zoom in, or Zoom out.**

(continued on next page)

FIGURE 13-26
The skeleton for the HTML file

```
<!DOCTYPE HTML PUBLIC
"-//IETF//DTD HTML//EN">
<HTML>
<HEAD>
<meta name="GENERATOR"
content="Microsoft&reg;
HTML Help Workshop 4.1">
<Title>Menu
Commands</Title>
</HEAD>
<BODY>


</BODY>
</HTML>
```

Later you will turn one of the phrases above into a link to another htm file.

10. After you enter the contents of the Help file, select **File | Save File As** in the menu bar. Enter the name: **MenuCommands** and click **Save**. This name must match the name supplied in the filename listed in the Table of Contents Entry.

11. Create htm files for the remaining menu items using the information contained in the table below. The process to follow is a) select **File | New**, b) select **HTML** from the New dialog box and click **OK**, c) enter a title for each entry as shown in the table and click **OK**, d) enter the body of the htm file as shown in the table, e) select **File | Save File As** and give the same filename given in the Table of Contents entry.

HTM FILES

TITLE	FILENAME	BODY
Draw the Graph	DrawtheGraph	Once the user has entered data for the function, this menu item draws the graph on the coordinate axis. The draw routine is also called by the Zoom menu items.
Clear	Clear	The Clear command clears all the text boxes used to enter data for the coefficients of the linear and quadratic functions and clears the picture box that represents the coordinate axis.
Zoom In	ZoomIn	The Zoom In command changes the scale of the coordinate axis. In effect, it allows you to zoom in on a graph. It does not allow you to change the center of the graph away from the origin, (0,0).
Zoom Out	ZoomOut	The Zoom Out command changes the scale of the coordinate axis. In effect, it allows you to zoom out on a graph. It does not allow you to change the center of the graph away from the origin, (0,0).

12. Now that all the topic files are saved you are almost ready to compile the Help file. First you must set the default file. If necessary, click the **Project** tab. Click the **Change project options** button and enter **MenuCommands.htm** for the name of the default file. Click **OK** to close the Options dialog box.

13. Click the **Project** tab (if necessary) and click the **Save all files and compile** icon. If you are prompted to save untitled html files that are already saved, click **Cancel** for each prompt.

14. Now that the Help file is compiled and saved, it is time to link it to the project. Leave the HTML Help Workshop open. Start Visual Basic and open the **Graphing** project. Right-click **Project1** in the Project Explorer. Select **Project1 Properties**. Select the **General** tab, if necessary.

Use the browse button (marked with an ellipsis) next to the Help File Name box to open the Help File window. Change the Files of type setting to **HTMLHelp Files (.chm)**. Navigate to the new help file, **GroundUp.chm** and select it from the list box. Click **Open**. The name of the file appears in the Help File Name box in the General tab of the Project Properties dialog box. Click **OK** to close the dialog box.

FIGURE 13-27
The HTML From the Ground Up Help System

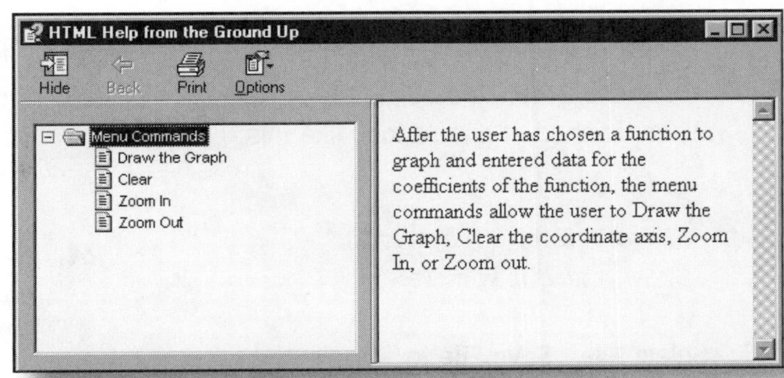

15. This kind of help is not context sensitive (although it could be made to be context sensitive) so be sure that the **HelpContextID** property of each menu item and control on the form is set to **0**. Save the project. Run the program. Press **F1**. The Help system starts and shows the entry for Menu Commands. See Figure 13-27. Click the plus symbol next to the Menu Commands to expand the list. Click each item to see if the correct Help topic text appears in the right window.

    To finish the project, in the following steps add the bold format to the Menu Commands heading and set up some links in the MenuCommands.htm file to the other Help files.

16. Close Help and stop the Visual Basic program. Do not close the Graphing project.

17. Return to the HTML Help Workshop. If you never closed it, just click its entry in the taskbar. If it is closed, load it and open the GroundUp Help project (the file with the .hhp extension).

18. Click the **Contents** tab and double-click the **Menu Commands** entry to open its HTML code on the right in the edit window. After the <HEAD> tag in the HTML code, press **Enter** and add the following entry, then press **Enter**.

```
<h1>Menu Commands</h1>
```

    The items in angle brackets are called *HTML tags* and tell the browser how to format text in the hypertext document. The h1 tag set the text between the tags to the Heading 1 font. The Heading 1 font is determined by the browser's default settings. The first tag, <h1> turns on the Heading 1 font and the second tag, </h1> turns the Heading 1 font off. Generally, a slash in the tag turns the setting off. Heading 1 is the largest, boldest font. For subtopics, use the <h2> tag.

19. Scroll down in the HTML code. Find the text within the body that says "Draw the Graph". You are going to turn this into a link to the Draw the Graph Help topic. Position the cursor just before the character D. Enter **<a** and press **Enter** then enter **HREF="DrawTheGraph.htm",** press **Enter** and enter **>**. The filename is part of the a tag. The a tag is used to set up a link. The link can be to a file, a URL on the Web or a particular named position

(continued on next page)

in a file or Web site. Following the text >Draw the Graph, insert the tag, **</a>**. When finished, it should look like this:

```
<a
HREF="DrawtheGraph.htm"
>Draw the Graph</a>,
```

20. Select **File | Save File** to save the new version of MenuCommands.htm.

21. Select the **Project** tab. Click **Save all files and compile** to rebuild the Help system. Cancel any prompts to save a file.

22. Use the taskbar to return to Project1 in Visual Basic (the Graphing project). Run the program. Press **F1**. Figure 13-28 shows the changes.

23. Click the link **Draw the Graph**. Notice that the index in the left window expands to show the Draw the Graph entry in the Table of Contents.

24. Close the Help window. Stop the Graphing program. Exit Visual Basic. Close the HTML Help Workshop.

FIGURE 13-28
The HTML Help from the Ground Up window showing the changes made to MenuCommand.htm

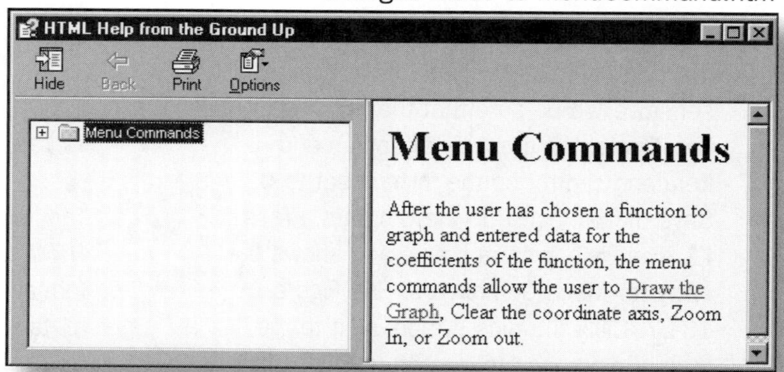

All the Help files in Windows 98 use the HTML Help System. Once you have a command of HTML, there is no limit to the connectivity you can put into your Help System. You can link directly to Web sites, images, or video. Help on the Web can be a way to keep users updated on the latest ways to use the application.

Someone with good writing and organization skills who can write good Help systems is invaluable to an organization.

Quick Check 13.d

1. If the HTML Help Workshop is not installed on your computer, you must download the product from ____________________.

2. It is possible to build a new HTML Help System from an existing ____________________ Help System.

3. Unlike the WinHelp Help System that uses a single topic file with Help topics separated by page breaks, the HTML Help System uses a separate ____________________ for each help topic.

4. When not using a context sensitive Help system, set the ____________________ to 0 for each control and menu item on the form of the application program.

5. The ____________________ brings together all the components of the Help system. It is the basis for building the compiled help file.

6. In HTML, the language used to build Web documents, items in angle brackets are called ____________________.

Summary

- The traditional Windows Help system, WinHelp, provides inter-linked Help topics with full-text search capabilities and tables of contents.
- The newer HTML Help System provides the same features as WinHelp but uses HTML to build each Help topic entry. HTML is the hypertext markup language used to build documents for the World Wide Web.
- To create context sensitive on-line help for your application:
  - create a topic file and save it in Rich Text Format.
  - compile the topic file in the Microsoft Help Workshop.
  - connect your application to the Help file.
- ToolTips are a valuable aid to the user and are very easy to use.
- The ScaleMode property allows choices among a number of predefined measuring standards: the twip, the pixel, the character, the millimeter, the centimeter, the inch, and the user defined mode.
- The Scale method is used to set a user defined measure for a form, picture box, or the printer. To use the Scale method, specify the coordinates of the top left corner of the object and the bottom right corner of the object.
- If no type is specifically declared in a variable declaration, the variables are of the Variant type.
- The PSet method has the following syntax:

  ```
  object.PSet [Step] (x, y), [color]
  ```

  It is used to draw a single point at coordinates (x,y) on the form or picture box.
- The CurrentX and CurrentY properties give the current graphic's position.
- The Line method has the following syntax:

  ```
  object.Line [Step] (x1, y1) [Step] - (x2, y2), [color], [B][F]
  ```

  The Line method is used to draw lines and boxes on a form or picturebox.
- Help files should be planned while the program is being written.
- The simplest kind of Help system to implement is What's This Help. In a way, it is a glorified ToolTipText system.
- To build a Help system start by creating a Help topic file in a word processor. Save the file in Rich Text Format.

- Use the Microsoft Help Workshop to compile the topic file and map information into a Help file that can be used by an appication.
- To initiate a footnote in Microsoft Word, position the cursor before the first letter of the Help topic and select **Insert | Footnote** from the menu bar. Use the pound sign (#) as a custom mark for the footnote. This identifies the footnote as a topic ID. Name each topic in the text of the footnote. Enter the topic ID name beginning with IDH_.
- To compile the Help file:
  - run the Help Workshop.
  - open a new project.
  - add the topic file to the project.
  - map each topic ID to a numeric ID.
  - click Save and Compile to build the Help file.
  - check the Help file before closing the Help Workshop.
- In the application, link the Help file to the project in the project's Property Pages. Change the BorderStyle property of the form to a Fixed style. Change the WhatsThisButton property and the WhatsThisHelp properties to True. Select the WhatsThisHelpID property of each control that gets Help and change the value of the property to match the Help topic's numeric ID.
- The WinHelp Help System is harder to set up than the What's This Help System, but the system is more powerful.
- The WinHelp Help System can use the same topic file as the What's This Help system.
- Keywords, used to build a Help index, are specified in a footnote that starts with the custom mark: k. Topic names are specified in a footnote that starts with the custom mark: $.
- Build a Table of Contents by linking topic titles to topic text with jumps. Set up a jump by following the topic title with a topic ID. Double-underline the topic title and format the topic ID as hidden text. To make a pop-up Help window, single-underline the topic title.
- The topic files used in the HTML Help System are normal HTML files. Use HTML to build files of any appearance and capability. To fully exploit the system, you must learn HTML code, although it is possible to use HTML documents created in any of the HTML editors, including Microsoft Word.
- The HTML Help System is a way to seamlessly provide Help in many forms to a user of an application program. The system may use images, multimedia, or Web sites to project Help.
- HTML is the hypertext markup language used to write Web documents.
- The HTML Help Workshop is available on the Web from the Microsoft Developer Network.
- The New Project Wizard in the HTML Help Workshop will help convert an old WinHelp Help System file to an HTML Help project.
- The HTML Help Workshop can build project files, text files, HTML files, a Table of Contents file, or an Index file.
- The format of the HTML Help Table of Contents file is different than the WinHelp Help System Table of Contents file.
- When using a non-context sensitive Help system, be sure the HelpContextID of each control and menu item is set to 0.

LESSON 13 REVIEW QUESTIONS

TRUE/FALSE

Circle the T if the statement is True. Circle the F is it is False.

T F 1. To create a Help topic file, use a word processor that can write an output file in Rich Text Format.

T F 2. HTML is the hypertext markup language used to build ActiveX documents.

T F 3. The easiest Help system is the WinHelp Help System: it is like a more extensive version of a ToolTip.

T F 4. The topic ID of a Help topic is stored in a footnote in the Help topic file.

T F 5. Each footnote used as a topic ID uses a special character: the dollar sign ($).

T F 6. Record jumps in the A footnotes for a topic title.

T F 7. Double-underline the topic title for a pop-up window.

T F 8. The WinHelp Help System uses the same Rich Text Format topic file as a What's This Help System.

T F 9. The HTML Help System uses the same Rich Text Format topic file to provide text for Help topics as the WinHelp Help System uses.

T F 10. The Table of Contents for an HTML Help project can be built within the HTML Help Workshop or included from an external file such as a Word topic file.

WRITTEN QUESTIONS

Write your answers to the following questions.

11. What are the similarities and differences between the What's This Help system and using ToolTips?

12. Describe the process of setting up a WinHelp Help System. Write a summary of the process, do not write a keystroke by keystroke description of the process.

13. What features of a topic file require the file to be saved in Rich Text Format instead of using a simple text editor like Notepad?

14. Each Visual Basic control has two properties that enable context sensitive Help for two different Help systems. What are the properties and their corresponding Help systems?

15. When building a file in Rich Text Format for the Help topic file used in the WinHelp System, a series of footnotes with custom marks are used. Make a table with two columns. In the first column put the custom mark. In the second column explain what the mark means.

16. A page break appears between each Help topic in a WinHelp topic file. What happens to each topic when the file is converted to use in an HTML Help System?

17. What are some of the advantages of using a Help system based on document created with HTML?

18. If not using context sensitive help, what precautions must you take in setting up the application program?

19. When should you start building a Help system for a project?

20. How do you set up a jump in a WinHelp Table of Contents?

LESSON 13 APPLICATION PROBLEMS

SCANS

Level One

THE GRAPHING PROJECT - ADDING A CIRCLE

Use the Graphing project of Step-by-Step 13.1 as a start for this program. Add a third tab to the TabStrip to enter data for drawing a circle on the graph. Add a new frame and three text boxes with appropriate labels. The Circle method has the following syntax:

```
object.Circle [Step] (x, y), radius, [color, start, end, aspect]
```

The coordinate (x,y) is the coordinate of the center of the circle. Radius is the value of the radius of the circle. The rest of the information is optional. Include the color parameter. Use QBColor( ) to provide a color for the circle. The user should enter coordinates x and y, and the radius r. The application should draw the graph in the picture box.

MORE WORK ON THE CIRCLE METHOD

Add another text box with an appropriate label to the frame dedicated to collecting input about the circle. Use this text box to get the aspect ratio from the user. See the Circle method syntax above to determine how to use the aspect ratio. Once you add this feature to the program, run the program and thoroughly explore what the aspect ratio does to the graph of the circle.

MORE HELP FOR THE GRAPHING PROJECT

Using the What's This Help System and the Help topic file created for the project in Step-by-Step 13.2, add a Help topic for the Circle tab. Like the Help topic for the linear and quadratic functions, describe the meaning of the values used to draw a circle.

Level Two

A NEW WINHELP SYSTEM FOR THE GRAPHING PROJECT

Write a new WinHelp Help System for the Graphing project. The old Help concentrated on the mathematics involved in the graphing project. Your new Help system should concentrate entirely on what the user enters to make the program work. Have a Help topic for each menu item as well as a Help topic explaining to the user how to enter values for each of the functions implemented in the program. Write a new topic file. Insert footnotes for topic ID, topic name, and keywords. Map the topic ID's to numeric values. Make the numeric values very different from the ones used in the text. Compile the topic file with a unique name. Link the new Help file with the project and set the HelpContextID property for each Help topic.

HTML HELP FOR THE GRAPHING PROJECT

Use the HTML Help workshop to convert the topic file used for the WinHelp System designed in Application 4 to an HTML Help file. Link the HTML Help to the project and thoroughly test it.

LESSON 13 PROGRAMMING AT WORK

SCANS

Adding Help

In this section, return to the Music Collection project of a few lessons ago. Add a context sensitive WinHelp Help system to the project to explain each of the menu items in the opening form. A What's This Help style Help system is not appropriate for this project because some of the forms have to be resizable.

The WinHelp Help system lets you build a fully cross-referenced system that is still context sensitive. A context sensitive Help system gives specific information about a menu item or control when the control has the focus and the user presses F1.

FIGURE 13-29
The Menu Editor showing the menu structure of frmMusic

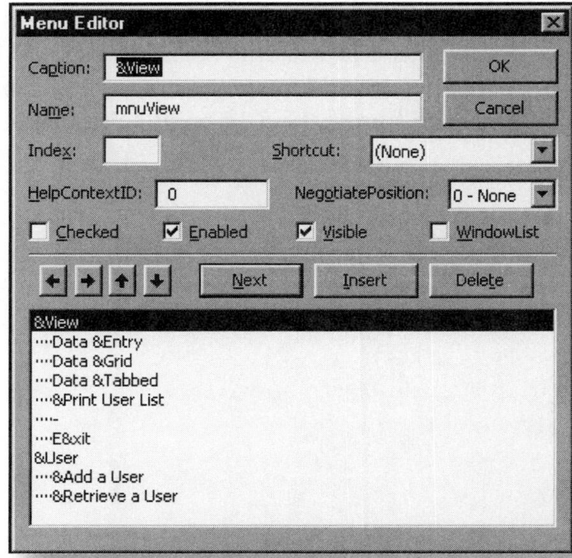

1. Run Visual Basic. Open the Music Collection Project you began in Lesson 4 and last saved in Lesson 10. The startup form is called frmMusic. Select this form in the Project Explorer and open the Menu Editor.

2. Figure 13-29 shows the Menu Editor of frmMusic. Your menu may not match exactly. Change the HelpContextID for each of the menu items listed in the table below. If your menu lacks an item in the table, just omit it.

HelpContextID	
CAPTION	**HELPCONTEXTID**
View	100
Data Entry	200
Data Grid	300
Data Tabbed	400
Print User List	500
User	600
Add a User	700
Retrieve a User	800

3. When the alterations are finished, make a note of the numbers assigned to the HelpContextID for each item. You need those numbers when you map the topicID of each Help topic to a menu item. Click **OK** to close the Menu Editor.

4. Open Microsoft Help Workshop to build the WinHelp style Help system. Select **File | New** to open the New dialog box. Select **Help Project** and click **OK**. Navigate to the same folder as the Music Collection project. Name the Help project file: **Mus13WinHelp** and click **Save**. The dialog box automatically supplies the file extension .hpj.

5. Leave the Help Workshop open. Open Microsoft Word. Insert the following text. Put a page break between each item in the file. The Help topics are brief. They are meant to be emblematic of what the actual text should be. Of course, page breaks are not shown in the table below. Add footnotes in the next step. Place the headings on the line above the topic text and format them 14 point bold. Indent the first line of topic text under each heading.

HELP TOPICS

HEADING	TOPIC TEXT
View	The View menu item organizes all the different views of the database included in the project.
Data Entry	The Data Entry view shows each of the fields of the database arranged on a form. From this form records may be viewed, added, or edited.
Data Grid	The Data Grid shows all the records at once in a grid format. Records may be viewed, added, or edited.
Data Tabbed	The Data Tabbed form shows the fields of each record divided into two tab areas. The first tab shows the basic information for each record and the second tab shows the details of the record. Records may be viewed and edited in this form.
Print User List	This item prints a hard copy of the list of recorded users along with their musical preference. It creates a form just to display the names and send the form to the printer to produce hard copy of the list.
User	The items in the User menu are used to add a new user and his or her musical preference to the list of users maintained by the database.
Add a User	The item calls the code to add a user to the list of user maintained by the program. The input area is an invisible frame on the startup form.
Retrieve a User	This item calls code to display the current user list. A user is selected from the list. The user's preference may be used in the Data Entry form to select a subset of all the records of the database.

6. Save the Help topic file. Save the file as a Rich Text Format file, .rtf, with the name **Mus13HelpTopic.rtf**.

7. Add footnotes to each of the Help topics. Use the # footnote for the TopicID. The first three letters of any TopicID are **IDH_**. Use the $ footnote for the Topic Name. Use the k footnote for a list of keywords separated by semicolons for each item. The table on the following page shows a set of possible values:

FOOTNOTES

Topic ID #	Topic Name $	Keywords (for the Index) k
IDH_View	View	views; project; database
IDH_Data	Data Entry	fields; records; viewed; added; edited
IDH_Grid	Data Grid	grid; fields; records
IDH_Tabbed	Data Tabbed	tabbed; tab; detail
IDH_Print	Print User List	print; user; preference
IDH_User	User	print; user; preference; prune; add; retrieve
IDH_Add	Add a User	add; user; preference
IDH_Retrieve	Retrieve a User	retrieve; user; preference

With practice, you can get into quite a rhythm entering each footnote. There are eight Help topics. Each gets three footnotes. Use the keyboard shortcuts instead of the mouse: Position the cursor in front of the first entry. Press Alt + n, to insert a footnote. Enter # for the Custom mark and press Enter. Enter the topic ID. Press Shift + F6 to return to the upper part of the document. The cursor is already positioned for the second footnote. Press Alt + i + n and enter $ for the Custom mark. Enter the topic name for the topic. Continue until all the footnotes are entered, then move on to the next topic.

8. Save the file. Be sure each Help topic is separated with a page break and that the file is in Rich Text Format.

9. Return to the Help Workshop. Click the **Files** button. Navigate to the topic file you created in Word and add it to the project.

10. Click **Map** and enter the numeric values for each topicID. Use the same values you entered into the HelpContextID for each item in step 2.

11. Click **Save and Compile**. Enter the name **Mus13 WinHelp.hlp** for the name of the Help file if you have not already named the file.

12. Once the file is compiled, return to the Music Collection Project. Right-click **Project1** in the Project Explorer and select **Project1 Properties**. In the **General** tab find the Help File Name text box and use the browse button (marked with an ellipsis) to navigate to the new Help file.

13. Save the project. Run the program. Select **View** from the menu bar. Position the pointer on **Data Tabbed**, but do not click the entry. Press **F1**. The Data Tabbed Help topic appears. Check the Index by clicking **Index** and use the index entries to access several different Help topics.

14. Close the Help window. Stop the program and exit Visual Basic.

You could spend a lot of time building a complete Help system for the project. This section just gets you started.

LESSON 14

DISTRIBUTION

OBJECTIVES

When you complete this lesson, you will be able to:

- Prepare a project for distribution.
- Compile a project.
- Use the Package and Deployment Wizard to package a standard EXE file for distribution.
- Install the packaged file in a system.
- Use the Add/Uninstall Utility to remove a project installation.
- Package an ActiveX control for distribution.
- Package a Help System for distribution.

Estimated Time: 5 hours

KEY TERMS

Machine Language
source code
Assembly Language
mnemonic
high-level programming language
memory-image file
Integrated Development Environment (IDE)
Package and Deployment Wizard (PD Wizard)
dependency
CAB file
Package folder
Shared file
Program Group
Internet Package
Intranet
digital signiture
GUID
container application
DAO drivers
scripting
cache

Preparing a Project for Packaging

How does a program run on a computer? The user does not care and should not have to know. To successfully package a project for distribution, you need to understand the fundamentals.

History

In the beginning there was machine code. *Machine Language* statements are the native language of the computer's processor. The statements are binary codes often expressed in base-16, hexadecimal. Each statement performs a small task like moving a piece of data, adding two values, or comparing two values.

Computers today are still programmed with binary codes. The path from the *source code* (a file of code statements) of a modern programming language to binary code understood by a processor is more complex than ever.

For a while, it was just a simple matter of translation. *Assembly Language* uses a *mnemonic*, a short descriptive syllable, to represent each machine language statement. There is a one to one correspondence between Assembly Language statements and Machine Language statements. Even so, there are features in Assembly Language that require more than one Machine Language statement to interpret it. Libraries of Machine Language statements are used to finish the translation from Assembly Language to object code, the pure Machine Language program run by the processor.

If it were easy to do, we would all still be programming in Assembly Language. One measure of programmer productively is measured in lines of code per day. Research shows that most programmers produce about the same number of lines of code whether they are writing in Assembly Language or a high-level language. A *high-level programming language* is less like the language of the processor and more like the language of the programmer. Consequently, each line of a high-level language usually accomplishes more than a line of Assembly Language. Using high-level programming languages, programmers are more productive.

Writing a program used to go like this:

- Create the source code of the program in a high-level language like Fortran or Cobol.
- Compile the source code into object code.
- Link the object code with one or more libraries of code snippets to resolve undefined terms in the object code.

The result is a *memory-image file* – the old name of a program in Machine Language ready to load into memory and run. If there is a mistake made, you go back to the beginning and re-edit the source code.

Today

As annoying as the procedure was (the cycle of edit-compile-link-test was endless), today's procedures are far more complex. The good news is that the procedures are largely automated.

BASIC was designed 35 years ago to simplify the process. Original BASIC is an interpreted language. You edit, run, test, and debug programs within a controlled programming environment. All the programming you have done thus far in Visual Basic is in this protected environment. Visual Basic has turned this environment into a programmer's heaven: debugging tools, Help systems, and tools for every purpose are part of the *IDE*, the *Integrated Development Environment*.

Why would anyone want to leave the IDE? As programmers we sometimes forget that someone eventually wants to run the programs we write. You do not ask a user to run Visual Basic, open a file and execute it by pressing F5. Instead you compile the program to an executable file and package it so it can run on another system.

In the old days, packaging meant resolving undefined terms in the system and language libraries. Today packaging means providing the run-time libraries and support files to enable a program to run. In addition, it means registering program components in the system registry.

Have you tried to remove an application by deleting its files from its directory? That process is doomed to failure because almost every application installs run-time libraries in the System directory. Which ones belong to the application? There is no easy way to tell. If the program was properly installed, its support files are listed in the Windows Registry. This allows the Uninstall program to get rid of an unwanted application.

Preparing the Project

A simple project needs no preparation. A more complex project may need some adjustment to run properly when taken from the controlled environment of Visual Basic and put onto another computer. One consistent problem is file access.

The early versions of the Music Collection project (See the Programming At Work exercises of most lessons) sometimes had trouble finding the MusCol.mdb database file. Connecting the ADODC Data Control to the database usually results in coding a specific file structure into the program. The next exercise investigates this problem and finishes by compiling the program.

STEP-BY-STEP 14.1a

1. Start Visual Basic. If you have access to the *Electronic Instructor* CD-ROM, copy the entire directory: **Lesson 6\Programming At Work** to a local drive and open the project **MusCol6.vbp** or use the most recent version of MusCol.vbp that you worked with in Lesson 13.

2. Click the **View Object** button in the Project Explorer (if necessary) to select the form, **frmDataEntry**. In this early version, there is no other form in the project.

3. Right-click the **ADODC Data Control** and select **ADODC Properties**. Click the **General** tab (if necessary). In the Source of Connection frame, click the Use Connection String option button if it is not already selected. There is already a complex entry in the text box. See Figure 14-1. Click the **Build** button to examine the structure of the connection string.

4. Click the **Connection** tab (if necessary). Examine the entry in the Database Name text box. Just the name of the database, MusCol.mdb, appears. Originally in Lesson 6, clicking the browse button next to the Use Con-nection String text box made the link between the database file and the Data Control. Click the browse button next to the filename now. The button is marked with an ellipsis. Navigate to the current location of **MusCol.mdb** and click the filename. Click **Open** to select the file and close the Select Access Database dialog box. A portion of the Data Link Properties window is shown in Figure 14-2.

   The database name now contains the complete path information to locate the database file. The figure shows the directory structure of the computer on which the application was developed. If you want to run the program on your computer, the directory structure of your disk must match that shown in the figure. If the path names do not match, the Data Control will not find the database file.

FIGURE 14-1
The Property Pages dialog box of the ADODC Data Control

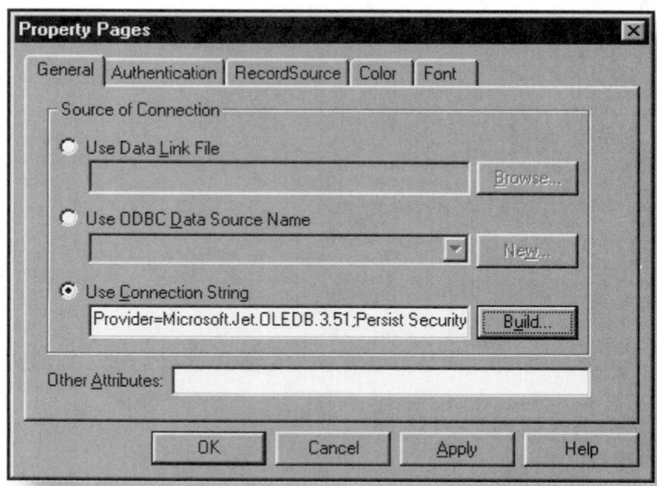

FIGURE 14-2
The Data Link Properties window showing the database name entry

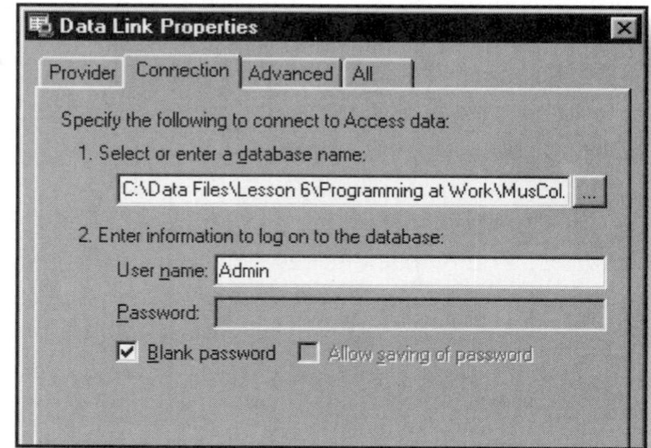

5. Click the **Test Connection** button near the bottom of the Data Link Properties dialog box. If the Data Control finds the database file, a message box appears with the message: Test connection succeeded. Click **OK** to close the message box, then click **OK** to close the dialog box.

   The simplest way to fix the file access problem is to put the database file in the project's home directory and make the home directory the default directory. When a file is opened or the Data Control seeks to establish a connection with a database and no pathname is specified, the default drive and directory is the first directory searched. To set the project's directory as the default directory, use the ChDir and ChDrive commands. Complete examples of the commands are ChDir App.Path and ChDrive App.Path. This uses the App object to determine the project's path.

6. Try an experiment. Save and run the program. The Music Collection project has the statements ChDir App.Path and possibly ChDrive App.Path in the Form_Load procedure. As soon you run the program, the default directory is set to be the project directory, the directory from which the project is loaded and run. If you did not run the program, the default directory remains the original directory from which Visual Basic is run. Stop the program and reopen the project without running the program again.

7. Select the form, right-click the **ADODC Data Control**, select **ADODC Properties**, select the **General** tab, click **Build**, and select the **Connection** tab. Edit the database name so that just the filename: **MusCol.mdb** appears in the text box. Click the **Test Connection** button. The error message in Figure 14-3 may appear.

8. Click **OK** in the Data Link Properties window to close it. Click **OK** to close the Property Pages dialog box.

9. Click **View Code** in the Project Explorer. Scroll to the Form_Load procedure. If ChDir App.Path are and ChDrive App.Path not the first two lines of code in the procedure, add them now.

10. Save and run the program. You may get an error message. The Data Control cannot find the file until the form is reloaded. Stop the program and run it again. This time, since the form has been reloaded, the default directory is changed to the project directory and the database file is found by the Data Control. All is well.

11. Stop the program but leave the project open for the next exercise.

FIGURE 14-3
The Microsoft Data Link Error message. Notice that the search directory is the directory from which Visual Basic is run

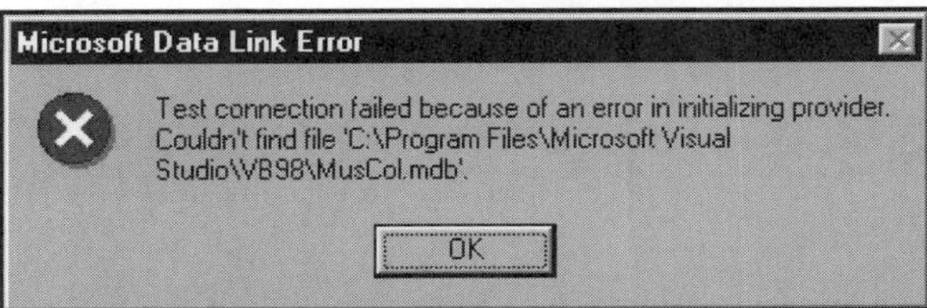

Other preparations for packaging your program involve putting yourself in the user's place. There is no debugging environment to depend on when a program is run as an executable file directly from the operating system. If there are any problems with the user interface, they must be addressed now. Can a user be reasonably expected to run your program without any assistance? If not, modify the user interface to provide the help they need. ToolTips and What's This Help come to mind as user aids.

STEP-BY-STEP 14.1b

1. The next step in preparing a file for packaging is to compile it to an executable file. If necessary start Visual Basic and open the version of the Music Collection project saved in the last exercise. The project should be in a local directory that accepts newly created files.

2. Before compiling the file, right-click the entry **Project1** in the Project Explorer. Select **Project1 Properties**. A number of items in the project properties are a concern when compiling and packaging a project. While developing a project, the project's name does not seem that important. When exporting a project to another computer, the project name, description, and version number are all important. In the General tab, enter **MusicCollection** for the Project Name. For the Project Description, enter **A program to maintain and display the items in a music collection**.

FIGURE 14-4
The Make tab in the Project Properties dialog box

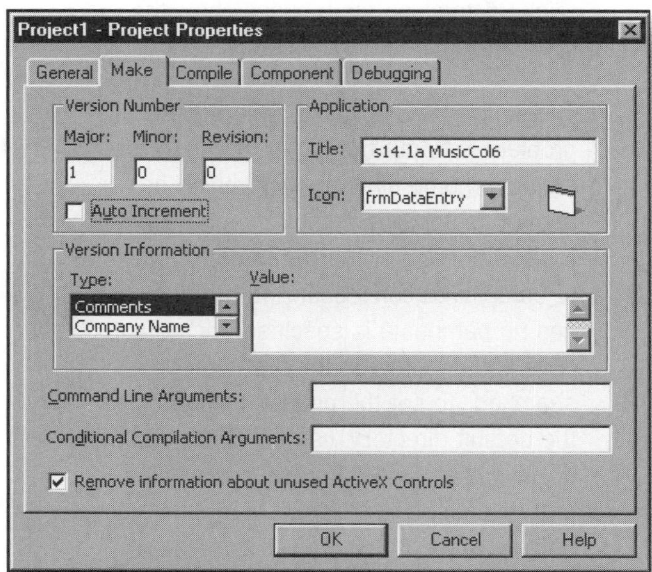

3. Click the **Make** tab. See Figure 14-4. In the Version number frame are three text boxes and a check box. The version number may be entered directly into the boxes or the Auto Increment check box may be clicked. Each new compile of the program ought to receive a new version number. For now, leave the default values.

4. Click the **Compile** tab. The default choices are best. See Figure 14-5.

   Compiling to Native Code means to convert the Visual Basic source code to machine language compatible with a PC. P-Code is an older slower system where Visual Basic code is compiled to an intermediate language, which is run by the Visual Basic Virtual Machine. The Virtual Machine program turns a PC into a P-code machine. This puts an extra layer of software between the application and the computer's hardware.

   Optimization is usually a trade-off: size for speed. If the executable code is optimized for speed, the executable file may be very large. If the executable code is optimized for size, the result is usually a program that runs slower. There is seldom a reason to minimize the size of a program. An exception occurs when you are compiling a program to run on a machine with limited memory. This is common in the world of embedded systems: a world of computers built into an appliance or machine tool dedicated to running a single program.

5. Click the **Component** tab. All the choices are dimmed. These options relate to applications compiled for use on the Internet or as an ActiveX component.

6. Click **OK** to close the Project Properties dialog box. Now it is time to compile the program.

7. Select **File | Make MusicCol6.exe** (or File | Make MusicCol.exe). If you are using a copy of the Music Collection program from the *Electronic Instructor* CD-ROM, there is probably a code number preceding the name of the file.

8. The Make Project dialog box appears prompting you to enter a filename for the executable file. Unless you want to save the executable file to another directory, click **OK** to accept Visual Basic's suggestions.

9. If necessary, click **OK** again to start compiling. Did you notice the Options button at the bottom of the Make Project dialog box? When the compilation is complete (no error messages appear), select **File | Make MusicCol6.exe** again. This time, click **Options**. The Music Collection – Project Properties dialog box appears. Just the Make and Compile tabs are present. If you had not set the version or the optimization before, this is your last chance. Click **Cancel** to close the Project Properties dialog box. Click **Cancel** to close the Make Project dialog box.

FIGURE 14-5
The Compile tab in the Project Properties dialog box

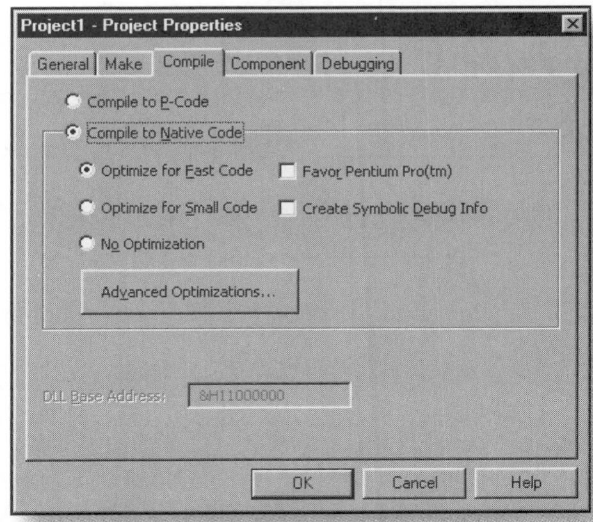

10. Save the program and exit Visual Basic.

11. Right-click the Start button in the task bar and select **Explore**. Navigate to the directory in which you saved the exe file. Find the file and double-click the file to run the program. Did you remember to move the MusCol.mdb database file to the directory? If not, you got an error message when you ran the program. Close the program. If necessary locate a copy of the **MusCol.mdb** file and copy it to the directory with the executable file. Run the program again. Use the program to view the records of the database. Click the Close box in the upper right corner of the form to exit the program. Close Windows Explorer.

Is that all there is to it? Can you copy the exe file (and the database file) to a diskette and transfer the program to another computer? Alas, no. The executable file still depends on various run-time libraries to execute. Without the libraries, you get one of those dreaded error messages that tell you that you are missing this or that DLL file.

In the next Step-by-Step exercise, you use the Package and Deployment Wizard to take care of all those nagging dependencies for you.

Quick Check 14.a

1. __________________ statements are the native language of the computer's processor.

2. A high-level programming language is less like the language of the processor and more like the __________________.

3. If a program is properly installed, its support files are listed in the __________________.

4. When the Data Control seeks to establish a connection with a database and no pathname is specified, the __________________ is the first directory searched.

5. __________________ is an older slower system where Visual Basic code is compiled to an intermediate language, which is run by the Visual Basic Virtual Machine.

6. Code optimization is usually a trade-off: __________________ for __________________ .

Using the Package and Deployment Wizard

You may already know how tough it is to move a program from one machine to another. As you work on solutions to various programs, you probably sometimes think it would be nice to run the program on another machine. Maybe you compiled the program, transferred the exe file to a disk and tried to run it at the second computer. The application works fine at the computer where it was developed, but fails at the second computer. If Visual Basic is installed on the second machine and the program is simple, it may run successfully. As soon as the complexity of the project reaches a certain point, transferring the program to a second computer fails.

You may not even be running the same version of Visual Basic. If you have version 5 at one computer and version 6 at another, files transfer one way but not the other. All this is fine because you are a programmer. In a worst case scenario, you can print the code on one machine and recreate the program on a remote machine no matter what version of Visual Basic is installed.

Programmers enjoy challenges up to a point. The point comes when it is time to deliver a program to a customer. When it is time to deliver a product, the customer expects a professional job. You cannot bring a program over on a disk, transfer the file, and then run back and forth for a day transferring DLL files from your development system to the customer's system.

The *Package and Deployment Wizard (PD wizard)* takes care of all the details of building an installation package for an application. It remembers what you forget to do. It ties up the package in a bow and coaches the user through the installation process. It even sets up an environment where you can easily make changes to the original program, recompile, and repackage the results.

In the Step-by-Step exercise that follows you revisit a program you worked on in lesson 9. It is a "simple" program: it has no special data files or DLL's. It converts measurements from one unit to another.

STEP-BY-STEP 14.2a

1. Start Visual Basic. Locate and open the **Convert** project developed in Lesson 9. If you have access to the *Electronic Instructor* CD-ROM, copy the project from **Lesson 9\Solutions\9-4Convert.vbp** to another directory on a local drive.

2. Run the program and test its operation. Stop the program.

   If there was ever a program that needed Help, this is it. As part of your preparations to package the program, write a short What's This Help system for the project.

3. The most mysterious buttons are those that appear in the toolbar. A ToolTip, however, handles each button. Each new conversion adds a button to the toolbar and builds a ToolTip for the button at the same time. You need Help text for each of the command buttons on the form and another connected to the text boxes. The Help topic for the text boxes describes how to enter a value, how to calculate a conversion, and how to eliminate the conversion from the form. Click the Windows **Start** button, click **Programs**, navigate to Microsoft Word and open it. Enter the following Help topics shown in the table below. Press **Enter** at the end of each topic and press **Ctrl + Enter** to separate each topic with a page break. Use an 11-point font size. Bold the headings and indent the first line of each paragraph of the topic text. When finished, save the file in rtf, Rich Text Format, with the name **ConvertHelp.rtf**. Save the file in the same directory as the Convert project.

4. In front of each heading add a topicID footnote to each of the three entries: **IDH_Conversion** for the first, **IDH_CalcButton** for the second, and **IDH_EnterValue** for the third. Use the pound sign as the identifying custom mark for the footnote. Save the file and exit Microsoft Word.

(continued on next page)

HELP TEXT

Topic	Text
Add a Conversion	Click this button to add a conversion to the form. You are prompted for three items; the units of the values (like in. or cm.) and the conversion factor (a numeric value). Once the values are entered, the form is enlarged, new text boxes are added, and a new button is added to the toolbar. To use the conversion, enter a value in either the left or right text box and press Enter.
The Calc Button	This button starts the Calculator accessory included with Microsoft Windows. Use the Calculator to build more complex conversion factors. A complicated conversion, like centimeters to miles, can also be added in steps: first centimeters to inches, then inches to feet, and finally feet to miles.
Enter a Value or Eliminate the Conversion	Use the text boxes to enter values to convert. Enter a value in either text box and convert to the other unit by pressing Enter. Eliminate a conversion from the form by double-clicking the left text box. Answer Yes to the prompt to remove the conversion.

5. Open Microsoft Help Workshop. If you have Visual Studio installed, click **Start** then select **Programs | Microsoft Visual Studio | Microsoft Visual Studio Tools | Help Workshop**. Otherwise, navigate to the location for the program and click it to load the Help Workshop.

6. Click the tip to close it. Select **File | New**. Select **Help Project** in the New dialog box and click **OK**. Click the **Files** button. In the Topic Files dialog box, click **Add**. In the Open dialog box, navigate to the Word document you saved, select the file, and click **Open**. Save the Help file as **Convert Whats This** and click **Save**. Click **OK** to close the Topic Files dialog box.

7. Click **Map** to open the Map window and click **Add** to add a mapping to the project. Did you make a note of the topicID's assigned in the footnotes? Enter the topicID, **IDH_Conversion** and a Mapped numeric value of **100** and click **OK**. Add **IDH_CalcButton** and a Mapped numeric value **200**. Add **IDH_EnterValue** and a Mapped numeric value of **300**.

8. Click **OK** to close the Map dialog box. Click **Save and Compile** to build the Help system.

9. You may want to leave the Help Workshop open in case you have to rebuild the system to correct an error. Return to Visual Basic. If necessary click **View Object** to view the Convert form. Select the form. In the Properties window, double-click the property **WhatsThisButton** to toggle its value from False to **True**. The **WhatsThisHelp** property also changes automatically. Change the **BorderStyle** property to **3-Fixed Dialog**.

10. Select **cmdAddConversion**. Change the value of **WhatsThisHelpID** to **100**. Select **cmdCalc**. change the value of **WhatsThisHelpID** to **200**. Select **txtLeft(0)**. Change the value of **WhatsThisHelpID** to **300**. Select **txtRight(0)**. Change the value of **WhatsThisHelpID** to **300**.

    What about the new text boxes created when conversions are added to the form? No problem. The new text boxes inherit the properties of the original.

11. Right-click **Project1** in the Project Explorer. Select **Project1 Properties**. Change the Project Name to **ConvertProject**. (The project name must be a single word.) Use the browse button (marked with an ellipsis) next to the Help File Name text box to navigate to the new Help system. This system uses compiled Help files with the hlp extension. This is the default. Select the name of the Help file in the Help File dialog box. Click **Open**.

12. In the Project Description enter **A project to convert measurements from one unit to another**. If there are changes to the Make or Compile tab, this is the time to make them. Click **OK** to make the changes.

13. Save and run the program. Click the What's This button (the question mark) and click a text box. Click the popup Help box to close it. Test the Help messages for other controls such as the command buttons. Add a conversion: **cm., in., 2.54**. Click **What's This** and click one of the new text boxes. Stop the program.

14. Select **File | Make Convert.exe** from the menu bar. In the Make Project dialog box,

click **OK**. A brief pause occurs while the application is compiled.

15. Save the project and exit Visual Basic.

16. Right-click the Start button and select **Explore**. Navigate to the home directory of the Convert project. Double-click **Convert.exe**. Try out the program by adding a conversion (**cm.**, **in.**, **2.54**) and testing it by entering a value and clicking the new toolbar button. Try out the Help system. Click the **What's This** button (the question mark) and click on a text box. The Help message, Enter a Value or Eliminate the Conversion, appears. Stop the program.

    The project is ready to package, right? When you used the browse button in the project Property Pages to link the Help file, did you paste the entire pathname of the Help file into the program? If so, the program is locked to a particular directory to use its Help file.

17. Use Windows Explorer to locate the Help file connected with the Convert project. It is named CONVERTWHATSTHIS.hlp. Move the file to a different directory. Run **Convert.exe**. Click the **What's This** button and click the **Add a Conversion** button. The error message in Figure 14-6 appears. Click **No**, then click **OK** for the next message. Exit the program.

18. The file is not ready to package. Start Visual Basic. Click the **Recent** tab and open the program. Right-click **ConvertProject** in the Project Explorer. Select **ConvertProject Properties**.

FIGURE 14-6
A Windows Help error message

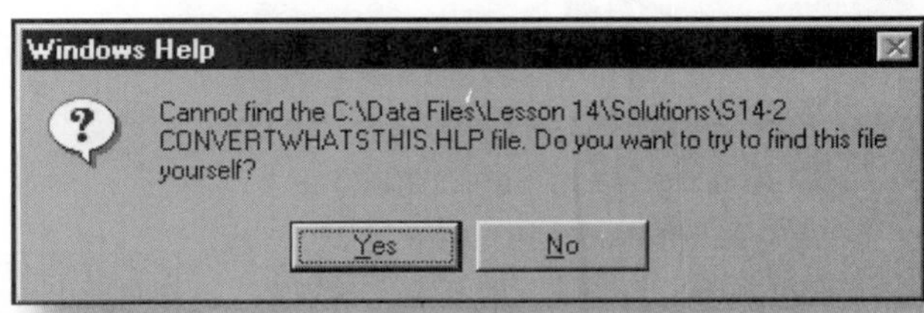

19. In the General tab of the ConvertProject Properties dialog box, edit the entry in the Help File Name text box. Completely eliminate the path information and leave just the name of the Help file in the text box.

20. Click **OK** to make the change and close the ConvertProject Properties dialog box. Select **frmConvert** in the Project Explorer and click **View Code**. Insert the lines **ChDir App.Path** and **ChDrive App.Path** in the code for **Form_Load**. This resets the default directory. Save the program.

21. Select **File | Make Convert.exe** from the menu bar and click **OK**. Visual Basic asks if you want to replace the existing file. Click **Yes**.

22. After the file is compiled, exit Visual Basic and run Windows Explorer (if it is not running). Navigate to the directory with Convert.exe. Be sure the Help file is in the same directory as the executable file. You may have to move the Help file back from another directory. Double-click **Convert.exe** to run the program. Use the Help system. When you confirm the system and the application are running correctly, exit the program. Close Microsoft Help Workshop and Windows Explorer.

Now you understand what a *dependency* is. The Help system cannot run if the application cannot find the file. The same is true of the DLL files. When packaging an application you must know and include its dependencies.

STEP-BY-STEP 14.2b

1. Start Visual Basic and open the **Convert** project. Select **Add-Ins | Add-In Manager** from the menu bar. Double-click the entry in the Add-In Manager for the Package and Deployment Wizard. The word **Loaded** appears in the Load Behavior column. Click **OK** to close the Add-In Manager. Select **Add-Ins | Package and Deployment Wizard**.

2. The Active Project text box lists the Convert project. Each of the three choices has an explanatory caption. The first mentions an Internet CAB file. "Cab" is short for cabinet. A *CAB file* holds not only the executable application file, but also all the support files needed to run the program. Click the **Package** icon to move to the next screen. If you have not recently compiled the project, the Wizard prompts you to compile it again. You may refuse the option if you know there are no changes in the project you want to package.

3. After a series of quick message boxes flash on the screen the Package and Deployment Wizard – Package Type window appears. See Figure 14-7. The picture in the upper left shows the three kinds of packages the Wizard can produce. The first creates a Standard EXE Setup program to install the application on another computer. The second shows a cabinet and a world icon. This represents the Internet Package. This choice is only available when packaging an ActiveX based project (see Lesson 15). The third shows a document icon that represents a Dependency file. This file is used to list information about the files needed to run the application. Select **Standard Setup Package** in the Package Type list box and click **Next**.

FIGURE 14-7
The Package Type dialog box of the Package and Deployment Wizard

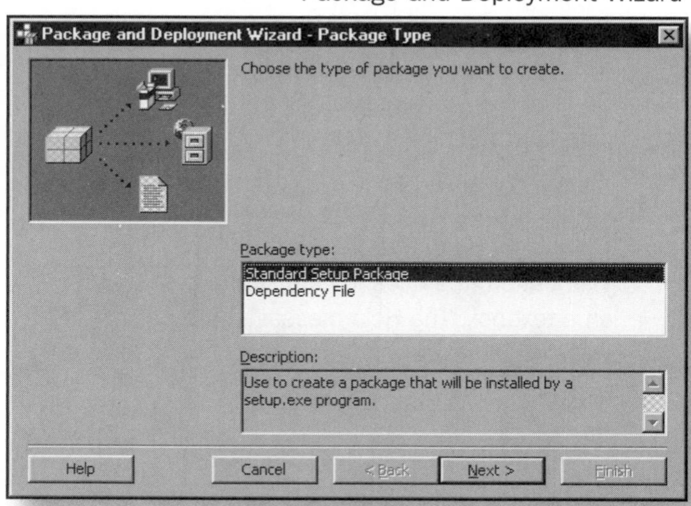

4. The Package Folder dialog box, shown in Figure 14-8, asks where you want the package. The *Package folder* is the default name of the directory created by the PD Wizard to hold the CAB file created for an application. This dialog box allows you to create a new folder or navigate to a network folder. Click **New Folder** and change the path to the location for your current lesson files. Be sure the path ends with \Package, then click **OK** to return to the Package Folder dialog box. Notice that the Finish button is present, but dimmed. If you had recorded a script file with all your preferences for packaging a project, you could let the script file take over by clicking Finish. Click **Next** to advance to the next dialog box. A

message box prompts you to create the folder. Click **Yes** to create the folder and advance to the next dialog box.

You may be prompted to browse for missing files Navigate to any missing files and click **Open**.

FIGURE 14-8
The Package Folder dialog box, showing the location of the folder and the new Package folder

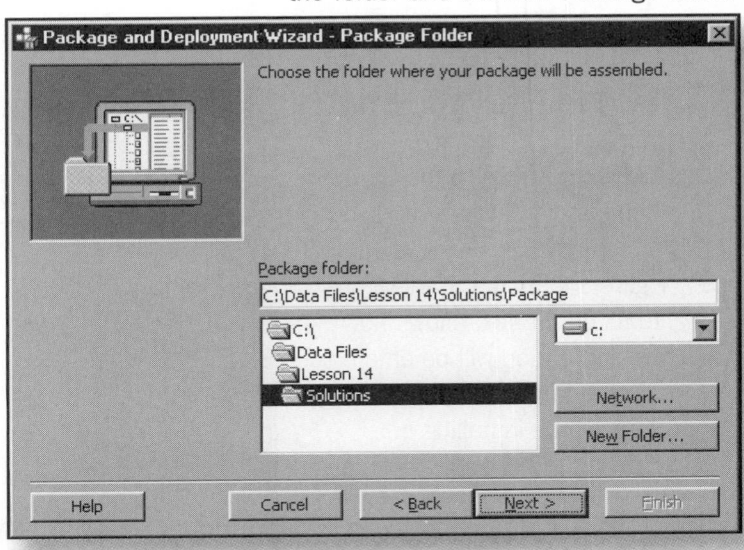

5. Figure 14-9 shows the Included Files window of the Wizard. A list of files necessary to install the application on another computer appears in the list box. The first file shown in the list below is MSCOMCTL.OCX. This file contains the definitions of the Microsoft Common Controls. The application uses a toolbar which is included in the Microsoft Common Controls. The compiled application appears along with the hlp file used to provide Help to the system. The Wizard takes care of most file dependencies, but if there is a file missing, add it with the Add button. Click **Next** to accept the other file choices and advance to the next dialog box.

FIGURE 14-9
The Included Files dialog box of the Wizard

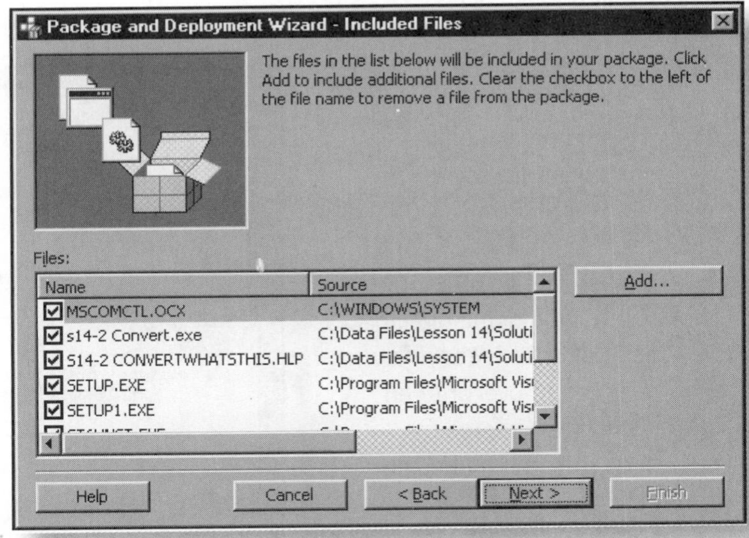

6. The Cab Options dialog box, in Figure 14.10, lets you package the application for distribution on diskettes or CD (or direct file transfer). If you choose Multiple cabs the application is split in pieces that fit using the media size you select in the combo box. A CAB file is a cabinet used to store the compressed file needed to run the application. Click **Single cab** (if necessary) and click **Next**.

(continued on next page)

7. In the Installation Title dialog box enter the following in the Installation title text box: **The Conversion Program**. Click **Next** to advance to the Start Menu Items dialog box.

FIGURE 14-10
The Cab Options dialog box

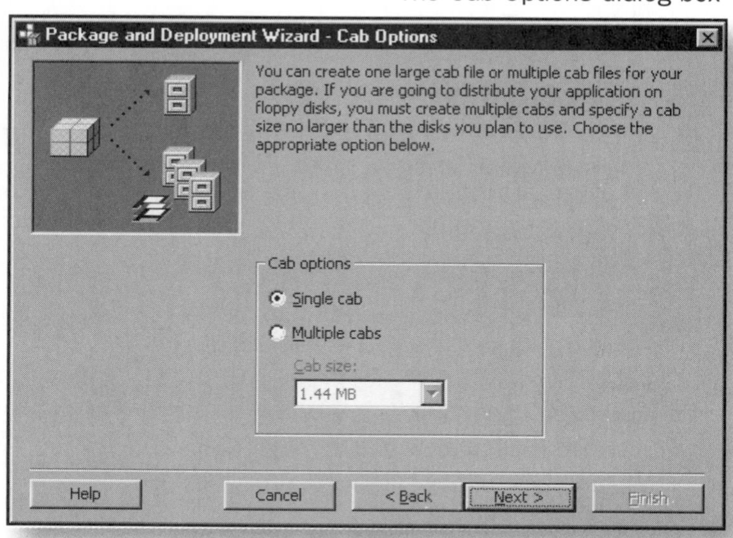

8. Figure 14-11, the Start Menu Items dialog box, shows how the application will be entered into the target computer's Start menu. Installing a shortcut to the program in the Start menu groups makes the program much easier to find. Although you may use the dialog box to make changes, click **Next** to accept the default arrangement.

FIGURE 14-11
The Start Menu Items dialog box

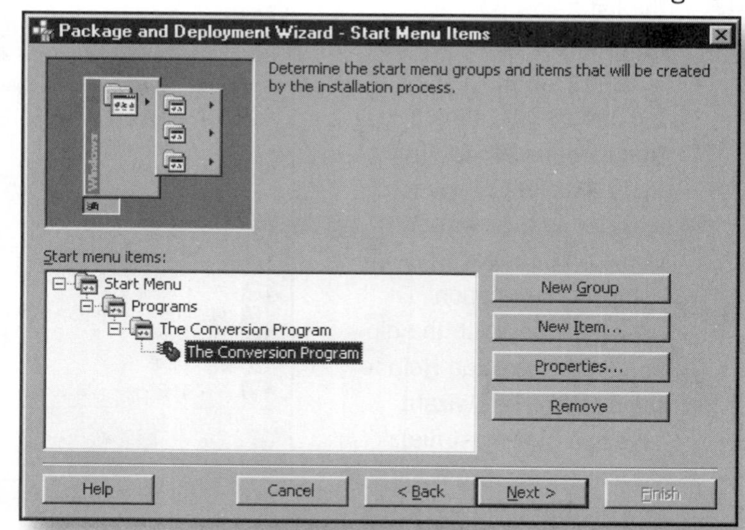

9. The Install Locations dialog box shows where the setup program will install the application and dependent files. The MSCOMTL.OCX file goes into the System folder. All other files go into the application's home directory. Click **Next**. Click **Yes** if you are asked to overwrite an existing file (created by another user in an earlier session).

10. Figure 14-12 shows the Shared Files dialog box. This dialog box is part of the plan of what happens when the application is uninstalled from the target machine. If a file is marked as a *shared file* it can be used as part of multiple applications. For instance, if the same Help file is to be used in more than one application it should be marked as a Shared file. As such, it is not removed from the target system until the last program that might use the file is removed from the system. Click **Next** to advance to the next dialog box. Do not check any files.

11. The Finished! window announces the completion of the information collection phase of the Wizard's job. This window lets you save the settings for later. Enter **Convert** as the script name. Click **Finish**.

12. The Packaging Report tells you where the CAB file for your installation package is saved. It also alerts you to a batch file (Convert.BAT) created in case you realize that there is a mistake. The batch file automates recreating the CAB file.

FIGURE 14-12
The Shared Files dialog box

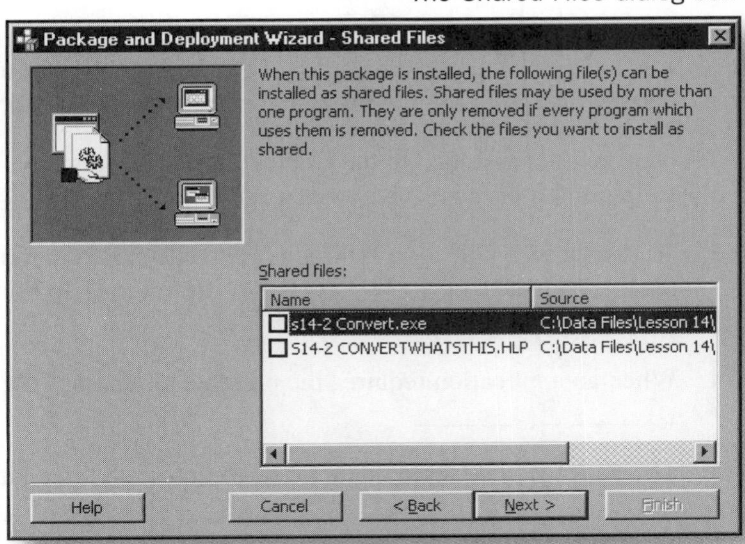

13. Click **Close** to close the report and click **Close** again to close the Package and Deployment Wizard.

14. Exit Visual Basic. Use Windows Explorer to view the directory listing for the files created by the Wizard. Three files and a folder appear in the Package folder.

    You can use the Setup.exe file later to install your application. The CAB file is a ZIP file that is literally the cabinet used to house the components of your application. The file Setup.lst contains information needed for the Setup program to do its work. You can view the file in any simple text editor like Notepad.

15. Open the Support folder by double-clicking its icon.

    This folder contains all the components used to build the CAB file. These are the files needed to support the application as it runs. Note the presence of the file Msvbvm60.DLL. This is the Microsoft Visual Basic Virtual Machine program. This provides run-time support for Visual Basic programs. Other files in the Support directory include the Help file and the batch file used to rebuild the CAB file if necessary.

    If the compiled application changes because features are added or corrections made, the CAB file must be rebuilt. To rebuild the CAB file, move the new EXE file into the Support directory. Double-click the BAT file. The old CAB file is overwritten by the modified file.

    Note the size of the CAB file. It is too large for a single 3.5" diskette. If you had clicked Multiple cab files earlier in the procedure you could have put each of the smaller files on a separate disk.

16. Close Windows Explorer.

The package is ready for distribution. In the next Step-by-Step exercise you install (and uninstall the application).

Quick Check 14.b

1. Just moving an application's __________________ file to another computer, probably will not enable you to run the program on the second machine.

2. New text boxes added to the Convert project at run-time, respond correctly to the What's This Help pointer because the new text boxes inherit __________________.

3. To enable an application to find its Help file stored in the same directory as the application itself, eliminate __________________ from the Help File Name text box in the application's Property Pages.

4. When an application requires the presence of another file to run properly, it is called a __________________.

5. The Package and Deployment Wizard can create three kinds of packages: __________________, __________________, and __________________.

6. The Package and Deployment Wizard uses a CAB file to __________________.

Installing and Uninstalling

Now that you have a CAB file, it is time to install and uninstall the application. Unfortunately, it is hard to completely test the installation process. It would be nice to install the application on a computer without any presence of Visual Basic. As soon as Visual Basic or applications written in Visual Basic are installed on a machine, a host of DLLs and OCXs are installed. When you install a new application, does it run because all of its dependencies are supplied by the CAB file? Or, does it run because it finds what it needs to run already installed in the Systems or Windows directory?

Before a program is installed, it must be distributed. You sidestep the problem by installing the application on the same machine where the CAB file and the installation file are built. You never have to transport the files. When distributing a file to another machine, you most cope with the details of putting the CAB file and installation program on storage media and moving the media to a different machine.

STEP-BY-STEP 14.3

1. Before you can install a program, you need to close all open applications. Some installations are lengthy and make a number of changes to the system. You would not want an installation to fail because you forgot to close Notepad. Close Windows Explorer, Notepad, and the Office Shortcut Bar (if it is open—click the multiple-colored square, then click Exit and click Yes).

2. Click the Windows **Start** button and select **Run**. Click **Browse**, navigate to the location of the new Package folder and double-click the exe file, then click **OK**. In the opening screen shown in Figure 14-13 click **OK** to proceed with the installation.

FIGURE 14-13
The opening screen of the Setup process

3. The next dialog box, shown in Figure 14-14 prompts you to change the directory in which the application is installed. Accept the default directory: Click the icon with the Tool Tip **Click here to begin Setup** in the left side of the dialog box. If instead, you choose to Exit the Setup program, you see a series of message boxes describing the bailout process. This is not the same as uninstalling an application, but it shows that even at this early stage of the process, a number of files have been installed.

FIGURE 14-14
The dialog box prompting for the directory in which to install the program

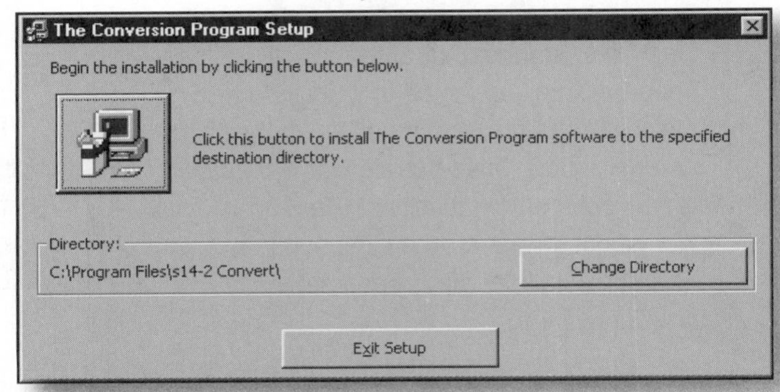

4. The next screen, shown in Figure 14-15, lets you choose a Program Group for the application. A *Program Group* is a group of related executable files. Program Groups determine what you see when you click the Start button. The Choose Program Group dialog box shows a new group for the application. Accept the default by clicking **Continue**.

5. A progress bar appears as the setup program unpacks the rest of the cabinet. Files are decompressed and copied to the destination directory. Setup alters the Start menu to reflect the new Program Group. Finally the message shown in Figure 14-16 appears. Click **OK**. The Setup program is finished and exits.

6. Click the **Start** button. Select **Programs | The Conversion Program | The Conversion Program**. Enter a value in the left text box marked ft. and press **Enter** or click the toolbar button. A value appears in the right text box. Click the **What's This** button in the upper right corner of the form. Click the left text box. The Help topic for the text boxes appears. Click the Help box to close it. Verify that Help is available for both text boxes and for the Add a Conversion and Calc buttons. Click **Add a Conversion**. Enter **cu. ft.**; **gal.**, and **7.5**. There are 7.5 gallons for each cubic

(continued on next page)

foot of liquid. Test the conversion by putting a value in either of the new text boxes and pressing **Enter** or clicking the second button on the toolbar. Double-click the left text box of the new conversion to remove it from the project. Click **Yes** to remove the conversion. Everything works normally. Click **Exit** to close the program.

7. Use Windows Explorer to navigate to the directory created by the installation program. Find it at C:\Program Files\Convert. View the directory of the Convert folder. Convert.exe is there, as is the Help file. The Uninstall log file contains information about the uninstall process. Double-click the filename to open the log file. If the file does not automatically open, you may be asked by the system to associate the file (and its extension) with an application. Open the file with Notepad. It may open automatically in the Help Workshop. Where it opens depends on what associa-tions have been set up on your system.

8. View the file, but do not modify the file. This gives you an idea of what needs to be done to both install and uninstall an application. Exit Notepad or the Help Workshop and close Windows Explorer.

9. Start the process of uninstalling the application by clicking the **Start** button. Select **Settings | Control Panel** to open the Control Panel. Figure 14-17 shows the Control Panel with Add/Remove Programs selected. (Note: On some systems, the Control Panel may be set up to display icons or file information rather than the simple list shown in the figure.) Double-click its entry to open the Add/Remove Programs Properties dialog box.

FIGURE 14-15
The Choose Program Group dialog box

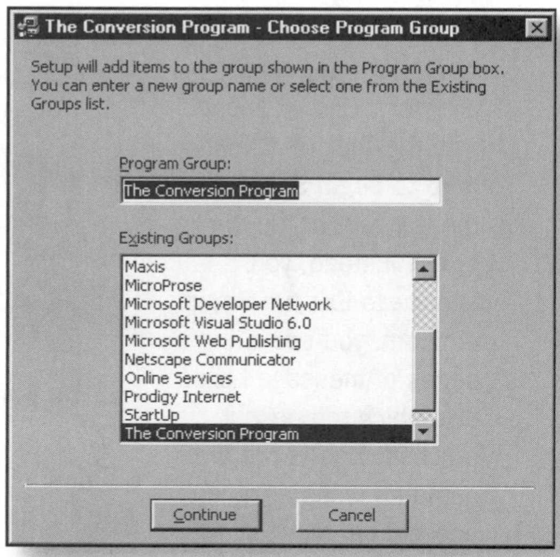

FIGURE 14-16
The Conversion Program Setup was successfully completed message

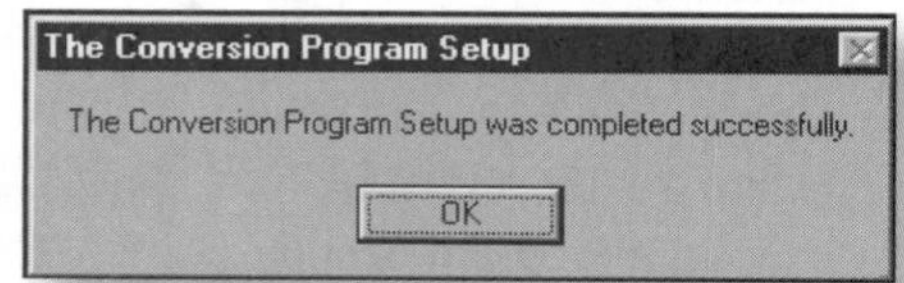

FIGURE 14-17
The Control Panel with Add/Remove Programs selected

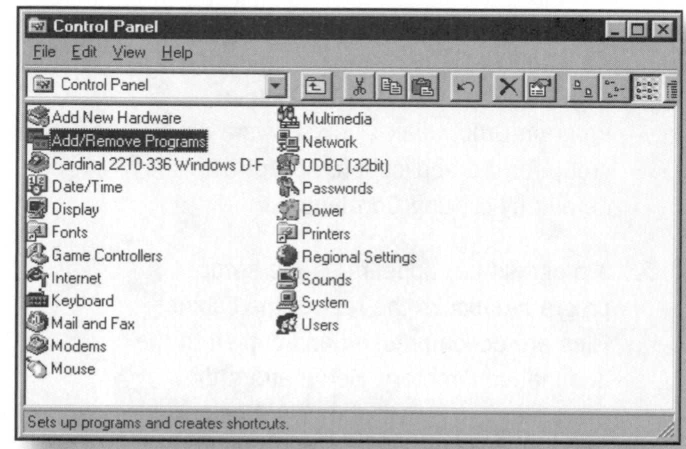

10. Figure 14-18 shows the Add/Remove Programs Properties dialog box with The Conversion Program selected. If necessary scroll in the list box and select **The Conversion Program**. As soon as a program is selected, the Add/Remove button is no longer grayed out. The message above indicates that the software can be removed automatically by Windows. The Windows Registry, along with the Uninstall log file created when the application was installed, has complete information about the dependencies of the applications listed. With complete information about dependencies, the entire application can be removed without leaving behind any stray files. DLLs and OCXs if not used by other applications are removed. If the Program Group is now blank, it is also removed.

FIGURE 14-18
The Add/Remove Programs Properties dialog box with The Conversion Program selected

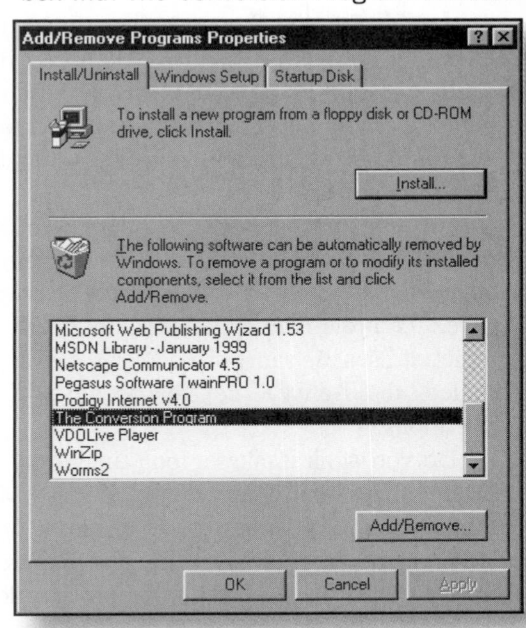

11. Click **Add/Remove**. A message appears prompting you for confirmation about the removal of the application. Click **Yes**. The Application Removal message box appears "Program installation removed". Click **OK**.

Close the Add | Remove Program Properties dialog box, the Control Panel, and the Explorer.

Going through the installation process yourself helps you understand what a user goes through when he opens a box of software and installs it. More complicated installations, like a new operating system, are far more complex and nerve-wracking. Although it rarely occurs, the fear is that something will happen in the installation or removal that somehow ruins your system. To prevent problems, be sure to follow the directions carefully.

Quick Check 14.c

1. When Visual Basic or applications written in Visual Basic are installed on a machine, a host of __________________ and __________________ are installed.
2. A __________________ organizes files in the Start menu.
3. Files that are used as a part of the installation of an application are distributed in __________________.
4. When the Conversion Program is installed, three files appear in its directory: __________________, __________________, and __________________.
5. Find the Add/Remove utility in __________________.

Packaging an ActiveX Control

In this Step-by-Step exercise you use the Package and Deployment Wizard to build an Internet package for an ActiveX control. You need Microsoft Internet Explorer to complete the lesson.

In Lessons 11 and 12 in the Programming At Work exercises, you built an ActiveX control capable of reading and searching Access databases. If you have not worked through these exercises, it is worth doing because the control you build is quite useful. You are going to use that control as the basis of this lesson.

An *Internet package* is quite an interesting thing. It is not primarily used to deliver the functionality of an ActiveX control over the Internet. That is, you do not use it to build more interesting Web pages, although it can be used that way. Use an Internet Package to install applications and ActiveX controls over a network, Internet or *Intranet.* An Intranet is a local implementation of the Internet. It uses the same protocols as the Internet for the transfer of documents and information. Once installed, the ActiveX control becomes a system resource, available for use in Web pages or applications.

Do you think it takes a long time for a Web page to load? Although not all Internet Packages are this large, how long would it take for an 8 Mb CAB file to be transferred to your system through the Internet? Getting the file to your system is only half the job. Internet Explorer handles the installation of components from the CAB file and prepares the system to use the components. Besides components from the CAB, file the installation process downloads a host of DLLs (if necessary) directly from the Microsoft Web site. At the end of the process, you have to reboot your computer.

Security

It is one thing for the Information Systems department of a company to distribute a new application through the company's Intranet to other company computers. It is another thing to install someone else's application from the Web onto your system. How can you be sure the installation will not damage your computer? There is no way to be sure. The security setting of the browser may not allow the installation of the ActiveX component at all. If it does, what problems are you inviting? Will other computer users trust your components enough to let them load? When installed, an ActiveX control has complete access to your system. That is why many browsers are set to reject such controls.

One way to provide some peace of mind for a user downloading your applications is to provide a digital signature. When you provide a digital signature with your application, you give the user a way to trace a path back to you or your company. You obtain the digital signature file from a company that provides a link from the user back to you if your control damages the user's system.

Once an ActiveX control is installed on the target system, it is called from a Web page with a *GUID*, a global unique identifier. A GUID is automatically assigned to every Visual Basic component, including ActiveX controls. You see a sample of the tag in the following Step-by-Step exercise.

STEP-BY-STEP 14.4a

1. Start Visual Basic. Open **SeeDatabase.vbp** from your own Lesson 12 Programming at Work files or from the *Electronic Instructor* CD-ROM: **\Data Files\Lesson 12\Programming at Work**. While under development, the project was part of a group that also contained a test bed project. The project group file has an extension of vbg. Do not load the group or the test project. Open just the project with the definition of the SeeDatabase control.

If you are using the file from the Electronic Instructor CD-ROM, after you open the file, select **File | Make SeeDatabase.ocx** and create the OCX file in the same folder as the VBP file. Select File | Open and reload the VBP file. Save changes if prompted.

2. Click the **Start** button on the toolbar or press **F5** to run the control. If the SeeDatabase Control Project Properties dialog box appears, click **OK**. An ActiveX control like SeeDatabase requires a *container application* in which to run. It cannot run independently. A container application, like Internet Explorer, provides a place for an ActiveX control to execute. Internet Explorer is launched and the ActiveX control is executed in that container.

3. In Internet Explorer, select **View | Source**. The source code of the HTML file displaying the ActiveX control appears. The <object> tag, shown below, shows the GUID of the ActiveX control. The alphanumeric characters shown may vary.

```
<OBJECT classid="clsid:AE4C18E4-0FBB-11D3-93BD-0C9F08C10000">
```

4. Close the HTML source code. Select **View | Internet Options** from the menu bar of the browser. Click the **Settings** button. Click the **View Objects** button. The Downloaded Program Files dialog box in Figure 14-19 shows files installed on the browser (if any). When the SeeDatabase control is downloaded and installed by the browser, it has an entry in this table. If you share a computer, an entry for SeeDatabaseControl may already be displayed. Your own copy can still be installed.

5. Select **File | Close** to close the Downloaded Program Files window. Click **OK** to close the Settings window. Click **OK** to close the Internet Options window. Select **File | Close** to close Internet Explorer.

6. You should be back in Visual Basic. If not, use the taskbar to return. Click the **End** button in the toolbar to stop execution of the control. Closing the browser did not stop the execution of the control. Select **Add-Ins | Add-In Manager**. In the Add-In Manager dialog box, double-click the entry for **Package and Deployment Wizard**. The word "loaded" should appear in the second column. Click **OK** to close the window. Select **Add-Ins | Package and Deployment Wizard**. If prompted, save the project.

(continued on next page)

FIGURE 14-19
The Downloaded Program Files dialog box

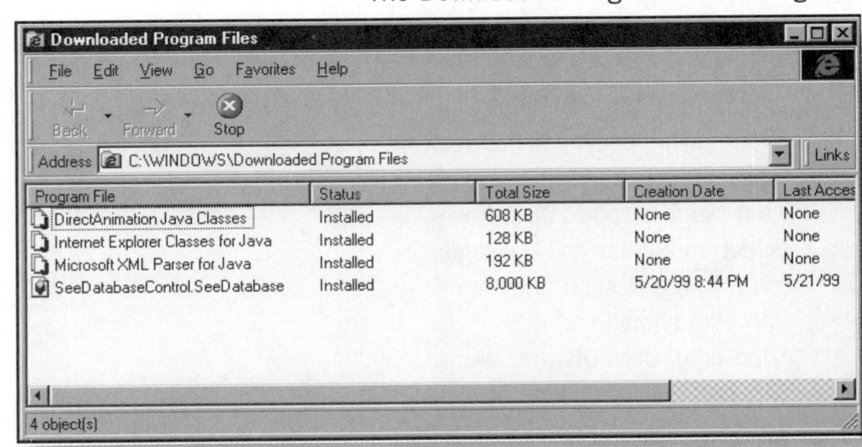

7. Click the **Package** icon in the opening screen of the Package and Deployment Wizard. The message box shown in Figure 14-20 appears prompting you to compile the control to an OCX file (or you may see a message asking if you want to recompile the OCX file; click **Yes** if you see this message). Click **Compile** to start the compilation process. In addition to compiling the control, dependencies are identified and the Wizard is initialized. The Packaging Script window may appear prompting you for the name of a script file. The script file, if it exists, is a compilation of choices made during a previous packaging session. Using a script file means you do not have to go through each screen of the Wizard making the same choices repeatedly. If necessary change the script to **SeeDatabase** (you may leave the s12 or s14 if you are using the file from the Electronic Instructor CD-ROM). Click **Next** to advance to the next screen. If prompted, include the file for the Property Page DLL.

8. In the Package Type list box of the Package Type dialog box, select **Internet Package** by clicking its entry with the mouse. Click **Next** to advance to the next screen.

9. The Package Folder dialog box prompts you for a destination folder for the packaged control. Navigate to a place where you want the files to go. Click **New Folder** and create the Package folder in the desired directory (the path should end with \Package). Click **OK**. The Wizard also creates a subfolder called Support. The CAB files, installation program, and uninstall file go into the Package folder and all the support files needed to rebuild the CAB file go into the Support folder. Click **Next** to advance to the next screen. Click **Yes** if you are prompted to create the folder.

10. The ActiveX control SeeDatabase uses DAO, Data Access Objects. *DAO drivers* are programs that make data sources available to DAO objects. The DAO Drivers dialog box lists all the DAO drivers installed on your system. Click the **double right pointing arrow**. All the entries of the left list box move to the right list box. See Figure 14-21 (your list may vary). Click **Yes** if you are prompted to distribute the Property Page DLL.

FIGURE 14-20
Package and Deployment Wizard message box

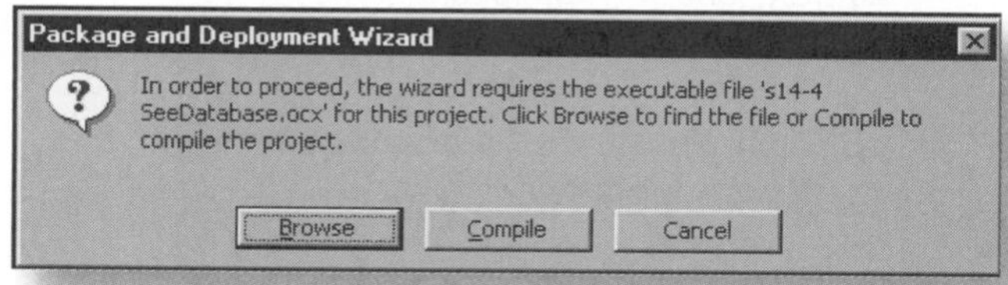

FIGURE 14-21
The DAO Drivers dialog box showing the selection of all the drivers

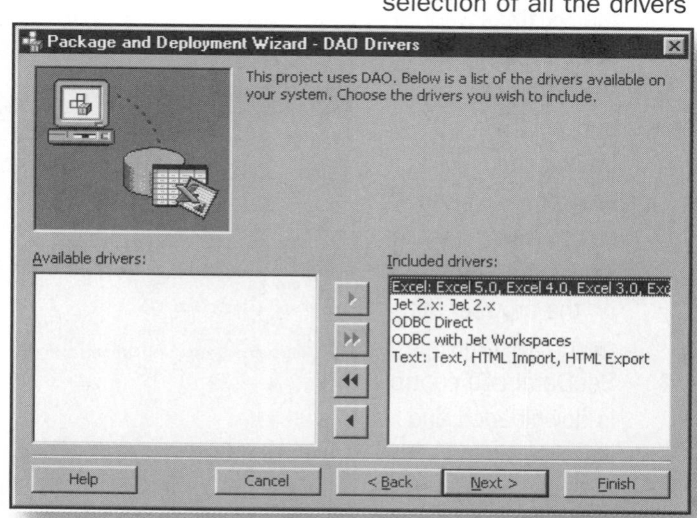

11. The Included Files window is usually a surprise. See Figure 14-22. Scroll through the list box noting the number, names, and sources of the included files. Each of these is either included in the CAB file or marked as a file necessary for the control to work. When the application is installed, the Setup program searches the target system for the presence of these files. If the files are present on the system they are only replaced if the files in the CAB are more recent versions. If the target system already has most of the files, the Setup can occur very quickly. The actual OCX file is not very large. It may be the only file transferred. Click **Next** to advance to the next step.

FIGURE 14-22
The Included Files dialog box

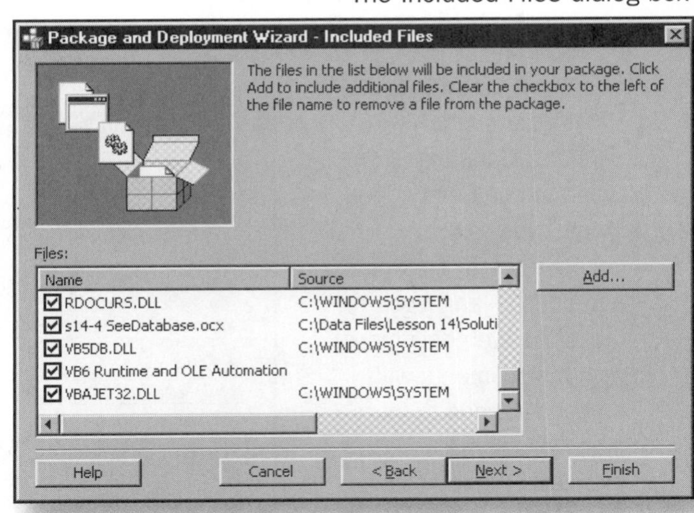

12. Figure 14-23 shows the File Source dialog box. A complete list of the files included in the package appears in the list box on the left (your list may vary). A file may be included in the package, but may not be included in the CAB file. Many files are downloaded directly from the Microsoft Web site. This ensures the most current copies of the files are installed on the target system. Select various files in the list box and note their sources. You can change the source, specify a new source, or request that all the DLLs be loaded into the CAB file. Scroll back to the top of the list and click the first entry. Click **Next** to accept the default settings and advance to the next step.

FIGURE 14-23
The File Source dialog box showing SeeDatabase.ocx selected in the list box

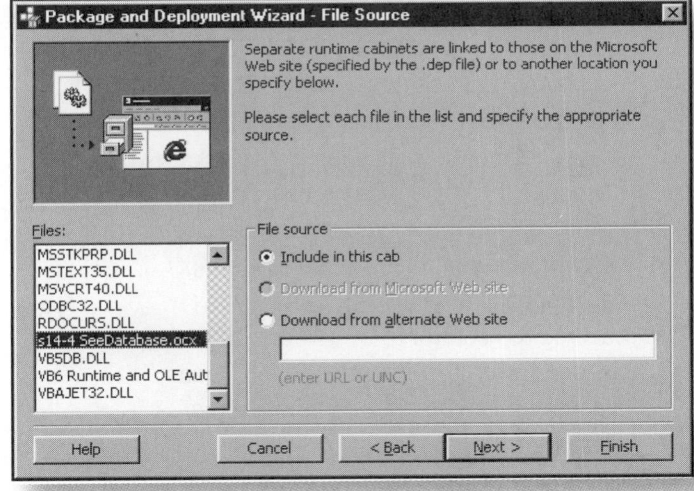

The Safety Settings dialog box shown in Figure 14-24 appears with the following message.

"Safety settings could not be determined for the following components."

What does "Safe for Scripting" mean? Hypertext Markup Language, HTML, is used to write Web pages. In its simplest form, it is used to format and present text and graphic information in a Web document. HTML language elements determine the appearance and

(continued on next page)

arrangement of information on the page. HTML also supports *scripting*. Scripting is program code embedded in the hypertext document. HTML authors use special languages to make the Web document active: documents with embedded code do not passively display information; they collect information or dynamically alter the appearance of a document.

FIGURE 14-24
The Safety Settings dialog box

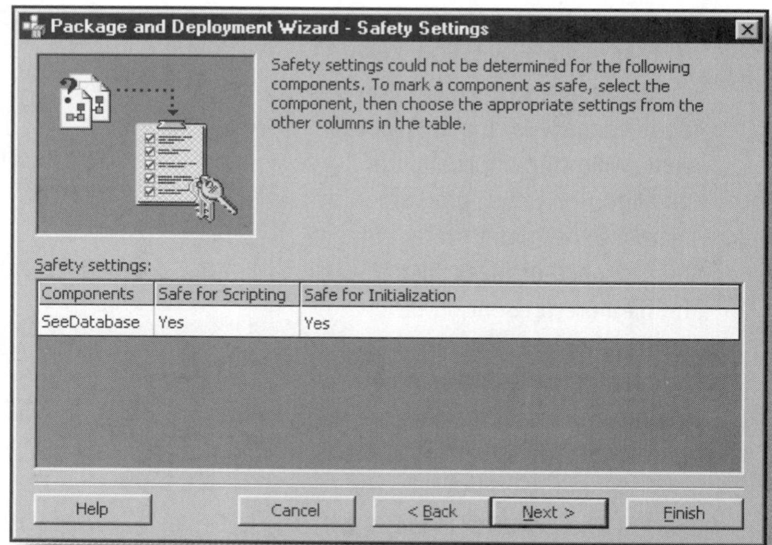

An ActiveX control embedded in an HTML document that writes a temporary file to the user's hard drive and erases it when it is finished is "safe for scripting" if the file's name is hard coded in the control. If the filename comes from a script, the control is not safe. A script could specify a name of a system file causing the control to overwrite a file needed to run the computer. That means a control could be used to damage the system on which it runs.

Another consideration is what kind of information does the control return to the Web server. Many Web pages query the user for information and return that information to the server. That is "safe" because the user volunteers the information. A control that searches the user's hard drive looking for particular documents and reporting information back to the server without the user's knowledge is unsafe.

"Safe for Initialization" means that no scripting used to initialize the control can cause the control to damage the target system even if the control is initialized with invalid data.

13. Click **Safe for Scripting** and if necessary alter its entry to **Yes**. Click **Safe for Initialization** and if necessary alter its entry to **Yes**. Is the control really safe? It is not always easy to tell. This control is used to display the contents of a database. It certainly can be used to display sensitive material on the target computer, but it has no capability to report the information back to the server. Click **Next** to move to the next step.

14. The Finished! window tells you the information needed to build the package is collected. It also lets you save the settings used in a script file. You should do this because the name is used when you want to deploy your application.

If necessary enter **SeeDatabase** for the Script name (if you are using the Electronic Instructor file, you may leave the s12 or s14). Click **Finish** to build the package. If you see a prompt to override, click **Yes**. Once the package is built, read the report and click **Close**. You are back to the opening screen of the Package and Deployment Wizard. Leave the Wizard open.

15. You are ready to deploy your package but first right-click **Start** and select **Explore** to open Windows Explorer. Navigate to the Package folder you created to hold the package. (If you did not change the path, the Package folder is most likely in C:\Program Files\Visual Studio\VB98). It contains two files and the Support folder. One file is the CAB file. It is compressed in WINZip format. The other is the sample HTML file created to show you how to call the control in a Web document.

16. Double-click the directory entry, **SeeDatabase.HTM**. Your default browser launches and tries to display the ActiveX control. If your default browser is Netscape, nothing happens. The page loads but Netscape does not support ActiveX objects. It is not a suitable container for your application. Before leaving Netscape view the page's source code by selecting **View | Page Source** from the menu bar. The code to run the control is there, it just does not work.

17. Close both the Page Source window and Netscape. Find and launch **Internet Explorer** (if it is not already running). If the sample Web page is not open, select **File | Open** from the menu bar in Internet Explorer. In the Open dialog box, click the **Browse** button. Navigate to the Package folder and select **SeeDatabase.HTM**. Click **Open** and **OK** to close the Open dialog box. Internet Explorer runs the Web page and the ActiveX control is running.

18. Click **Load DB** on the control and navigate to the **Biblio.mdb** database (It is probably located in C:\Program Files\Microsoft Visual Studio\VB98) or you can open a copy from the Electronic Instructor CD-ROM. Select and open the file. Test the control by searching the database for a particular author. To search click a field name (contained in a label) and follow the directions.

19. Select **View | Source** to view the source code for the Web page. Following the <BODY> tag is a comment tag: <!—. Everything in this tag is ignored (unless it is a script) until the closing tag. Although a particular file may be required to run your control, you may not be permitted to distribute the file without a license. In the comment are instructions on how to create a license package file. The rest of the file contains the call to the ActiveX control. This page is the starting point for designing your own page that uses the SeeDatabase control. Select **File | Exit** to close the Source code view and return to Internet Explorer. Close Internet Explorer and Windows Explorer.

The next step is to simulate deployment of the package and install the package on your machine. This is not much different than giving yourself a blood transfusion.

STEP-BY-STEP 14.4b

1. The Package and Deployment Wizard was open when you left on a tour of your hard drive and browser. If it is not open, return to Visual Basic and run the Wizard from the Add-Ins menu.

2. Click the **Deploy** icon on the opening screen of the Wizard. As usual, the first screen may ask you to choose an existing Deployment script. Select **(None)** if necessary and click **Next** to go to the next step.

3. In the Package to Deploy dialog box, select **SeeDatabase** from the Package to deploy combo box. Click **Next** to move to the next step.

4. Figure 14-25 shows the Deployment Method dialog box. Select **Folder** from the Deployment method list box. Use this selection to deploy your application to a network. The Web Publishing selection prepares the package for deployment to a Web server. Click **Next** to move to the next step.

5. Figure 14-26 shows the Folder dialog box. If you click the Network button, you can browse the network drives looking for a place to deploy your application. In a business network there would be a special folder in a common drive dedicated to such packages. If you have access to a network, it would be ideal to deploy the package to a network drive and install it in a machine with no installation of Visual Basic. You would be able to see each of the DLLs downloaded and installed. For this exercise, find a place on your local drive and create a new folder named **Deploy** with the New Folder button, then click **OK** and click **Yes** to create the folder. Click **Next** to move to the next step.

6. You are, once again, at the Finished! dialog box. Change the script name to **SeeDatabase** and click **Finish**. If you are prompted to overwrite an existing file click **Yes**. The Deployment Report shows that two files are copied, the CAB file and the HTM file. Click **Close** to close the report window.

7. Close the Package and Deployment Wizard. Exit Visual Basic. Run Internet Explorer. You do not need to sign on to the Internet. If prompted, click **Stay Offline**. If you are signed on automatically when you run Internet Explorer, select **File | Work Offline**. Select **View | Internet Options** to open the Internet Options dialog box. Click **Settings**, then click **View Objects** to view the objects installed by Internet Explorer. Confirm that SeeDatabase is not among

FIGURE 14-25
The Deployment Method dialog box

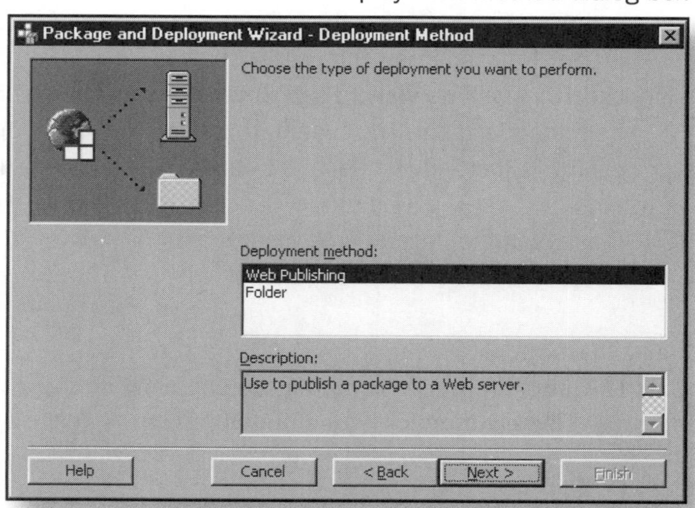

the installed objects. Close the Downloaded Program Files window by clicking the **Close** button in the upper right corner. Click **OK** to close the Settings window. Do not close the Internet Options window.

8. You want to load a fresh copy of the Web page that uses the SeeDatabase control, so clear the *cache*, the storage area used to store recently used Web pages. To clear the cache click **Delete Files** in the Internet Options dialog box. Click **OK** in the Delete Files dialog box. Click **OK** at the bottom of the Internet Options dialog box to close it.

9. Select **File | Open**. In the Open dialog box, click the **Browse** button. Navigate to your Deploy folder. Select **SeeDatabase.HTM** and click **Open**. Click **OK** in the Open dialog box to launch the Web page. The page opens almost immediately. Has the browser already installed the control? No, the browser is too smart for that. The browser uses the original copy of SeeDatabase.ocx to bring up the Web page. Close Internet Explorer.

10. To really test the browser's ability to install a control from its CAB file, use Windows Explorer to navigate to the folder of the original SeeDatabase.ocx file. Right-click the filename and select **Rename**. Change the name to **SeDatabase.ocx**. This prevents the browser from finding the control. When you are done with this experiment, return to the filename in Windows Explorer and restore the missing "e". Without the missing letter, the filename no longer matches its entry in the Windows Registry. This prevents applications from finding the control.

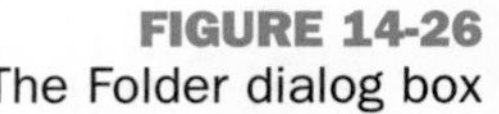

FIGURE 14-26
The Folder dialog box

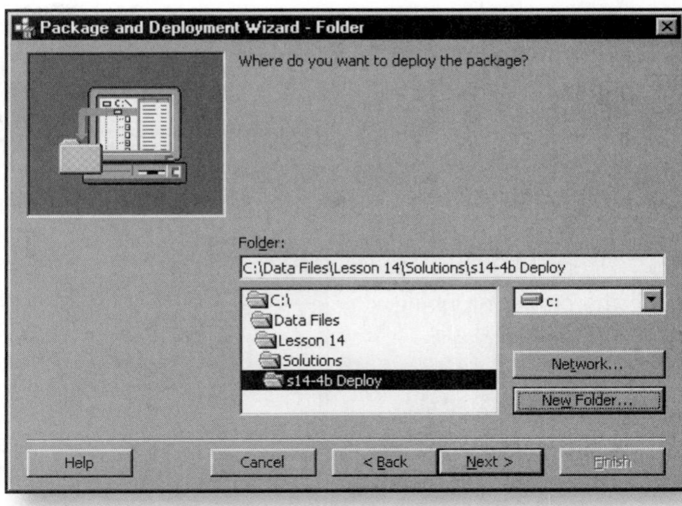

11. Open Internet Explorer. Select **File | Open**. In the Open dialog box, click the **Browse** button. Navigate to your Deploy folder. Select **SeeDatabase.HTM** and click **Open**. Click **OK** in the Open dialog box to launch the Web page. This time the page takes much longer to load. Finally the SeeDatabase control appears.

12. Leave Internet Explorer open and open Windows Explorer. Navigate back to the location of the original SeeDatabase.ocx. Has the file been restored? It has not. Where was the control installed? Return to Internet Explorer.

13. Select **View | Internet Options**. Click **Settings** to open the Settings window. Click the **View Objects** button. The Downloaded Program Files window appears. A program file named SeeDatabaseControl.SeeDatabase has been installed. Its file size is roughly the size of the CAB file created by the Package and Deployment Wizard. Figure 14-27 shows the window.

(continued on next page)

14. Close the Downloaded Program Files window, the Settings dialog box and the Internet Options dialog box.

15. Figure 14-28 shows the browser running the SeeDatabase control. The display shows an entry from Biblio.mdb. Click **Load DB**, locate and open **Biblio.md** and test the control.

16. Close Internet Explorer. In Windows Explorer, locate **SeDatabase.ocx** and rename it **SeeDatabase.ocx**, then close Windows Explorer.

FIGURE 14-27
The Downloaded Program Files dialog box showing SeeDatabaseControl.SeeDatabase

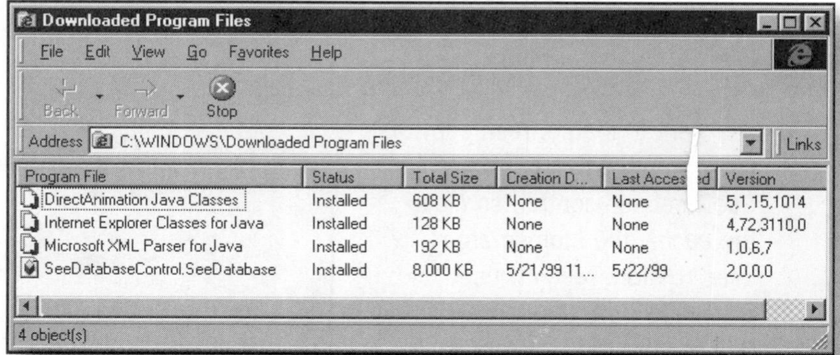

FIGURE 14-28
Internet Explorer showing SeeDatabase.HTM. The SeeDatabase control shows an entry from the Biblio.mdb database

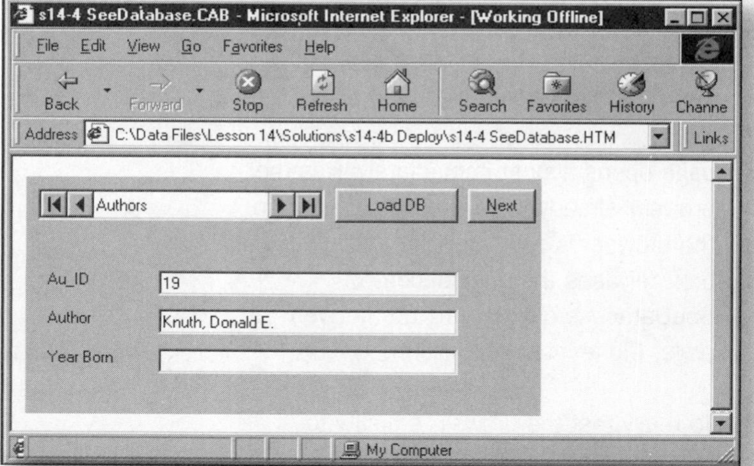

The SeeDatabaseControl.SeeDatabase may not show up in the Downloaded Program Files window. Close the Downloaded Program Files window, the Settings dialog box, and the Internet Options dialog box. Reopen each. The file should appear. If it did not, the browser is still using some copy of SeeDatabase.ocx to enable the Web page.

To see the full power of the system you have to install the control in an environment that has none of the support files installed. The process takes much longer. The first roadblock you find in such an experiment relates to the Browser Security Settings. Figure 14.29 shows the Security tab of the Internet Options window. You may define different levels of security for different zones. The zones are Local Intranet zone, Trusted sites zone (shown), Internet Zone, and Restricted sites zone. As components of the application are downloaded and installed, the user is queried whether or not to accept each part.

FIGURE 14-29
The Security tab of the Internet Options dialog box

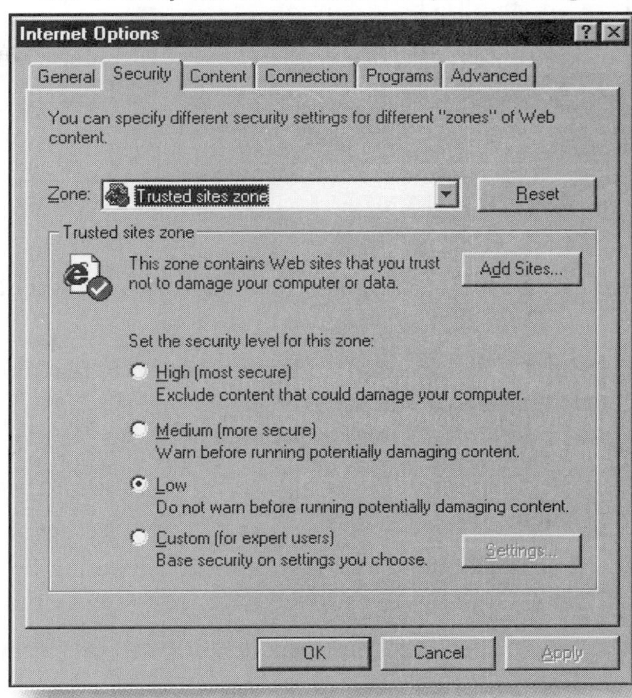

At the highest setting, ActiveX controls, because of their potential to damage the target system, are not accepted. Some viruses are delivered as ActiveX controls in Web pages downloaded from the Internet. It may be possible for a hacker to supply a phony digital signature for an ActiveX control. If so, your browser may accept the control when it should not.

When loading the control on a system with none of the support files, each file from the CAB is downloaded and installed. Then each DLL file from the Microsoft Web site is downloaded and installed. The browser installs the components of the Data Access system.

If working over a slow Internet connection, the time it takes for a full installation is very long. Once the components are installed, everything works quickly.

This is a great system for delivering programs through a network, Intranet, or the Internet. First time through, bring a book to read and be prepared to lower your browser's security level.

Quick Check 14.d

1. An ____________________, built by the Package and Deployment Wizard, is used to install an application through a network, the Internet, or an Intranet.

2. One way to provide some peace of mind for a user downloading your applications is to provide a ____________________.

3. An ActiveX control requires a ____________________ in which to run. It cannot run independently.

4. When an application is installed, the ____________________ searches the target system for the presence of files required to run the application.

5. ____________________ is program code embedded in a hypertext document. HTML authors use special languages to make Web documents active.

6. Two files are created when the Package and Deployment Wizard is finished building an Internet Package: a compressed ____________________ and a ____________________.

Summary

- Machine Language statements are binary codes that instruct a processor to execute simple mathematical and logical operations.
- Assembly Language statements are short mnemonics that represent individual machine language statements.
- A high-level programming language is less like the language of the processor and more like the language of the programmer. Visual Basic is an example of a high-level programming language.
- The IDE, Integrated Development Environment, is an ideal environment in which to program. Help and debugging tools make it easy to fix problems.
- Visual Basic programs can be compiled to executable files that run outside the Visual Basic IDE.
- Packaging a program means providing the run-time libraries and support files to enable a program to run outside the Visual Basic environment. It also means registering program components in the system registry.
- Use ChDir App.Path and ChDrive App.Path in the project's code to change the default drive and directory to the drive and directory in which the application is saved.
- Prepare a program for packaging by resolving any file access and user interface problems. Set the project name, version number, and optimization.
- To make a database connection independent of a particular path, remove the path information from the database name text box. The database name text box is in the Data Link Properties dialog box of the project's Property Pages.
- Although an EXE file is compiled and ready to run in the machine's native code, it requires the presence of a number of other files to run outside the Visual Basic environment.
- "Cab" is short for cabinet. A CAB file holds not only the executable application file, but also all the support files needed to run the program.
- The Package and Deployment Wizard produces three kinds of packages:

  The first creates a Setup program to install the application on another computer.

  The second shows a cabinet and a world icon. This represents the Internet Package. This choice is only available when packaging an ActiveX based project (see Lesson 15).

  The third shows a document icon that represents a Dependency file. This file is used to list information about the files needed to run the application.

- The Package and Deployment Wizard can package a program for distribution in two forms. The first is a single large CAB file. This is suitable for writing to any high capacity storage media, like a CD. The second form is several small CAB files. Transfer these files to individual diskettes.
- The Package and Deployment Wizard includes the Microsoft Visual Basic Virtual Machine DLL, Msvbvm60.DLL. This provides run-time support for Visual Basic programs.
- Program installation is preceded by program distribution.
- Double-click setup.exe to start the installation procedure. Most of the time, accepting the defaults presented by the Setup program is a good idea.
- The Setup program requests that all other applications be closed before an installation is attempted.
- The user is guided step-by-step through the application installation procedure by the Setup program.
- Once installed, a new Program Group, accessible from the Start menu, is created for the application. You do have the option of adding the application to an existing Program Group.
- To uninstall an application, open the Control Panel and select Add/Remove Programs. Follow the simple instructions to completely remove an application from the system. Besides removing the main files in the application's folder, DLL's and OCX's, if not used by other applications, are removed. If a Program Group was created with the installation, it is removed.
- An Internet Package is used to install applications and ActiveX controls over a network, Internet or Intranet.
- Once installed, the ActiveX control becomes a system resource, available for use in Web pages or applications.
- Some necessary components of an Internet Package are downloaded directly from the Microsoft Web site.
- Use a digital signature to sign applications delivered over the Internet. The digital signature makes a link back to you or your company if the control damages the target system.
- Use a container application to run components like ActiveX controls that cannot run on their own.
- Setup programs, used to install applications, look for the presence of required files and install only those files that are out of date or missing.
- Scripting is program code embedded in the hypertext document. Scripting makes Web documents active: documents with embedded code do not passively display information; they collect information or dynamically alter the appearance of a document.
- A control is "safe" if two conditions are met:

  if the file name is hard coded in the control and the control does not write files to the host system based on filenames provided by a scripting language.

  if the control does no damage to a host system even if initialized with invalid data.
- Internet Explorer installs applications from an Internet Package. Netscape does not support ActiveX objects.

LESSON 14 REVIEW QUESTIONS

TRUE/FALSE

Circle the T if the statement is True. Circle the F is it is False.

T F 1. Machine code statements are closer to the language of the programmer than to the language of the processor.

T F 2. Code optimization is usually a trade-off between speed and size.

T F 3. The executable file created by the Make option in the File menu builds an executable file that can be moved to another machine and run outside the Visual Basic environment with no additional files.

T F 4. A CAB file holds only the executable file of an application program.

T F 5. The Package and Deployment Wizard produces three kinds of packages: the Standard Setup program, an Internet version, and a Dependency file.

T F 6. Run an application's setup program by clicking the Start button and selecting the new program's name from the Programs menu.

T F 7. Uninstall an application by selecting Add/Remove Programs from the Control Panel.

T F 8. An application installed from the Internet may require support files downloaded from the Microsoft Web Site.

T F 9. The Package and Deployment Wizard provides a digital signature for your Internet Packages.

T F 10. If you install an ActiveX component on a machine that already has Visual Basic installed, it is likely that the installation process will take longer than normal.

WRITTEN QUESTIONS

Write your answers to the following questions.

11. What is the relationship between Machine Language and Assembly Language?

12. What steps should you take before you compile a program to an executable file?

13. How do you remove the path information from a Data Control's connection string?

14. Explain what "CAB" means and for what it is used.

15. Describe what choices are made in the Cab Options dialog box.

16. What does the file Msvbvm60.DLL do?

17. Why is it important to use the Uninstall procedure instead of just deleting the application's files?

18. How is an Internet Package different from a regular Setup file?

19. What is a digital signature?

20. What two criteria are used to determine if an ActiveX control is safe?

LESSON 14 APPLICATION PROBLEMS

Level One

COMPILE YOUR OWN APPLICATION

Pick a programming problem competed in a previous lesson such as the Payments project in Lesson 7. Prepare the project for compilation by giving it a project name and description as well as resolving any file access or user interface problems. Compile the file. Exit Visual Basic. Test the result to make sure the executable file works properly. If possible, put the executable file on a disk and move the executable file to another computer. Test the program on the other computer. Answer this question if you can: Does it make a difference if the other computer has Visual Basic installed?

PACKAGE YOUR OWN APPLICATION

Package the program used in the first application above as a Standard Setup Package. Be sure any dependencies are handled properly. Run the Wizard twice, once to create a single cab file and again to create multiple cab files for 1.44mb diskettes.

INSTALLING YOUR APPLICATION

Install the application you packaged in the problem above to a new folder. Once the application is installed, test it to be sure it is running correctly. Use Add/Remove Programs from the Control Panel to remove the application.

Level Two

AN INTERNET PACKAGE

Create an Internet package for one of the ActiveX controls created in Lesson 11 such as the LoanCalculator control. Enter the project's Properties Pages dialog box and give the project a name and description. Compile the control before starting the Wizard. Save the package in a new folder.

INSTALLING THE INTERNET PACKAGE

Install the Internet Package created in the fourth application above on your own system. Before you start the process, change the name of the OCX file created when the control was compiled. This should ensure the Internet Package is installed by the browser. When you are satisfied that the control installed correctly, delete all the files and folder created in the process of installation and packaging.

INSTALLING THE INTERNET PACKAGE ON THE INTERNET (OPTIONAL)

If you have access to the Internet and have a Web page, deploy the Internet Package to your Web site. Upload the files to the Web site using the upload utilities provided by your Internet Service Provider. Although the sample used in the text generated an 8mB CAB file, the ActiveX control in Lesson 11 creates far smaller CAB files. The Loan calculator control created in Step-by-Step 11.3 creates a CAB file that is about 14k. Since the control has no digital signature, you will have to lower the security standards quite a bit to persuade Internet Explorer to download the control.

When uploading files to a Web site, filenames must conform to Internet Standards. The extended filenames allowed in Windows will not work. If you have used filenames with spaces, go back, rename, and recompile the project with a different filename.

LESSON 14 PROGRAMMING AT WORK

SCANS

In this section, package the Music Collection project started in Lesson 4 and last updated in Lesson 13, for network distribution. As a large, complex application, it is good test of the Packaging and Deployment Wizard. Most of the file access issues were handled long ago.

1. Start Visual Basic. Open the **Music Collection** program you revised in Lesson 13. If you do not have a copy with the current revisions, use the Electronic Instructor CD. Move the entire Programming at Work folder from the Lesson 13 files on the Electronic Instructor CD to a spot on a drive where you have read and write privileges. Open the application. Run the application to confirm it works as expected. Test the Help system. Stop the program.

You may try to load the project directly from the CD. If you do, take the following steps. First, resave each of the form and code modules individually to the new folder. Once all the modules are saved, resave the project file. Second, copy the database, MusCol.mdb, and user file, MusListnrs.dat, to the new folder. Finally, move the Help file to the new folder. It is much easier to copy the entire folder from the CD to a new folder.

2. Right-click **Project1** in the Project Explorer. Change the Project Name to **MusicCollection**. Make sure to strip any path information from the Help file, leaving just the file name. You want the application to find the Help file in the same folder as the application. Change the Project Description to **The Music Collection Database program**. See Figure 14-30 to see the Project Properties dialog box with the changes. Open the Code window for frmMusic and if necessary add the ChDrive App.Path and ChDir App.Path statements to Form_Load.

3. Select **Add-Ins | Add-In Manager**. Double-click the **Package and Deployment Wizard**. The word "Loaded" should appear in the second column. Click **OK**.

4. Select **Add-Ins | Package and Deployment Wizard**. Once you make alterations, the Wizard prompts you to save the changes before the Packaging begins. See Figure 14-31.

5. Click **Yes** to save the project. Click the **Package** icon in the opening screen of the Wizard. The Wizard may prompt you to recompile the project. See Figure 14-32. Click **Yes** to recompile the project.

6. In the Package Type window select **Standard Setup Package**. Click **Next**.

7. The Package Folder dialog box prompts you for a destination folder. The path to the application is shown in the window. In the text box is the path to the folder that holds the application, but there is an additional level. The complete path shows an additional folder, the Package folder. Click **Next**. The Wizard asks if you want to create the Package folder. Click **Yes** to create the Package folder. If a dialog box about missing files appears, add them and click **OK**.

8. The Included Files dialog box shows the files included in the CAB file. Click **Add**. Add the datafile **MusCol.mdb** to the file list. Click **Add**. Add the datafile **MusListnrs.dat** to the file list. Click **Next**.

9. In the Cab Options dialog box, select **Single cab** and click **Next**.

10. In the Installation Title dialog box, enter **MusicCollection** (if necessary) in the Installation Title text box. Click **Next**.

FIGURE 14-30
The Project1 – Project Properties dialog box showing changes

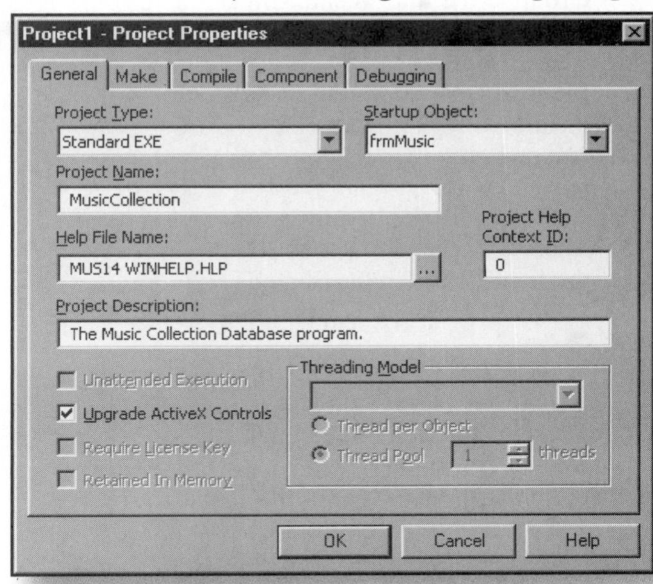

FIGURE 14-31
A message from the Wizard prompting you to save your project

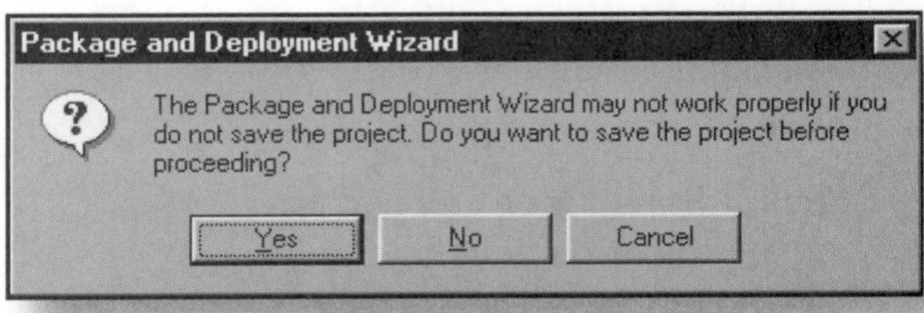

FIGURE 14-32
A message from the Wizard prompting you to recompile your project

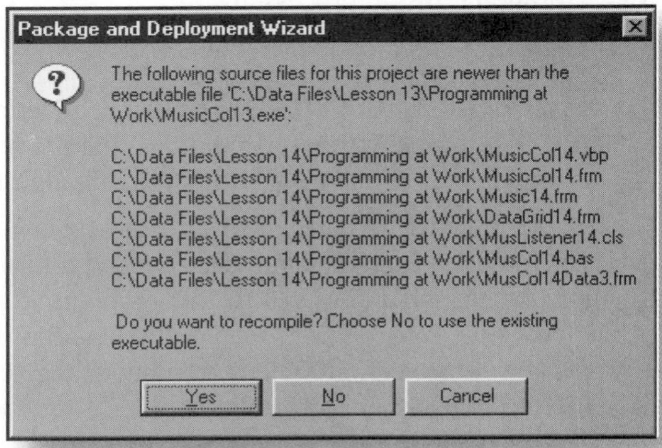

11. Figure 14-33 shows the addition of the MusicCollection Program Group to the Start menu. Click **Next**.

12. Figure 14-34 shows the install location of the various components of the application. Click **Next**.

13. There is no need to check any of the items listed in the Shared Files dialog box. Click **Next**.

14. In the Finished! dialog box, change the Script name to **MusicCollection14** and click **Finish**. If necessary, click **Yes** to overwrite the existing file.

15. Click **Close** to close the report window and then click **Close** again to close the Package and Deployment Wizard.

16. Exit Visual Basic. If you do not exit Visual Basic at this time, the installation will not work.

17. Close all open applications. Select **Start | Run** and navigate to the folder holding the CAB and Setup files. The CAB file is larger than 10 megabytes. Double-click **setup.exe** to start the installation process.

18. During the Install process always accept the defaults. When the setup is complete, click **Start | Programs | MusicCollection | MusicCollection** to run the program. Click **View** on the menu bar. Select a menu item without clicking the mouse and press **F1** to activate the item's Help topic, then close the Help. Continue running the program to test each form. Stop the program.

FIGURE 14-33
The Start Menu Items dialog box

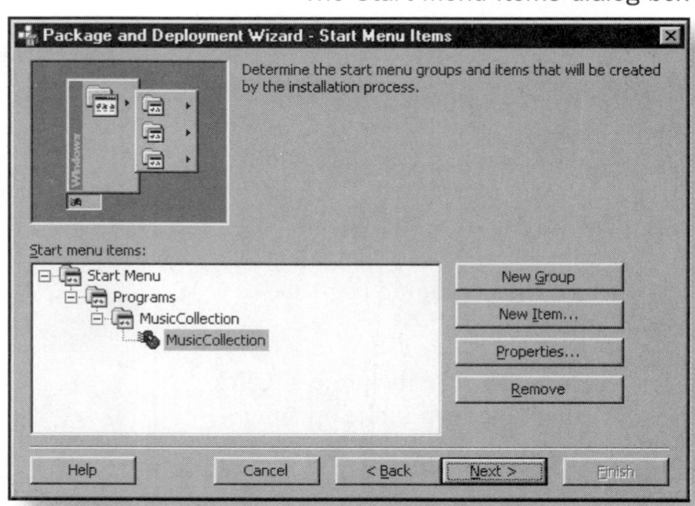

FIGURE 14-34
The Install Locations dialog box

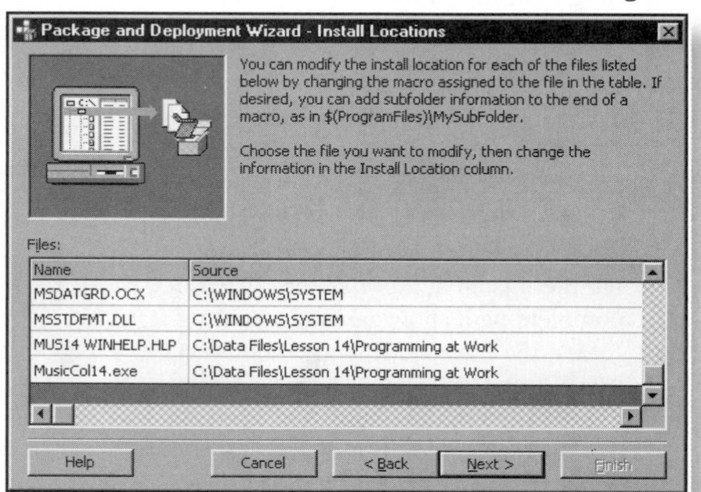

Sometimes it is good when something goes wrong. For instance, if you forget to add the database file, the program cannot find needed information. You can transfer a copy of the datafile to the directory, but that does not fix the problem. You have to rebuild the Package. Run the Wizard again. This time remember to include the datafile. Running the Wizard over and over again to fix errors makes you very proficient at running the program. With all that experience, you will not hesitate to package files using the Wizard.

ACTIVEX DOCUMENTS

OBJECTIVES

When you complete this lesson, you will be able to:

- Describe the differences between a Standard EXE project and an ActiveX document.
- Write applications as ActiveX documents.
- Package an ActiveX document for distribution.
- Use the PropertyBag object to store information.
- Use the ActiveX Document Migration Wizard to translate Standard EXE projects into ActiveX documents.

KEY TERMS

ActiveX Document
User Document
FTP
Initialize
Init Properties
ReadProperties
WriteProperties
AsyncReadComplete
AsyncRead
Property Bag
Property Changed
ActiveX Document Migration Wizard (ADM Wizard)
Hyperlink object
AsyncProp object

Your First ActiveX Document

The Internet is huge, and it is getting more pervasive every year. More people have email addresses. Many have Web sites. Some use the Internet to make long distance telephone calls. Others use it to listen to the radio or watch TV. The day is coming when household appliances will use the Internet to communicate.

With each software update, your desktop is more integrated with the Internet. Microsoft Word doubles as a browser. Your browser doubles as a text editor. Windows Explorer uses a browser interface. Most Microsoft products can write output files in HTML. The files are suitable for Web publishing.

If everything on the desktop is a browser, you should be able to write applications that run in browsers. That is exactly what an *ActiveX Document* is; it is an application that runs in a browser.

Writing an ActiveX Document is no more difficult than writing a Standard EXE. Instead of a form, your palette is a *User Document*. A User Document looks like a form without its frame. Without a frame, there is no place to display a menu bar. However, pop-up menus work well in a user Document and with a little persuasion, the container program will show a User Document's menu in its menu bar. The User Document does not have a Load or Activate event, but it does have an Initialize event that accomplishes the same purpose.

You normally do not use multiple forms with an ActiveX Document. An ActiveX Document is a Web page. Web pages do not have multiple forms, but a Web page can easily link to another page. To navigate from one user document to another, use a hyperlink object.

One of the biggest benefits of writing ActiveX Documents to create Web applications is the Visual Basic IDE, Integrated Design Environment. Debugging and trouble-shooting ActiveX Documents is as easy as fixing regular Visual Basic applications. You can set breakpoints, examine the values of variables, set watch expressions, and single-step through your code.

When you run the ActiveX Document, Internet Explorer automatically launches to execute your application. You test the application in a live browser environment. When you are done testing, use the Package and Deployment Wizard to prepare the application for Web or network uploading.

In this lesson, you explore ActiveX Documents. You look at writing simple applications, using the Package and Deployment Wizard to prepare the application for distribution, and use the ActiveX Document Migration Wizard to convert existing Standard EXE projects to ActiveX Documents.

In the first exercise, build a simple application to solve triangles. When the application is running, the user enters the three sides of a triangle. The program calculates and displays the area, and the angle measure of each of the three angles of the triangle. If the user enters three values that do not make a triangle, like 4, 5, and 10, an error event is raised.

Start by creating a class. Classes are a good way to encapsulate data, methods, and events. Call the Triangle class to do most of the work of the program. It uses three Private variables for the sides of the triangles and three more for the angles. Methods of the class calculate the area of the triangle and the measure of an angle. An error event alerts the calling program when invalid values are entered for the lengths of the sides.

STEP-BY-STEP 15.1

1. Start Visual Basic. Select **ActiveX Document Exe** and click **OK.** See Figure 15-1.

2. A blank work area surrounded by the normal Visual Basic work environment greets you. Double-click the **User Documents** folder in the Project Explorer. Double-click the **User Document** icon. The User Document Designer appears in the work area. Save the User Document as **TriangleSolver** and save the project as **Triangle Master**.

FIGURE 15-1
The New Project Window with ActiveX Document EXE selected

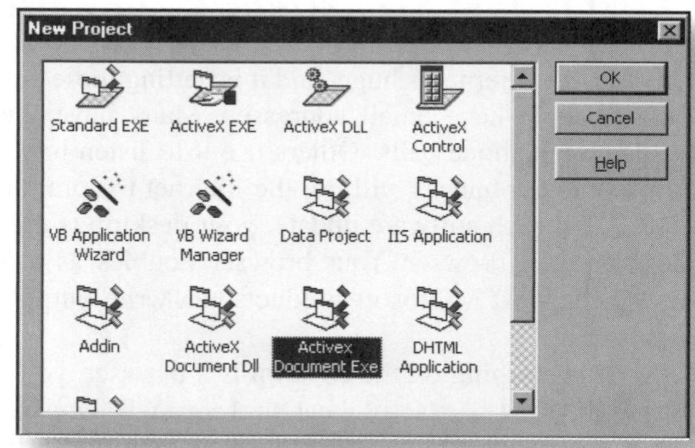

3. Click the **Name** property of the User Document in the Properties window and change the name to **TriangleSolver**.

4. Right-click **Project1** in the Project Explorer and select **Project1 Properties**. In the General tab, change the Project Name to **TriangleMaster**. Add the following line to the Project Description: **The TriangleMaster finds the area and angles of scalene triangles**. Click the **Make** tab and enter the name **TriangleMaster** in the Title box. Click **OK** to accept the changes

and close the Property Pages dialog box.

5. Before work begins on the user interface, create the Triangle class. Select **Project | Add Class Module**. Select the Class Module icon from the Add Class Module window shown in Figure 15-2. Click **Open**. Save the class as **Triangle.cls**.

6. Click the **Name** property in the Properties window and enter the name **clsTriangle**. In the General Declarations section of the class definition, enter the declarations for the Private variables representing the lengths of the sides and the measures of the angles of the triangle.

```
'Declare variables for lengths
'of sides and measures of angles
'of triangle
Option Explicit
Private a As Double
Private b As Double
Private c As Double
Private AngA As Double
Private AngB As Double
Private AngC As Double
```

Option Explicit sets the program environment to require variable declarations.

7. Following these lines in the General Declarations section, enter the line shown in **Code Step 7** to declare an event of clsTriangle: an event that fires in the application if the program detects an invalid triangle.

FIGURE 15-2
The Add Class Module with the Class Module icon selected

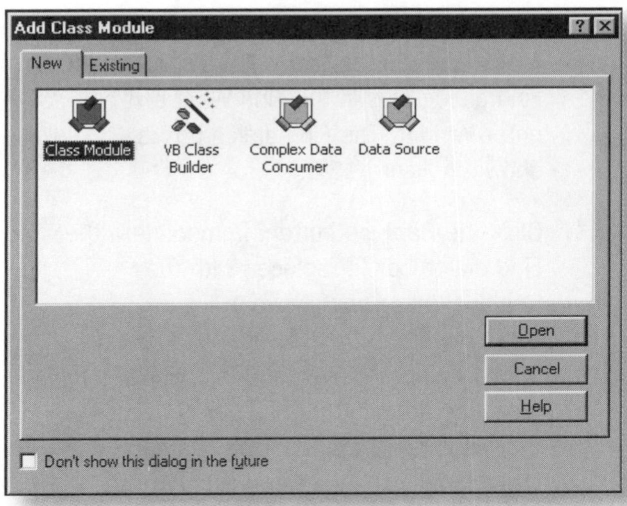

The last time you used code like this, (back in Lesson 8) you also passed the object that caused the error as a parameter back to the program. The program code filled the offending field with an "Error" entry. In this project, if the user enters bad data, the program displays a message but takes no corrective action with the triangle object itself. Thus, the object is not passed as a parameter.

8. From the menu bar, select **Tools | Add Procedure**. In the Type frame of the Add Procedure dialog box, click the **Property** option. In the Name text box, enter **SideA**. Click **OK** to close the dialog box. This creates the property procedures for SideA. Repeat the process for **SideB** and **SideC**.

9. In the **Get** procedure of **SideA**, enter the line: **SideA = a**. In the other **Get** procedures, enter the lines: **SideB = b** and **SideC = c**.

(continued on next page)

CODE STEP 7

```
Public Event BadEntry(ByVal sMessage As String)
```

10. To change Variant to Double in all the procedures, press **Ctrl + F**. This opens the Find dialog box. In the Find What text box, enter **Variant**. The Find dialog box is shown in Figure 15-3.

FIGURE 15-3
The Find dialog box showing the word Variant in the Find What text box

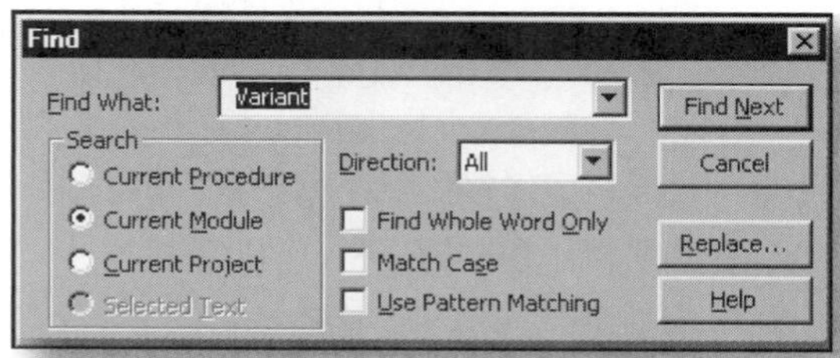

11. Click the **Replace** button. Immediately, the Find dialog box is replaced with the Replace dialog box shown in Figure 15-4. Enter **Double** in the Replace With text box. Click **Replace All**. Visual Basic displays a message showing the number of items that were replaced. Click **OK.** Replace **vNewValue** with **NewValue** (without the lowercase v) in each parameter list of the Let procedures. Click **OK** in the message box, then close the Replace dialog box.

FIGURE 15-4
The Replace dialog box showing the word Double in the Replace With text box

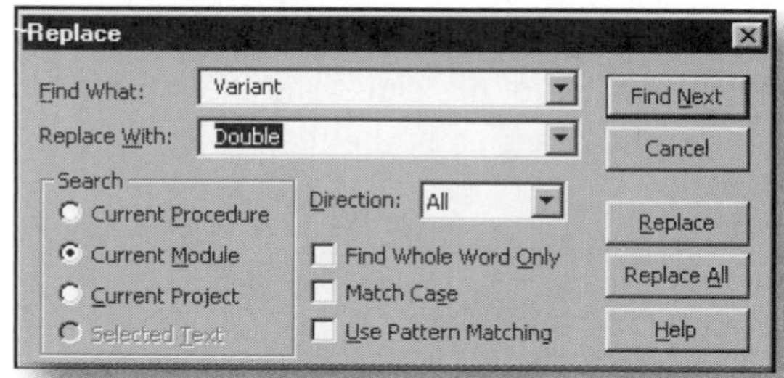

NOTE:

As an alternative to opening the Find dialog box and clicking Replace, press Ctrl + H to open the Replace dialog box directly.

12. In each **Let** procedure, enter a line like this: **a = Abs(NewValue)**. If the user enters a negative number, which is unlikely but possible, the program just changes the entered value to a positive value. No error event is raised.

13. An internal function checks the values entered by the user to see if they constitute a valid triangle. Select **Tools | Add Procedure** from the menu bar. In the Add Procedure dialog box, click **Function** in the Type frame, **Private** in the Scope frame, and enter **Valid** in the Name dialog box. Click **OK** to add the procedure. Add **As Boolean** following the parentheses after the function name. No parameters are passed to the function. The variables checked in the function are visible throughout the module. Valid is not a Public function. So there is no good reason to pass the lengths of the sides of the triangle as parameters to the function.

14. In **Private Function Valid( ) As Boolean** enter the comment and the line of code shown in **Code Step 14**.

This line is different and interesting. It implements the triangle inequality. The triangle inequality states the sum of the

CODE STEP 14

```
'Triangle inequality statement
Valid = a < b + c And b < a + c And c < a + b
```

lengths of any two sides of a triangle must be greater than the length of the third side. Each expression (for example a < b + c) tests a different combination of sides. When evaluated, the entire expression returns a True or False. Each of the three inequalities returns a Boolean value. The And operator joins the Boolean values together. If the triangle is valid, all three expressions are True. "True And True And True" results in True. Return that value as the value of the function. If even one of the expressions is False, the And statement is False. Return False as the value of the function. How would you rewrite the statement as an If Then statement?

15. You do not need to use the Tools | Add Procedure menu selections to start a new procedure. Just enter the function that is shown in **Code Step 15** into the space below the Valid function. Be sure to include both the first and last lines shown.

Call the function in code like this: assume t1 is a triangle object. The area of t1 is t1.Area( ). The function first checks to see if the lengths representing the sides form a valid triangle. If they are not, the RaiseEvent statement fires the BadEntry event of the triangle object in the main program. If the sides form a valid triangle, calculate the triangle's area with Hero's Formula. The variable name "Semi" stands for the semi-perimeter, which is half the perimeter of the triangle. In the formula below, *s* is the semi-perimeter. The formula to calculate the area is:

$$\sqrt{s(s-a)(s-b)(s-c)}$$

Hero's formula finds the area of any triangle as long as you know the lengths of the three sides.

16. Use another function to calculate the angles. To write a function that works for all three angles, you have to rearrange the sides in the equation used in the calculation. Compute the measure of the angle with the Law of Cosines. If given the three sides of a triangle, the law first finds the cosine of an angle. Then, from the cosine, find the measure of the angle. The code uses a few math tricks. First, there is no Arccosine function, a function to find the measure of an angle from the cosine of the angle. There is only an Arctangent function, named Atn( ). To use the Atn( ) function, convert the cosine calculated by the Law of Cosines into the equivalent tangent value. The Atn( ) function returns the measure of an angle with the given tangent, but the measure is expressed in radians. A line of code below converts the radian measure of the angle to degrees. Visual Basic does not include a constant

(continued on next page)

CODE STEP 15

```
Public Function Area() As Double
  If Not Valid() Then
    RaiseEvent BadEntry("Your entry is not a valid triangle.")
  Else
    'Calculate the triangle's area
    Dim Semi As Double
    Semi = 0.5 * (a + b + c)
    Area = Sqr(Semi * (Semi - a) * (Semi - b) * (Semi - c))
  End If
End Function
```

for Pi, but by using the expression 4 * Atn(1) you get a very close approximation. (Trig learners should figure out why this works). Enter the code shown in **Code Step 16**: be sure to include the first and last lines of the procedure (the last line may already be added when you press Enter at the end of the first line.) Click the **SaveProject** button on the toolbar.

Some programmers are reluctant to use the Variant type unless one of its special forms is needed: dates and times, for instance. Variables of the Variant type take up more memory than a specifically typed variable. Operations involving variables of the Variant type may take more time to execute than the equivalent operation involving variables declared with a specific type. However, the Variant type is closer to the original intent of the BASIC programming language in the sense that it relieves the user of worry about mixing variable types in expressions. Some would say that programmers ought to worry about stuff like that. It seems silly though, to generate an error when a program statement compares a character type with a one-character string. In this application, the operations are not repeated thousands of times in a loop, so time is not an issue. The variables do not occupy thousands of positions in an array, so space is not an issue.

CODE STEP 16

```
Public Function AngleA(AngleNo As Integer) As Double
  If Not Valid() Then
    RaiseEvent BadEntry("Your entry is not a valid triangle.")
  Else
    Dim AngleInRadians As Double
    Dim x As Double, y As Double
    Dim r, s, t   'Use the Variant type
    'The user sends a parameter telling which angle to calculate.
    Select Case AngleNo    'short for: angle number
      Case 1
        r = a: s = b: t = c   'shuffling the sides
      Case 2
        r = b: s = a: t = c   'to generate each of the
      Case 3
        r = c: s = a: t = b   'three angles
    End Select
    x = (s * s + t * t - r * r) / (2 * s * t)
    If x <> 0 Then
      y = Atn(Sqr(1 - x * x) / x)
      If y < 0 Then y = y + 4 * Atn(1) 'If the angle is negative
      AngleA = y * 180 / (Atn(1) * 4)  'convert to degrees.
    Else     'If the cosine is 0, then the angle is 90 degrees.
      AngleA = 90
    End If
  End If
End Function
```

The expression, Sqr(1 - x * x) / x, in the Atn( ) function converts the cosine, x, to the equivalent tangent. (Trig learners should figure out why.)

17. Double-click **TriangleSolver** in the Project Explorer to view the User Document. The User Document provides the interface for the user. The user enters three values for the lengths of the sides of the triangle. The code then calculates the area of the triangle and the three angles of the triangle. Once calculated, the values are displayed in labels on the User Document.

18. Use the Line tool in the toolbox to draw a triangle on the User Document. One way to do it is to double-click the Line tool to put a line segment on the User Document. Use the mouse to drag the handles of the line segment into position.

19. Draw three text boxes into positions adjacent to the three sides of the triangle. Name the text boxes, **txtSideA**, **txtSideB**, and **txtSideC**. Clear the Text property of each text box. For the sake of consistency, you may want to prepare a single text box then copy and paste it twice. This creates three identical text boxes. If you do create the text boxes this way, do not create a control array.

20. Put a label over each text box. Change the captions of the labels to **Side a**, **Side b**, and **Side c**. It is customary to name the sides of a triangle with lowercase characters and the vertex points (the corners) with uppercase characters. The names of the labels do not matter.

21. Position a label near each vertex of the triangle. Name the labels, **lblAngleA**, **lblAngleB**, and **lblAngleC**. Put a label in the center of the triangle. Name the label **lblArea**. Change the captions of the labels to **Angle A**, **Angle B**, **Angle C**, and **Area**. Change the BorderStyle property of each of the labels to **1-Fixed Single** by double-clicking the Border Style property. Position the labels that name the vertices so that Angle A is opposite the Side a text box. Check Figure 15-5 to confirm the placement of the labels and text boxes.

22. Put two command buttons on the User Document. Change the names of the command buttons to **cmdCalculate** and **cmdClear**. Change the captions of the buttons to **Calculate** and **Clear**. See Figure 15-5 to view the complete User Document.

23. Right-click the body of the User Document and select **View Code** in the pop-up menu. In the General Declarations section enter the following line;

```
Dim WithEvents t1 As clsTriangle
```

To declare an object that responds to events, you must declare the variable in the General Declarations section of the Code window. You cannot use the WithEvents keyword in a declaration inside an event

(continued on next page)

FIGURE 15-5
The complete User Document Designer showing the placement of controls

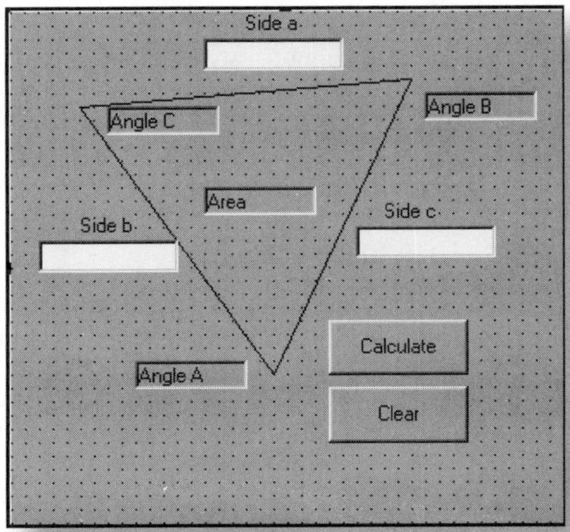

procedure. This statement declares a variable t1 as a clsTriangle type.

24. Enter the code shown in **Code Step 24** in **cmdCalculate_Click**.

To set an object equal to another object or, as in the code above, to create a new clsTriangle object and set it equal to the variable t1, precede the assignment statement with the keyword Set.

If there is an error converting the contents of a text box, the error handler code is called. Once the lengths of the sides have been assigned to the triangle object, calculate the area of the object by calling the Area method of the object. The value returned by the method is assigned to lblArea. The Angle( ) method is called to calculate each of the angles. The parameter sent to the Angle method determines the angle calculated. The method returns the degree measure of a particular angle. That value is assigned to the appropriate label.

25. Save the program. There is another line or two of code to enter, but leave the Code window open for now and run the program by pressing **F5**. The TriangleMaster – Project Properties dialog appears. It appears so you can tell the program how to run the new application. Compare your settings with the ones shown in Figure 15-6. If TriangleSolver does not appear in the Start Component combo box, check to be sure that you changed the name of the User Document to TriangleSolver in the Properties window. Click **OK** to run the browser. Internet Explorer launches with your application. Enter **3**, **4**, and **5** for the lengths of the sides of the triangle. Click **Calculate**. The area of the triangle appears in the center and the measures of the angles appear at the corners. A 3, 4, 5 triangle is a right triangle, so it is easy to calculate the area in your head: it is one half the product of 3 and 4: 6. Test the program for several more triangles. Close the browser to exit the program and click the **End** button to stop the program in Visual Basic.

CODE STEP 24

```
Set t1 = New clsTriangle
   'Declare an object.
   On Error GoTo errorhandler
   With t1
      .SideA = CDbl(txtSideA)   'Read the text boxes.
      .SideB = CDbl(txtSideB)
      .SideC = CDbl(txtSideC)
      lblArea = t1.Area         'Calculate the area.
      lblAngleA = .AngleA(1)   'Calculate each of the angles.
      lblAngleB = .AngleA(2)
      lblAngleC = .AngleA(3)
  End With
  Exit Sub
errorhandler:
   MsgBox "Illegal Entry"
```

26. In the **Private Sub t1_BadEntry(ByVal sMessage As String)** procedure, enter the following line of code:

```
MsgBox sMessage
```

27. Remember Lesson 9? Lesson 9 dealt with collections. To clear the labels and text boxes on the User Document, use the Controls collection. Enter the code shown in **Code Step 27** in **cmdClear_Click**.

    Count the number of lines. Six lines of code used to clear six text boxes and labels. You could write six assignment statements, but using the Controls collection is more interesting.

28. Save and run the program. Enter the lengths **5**, **6**, and **12**. Click **Calculate**. An error message alerts you to the illegal triangle. You see the error message several times. The error is generated each time the Area or the AngleA functions are called. As Public functions available for the programmer to use together or separately, each must check the triangle and raise the error event.

29. Close the browser to stop the program. Click the **End** button to stop the program in Visual Basic. Leave the project open.

CODE STEP 27

```
'Clear the labels and text boxes
Dim CtrlObj As Control
For Each CtrlObj In Controls
    If TypeOf CtrlObj Is TextBox Or _
       TypeOf CtrlObj Is Label Then
         CtrlObj = ""
    End If
Next CtrlObj
```

FIGURE 15-6
The Project Properties window

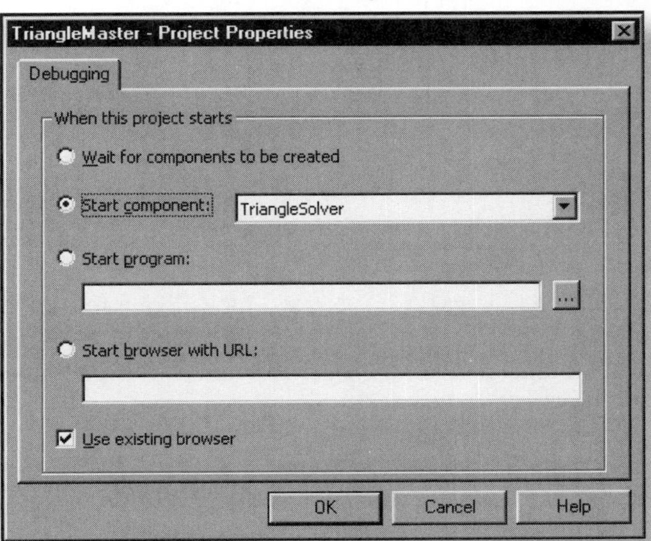

Have you ever opened a Visual Basic form file in Notepad? A form file is a text file! It contains information about each control and the code from each event procedure. When you save the User Document, it is saved with a .dob extension. Open this file in Notepad and you find it too is a text file. Graphic elements of a Standard form (like bitmaps) are stored in a file with an extension of .frx. Graphic elements of a User Document are stored in a file with an extension of .dox. The .dob file and the .dox file together completely define a User Document. When compiled, the User Document is saved as a .vbd file. In addition, an ActiveX .dll or ActiveX .exe accompanies the .vbd file.

As you know from the last lesson, the application is not ready for distribution. In the next exercise, you prepare the ActiveX Document for Web distribution. In this Step-by-Step exercise, you practiced creating a class. As you get more comfortable with creating classes, you will find yourself using them for everything.

Quick Check 15.a

1. An __________________ is an application that runs in a browser.
2. The __________________ looks like a form without its frame.
3. Unlike a form, the User Document Designer does not have a __________________ event.
4. Hero's formula finds the __________________ of any triangle as long as you know the lengths of the three sides.
5. To find an angle of a triangle given its sides you must use the __________________ function.
6. To declare an object and enable events defined for the object, use the keyword __________________ in the object's Dim statement in the General Declarations section.

Putting the Application on the Web

The next step is to publish the application. First, use the *Package and Deployment Wizard (PDWizard)* to prepare the application for distribution. Then upload the package to a Web site and test it.

STEP-BY-STEP 15.2

1. If necessary start Visual Basic and open the **TriangleMaster** project.
2. Select **Add-Ins | Add-In Manager**. Double-click the **Package and Deployment Wizard** in the Add-In Manager. The word "Loaded" must appear in the second column of the list box. Click **OK**.
3. Compile the project. Select **File | Make TriangleMaster**. Navigate to the drive where you want to store the file. Delete any path in the File name box and use only the File name. If you used any special characters or spaces in the name, remove them now. When the filename in the Make Project dialog box is correct, click **OK**.
4. Select **Add-Ins | Package and Deployment Wizard**. Before the PDWizard runs, the error message shown in Figure 15-7 may appear. The message appears even if you saved the project moments before. Click **Yes**, just to be safe.
5. Confirm that the name of the TriangleMaster project is displayed in the Active project text box at the top of the

opening screen of the PDWizard. Click the **Package** icon.

FIGURE 15-7
The Save the Project message from the Package and Deployment Wizard

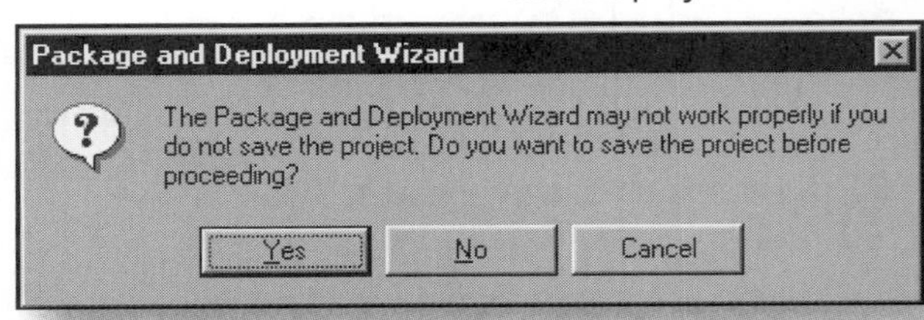

6. Figure 15-8 shows the Compile the Project error message. (You may see a message to recompile instead of the message to compile). This shows because the project files are now newer than the compiled version you made moments ago. Click **Compile** (or click **Yes** if prompted to recompile).

FIGURE 15-8
The Compile the Project message from the Package and Deployment Wizard

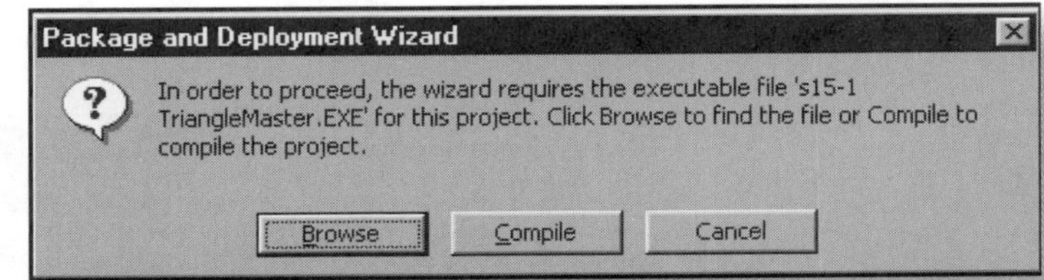

7. Again the Save the Project message may appear. Click **Yes**. Finally, the Package Type dialog box of the PDWizard appears. Select **Internet Package** in the Package Type list box. Click **Next** to advance to the next screen.

FIGURE 15-9
The Package Folder dialog box

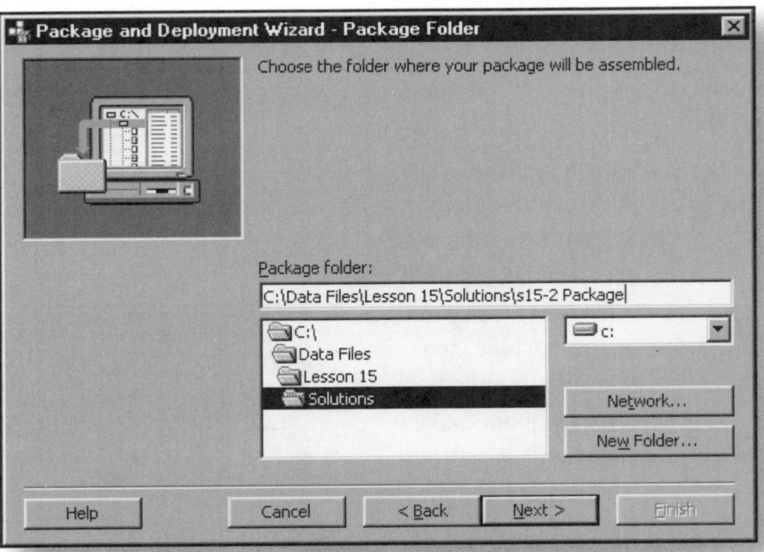

8. The Package Folder screen of the PDWizard prompts you to create a folder named Package. It is a good idea to let the PDWizard create a new folder for the Internet Package. Figure 15-9 shows the Package Folder dialog box. Click the **New Folder** button if necessary to change the path and click **OK**. Click **Next**.

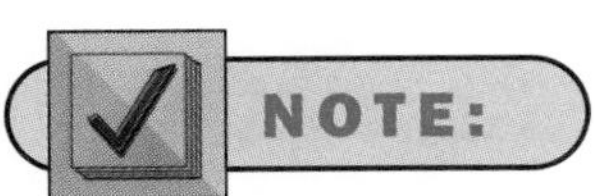

The figure shows the same directory name as that used on the Electronic Instructor CD. Most files are named with a convention that is a combination of the lesson number, the exercise number, and the real name of the application. Unfortunately, the file names, while perfectly good file names in the Windows Operating System, do not work on the Internet. Alter the Package name to fit the Internet style of naming: no spaces, no special characters.

(continued on next page)

9. Figure 15-10 shows the "Do you want to create it?" message box. Click **Yes**.

FIGURE 15-10
The Do you want to create it? Message box

10. A second message appears. This message asks whether the application will be used as a Remote Automation (RA) server. Click **No**.

11. Figure 15-11 shows the first of three error messages concerning missing DLLs. Click **OK** to proceed without the missing files.

FIGURE 15-11
The Missing Files message box

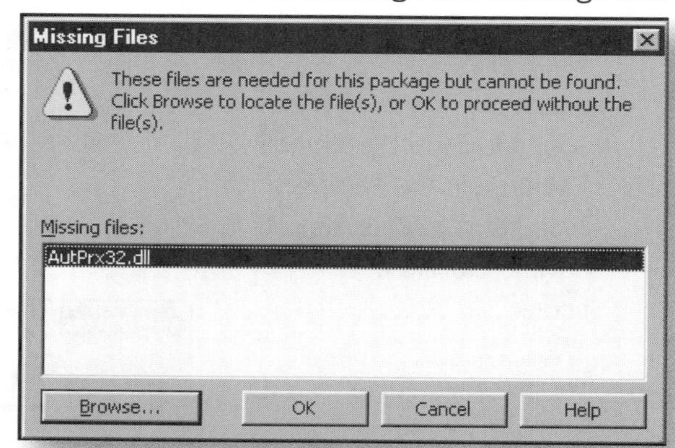

12. The Included Files dialog box shown in Figure 15-12 is more reassuring. It shows the files that are included in the Internet package. Click **Next**.

13. The File Source dialog lets you set the source of the files included in the Internet Package. You want to minimize the size of the CAB file, since that is what goes into the Web site. The TriangleMaster application is included in the CAB file, but the VB6 Runtime and Automation file is downloaded as needed from the Microsoft Web site. If the file is already present on the target machine, the file is not downloaded. Click **Next** without making any changes.

FIGURE 15-12
The Included Files dialog box

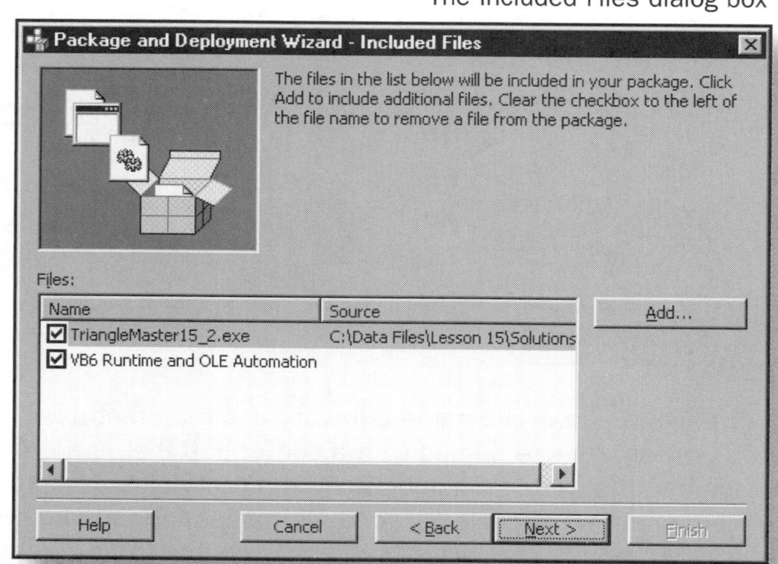

14. The Safety Settings dialog box lists the components of the application. There are two: the class module that defines the triangle class and the TriangleSolver application itself. It is likely that no browser will download the application unless it is

marked safe. The document is safe in that it does not collect information from the user and it does not write new files to the local drive. Select the **Components** column by clicking the column heading. The TriangleSolver component is selected. Click the **Safe for Scripting** column. Click the current entry (**No**). The list arrow appears. Select **Yes** from the list. Click **Safe for Initialization**. Click **No** then click the list arrow. Select **Yes**. Repeat the process for the other component. See Figure 15-13. Click **Next**.

It was not possible to select the first component in the test program, clsTriangle, but it was possible to change the Safety settings.

15. In the Finished! dialog box, change the Script name to **TriangleMaster**. Click **Finish**. Click **Close** to discard the report. Leave the PDWizard open.

What happens next depends on whether you have a Web site or not and what kind of access you have to the Web site. Before uploading the Package to a Web site, look at the package created by the PDWizard.

16. Right-click the Windows **Start** button and select **Explore** to open Windows Explorer. Navigate to the Package directory created by the PDWizard. There are three files in the directory:

How did it go? Did the PDWizard create the CAB file? If something goes wrong, it is easy to back up and start again. Sometimes errors can be corrected by clicking the Back button and returning to an earlier dialog box. Sometimes you need to cancel the whole process and start over. The next time through everything goes a lot more quickly. You may need to open Windows Explorer and delete the folder created by the Wizard. You may need to go back and rename your project. Starting over is not a problem.

TriangleMaster.CAB, TriangleMaster.HTM, and TriangleSolver.VBD. A .VBD file is a compiled ActiveX Document file. It is equivalent to an EXE file. These three files must be saved on the Web site to run the application. A Support folder is also created with files necessary to run the application. Close Windows Explorer.

(continued on next page)

FIGURE 15-13
The Safety Settings dialog box

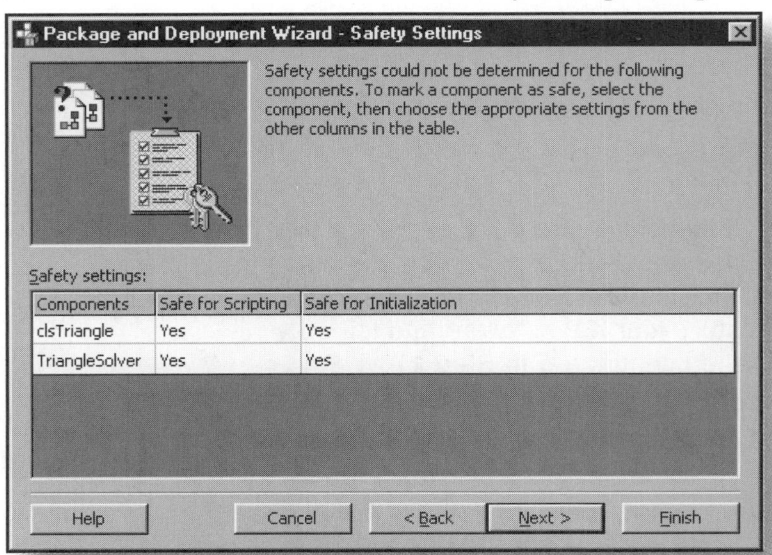

In the last lesson, you packaged an ActiveX control for the Internet. The packaging process also created an HTML file. That file called the ActiveX control in an Object tag using the control's GUID, Global Unique Identifier. The HTML file created for the ActiveX Document is different. It calls the compiled ActiveX Document, the file with the .VBD extension.

Herein lies a difficulty. To post these three files to a Web site in GeoCities, you must use their File Manager upload command. Unfortunately, the GeoCities File Manager will not upload a file with a .VBD extension. If you upload the file with an .HTM extension, the file does not work because the browser does not know how to execute the file: it tries to execute it as an HTML file. The GeoCities File Manager does not allow a name change to the file that changes the extension to .VBD. The program does not run from a GeoCities Web site. However, follow the steps below to see how to post the file to a different Internet Web site.

If launching Internet Explorer does not automatically log you onto your Internet Service Provider (ISP), start your ISP software and log on, then continue with Step 17.

17. Return to Visual Basic. In the steps above, you left the PDWizard open. If it is closed, open it by selecting **Add-Ins | Package and Deployment Wizard**. (If Visual Basic was closed, run the Add-Ins Manager to add the Package and Deployment Wizard to the project first.)

18. Select the **Deploy** icon by clicking the icon with the mouse. If you see a Deployment Script dialog box, leave the Deployment Script empty and click **Next**.

19. The Package to Deploy dialog box lets you choose a package to deploy. The TriangleMaster project is listed in the Package to Deploy text box. Click **Next**.

20. Figure 15-14 shows the Deployment Method dialog box. Select **Web Publishing** as shown in the figure. Click **Next**.

FIGURE 15-14
The Deployment Method dialog box showing the select of Web Publishing

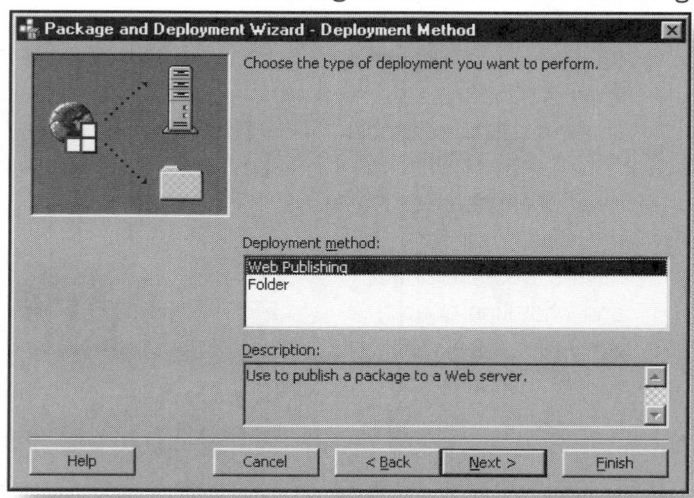

21. The Items to Deploy dialog box lists the components of the Internet package to upload to the Web. To remove an item, click its check box. In this case, confirm that all three files are checked and click **Next**. See Figure 15-15.

22. The Additional Items to Deploy dialog box gives you the opportunity to add files to the list of files to deploy. You could add a Help file or an additional datafile that the PDWizard did not detect as a dependency. Click **Next**.

FIGURE 15-15
The Deploy dialog box showing the three files of the Package to deploy

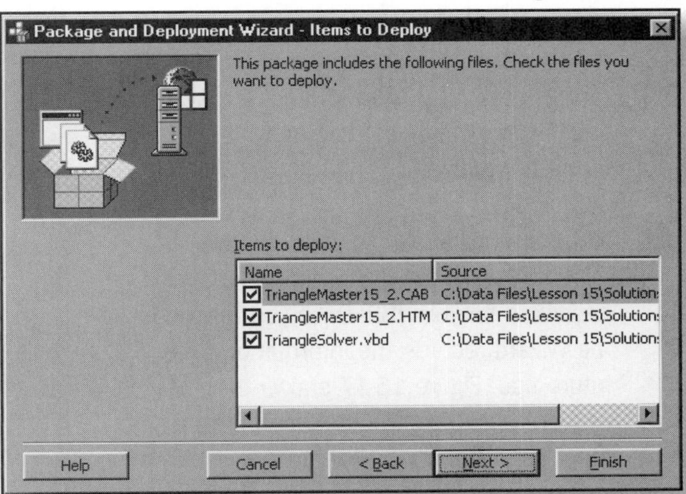

23. If you are a member of an Internet Service Provider (ISP), you may already have a Web site. If you have no Web site, check the simple steps on the ISP's Web site on how to make one if you are a member. To upload files to your Web site, the instructions may say to run your *FTP* program. FTP stands for file transfer protocol. You may not have an FTP program: that is OK because the Deployment Wizard acts as an FTP agent.

FIGURE 15-16
The Web Publishing Site dialog box showing the URL for a web site

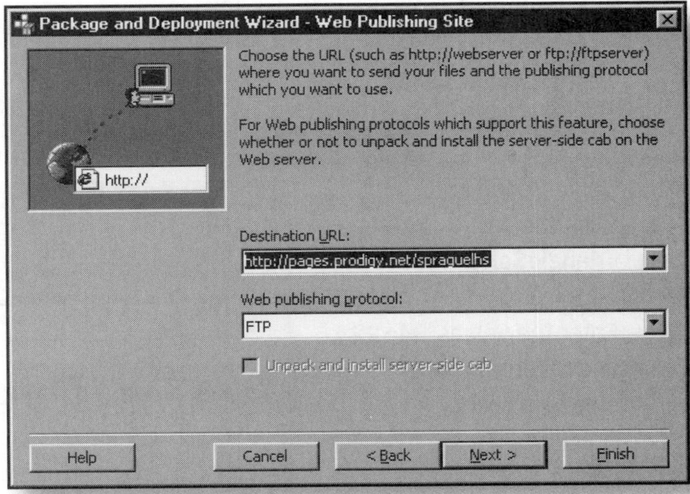

24. The Web Publishing Site dialog box asks you to supply the Web location of the site to which you want to upload the Package. Figure 15-16 shows the author's URL as the destination. Put the URL of your own Web site in the Destination URL text box. Change the Web publishing protocol to **FTP**. Click **Next**. This dialog box will look the same (except for the URL) no matter who provides space for your Web site.

A message appears that the URL and protocol can be saved in the registry. Click **No** unless your instructor gives you permission to save this information. If you click **No**, you must enter the URL and protocol each time you upload a package.

25. In the Finished! dialog box, enter the name **TriangleMasterWeb1** in the Script name text box. If you publish your application on more than one Web site, you want to save the information for each upload in a different script. Click **Finish**.

(continued on next page)

26. If your connection to the Web is active, the PDWizard can deploy the files without further delay. If you are offline, the system seeks to connect you. Log on to the Web in the normal way.

27. If you are not already signed on, the PDWizard asks for your login name and password for your ISP. Once you respond, the Wizard records the information for future use. Figure 15-17 shows the Deployment Report. Click **Close** for the report and close the Wizard.

28. Launch Internet Explorer to test the new Web page. Type your URL in the Address combo box and press **Enter**. Figure 15-18 shows the index for the URL used in the example. Click **TriangleMaster.HTM**. The HTM file contains a link to the .VBD (Visual Basic Document) file. Click the link, **TriangleSolver.vbd**.

29. Enter the values **34**, **22**, and **27** for the three sides and click **Calculate**. Figure 15-19 shows the running application. Click **Clear**. Close the Internet Explorer browser and close your Internet connection. Leave Visual Basic open.

FIGURE 15-17
The Deployment Report showing the transfer of files from your local drive to your web URL

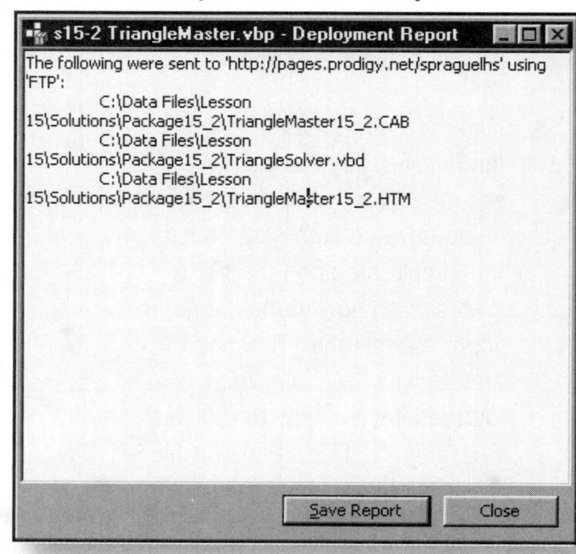

FIGURE 15-18
The Index for http://pages.prodigy.net/spraguelhs showing the files uploaded from the Package and Deployment Wizard

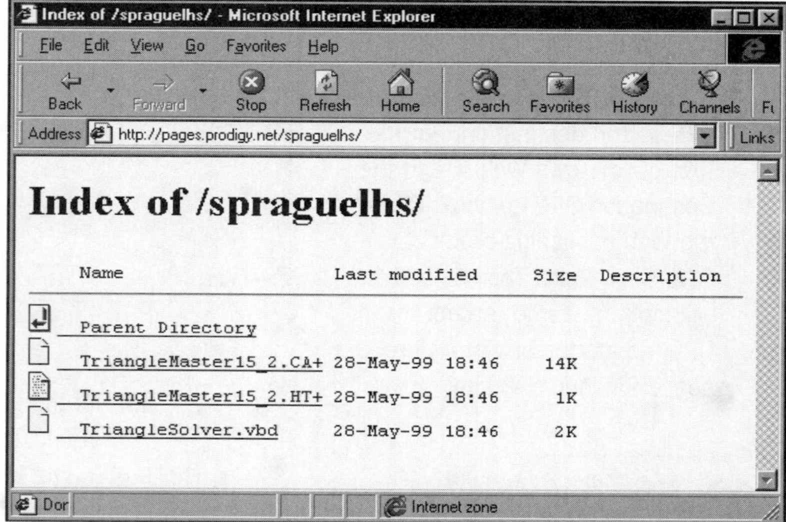

Do not remove the Package until the end of the lesson."

FIGURE 15-19
The TriangleMaster application

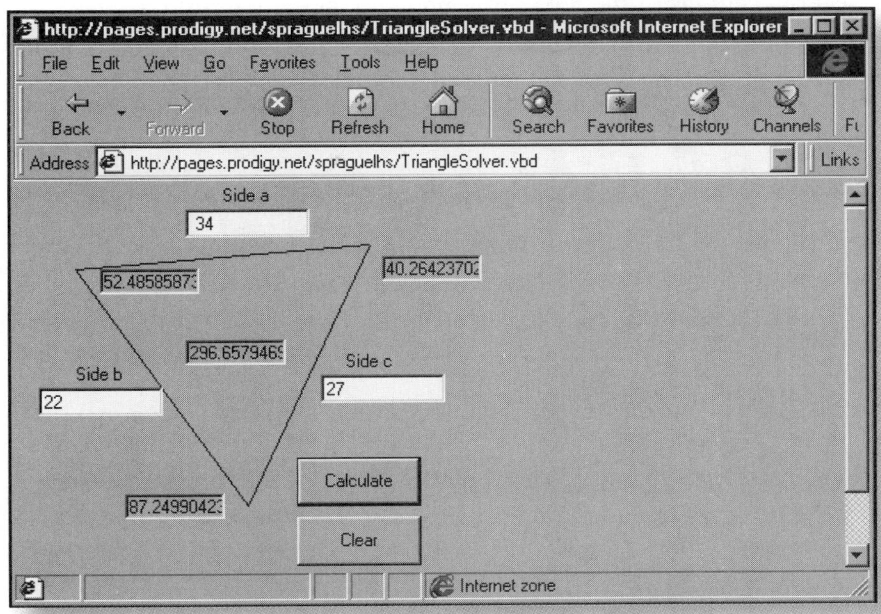

The preceding operation was deceptively easy. Running the application on your own system is always easier than running it on another system. Your system already has all the support files installed. To run this on a different system requires the following.

- Lower the browser's security. In the Internet Explorer browser select **View | Internet Options** and click the **Security** tab to view the security settings.
- For each zone listed in the Zone combo box, select Low security. Without these settings, ActiveX controls and documents may not be loaded and run by the browser. With a higher setting, your browser may offer to download the .VBD file or ask in what application you want the file opened. If that happens, you are on the wrong track. Change the security settings and reload the page. Even with security lowered, you are likely to get an error message like the one shown in Figure 15-20.
- You may have to restart the browser for the new security settings to take effect.
- Once the security issues are resolved, the browser will install the TriangleMaster application. This requires downloading files from the Microsoft Web site and installing them on your system.

FIGURE 15-20
The Security Warning message

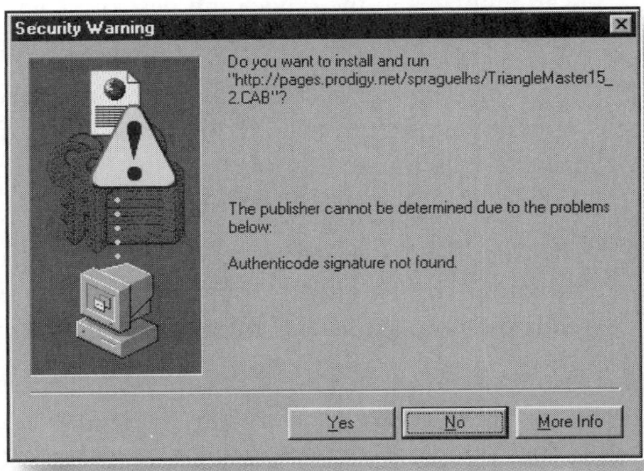

- When the installation is complete, you are instructed to restart the system.
- Reset the Security settings of the browser to protect your system from ActiveX viruses.

Installation is not as smooth as it could be, especially at the browser end of things. This is the future, though: applications written for and delivered through the Web.

Quick Check 15.b

1. Before the Package and Deployment Wizard can package an application for Internet distribution, the application must be ________________.
2. Internet file names should have no ________________ and no ________________.
3. No browser will download an ActiveX Document unless it is marked as ______________.
4. If the Package and Deployment Wizard reports an error or the Internet Package is not built correctly, it is easy to ________________.
5. A ________________ file is a compiled ActiveX Document file. It is equivalent to an EXE file.
6. FTP stands for ________________.

Refining Your Project

Before you can refine your project, you need to understand the differences between an ActiveX Document and the form used in a Standard EXE. A Standard EXE is a stand-alone program. An ActiveX Document always runs in a container. This difference is reflected in the events to which each responds. The User Document does not support the following familiar events of a form: Activate, Deactivate, Load and Unload. The User Document does support the following additional events.

- The *Initialize event* occurs whenever an instance of the User Document is created. Notice the use of the "object" language. Think of the User Document as an object that is created when a user navigates to the object and destroyed when the user leaves the object. Code in the Initialize event is always the first code to execute when the User Document is created.
- The *InitProperties event* occurs when an instance of the User Document is first created. If property values are saved in the PropertyBag for future use, the InitProperties event does not execute with the next instance of the User Document. If properties are saved in the PropertyBag, the ReadProperties event occurs instead.
- The *ReadProperties* event occurs when an instance of the User Document is created and properties from a previous run have been stored. Use this event to execute code that actually reads the property values from the PropertyBag.
- The *WriteProperties* event occurs when the User Document is terminated by the container application. If any property has changed, the WriteProperties event fires. This is not a method, it does not write properties to the PropertyBag for you. You supply the code in this event to save the properties in the PropertyBag. More on this later in the lesson.

- The Terminate event fires as the User Document is terminated. The User Document terminates in Internet Explorer 4 and 5 as soon as the user navigates to another page. Use this event to clean up all outstanding global object references. Set objects to Nothing to free up memory. Global object references are used by User Documents to communicate with each other.
- The Show event occurs whenever the user navigates to the User Document. Use this event to check for messages from other documents in global object references. The Show event occurs after the User Document is established in its container.
- The Hide event occurs whenever the user navigates from the User Document to another document. It also fires just before a Terminate event.
- The EnterFocus event occurs when the User Document receives focus. Receiving and losing focus occurs when more than one window of the container application is open. Focus can shift back and forth between windows. Code in the focus events executes when there is a change.
- The ExitFocus event occurs when the User Document loses focus.
- The *AsyncReadComplete* event occurs when an asynchronous read request is complete. Asynchronous activities occur at the same time. A Web page can send a request to download an image while still responding to events generated at the page itself. The request to download a file is made using the Document's *AsyncRead method*. When the image download is complete, the AsyncReadComplete event fires.

When a User Document with no saved properties is instantiated, the following events fire: Initialize, InitProperties, Show, and EnterFocus. If properties have been saved, the following events fire: Initialize, ReadProperties, Show, and EnterFocus.

In the following Step-by-Step exercise, add features to the TriangleMaster project developed in the first exercise.

STEP-BY-STEP 15.3a

1. If necessary start Visual Basic and open **TriangleMaster ActiveX Document**.

2. Start the modifications by adding an About form to the project. At the same time, add a menu to call the form. Select **Project | Add Form**. Click the **About Dialog** icon in the Add Form window. See Figure 15-21. Click **Open**.

3. The default About Dialog form is shown in Figure 15-22. Click the label with the caption **Application Title** on the form. Enter a new title **TriangleMaster** in the Caption property of lblTitle. Click the label with the name lblDescription and caption App Description. In the Caption property of the label enter the following: **The TriangleMaster application solves a triangle given the lengths of the three sides**. Change the caption of lblDisclaimer, (with the caption Warning) to **All angle measures are reported in degrees**. Leave the default name of the form, frmAbout, unchanged.

4. In the Project Explorer, click the icon for the TriangleSolver document. Click the **View Object** icon in the Project Explorer. The User Document Designer of the TriangleMaster project appears in the work area. Click the icon for the **Menu Editor** on the toolbar. Enter the menu entries shown in the table on the following page to add an item to the User Document's menu.

(continued on next page)

The most important property is the NegotiatePosition property. If this is not set to a non-zero value, the menu is not added to the container's menu bar.

5. Click **OK** to close the Menu Editor. Right-click the body of the User Document Designer and select **View Code** from the pop-up menu. In **mnuAbout_Click** enter the following line of code:

```
frmAbout.Show vbModal
```

A modal form cannot be sidestepped or dismissed by the user without a proper response. For the About form, the proper response may be a click on the OK button, but until that is done, no other action can occur.

6. In **UserDocument_Initialize** enter the following line: **App.Title = "TriangleMaster"**. Click the **SaveProject** button on the toolbar. Save the About form with the suggested name.

7. Click the **Start** button on the toolbar to run the program. Internet Explorer launches and displays the TriangleMaster application. Select **Help** in the browser's menu bar. The last entry in the menu is TriangleSolver Help. Select this item. A submenu appears with the item About TriangleMaster. Select this item. The About form in Figure 15-23 appears.

FIGURE 15-21
The Add Form window showing the selection of the About Dialog form

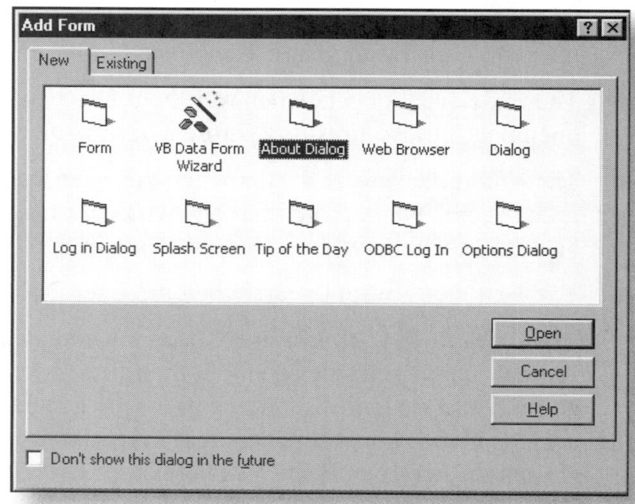

FIGURE 15-22
The About Dialog form shown before change

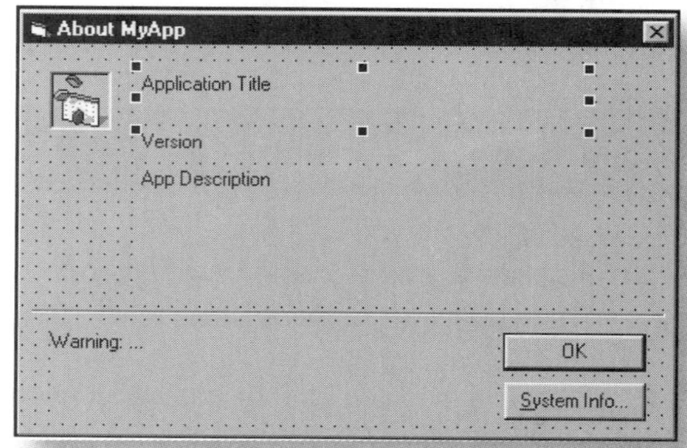

8. Click **System Info** to look at Microsoft System Information. Do not make any changes. Select **File | Exit** to close the

MENU ENTRIES

CAPTION	NAME	NEGOTIATEPOSITION
&Help	mnuHelp	3-Right
....About TriangleMaster	mnuAbout	0-None

System Information dialog box. Click **OK** to close the About box. Close the browser. Stop the program. Save all project files. Leave the project open.

FIGURE 15-23
The About Form of the TriangleMaster application

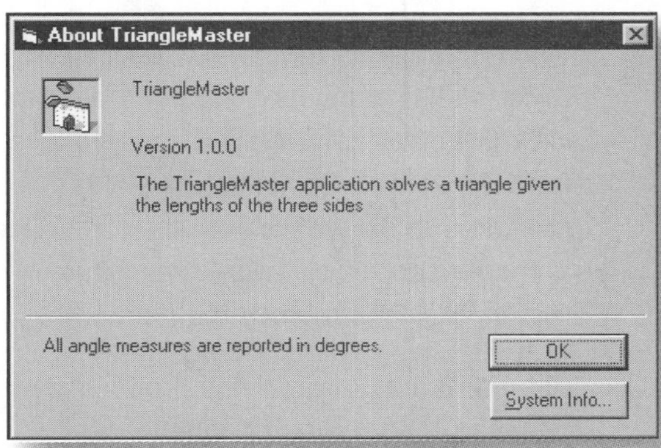

When the user leaves TriangleMaster, all data is lost. Save information from run to run using the *PropertyBag* object. Use the *PropertyChanged method* to signal the container application when the value of a property changes. When the application is shutting down, because either the user is navigating to another Web page or the container is closing, code in the PropertyBag's WriteProperties method writes the values of changed properties to the PropertyBag. When the application starts or when a user navigates to the document, use the PropertyBag's ReadProperties method to read property values from the PropertyBag and initialize the properties of the ActiveX Document.

STEP-BY-STEP 15.3b

1. If necessary, start Visual Basic and open **TriangleMaster**. Click **TriangleSolver** in the Project Explorer. Click the **View Code** button to open the Code window of the User Document.

2. Use the Object list box at the top of the code window to select **txtSideA**. If necessary use the Procedure list box to select the **Change** event. Enter the following code in **txtSideA_Change:**

   ```
   PropertyChanged "txtSideA"
   ```

   Put similar lines of code in **txtSideB_Change** and **txtSideC_Change**.

3. Select **UserDocument** in the Object list box. Select the **WriteProperties** event procedure of the User Document. The PropBag parameter of the event procedure exposes the PropertyBag. Enter the code shown in **Code Step 3** in **Private Sub UserDocument_WriteProperties(PropBag As PropertyBag)** to save the values of the lengths of the three sides.

   The three parameters of the WriteProperty event are the name of the property, a string, the value of the property (read directly from the text box) and an optional default value for the property.

4. Using the Procedure list box, select the **ReadProperties** event procedure of the User Document. Enter the code shown in **Code Step 4** in **Private Sub UserDocument_ReadProperties(PropBag As PropertyBag)**.

5. Save and run the project. Enter the values **33**, **49**, and **55**, for the lengths of the three sides of the triangle. Click the **Calculate** button.

6. The filename listed in the Address combo box at the top of the browser is the name of the temporary .VBD file created when

(continued on next page)

Visual Basic runs the ActiveX Document. Click the list arrow for the combo box and click any other item. As you navigate away from the ActiveX Document, you are prompted to save data from the form. This is the PropertyBag at work. See Figure 15-24. Click **Yes** to save the data.

7. Use the **Back** button of the browser to return to TriangleMaster. When TriangleMaster restarts, it executes the UserDocument's ReadProperties event. This event reads the values of the properties and initializes the text box. Close the browser and stop the program.

8. To confirm that the ReadProperties event is really working, change its code to shuffle the values of the text boxes. Change the code in **Private Sub UserDocument_ReadProperties(PropBag As PropertyBag)** to the code shown in **Code Step 8**. This code sets each of the text boxes to the former value of txtSideA. Do *not* save this change.

FIGURE 15-24
The "This document has been modified" message box

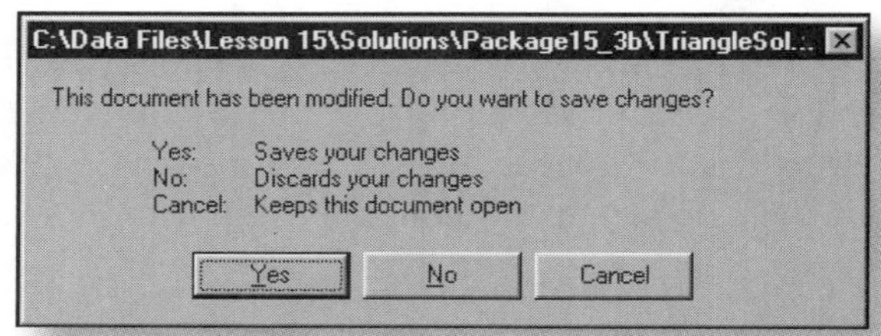

9. Run the program. Once the application launches in the browser, enter the values **33**, **49**, and **55** for the lengths of the sides of the triangle and click **Calculate**. Use the Address combo box to navigate to any other directory. Click **Yes** when prompted to save this. Use the **Back** button of the browser to return to TriangleMaster. All three text boxes should have the value 33. Close the browser.

10. Stop the program without saving the latest changes. Leave Visual Basic open.

CODE STEP 3

```
PropBag.WriteProperty "txtSideA", txtSideA.Text
PropBag.WriteProperty "txtSideB", txtSideB.Text
PropBag.WriteProperty "txtSideC", txtSideC.Text
```

CODE STEP 4

```
txtSideA = PropBag.ReadProperty("txtSideA")
txtSideB = PropBag.ReadProperty("txtSideB")
txtSideC = PropBag.ReadProperty("txtSideC")
```

CODE STEP 8

```
txtSideA = PropBag.ReadProperty("txtSideA")
txtSideB = PropBag.ReadProperty("txtSideA")
txtSideC = PropBag.ReadProperty("txtSideA")
```

Any time the TriangleMaster application is run, property values are read from the PropertyBag to initialize the lengths of the sides of the triangle. So the PropertyBag lets you initialize properties to their most recent values.

Quick Check 15.c

1. The ________________ event of a User Document takes the place of the Load event for a standard form.

2. When adding a menu to a User Document, the ________________ property must be set or the menu will not be added to the container's menu bar.

3. Use the PropertyBag when you want to ________________.

4. To inform the container of a change in the value of a property, use the ________________ method.

5. When the user navigates away from a User Document where a property has been changed and the proper notification is given to the container about the change, the ________________ event of the User Document fires.

6. Once a property is stored in the PropertyBag, the ________________ event of the User Document is executed when the Document runs.

Using the ActiveX Document Migration Wizard

In this section, use the *ActiveX Document Migration Wizard, (ADMWizard)*, to convert an existing Standard EXE application to an ActiveX Document. The Wizard does not convert the entire application to an ActiveX Document application, but it does convert the form, the heart of the project, into an ActiveX Document. Once that conversion is complete, finishing the project is just a matter of tying up loose ends.

In Lesson 13, a graphing application was used to illustrate the Help system. In the first application problem at the end of the lesson, the basic program was modified to draw circles. That program is used in this exercise. If you do not have that particular program, substitute any Standard EXE project or any version of the graphing application. Find the complete solution to the application problem on the *Electronic Instructor CD*. This program was chosen because it contains elements not yet used in an ActiveX Document. It uses graphics methods and the TabStrip control.

STEP-BY-STEP 15.4a

1. If necessary start Visual Basic and open the **Graphing** project from Lesson 13, Application Problem 1. (If you use Problem 5 open the Project's Property Pages and delete the name in the Help File Name box.) Do *not* save changes to TriangleMaster if prompted. Run the **Graphing** program to remind yourself what the program does. Stop the program.

2. Select **Add-Ins | Add-In Manager** from the menu bar. In the Add-In Manager, double-click **VB6 ActiveX DOC Migration Wizard**. The word "Loaded" must appear in the second column of the list box. Click **OK** to close the Add-In Manager.

3. Select **Add-Ins | ActiveX Document Migration Wizard** in the menu bar. Figure 15-25 shows the opening screen of the Wizard. Click **Next** to move to the next step.

4. The Form Selection window lets you choose which forms to convert to ActiveX Documents. This project has a single form. Click its check box and click **Next** to move to the next step. See Figure 15-26.

FIGURE 15-25
The Introduction Screen of the ADMWizard

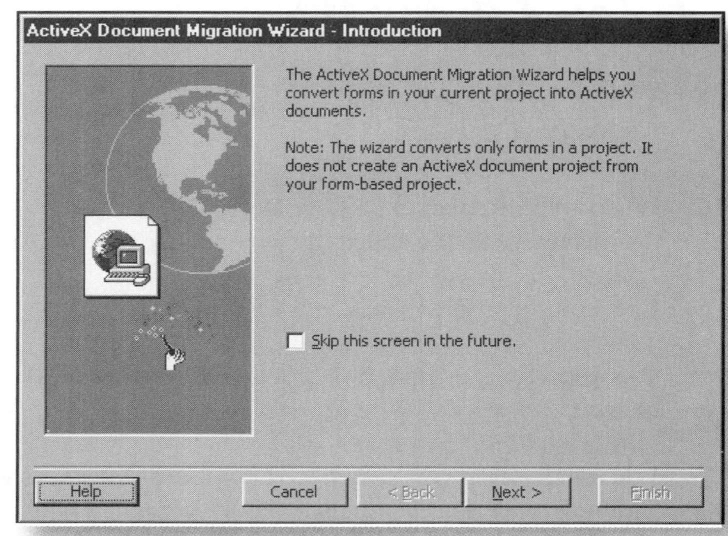

FIGURE 15-26
The Form Selection screen of the ADMWizard

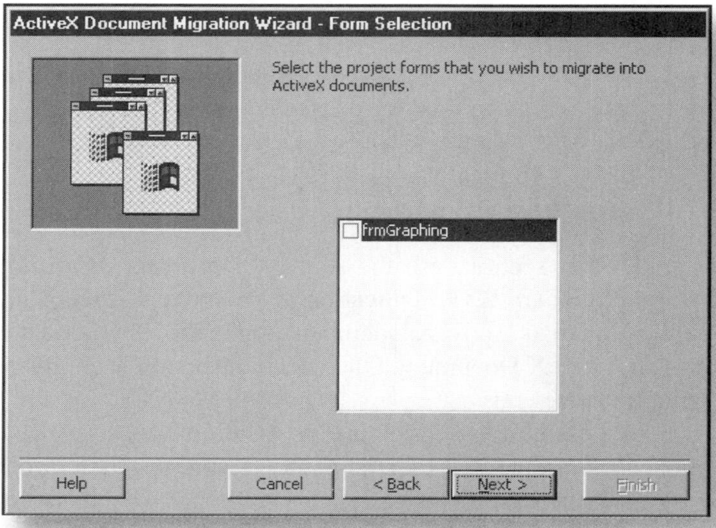

5. The Options screen lets you set certain preferences. A Standard form responds to events that do not exist in an ActiveX Document. The Wizard can identify those statements and comment them out by inserting a single quote character before the first character of the statement. Statements targeted by the Wizard include any reference to the Load and Unload events of a form. The statements Form.Show and Form.Hide are commented out not because of the Show and Hide

methods which do work for the UserDocument, but because of Form. The Wizard is limited; it can comment out code but it cannot supply something to take that code's place. Click the "**Comment out invalid code**" check box.

6. If checked, the second option, "Remove original forms after conversion", removes the converted form from the original project when the conversion is complete. What this is really asking is whether you want a project with both the original form and the ActiveX Document in it. This process does not alter the original project with its original form because when you save the new project you will change its name. The original project still exists in an unaltered state. There is no reason to have a project with both the original form and the new User Document. Click the **Remove original forms after conversion** check box.

7. The default, Convert to an ActiveX EXE is the correct choice in the "Your Project Type is invalid" frame. Click **Next** to move to the next step.

8. Figure 15-27 shows the Finished! screen of the ADMWizard. The default setting, Yes, generates a summary report for you to view and save. The "Save current settings as default" check box, if selected, will save your choices and make them the default choices for subsequent runs of the Wizard. Click **Finish**. (do not check Save current settings as default).

9. Remember that the Wizard is looking for code incompatible with a User Document. The error message shown in Figure 15-28 is displayed. Click **OK**.

10. Figure 15-29 shows the last message from the ActiveX Document Migration Wizard. Click **OK** to close the message.

11. Read the Summary Report. It tells you about the limitations of the conversion process and tells you how to test the result of the conversion. Click **Close** (or Save) to close the Summary Report.

12. Click the **Start** button on the toolbar to test the project. The Debugging tab of the Project1 Project Properties appears prompting you to enter a Start Component. Accept the default by clicking **OK**. See Figure 15-30.

(continued on next page)

FIGURE 15-27
The Finished! screen of the ADMWizard

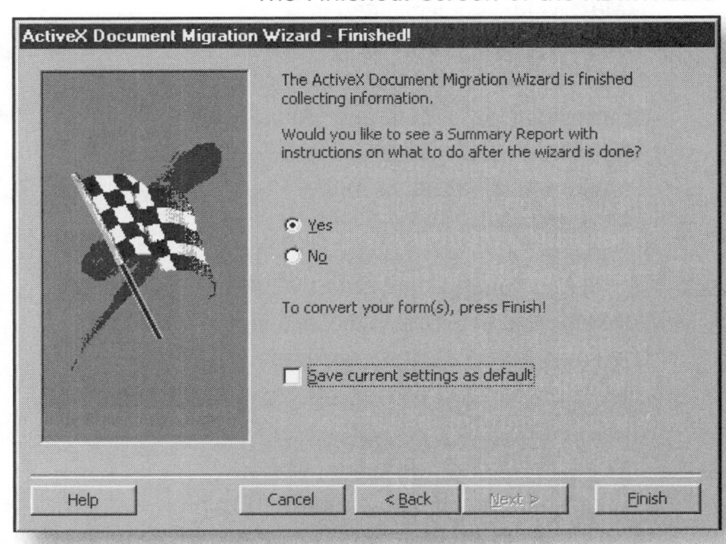

FIGURE 15-28
The Invalid Code message from the ADMWizard

13. Internet Explorer launches and displays the Graphing project. The Graph menu appears in the menu bar of the browser. That means the Wizard has changed the value of the NegotiatePosition property of the Graph item in the menu to a non-zero entry. Click each of the tabs. Each tab presents different data appropriate for lines, parabolas, and circles. The Zoom In and Zoom Out buttons call the graphing routine. With any of the three tabs showing, click the **Zoom In** button or select **Graph | Draw the Graph** from the menu bar. Instead of a graph, a Division by zero error message appears.

14. Click **Debug** to find the error. The line picGraph.Scale (-xMax, yMax)-(xMax, -yMax) is highlighted in yellow. It is the source of the error. Hover the mouse pointer over each of the variables: **xMax**, and **yMax**. The value of each is zero! Something in the initialization of the variables has failed.

15. In the original application, the values for xMax and yMax are initialized in the Form_Activate event procedure. This is converted by the Wizard to the UserDocument_Activate event procedure. Click **frmGraphing.vbd** on the taskbar and close the Internet Explorer browser. Click the **End** button on the toolbar to stop execution of the program.

16. If necessary, open the Code window. In **Private Sub UserDocument_Activate( )** insert the following line just before the lines that initialize the Max variables.

```
MsgBox "Initializing the Max variables."
```

FIGURE 15-29
The ActiveX Document Created screen at the end of the conversion procedure

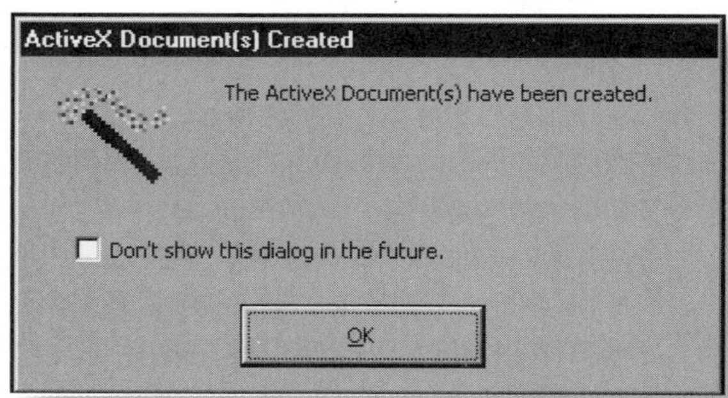

FIGURE 15-30
The Debugging Tab of the Project1 Project Properties

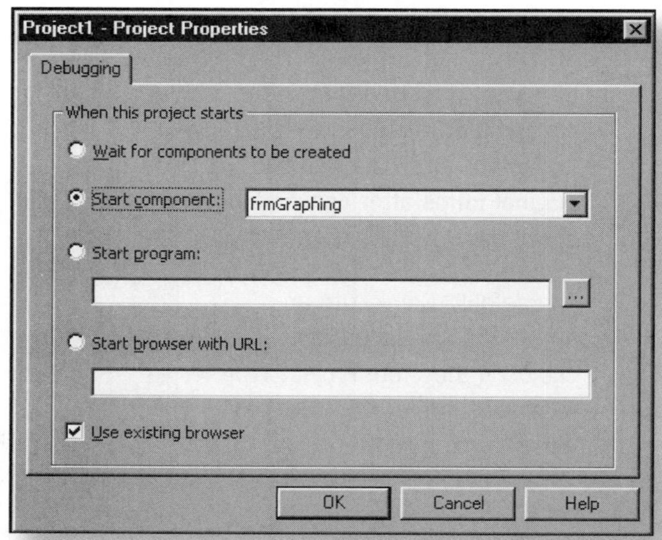

17. Save and run the program. If the Activate event works, the message box should appear. It does not appear. The Activate event is not a valid event for the User Document. This is not a surprise: the Activate event does not appear in the list of User Document events given in the previous exercise. The Initialize event should be used instead.

18. Close the browser and stop execution of the program. Cut the code in the **UserDocument_Activate** event and paste it into the **UserDocument_Initialize** event.

19. Save and run the program. This time the message box appears before the browser window appears (It may appear so quickly that you do not see it). The actual project does not even appear; an hourglass appears in the blank browser window. The Initialize event of the UserDocument fires before the browser even appears. Click **Project 1** on the taskbar and click **OK** in the message box. In the browser click **Zoom In** or select **Graph | Draw the Graph**. A graph appears in the picture box. Click the **Quadratic** tab. Click **Zoom In**. Click **Zoom Out** two or three times. Click the **Circle** tab. Click **Zoom In**. Close the browser and click **OK** in the message box. Stop execution of the program.

20. In the Project Explorer, right-click **Project1** and select **Project1 Properties**. Change the Project Name to **Graphing**. Add the following line to the Project Description: **The Graphing program draws graphs of lines, parabolas, and circles**. Delete the Help File name if any.

21. Click the **Make** tab and confirm that the Wizard has provided an appropriate title for the project. If not, enter the title **Graphing**. Click **OK** to close the Properties window.

22. Click the UserDocument (still called **frmGraphing**) in the Project Explorer and click the **View Object** button.

FIGURE 15-31
The Menu Editor showing the change to the Graph entry

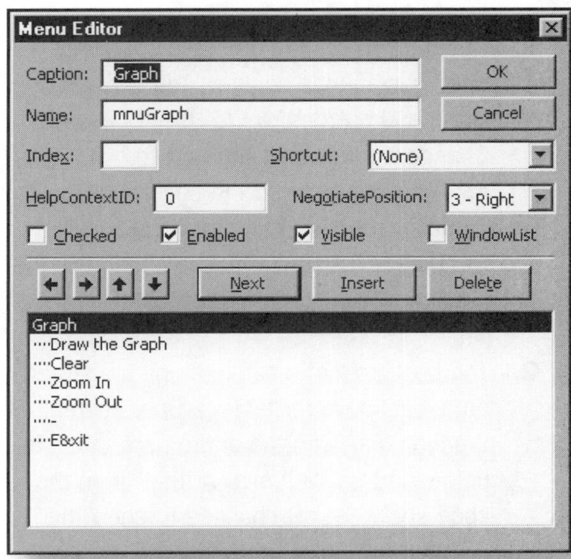

23. Right-click the body of the UserDocument and select **Menu Editor**. Figure 15-31 shows the change made to the menu by the Wizard. The NegotiatePosition property of the Graph menu item is changed from 0-None to 3-Right. Select the separator entry in the menu and click the **Delete** button. Select the Exit entry in the menu and click the **Delete** button. Click **OK** to close the Menu Editor and save the changes.

24. Open the Code window and delete or comment out the message box statement inserted into the **UserDocument_Initialize** event.

25. Save the form and the project with a new name. Leave the project open.

Two things are left to do: use the AsyncRead method and a hyperlink object. The AsyncRead method initiates a file download. A *hyperlink object* is used to navigate to filenames or URLs and is part of the User Document. In the next exercise add two command buttons to the User Document. The first calls an image using the AsyncRead method. When the read is complete, as determined by the AsyncReadComplete event, the image is transferred to the background of the User Document. The second command button uses a hyperlink object to navigate to another User Document.

STEP-BY-STEP 15.4b

1. Use the Project Explorer to display the User Document Designer. Add two command buttons to the User Document. Change the name of the first to **cmdBackground** and the second to **cmdLink**. Change the caption of the first to **Add Background** and the caption of the second to **Link to TriangleMaster**.

2. The background image is a .jpg file stored on a local drive for testing. Once tested, the file along with the entire application is uploaded to a Web site. At that time, the code shown below changes to show the picture's URL, not its pathname. Use the Image04.jpg file supplied on the *Electronic Instructor CD*, or find your own image file. Enter the line of code shown in **Code Step 2** in **cmdBackground_Click**. (Substitute the correct path for the image).

   AsyncRead has the following syntax:

   object.**AsyncRead** *Target*, *AsyncType* [, *PropertyName*], [*AsyncReadOptions*]

   The object is the UserDocument. The Target is the file's pathname or URL. AsyncType is an integer that describes the kind of data being downloaded. The PropertyName is a tag used to identify the file when two or more files are downloading at the same time. It is omitted in this application because only one file is downloaded. AsyncReadOptions specifies other options for AsyncRead that are not explored here.

3. The AsyncRead method initiates the file download. Once downloaded, the file itself is available through the *AsyncProp object*. This object is exposed through the parameter list of the AsyncReadComplete event. Enter the code shown in **Code Step 3** in **UserDocument_AsyncReadComplete (AsyncProp As AsyncProperty)**.

4. Save and run the program. Click the **Quadratic** tab and click **ZoomOut** several times. Once the application is running, click the **Add Background** button. Figure 15-32 shows the result.

5. Close the browser and stop the execution of the application.

6. Enter the lines of code shown in **Code Step 6** in **cmdLink_Click**. This code navigates to the TriangleMaster.vbd file (substitute the correct path). It depends on the presence of a copy of

CODE STEP 2

```
UserDocument.AsyncRead "C:\TEMP\IMAGE04.JPG", vbAsyncTypePicture
```

CODE STEP 3

```
Set UserDocument.Picture = AsyncProp.Value
```

CODE STEP 6

```
UserDocument.Hyperlink.NavigateTo _
  "c:\temp\TriangleSolver.vbd"
```

TriangleSolver.vbd in "c:\temp" (or the location you specify).

7. Save and run the program. Click the Quadratic tab and click **Zoom Out** several times. Once the application is running, click the **Add Background** button Click **Link to TriangleMaster**. The ActiveX Document, TriangleSolver.vbd, executes showing you the familiar triangle program. Click the **Back** button to return to the Graphing application.

FIGURE 15-32
The Graphing application showing the background picture, the final placement of controls and a parabola in the picture box

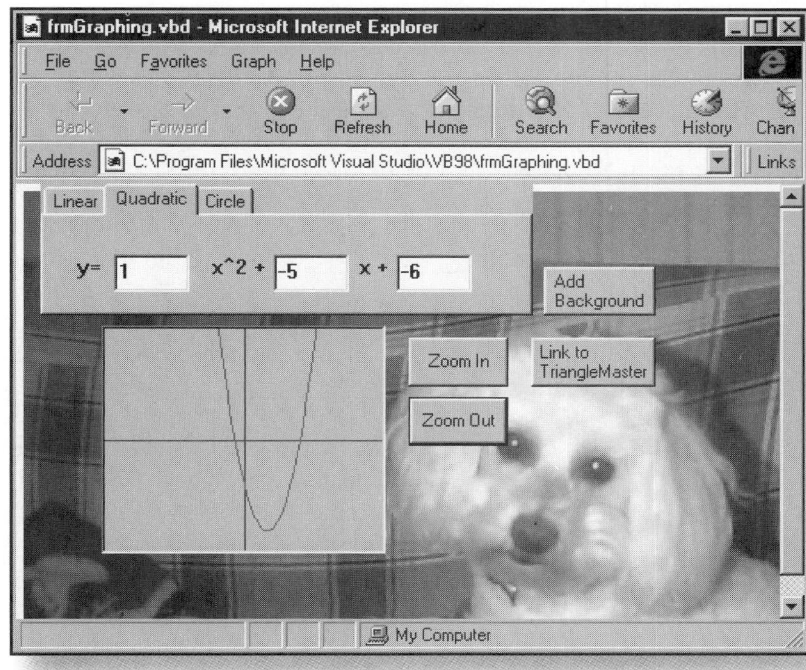

8. Close the browser and stop the program, then exit Visual Basic.

What can you do with the Hyperlink object? Start with the NavigateTo method. Examine the syntax for the method below.

object.**NavigateTo** *Target* [**,** *Location* [, *FrameName*]]

The object is the UserDocument.Hyperlink. Target is the URL or pathname of the destination. Location is optional. If present, it specifies a particular place within the document to which to jump. Many HTML documents use frames. If the optional FrameName is specified, the jump is made to that frame of the document.

The browser maintains a history list of URLs visited by the user. The GoForward method navigates to the next URL in the history list. The GoBack method of the User Document returns to the most recently visited URL in the history list. It sounds funny to navigate to the next item in the history list, but the user can move through the history list in both directions. Of course, the user cannot go to the next item in the list unless they have first navigated to one of the previous entries in the history list.

Except for the unexpected conversion of Form_Activate to the non-existent UserDocument_ Activate, the conversion from Standard EXE to ActiveX Document went quite well. Even the menu was altered to work along with the container's menu. The ease of conversion means you have a whole new source of Web (almost) ready applications: your Standard EXE applications.

Quick Check 15.d

1. ADMWizard stands for ___________________.
2. When adding an Add-In in the Add-In Manager the word ___________________ must appear in the second column next to the Add-In before closing the Add-In Manager.
3. The Form Selection window in the ADMWizard lets you choose which forms to convert to ___________________.
4. The ADMWizard will ___________________ code that is incompatible with a User Document.
5. Instead of the Activate event used in a Standard EXE, a programmer using an ActiveX Document should use the ___________________ event.
6. When the AsyncRead method has completed its job of downloading a file, the file is available in the ___________________ object.

Summary

- An ActiveX Document is an application that runs in a browser.
- The palette on which an ActiveX Document is drawn is the User Document Designer. It replaces the form used in the Standard EXE. The User Document Designer has no menu bar but can use pop-up menus. The User Document does not have a Load or Activate event but does have an Initialize event.
- Like other Web documents, ActiveX Documents call each other with Web addresses.
- Classes are a good way to encapsulate data, methods, and events.
- An And statement is True if all parts of the statement are True.
- Visual Basic does not have an Arccosine function. Use the Arctangent Atn( ) function. Convert the cosine into the equivalent tangent value.
- Although Visual Basic does not define a constant for Pi, the expression 4*Atn(1), within the limits of the double type, is a close approximation to Pi.
- The Variant type is a way to make life easier for the programmer. There are applications where there is a time or space penalty for using variants, but many times the Variant type gives the programmer more flexibility.
- To declare an object variable with the class's events enabled, use the Dim With Events statement in the General Declarations section of the code, not inside an event procedure.
- The User Document is saved with a .dob extension. Like a Visual Basic form file, the User Document is a text file that can be opened in Notepad. Graphic elements of a User Document are stored in a file with an extension of .dox. When compiled, the User Document is saved as a .vbd file. An ActiveX .dll or ActiveX.exe accompanies the .vbd file.
- File naming conventions are different for Windows and for the Internet. To copy files to the Internet omit spaces and special characters from filenames.
- It is likely that no browser will download the application unless you set Safe for Scripting and Safe for Initialization to Yes. To lower the browser's security, select View | Internet Options | Security and select Low security.

- Backing up or starting over is easy when using the Package and Deployment Wizard.
- A .vbd file is a compiled ActiveX Document file. It is equivalent to an EXE file. To run the application, the .vbd file, the .CAB File and the .HTM files must be saved on the Web site.
- Not every Web site provider on the Web (for example, GeoCities) allows ActiveX Documents.
- The PDWizard can use FTP, File Transfer Protocol, to upload files to the Internet.
- If you publish your application on more than one Web site, save the information for each upload in a different script.
- The User Document has many similarities to the Standard EXE form, but there are some differences. A User Document must run in a container like Internet Explorer. There are many differences in events, especially events that fire as the User Document is run or is stopped.
- A menu attached to a User Document can be displayed in the menu bar of the container. The most important property to set is the NegotiatePosition property. If this is not set to a non-zero value, the menu is not added to the container's menu bar.
- The PropertyBag, when supported by the container application, stores values of properties as they change at run-time. The values can be recalled from the PropertyBag when the User Document starts executing. The Property Changed method signals the container application when the value of a property changes.
- The ActiveX Document Migration Wizard converts forms from Standard EXE projects into ActiveX Documents.
- In the conversion process, the ADMWizard comments out code that is incompatible with the UserDocument object, but it cannot replace it with correct code.
- The ADMWizard automatically corrects menus in a form so that they appear in the menu bar of the container application.
- The AsyncRead method initiates a file download. It can be used for images in a User Document. The AsyncProp object exposed to the programmer through the AsyncReadComplete event procedure contains the downloaded file in its Value property.
- A hyperlink object has three methods that allow a user to navigate through the Internet, the NavigateTo method, the GoForward method and the GoBack method.

LESSON 15 REVIEW QUESTIONS

TRUE/FALSE

Circle the T if the statement is True. Circle the F is it is False.

T F 1. To declare an object that responds to events, put code into the Document's Load event.

T F 2. Once the PDWizard starts building a package for distribution, there is no way to stop the process.

T F 3. The PDWizard puts three files into a Package folder: a Cab file, an HTML file to call the ActiveX Document and the ActiveX Document itself.

T F 4. A User Document can run as a stand-alone application.

T F 5. Put startup code for a UserDocument in the document's Activate event.

T F 6. The AsyncReadComplete event occurs when an asynchronous read request is complete.

T F 7. It is not possible to add a form to an ActiveX Document.

T F 8. A User Document menu will not appear in the container's menu bar unless the NegotiatePosition property is set to 0-None.

T F 9. Use the PropertyBag object to store the values of properties that change while the application is running.

T F 10. Use a hyperlink object to download picture files from the Internet.

WRITTEN QUESTIONS

Write your answers to the following questions.

11. Describe the Triangle class created in Step-by-Step 15.1. What kinds of things are there in the class? Give a short description of each.
12. What has to be done to the Internet Explorer to allow it to run an ActiveX Document?
13. What is FTP and for what does the PDWizard use it?
14. What does it mean when we say, "A User Document must run in a container"?
15. Name three events that are present in a User Document that are missing from a Standard EXE.
16. How do you cause a User Document menu to appear in the menu bar of the container?
17. Describe the process of using the PropertyBag to store a changed property value. In your answer, mention all the relevant methods and events by name.
18. What kinds of changes are made when converting a Standard EXE form to an ActiveX Document?
19. Describe how to use a hyperlink object to navigate from one ActiveX Document to another.
20. How do you display a picture in the background of a User Document?

LESSON 15 APPLICATION PROBLEMS

Level One

THE PHOTO COST PROGRAM

Write an ActiveX Document to calculate the cost to the customer of photo services provided by a wedding photographer. The photographer charges for prints according to the table on the following page.

PRINT COSTS	
SIZE	COST
Four by Six	$1
Five by Seven	$2.50
Eight by Ten	$4.50
Eleven by Fourteen	$9.00

The User Document should show a text box for each print size. The user uses the text boxes to enter the number of prints of each size. A Calculate button displays the total cost calculated using the table above. A second command button clears the text boxes. For this program, just run the User Document from within Visual Basic. It will open in the Microsoft Internet Explorer browser. Do not use the Package and Deployment Wizard to package and deploy the project.

COMPILING, PACKAGING, AND DEPLOYING THE PHOTO COST PROGRAM

Compile the program. Run the Package and Deployment Wizard to package the project and deploy it to a Web site. Run the program from the Web site to be sure it works properly.

ADDING AN ABOUT FORM

Add an About form to the Photo Cost program. Add a menu to the User Document to call the About form from the menu bar. Compile the program again. Run the Package and Deployment Wizard again to repackage and re-deploy the project to a Web site.

Level Two

SAVING THE NUMBERS

Add the code required to save the print quantities entered in the text boxes in the PropertyBag when the user navigates away from the document or closes the browser. Use the stored values to initialize the text boxes the next time the application is run. For this program, just run the User Document from within Visual Basic. It will open in the Microsoft Internet Explorer browser. Do not use the Package and Deployment Wizard to package and deploy the project.

ADDING A BACKGROUND AND A LINK

Add a button to add a background to the Photo Cost program. Also add a button to link to the TriangleMaster program. Use c:\temp or whatever directory your TriangleSolver.vbd and IMAGE04.JPG files are stored in from Step-by-Step 15.4b. For this program, just run the User Document from within Visual Basic. It will open in the Microsoft Internet Explorer browser. Do not use the Package and Deployment Wizard to package and deploy the project."

There is no flexibility about case in URL's. The filename IMAGE04.JPG must be reproduced exactly. It is easy to assume that exact matches are not necessary because the Web seems so friendly.

DISTRIBUTING TO THE INTERNET (OPTIONAL)

If you have access to Prodigy, change the path for IMAGE04.JPG to the URL http://pages.prodigy.net/spraguelhs/IMAGE04.JPG and change the TriangleMaster path to http://pages.prodigy.net/spraguelhs/TriangleSolver.vbd. Compile the project. Create and deploy the package to your Web site.

LESSON 15 PROGRAMMING AT WORK

SCANS

In this section, turn the Music Collection project into ActiveX documents. Each form becomes an independent ActiveX Document. This profoundly affects program design. You are used to thinking of each form as dependent upon a main form that organizes the user's access to the project. When each form is a separate document, there is no telling how a user might navigate to each document. A user might begin at a "Startup" form, but subsequent access to the individual forms might originate anywhere. In particular, a user might access a document directly by entering the URL or navigate to the document through the history list.

In the Music Collection project, these design issues are not a problem. To some extent, the entire project is a collection of independent forms. Dividing them into stand-alone projects and revising the main form as an overall organizer is easy.

There are four forms in the project. These become four separate ActiveX projects. Rather than store them all in the same folder, once the ActiveX Document Migration Wizard has converted the forms to their ActiveX Document equivalents, move each to a new folder and build a new ActiveX Document EXE project around it. In this activity, you will only create the ActiveX Document for the Data Entry form.

1. Start Visual Basic and open the most recent version of the **Music Collection** project.

2. Since you are going to alter the project, you may want to resave the entire project in a new folder with all new names. To save the project with new names right-click **frmDataEntry** in the Project Explorer. Select **Save frmDataEntry.frm As** from the pop-up menu. Change directories. Enter a new name for the form. Repeat the process for each of the form modules, the code module, and the class module. Finally, select **File | Save Project As** and change the name of the project.

3. The Music Collection project had four forms, one class module and one code module. Select **Add-Ins | Add-In Manager** from the menu bar. Double-click the **ActiveX Doc Migration Wizard**. Be sure that the word Loaded appears in the second column next to the entry. Click **OK** to close the Add-Ins Manager.

4. Select **Add-Ins | ActiveX Document Migration Wizard** from the menu bar. Click **Next** to move past the Introduction window to the Form Selection window.

5. Select each of the four forms. See Figure 15-33. Click **Next** to move to the next step.

6. In the Options window check "Comment out invalid code?" and "Remove original forms after conversion?". Click **Finished**. The Wizard reports that code is commented out in each of the four documents. Click the **Save** icon in the toolbar to save the altered project.

7. Run Windows Explorer. Create a new folder for the DataEntry document. Call the folder **DataEntry**. Copy **frmDataEntry.dob**, **frmDataEntry.dox** (if it exists) and **MusCol.mdb** to the DataEntry folder. Leave Windows Explorer open for future use.

FIGURE 15-33
The Form Selection window showing all four forms selected

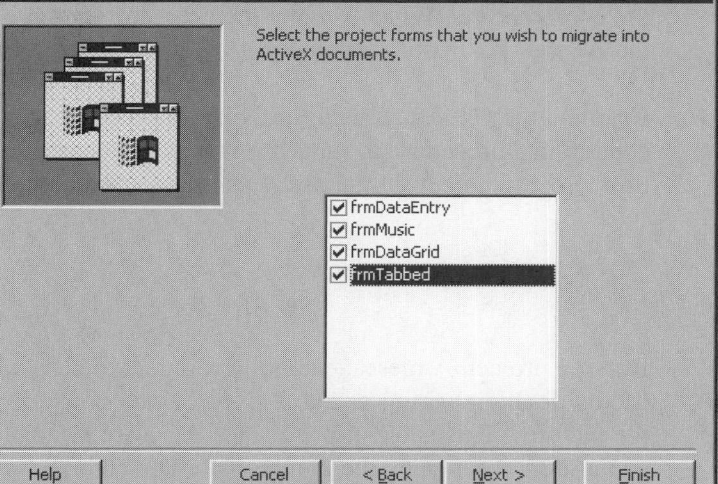

8. Return to Visual Basic.

9. Select **File | New Project** from the menu bar. Click **ActiveX Document Exe** from the New Project window. Click **OK** to close the window.

10. Select **Project | Add User Document** from the menu bar. Click the **Existing** tab, navigate to the DataEntry folder, and select **frmDataEntry.dob**. Click **Open** to close the dialog box. Check the Project Explorer for the newly added document.

11. Right-click **UserDocument1** and select **Remove UserDocument1** to remove the document from the project.

12. Click the Start button on the toolbar or press **F5** to run the program. The Project Properties window opens. The default Start component is frmDataEntry. It is the only choice. Click **OK** to accept the choice. The error message shown in Figure 15-34 may appear. Click **OK**.

FIGURE 15-34
The Errors During Load message box

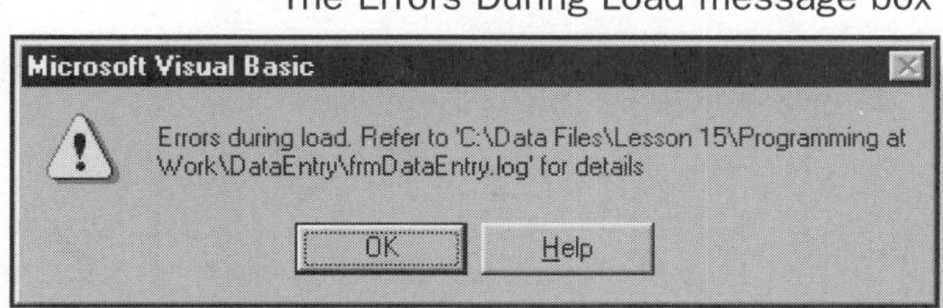

13. It runs! Well, it seems to run. If you start clicking buttons, you find most of the buttons do not work and some crash the program. It does display the records of the database and it does update the records when you edit a field. Close the browser. Click the **Stop** button in the toolbar to stop execution of the program.

14. Before fixing any of the errors, right-click **Project1** in the Project Explorer and select **Project1 Properties**. Change the Project Name to **DataEntry**. Click the **Make** tab and change the Title to **MainDataEntry**. Click **OK** to close the Property Pages dialog box.

15. Select **frmDataEntry** in the User Documents folder in the Project Explorer. Click the **View Code** icon. Examine the Form_Load event procedure. Although present it does not execute because the UserDocument does not have a Load event. The code in the procedure initializes the combo boxes. When running the program you may have noticed that when you opened the combo box list, it was empty.

16. Examine the UserDocument_Initialize event procedure. It is possible that the Wizard writes code to this procedure to initialize the User Document. The procedure is empty. In the Private Sub UserDocument_Initialize( ) event procedure, add the lines:

    ```
    ChDrive App.Path
    ChDir App.Path
    Call Form_Load
    ```

17. Run the project. A message about errors recorded in a log file appears. (If you open the log file by double-clicking its entry in the Windows Explorer, you find entries about the failure of the pictures. This is no surprise since there are three black holes where the icons are supposed to be.) Open the combo lists. The code in the Form_Load event initializes the combo boxes. Close the browser. Click the **End** button on the toolbar to stop execution of the program. Return to the Code window.

18. In the Private Sub cmdRecord_Click( ) event procedure, remove the constant parameter **adAffectAll**. Tests show this is not necessary and does not work in this environment.

    As you look over the code, you find some that do nothing, like Private Sub cmdReturn_Click( ). All the statements are commented out. Other code causes the system to crash. The Prune function refers to a variable CurrentUser that does not exist in the context of this project. There is a way to communicate between documents, but that does not solve the problem, because there is no guarantee that the CurrentUser variable will be initialized by the other document.

19. In Private Sub Toolbar1_ButtonClick(ByVal Button As MSComctlLib.Button), comment out or remove the following code:

    ```
    Case "Prune"
        If CurrentUser.NickName <> "" Then
          datCollectionRS.RecordSource = CurrentUser.PruneSQL()
          datCollectionRS.Refresh
        End If
    ```

    When other components of the project have been turned into independent ActiveX Documents, you may want to add code to the Private Sub cmdReturn_Click( ) event using the Hyperlink object and the NavigateTo method to link to another document. For now, leave the code the way it is.

20. Use the Project Explorer to display the User Document. Right-click the toolbar. Select **Properties** from the pop-up menu to open the toolbar's Property Pages. Open the list box in the ImageList combo box. Select **<None>**. The ImageList must be disconnected from the toolbar before it can be altered.

21. Click the **Buttons** tab and navigate to the Prune button. Click **Remove Button** to remove the Prune button from the toolbar. Click **OK** to close the Property Pages dialog box.

22. Right-click the body of the User Document and select **Menu Editor**. The menu commands do not include a command for Prune and the rest of the commands are OK. Select **Command** and click the Visible option to make the menu visible. The Wizard has already altered the NegotiatePosition property. The menu should be visible in the menu bar of the browser the next time you run the program. Click **OK** to close the Menu Editor.

23. Right-click the ImageList control and select **Properties** to enter the control's Property Pages. Click the **Images** tab. Click the first picture. Click **Remove Picture**. Continue to click **Remove Picture** until all the entries have been removed. Click **Insert Picture** and add four pictures to the ImageList control. Make a note of which picture will go with which button in the toolbar: Record, Clear, Return, and Refresh. Click **OK** to close the Property Pages dialog box.

24. Right-click the Toolbar and select **Properties**. In the General tab, open the list for the ImageList combo box and select **DataEntrySupport**.

FIGURE 15-35
Zoom Dialog Box

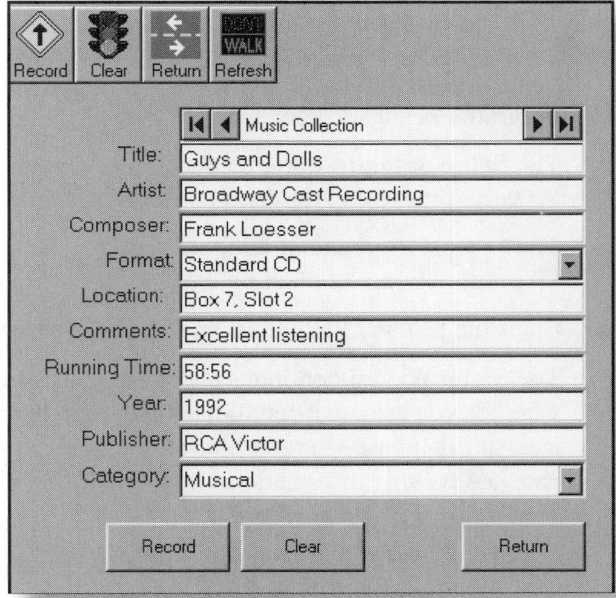

25. Click the **Buttons** tab. Change the **Image** property of each button entry to the image numbers recorded in the step above. Click **OK** to accept the changes.

26. Run the program. Test all the functions. Click **Clear**. Add a new entry. Copy the data from Figure 15-35. Click **Record**. Navigate through the records. It is not visible in the figure, but the project's menu appears in the menu bar of the browser. Close the browser.

27. Save and compile the project.

Once the project is compiled, the Document's .vbd and .exe files are available. The project can be packaged and deployed to the Web.

APPENDIX A

Getting Around Windows 98

Once upon a time, it was said, "If you want to upgrade your operating system, buy a new computer." And although the way is not always straight and smooth, the old saying is no longer true. It is easier than ever to upgrade your operating system.

In this section, you look at the essentials of getting up and running with Windows 98.

Upgrading to Windows 98

If you are upgrading from Windows 3.1 to Windows 98, you need more than a paragraph or two because you probably need to upgrade your hardware as well as the operating system. For those moving from Windows 95 to Windows 98 however, here is a brief summary of the process:

- Insert your Microsoft Windows 98 Upgrade CD in the CD-ROM drive. If the install program does not start by itself, click Start and select Run. Use the Browse button to navigate to the CD-ROM drive and select setup.exe. Click OK to run the Setup program.
- From this point on, there are very few decisions to make. Most of the responses required by you involve clicking the Next button. If you are not there to click the button, the Setup program does it for you.
- The Setup program starts by checking your system and preparing the Setup Wizard. The Setup Wizard guides you step-by-step through the installation process.
- The License Agreement window displays the agreement. Accept the agreement by clicking the I Accept option and clicking Next.
- Enter the product key found on the disk sleeve.
- The Setup Wizard continues checking your system. One of the things it is checking for is whether you are qualified to use the Upgrade disk instead of a full installation disk. The Registry database—a record of all the applications registered to run on the system—is checked for this information.
- Setup prepares the Window directory and checks the system for sufficient drive space for the installation. It also checks for "Installed Components." Installed Components are pieces of the operating system that may already be installed.
- Setup prompts you to save the old system files. It is always a good idea not to burn the bridges behind you. If there is a serious problem with the Windows 98 installation, saving the old System files provides a way to restore the old system.
- Setup asks for your geographic location to customize operating system settings such as time and money that are expressed differently in different countries. Windows 98 adapts to your location.
- Setup prompts you to insert a disk and then creates a Startup disk. This disk allows you to restart the system if something goes wrong with the installation. It may seem that the Wizard is taking many precautions. The precautions are taken, not because the installation is prone to

failure, but because there is a possibility of failure. The precautions should make you feel better, not apprehensive.

- Once Setup starts copying files, you can take a break. It takes several minutes to complete copying Windows 98 to your hard drive. Setup gives a good time estimate, so you will know how much time you have. While the files are being copied, a commercial for Windows 98 runs to inform you of new features.
- When the Wizard finishes copying files, Setup configures the hardware and finalizes the settings. None of this requires your input.
- Eventually, the system reboots and Windows 98 starts.

Running Programs from the Start Menu

Programs installed with a Setup program are usually listed in the Start menu. Figure A-1 shows that Notepad, a simple text editor, is selected. To start Notepad, single-click the **Start** button on the left side of the taskbar. The taskbar is found along the bottom edge of the screen. If the taskbar is not visible, move the mouse pointer to the bottom edge of the screen and it will appear. Point to Programs. It is not necessary to click Programs, because another menu appears as soon as you position the mouse pointer over the word Programs. From this submenu, point to Accessories. Another submenu appears. Click Notepad and the application starts executing. Close a program by clicking the Close box (the one with an *X*) in the upper right corner of the application.

FIGURE A-1
Selecting an application from the Start menu

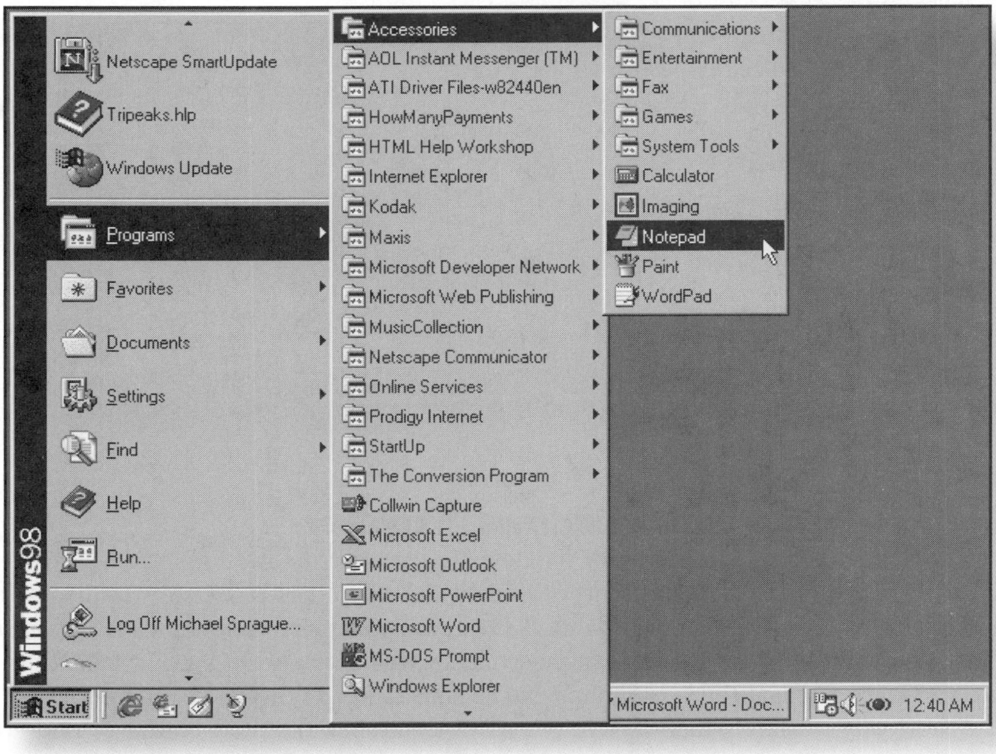

If you have a Windows keyboard with a special Start key, you can press the Start key (usually marked with the Windows logo) rather than using the mouse. Then you can press the up and down arrow keys to select Programs and press the right arrow key to open the submenu. For example, you can press the up arrow key to select Accessories, press the right arrow key to open the Accessories sub-menu, press the down arrow key to select Notepad, and then press Enter to start the application.

Most Windows programs can be started and run without the mouse, but using the keyboard instead of the mouse is not always intuitive.

You can click Start | Documents to open a menu of recently used documents. The term Documents is used loosely to include any file recently used. Visual Basic programs, image files, and other executable files may appear in the menu. Locate a file in the menu and click its entry to start the application needed and open the file.

You can click Start | Favorites to open a menu of saved favorite Web sites. Click an entry to launch a browser. Windows automatically connects you to your Internet Service Provider.

You can click Start | Settings to open a menu of utilities. Click Control Panel. The Control Panel, shown in Figure A-2, contains a number of utilities. Double-click an icon to run one of these utilities.

FIGURE A-2
The Control Panel

Starting Programs with Windows Explorer

Another way to start programs is with Windows Explorer. Windows Explorer is a window into your hard drive since it displays the contents of folders and subfolders in a variety of display modes. Not only can it display files, it can also be used to start applications. Sometimes it is necessary to start applications from Windows Explorer because the application may not appear in the Start menu. Executable versions of Visual Basic programs can be started from Windows Explorer.

The easiest way to start Windows Explorer is to right-click the Start button. A pop-up menu appears with the menu selections: Open, Explore, and Find. (It may have additional selections.) Click Explore. Windows Explorer starts, as shown in Figure A-3. The left pane shows the arrangement of folders on a drive. The right pane shows the contents of the selected folder.

FIGURE A-3
Windows Explorer showing the contents of the Start Menu folder

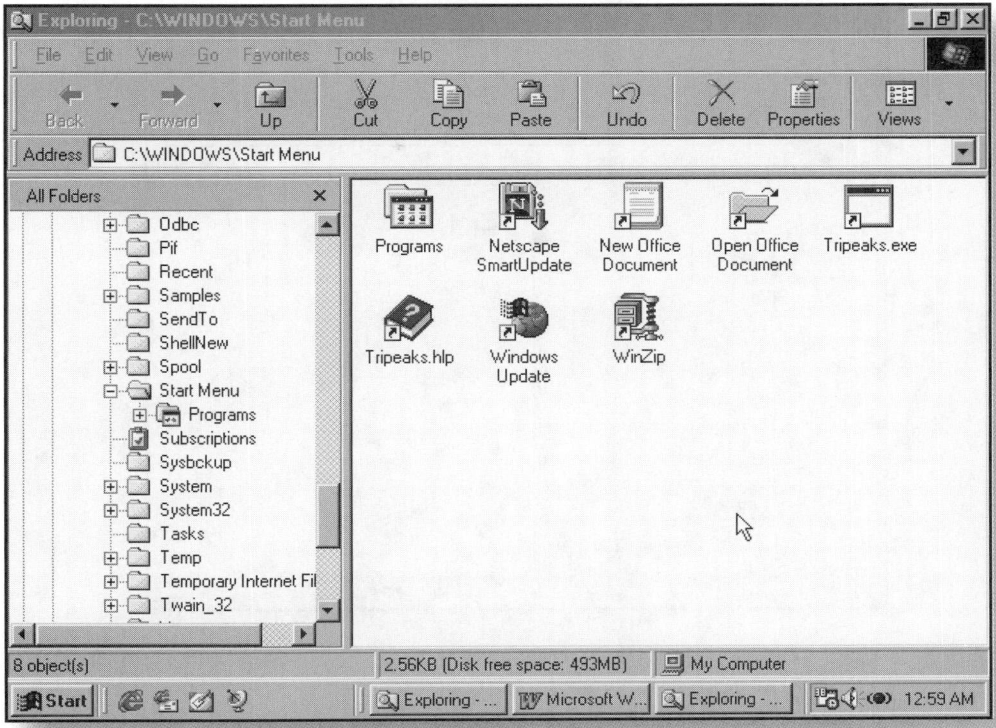

To start the Notepad application from Windows Explorer, you must locate the .EXE file in a folder. Once the file is found, you start the application by double-clicking its entry in the folder.

Finding a File

To find a particular file, you can explore the drive by clicking folders in the left pane of Windows Explorer, or you can search the drive, using the Find utility. The Find utility searches each folder on the drive looking for the file or files you specify in the Find window. There is more than one way to start the Find utility. One way is to right-click the Start button and select Find from the pop-up menu. Another way to start Find is to right-click a folder in the left pane of Windows Explorer. If you want to search a whole drive, right-click the icon for the drive as shown in Figure A-4.

FIGURE A-4
Right-clicking the drive icon

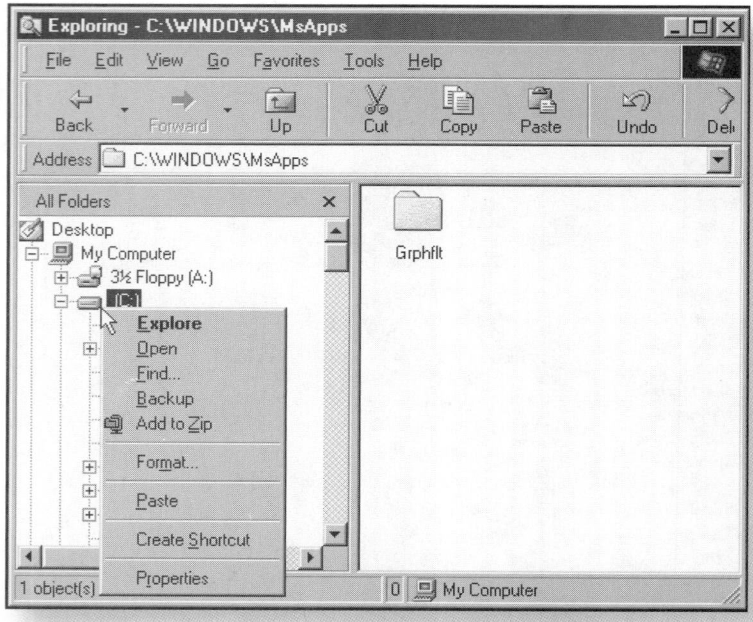

Next select Find from the pop-up menu. In the Find dialog box, enter Notepad.* (or the filename of the file you need) in the Named box. The asterisk is a wildcard symbol. It instructs the Find utility to find all the files with the name Notepad. If you want the Find utility to search all subfolders, be sure to check the Include subfolders check box by clicking it. Then click Find Now to initiate the search (see Figure A-5).

FIGURE A-5
The Find dialog box showing the entry for Notepad.*

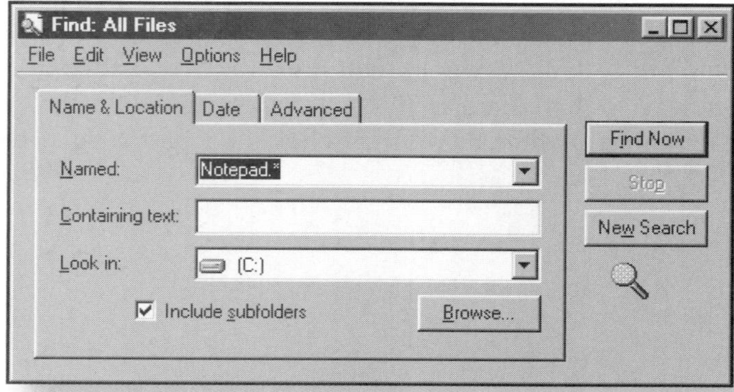

In a few moments, a list of every file with the name Notepad is listed in an expanded Find dialog box. The executable file is the one with the EXE extension. The result of the search is shown in Figure A-6.

FIGURE A-6
The result of the search for Notepad.*

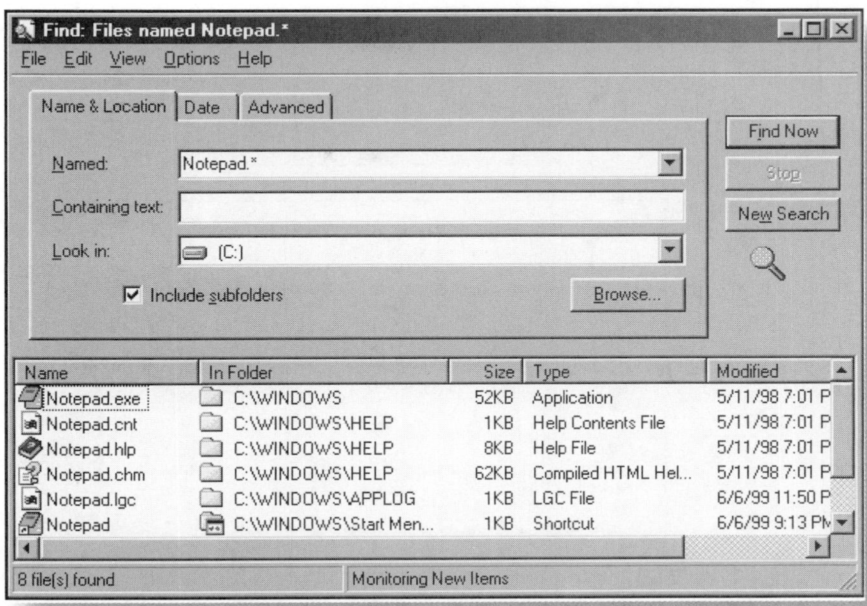

When the file is found, the Find utility displays a great deal of information about the file. The path of the file, listed in one column of the window, is often too long to be read. You can adjust the width of the columns by clicking and dragging the column dividers in the top row of the display. With the path information you can return to Windows Explorer and locate Notepad.exe. Once located, double-click its entry to launch the application.

You can also double-click its entry in the Find window and launch the application directly through the Find utility. This is like calling directory assistance and letting them connect you without writing the number down.

Using My Computer

Another way to view files and start applications is by using My Computer. You can find the My Computer icon on the desktop. Double-click the icon to start My Computer and show the contents of a single folder. Double-click folders in the display area to open other folders. With its default settings, My Computer creates a new window for each folder, leaving your screen cluttered with windows.

Once you find an application, double-click its entry to start the application, as shown in Figure A-7.

FIGURE A-7
My Computer showing multiple folder windows open

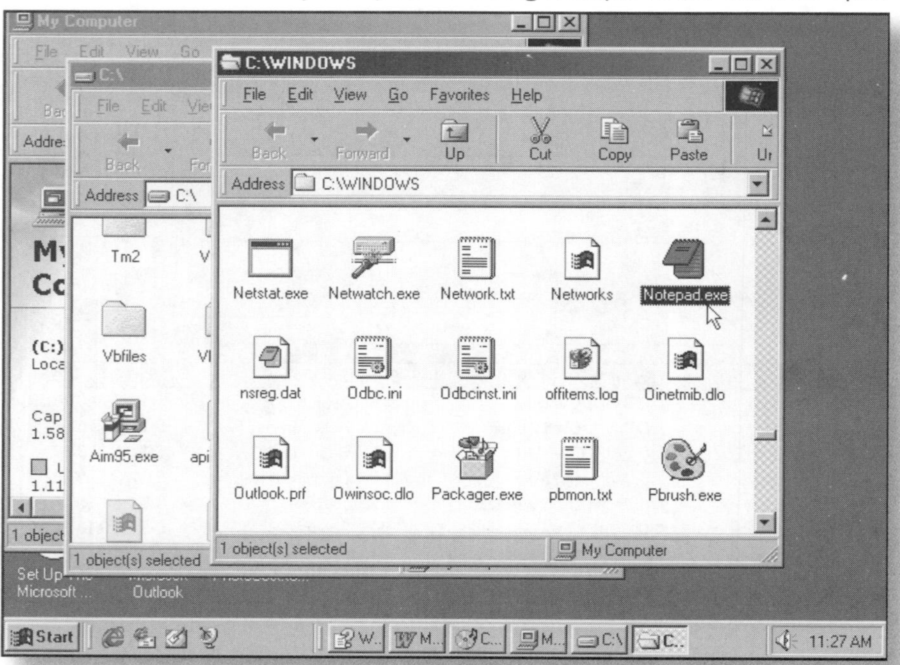

Deleting Files

In either Windows Explorer or My Computer you delete a file by right-clicking its entry. Then in the pop-up menu that appears, choose Delete to send the file to the Recycle Bin. Figure A-8 shows the options available in the pop-up menu.

To delete multiple files, you can drag a box around the files with the mouse. This is analogous to selecting text in a word processing document. You click at one corner of the area and drag the mouse pointer diagonally. If you click on or very near an icon, you drag the icon to a new position, so be sure and click between icons to select them. Another way to select multiple items is to hold down the Ctrl key and click each item you wish to select. Once a number of items is selected, right-click one of the selected items and select Delete from the pop-up menu.

You can select all the items in a window by pressing Ctrl + A or by clicking the Edit menu and selecting Select All.

FIGURE A-8
The pop-up menu that appears when you right-click an entry in My Computer or in Windows Explorer

Copying and Moving Files

To move a file from one folder to another in Windows Explorer, you start by selecting the source folder in the left pane of the Explorer. The contents of the folder appear in the right pane. Select the file to move with a single click. In the left pane, you click the plus symbol to the left of a folder icon to show the folders in the next lower level. Once the destination folder appears in the left pane (it may appear without any navigation), click and drag the icon of the file to be moved and drop it on the destination folder.

To copy a file from one folder to another, use the same procedure but press and hold the Ctrl key while dragging the file icon.

How Much Space is Left?

To find out how much disk space is left on a drive, right-click the drive icon in Windows Explorer. Select Properties. A pie chart representing disk usage appears. A sample is shown in Figure A-9.

Returning to the Desktop

One of the most useful new features of Windows 98 is the Quick Launch toolbar on the taskbar. This toolbar has buttons for commonly used applications and utilities. The Show Desktop button minimizes all the open applications and lets you view the desktop. This makes it easy to start applications that have shortcut icons on the desktop. The Show Desktop icon looks like a desktop blotter with a pad of paper and a pencil.

FIGURE A-9
The Properties dialog box of Drive C showing disk usage

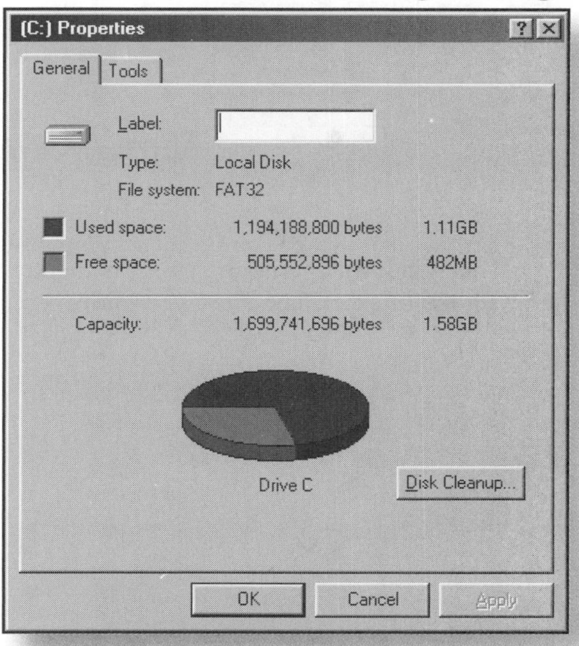

Help

Books are written about Windows 98 and all the ways to use it. A book about Windows 98 was transferred to your local drive when you installed it called Windows Help.

You can press F1 with the mouse pointer anywhere on the desktop to open Windows Help. Use the Contents tab to navigate to Help articles on particular subjects. Use the Index tab to find articles about specific topics.

Figure A-10 shows the Contents tab with an article about dragging and dropping within the Start menu displayed in the right pane.

FIGURE A-10
The Help window

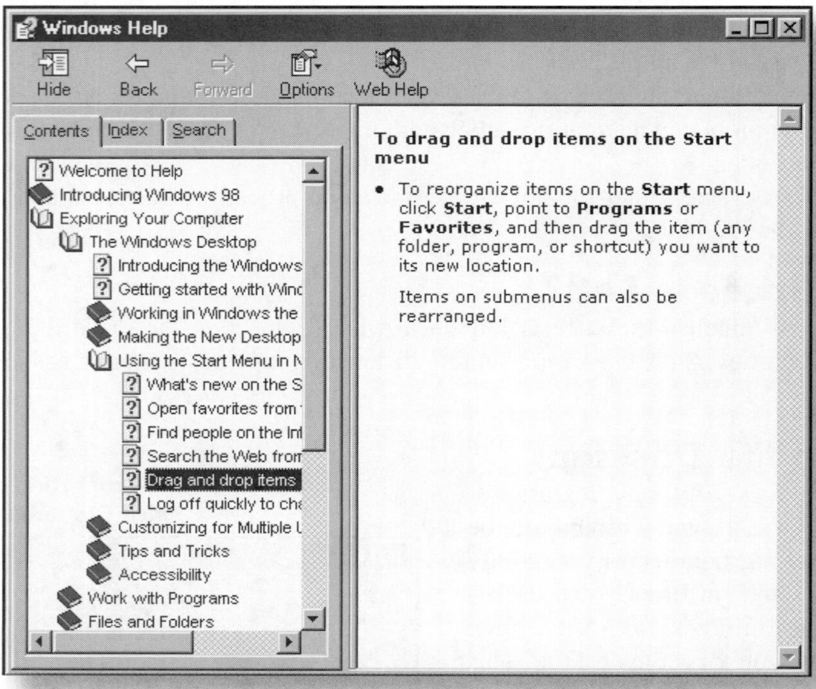

The Windows operating system is the key to integrating desktop applications with each other and with the Internet. The more you know about it, the better Visual Basic programmer you will be.

APPENDIX B

Installing Visual Studio 6.0 Professional

Installing Visual Studio Professional is a two-stage process. First, you install the Visual Studio programs. Then you install the Microsoft Developer Network (MSDN) Library. The MSDN Library is a collection of Help files, books, and articles about Visual Studio.

Before you begin the installation, you may have to uninstall one or more programs to make room for Visual Studio and the MSDN Library. You should always uninstall previous versions of Visual Studio before installing a new one. To uninstall programs, click Start, then select the Settings | Control Panel. In the Control Panel, double-click Add/Remove Programs. A window like the one in Figure B-1 appears.

FIGURE B-1
The Add/Remove Programs Properties window showing MSDN Library –January 1999 selected

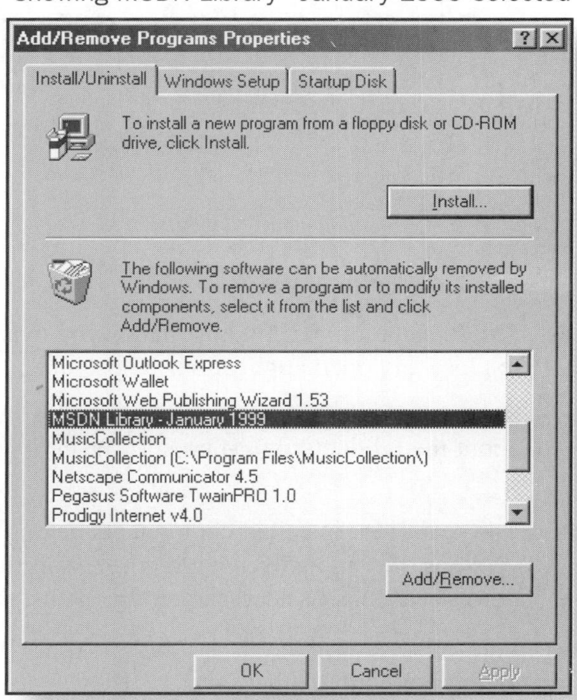

Click Add/Remove and follow the directions to remove the selected application. This is the only way to completely remove an application. Today, every installation saves files scattered through many folders. Merely deleting a folder for an application does not completely remove the application from the system. Each installation or removal ends in a reboot.

- To begin the installation, carefully remove the Microsoft Visual Studio 6.0 Professional Edition Disk 1 from its case and insert it in the CD-ROM drive. The Installation Wizard opening screen displays. Click Next.
- Accept the License Agreement by clicking I accept the agreement and clicking Next.
- Enter the product's ID number. This number is located on a sticker marked CD Key: on the back of the case. Your name should appear in the Name box. If it does not appear, enter it. Click Next.
- Click the Install Visual Studio 6.0 Professional Version option and click Next.
- The Choose Common Install Folder window appears, as shown in Figure B-2. This window prompts you to confirm the names and location of the folders created for the installation. It also gives information about space required and space available on the drive. Click Next to accept the path name or change the path, if necessary, and click Next.

FIGURE B-2
The Choose Common Install Folder window

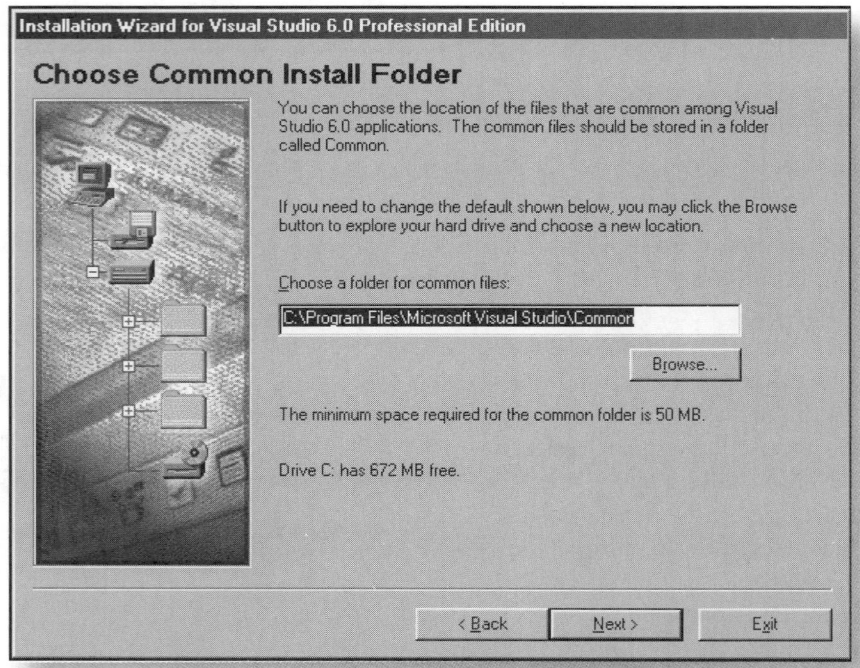

- The Installation Wizard now hands you over to the Setup Wizard whose first job is to tell you to close any open applications. Close open applications and click Continue.
- The next window shows your Product ID number. You need this number to communicate about the product with Microsoft. Write it down on the registration card and in the CD case. Click OK.
- The search for installed components begins. The Setup Wizard searches for up-to-date versions of components that are necessary for the installation. If your system already has the newest versions of necessary components, they are not recopied.
- Figure B-3 shows the dialog box with the button to click to begin the installation. Click the button to proceed.

FIGURE B-3
The Start Installation dialog box

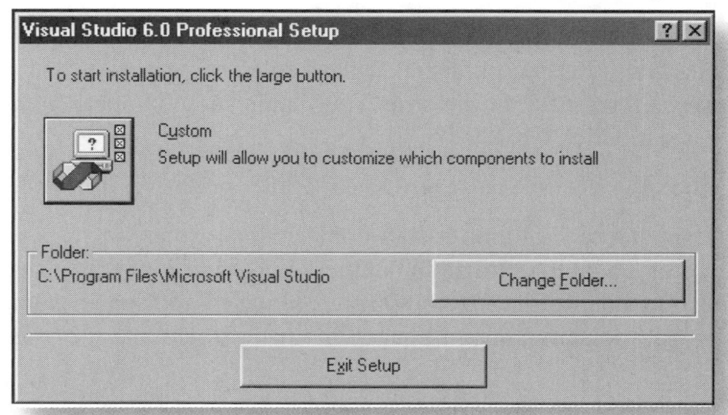

- Figure B-4 shows the Custom installation dialog box with several selections chosen. If you do not need Visual C++, click its entry to remove it from the list of selected items. It is huge and you may not have enough disk space. You can always add just this component if you need it later. Once your selections are made (they do not need to match the figure, although these settings are recommended), click Continue.

FIGURE B-4
The Custom installation dialog box

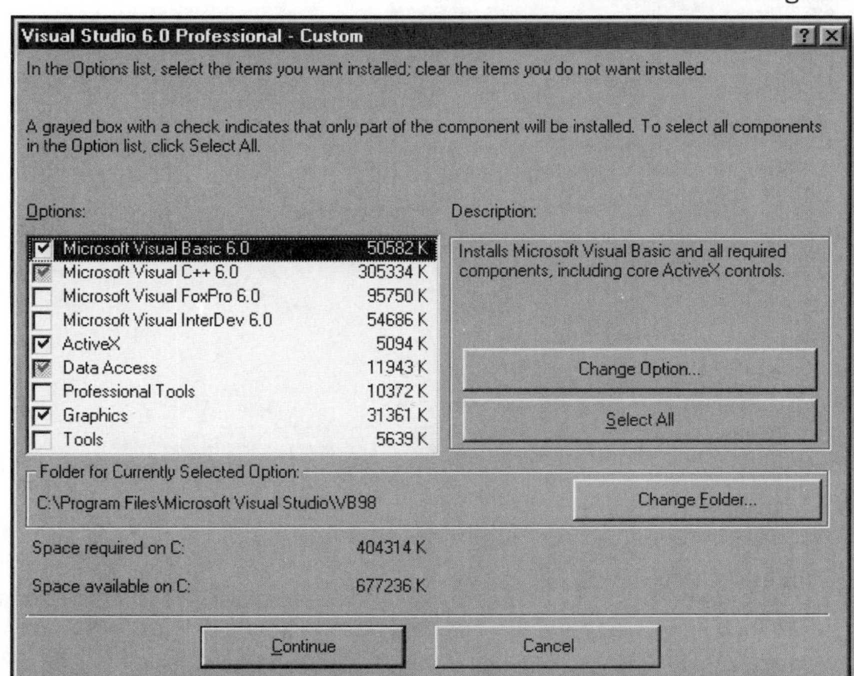

- The advertisement begins as files are transferred from the CD to your local drive. A progress bar in the lower right corner keeps you informed about the progress of the installation. Once the file transfer is complete, the screen may show no activity for some time. Be patient. The Setup Wizard is manipulating your system. When finished you are rewarded with the message shown in Figure B-5. Click OK.

FIGURE B-5
The Setup was completed successfully message

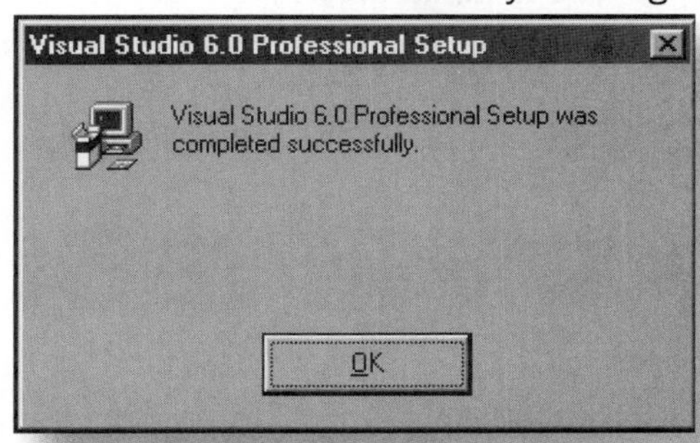

- Immediately following the successful installation of Visual Studio 6.0 Professional, you are prompted to install the MSDN Library. These are your Help files. Figure B-6 shows the opening window. Make sure the Install MSDN box is checked and click Next to proceed with the installation.
- The "Locate Microsoft Developer Network Disk 1" dialog box that appears reminds you to insert the disk in the CD-ROM drive. Once the disk is inserted, click OK.

FIGURE B-6
The Install MSDN opening screen

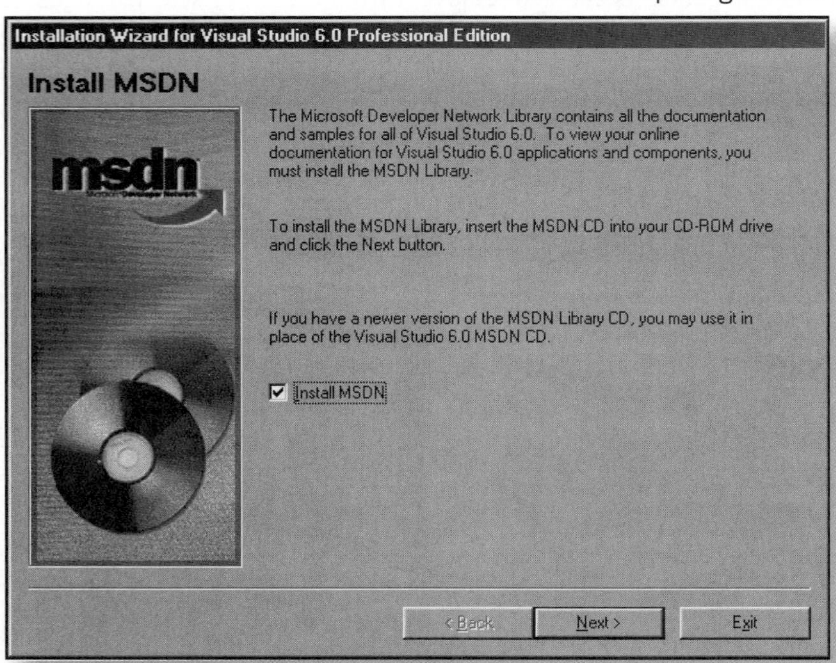

- Click Continue to advance to the Product ID window. Copy the ID number and click OK.
- The Search for installed components phase ends in the appearance of the License Agreement window. Click I Agree to accept the terms of the license.
- The Installation window shown in Figure B-7 appears. It shows the three installation options. The Typical option uses minimal local drive space, but it requires the presence of the CD for any Help to appear. The Custom option is probably the best if you have limited drive space, but do not always want to have the CD in the drive. The Full option, the best choice if you have the space, installs the entire library. It takes 800Mb.
- Select the second choice, Custom, by clicking its icon to see the choices you can make.

FIGURE B-7
The Installation window

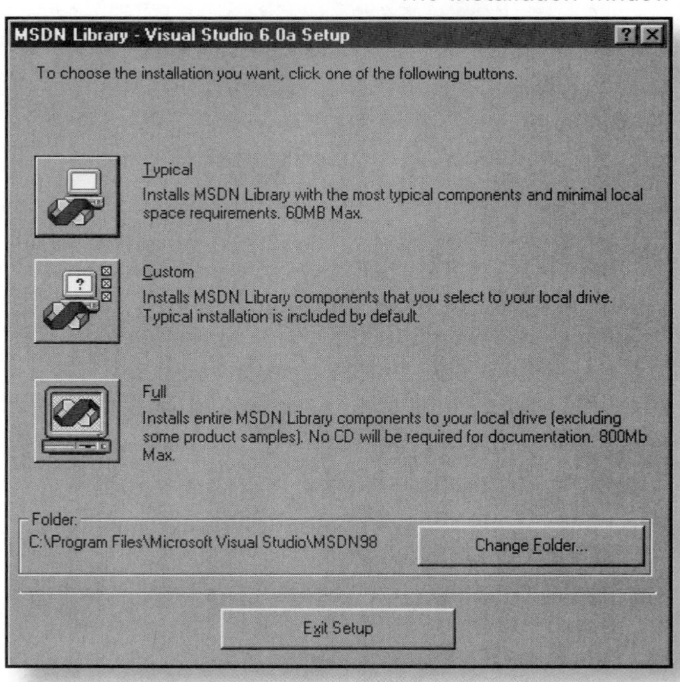

- Figure B-8 shows the choices you made in the Custom installation window. Besides the choices you see in the Figure, Visual J++ Documentation, and Product Samples were added as well as the last item in the list (not shown), All Other Files. If you have the room, there are interesting files in this last section. Keep a careful eye to the space requirements and space available figures shown in the lower half of the window. Click Continue when you have finished. During the file transfer, you will be prompted to insert Disk 2 of the MSDN Library.

FIGURE B-8
The Custom installation window showing a few of the selections

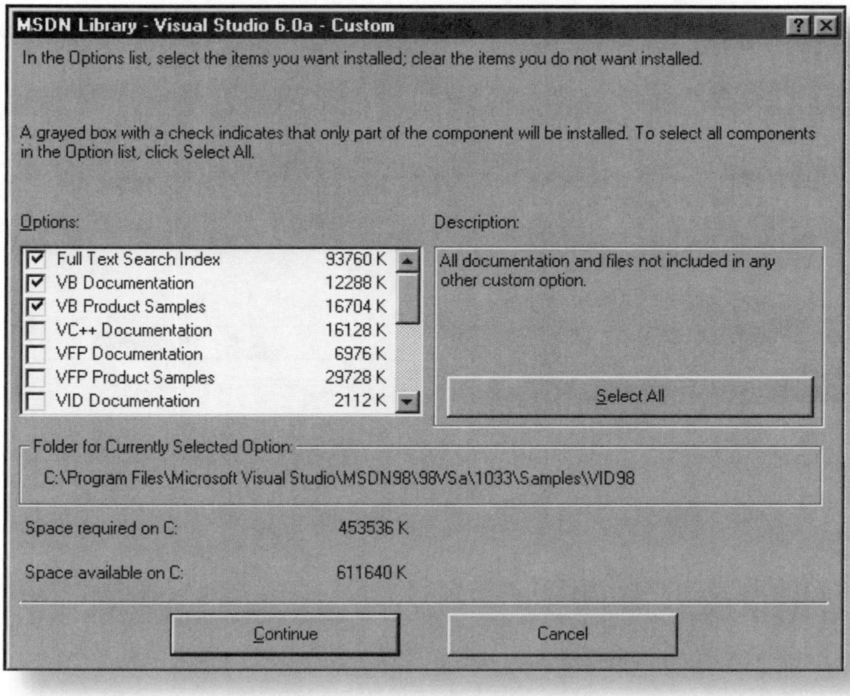

MSDN Library - Visual Studio 6.0a - Custom

In the Options list, select the items you want installed; clear the items you do not want installed.

A grayed box with a check indicates that only part of the component will be installed. To select all components in the Option list, click Select All.

Options:

☑	Full Text Search Index	93760 K
☑	VB Documentation	12288 K
☑	VB Product Samples	16704 K
☐	VC++ Documentation	16128 K
☐	VFP Documentation	6976 K
☐	VFP Product Samples	29728 K
☐	VID Documentation	2112 K

Description:
All documentation and files not included in any other custom option.

Select All

Folder for Currently Selected Option:
C:\Program Files\Microsoft Visual Studio\MSDN98\98VSa\1033\Samples\VID98

Space required on C: 453536 K

Space available on C: 611640 K

Continue Cancel

- When the library is successfully installed, you are prompted to add Other Client Tools. Click Next to advance to the Server Setups screen. Click Next.
- Finally, you are prompted to register Visual Studio. Figure B-9 shows the "Register Over the Web Now!" screen. Registering your software is a good idea. Click Finish to connect to the Web and go to the registration Web site, or click Exit to exit without registering.
- Click Start. Select Programs | Microsoft Visual Studio 6.0 | Microsoft Visual Basic 6.0. Select Standard EXE. Select Help | Contents from the menu bar. Navigate around the Help screen to make sure everything is working. Close Visual Basic by selecting File | Exit from the menu bar.

FIGURE B-9
The Register Over the Web Now! screen

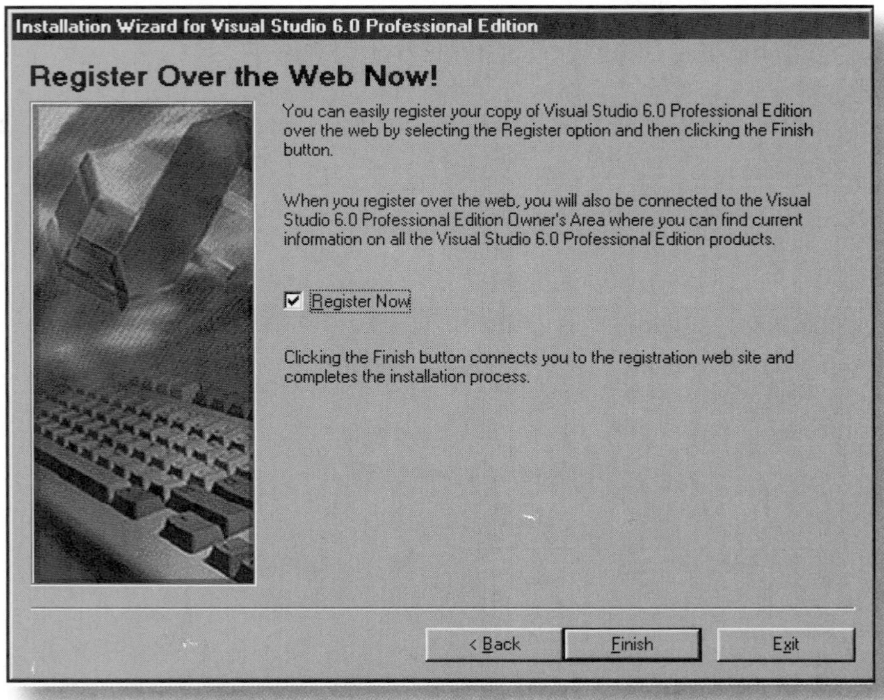

You may repeat the installation process to add components that were omitted. All of the MSDN Library material is available as long as you keep the CDs on hand.

GLOSSARY

A

Abs function A function that finds the absoluted value of the difference so a positive value is always displayed.

access keys Allow the user to open a menu and then access a menu command. This is done by pressing the Alt+letter key.

ActiveX Control Interface Wizard The ActiveX Control Interface Wizard automates the process of designing new ActiveX controls.

ActiveX controls ActiveX controls are used by Microsoft programs to package commonly used data structures and methods so they may be shared among applications.

ActiveX Data Objects Microsoft's newest way to access data from a Visual Basic program.

ActiveX DLL An ActiveX DLL is a resource for application programs. It provides class definitions to projects.

ActiveX Document Migration Wizard (ADM Wizard) The ADM Wizard converts an existing Standard EXE application to an ActiveX document.

ActiveX Document An ActiveX Document is an application that runs in a container application like a browser.

Add method The Add method adds an object to a collection.

algorithm An algorithm is a Step-by-Step exercise solution to a problem.

API API is the Application Programming Interface. The API is a set of routines used by an application to access and execute the procedures of a computer's operating system.

App Object App is a system object that contains information about the currently running project.

array An array is a list of values referred to by a single variable name. Values in an array may be numbers or strings, or may represent complex data types that include many pieces of information.

ASCII code The ASCII code is a numerical code that represents each character as a value. "A" is 65. "a" is 97. The space character is 32.

Assembly Language Assembly language uses a mnemonic, a short descriptive syllable, to represent each Machine Language statement. There is a one to one correspondence between Assembly Language statements and Machine Language statements.

assignment operator The equal sign assigns the value of the expression on the right to the variable on the left.

assignment statement An expression that assigns the value on the right to the object on the left.

asynchronously Asynchronous events can happen simultaneously. Synchronous event have to occur in the proper order. One has to finish before another can start.

AsyncProp object This object receives files downloaded by the AsyncRead method.

AsyncRead method The Async-Read method initiates a file download.

AsyncReadComplete event The AsyncReadComplete event occurs when an asynchronous read request is complete.

B

base-16 A number system based on powers of 16 instead of powers of 10. Because 16 is 2 raised to the 4th power, its relationship with the binary number system is very close. Translation between the two bases, 16 and 2, is fast and easy.

binary file A file where the data is stored in its native binary form. For instance, a number like 17 is not stored as two characters: "1" and "7". It is stored as a pure binary number. Binary files are often more compact than files that store everything as an ASCII character.

Boolean or logical expression A Boolean or logical expression is an expression that, when evaluated, results in a True or False.

boundary conditions The upper and lower limits of the acceptable input values. The boundary conditions frequently cause program errors.

branch A branch of a tree is an item in the tree that is neither a root nor a leaf.

break mode The execution of a program in break mode is paused. While in break mode, variables can be examined and changed.

breakpoint A breakpoint is a spot in the code at which the program pauses.

bugs Bugs are errors in program code.

Business Rule A business rule is a rule or procedure used to run a business. Rules may used to determine pay or vacation or disciplinary action. Rules built into classes are easy to maintain and modify.

Buttons Collection The Buttons Collection is a collection of the buttons on a toolbar. The collection is like an array. The Buttons Collection is used when individual buttons of the Toolbar have to be accessed.

ByVal The ByVal keyword is used in parameter lists to indicate which variables are sent by value instead of by reference. Variables sent by value cannot be permanently changed in the calling program.

C

CAB file "Cab" is short for cabinet. A cab file holds not only the executable application file, but also all the support files needed to run the program.

cache The cache in Internet Explorer is the storage area used to store recently used Web pages.

cascade Separate documents are displayed in separate windows with part of the windows overlapping.

ChartData property ChartData is a property of the MSChart control. It is loaded with the contents of an array that contain both the labels for the data and the data itself.

ChDir App.Path A statement that changes the default directory to the path where the running application is saved.

ChDrive App.Path A statement that changes the default drive to the drive where the running application is saved.

children A node's descendants are its children. A single item descended from another is referred to as a child.

Circle method The Circle method draws a circle or an ellipse that can be filled with color.

Class module A Class module is used to contain the definitions of one or more class definitions.

Close Close [#]filenumber Closes the file associated with channel filenumber.

Collection A collection is itself an object that contains a number of related objects.

ColumnHeaders collection A collection of ColumnHeaders used by the ListView control.

Common Dialog Control Microsoft's built-in control for letting a programmer include standard Windows dialog boxes in his program. The ShowFont method, for example, displays the Font dialog. ShowOpen displays the Open a File dialog.

compile Compiling is turning source code into object code and ultimately into machine code. Once an ActiveX control is compiled is runs faster but it is no longer possible to modify the control without returning to its source code.

Component Object Model (COM) COM allows programmers to build applications and systems from components supplied from many sources.

concatenation String concatenation is joining two strings together end to end. The catenation operator is the ampersand, (&).

constant Values in the program that never change.

container application A container application, like Internet Explorer, provides a place for an ActiveX control to execute.

Controls collection The Controls collection is a collection that contains each of the controls on a particular form.

controls Objects such as buttons, boxes, and scroll bars placed on a form as the user interface.

Count property The Count property reports the number of objects in a collection.

cross-platform A program that can run on more than one platform is a cross-platform program.

D

DAO drivers DAO drivers are programs that make data sources available to DAO objects.

Database A record is one complete entry in a table.

Data control A Data control links a database file with a Visual Basic project.

Data Encapsulation Data Encapsulation is hiding data and methods from the user and even the programmer. This prevents accidental changes to the data.

data hiding Data hiding is protecting data from users and programmers. Information that can be hidden is used "behind the scenes". The information doesn't have to be directly available to a calling application.

data source name (DSN) DSN is an ODBC term for the collection of information used to connect your application to a particular ODBC database. The DSN is usually stored in the Windows registry and it allows your application to connect to the ODBC database.

data structure A data structure is way to organize data.

data type Determines the type of data a variable can hold.

DataField property A property of a data bound control that specifies which field is to be displayed in the control.

DataSource property A property of a data bound control that specifies where the data is to come from.

debug Debugging is ridding code of errors.

definite loop A program loop where the starting and ending points and the number of repetitions is know before the loop is executed.

dependency A dependency is a file that is a necessary part of an application. A Help file is a dependency. Such files must be included when building an installation program for an application.

digital signature Providing a digital signature allows the user to trace a path back to you or your company if your control damages the user's system.

Dynamic Link Library (DLL) A Dynamic Link Library is a collection of executable code definitions for running applications. Not all code needed to execute a program is in the program itself. DLL's provide the missing code.

dynaset A dynaset is a kind of Recordset. It is a set of pointers that point to particular fields of particular records from particular tables. A dynaset may be all the records of a particular table, or it may combine records and fields from several tables.

E

element or member The items in an array are called the elements or members of the array.

element In the For Each element In group statement element is an object variable.

End statement Code that terminates the program.

Enter Focus event The Enter Focus event occurs when the User Document receives focus.

Err and Error Err and Error are system variables that contain an errors number and description for the last run-time error.

Err object The Err object contains a recently occurring run-times error's number, description, source, and other information.

error log or log file An error log or log file is a simple text file used to store information about a program's run-time errors.

error trapping An error trap responds when an error occurs. The flow of program execution can be sent to special code written to handle the error, the program can end, or the program can skip the offending statement and try to continue.

error-handler The OnError statement alerts Visual Basic to watch for any run-time errors in the code. If an error occurs the OnError statement sends program code to an error-handling routine to dertmine how to handle the error.

event driven Event driven applications execute code in response to an event, such as a mouse click. Every form and control in Visual Basic has a predefined set of events.

event procedure An event procedure is a subroutine connected with an object like a text box or command button. It is executed when a particular event associated with the object occurs.

Exit Focus event The Exit Focus event occurs when the User Document loses focus.

F

family metaphor

A tree is sometimes described with a family metaphor: items in the tree have parents, children, and siblings.

field A field is one whole piece of information, like a first name or an age.

file extension Appear after the file name of most documents or saved files. It tells the user and computer what type of file is being used.

fixed-length string A String data type whose length is fixed by an integer value less than or equal to 65,535. The length is fixed in the variable declaration.

flag A variable used to indicate the state or occurrence of an action or condition. A flag variable is usually defined as the Boolean type.

For Each statement The For Each statement is a special version of the For statement used for processing the items in a collection.

Forms collection The Forms collection is a collection whose elements represent each of the loaded forms of an application.

forms The main object on which you design the user interface.

FreeFile function Keeps track of which numbers have been used and provides a free channel number when called.

FTP File Transfer Protocol.

G

General Declarations A part of the code associated with a form or code module. Declarations made in this section are available in all the procedures defined within the module.

Get Get is the name of a kind of property procedure defined in a class that gets a value from the object and reports the value of the object to the calling program. The Get procedure is called when the user wants to read a property.

Graphical User Interface (GUI) a user interface based on graphics (icons and pictures and menus) instead of text; uses a mouse as well as a keyboard as an input device.

group In the for Each element In group statement group is a collection.

GUID GUID stands for global unique identifier. One is automatically assigned to every Visual Basic component, including ActiveX controls. Use the GUID to call the control in an <object> HTML tag in a Web page.

H

handle A handle is an integer value assigned to forms and many controls. The value of the integer is defined by the operating environment and is unique for each control and form.

hard coded Hard-coded values are written into the program code, not entered by the user.

HelpContextID The HelpContextID property connects a control with a Help topic when using WinHelp.

hexadecimal Another term for base-16. Hex is short for hexadecimal. Values in hexadecimal are identified by the &H prefix.

Hide event The Hide event occurs when the user navigates from the User Document to another document.

high-level programming language A high-level programming language is less like the language of the processor and more like the language of the programmer.

HTML Help System The HTML Help System is part of a strategy to make information available to the user in a seamless natural way. It provides Help based on HTML documents: the same documents used in the World Wide Web on the Internet. It provides the same features as WinHelp but uses HTML to build each Help topic entry.

HTML tags HTML instructions to tell the browser how to format text in the hypertext document.

HTML HTML is the hypertext markup language used to build the inter-linked documents for the World Wide Web.

hWnd property The name of the property containing a form's or control's handle.

hyperlink object An object used to navigate to filesnames or URLs. It is part of the UserDocument.

I

ImageList control A resource of images for the Toolbox control. It is not visible on the form when the program is running.

indefinite loop Indefinite loops are sections of code whose repetitions are determined by conditions within the loop itself.

index or subscript The items in an array are referred to by the name of the array along with a number called an index or subscript.

indexed fields Special lists that maintain an ordering of records based on particular fields.

Inheritance Inheritance is when a new class is defined to inherit all the properties and methods of an existing class.

INI files Text files used to store application configuration information.

Initialize event The Initialize event occurs whenever an instance of the User Document is created or when a UserControl is put onto an application's form. Code in this event is the first to execute when a User Document is created.

Initialize The initialize event occurs whenever an instance of the User Document is created or when a User Control is put onto an application's form. Code in this event is the first to execute when a User Document is created.

InitProperties event An event of the UserDocument that fires when the application is started, but only if no properties have been saved in the PropertyBag. If property values are saved in the PropertyBag the ReadProperties event occurs instead of the InitProperties event.

Input Function Input(number, [#]filenumber) The Input function collects number characters from the file associated with channel filenumber. The number sign is optional.

InputBox Function variable = InputBox(prompt [, title] [, default]) A dialog box to collect up to 255 characters entered from the keyboard. Return a string or variant type.

instance An instance is an object created from a class.

Integrated Development Environment This environment is provided when you launch Visual Basic. It consists of menu bars, context menus, toolbars, a toolbox, the Properties window and the Project Explorer.

InterCap naming convention The InterCap naming convention is to names variables and objects by capitalizing first letters of words that make up the name.

Internet Browser The Internet Browser, a piece of software used to view specially encoded Internet documents, is one of the most important pieces of software on your computer.

Internet Package A package created for an application or ActiveX component that allows the program to be installed over a network, Internet or Intranet.

Internet Server A computer that give Internet access to a network of computers.

Intranet An Intranet is a local implementation of the Internet. It uses the same protocols as the Internet for the transfer of documents and information.

Item method The Item method retrieves a single object from the collection.

J

Jet database engine The software engine that builds and modifies a database.

jumps Links you click to "jump" from one area to another related area in a browser or Help file.

K

keyword Words that have special meaning in a programming language.

L

leaf An item in a tree with no branches.

Let The Let property procedure converts or processes property information entered by the user and saves it as a property of the object created by the class. The Let procedure is called when the user wants to set a value for a property.

lifetime The lifetime of a variable is when it does and does not hold valid values.

Line method The Line method draws a line from one pair of coordinates to another or draws a box that can be filled with color.

linear search The code of a linear search examines each element of an array in order from first to last.

List method The List method of the list box returns the line selected by the ListIndex property.

ListImages collection A collection of images used by the ImageList control.

ListIndex property The ListIndex property of a list box is set to the index number of the entry clicked by the user. If no item is selected, the ListIndex property is set to –1.

ListIndex When applied to a combo box, the ListIndex method selects a particular item from the list and inserts that item in the combo box's Text property.

load and unload forms Forms are loaded into memory and on the screen when a program starts. Code unloads them from memory and the screen at the appropriate time.

LOF( ) The Length Of File Function returns a value equal to the number of characters in a file.

M

Machine Language Machine Language is the programming language made up of machine codes. Machine code statements are the native language of the computer's processor. The binary code is directly understood by the microprocessor. Machine language statements are often expressed in base-16.

Make command The Make command in the File menu builds executable files from project files.

member A member of an ActiveX control is a property, method, or event of the control.

memory-image file The memory-image file is the old name of a program in Machine Language ready to load into memory and run.

menu control array A menu control array is a number of menu items with the same name, but unique Index numbers. Each element of a menu control array must be part of the same menu.

Menu Editor A tool that allows you to create new menus and edit existing menus.

menus Are used in most Windows programs to access a variety of commands. The Menu bar is located under the title bar.

messages To communicate with an object a programmer writes code that send messages to the objects. The message instructs the objects what operations to perform on themselves.

Microsoft Help Workshop An application to compile Help files from topic files, mappings, and other data.

mnemonic A mnemonic is a short descriptive syllable used to represent each Machine Language statement.

modal A dialog box made modal must be clicked before any other activity can be processed.

Mod The Mod operator divides one whole number by another and returns the remainder of the division.

modules Programs are composed of one or more independent modules that are not combined until the program is linked together.

MSChart control A control used to display a graph of data provided by a program.

MsgBox function variable = MsgBox(prompt [, buttons] [, title] [, helpfile, context]) A dialog box that lets the program communicate a message with user and get (or ignore) a simple response.

Multiple Document Interface (MDI) Allows you to creat an application that has many forms contained within one main form.

N

New keyword The New keyword creates a new instance of an object.

New The New keyword is used to declare a new instance of a class.

node A node is an item in a tree.

Nodes collection A collection of nodes used by the TreeView control.

null string Two adjacent double quote characters. Another definition for the null string is the empty string. It is used to blank any object, like a label or text box that takes displays or enters a string.

O

Object Browser The Object Browser lets the programmer inspect classes and the properties and methods associated with objects created with each class.

object model An object model is a diagram that represents the hierarchical organization of classes and objects.

Object Oriented Programming Object Oriented Programming (OOP) revolves around building objects that contain both data and the operations performed on the data.

object An object is anything that has properties attached to it. A form, a message box and a list are all considered objects.

OCX OCX is the file extension of the compiled files created when the Make command is executed on an ActiveX control.

ODBC driver ODBC is an acronym for Open Database Connectivity. It is an interface providing a common language for Windows applications to gain access to a database.

Open Statement Open pathname For mode As [#]filenumber Open a file to access its contents. If the Mode is Input, the file is opened to import data to the program. If Mode is Output, the file is created or overwritten with data from the program. If the Mode is Append, data is added to the currently existing data in the file. The filenumber is a number assigned to the channel used by the program to access the data.

operator overloading When existing operators have more than one function depending on the context, it is called operator overloading. You can overload operations when you define new classes.

Option Explicit The Option Explicit statement in the General Declarations section of a module requires variables names to be declared before they are used in code.

P

Package and Deployment Wizard (PD Wizard) The package and Deployment Wizard builds an installation package for an application.

Package folder The default name of the directory created by the package and Deployment Wizard to hold the cab file created for an application.

Panels collection A collection of panels used by the StatusBar control.

panels An entry in the StatusBar control.

parallel arrays Parallel arrays use the same index value to indicate related values stored in separate arrays.

parameter A parameter is a variable listed in the top line of a subroutine that lets the subroutine communicate with other procedures or functions.

parents A node's parent is the item preceding it in the Tree hierarchy.

parsing Parsing is separating commands and information from strings that come from the keyboard or text files. A number of string functions are designed to help the programmer parse strings. For instance, if the command is Drop the Amulet, the command Drop is parsed from the string and interpreted as a command to the program.

personal library A collection of forms and code that can be reused when creating new programs.

platform A platform is a combination of computer hardware and operating system. A Mac running OS8 is a platform. A Sun workstation running Solaris is a platform.

Polymorphism Polymorphism is giving two or more definitions to the same operator or method. The program tells the difference between the two by the context in which it is found.

Pop-up menu A menu designed in the Menu Editor, but usually displayed as a result of right-clicking the mouse on an object.

Print # Statement Print #filenumber, [outputlist] The Print # statement prints an outputlist to a file associated with the filenumber. The number sign (#) is not optional. The outputlist is a list of expressions, variables, or strings.

Printers collection The Printers collection is a collection of all the installed printers.

profile A profile stores choices made in the course of executing a wizard. These choices can be recalled if the wizard is need again to build a similar form.

program flow Program flow means the order in which statements are executed.

Program Group A Program Group is a group of related executable files.

project group A project group allows two or more projects to be open at the same time. It is a perfect way to test ActiveX controls while they are being designed. One project is designated as the startup project.

Property Changed The Property Changed event signals the container application when the value of a property changes.

Property Pages Many controls have many properties. Too many to access in the Properties window. The Property Pages organize the properties to make it easy to interact with the control at design-time.

PropertyBag The PropertyBag is used to store initial values for properties from run to run.

PropertyChanged The PropertyChanged event signals the container application when the value of property changes.

PSet method The PSet method plots a single point on an object at specified coordinates.

R

Random access file Stores information in pieces called recards. Each record is exactly the same length.

ReadProperties event The Read Properties event occurs when an instance of the User Document is created and properties from a previous run have been stored.

Record A record is one complete entry in a table.

Recordset A Recordset is a collection of records of a database.

reentrant Reentrant code means the code can be loaded and run from anywhere in memory. Code that contains references to specific memory addresses, not just an address specified in relation to a base address, is not reentrant.

References References are resources available to a project. A DLL is a reference.

relational operators A relational operator compares two expressions are returns a True or False. For instance, <=, less-than-or-equal, compares the expression on the left to the expression on the right. If the expressions represent numbers, an expression using <= is True if the value of the left side expression is less than or equal to the value of the right side expression.

Remove method The Remove method deletes an object from a collection.

reusable code Reusable code is code that can be used in more than one project. One goal of programming is to write reusable code to save work.

Rich Text Format (RTF) Saves all formatting. Converts formatting to instructions that other programs, including compatible Microsoft programs, can read and interpret.

robust The word robust means durable, tough, strong. A program's robustness refers to the program's ability to cope with or recover from error conditions.

root The root of the tree is its first node or item in the hierarchy of the tree.

run-time error An error that occurs while a program is running. If not properly trapped, such an error will crash the program.

S

Scale method The Scale method is used to set a user defined measure for a form, picture box, or the printer. To use the Scale method specify the coordinates of the top left corner of the object and the bottom right corner of the object.

ScaleMode property The ScaleMode property allows choices among a number of predefined measuring standards: the twip, the pixel, the character, the millimeter, the centimeter, the inch, and the user defined mode.

scope The scope of a variable is a variable's visibility and its lifetime.

scripting Scripting is program code embedded in the hypertext document.

sentinel A sentinel value is a special value entered by the user as a signal that the input to the program is complete.

separator bar A horizontal line used in menus to separate menu commands into logical groups.

sequential file A file, usually of characters, that is built character by character in order from first to last. To access the last character, all the preceding characters must be read.

Set keyword The Set keyword is used in an assignment statement to assign an object to an object variable.

Set Set is used at the beginning of an assignment statement that gives a value to an object variable.

shared files If a file is a shared file it can be used as part of multiple applications. For instance, if the same Help file was used in more than one application it should be marked as a shared file.

Shell command The Shell function runs an executable program. It returns a double value that represents the program's task ID number.

shortcut keys Run a menu command immediately after the shortcut key combination is pressed. Eg. Ctrl+C for the Copy command.

Show event The Show event occurs whenever the user navigates to the User Document.

siblings Two or more items with the same parents are siblings.

snapshot A snapshot is a copy of a Recordset. It cannot be updated, but like a dynaset, it may be drawn from several tables.

source code Source code is a file of statements in a computer language that together make a program.

Standard module A Standard module is used to hold code that is accessed by other modules in the project. The procedures and functions in a standard module are not linked to particular events or controls on a form. The module itself does not have a form.

Static variables A variable whose value persists beyond the end of the event procedure.

Step Into The Step Into option steps into any procedure or function called in the code and executes it line by line.

StrConv( ) Used with the vbProperCase constant, this function converts a string entered by a user into a string where the all the characters are lowercase except the first character. The first character of the converted string is uppercase.

Stretch property A property of the image control. When True, an image is stretched or shrunk to fit the size of the image control.

subroutine A subroutine is a self-contained portion of a complete program. It usually has a single task. An event procedure is a subroutine.

syntax errors Syntax errors occur when mistakes are made in the structure of a statement. The most common syntax error is misspelling.

syntax The construction of a statement is called the statement's syntax.

T

Terminate event The Terminate event fires as the User Document is terminated. In Internet Explorer this event fires when the user navigates to another page.

The Integrated Development Environment (IDE) The Integrated Development Environment is the environment in which programmers create, run, test, and debug programs. This environment is provided when you launch Visual Basic. It consists of menu bars, menus, toolbars, a toolbox, the Properties window and the Project Explorer.

tile To display more than one document in separate windows at the same time.

ToolTip When a user briefly rest the mouse pointer over a button a ToolTip appears, displaying the name of the button.

topic file The topic file contains text and graphics used to explain a feature or instruct the user in how to use the application. It is saved in Rich Text Format.

topic ID A topic ID is a string that identifies a Help topic or identifies a location within the topic to display.

tree metaphor The items in a TreeView control are sometimes referred to using the tree metaphor: one root, branches, leaves.

twip A unit of graphical measurement. 1,440 twips equal one inch and 567 twips equal one centimeter.

two dimensional array An array that stores data in table form. It requires two index values; a row and a column.

U

User Defined Type (UDT) A UDT, is a datatype designed by the programmer. It contains fields of built-in types or other UDT's. Variables and arrays of the new datatype can be declared and used in programs. UDT's are usually defined with the Public keyword in the general declarations section of a Standard module.

User Document Designer The palette on which an ActiveX Document is built.

user interface The user interface is how the user will interact with the program. It is what the user types and clicks. It is what the user sees as output.

UserControl The UserControl object is the key part of an ActiveX control. It is the body used as the foundation of the control.

V

variable A named storage location used to hold data that changes as the program runs.

variable-length string A String data type whose length varies with the data it is used to store. A variable-length string has a maximum length of about 2 billion characters.

Virtual Machine A Virtual Machine is a computer built of software. Virtual Machine software allows programs not normally supported by a particular platform to run.

VisData A short form of the name: Visual Data Manager, a program used to create, modify, and display database files.

visibility The visibility of a variable defines where in the project the value of the variable is available to use or change. A private variable declared with a Dim statement in one event procedure is not visible in any other procedure.

Visual Basic for Applications (VBA) VBA is the language used to program in most Microsoft applications.

W

Watch expression A Watch expression is a variable or expression used to display a value when the program enters break mode.

Watch window The Watch window is used to specify the conditions that lead to a program break.

WAV sound files Sound files with small snippets of sound. Typically used to accompany various Windows actions. They can be used in Visual Basic programs through an API function.

What's This Help A Help system similar to a more comprehensive ToolTip.

WhatsThisHelpID The WhatsThisHelpID property is used to connect a control with a Help topic. It is used when the What's This Help system is active.

Win32api.txt A file of Declare statements, Constants, and Type declarations applying to API calls. It is supplied with Visual Basic.

Windows Common Controls A collection of controls that commonly appear in Windows programs, giving those programs the customary look and feel of a Windows program.

Windows Registry The Registry is a database maintained by the Windows operating system. It contains configuration information about the Windows operating system, all applications, and even ActiveX controls and databases.

WinHelp The traditional Windows Help system, WinHelp, provides inter-linked Help topics with full-text search capabilities and tables of contents.

World Wide Web A collection of inter-linked documents stored on computers all over the world.

WriteProperties event An event used to execute code to store current property values in the PropertyBag when the User Document is terminated by the container application.

Z

ZOrder Every form is organized into three view planes. The top plane has: ZOrder of zero. Setting a control's ZOrder to zero usually brings it to the forefront and it becomes visible to the user.

INDEX

A

B

G

H

I

J

K

L

M

N

O

S

T

U

V

W

Z